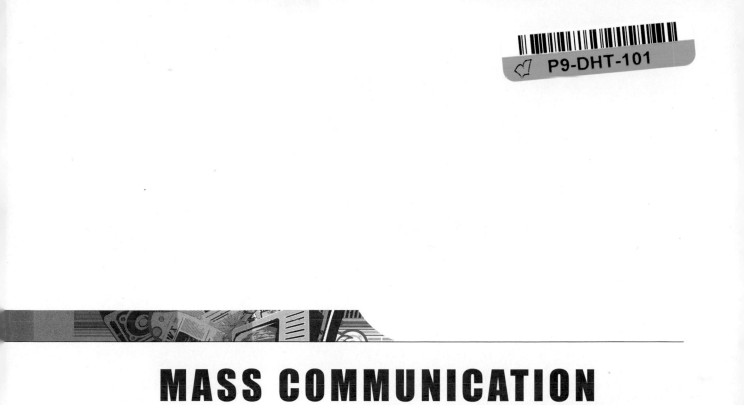

# MASS COMMUNICATION

# MASS COMMUNICATION
## Living in a Media World

THIRD EDITION

## RALPH E. HANSON
**University of Nebraska at Kearney**

CQ PRESS

A Division of SAGE
Washington, D.C.

CQ Press
2300 N Street, NW, Suite 800
Washington, DC 20037

Phone: 202-729-1900; toll-free, 1-866-4CQ-PRESS (1-866-427-7737)

Web: www.cqpress.com

Cover design: Matthew Simmons, Myself Included Design
Front cover image: iStockphoto.com
Back cover photo: Joel Beeson
Typesetting: C&M Digitals (P) Ltd.

♾ The paper used in this publication exceeds the requirements of the American National Standard for Information Sciences—Permanence of Paper for Printed Library Materials, ANSI Z39.48-1992.

Printed and bound in the United States of America

14   13   12   11   10        1   2   3   4   5

**Library of Congress Cataloging-in-Publication Data**
Hanson, Ralph E.
Mass communication : living in a media world / Ralph E. Hanson. — 3rd ed.
     p.  cm.
Includes bibliographical references and index.
ISBN 978-1-60426-600-9 (pbk. : alk. paper)  1.  Mass media.  I.  Title.

P90.H314 2010
302.23—dc22
                                                                    2009053989

*To Pam, Erik, and Andrew*

# About the Author

Ralph E. Hanson is professor and chair in the communication department at the University of Nebraska at Kearney, where he teaches courses in writing, blogging, reporting, and mass communication. Previously, he was on the faculty at West Virginia University and Northern Arizona University. He has been teaching introduction to mass communication for more than a decade, and he has worked extensively on developing online courses and degree programs. Hanson has a bachelor's degree in journalism and anthropology from Iowa State University, a master's degree in journalism from Iowa State, and a doctorate in sociology from Arizona State University. When Ralph is not out on his motorcycle, he is blogging on mass communication issues at http://ralphehanson.com. He Twitters as ralphehanson.

# Brief Contents

# Contents

# Preface

The media world we inhabit is a constantly changing place. The world I inhabited growing up in the 1960s with three broadcast networks, landline phones with expensive long distance, AM radio, and family-owned newspapers had changed dramatically by the time the first edition of this book came out in 2004. Then there were four major broadcast networks, cable television was a dominant force, FM ruled radio broadcasting, cell phones had become commonplace, and newspapers were largely owned by major corporations.

Now, with the third edition of *Mass Communication: Living in a Media World* coming out, the rate of change continues to accelerate. As I write this in the winter of 2009–2010, the nation's largest cable and Internet provider is in the process of buying NBC, one of the original broadcast television networks; music is moving from terrestrial broadcast stations to digital satellite and Internet-based delivery systems; mobile phones are becoming a hub for delivery of a wide range of media from text messages to television shows; and newspapers are shutting down or looking for new ways of making money through electronic delivery. Even as this book goes to press, intense speculation surrounds what the winning platform will be for delivering electronic books. (Right now, Amazon's Kindle is leading devices from Sony and Barnes & Noble, but Apple's new iPad tablet computer is assumed by many to be the next big thing for electronic publishing.)

Yet with all this change taking place, some things remain constant. Many of the defining moments of our lives continue to come from our shared experiences with the media. It could be the death of a global pop star witnessed through wall-to-wall television coverage, the thrill of a sports victory viewed streaming on the Internet, the blockbuster movie as the backdrop to a first date, or hearing a song from the summer you turned sixteen.

For my generation, it was the moon walk. Parents all across the United States let their nine-year-olds stay up way past their bedtimes to watch on television the biggest show of their lives—*Apollo 11* astronaut Neil Armstrong setting foot on the moon. More recently my journalism students bring up the Oklahoma City bombing, the first Gulf War, or the explosion of the space shuttle *Challenger*. On September 11, 2001, my fifth-grade son and his classmates sat mesmerized by news coverage of the airplanes crashing into the World Trade Center twin towers, the Pentagon, and a field in southwestern Pennsylvania. Some parents questioned whether their children ought to have watched these events, but my son said, "We begged the teacher to keep the TV on. We had to know."

Then there are the myriad trivial aspects of everyday life that come from our time with the media: the perfect pair of vintage Levi's found in the shopping magazine *Lucky*, William Shatner's version of the song "Common People" on the Coverville podcast, or arguments about the merits of the Bowl Championship Series versus a college football playoff on the Internet.

In my first job as a college professor, I taught a course in media effects. On the first day of class, a student raised his hand and asked, "When do we get to the part where we talk about how television turns people into zombies?" His question has stayed with me through the years because it represents the view many people have about the media. The student's attitude has been fostered by media critics who have an agenda—getting elected to office, getting a regulation approved, promoting a product, or even pushing a moral choice. I have long taken the view that the successful study of mass communication is also a journey of self-awareness. We are students of media and also players in a media world.

A study conducted by Fairfield Research suggests that Americans spend nearly 70 percent of their waking hours in contact with one mass medium or another. The media are a central aspect of our lives, and many worry about the influence of these institutions.

This book views the media in our world not as isolated institutions that somehow "do something" to us, but rather as forces that are central to how we live, work, and play. The media are not outside influences; they are part of who we are. To emphasize this perspective, key topics including diversity, media effects, and ethics are incorporated throughout the book, though there are separate chapters on media effects and on media ethics. In this third edition of *Mass Communication: Living in a Media World*, I have worked to address fully the changes taking place since the turn of the twenty-first century. Issues such as the collapse of the newspaper industry, the rise of mobile media, the growth of integrated marketing communication, the emergence of video games as a mass medium, and the continuing consolidation of media ownership have been integrated throughout the book. The book is also technologically savvy, assimilating the presence of digital media into the text as seamlessly and boldly as these same media have permeated our daily lives.

My students over the years have told me that they remember information better if it is presented as a story, and I strive to be a storyteller. The narrative style of this book will help motivate students to do the reading and facilitate their recall of the material. Many of the "Test Your Media Literacy" exercises are based on writing assignments I've used in large lecture sections of my class, as well as in more writing-intensive online and small lecture sections. These exercises connect the material from the book to the media that students use every day, and students say that these assignments make them really think about how they experience the media.

# ABOUT THE THIRD EDITION

From mobile media devices to digital cable, the pervasiveness of mass communication in our daily lives complicates our ability to understand the media's rich history of technical, cultural, sociological, political, economic, and artistic achievements. *Mass Communication: Living in a Media World* reveals the forces that drive the industry while at the same time motivating readers to think critically about how they consume media. It uses compelling stories and examples drawn from everyday life. Readers are encouraged to consider the media industry from the inside out and, in so doing, to explore the many dimensions of mass communication that operate in our society.

My chief goal in writing this third edition, in addition to comprehensively updating the material, was to reflect the big changes taking place within the media industry while continuing to strengthen the media literacy focus of the second edition. Here's what's new:

1. *A revised chapter on the news industry.* Chapter 6, on newspapers, has been renamed "Newspapers and the News." Of course, the chapter discusses the many changes in the newspaper industry, with profitability declining and a significant number of papers going out of business. But it also looks at how the news business is changing, with newspapers and other news organizations becoming "brands" rather than delivery systems tied to a particular medium. The chapter also brings together news media history that was formerly spread across several chapters. So we now see the rise of radio and television news in context with the changes that took place in newspapers in the 1930s, 40s, 50s, and 60s.

2. *A comprehensive look at mobile media throughout the book.* Mobile phones, smart phones, iPods, Blackberries, iPhones, and netbooks are all becoming significant ways for people—especially young people—to access media content on the go. We used to think of online media as something that was accessed over the Internet using computers hooked up to wires. Increasingly, however, people are accessing media content using mobile devices rather than place-based media. Chapter 10, "The Internet: Mass Communication Gets Personal," looks at the birth of Twitter and how it has expanded the connection between mobile media and the Internet. Chapter 15, "Global Media: Communication Around The World," looks at how mobile social media was the major channel for news flowing out of India during the Mumbai terror attacks in 2008.

3. *A new section on integrated marketing communication.* Chapter 11, on advertising, has been updated to include a new section on integrated marketing communication (IMC). IMC is a growing approach to strategic communication that integrates advertising, public relations, sales promotion, and interactive media. The section examines how Denny's

restaurants used a Super Bowl–based IMC campaign in 2009 to help draw lapsed customers back to the chain.

4. *A new section on video games as mass communication.* Video game consoles have become a major channel for delivering media content, including game-based advertising, worldwide interaction, and elaborate games that can out-gross major movies. In recognition of this shift, I include a new section on the influence of consoles and video games in Chapter 10, "The Internet: Mass Communication Gets Personal."

5. *A reorganization of Part I—Introduction to the Media.* "Mass Communication Effects: How Society and Media Interact" is now Chapter 2, and "The Media Business: Consolidation, Globalization, and the Long Tail" is now Chapter 3. Switching the order of these chapters was made at the suggestion of several users who said that the media and society chapter fit better immediately following the introduction to media literacy in Chapter 1. This also puts the chapter on the media business directly before the individual media chapters.

A number of key features of the book remain the same:

1. *The Seven Truths "they" don't want you to know about the media.* Throughout all fifteen chapters, the Seven Truths remind students about the media literacy principles laid out in Chapter 1. These concepts deal with what the media are, who controls the media, how media content is selected, why the media behave the way they do, and how society and the media interact with each other. The Seven Truths are as follows:

   ■ Truth One: The media are essential components of our lives.

   ■ Truth Two: There are no mainstream media.

   ■ Truth Three: Everything from the margin moves to the center.

   ■ Truth Four: Nothing's new: Everything that happened in the past will happen again.

   ■ Truth Five: New media are always scary.

   ■ Truth Six: Activism and analysis are not the same thing.

   ■ Truth Seven: There is no "they."

   The truths are presented in depth in the last section of Chapter 1, and they recur, where relevant, in the subsequent chapters to remind students of these concepts and also to serve as a springboard for discussions or for writing assignments. The truths emerged over several years as I found certain key ideas coming up repeatedly in my class lectures. For example, in Chapter 2, on media effects, students look at different types of bias that can appear in the media that go beyond the "liberal versus conservative" debate and are reminded of *Truth Six: Activism and analysis are not the same thing.* They are encouraged to look at who is charging the media with bias, and to ask what their motivations are for making such charges. Chapter 3, which looks at the media business, uses *Truth Seven: There is no "they"* to take students beyond the simplistic question of whether Big Media control society and move them onto a more complex inquiry into who controls the media and their content. The Seven Truths were introduced in the second edition and have proved to be one of the book's most popular features.

2. *The significance of long-tail media economics.* As important as the big media companies are, the so-called long-tail media are continuing to turn the industry on its head. Unlike the big companies, which try to focus on selling a limited number of blockbuster movies, books, CDs, or programs to a large number of people, long-tail media provide a huge range of specialized content to smaller groups, which in the aggregate constitute a large number of people. The concept of long-tail media has been popularized by *Wired* magazine editor Chris Anderson, and this third edition contains expanded discussion of how the long tail affects just about every aspect of the media business. The concept of the long tail is discussed in depth in Chapter 3, on the media business, and is then expanded upon throughout the remaining chapters. For example, in Chapter 7, "Audio: Music and Talk Across Media," we look at how established musician Katrina Leskanich, formerly of Katrina and the Waves, and the local West Virginia band Erik Goes to Germany use the same tools in the long-tail part of the audio industry to promote and distribute their music. And in Chapter 4, "Books: The Birth of the Mass Media," we examine how e-book readers such as Amazon's Kindle are enhancing the distribution of self-published books.

3. *Each chapter still features people-focused opening vignettes that make key pedagogical points.* The opening chapter starts off with a look at how the news of Michael Jackson's death broke first online and then went on to dominate legacy media coverage for weeks to come; the movie chapter now opens by discussing how Atlanta-based filmmaker Tyler Perry has quietly become the sixth highest paid person in Hollywood with his string of hit movies about African American families and faith; and the media law chapter begins with the little-known story of how Barbara Ringer created modern copyright law.

4. *Discussions of media effects, diversity, and ethics are woven into every chapter.* These central themes of *Mass Communication: Living in a Media World* are too important to be isolated in a single chapter. Diversity in the media is covered in two ways—by discussing the importance of women

and minorities in both the business and content sides of the media, and by looking at the roles the media have played in social change. For example, Chapter 6, "Newspapers and the News," has sections devoted to minority, gay, and alternative news outlets; Chapter 7, "Audio: Music and Talk Across Media," looks at how rock 'n' roll brought black and white music traditions together; and Chapter 9, "Television: Broadcast and Beyond," looks at the growing roles of racial and ethnic minorities in broadcasting, including the role of the Spanish-language television network Univision—the nation's fifth-largest broadcast network—and of cable network Black Entertainment Television. The book also looks at the role of the media in social change. For example, Chapter 12, "Public Relations: Interactions, Relationships, and the News," has a section examining how civil rights leaders such as Martin Luther King Jr. used public relations techniques in the 1950s and 1960s to further their cause.

5. *Comprehensive coverage is offered at a manageable length.* The book is still fifteen chapters long to avoid bloat and to fit a standard semester schedule for both teachers and students.

6. *Great content at a reasonable price.* One of the most important continuing features for the third edition is its price. New copies of the third edition of *Mass Communication: Living in a Media World* will likely cost students less than used copies of most competing titles. And even with this significant price advantage, the book covers topics in greater depth and still offers a rich assortment of photos, tables, and figures. The only thing not included is full-color glitz.

## ORGANIZATION

The book is organized into five parts, each examining critical dimensions that comprise the world of mass communication:

*Part I: Introduction to the Media* presents the institutions, social effects, and business of the media. Chapter 1, "Living in a Media World," discusses the communication process, the development of mass communication, the concepts of media literacy, and the Seven Truths. Chapter 2, "Mass Communication Effects: How Society and Media Interact," looks at the history of media effects, ways of approaching media effects, and theories of media and society. Chapter 3, "The Media Business: Consolidation, Globalization, and the Long Tail," examines how the media developed as a business in the United States, takes a unique in-depth look at each of the world's six biggest media companies, and then turns to how new media production and distribution techniques are bringing massive changes to the industry.

*Part II: Print Media* explores what has traditionally been the paper-oriented print media. Chapter 4, "Books: The Birth of the Mass Media," examines the development of mass literacy and mass communication, the development and influence of print, and the future of the book industry. Chapter 5, "Magazines: The Power of Words and Images," covers the many types of specialized magazines as well as idealized images of men and women presented in magazines, the conflict between advertisers and editorial content, controversial teen magazines, and the future of the magazine industry. Chapter 6, "Newspapers and the News: Reflection of a Democratic Society," takes a comprehensive look at the history of the news industry, including radio and television, as well as newspapers. It examines how the newspaper and news industry is changing to match the changing media and economic environments. It looks at the role of newspapers and the news in a democratic society but also considers their entertainment functions and the relevance of newspapers in the information age.

*Part III: Electronic Media* covers the media of sound and motion. Chapter 7, "Audio: Music and Talk Across Media," looks at how the digital revolution has brought together terrestrial radio, satellite radio, podcasting, Webcasting, digital downloads, file sharing, and the recording industry into a converged medium. The chapter includes material on the racial integration of music and the role of music in the lives of young people. It takes an extensive look at how long-tail media tools are making widespread distribution of music available from lesser-known artists. Chapter 8, "Movies: Mass Producing Entertainment," addresses the continual conflict among the movie industry, its varied audiences, and the desire of different groups to control the content of movies. It also looks at how digital technology is changing the production, financing, and promotion of movies. Chapter 9, "Television: Broadcast and Beyond," considers television as two distinct media—broadcast and cable/satellite. Among the topics covered in the chapter are concerns about diversity of television content, control of the industry, the influence of television on society, and how digital technology is forcing television networks to radically change their methods of distributing programs to viewers. Chapter 10, "The Internet: Mass Communication Gets Personal," looks at the revolutionary new medium that is now reaching the majority of American homes. This chapter focuses on how the Internet makes use of virtually every level of communication, how it puts consumers in control of what materials they choose to see, how online searching is becoming a new medium of targeted communication, and how long-tail technology is changing how we select and receive news. It also looks at the emergence of video games as a new form of mass communication and the role of mobile media in delivering interaction with online content.

*Part IV: Strategic Communication* covers the advertising and public relations industries. Chapter 11, "Advertising: Selling a Message," explains how advertising, national media, and nationally available products all evolved together; the elements of the advertising process; the roles advertising plays in a media society; and how digital technology is forcing changes to the traditional separation of programming and advertising. It also looks at the emergence of integrated marketing communication and the growing use of advertising to highly targeted audiences using mobile devices. Chapter 12, "Public Relations: Interactions, Relationships, and the News," looks at the public relations process, the various publics organizations need to work with, the symbiotic relationship between the news and the public relations industry, and the use of public relations in political activism.

*Part V: Regulation and Control of the Media* looks at the institutions, conventions, and rules that regulate and control the media in the United States and around the world. Chapter 13, "Media Law: Free Speech and Fairness," delves into the development and power of the laws that regulate the communication industry in the United States, as well as the limitations on free speech that have come about in the post-9/11 era. Chapter 14, "Media Ethics: Truthfulness, Fairness, and Standards of Decency," discusses the basic philosophical underpinnings of media and journalistic ethics. It then addresses how these principles apply to the news, entertainment, advertising, and public relations industries. The book concludes with Chapter 15, "Global Media: Communication Around the World." This chapter critiques normative theories of the press from around the world and then looks at how the media operate around the globe. It also looks at how emergent mobile technology is changing how news flows around the world.

Most of the chapters about the individual print or electronic media are organized around the same basic structure. Following an opening vignette and chapter timeline come four major sections:

- The first section looks at how the medium developed along with major changes in society and culture. More than a history of the medium, this section considers how societal, cultural, and technological elements came together to create the medium we have today.

- The second section focuses on how the medium operates within the business and social world. This section looks at why the media behave the way they do within our economy.

- The third section turns to current issues and controversies between the medium and society. These often include issues surrounding media effects, such as the concern about the influence of fashion magazines on young women's body image, or the influence of rock and rap lyrics on listeners.

- The fourth section looks at the future of the medium, including the effects of digital technology and the long tail.

# SPECIAL FEATURES OF THE TEXT

■ *Chapter-opening vignettes.* Chapters open with an intriguing story about people in the media. Drawn from newsworthy events, these accounts provide a powerful narrative thread exemplifying the major themes of each chapter. They convey the excitement and relevance of media studies and critical inquiry by way of those whose lives have been profoundly affected by the media. For example, the opening vignette in Chapter 3 looks at how Apple founder Steve Jobs took his company from being a failing computer manufacturer to a major media player; Chapter 4 looks at how authors James Frey and Margaret Seltzer built best-selling memoirs out of a fabric of lies, and how they were found out. Chapter 6 tells how the staff of the New Orleans *Times-Picayune* rode out Hurricane Katrina so that they could continue to turn out a newspaper throughout the United States' worst weather disaster in modern times. Chapter 9 recounts how *Daily Show* host Jon Stewart continues to skewer cable news hosts by asking them the pointed questions no one else will. Chris Martin, vice president for university relations for West Virginia University, is profiled in Chapter 12. Her story demonstrates how online and mobile media have changed the practice of public relations.

■ *Chapter timelines.* The history of mass media is an engaging storyline that defines the industry. Major events in the development of mass communication are summarized in an illustrated timeline in each chapter and placed within the context of other major historical dates. This approach allows students to integrate their knowledge of world history with the parallel development of mass media. The timelines preview important dates in mass media history that are detailed elsewhere in the chapter.

■ *"Test Your Media Literacy" boxes.* Introductory texts often are loaded with sidebars and boxes that feature anecdotal information or stories. While this material is interesting, students see it as expendable—as portions of the chapter that provide relief from heavy reading. They simply skip the boxes because they're rarely ever tested on them. In an effort to streamline the text and encourage critical thinking, I created one set of boxes directly relevant to the theme of the book. The idea is to cultivate critical media consumers, and there is no better way to do so than to model this type of critical thinking. The "Test Your Media Literacy" feature presents students with current research, interviews, or noteworthy events relating to the practice of mass communication and combines them with a set of questions that challenge students to evaluate and analyze the story. Questions model critical thinking by asking the following types of questions: Who is the source? What is he/she saying? What evidence is there? What do you and your classmates think about the topic? The readings are engaging and fun, but more important, the questions get students to do more than summarize—they encourage them to think. In addition, the readings are supplemented with up-to-the-minute additions and further related information through my blog at http://ralphehanson.com.

- *Key terms.* I have paid particular attention to presenting understandable and accurate definitions of all key terms. These boldface terms are defined in the margins. Furthermore, a list of key terms—with page references—comes at the end of each chapter to make the terms easy to locate. Finally, the comprehensive glossary at the back of the book includes the definitions of all of the textbook's key terms.

- *Chapter summary.* Each chapter concludes with a brief recap of important points to assist students in reviewing important themes, events, and concepts.

- *Concept review.* Central concepts are listed at the end of each chapter, providing students with a mini study guide. The central concepts are ideas that go beyond one or two vocabulary words and may be developed throughout an entire section or chapter.

- *Notes.* A comprehensive chapter-by-chapter list of endnotes is provided at the conclusion of the book.

- Living in a Media World *blog.* Since 2004, I've been writing the blog *Living in a Media World,* which covers the entire field of mass communication. Located at **http://ralphehanson.com,** *Living in a Media World* has been linked to by national Web sites, including FishbowlDC, Wonkette, Gawker, Eat The Press, and *USA Today*'s On Deadline. One of the biggest benefits to you from the blog is that it provides a single destination for up-to-date material on the topics covered in this book. As I write this, Comcast is working on its purchase of NBC Universal from General Electric. You'll be able to follow this story as it develops, along with breaking stories on new media devices, closing media, changes to the music industry, new trends in advertising, and developments in social media. Among the many topics I've covered are deliberate disruptions on live television to grab media attention, the debate over model size taking place in fashion/beauty/lifestyle magazines, and how journalists love the number 50,000. (Hint: Any time a journalist uses the number 50,000, you can bet that he's guessing at how many of something there are.) The blog is also a great source of images, sound, and video to use in your classes.

  Along with the lively commentary and news you would expect from a blog, my site also has an entire section devoted to this book. Instead of including rapidly dated Web links within the text of the book, students and teachers can find chapter-by-chapter entries of supplemental readings and links tied to exercises and topics in the book (including the full story on the number 50,000!). So check out the link at the top of my blog. By the way, this will not be a static set of links. They'll be updated regularly with new developments in the media world.

# ANCILLARIES

## Student Companion Web Site

CQ Press has created a student Web site customized to the text that provides chapter summaries, objectives, and review questions with response boxes so that students can e-mail answers to their instructors for credit or for a grade. There are also key-term interactive flashcards, self-grading quizzes (with the ability to e-mail quiz results to a professor), and annotated Web-linked activities and critical-thinking exercises like those found in the "Test Your Media Literacy" boxes, for which, again, students can e-mail their findings and responses to an instructor. On the home page, users will find two incredibly useful resources. One is a link (and RSS feed) to daily headlines from the *New York Times* and *USA Today*. These headlines are updated whenever new stories are posted to the site and provide students with a snapshot of important media news each day. The other is a one-of-a-kind video that takes students on a media tour inside the converged newsroom of *USA Today*. With reporter (and CQ veteran) David Rapp working with a team at *USA Today*, viewers can follow a story from inception to final product, with its print and online publication. The idea is to show the dynamic newsmaking process as it happens today—while looking over the shoulders of reporters, editors, and graphic designers—rather than sitting through an interview with a talking head. You can find all these resources at **http://masscomm.cqpress.com.**

## Instructor Resources

Additional electronic resources have been developed specifically for the instructor, including

- *Instructor's Resource Manual.* Over the years, I have taught an introduction to mass communication course as a small lecture class, as a large lecture class (350 students at 8:30 in the morning), and as an online extended learning class. I have written the *Instructor's Resource Manual* based on these different formats. It contains links and suggestions for up-to-date teaching materials, lecture starters tied to the chapters that go beyond what's in the book, learning objectives, additional exercises, suggestions for using the Seven Truths in class, homework ideas (along with suggestions for grading them!), teaching outlines, and alternative approaches to organizing the class.

- *Computerized test bank.* This is a testing resource with more than 800 multiple-choice, true/false, fill-in-the-blank, short-answer, and essay questions. The test bank, written by me, provides many multiple-choice and true/false questions to test students' critical-thinking skills along with their recall of factual knowledge. These questions come formatted, ready to go into the test-generating software Respondus, which many teachers use to put together exams for online classes. Many of the questions have been tried out over the past year by students in my own introductory courses. The test bank has been updated fully to reflect the changes in the third edition.

- *PowerPoint lecture slides.* The PowerPoint slides feature lecture points that follow the chapter structure of the book.

# ACKNOWLEDGMENTS

I want to thank all my students at the University of Nebraska at Kearney for letting me test out materials from this book on them. They have always been more than willing to tell me what works and what doesn't. I would also like to thank the many journalists and media professionals who spoke with me about what they do, particularly Cody Cheesebrough, founder of the band Erik Goes to Germany; Brian Ibbott of Coverville Media; Chris Martin, vice president for university relations at West Virginia University; as well as journalists Danny Glover and Jeff Young. I would like to express a special thanks to the University of Nebraska at Omaha graduate student Charley Reed for his research work on video games as mass media and on news coverage of the 2009 Iranian elections. I would also like to thank the many professors who use this book and who have provided me with invaluable feedback, particularly Chris Allen, Dolores Hill Sierra, and Brian Steffen.

A panel of expert reviewers was instrumental in shaping the direction of this book, and I wish to thank them:

Herbert Amey, *Ohio University*

Frederick R. Blevens, *Florida International University*

Joan Blumberg, *Drexel University*

Jeff Boone, *Angelo State University*

Larry L. Burriss, *Middle Tennessee State University*

Meta G. Carstarphen, *University of Oklahoma*

Tom Clanin, *California State University–Fullerton*

Lance Clark, *Huntington University*

Barbara J. DeSanto, *Maryville University*

Roger Desmond, *University of Hartford*

Jules d'Hemecourt (late), *Louisiana State University*

Michael Eberts, *Glendale Community College*

Anthony J. Ferri, *University of Nevada–Las Vegas*

Fred Fitch, *Eastern Kentucky University*

Jennifer Fleming, *California State University–Long Beach*

Donna Gough, *East Central University*

Meredith Guthrie, *University of Pittsburgh*

Louisa Ha, *Bowling Green State University*

Wendy J. Hajjar, *Tulane University*

Elizabeth Blanks Hindman, *Washington State University*

Sharon Hollenback, *Syracuse University*

Patricia Holmes, *University of Louisiana–Lafayette*

James L. Hoyt, *University of Wisconsin*

Kim Landon, *Utica College*

Phyllis Larsen, *University of Nebraska–Lincoln*

Martin P. LoMonaco, *Neumann University*

Alfred L. Lorenz, *Loyola University*

Karen Smith McGrath, *College of Saint Rose*

Michael Meadows, *Griffith University*

Eileen R. Meehan, *Southern Illinois University–Carbondale*

Steve Miller, *Livingston College of Rutgers*

James C. Mitchell, *University of Arizona*

Andrew Moemeka, *Central Connecticut State University*

Jennifer Mullen, *Colorado State University–Pueblo*

Robin Newcomer, *Olympic College*

Sandy Nichols, *Towson University*

Mark Plenke, *Normandale Community College*

Felicia Jones Ross, *Ohio State University*

Marshel D. Rossow, *Minnesota State University*

Enid Sefcovic, *Broward College*

Danny Shipka, *Louisiana State University*

Cathy Stablein, *College of DuPage*

Venise Wagner, *San Francisco State University*

Hazel Warlaumont, *California State–Fullerton*

Patsy G. Watkins, *University of Arkansas*

Mark West, *University of North Carolina–Asheville*

Jan Whitt, *University of Colorado–Boulder*

Marvin Williams, *Kingsborough Community College*

David Wolfe, *Mountain View College*

I owe a great debt to people at CQ Press who are not afraid of trying something different—an introduction to mass communication textbook with greater depth and a significantly lower price for students. I would like to thank John Jenkins, president and publisher; Brenda Carter, executive director of college publishing; Charisse Kiino, editorial director, college publishing; and Matthew Simmons of Myself Included Design, the designer of the book's cover. I would also like especially to give thanks to Dwain Smith, development editor; Amy Marks, copy editor; Christina Mueller, photo researcher; and Gwenda Larsen, production editor, who have been so patient with me over the past several months.

Finally, I would like to thank my wife, Pam; my sons, Erik and Andrew; my parents, Roger and Marilyn; and my mother-in-law, Barbara Andrews.

*Ralph F. Hanson*

# MASS COMMUNICATION

# Living in a Media World

**On Thursday,** June 25, 2009, *Washington Post* media reporter Howard Kurtz used the microblogging tool Twitter to announce his current status: "Slow morning. No new Iran protests, no new sex scandals. Might have to do some reporting." But by late afternoon Kurtz, and virtually every other reporter on the planet, would have put aside the contested Iranian election and a scandal surrounding the South Carolina governor to report on the sudden death of superstar Michael Jackson. For the next two weeks, the death of the self-proclaimed King of Pop would dominate the news industry. But it would also provide stark evidence of the rapidly changing media world we all live in.

Jackson was fifty years old at the time of his death, and he had been a star for more than forty years. He has been credited with helping to create the current era of popular music in which stars need to be great dancers and performers as well as being gifted musicians. He also had generated a fandom that transcended age, race, and nationality.[1] Jackson was undoubtedly a superstar in the music, video, and pop culture world. He had sold 750 million albums—that means 2.5 albums for every man, woman, and child in the United States.[2] But in addition to being famous for groundbreaking albums and music videos, Jackson also was famous for his eccentricities and infamous for charges of child molestation.

**R.I.P. Michael Jackson 1958-2009**

**Michael Jackson Dies**

Posted Jun 25th 2009 5:20PM by TMZ Staff

We've just learned **Michael Jackson** has died. He was 50.

Michael suffered a cardiac arrest earlier this afternoon at his Holmby Hills home and paramedics were unable to revive him. We're told when paramedics arrived Jackson had no pulse and they never got a pulse back.

A source tells us Jackson was dead when paramedics arrived. A cardiologist at UCLA tells TMZ Jackson died of cardiac arrest.

Once at the hospital, the staff tried to resuscitate him but he was completely unresponsive.

...rce inside the hospital told us there was "absolute ... after Jackson arrived. People who were with the ...re screaming, "You've got to save him! You've got

...e staff members at Jackson's home called 911

**EXCLUSIVE**

The news of Jackson's death broke in a way that was as controversial as his life. The story of his cardiac arrest and subsequent death was first reported by the tabloidy TMZ.com, a celebrity gossip Web site owned by two divisions of Time Warner. TMZ's initial post of Jackson's death went up at 5:20 p.m. eastern time, six minutes before the coroner officially declared Jackson dead, and more than an hour before most other news outlets would report the King of Pop had died.[3]

Jackson's death led to a ripple that could be felt across the Internet:

- The average load time for stories at news Web sites doubled.
- Online fights emerged over whether Jackson's Wikipedia page would list him as alive or dead.

- Twitter saw a doubling of the normal level of tweets per second being posted.
- AOL's instant messaging service went down for forty minutes after Jackson died because of the huge amount of traffic Jackson's death generated.[4]

Legacy media outlets, such as the major television networks, were reluctant to attribute to TMZ, looking instead for what they saw as better sources of the news. "There's still this residual . . . instinct to think 'Oh, it's just TMZ, let's wait for The Associated Press or *The New York Times* or *The Los Angeles Times* before we can say it's true,'" said press critic and journalist Kurt Anderson. "I don't think in, say, five years, that this will be the case."[5]

TMZ was founded in 2005 and is owned by the same folks who own *Time*, *Sports Illustrated*, CNN, and *People*. This was not the first big scoop for the upstart site. It broke the stories of misbehavior by actors such as Mel Gibson, Alec Baldwin, and Christian Bale, and many people turned to it for news when Anna Nicole Smith died in 2007. The site has been accused by critics of paying for information, something that is generally frowned on in journalism circles, though the practice is common enough in the celebrity tabloid business.[6]

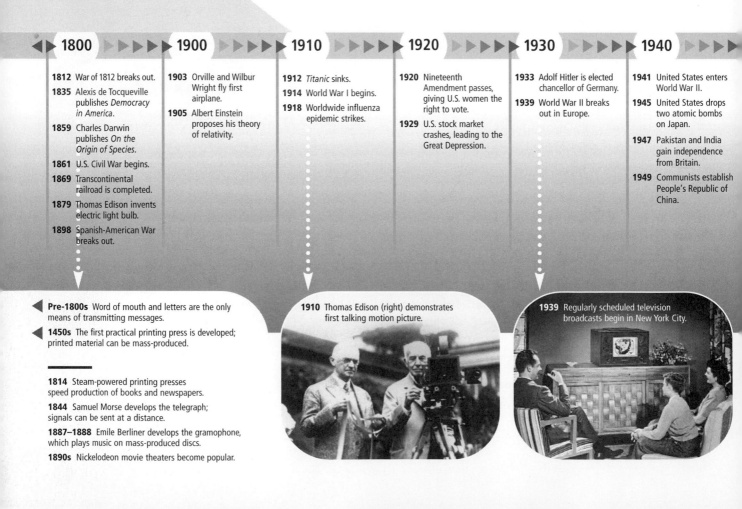

| 1800 | 1900 | 1910 | 1920 | 1930 | 1940 |
|---|---|---|---|---|---|
| **1812** War of 1812 breaks out. | **1903** Orville and Wilbur Wright fly first airplane. | **1912** *Titanic* sinks. | **1920** Nineteenth Amendment passes, giving U.S. women the right to vote. | **1933** Adolf Hitler is elected chancellor of Germany. | **1941** United States enters World War II. |
| **1835** Alexis de Tocqueville publishes *Democracy in America*. | **1905** Albert Einstein proposes his theory of relativity. | **1914** World War I begins. | **1929** U.S. stock market crashes, leading to the Great Depression. | **1939** World War II breaks out in Europe. | **1945** United States drops two atomic bombs on Japan. |
| **1859** Charles Darwin publishes *On the Origin of Species*. | | **1918** Worldwide influenza epidemic strikes. | | | **1947** Pakistan and India gain independence from Britain. |
| **1861** U.S. Civil War begins. | | | | | **1949** Communists establish People's Republic of China. |
| **1869** Transcontinental railroad is completed. | | | | | |
| **1879** Thomas Edison invents electric light bulb. | | | | | |
| **1898** Spanish-American War breaks out. | | | | | |

**Pre-1800s** Word of mouth and letters are the only means of transmitting messages.

**1450s** The first practical printing press is developed; printed material can be mass-produced.

**1814** Steam-powered printing presses speed production of books and newspapers.

**1844** Samuel Morse develops the telegraph; signals can be sent at a distance.

**1887–1888** Emile Berliner develops the gramophone, which plays music on mass-produced discs.

**1890s** Nickelodeon movie theaters become popular.

**1910** Thomas Edison (right) demonstrates first talking motion picture.

**1939** Regularly scheduled television broadcasts begin in New York City.

Terrence Samuel, an editor for TheRoot.com, notes that although TMZ is not a traditional news outlet, it got the scoop on Jackson using traditional techniques: "In some ways, despite all the tweeting and Facebooking, what you had here was a very old-time media scoop where somebody had better sources."[7] *Rolling Stone* contributing editor Touré says that journalists and the public are going to have to get used to getting news from a much wider range of sources than in the past. "The mode of delivery doesn't make it not journalism or journalism," he says. "A tweet can be journalism. . . . TMZ was ahead of the story and they were right. And if that doesn't validate them, what will?"[8]

For the next two weeks, news about Jackson's death was unavoidable. According to the Project for Excellence in Journalism, during the day following Jackson's death, 60 percent of the news coverage was about Jackson. And that does not include the prime-time coverage of Jackson on the broadcast television networks. On the cable news networks, 93 percent of the coverage from the time of Jackson's death on Thursday through Friday night was of Jackson.[9] Although his dominance slipped a bit the following week, Jackson's death was still the biggest story on television.

## ▶▶ 1950 ▶▶▶▶▶ 1960 ▶▶▶▶▶ 1970 ▶▶▶▶▶ 1980 ▶▶▶▶▶ 1990 ▶▶▶▶▶ 2000 ▶▶▶▶

**1950** Korean War begins.

**1953** Francis Crick and James Watson discover structure of DNA.

**1957** Soviet Union launches spacecraft *Sputnik I*.

**1963** Martin Luther King Jr. delivers "I Have a Dream" speech during Washington, D.C., civil-rights march.

**1969** Neil Armstrong walks on the moon.

**1974** U.S. president Richard Nixon resigns due to Watergate scandal.

**1975** Vietnam War ends.

**1977** Apple II personal computer is introduced.

**1978** First test-tube baby is born.

**1983** First HIV/AIDS cases are documented.

**1985** Ozone hole is discovered over Antarctica.

**1986** Space shuttle *Challenger* explodes.

**1989** The Berlin Wall falls.

**1991** Soviet Union disbands.

**1993** European Union is formed.

**1994** Nelson Mandela is elected president of South Africa.

**1997** Diana, Princess of Wales, dies in car accident.

**2001** Al Qaida attacks World Trade Center and Pentagon.

**2003** United States invades Iraq.

**2003** Human genome project is completed.

**2005** Terrorists bomb London's transport system.

**2005** Hurricane Katrina hits the U.S. Gulf Coast.

**2008** Barack Obama is elected U.S. president.

**1969** The first computers are connected to the fledgling Internet.

**1984** Apple introduces its latest generation of personal computers—the Macintosh—with a memorable Super Bowl ad.

**1991** The World Wide Web is publicly released.

**2001** Apple unveils the first iPod.

**2004** Mark Zuckerberg (pictured) founds Facebook.

**2008** American consumers spend more time with media they pay for than with advertising-supported media.

Was the Jackson story over-covered? Perhaps, but as *Time* magazine founder Henry Luce has been credited with saying, "People make news, and dead people make more news, and dead superstars make even more news."[10] The wall-to-wall coverage of Jackson's death hasn't always been the standard for celebrity deaths. As Emily Hedges of the Newseum points out, *The CBS Evening News* didn't report Elvis' death until six-and-a-half minutes into the evening newscast.[11]

Regardless of critics charging that television, in particular, over-covered the Jackson story, there can be no doubt at all that the public was interested. The three prime-time specials that aired on CBS, NBC, and ABC the night Jackson died drew a total audience of 21.3 million viewers. That compares to 8.2 million viewers for a *CSI: Miami* rerun a week earlier, or 4.7 million people for a health care special by President Barack Obama.[12] Jackson's memorial service drew more than 31 million viewers spread across eighteen networks that carried the event live. In addition to the television viewership, MSNBC had 19 million video streams fed by its Web site the day of the service, a record for the news site, and CNN had more than 4 million streams going out during the service. ABC News had close to 6 million streams, and FOXNews.com had more than 3 million.[13]

Jackson's death will have a lasting impact on a number of levels. At its most obvious, Jackson's death was the loss of an amazing, if controversial, talent. Jackson's album *Thriller* and the groundbreaking videos that accompanied it changed the face of popular music. But the reports of his death were funneled to an online and mobile generation through channels that were not even thought about when Jackson's career began. In the week's following Jackson's death, TMZ continued to scoop the so-called mainstream media with accurate details about the police investigation of the cause of Jackson's death.[14]

# LEVELS OF COMMUNICATION

As the flow of news about Michael Jackson's death illustrates so clearly, we no longer rely just on conventional media to engage in the various levels of communication. While television, newspapers, and radio are still significant, they are increasingly being supplemented by channels that allow people to engage in multiple levels of communication at once.

Communication graduate student Charley Reed communicates a lot, and that communication is often flowing through Facebook, the popular social networking Web site. He uses it to plan social events, talk with his friends and professors, and even drop birthday present hints to his parents. "When I go on Facebook, I'll check whether anyone has responded to a wall post or commented on my status," Charley says. "Next, I'll go through the news feed to see what people are up to. Then the last thing I'll do is change my status before I leave. I try to avoid the Twittering approach for my status; I know how annoying that can be to people. One of the last ones I did was on the song "Grounds for Divorce" by the British band Elbow. It was the theme song for the video game *Left for Dead*, and it reminded me that I used to listen to the band a few years ago, and it got me listening to the band again."[15]

When Charley logs on to Facebook, he's engaging in almost every possible level of communication, but before we try to analyze the levels of communication Charley is using, we need to define what communication is. Media scholar George Gerbner provides a simple definition: **Communication** is "social interaction through messages."[16] More plainly put, communication is how we interact with our entire world, whether through spoken words, written words, gestures, music, paintings, photographs, or dance. The important point is that communication is a *process*, not a static thing. Communication is an interaction that allows individuals, groups, and institutions to share ideas.

Media scholar and theorist Denis McQuail suggests that the various levels of communication can be viewed as a pyramid with a large base of intrapersonal communication where everyone is sending messages, building up to a peak of mass communication, at which a relatively small number of organizations or individuals are transmitting messages (see Figure 1.1).[17]

## Intrapersonal Communication

Communication at its most basic level is **intrapersonal communication**, which is really communication within the self. This is how we think and how we assign meaning to all the messages and events that surround our lives. It ranges from the simple act of smiling in response to the smell of a favorite food coming from the kitchen to the complex reaction to an unexpected proposal of

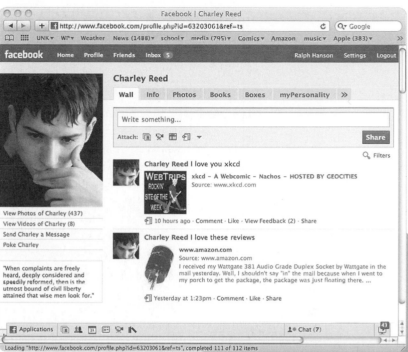

College student Charley Reed can communicate with his classmates, friends, and professors through his Facebook page.

**communication**

How we socially interact at a number of levels through messages.

**intrapersonal communication**

Communication you have with yourself. How you assign meaning to the world around you.

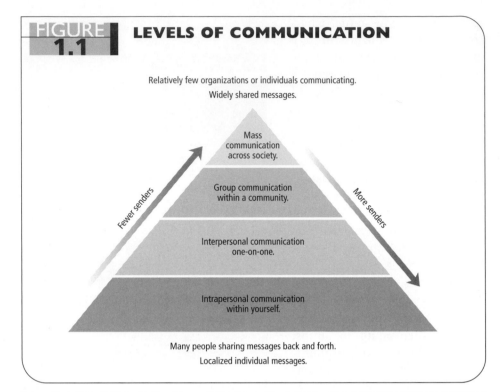

## FIGURE 1.1 LEVELS OF COMMUNICATION

Relatively few organizations or individuals communicating.
Widely shared messages.

Fewer senders

More senders

Mass communication across society.

Group communication within a community.

Interpersonal communication one-on-one.

Intrapersonal communication within yourself.

Many people sharing messages back and forth.
Localized individual messages.

*Source:* Denis McQuail, *McQuail's Mass Communication Theory*, 5th ed. (London: Sage Publications, 2005), 18. Reproduced by permission of Sage Publications. Copyright © Denis McQuail, 2005.

marriage. Feedback, or the response from the receiver of the message, is constant because we are always reflecting on what we have done and how we will react. Intrapersonal communication is the most prevalent form of communication and is, therefore, at the base of the pyramid. When Charley debates with himself as to whether a post about a personal relationship is really appropriate, he's engaging in intrapersonal communication.

## Interpersonal Communication

The next level on the pyramid is **interpersonal communication**, or one-on-one communication: "the intentional or accidental transmission of information through verbal or nonverbal message systems to another human being."[18] Interpersonal communication can be a conversation with a friend or a hug that tells your mother you love her. Like communication with the self, interpersonal communication is continual when others are around because we constantly send out messages, even if they consist of nothing more than body language indicating that we want to be left alone.

Interpersonal communication provides many opportunities for feedback. Your friend nods, raises an eyebrow, touches you on the arm, or simply answers.

**interpersonal communication**

Communication, either intentional or accidental, between two people. It can be verbal or nonverbal.

Not all interpersonal communication is done face-to-face, however. A telephone conversation, an instant message, an e-mail, even a greeting card can be interpersonal communication, though at a somewhat greater emotional distance than in a face-to-face conversation. When Charley sends a personal message over Facebook, sends an e-mail to a professor about a homework assignment, or talks to his roommate over breakfast, he's engaging in interpersonal communication.

## Group Communication

**Group communication** is near the top of the pyramid and has reached a level of unequal communication in which one person is communicating with an audience of two or more people. Group communication often has a leader and is more public than interpersonal communication. In a small group—say, a family at the dinner table or a coach with a basketball team—each individual has an opportunity to respond to the leader and is likely to do so. In a large group—like a 350-student lecture section of a university class—each individual still has an opportunity to respond but is unlikely to do so. Other situations test the boundaries of group communication, such as a Paul McCartney concert at a baseball stadium. With the amplifiers and multiple video screens, there is a high level of communication technology and limited possibilities for audience members to provide direct feedback to the performers, but there is still interaction between Sir Paul and the audience. Charley engages in group communication when he participates in a class discussion, cheers at a hockey game, or leaves a status update on his Facebook page. For example, he left an enthusiastic status update about the band Mastodon. His parents saw the update and bought him tickets to an upcoming Mastodon concert for his birthday.[19]

**group communication** Communication in which one person is communicating with an audience of two or more people. The roles of communicator and audience can be changing constantly.

**mass communication** When an individual or institution uses technology to send a message to a large, mixed audience, most of whose members are not known to the sender.

## Mass Communication

**Mass communication** is the pinnacle of the communication pyramid; it is a society-wide communication process in which an individual or institution uses technology to send messages to a large mixed audience, most of whose members are not known to the sender. Nationally broadcast speeches by politicians, stories about crime in the newspaper, and popular new novels are all forms of mass communication. These communications are fundamentally different from the forms described previously because the sender is separated in space, and possibly in time, from the receiver. Also, the audience is not really known to the communicator. When a communicator appears on television or writes an article for a newspaper, he or she doesn't know who will be listening or reading. What is more, the audience consists of many types of people. It might contain a young man in prison, an old woman in a nursing home, a child eating Cheerios for breakfast, or Charley getting ready to go to school. The message is communicated to all these people and to thousands or millions of others.[20]

Traditionally, mass communication has allowed only limited opportunities for feedback because the channels of communication are largely one-way—but with the rise of interactive communication networks, the opportunities for feedback are growing rapidly. Charley consumes a wide range of mass communication during his day, including watching the television series *House*, watching cable's *Adult Swim*, reading media theorist Marshall McLuhan, and discussing the band Elbow on Facebook.

## A Mix of Levels

The distinctions among the various levels of communication are useful, but don't assume that every instance of communication can automatically be placed in one category or another. In reality, there are frequent crossovers in the levels of communication. Consider the Internet: You can share information with a friend via e-mail. Through a Web-based journal, you can share your thoughts and interact with friends. With a listserv, an employer can communicate with employees throughout the world. And through Web sites and podcasts, messages can go out to the entire world. The same is true of a newspaper, in which a classified ad can carry a proposal of marriage, a notice of a group meeting, or a political manifesto. When Charley goes out to dinner with friends, they cheer when the hockey game being shown on the television gets exciting and talk about the game with each other, thus engaging in mass and group communication at the same time.

The purpose of this book is to help you better understand mass communication and the mass media. In the fifteen chapters of this book, we look at a variety of topics:

- The institutions that make up the media and how they function in and affect our society.
- Who owns and controls the media business.
- The media themselves, including books, magazines, newspapers, radio, recorded music, movies, television, and the Internet.
- The industries that support the media, including advertising and public relations.
- The laws and ethics that regulate and control the media.
- The roles the media play in countries and cultures around the world.

By the time you are finished, you will better understand what the media are, why they function as they do, and what roles they play in your life.

# ELEMENTS OF MASS COMMUNICATION

Although people often use the terms *mass communication* and *mass media* interchangeably, they are significantly different concepts. Mass communication is a process, whereas the **mass media** are simply the technological tools used to transmit the messages of mass communication.[21] Earlier in this chapter we defined *mass communication* as a society-wide communication process in which an individual or institution uses technology to send messages to a large mixed audience, most of whose members are not known to the sender. Let's now take a closer look at all the players in the mass communication process and at several models that describe how these elements interact with each other.

## The Players in the Mass Communication Process

There is an old way of describing mass communication known as the **Sender Message Channel Receiver (SMCR) or transmission model**. This transmission model does not do justice to the complexity of the mass communication process because it tends to portray mass communication as a largely one-directional flow of messages from the sender to the receiver rather than as a complex interaction where senders and receivers are constantly changing places. But the model is still useful in helping to identify all the players we will be working with throughout this text.

*The Sender.*    When critics talk about "the media" as a potent force, they are often talking about the ability of a few large corporations to control the messages that go out through the various channels of mass communication. These corporations, which are discussed in depth in Chapter 3, are the major senders in the mass communication process. They are the large, bureaucratic organizations that produce the complex messages we receive through the mass media, and they employ large numbers of people. If you look at the credits of a major movie, you'll see hundreds, if not thousands, of names listed. Even a relatively straightforward medium like a newspaper requires a substantial staff of writers, editors, graphic artists, photographers, computer specialists, printers, truck drivers, delivery people, janitors, librarians, circulation clerks, accountants, advertising salespeople, business managers, and a publisher.

As you may have already figured out, there are many more senders in addition to the major corporations. For example, although the majority of the most frequently visited Web sites are produced by large media organizations, the Internet has given rise to smaller, more intimate media without the accompanying structure and staff. For example, FiveThirtyEight.com, which had an impressive record in predicting the 2008 presidential primaries and general election, is operated by baseball and political statistician Nate Silver, assisted by one other person. (In case you were wondering, 538 is the total number of votes in the Electoral College.)[22] You may have acted as a "sender," too, just as

**mass media**
The technological tools, or channels, used to transmit the messages of mass communication.

**Sender Message Channel Receiver (SMCR) or transmission model**
A dated model that is still useful in identifying the players in the mass communication process.

Charley does when he writes an occasional guest post to your textbook author's blog.

Mass communication has generally been thought of as one-on-many communication, with few senders and many receivers, in contrast to interpersonal communication, which involves roughly equal numbers of senders and receivers. Sociologist C. Wright Mills wrote that the real power of the mass media is that they can control what topics are being covered and how much attention they receive. The most significant change brought about by the media in the United States, he said, was that public communication became a matter of sending information to a large number of receivers, rather than a dialogue between roughly equal numbers of senders and receivers.[23]

The balance of power between senders and receivers in the mass media has started to change in recent years, however, with the rise of bloggers as a force in the news business. **Bloggers** are people who post their thoughts on a regularly updated Web site. Bloggers started receiving significant notice in September 2004 when CBS's *60 Minutes* ran a story that supposedly showed that President George W. Bush had been criticized by his superior officer for poor work during his National Guard service. Within minutes of the story's airing, conservative bloggers, including those at Power Line and Little Green Footballs, started questioning the story, most notably because the memos used to support the allegations were forgeries. *CBS Evening News* anchor Dan Rather eventually had to resign over the resulting scandal, and bloggers started serving as a major source of media criticism whose voices could be heard as loudly as those in the mainstream media.[24]

*The Message.*    The **message** is the content being transmitted by the sender and reacted to by the receiver. Before a message can be transmitted, it must be encoded. **Encoding** requires at least two steps. First, the sender's ideas must be turned into a message: A script for a broadcast is drafted, a graphic is created, or a newspaper story is written. Then the message must be prepared for transmission: The script is taped and sent out over the air, the graphic is placed on a Web page, or the newspaper is printed.

Mass communication messages are transmitted rapidly to the receivers. Audience members can receive the message simultaneously, as they would in the case of a radio broadcast; at similar though not identical times, as in the case of a newspaper or magazine; and occasionally over an extended period, as in the case of a CD, movie, or video. In addition to being transmitted rapidly, mass communication messages are available to a wide audience. Mass communication messages also tend to be transient—here today and gone tomorrow. The newspapers and magazines are recycled, a new movie is showing at the theater, or a broadcast ends and a new one airs the next day. Even though the message can be stored in the form of a computer file or videotape, it is generally replaced when something new comes along. The receiver's attention fades even if the physical item remains.

**bloggers**
People who post their thoughts, typically with the most recent posts at the top of the page, on a regularly updated Web site.

**message**
The content being transmitted by the sender to the receiver.

**encoding**
The process of turning the sender's ideas into a message and preparing the message for transmission.

TEST YOUR MEDIA LITERACY

## When Media Coverage Is a Life or Death Issue

Jon Krakauer was out of his tent and on his way to the top of Mount Everest several hours before dawn on Friday, May 10, 1996. The journalist was just one of dozens of climbers trying to reach the summit at 29,028 feet. Climbing Everest had been a lifelong dream for Krakauer, and an assignment for *Outside* magazine had made it possible.

Krakauer reached the summit at 1:12 p.m., and after a brief stay at the top he started on the long way back down. But during his descent a surprise snowstorm rolled in. At 6:45 p.m., just as it was getting dark, Krakauer stumbled back into camp and collapsed in his tent. Others in his party weren't so fortunate. By the time the storm cleared, eight of the climbers on the world's tallest mountain were dead, including guides Rob Hall and Scott Fischer.

Despite Mount Everest's remote location on the border between Nepal and Tibet, the world watched the tragedy unfold through Web sites, newspapers, television, magazines, and eventually even a major motion picture. In May of each year, Everest Base Camp becomes media central as climbers attempt to reach the summit and journalists show up to cover them, in part because of the high degree of risk involved. During a typical year, six to ten people will die on the mountain.[1]

To complete his assignment of researching and writing a story about the commercialization of Mount Everest, Krakauer climbed the peak as a paying customer of Hall. Krakauer was not the only journalist on the mountain on the day of the snowstorm. Climber Sandy Hill Pittman was sending daily dispatches to NBC's Web site via satellite phone and yak courier; reporter Jane Bromet of *Outside Online,* a Web magazine, was covering the climb from Everest Base Camp; a South African newspaper was sponsoring another expedition; and an IMAX film crew was shooting a documentary about climbing the peak. The IMAX team, led by filmmaker and professional climber David Breashears, produced the movie *Everest*, which became the most successful large-format IMAX film ever and one of the top films of 1997. And this is not an exhaustive list of the reporters, photographers, and filmmakers who were present.

Krakauer says that because of the media coverage, thousands of people around the world knew more about what was happening on the mountain than did the people who were climbing: "A teammate might call home on a satellite phone, for instance, and learn what the South Africans were doing at Camp Two from a spouse in New Zealand or Michigan who'd been surfing the World Wide Web."[2]

This is not to say that the presence of journalists was entirely negative. Krakauer credits the well-equipped, well-prepared IMAX film crew with providing much-needed help and bottled oxygen to the other struggling

**MORE online**

You can find several readings about Jon Krakauer, his book *Into Thin Air,* and the film *Everest* at **http://ralphehanson.com.**

groups after the storm. Even though their help could have jeopardized their $5.5 million film, the crew put down their cameras and simply worked at saving lives.[3]

## Who is the source?

How do you think that Jon Krakauer's background—as a well-known outdoors journalist who writes both books and articles for national magazines—and close involvement in the story shaped his version of what he saw? Was he an unbiased observer? Were his observations "fair" and accurate? What factors could have interfered with his ability to observe accurately?

## What were the consequences of Krakauer's actions?

Do you think that the presence of Krakauer and other journalists on the mountain changed the actions of the guides and the other climbers? Was it fair to the other climbers to have a journalist observing them during the expedition? Or should they have expected the media attention, given what they were attempting? Was Krakauer in any way responsible for what happened to the other climbers? Why or why not?

## What was the lasting impact of Krakauer's book and the IMAX *Everest* film?

Have you read *Into Thin Air* or seen the IMAX *Everest* film? If so, what made you choose them? How did they make you feel? Why do you think people are drawn to stories about adventure and disaster? What do people get out of these stories? Does hearing the story about what happened on Everest make you more or less interested in going on a big adventure?

## Is it wrong for journalists to profit from disasters?

Although Krakauer was a successful author and journalist prior to writing *Into Thin Air*, the book made him a large amount of money and brought him national attention. He has since endowed a foundation to help the indigenous people of the Himalayan Mountains with some of the royalties from the book. Given that Krakauer makes a living as an author and journalist, do you see anything wrong in his profiting from writing about a tragedy? What are the arguments for and against this? If he could not have profited from writing the story, would we have had as complete of a report of what happened? Does the fact that the *Everest* film crew rescued people first give them more of a right to profit from covering the disaster?

[1] David Pugliese, "A Mountaineer's Perspective," *Ottawa Citizen,* May 18, 2002, A13.

[2] Jon Krakauer, *Into Thin Air: A Personal Account of the Mount Everest Disaster* (New York: Villard, 1997), 114.

[3] B. Coburn, *Everest: Mountain Without Mercy* (Washington, D.C.: National Geographic Society, 1997).

Production of mass communication messages is generally expensive. The average cost of producing a studio movie in 2007 was $70.8 million, and advertising it added $25.7 million, according to figures by the Motion Picture Association of America.[25] Thirty seconds of commercial time during the 2009 Super Bowl can cost as much as $3 million. (That's $100,000 per *second*!)[26] The global television rights for the 2006 FIFA World Cup held in Germany sold for £1.2 billion (more than $1.5 billion).[27] But, again, if people do not seek to make money with their messages, they can reach a large audience through the Internet at a relatively low cost.

What do all these messages mean? According to media scholar James Potter, the meaning of messages depends on who is receiving them and what kinds of media literacy skills they can use to decode them. Potter writes that people with low levels of media literacy will look at the surface meanings in media content, whereas those with higher levels of media literacy can interpret messages from a wide range of perspectives with many choices of meanings.[28] For example, Jon Krakauer's book about the disaster that befell a group of Mount Everest climbers in 1996, *Into Thin Air*, can be read as a simple adventure story, an allegory of the battle between man and nature, or a study on obsession. (See box, "Test Your Media Literacy: When Media Coverage Is a Life or Death Issue.") Which of these interpretations is correct? Although *Into Thin Air* is most emphatically an adventure story, it also tells of Krakauer's struggle with the mountain and the weather, and it discusses why people are drawn to dangerous activities like mountain climbing.

*Members of the IMAX expedition filming the documentary* Everest *reach the summit after abandoning their first summit attempt in order to help rescue other climbers.*

*The Channel.* The **channel** is the medium used to transmit the message. Recall that a mass medium is a technological tool. Think about a newspaper. It consists of black and colored ink printed on relatively low-quality paper. It is portable, readily available, and cheap. An article can be clipped from the paper and placed in a pocket. A newspaper also provides local and regional news in greater depth than is possible with almost any other medium.[29]

Print media include books, magazines, newspapers, billboards, and posters. Audiovisual media include radio, sound recordings, broadcast television, cable and satellite television, and video recordings. Interactive media include the Internet, mobile phones, and video games.

What about cell phones, faxes, letters, and e-mail? Do they fit in as channels of mass communication? Although e-mail is not generally considered to be a mass medium, an unsolicited commercial e-mail, known as *spam*, could satisfy

**channel**
The medium used to transmit the encoded message.

at least part of the definition of mass communication, since spam is distributed widely to a large, mixed, and anonymous audience. News reports and sports scores arriving via a small screen on a mobile phone would also seem to qualify. But our phone calls and e-mails from friends are generally interpersonal communications, unless we post them to a blog for everyone to see.

The nature of the channel used to transmit a message can change the meaning of the message. Take, for example, the daily news. On the radio, the news is something happening in the background; read in a newspaper, news is something that demands your undivided attention. But can you call it news when it is presented by a naked man or woman on the Naked News Web site? A dramatic speech given by a great orator on television will likely be much more influential than a transcript of the speech that's published on the Internet the next day.

*The Receiver.* The **receiver** is the audience for the mass communication message—that is, the people who are receiving and decoding the message. **Decoding** is the process of translating a signal from a mass medium into a form that the receiver can understand. The term *mass* can have at least two meanings when referring to audiences. In one sense, the term refers to the mix of ordinary people who receive the message—"the masses." In the second sense, the term refers to the size of the audience. The concept of mass, or popular, taste is an old one, but the concept of a massive, or large, audience developed in the twentieth century. The mass audiences reading major newspapers, listening to the radio, watching network television, or going to the movies are much larger than the crowds of people that gather for events such as political rallies or rock concerts. They form a **heterogeneous audience**—an audience made up of a mix of people who differ in age, sex, income, education, ethnicity, race, religion, and other characteristics. As with size, heterogeneity is a matter of degree. A small-town radio station is likely to reach an audience whose members are more similar than those listening to a station in a major urban area.

Receivers don't always get a clear message from the sender, however. Several types of **noise** can interfere with the delivery of the message. There is semantic noise, when the receiver does not understand the meaning of the message, such as when you can't understand the lyrics on a Latin music channel because you don't speak Spanish; mechanical noise, when the channel has trouble transmitting the message, such as when a thunderstorm produces too much static for you to hear the score of a baseball game being broadcast on an AM radio station; and environmental noise, when the action and sounds surrounding the receiver interfere with the reception of the message, such as when your roommate's loud stereo keeps you from concentrating on your introduction to mass communication textbook.

The receivers of a mass communication message have traditionally been seen as an **anonymous audience**. This means that the sender does not personally know all, or even most, of the people receiving the message. This doesn't mean

**receiver**
The audience for the mass communication message.

**decoding**
The process of translating a signal from a mass medium into a form that the receiver can understand and then interpreting the meaning of the message itself.

**heterogeneous audience**
An audience made up of a mix of people who differ in age, sex, income, education, ethnicity, race, religion, and other characteristics.

**noise**
Interference with the transmission of a message. This can take the form of semantic, mechanical, or environmental noise.

**anonymous audience**
An audience the sender does not personally know. These are not anonymous, isolated people who have no connection to anyone else; they simply are anonymous in their audience status.

that the audience consists of isolated people who have no connection to anyone else; audience members simply don't expect the sender to know who they are. But with the increasing number of channels available for audience members to send feedback to the senders—through the Web, e-mail, faxes, text messages, and phone calls—audience members typically on the receiving end are becoming senders themselves, and are becoming better and better known to the original senders. Sometimes, in the case of reality TV programs such as *American Idol*, audience members become active participants by voting on who should advance to the next level of the competition.

*Smartphones, such as RIM's BlackBerry, are used by young people as their standard way to go online.*

## Contemporary Models of Mass Communication

Though the transmission model (SMCR) is useful for laying out the various elements of the mass communication process, it does not explain how mass communication works in our lives. It focuses primarily on the process of transmitting messages largely from the point of view of a sender trying to have an effect on the receiver. Media scholar Denis McQuail lays out three contemporary models that help us answer three different questions about the nature of mass communication:[30]

*Ritual Model.*    Whereas the transmission model looks at how a message is sent, the ritual model puts audience members at the center of the equation. The **ritual model** looks at how and why audience members (receivers) consume media messages. The ritual model suggests that we watch a program like *American Idol* not so much to learn about aspiring singers or to receive advertising messages but rather to interact in a shared ritual with family and friends. This ritual is then extended through television to other groups of people all across the United States. Media consumption, going beyond simply delivering messages, thus becomes a shared experience that brings us together as a people. For example, when Michael Jackson died, more than 30 million people watched his memorial service on television, and nearly that many viewed some of it using streaming video on their computers.[31] That made Jackson's memorial service one of the most shared experiences for Americans, other than the Super Bowl, in 2009.

**ritual model**
A model of the mass communication process that treats media use as an interactive ritual engaged in by audience members. It looks at how and why audience members (receivers) consume media messages.

## TEST YOUR MEDIA LITERACY

### Can Television Take Anything Seriously?

In his book *Amusing Ourselves to Death,* media scholar Neil Postman argues that the primary effect of television is that it changes how people see the world; that is, with television, people start viewing everything as entertainment. Young people get their news in a comedy format, watching *The Daily Show* the same way they watch MTV. They learn about politics on the same channel that shows a professional football game.[1]

In an interview with Robert Nelson for the *Civic Arts Review,* Postman described the major point of *Amusing Ourselves to Death*:

> Television always recreates the world to some extent in its own image by selecting parts of that world and editing those parts. So a television news show is a kind of symbolic creation and construction made by news directors and camera crews....
>
> Americans turn to television not only for their light entertainment but for their news, their weather, their politics, their religion, their history, all of which may be said to be their furious entertainment. What I'm talking about is television's preemption of our culture's most serious business. It is one thing to say that TV presents us with entertaining subject matter. It is quite another to say that on TV all subject matter is presented as entertaining and it is in that sense that TV can bring ruin to any intelligent understanding of public affairs....
>
> And stranger still is the fact that commercials may appear anywhere in a news story, before, after or in the middle, so that all events are rendered essentially trivial, that is to say, all events are treated as a source of public entertainment. How serious can an earthquake in Mexico be or a hijacking in Beirut, if it is shown to us prefaced by a happy United Airlines commercial and summarized by a Calvin Klein jeans commercial? Indeed, TV newscasters have added to our grammar a new part of speech altogether. What may be called the "now this" conjunction. "Now this" is a conjunction that does not connect two things but does the opposite. It disconnects. When newscasters say, "Now this," they mean to indicate that what you have just heard or seen has no relevance to what you are about to hear or see. There is no murder so brutal, no political blunder so costly, no bombing so devastating that it cannot be erased from our minds by a newscaster saying, "Now this." The newscaster means that you have thought long enough on the matter, let's say 45 seconds, that you must not be morbidly preoccupied with it, let us say for 90 seconds, and that you must now give your attention to a commercial. Such a situation in my view is not news. And in my opinion it accounts for the fact that Americans are among the most ill informed people in the Western world.[2]

**MORE online**

You can find a link to the rest of the interview at **http://ralphehanson.com.**

• • • • • • • • • • • • • • • • • • •

### Who is the source?

Neil Postman (1931–2003), a prominent American educator, media theorist, and cultural critic, founded the media ecology program at New York University and chaired the NYU Department of Culture and Communications.

Postman wrote eighteen books and more than 200 magazine and newspaper articles for such periodicals as the *New York Times Magazine, Atlantic Monthly, Harper's,* and the *Washington Post.* He edited the journal *ETC.: A Review of General Semantics* and was also on the editorial board of *The Nation.*

### What is he saying?

Postman argues that the primary effect of television is that it changes how people see the world; that is, with television, people start viewing everything as entertainment. In comparison, think about your own viewing habits. Do you watch the news the same way you watch MTV? Or learn about politics on the same channel that shows *Survivor*? Or see news about the war in Iraq, followed by a commercial for Domino's Pizza?

### What kind of evidence does the book provide?

What kind of data does Postman provide to support his arguments? What kind of evidence is needed to bolster these claims? Is there evidence that disputes his claims? How do you think Postman's background is likely to have shaped his view of television?

### How do you or your classmates react to Postman's arguments?

What does the title—*Amusing Ourselves to Death*—mean to you? Do you feel that television trivializes important issues or makes them more palatable? Have you noticed similar effects in yourself as described by Postman? Do you notice differences in how news anchors make the transition from news to commercials, and back again? Are the stories before and after the break any different from stories during the rest of the newscast?

### Does it all add up?

Do you believe that Postman's arguments are true today? In a study conducted in 2000, researchers found that 75 percent of television viewers under the age of thirty watch the news with the remote in their hands, ready to change channels if they get bored for a moment or two. Do you think that the data from this study support Postman's claims? Why or why not? Think back to the material about news coverage of Michael Jackson's death at the beginning of the chapter. Do you think that Jackson's death was newsworthy enough to merit the coverage it received? Or were the cable news channels just trying to entertain their viewers?

[1] Neil Postman, *Amusing Ourselves to Death: Public Discourse in the Age of Show Business* (New York: Penguin Books, 1985).

[2] Robert Nelson, "Television and the Public Decline of Public Discourse," *Civic Arts Review,* vol. 3: 1990, 1. Excerpt used with permission.

*Publicity Model.*   Sometimes media messages are not trying to convey specific information as much as they are trying to draw attention to a particular person, group, or concept. According to the **publicity model** the mere fact that a topic is covered by the media can make the topic important, regardless of what is said about it. For example, when Janet Jackson displayed her breast during the 2004 Super Bowl, there were all sorts of charges that broadcast network CBS was

**publicity model**
A model of the mass communication process that looks at how media attention can make a person, concept, or thing become important, regardless of what is said about it.

| TABLE 1.1 MASS COMMUNICATION MODELS | | |
| --- | --- | --- |
| **Models** | **Orientation of sender** | **Orientation of receiver** |
| **Transmission model** | Transfer of meaning | Cognitive processing |
| **Ritual model** | Performance | Shared experience |
| **Publicity model** | Competitive display | Attention-giving spectatorship |
| **Reception model** | Preferential encoding | Differential decoding/construction of meaning |

*Source:* Denis McQuail, *McQuail's Mass Communication Theory,* 5th ed. (London: Sage Publications, 2005). Reproduced by permission of Sage Publications. Copyright © Denis McQuail, 2005.

lowering the moral standards of America's young people. But the major effect of Jackson's stunt was that the Federal Communications Commission (FCC) adopted increasingly strict rules on broadcast decency. As a result, at least twenty ABC affiliates refused to air the World War II movie *Saving Private Ryan* the following November for fear that they would be fined for all the bad language contained in the movie. Concerns about changing television standards had existed for several years prior to Jackson's flashing Super Bowl viewers, but the attention Jackson brought to the issue put broadcast decency in the limelight.[32]

*Reception Model.* The **reception model** moves us out of the realm of social science analysis and into the world of critical theory. Instead of looking at how messages affect audiences or are used by the senders or receivers, the reception model looks at how audience members derive and create meaning out of media content. Rather than seeing content as having an intended, fixed meaning, the reception model says that each receiver decodes the message based on his or her own unique experiences, feelings, and beliefs. You can take a single news story, show it to liberal and conservative observers, and both will claim that it is biased against their point of view. In fact, a 1982 study showed the more that journalists tried to present multiple sides of an issue, the more partisans on either side of the issue viewed the story as biased.[33]

**reception model**
A critical theory model of the mass communication process that looks at how audience members derive and create meaning out of media content as they decode the messages.

# EVOLUTION OF THE MEDIA WORLD

Where did our media world come from? Is it just a product of the late twentieth century, with its constant flow of print and electronic messages? Not really. The world of interconnected and overlapping communication networks that surrounds us has been evolving for hundreds of years. Before the advent of the mass media, people interacted primarily face-to-face. Most of the time they interacted only with people like themselves and had little contact with the outside world. But people gradually created communication networks that used first interpersonal channels, then print media, electronic media, and, most recently, interactive media. This section examines how various communication networks have grown over the centuries to form the media world in which we now live.

## Before Print: Pre–Mass Media Communication Networks

The first major communication network in the Western world predates the mass media and was developed by the Roman Catholic Church in the twelfth, thirteenth, and fourteenth centuries. During that period messages flowed from the Vatican in Italy through the cardinals and bishops, to priests in cathedrals and villages throughout Europe, and finally to their congregations through sermons from the pulpit.[34] Although the process started as group communication, the messages moved through so many groups that they eventually became a rudimentary form of mass communication.

## Print: Arrival of the Book

The first major expansion in communication beyond the Church was the development of the printing press—in particular, the invention of movable type in the 1450s—and the subsequent mass production of printed materials. Mass printing made it possible for major social changes, such as the Protestant Reformation, to spread from their country of origin to the rest of Europe and the world. Transmitting messages to a larger audience became easier and cheaper with the birth of the printing press, which led to the publication and widespread dissemination of books, magazines, newspapers, pamphlets, and maps.

Although the printing press allowed for the mass production of information, printing was still relatively slow and publications remained fairly expensive. The addition of steam power to the printing press in 1814 dramatically increased the rate at which printed material could be reproduced. Revenues from advertisements of the new goods mass produced in the factories helped drive down the cost of newspapers and magazines, thus spreading the communication net ever wider.

## Electronic Networks: Telegraph, Gramophone, Radio, Movies, and Television

The advent of electronic communication made the media world much more complex, beginning in 1844 with the opening of the first telegraph line, from Baltimore to Washington, D.C. For the first time, the communication network extended beyond personal limitations. Before the development of the telegraph,

THE LAYING OF THE CABLE—JOHN AND JONATHAN JOINING HANDS.

*This wood engraving from the 1860s celebrates the completion of the transatlantic telegraph cable, which allowed messages to cross the ocean almost instantaneously.*

sending a message from one place to another meant that the paper it was written on had to be carried physically from one location to another; this limitation made the fastest form of communication dependent on the fastest form of transportation. But the telegraph wire enabled a message to span a great distance almost instantaneously. In 1866, telegraph cables spanned the Atlantic Ocean, overcoming a seemingly insurmountable barrier that had long hindered transoceanic communication. Instead of sending a message on a two-week journey by boat across the ocean and waiting for a reply to come back the same way, two people on opposite sides of the ocean could carry on a dialogue via telegraph.

In the 1880s Emile Berliner invented the gramophone, or phonograph, which played mass-produced discs containing about three minutes of music. Just as printed books made possible the storage and spread of ideas, so the gramophone allowed musical performances to be captured and kept. Before the development of the gramophone, the only way to hear music was to go to a concert or perform it oneself.

The invention of radio in the late nineteenth century freed electronic communication from the limits imposed on it by telegraph wires, and the media world grew in complexity once again. Messages could come into the home at any time and at almost no cost to the receiver. All that was needed was a radio set to receive an endless variety of cultural content, news, and other programming.

Movies were first shown at nickelodeon theaters in the late 1890s and early 1900s, and were produced by an entertainment industry that distributed films worldwide. Young couples on a date in London, Ohio, and London, England, could see the same movie, copy the same styles of dress, and perhaps even practice the same kisses they had seen in the movie. With radio and the movies, the media world became a shared entertainment culture produced for profit by major media corporations.

In 1939, patrons in New York's neighborhood taverns no longer had to settle for radio broadcasts of Yankees games being played at the Polo Grounds. Instead, a small black-and-white television set located on a pedestal behind the bar showed a faint, flickering image of the game. What would this new medium bring? A new era of accessible education? High-level political debate to enlighten the masses? Clowns being hit in the face with pies? After a series of delays caused by World War II, television surpassed radio in popularity. It also became a light-ning rod for controversy as people stayed home to watch whatever images it would deliver.

## The Internet: Interactive Communication

After several decades of television, people had gotten used to the idea that news, information, and entertainment could be delivered almost magically into their homes, although they could do little to control the content of this medium other than change channels. Then a new medium emerged, one that made send-ers and receivers readily interchangeable. The Internet became a full-fledged mass communication network in the 1990s (though many people were unaware that the first nodes of this new medium were being linked together as far back as 1969). Rather than simply making it easier for individuals and organizations to send messages to a mass audience, the new computer networks were designed for two-way communication. Reversing a centuries-old trend, they allowed audience members to send messages back to the original senders. Audience members were becoming message providers themselves.

The Internet's interactivity was a culmination of a trend toward giving audi-ence members new controls over their media. The growth of cable and satellite television, along with the videocassette recorder (VCR), had already given view-ers more choices and more control; and the remote control allowed them to choose among dozens of channels without leaving their chairs.

The implications of interactivity are significant. Whereas the commercial media have come to be controlled by a smaller and smaller number of large corporations (see Chapter 3), an important channel of mass communication is open to ordinary people in ways that were never before possible. With a trivial investment in a computer and an Internet connection, individuals can grab the spotlight with news and entertainment on the World Wide Web.

Consider the example of the artist Jeph Jacques, creator of the popular Web comic *Questionable Content*. Started in 2003, the comic features characters such as library-assistant and indie-music geek Martin; his former-goth, coffee-shop-owning girlfriend, Dora; and his AnthroPC robot, Pintsize. The strip takes place in a location that looks a lot like Northampton, Massachusetts, and gives a slice-of-life storyline dealing with Martin, Dora, and the customers at Dora's shop, Coffee of Doom. Although the strip started out small, Jacques's Web site draws as many as 200,000 unique visitors daily, and it produces enough income to support Jacques and his wife, Cristi.[35] "My wild fantasy about the massive success of the comic was, wow, maybe sometime 10,000 people will be reading it every day," Jacques told the *Boston Globe*. Jacques's income comes from a combination of merchandise such as T-shirts, posters, and tote bags, along with advertising on the site. It's worth noting that given the subject matter and language in *Questionable Content*, Jacques could never move his comic to a newspaper or even an alternative weekly paper. Jacques is happy with having

Questionable Content *creator Jeph Jacques poses with his Web comic characters Dora (left) and Faye (right).*

his comic online and getting the high level of feedback that he gets from a Web forum connected to his site. As he wrote in a blog post about Web comic economics, "You have to adapt to your medium and its potential audience, and if you can't do that then all the business acumen in the world won't help you make a living."[36] (You can find a link to *Questionable Content* along with other Web comics at http://ralphehanson.com.)

Audience participation in the communication network can have economic effects as well. For example, fans talking about movies on the Internet were credited with making the tiny-budget indie movie *The Blair Witch Project* an enormous success with their positive comments, and with destroying the chances of the big-budget, studio-produced *Batman & Robin* with their criticism.[37] Cult-movie director Kevin Smith (*Clerks, Dogma*) even used online fans as the subject of his 2001 film *Jay and Silent Bob Strike Back*.

The increased participation of audience members in the media world is not just a low-budget Internet phenomenon. Fox's popular *American Idol* has audience members vote via text messages on who will advance to the next round, and news programs on CNN routinely feature e-mails from viewers. On a more serious level, C-SPAN's morning talk show *Washington Journal* features a host, a guest or two, and questions called in, faxed, or e-mailed by viewers. The real host and guests are the audience rather than the panelists on the show.

Some critics would argue that the growth of cable television stations, Web sites, and new magazines creates only an illusion of choice because a majority of the channels are still controlled by the same five or six companies.[38] Even so, it is a new media world, one in which audience members are choosing what media content they will consume and when they will consume it. It's a world that even media giants are having to adjust to.

## Media Consumption

The number of distinct media outlets is huge. According to the most recent figures, there are approximately 1,408 daily newspapers, 6,700 weekly newspapers, 20,000 magazines, 13,000 radio stations, 2,200 broadcast television stations, at least 580 cable networks, 2,700 book publishers, 7 major movie studios (along with a number of smaller ones), and 39,000 movie screens in the United States alone.[39]

Consumption trends vary among different media. Consider a few examples:

- The newspaper business has fewer newspapers and readers than in the past. In 1970, there were 63 million households in the United States and 62 million issues of daily papers were sold. By 2008, circulation had dropped to 49 million, but the number of households had grown to 117 million.[40] Despite declines in circulation and revenue, newspapers are still profitable. They simply are not making the level of profits they've made in years past. With their online editions, newspapers are in the process of redefining themselves from being in the business of delivering news printed on cheap pulp paper to companies that deliver in-depth news coverage using a range of formats from ink-on-paper, to Web pages, to mobile phone screens. Nevertheless, ink-on-paper editions are still responsible for most of the newspaper business revenue.[41]

- Magazines make about $7 billion a year in subscription revenue and about $3 billion in single copy sales for a total of about $10 billion in circulation revenue. They also bring in about $12.9 billion in advertising revenue. Of all the companies that publish magazines, the top four account for more than 70 percent of the revenue. On average, American adults read between eight and nine magazines a month.[42]

- The Big Four television networks (NBC, CBS, ABC, and Fox) still receive 40 percent of all television advertising revenue, and their profits have averaged 25 percent a year. But like newspaper readers, viewers of network television are getting older, and marketers want to reach younger audiences. From 1994 to 2004 the network broadcasters' share of the television audience declined from 69 percent to less than 50 percent.[43] Many viewers are also attracted to the Spanish-language Univision, which in 2000 became the fifth largest network in the United States.[44] The new CW network, built out of the remains of startup networks The WB and UPN, was giving Univision some competition to be the fifth largest network as of

*Fox's popular TV program American Idol, hosted by Simon Cowell, depends on audience votes to help determine the singing contest's winners.*

2006, but both Univision and The CW are much smaller than the Big Four, attracting at best one-third of the audience that any of the larger networks draw.

■ The Internet, videos, and video games are stealing adults away from television. People are still spending time in front of their sets, but they are not necessarily watching cable or broadcast programming.[45] Not only are DVDs and video games taking up television time, but people are now watching television shows delivered over the Internet. Networks are streaming such popular shows as *Big Brother, CSI, Grey's Anatomy, Desperate Housewives,* and *Heroes* to viewers for free from their Web sites.

■ Advertising revenue has been declining in recent years for newspapers, consumer magazines, radio, and broadcast television. It is expected to be climbing in mobile media and the Internet. Overall, the media industry is projected to be one of the fastest growing industries in the United States in the coming years.[46]

■ In 2008, consumers spent more time with media they paid for than with media supported primarily by advertising. This means that books, movies, and cable television are growing in importance, whereas ad-supported media like broadcasting, newspapers, and magazines are declining.[47]

# UNDERSTANDING THE MEDIA WORLD

Most people have ambivalent feelings about their high levels of media use. The convenience of the cell phone is offset by the fact that it makes one available to others at all times. The wide selection of programming on cable television is wonderful, but the content on some of those channels can be disturbing. It is liberating to be connected to the entire industrialized world through the Internet, but the risk of invasion of privacy is troubling. This section discusses the concept of media literacy and examines some common misconceptions about the mass media. It also examines in detail "Seven Truths" about mass media and mass communication that are at the center of this book's look at media literacy.

## Defining Media Literacy

**media literacy**
Audience members' understanding of the media industry's operation, the messages delivered by the media, the roles media play in society, and how audience members respond to these media and their messages.

The term **media literacy** refers to people's understanding of what the media are, how they operate, what messages they are delivering, what roles they play in society, and how audience members respond to these messages. Media scholar James Potter writes that people with high levels of media literacy have a great deal of control over the vision of the world they see through the media and can decide for themselves what the messages mean. In contrast, those with low levels of media literacy can develop exaggerated impressions of problems in society, even when those impressions conflict with their own experience. For example, media consumers who spend large amounts of time watching television often perceive society as far more dangerous and crime-ridden than it is because that's the image they see on television.[48] Potter says that too often consumers with low levels of media literacy assume that the media have large, obvious, and largely negative effects on other people but little or no effect on themselves. Finally, those with low levels of media literacy tend to blame the media for complex social problems such as teen pregnancy or school violence.

Potter has identified four basic dimensions of media literacy: cognitive, emotional, aesthetic, and moral.[49] Let's take a closer look at each of these dimensions.

*The Cognitive Dimension.*    The cognitive dimension of media literacy deals with the ability to intellectually process information communicated by the media. This can involve interpreting the meaning of words on a printed page, appreciating the implications of ominous music in a movie, or understanding that a well-dressed character in a television show is wealthy. For example, the hardcover edition of Jon Krakauer's book *Into Thin Air* featured a series of ominous woodcuts at the beginning of each chapter. These illustrations may be viewed simply as decorations at the beginning of each chapter or interpreted as foreshadowing the suffering and peril to come.

The cognitive dimension also includes the skills necessary to access the media: using a computer, accessing high-definition programming on your new HDTV, or finding a book in the library. All of these are learned skills. We learn to read in school, learn the meaning of musical cues from movies we've seen, and learn how to navigate the Internet through repeated practice.

*The Emotional Dimension.*    The emotional dimension of media literacy covers the feelings created by media messages. Sometimes the emotions can be overwhelming; examples include the fear of a young child watching a scary movie or the joy of a parent watching a news story about a child's being rescued. People often spend time with songs, movies, books, and other media specifically to feel the emotions they generate.[50] *Titanic* became the all-time box office champion in large part because of the young women who went to see the movie again and again to experience the emotional release it provided.[51] And it is unlikely that either the IMAX documentary *Everest* or Krakauer's *Into Thin Air* would have been such commercial successes were it not for the gut-wrenching emotions created by both the deaths and the dramatic rescues of the climbers on the mountain.

*The Aesthetic Dimension.*    The aesthetic dimension of media literacy involves interpreting media content from an artistic or critical point of view. How well is the media artifact produced? What skills were used in producing it? How does it compare in quality to other similar works? Understanding more than the surface dimensions of media content can require extensive learning. *Into Thin Air* was unquestionably a commercial success, and it was largely a critical success as well. But it was also controversial; several critics suggested that Krakauer had overdramatized the events that took place on Everest and unfairly portrayed one guide as a villain rather than a hero.[52] It is through such critical debate that alternative views and understandings of media content emerge.

*The Moral Dimension.*   The moral dimension of media literacy consists of examining the values of the medium or the message. In a television situation comedy, for example, an underlying message might be that a quick wit is an important tool for dealing with problems and that problems can be solved in a short time. In an action movie, the moral lessons may be that violence and authority are needed if one is to succeed and that the world is a mean and dangerous place. The moral message of most advertisements is that problems can be solved by purchasing something.[53] Among the great many moral issues raised by *Into Thin Air* is the message that the presence of the media changes the nature of an event.

## Seven Truths About the Media "They" Don't Want You to Know

Media literacy is a tricky subject to talk about, because few people will admit that they really don't understand how the media operate and how messages, audiences, channels, and senders interact. After all, since we spend so much time with the media, we must know all about it, right? As an example, most students in an introduction to mass communication class will claim that the media and their messages tend to affect other people far more than they affect themselves. The question of media literacy can also become a political question, for which the answer depends on whether you are a liberal or a conservative, rich or poor, young or old. But the biggest problem in the public discussion of media literacy is that certain routine issues get discussed again and again, while many big questions are left unasked.

Consider some of the things we think we know about the media: "The news media are hopelessly liberal. . . ." "Watching too much television turns children into overweight zombies, or else it makes them violent. One or the other. . . ." "Reading too many fashion magazines makes young women anorexic. . . ." "The mainstream media cover up stories they don't want us to know about. . . ." "Our media are run by giant corporations that seek world domination. . . ." How do we know these things? Well, people on the media tell us they are so! And they wouldn't say these things if they weren't true, would they?

But there are several things we don't hear about the media. Perhaps it's because there is no one out there who can attract an audience by saying them.

Or maybe it's because the ideas are complicated, and we don't like complexity from our media. Or maybe it's because "they" (whoever "they" may be) don't want us to know them.

So here are seven truths about the media that "they" don't want you to know. These key issues of media literacy that don't get the discussion they deserve provide a foundation for the rest of the chapters in this book. (And just who are "they?" Wait for Truth Seven.)

*Truth One: The Media Are Essential Components of Our Lives.* Critics often talk about the effects the media have on us, as though the media were

> ## Seven Truths "They" Don't Want You to Know About the Media
>
> - **Truth One:** The media are essential components of our lives.
>
> - **Truth Two:** There are no mainstream media (MSM).
>
> - **Truth Three:** Everything from the margin moves to the center.
>
> - **Truth Four:** Nothing's new: Everything that happened in the past will happen again.
>
> - **Truth Five:** New media are always scary.
>
> - **Truth Six:** Activism and analysis are not the same thing.
>
> - **Truth Seven:** There is no "they."

something separate and distinct from our everyday lives. But conversations with my students have convinced me otherwise. Every semester I poll my students as to what media they have used so far that day, with the day starting at midnight. I run through the list: watching MTV, logging onto Facebook, listening to the radio, checking the weather on the Weather Channel, reading *USA Today,* reading *Cosmopolitan,* reading the latest James Patterson novel, listening to an iPod. . . . In fact, media use is likely to be the most universal experience my students will share. I recently found that more of my morning class students had consumed media content than had eaten breakfast. Are the media an important force in our lives? Absolutely! But the media are more than an outside influence on us. They are a part of our everyday lives.

Think about how we assign meanings to objects that otherwise would have no meaning at all. Take a simple yellow ribbon twisted in a stylized bow. You've seen thousands of these, and most likely you know exactly what they stand for—Support Our Troops. But that hasn't always been the meaning of the symbol.

The yellow ribbon has a long history in American popular culture. It played a role in the rather rude World War II–era marching song "She Wore a Yellow Ribbon." The ribbon was a symbol of a young woman's love for a soldier "far, far away," and the lyrics mention that her father kept a shotgun handy to keep the soldier "far, far away." The yellow ribbon was also a symbol of love and faithfulness in the John Ford film *She Wore a Yellow Ribbon.* In the 1970s, the ribbon became a symbol of remembering the U.S. staff in the Iranian embassy who had been taken hostage. This meaning came from the song "Tie a Yellow Ribbon 'Round the Old Oak Tree," made popular by the group Tony Orlando and Dawn. The song tells about a prisoner coming home from jail hoping that his girlfriend would remember him. She could prove her love by displaying the yellow ribbon.

*A volunteer carries a red ribbon, the international symbol of AIDS awareness, on World AIDS Day in Calcutta, India. The ribbon's meaning is recognized worldwide through its appearances in the mass media.*

The prisoner arrives home to find not one but 100 yellow ribbons tied to the tree. The display of yellow ribbons tied to trees became commonplace in newspapers and television news stories on the ongoing hostage crisis after the wife of a hostage started displaying one in her yard.

Then, during the 1990–1991 Persian Gulf War, Americans were eager to show their support for the troops fighting overseas, even if they did not necessarily support the war itself. During the early 1990s the stylized ribbon started to become institutionalized as a symbol of support. The yellow "Support Our Troops" ribbon was followed by the red ribbon of AIDS awareness, the pink ribbon of breast cancer awareness, and ribbons of virtually every color on every issue. And how do we know the meanings of these ribbons? We hear or see them being discussed through our media. The meanings are assigned by the creators of the ribbon, but the success of the ribbon depends on the meanings being shared through the media. So, do the media create the meanings? Not really. But could the meanings be shared nationwide without the media? Absolutely not. The media may not define our lives, but they do help transmit and disseminate shared meanings from one side of the country to the other.[54]

*Truth Two: There Are No Mainstream Media (MSM).* We often hear charges related to perceived sins of the so-called mainstream media (MSM). But who exactly are these mainstream media? For some the MSM are the heavyweights of journalism, especially the television broadcast networks and the major papers such as the *New York Times.* For others, the MSM are the giant corporations who run many of our media outlets. New York University journalism professor and blogger Jay Rosen says that the term MSM is often used to refer to media we just don't like—a "them."[55] It isn't always clear who constitute the MSM, but in general we can consider them to be the old-line big business media—newspapers, magazines, and television.

But are these old media more in the mainstream than our alternative media? Look at talk radio. Afternoon talk radio is dominated by conservative political talk show hosts such as Rush Limbaugh and Sean Hannity. Limbaugh, in particular, is fond of complaining about how the MSM don't "get it." But how mainstream are the MSM? On a typical evening, CNN will have approximately 1.05 million viewers of its evening programming, Fox News will have 1.79 million viewers, MSNBC will have 889,000, and the individual broadcast network newscasts will have 6 to 8 million viewers. The Rush Limbaugh show, on the other hand, averages somewhere between 14 and 25 million listeners a week.[56] (Note that television audiences and radio audiences are measured differently.) So who is more mainstream? A popular afternoon radio host with a large daily audience or a television news program with a much smaller audience? Daily Kos, a leading liberal political blog—and one of the most-read blogs on the Internet—attracts more than 4 million views per month. Again, these numbers are not directly comparable with television ratings, but they are substantial. The Internet video site YouTube streams approximately 100 million videos a day and has been acquired by Internet advertising giant Google. No one video gets a particularly large viewership, but the combined total is massive.[57] (For more on YouTube's explosive popularity, see Chapter 3.)

So it is largely meaningless to describe one medium as mainstream and another as nonmainstream. They are all significant presences in our world.

This is not to say that our media are not giant businesses. Even the alternative press is a big business these days. New Times Newspapers, the publisher of eleven alternative weekly newspapers, purchased Village Voice Media in October 2005. This gave a single company control of alternative weekly newspapers and Web sites in at least 15 of the biggest U.S. markets. (Although New Times bought the Village Voice, the new company operates under the Village Voice Media name.) In addition to publishing alternative newspapers, Village Voice Media sells advertising for 35 additional weekly newspapers and more than 1,500 college papers.[58]

Can we distinguish between old and new media? Perhaps. Can we argue that our alternative sources of news and entertainment are any less significant than the traditional ones? Absolutely not.

*Truth Three: Everything From the Margin Moves to the Center.*    The mass media, both news and entertainment, are frequently accused of trying to put forward an extremist agenda of violence, permissiveness, homosexuality, drug use, edgy fashion, and nonmainstream values.

People in the media business, be they entertainers or journalists, respond with the argument that they are just "keeping it real," portraying the world as it is by showing aspects of society that some people want to pretend don't exist. They have no agenda, the argument goes; they just want to portray reality.

Now it is true that much of what the media portray that upsets people is real. On the other hand, it is a bit disingenuous to argue that movie directors and musicians are not trying for shock value when they use offensive language or portray stylized violence combined with graphic sexuality. Think back to any of a number of recent horror movies. We all know that teenagers routinely get slashed to ribbons by a psycho killer just after having sex, right? Clearly movie producers are trying to attract an audience by providing content that is outside of the mainstream.

The problem with the argument between "keeping it real" and "extremist agenda" is that it misses what is actually happening. There can be no question that audiences go after media content that is outside of the mainstream. By the same token, the more nonmainstream content is presented, the more ordinary it seems to become. This is what is meant by Truth Three—one of the mass media's biggest effects on everyday life is to take culture from the margins of society and make it into part of the mainstream, or center. This process can move people, ideas, and even individual words from small communities into mass society.

We can see this happening in several ways. Take the grunge band Nirvana. Founded in 1987 by Kurt Cobain and Krist Novoselic, the band brought the 1970s British punk sound to a mass American audience, and their breakout album *Nevermind* sold 10 million copies. Cobain could not cope with the fact that his antiestablishment message was making him a part of the establishment. Following a lengthy battle with drug use and depression, he committed suicide in 1994. The problem that Cobain and other punk and grunge rockers encountered was that themes of alienation resonate strongly with young people, leading the artists to experience the kinds of success that they were rebelling against. Rebels don't sell out, they simply become part of the mainstream, whether they want to or not.[59]

Or consider the children's show *Shining Time Station*, featuring the lovable Thomas the Tank Engine and his train friends. The show also features a live-action Mr. Conductor, first played by Beatles drummer Ringo Starr, and then by comic George Carlin. Carlin's position as a wholesome children's show host was particularly surprising, given that he built his fame on the wildly offensive comedy routine "Seven Words You Can Never Say on Television." But the process shouldn't be surprising. Both Starr and Carlin started out as counterculture figures who made worldwide reputations for themselves through media portrayals. Then, as their fans grew older and had children of their own, these counterculture figures became mainstream. (You can find a link to Carlin's "Seven Words" routine and a sample of his appearances on *Shining Time Station* at http://ralphehanson.com.)

An alternative approach is to look at how the media accelerate the adoption of activist language into the mainstream. Take the medical term "intact dilation and extraction" that describes a controversial type of late-term abortion. A search of the Lexis-Nexis news database shows that newspapers used the medical term only five times over a six-month period. On the other hand, "partial-birth abortion," the term for the procedure used by abortion opponents, was used in more than 125 stories during the same time period. Opponents even got the term used in the title of a bill passed by Congress that outlawed the procedure, thus moving the phrase into the mainstream through repeated publication of the bill's name.

This process is not a product of a liberal or conservative bias by the news media. It's simply a consequence of the repeated use of the term in the press.

*Truth Four: Nothing's New: Everything That Happened in the Past Will Happen Again.*    Truth Four is a little different than the oft-repeated slogan "Those who ignore the past are doomed to repeat it." Instead, it says that media face the same issues over and over again as technologies change and new people come into the business.

The fight between today's recording companies and file sharers has its roots in the battle between music publishers and the distributors of player piano rolls in the early 1900s. The player piano was one of the first technologies for reproducing musical performances. Piano roll publishers would buy a single copy of a piece of sheet music and hire a skilled pianist to have his or her performance recorded as a series of holes punched in a paper roll. That roll (and the performance) could then be reproduced and sold to anyone who owned a player piano without further payment to the music's original publisher.[60]

Then again in 1984, Sony successfully defended a lawsuit from Universal Studios, by arguing that it had a right to sell VCRs to the public even though the video recorders could be used to duplicate the studio's movies because there were legitimate, legal uses for the technology. Before long the studios quit trying to ban the VCR and started selling videocassettes of movies directly to consumers at reasonable prices. All of a sudden the studios had a major new source of revenue.[61]

More recently the recording industry has done its best to force consumers to buy their music on little plastic discs, having gotten the courts to levy large fines against consumers who are "sharing" copyright music over the Internet. In the meantime, Apple sells millions of songs a week through its online iTunes music store for an average price of ninety-nine cents. And as of fall 2006, Apple and Amazon have started to sell movie downloads through their online stores, a step that has the movie industry worried.

*Truth Five: New Media Are Always Scary.*    Concern about how new media will affect our lives is nothing new. Known as the legacy of fear, it dates back at least to the early twentieth century.

In the 1930s there was fear that watching movies, especially gangster pictures, would lead to precocious sexual behavior, delinquency, lower standards

*Congressional hearings in the 1950s about horror comics, such as those pictured here, show how adults are always concerned about the possible effects of new media on children.*

and ideals, and poor physical and emotional health. The 1940s brought concern about how people would react to radio programs, particularly soap operas.[62]

Comic books came under attack in the 1950s. The notion that comic books were dangerous was popularized by a book titled *Seduction of the Innocents,* by Dr. Fredric Wertham, who also testified before Congress that violent and explicit comic books were a cause of teenage delinquency and sexual behavior. The industry responded to the criticism by forming the Comic Code Authority and ceasing publication of popular crime and horror comics such as *Tales From the Crypt* and *Weird Science.*

The 1980s and 1990s saw controversies over offensive rap and rock lyrics.[63] These controversies reflected widespread concern about bad language and hidden messages in songs. In 2009, pop star Britney Spears had the not-hidden allusion to the "F word" in her song and video *If You Seek Amy.* If you speak the title aloud, it sounds like you are spelling out F U . . . well, you get the picture. Critics were, of course, shocked and dismayed about this example of a pop star lowering public taste. Of course, Spears didn't really create her naughty little lyric on her own. Aside from a host of rock and blues singers who have used similar lines, *Slate* writer Jesse Sheidlower notes that James Joyce used the same basic line in *Ulysses,* when he has a group of women sing:

> If you see kay
> Tell him he may
> See you in tea
> Tell him from me.

A careful reading of the third line will let you find a second hidden obscenity, as well.[64]

Numerous media critics and scholars have argued that television and movies present a distorted view of the world, making it look like a much more violent and dangerous place than it is. More recently, wireless telephones have been blamed for a range of social ills, from car accidents caused by distracted drivers to promiscuity caused by sexually explicit mobile phone text and photo messages.

The idea that new media are always scary applies as much to media companies as it does to audience members. Newspaper publishers were frightened that radio stations would steal away all their readers in the 1920s and 1930s. Record companies were also afraid that radio would steal away all the customers who were paying for record albums. And as we've seen earlier in this chapter, the movie industry, the television industry, and the music industry are terrified of what the Internet is doing to their business.

Why has there been such long-running concern about the possible effects of the media? Media sociologist Charles R. Wright says that people want to be able to solve social ills, and it is easier to believe that poverty, crime, and drug abuse are caused by media coverage than to acknowledge that their causes are complex and not fully understood.[65]

Writing in 1948, sociologists Robert Merton and Paul Lazarsfeld identified four major aspects of public concern about the media:

- Concern that because the media are everywhere, they might be able to control and manipulate people. This is a large part of the legacy of fear.

- Fear that those in power will use the media to reinforce the existing social structure and discourage social criticism. When critics express concern about who owns and runs the media, this is what they are worried about.

- Fear that mass entertainment will lower the tastes and standards for popular culture by trying to attract the largest possible audience. Criticism of action movies, soap operas, and wrestling as replacements for healthier entertainment such as Shakespeare's plays is at the heart of this concern.

- The belief that mass entertainment is a waste of time that detracts from more useful activities. When your mother told you to turn off the television set and go outside, this was her concern![66]

*Truth Six: Activism and Analysis Are Not the Same Thing.*    The five truths we've examined so far lead us to the conclusion of Truth Six—critics of the mass media are not necessarily interested in giving an honest analysis of how the media affect the public at large. Instead, critics may have an agenda that has nothing to do with the nature of our mass media. When senators hold hearings

## TEST YOUR MEDIA LITERACY

### Children's Media Use

Teens are significant media users. According to the 2005 study *Generation M: Media in the Lives of 8–18 Year-Olds,* U.S. children spend an average of 6.5 hours a day using media, more time than they spend doing anything else other than sleeping.[1] There are also a lot of stereotypes about teen media use that may or may not be supported by evidence. Recently the Nielsen Company, the same folks who do the ratings that tell us how many people are watching television programs, surveyed teens and discovered that they are not always that much different from adults in how they use the media, though a few stark differences were found. In their 2009 study of teen media use,[2] the ratings company found:

- Teens are not giving up on television. Their viewership is up 6 percent over the last five years.

- Teens love the Internet, but they spend less time there than adults. Teens spend an average of 11 hours and 32 minutes on the Internet per month compared to 29 hours and 15 minutes for adults.

- Teens watch less online video than adults but are more engaged in the online ads. The study found teens recall online ads better than televised ads.

- Teens like all types of video games, including music games, racing games, and violent games.

- Teens' taste in media content is not that different from their parents. *American Idol* was their favorite television show and Google their most used Web site.

| Medium | Usage per day |
|---|---|
| Television | 3 hours, 20 minutes |
| Internet | 23 minutes |
| Console gaming | 25 minutes |
| Text messages | 96 sent or read |
| Audio MP3 | 1 in 2 used |
| Mobile Web | 1 in 3 used |
| Newspapers | 1 in 4 read |
| Video player | 1 in 4 used |

The one stereotype that might be correct is that young people love mobile media. The study found that 77 percent of teens have their own mobile phone and an additional 11 percent borrow one on a regular basis. In addition,

**MORE online**

You can download the entire study at **http://ralphehanson.com.**

83 percent of teens with mobile media use text messages, and 56 percent use MMS/picture messaging. The typical teen with a mobile phone sends 2,899 text messages per month but makes 191 calls. And according to Nielsen's survey, two-thirds of teens prefer texting to calling. But in addition to texting and phoning, teens also download ringtones, instant message, use mobile Web, download games and messages, use video messages, and watch mobile video.

There's been a wide range of responses to these trends. Most high schools have restrictions on mobile phone use, and close to two-thirds of teens say their parents have put at least one restriction on their mobile use.

## Who is the source?

The Nielsen Company is a major media research company devoted to helping advertisers find the best media to use to reach consumers. How do you think the Nielsen Company funded the study? How might this influence the findings and analysis? Who is the intended audience for this study?

## What is the report saying?

What are some of the stereotypes that Nielsen says adults have about teen media use? Which of them does the study support? Which does the study reject?

## What kind of evidence does the study provide?

What kinds of data do the researchers use? Are those data sufficient to support the assumptions and thereby the recommendations? Are the stereotypes they suggest that adults hold real?

## How do you or your classmates react to the Nielsen Company findings?

Do you think the results of the study accurately describe how you and your friends use media? How do you think your media use differs from how your parents use media? Who or what organizations may benefit from these findings? How might they change media usage in children? What questions are left unanswered? How does your media use compare with that of the young people in the study? How much time do you spend with the various media over the course of a week?

## How were media used in your home?

What controls over media use did you have growing up? Did you have television or Internet access in your own room? Were any limits placed on how you could use your mobile phone? If so, what were they? Do you think these limits (or the lack of limits) had any effect on how you use media or your mobile phone now?

[1] Donald F. Roberts, Ulla G. Foeher, and Vicky Rideout, *Generation M: Media in the Lives of 8–18 Year-Olds* (Henry J. Kaiser Family Foundation, 2005).

[2] Nielsen Company, "How Teens Use Media: A Nielsen Report on the Myths and Realities of Teen Media Trends," 2009, http://blog.nielsen.com/nielsen-wire/reports/nielsen_howteensusemedia_june09.pdf.

on violent video games and television programming, they may well be concerned about the effects of electronic violence on children. But they may also be trying to show that they are concerned about America's children, or that they are getting tough on violence, or that they want to lend support to a cause that their contributors feel strongly about. Take as an example the following excerpts from a press release supporting a bill that would limit "gratuitous and excessive" television violence:

> "Increasing fines is an important way to tell broadcasters that we are serious about taking action against indecent material," [the senator] said. "For the sake of our children, we are not going to tolerate indecency, which seems to appear at all hours of the day on more TV channels than ever. We know from numerous studies that such gratuitous and graphic programming negatively affect our children.
>
> "But it's not enough to increase fines. We need to take on this problem in a truly comprehensive and systematic way that will enable us to diminish the appetite that television producers have for producing shows full of sex and violence. Instead of merely reacting to one or two high profile incidents, we need to preempt these incidents by fundamentally transforming the culture of programming. Only then will we be able to give parents more control of what their children are watching.
>
> "That's what . . . parents want. I hear over and over from them that they are very concerned about what their children are watching. I believe we have a moral imperative to meet this issue head on."
>
> [The senator's] bill enjoys wide support from a variety of groups, including: Parents Television Council, Benedum Foundation, Children Now, Children's Media Policy Coalition, Kaiser Family Foundation, National Association for Family and Community Education, National Coalition for the Protection of Children and Families, and the National Institute on Family and the Media.[67]

Look through the quotes for the signs of activism: "for the sake of our children," "that's what parents want," "the bill enjoys wide support from a variety of groups." Although the senator sponsoring the bill certainly is concerned about the issue of television violence, he has also through this criticism of media violence managed to ally himself with parents and several significant organizations in a way that is relatively safe.

As media consumers, whenever we hear criticism of the media, we ought to ask ourselves, "What is the critic's agenda?"

***Truth Seven: There Is No "They."***    If you listen to media criticism for long, you will hear a pair of words used over and over again: *they* and *them.* It is easy to take potshots at some anonymous bogeymen—*they*—who embody all evil. I even engaged in it at the beginning of this section with the title "Seven truths 'they' don't want you to know about the media."

So who are *they?* No one. Everyone. A nonspecific other we want to blame. Any time I used "they" in a news story, my high school journalism teacher would always ask who "they" were. And that's what you need to ask whenever you hear criticism of the media. It isn't that the criticism is not accurate. It very well may be. But it probably applies to a specific media outlet, a specific journalist, a certain song, or a particular movie. But we can make few generalizations about an industry so diverse that it includes everything from giant corporations producing the $220 million *Superman* movie to kids blogging on LiveJournal. There's a lot of media out there, but no unified *them.*

## CHAPTERSummary

Communication takes place at a number of levels, including intrapersonal (within the self), interpersonal (between individuals), group (between three or more individuals), and mass (between a single sender and a large audience). Mass communication is a communication process that covers an entire society, in which an individual or institution uses technology to send messages to a large, mixed audience, most of whose members are not known to the sender. Mass communication can be examined in terms of the process of transmission; the rituals surrounding its consumption; the attention messages draw to persons, groups, or concepts; or how audience members create meaning out of media content.

The first communication network was developed by the Roman Catholic Church, which as early as the twelfth century could send messages reliably throughout Europe. In the mid-fifteenth century, the development of printing made it possible for books and other publications to be mass produced for the first time, leading to numerous cultural changes. Books, magazines, newspapers, and other printed forms became readily available, although they were expensive before steam-driven printing presses became common in the nineteenth century.

The electronic media emerged in the mid-nineteenth century with the invention of the telegraph, followed by recorded music, radio, movies, and television. These media allowed popular culture to be produced commercially and to be delivered easily and inexpensively into people's homes. The first interactive digital communication network, the Internet, was developed starting in the late 1960s but wasn't available to the general public until the 1990s. The Internet added a return channel to the mass communication process, initiating a much higher level of audience feedback. The Internet also allowed individuals to disseminate their own ideas and information without the costs of a traditional mass medium.

The rapid growth of the mass media has led the public and media critics to raise questions about the effects various media might have on society and individuals. Scholars have suggested that the best way to control the impact of the media in our lives is to develop high levels of media literacy—an understanding of what the media are, how they operate, what messages they are delivering, what roles they play in society, and how audience members respond to these messages. Media literacy includes cognitive, emotional, aesthetic, and moral dimensions.

Your text suggests that the following seven principles can guide your understanding of how the media operate: (1) The media are essential components of our lives; (2) there are no mainstream media; (3) everything from the margin moves to the center; (4) nothing's new—everything that happened in the past will happen again; (5) new media are always scary; (6) activism and analysis are not the same thing; and (7) there is no "they."

## KEYTerms

## CONCEPT Review

Levels of communication

Mass communication versus mass media

Elements of the mass communication process

Models of mass communication: transmission, ritual, publicity, and reception

Pre–mass media communication networks

Print media

Electronic networks

Interactive communication

Media consumption levels

Media literacy and its dimensions

Seven truths about the media

# Mass Communication Effects

## How Society and Media Interact

**The opening of** the YouTube video is instantly familiar—Apple's iconic "1984" Super Bowl commercial featuring dark Orwellian imagery created by famed director Ridley Scott streams out. But what's going on here? Instead of television screens filled with Big Brother spouting ideology at the colorless marching drones, it's Hillary Clinton's face and voice from her presidential campaign announcement video. At the close of the video comes the text, "On January 14th, the Democratic primary will begin. And you'll see why 2008 won't be like '1984.'" The one-minute clip then ends with a letter "O" stylized to resemble the rainbow Apple logo, above the Web address of rival Democratic presidential hopeful Barack Obama.

The mash-up video appeared to come from Obama's campaign, though of course it didn't. But it's a fascinating look at how user-created video sites such as YouTube changed the nature of the 2008 presidential campaign. You had a zero-cost distribution network through which individual people enthralled by the video distributed it virally through blogs and e-mails. Messages were going out that no candidate financed or approved.

Once posted, the video became one of the hottest user-created videos on the Web. Over an eighteen-day period the clip was viewed more than 2.5 million times, and over the course of the 2008 campaign it was viewed more than 4 million times.

There was endless speculation about who created it and, just as important, why. The user name of the video poster was "ParkRidge47," a subtle poke at Senator Clinton, who was born in 1947 and was raised in the Park Ridge, Illinois, area.[1]

The response to the video was fascinating. Obama, appearing on the *Larry King Live* show, denied having anything to do with the video, but he spoke admiringly about it:

> [W]e knew nothing about it. I just saw it for the first time. And, you know, one of the things about the Internet is that people generate all kinds of stuff. In some ways, it's—it's the democratization of the campaign process. . . . But it's not something that we had anything to do with or were aware of and that frankly, given what it looks like, we don't have the technical capacity to create something like that. It's pretty extraordinary.[2]

**Phil de Vellis**

The accusations and rumors about the identity of the creator were all over the place. Of course, some fingered the Obama campaign, while others accused Republican activist groups similar to Swift Boat Veterans for Truth (who helped sink John Kerry's presidential campaign in 2004). Eventually the liberal-leaning Web site the Huffington Post tracked the video back to Phil de Vellis, who had been an Internet consultant for an Ohio Democratic Senate candidate and also worked for a Democratic Internet consulting firm.[3] In his own post on Huffington's blog, de Vellis acknowledged creating the video:

> I made the "Vote Different" ad because I wanted to express my feelings about the Democratic primary, and because I wanted to show that an individual citizen can affect the process. There are thousands of other people who could have made this ad, and I guarantee that more ads like it—by people of all political persuasions—will follow.
> This shows that the future of American politics rests in the hands of ordinary citizens. . . . This ad was not the first citizen ad, and it will not be the last. The game has changed.[4]

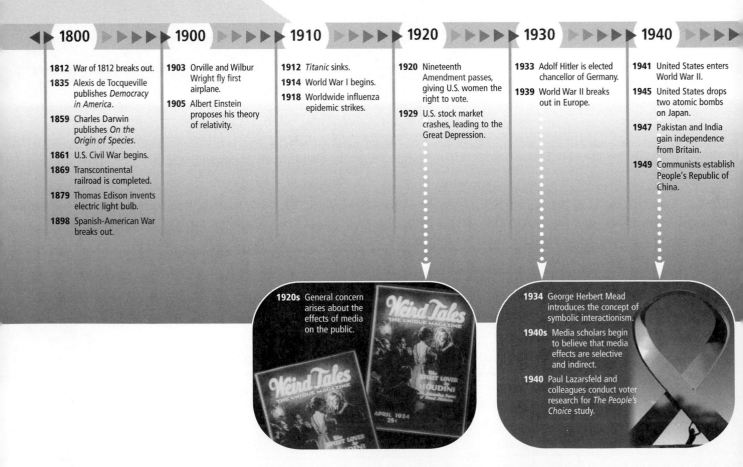

**1800** ▶▶▶▶▶ **1900** ▶▶▶▶▶ **1910** ▶▶▶▶▶ **1920** ▶▶▶▶▶ **1930** ▶▶▶▶▶ **1940** ▶▶▶▶

**1812** War of 1812 breaks out.

**1835** Alexis de Tocqueville publishes *Democracy in America*.

**1859** Charles Darwin publishes *On the Origin of Species*.

**1861** U.S. Civil War begins.

**1869** Transcontinental railroad is completed.

**1879** Thomas Edison invents electric light bulb.

**1898** Spanish-American War breaks out.

**1903** Orville and Wilbur Wright fly first airplane.

**1905** Albert Einstein proposes his theory of relativity.

**1912** *Titanic* sinks.

**1914** World War I begins.

**1918** Worldwide influenza epidemic strikes.

**1920** Nineteenth Amendment passes, giving U.S. women the right to vote.

**1929** U.S. stock market crashes, leading to the Great Depression.

**1933** Adolf Hitler is elected chancellor of Germany.

**1939** World War II breaks out in Europe.

**1941** United States enters World War II.

**1945** United States drops two atomic bombs on Japan.

**1947** Pakistan and India gain independence from Britain.

**1949** Communists establish People's Republic of China.

**1920s** General concern arises about the effects of media on the public.

**1934** George Herbert Mead introduces the concept of symbolic interactionism.

**1940s** Media scholars begin to believe that media effects are selective and indirect.

**1940** Paul Lazarsfeld and colleagues conduct voter research for *The People's Choice* study.

The amazing thing was how easy it was for de Vellis to produce the ad. He told *Vanity Fair's* James Wolcott, "I made the ad on a Sunday afternoon in my apartment using my personal equipment (a Mac and some software), uploaded it to YouTube, and sent links around to blogs."[5] Prior to becoming a full-time political consultant, de Vellis was a freelance video editor and graphics designer in Los Angeles. He has a bachelor's degree in history from the University of California, Los Angeles. After de Vellis was outed as the creator of "Vote Different," he was terminated by his employer, Blue State Digital, but he was soon hired to be the vice president of new media for Murphy Putnam Media.

De Vellis was correct when he said that the political advertising game had changed. During the general election campaign, the best video supporting Obama came not from the campaign but rather from Will.i.am of the Black Eyed Peas. The video "Yes We Can" features speeches by Obama overlaid by a wide range of popular performers singing and speaking. Like "Vote Different," it was created as a personal project by a skilled media professional with no connection to the campaign. Numerous advertising

## 1950 ▶▶▶▶▶ 1960 ▶▶▶▶▶ 1970 ▶▶▶▶▶ 1980 ▶▶▶▶▶ 1990 ▶▶▶▶▶ 2000 ▶▶▶▶

**1950** Korean War begins.

**1953** Francis Crick and James Watson discover structure of DNA.

**1957** Soviet Union launches spacecraft *Sputnik I*.

**1963** Martin Luther King Jr. delivers "I Have a Dream" speech during Washington, D.C., civil-rights march.

**1969** Neil Armstrong walks on the moon.

**1974** U.S. president Richard Nixon resigns due to Watergate scandal.

**1975** Vietnam War ends.

**1977** Apple II personal computer is introduced.

**1978** First test-tube baby is born.

**1983** First HIV/AIDS cases are documented.

**1985** Ozone hole is discovered over Antarctica.

**1986** Space shuttle *Challenger* explodes.

**1989** The Berlin Wall falls.

**1991** Soviet Union disbands.

**1993** European Union is formed.

**1994** Nelson Mandela is elected president of South Africa.

**1997** Diana, Princess of Wales, dies in car accident.

**2001** Al Qaida attacks World Trade Center and Pentagon.

**2003** United States invades Iraq.

**2003** Human genome project is completed.

**2005** Terrorists bomb London's transport system.

**2005** Hurricane Katrina hits the U.S. Gulf Coast.

**2008** Barack Obama is elected U.S. president.

**1964** Marshall McLuhan theorizes that the medium is as important as the message that it sends.

**1967** George Gerbner begins his studies of violence on television.

**1968** Donald Shaw and Maxwell McCombs study agenda setting among uncommitted voters in the 1968 presidential election.

**1979** Herbert Gans finds a bias in the media towards enduring American values.

journalists, including *Ad Age*'s Bob Garfield and *Business Week*'s David Kiley, called "Yes We Can" the best marketing message of 2008.[6] (You can see the "Vote Different" and "Yes We Can" videos at http://ralphehanson.com.)

Clay Johnson, the head of Blue State Digital, in an interview conducted before de Vellis was revealed as the video's creator, spoke to the challenges of user-created video. "The real trouble . . . is that as people get more sophisticated in producing these videos, you're going to see a very large blur in what's official and what's not."[7]

In this simple statement, Johnson is putting forward Truth Two—There are no mainstream media; Truth Three—Everything from the margin moves to the center; and, by implication, Truth Five—New media are always scary. The "Vote Different" and "Yes We Can" videos show how new tools, such as YouTube videos, are becoming a growing part of the political process. What makes user-produced videos so scary to those in the business of politics is that the videos can't be controlled. They aren't yet regulated—at least as of this writing—by the Federal Election Commission; they can be produced by anyone with talent and a halfway-decent computer; and they can reach a worldwide audience almost instantly at little cost to the producer. In this chapter we look at how our understanding of media effects have evolved over the past century, and consider several approaches to studying media effects. Finally, we look at how media effects can be analyzed within the realm of politics.

# HISTORY OF MEDIA EFFECTS RESEARCH

As we discussed in Chapter 1 in the section on media literacy, media consumers often assume that the media have large, obvious, and generally negative effects on people, and look to blame the media for complex social problems.[8] In this section we look at how our understanding of media effects has evolved and changed over the past 200 years.

## Rise of Mass Society

Prior to the 1800s, most people in Europe and North America lived in rural communities where their neighbors were likely to be similar in ethnic, racial, and religious background. People knew their neighbors, and their neighbors knew them. There were only limited opportunities for people to change their station in life or to learn much about the outside world. But with the rise of the Industrial Revolution in the nineteenth century, we started to see a massive level of migration from the rural areas into the cities, and from various countries to the United States. As people moved into the cities, they started working for wages in factories with people who were quite different from them. With industrialization, people went from small, close-knit communities where they knew everyone to a mass society where they learned about the world from mass media sources such as the new inexpensive newspapers, magazines, and paperback novels.[9]

At the end of the nineteenth century, people came to believe that the traditional ties of church, community, and family were breaking down and losing their power to influence people. The comfortable local community was being replaced by something impersonal, complex, and removed from the traditions that had previously held people together. Concerned observers noted that people seemed to be alienated, isolated, and interchangeable members of a faceless mass audience, separated by the decline of the family and the growth of technology. So what held this new, mass society together?[10] The increasingly frequent answer was that the mass media would replace the church, family, and community in shaping public opinion.[11] (For additional discussion of the growth of the mass media from its origins in the 1400s to the present day, see Chapter 1.)

## Propaganda and the Direct Effects Model

Fears that media messages would have strong, direct effects on audience members grew out of propaganda efforts by all combatants during World War I and by Nazi Germany and Fascist Italy in the 1930s. Critics worried that mass media messages would overwhelm people in the absence of the influences of family and community. With traditional social forces in decline, it was inevitable, critics feared, that the media would become the most powerful force within society.

This argument viewed audience members as passive targets who would be hit or injected with the message, which, like a vaccine, would affect most people in similar ways. But research looking for powerful direct effects leading to opinion and behavioral changes generally came up short. In fact, in the 1940s and 1950s researchers sometimes doubted whether media messages had any effect on individuals at all.[12] Although most scholars now focus on the media's indirect effects on society rather than their direct effects on individuals, they remain concerned about how the media influence individuals.

The big problem is that the direct-effects approach viewed media messages as a stimulus that would lead to a predictable attitudinal or behavioral response with nothing intervening between sender and audience. But although people have a shared biological heritage, they have different backgrounds,

*Allied propaganda posters designed to build support for World War I weren't afraid to make use of strong negative stereotypes of the Germans.*

needs, attitudes, and values. In short, everyone has been socialized differently. The indirect-effects approach still looks at the effects that messages have on individuals, but it accounts for the fact that audience members perceive and interpret these messages selectively according to individual differences. Because people's perceptions are selective, their responses to the messages vary as well. A person who is preparing to buy a car, a person who just bought one, and a person who doesn't drive will each react differently to an automobile commercial.

## Voter Studies and the Limited Effects Model

During the 1920s and 1930s, coinciding with the uses of propaganda by the Nazis, Italian Fascists, and Soviets, many critics worried that the media might be responsible for powerful, direct effects on the public. Their general worries about the media extended to the possible effects of political campaign messages. Critics, considering recent urbanization and the decline of traditional institutions, feared that political media campaigns would "inject" people with ideas that would lead to the message creator's desired actions, such as supporting a particular candidate, ideology, or point of view. This model of powerful direct campaign effects was largely discredited by voter studies in the 1940s and 1950s, but it remains important because many people still believe that it is accurate.[13]

**The People's Choice.**   One of the first large-scale social-scientific studies of campaign influences was *The People's Choice* study of the 1940 U.S. presidential election contest between Democrat Franklin D. Roosevelt and Republican Wendell Willkie. A team of researchers led by Paul Lazarsfeld looked at how voters in Erie County, Ohio, decided which candidate to vote for. Lazarsfeld's team found that people who were highly interested in the campaign, and paid the most attention to media coverage of it, were least likely to be influenced. Why? Because they had decided whom they supported before the campaign had even begun.[14]

In contrast, voters who decided at the last minute usually turned to friends or neighbors, rather than the media, for information about the campaign. In general, they turned to people who followed the campaign closely, the ones whom Lazarsfeld called opinion leaders.

**opinion leaders**
Influential community members who invest substantial amounts of time learning about their own area of expertise, such as politics. Less well-informed friends and family members frequently turn to them for advice about the topic.

**Opinion leaders** are influential community members—friends, family members, and coworkers—who spend significant time with the media. Lazarsfeld suggested that information flows from the media to opinion leaders, and then from opinion leaders to the rest of the public. Keep in mind that the opinion leaders are ordinary people who are simply very interested and involved in a topic. Although this finding was not expected, it should not be terribly surprising that interpersonal influence is more important than the media. The idea here is fairly simple: People in groups tend to share opinions with one another, and when they want reliable information, they go to the people they know. With the lengthy campaigns today, people find it easier to turn to interpersonal sources than the wealth of media information. Yet this trend is nothing new. Although many people believe that our election campaigns are starting earlier and earlier every election cycle, presidential candidate William Jennings Bryan started his campaign for the 1900 election one month after the election of 1896![15] Even as early as the 1830s, when the penny press was just getting started, presidential campaigns could run as long as two years.

*The People's Choice* study, as well as other early voter studies, found that campaigns typically reinforced existing political predispositions and that few people changed their minds about whom they were going to support. There are several reasons for this:

The People's Choice *study examined how voters made up their minds during the 1940 presidential election between the Republican candidate Wendell Willkie (pictured standing, center front) and the Democratic incumbent, Franklin D. Roosevelt.*

- The voters who start off with strong opinions are unlikely to change them.

- The voters who pay the most attention to a campaign are those with the strongest political views; thus, they are the least likely to change their opinions.

- The most persuadable voters (those who are least informed) are not likely to pay attention to political communication and therefore are not strongly influenced by media coverage of the campaign.[16]

## The Importance of Meaning and the Critical/Cultural Model

Up through the 1940s, most of the research on the mass media focused on direct and indirect effects of media messages on the behaviors of groups and individuals. But another school of thought looks at how people use media to construct their view of the world rather than looking at how media change people's behaviors. Instead of using the quantitative data analysis of the voter studies, the critical/cultural approach takes a more qualitative examination of the social structure in which communication takes place. It considers how meaning is created within society, who controls the media systems, and the roles the media play in our lives. Instead of looking at how messages affect people, it looks at how people use and construct messages.[17]

Under the critical/cultural approach, ordinary people were seen as moving from being information providers to information receivers, with only limited opportunities to answer back to the ideas being provided by the people in power. Thus the mass media become a tool for controlling the flow of information and the topics that can be discussed.[18] As we discuss in Chapter 3, with increasing media consolidation, more and more of our media are owned by fewer and fewer companies, so that there is an increasing level of control of what topics can be discussed and debated. Critical theorists would argue that the subjects that get covered are those in the best interests of the advertisers who support the media and the companies that own them.[19]

An example of the critical/cultural approach is the charge, leveled by many critics, that the disappearances of attractive, wealthy white women attract much more media attention than do disappearances of women of color, or those who are poor. Consider the case of Lakesha Parker, a 33-year-old African American woman who was murdered by persons unknown in an elementary schoolyard in inner-city Washington, D.C., in 2005. Haven't heard of Lakesha Parker? Her murder and the surrounding mystery got written up by *Washington Post* columnist Colbert I. King, and the case received a three-paragraph mention in a *Post* crime roundup story. Her murder got no attention from Fox News, CNN, MSNBC, or any other media outlet outside Washington, D.C. Four years later, her murder was still listed as an unsolved cold case.[20] Compare her story to that of Laci Peterson. The wealthy, pregnant white woman was murdered in 2002; by 2005, she had long been buried, and her husband had been convicted of the crime. Yet at the time Parker was killed, a Google news search could still find 275 stories about the Peterson case.

A similar media silence characterized the 2004 disappearance of 24-year-old Tamika Huston, an African American woman from Spartanburg, South Carolina. Her case received one or two mentions on Fox News, but it was noted mostly in stories about how disappearing black women are ignored, while stories about white women and girls, such as the "runaway bride" and missing teenager Natalee Holloway, get story counts in the hundreds or thousands. Keith Woods, an expert on diversity issues at the Poynter Institute, a journalism think tank, says stories about minority women tend to get lost because reporters are more likely to report about people they see as being like themselves. And since most newsrooms tend to be disproportionately white and middle class, the disappearance of a white woman is seen as a bigger story. This control over which stories are reported means that the public at large is not aware that African American women are disproportionately more likely to disappear than white women.[21] (For more about the so-called missing white women syndrome, go to http://ralphehanson.com.)

# EFFECTS OF THE MEDIA IN OUR LIVES

Media scholars throughout the twentieth century who studied the effects of the mass media on individuals and society questioned several aspects of the media, including the messages being sent, the media sending them, the owners of the media, and the audience members themselves.[22]

## Message Effects

Not surprisingly, the earliest concerns about the effects of mass communication focused on how messages might change people's behaviors, attitudes, or beliefs. These message effects can take a variety of forms.

*Cognitive Effects.* The most common and observable message effect is on the short-term learning of information. This can be as significant as learning about a new medical treatment or as trivial as remembering the lyrics to a popular song. The amount of learning that takes place from media content depends largely on the motivation level of the person consuming the media. Political scientist Doris Graber found that people who want to be able to talk intelligently with others about media content (whether it is the news, a sporting event, or an entertainment program) learn much more from the media than people who are simply seeking entertainment. Research also shows that people learn more from people they identify with and pay more attention to political commentators they agree with than ones they dislike.[23] Hence the most popular political radio talk shows, such as those hosted by conservatives Rush Limbaugh and Sean Hannity, argue a single and consistent point of view rather than providing a range of views.[24]

*Attitudinal Effects.* People can develop feelings about a product, an individual, or an idea on the basis of media content. Viewers might decide that they like a new product, political candidate, or hairstyle because of what they have seen in a television commercial, a news broadcast, or a sitcom. Typically it is much easier to get people to form new opinions than to get them to change existing ones.[25] For example, political advertising generally tries to change the opinions of uncommitted voters rather than those of voters who already have strong political loyalties. In the 2008 presidential campaign, the Obama campaign frequently targeted young voters who had less established political loyalties with ads found on Comedy Central to VH1 to Xbox Live video games.[26] (For more on advertising in video games, see Chapter 10.)

*Behavioral Effects.* Behavioral effects include actions such as clipping a coupon from a newspaper, buying a product, making a phone call, or voting for a candidate. They might also include imitating attractive behaviors (for example, dressing a certain way). Behavioral effects are in many ways the most difficult to achieve because people are reluctant to change their behavior. Sometimes, however, people go to the media deliberately looking for behavior to copy, as when a child watches an episode of *Batman* and then imitates it in play, or when a teenager watches a movie to learn how to behave on a date.[27]

*Psychological Effects.*    Media content can inspire fear, joy, revulsion, happiness, or amusement, among other feelings.[28] A major psychological effect of media content, especially violent or erotic material, is arousal. Symptoms of arousal can include a rise in heart rate, adrenaline levels, or sexual response. Seeking a psychological response is a common reason for spending time with the media, whether the response sought is relaxation, excitement, or emotional release. Arousal can come from content (action, violence, sexuality, loud music or sound) and from style (motion, use of color, the rate and speed at which new images appear). Notice that music videos, which often offer little in terms of learning, provide many of these elements.[29] Contemporary composer John Adams talks about how his Pulitzer Prize–winning composition about the September 11, 2001, attacks, "On the Transmigration of Souls," makes people feel:

> Modern people have learned all too well how to keep our emotions in check, and we know how to mask them with humor or irony. Music has a singular capacity to unlock those controls and bring us face to face with our raw, uncensored, and unattenuated feelings. That is why during times when we are grieving or in need of being in touch with the core of our beings we seek out those pieces which speak to us with that sense of gravitas and serenity.[30]

You can find a link to the complete interview and excerpts from Adams's music at http://ralphehanson.com.

## Medium Effects

As mass media consumption grew in the 1950s, scholars also started paying more attention to the particular medium being used to transmit messages. Until the 1950s, most of the media effects research focused on the interactions among the sender, the message, and the receiver, ignoring the influence of the medium itself. But the medium used to communicate is crucial. Canadian communication researcher Marshall McLuhan argued that the medium used for transmission can be as important as the message itself, if not more so. McLuhan is best known for his statement "The medium is the message," by which he meant that the method of message transmittal is a central part of the message. For example, television does an excellent job of transmitting emotional messages because it includes both visual (explosions, luxury interiors) and audio (laugh tracks, scary music) cues along with words. And consider technology that enhances the sound of movies: Surround sound systems are designed to create a realistic experience by surrounding viewers with five distinct sound channels as well as shaking them with a deep bass channel. The goal is not to transmit the message better but rather to create a more overwhelming experience. (Think of how the impact of a summer blockbuster film would be diminished if the sound were turned down.) The same is true of large-screen high-definition television sets. Books and newspapers, in contrast, are much better at transmitting complex rational information because these media allow us to review the information and consider its meaning at our own pace.[31] The Web excels at providing obscure materials that appeal to a limited, widely dispersed audience, and it makes it easy for receivers to respond to what they've seen or heard.

*Canadian media scholar Marshall McLuhan is best remembered for his statement, "The medium is the message." He argued that the way a message is transmitted can have as big an impact as the content of the message.*

Media scholars now recognize that communication technology is a fundamental element of society and that new technologies can lead to social change.[32] Media sociologist Joshua Meyrowitz, for example, argues that the existence and development of various media can lead to radical changes in society. He writes that the development of publishing and books in the sixteenth century made it easy for new ideas to spread beyond the person who originated them and that this tended to undermine the control of ideas by both the monarchy and the Roman Catholic Church.[33] As can be seen by the "Vote Different" ad discussed at the beginning of the chapter, the existence of the Internet now allows anyone to create and spread political messages, not just those with the resources to command the attention of the traditional media.

Meyrowitz also identifies some social effects of particular media. In *No Sense of Place*, he argues that the major effect of print as a medium is to segregate audiences according to education, age, class, and gender. For example, a teenager needs to be able to read at a certain level to understand the content of a magazine targeted at young women or young men—content that a young child would be unable to comprehend. In contrast, electronic media like television tend to cross the demographic boundaries. A child too young to read a magazine or book can still understand at least some of the information in a television program targeted at adults.[34] This is why parent groups and childhood educators pushed to have early evening programming on television contain more "family-friendly" programs and why parents seek to restrict certain Internet sites on a family computer.

The importance of the particular medium used to convey a message applies at every level of communication, from intrapersonal (How is an audio journal different from a written one?) to interpersonal (How is a phone call different from an e-mail?) to mass (How is a book different from a movie?).

## Ownership Effects

Instead of looking at the effects of media and their messages, some scholars examine the influence of those who own and control the media.[35] These critical scholars are concerned because owners of media determine which ideas will be produced and distributed by those media.

In the United States, the majority of media outlets are owned by six giant multinational companies: Time Warner, Disney, News Corporation, Viacom/CBS, Bertelsmann, and General Electric. Some observers, like the German academic and sociologist Jürgen Habermas, fear that these corporations are becoming a sort of ruling class, controlling which books are published, which programs are aired, which movies are produced, and which news stories are written.[36] As we discuss in Chapter 3, Rupert Murdoch's News Corporation has at times dropped publication of books critical of the Chinese government and removed channels such as the BBC from its satellite service in China in order to please the communist government there.[37]

Media critic and former newspaper editor Ben Bagdikian suggests that the influence of media owners can be seen in how the news media select stories to be covered. He argues that large media organizations will kill news stories and entertainment programs that don't reflect well on the corporation. The roots of this tendency go back to when captains of industry such as J. P. Morgan and the Rockefellers bought out magazines that criticized them in order to silence their criticism. What we end up with, Bagdikian says, is not the feared bogeyman of government censorship, but rather "a new Private Ministry of Information and Culture" that gives corporations control over what we will see, hear, or read.[38] Increasingly, however, the new alternative media are providing channels that allow consumers to bypass big media controls.[39] (See the section on long-tail media in Chapter 3 for more on how these new channels are enabling anyone who wants to distribute content to do so on a large scale.) Bloggers such as Red State or the Daily Kos give voice to issues from a partisan point of view with no controls at all other than those the authors choose to employ.

## Active Audience Effects

Some of the early fears about the effects of the media on audience members arose from the belief that the audience truly was a faceless, undifferentiated mass—that the characteristics of the audience en masse also applied to the audience's individual members. Early critics viewed modern people as alienated and isolated individuals who, separated by the decline of the family and the growth of a technological society, didn't communicate with one another. After World War II, the concept of the mass audience began to change as scholars came to realize that the audience was made up of unique members who respond as individuals, not as undifferentiated members of a mass.[40]

Today communicators, marketers, and scholars realize that individuals seek and respond to different messages at different times and for different reasons. Therefore, they divide audiences on the basis of **geographics**, or where people live; **demographics**, or their gender, race, ethnic background, income, education, age, educational attainment, and the like; or **psychographics**, a combination of demographics, lifestyle characteristics, and product usage. Hence a young woman buying a small SUV to take her mountain bike out into the mountains will respond to a very different kind of advertising message than a mother seeking a small SUV so that she can safely drive her child to school during rush hour in the winter.

Audiences can also be classified by the amount of time they spend using media or by the purposes for which they use media. Each segment of the media audience will behave differently. Take television viewing as an example. Some people tune in daily to watch their favorite soap opera and won't change channels for the entire hour. This is known as appointment viewing. Others surf through a number of channels using the remote control, looking for something that will capture their interest. Still others switch back and forth between two channels. With regard to television, the concept of a mass audience consuming the same content at the same time existed to some extent from the 1950s to the 1970s, when the vast majority of viewers had access to only three broadcast networks, but that concept broke down completely with the advent of cable, satellite, multiple broadcast networks, TiVo, DVDs, and VCRs.

Media scholar James Potter suggests that the media audience resembles a pyramid. (Remember the pyramid figure in Chapter 1?) At the peak of the pyramid we are all consuming the same messages, such as the horrifying reports of the September 11, 2001, terrorist attacks. At the base of the pyramid we are all different, consuming what interests us personally, such as when we surf the Internet. In between the narrow top and the wide base are the various audience segments that the media and advertisers are trying to reach.[41]

In addition to recognizing that different people use the media in different ways, scholars have realized that mass communication messages are generally mediated through other levels of communication. One reason this book discusses intrapersonal, interpersonal, and group communication as well as mass communication is that these levels all come into play in how mass communication operates. People discuss political news with one another, cheer together for their favorite teams while watching a hockey game on television, and think

**geographics**
The study of where people live; a method typically used to analyze potential markets for products and programs.

**demographics**
The study of audience members' gender, race, ethnic background, income, education, age, educational attainment, and the like; a method typically used to analyze potential markets for products and programs.

**psychographics**
A combination of demographics, lifestyle characteristics, and product usage; a method typically used to analyze potential markets for products and programs.

about how stock market information is going to affect their investment plans. A young man's reaction to a love scene in a movie will differ when he watches it with other young men, with his girlfriend, or with his parents.[42]

# THEORIES OF MEDIA AND SOCIETY

There is a scene in *Star Wars: The Empire Strikes Back* where Luke Skywalker is nervous about entering a cave beneath a tree in the Dagobah jungle. He asks Master Yoda, "What's in there?" To which Yoda replies, "Only what you take with you." And so it is with mass communication. What we find with mass communication research depends in large part on the theory base we take with us and the questions the theories suggest we pose. It's not so much that different approaches to research give us different answers, as it is that they take us to different questions. In this section we look at several of the theoretical approaches to mass communication and the types of questions they raise.

## Functional Analysis

The effects of the media are not limited to those on individuals or groups. Some of the media's most significant effects reach society as a whole.

According to media scholar Harold Lasswell, the mass media are simply an extension of basic functions that society has always needed. Earlier societies had priests, town criers, storytellers, bards who sang ballads, and travelers who brought news from distant lands.[43] Communication can be functional or dysfunctional, but in either case it operates within the social system.[44] For example, some people respond inappropriately to the news of approaching danger. Instead of going to the basement during a tornado warning, a functional response, they go outside with their video cameras to get footage of the storm, a dysfunctional response. In both cases, they are responding to the news of the storm.

Lasswell wrote that the media perform three major social functions:[45]

1. Surveillance of the environment, looking for both threats and opportunities.

2. Correlation of different elements of society, allowing segments of society to work together.

3. Transmission of culture from one generation to the next.

To these three, media sociologist Charles Wright adds the function of entertainment.[46] Let's look more closely at each of these functions.

*Surveillance of the Environment.*    Much of what we know about the world we learn from the media through the process of **surveillance**. The media show us what is happening not only within our own culture but in other societies as well. Our only other sources of knowledge about the world are our own direct experiences and the direct experiences that others share with us.

The constant flow of information from the media allows us to survey our surroundings. It can give us warnings of approaching danger—everything from changes in the weather, to earthquakes, to violence in the streets. This flow of information is essential for the everyday operation of society. The stock markets depend on the business news, travelers depend on weather forecasts, and grocery shoppers depend on knowing what's on special this week.

Surveillance can also serve to undermine society. For example, when people in poor nations see media images of what life is like in the United States and other industrialized Western nations, they may become dissatisfied with the conditions of their own lives, and this may lead to social unrest and violence. News about violence may also make people more fearful for their own safety.

Surveillance is not just for the masses. Government and industry leaders worldwide watch CNN or C-SPAN or read the *New York Times* or the *Financial Times* to know what other government leaders are saying and thinking.

News can also give status to individuals. Because media coverage exposes them to large audiences, they seem important. This process is known as **status conferral**. Thus the U.S. president's press spokesperson becomes famous and important simply because he or she is speaking with the media.[47] Think about the level of coverage that the death of Anna Nicole Smith generated in the winter of 2007. Smith's main claim to fame seems to have been being a *Playboy* Playmate of the Year, marrying a wealthy old man, and engaging in a particularly nasty estate battle with the old man's other heirs after he died. She was certainly not a popular culture figure at the level of Michael Jackson. Yet she had been in the news continually, apparently famous for being famous. When she died, for two days afterward, her story consumed 50 percent of the airtime on cable news channels.[48]

*Correlation of Different Elements of Society.*    **Correlation** is the selection, evaluation, and interpretation of events to impose structure on the news. Correlation is accomplished by persuasive communication through editorials, commentary, advertising, and propaganda. Through media-supplied correlation we make sense out of what we learn through surveillance. It puts news into categories and provides cues that indicate the importance of each news item. Does it appear on the front page of the newspaper? Is it the first item on the broadcast? Is there a teaser on the magazine cover promoting the story?

**surveillance**
How the media help us extend our senses to perceive more of the world surrounding us.

**status conferral**
The process by which media coverage makes an individual gain prominence in the eyes of the public.

**correlation**
The process of selecting, evaluating, and interpreting events to give structure to the news. The media assist the process of correlation by persuasive communication through editorials, commentary, advertising, and propaganda, and by providing cues that indicate the importance of each news item.

*Kourtney, Kim, and Klohé Kardashian, and their mother, Kris Jenner (left to right), are famous primarily for showing up at media events. Their fame is an example of media status conferral.*

Although many people say that they would prefer just the facts, virtually the only news outlet that provides no interpretation of events is the public affairs network C-SPAN, which has rigid rules governing how every event is covered. Far more viewers choose to go to the broadcast networks or cable news channels, which provide some interpretation, rather than the relatively dry, "just the facts" C-SPAN.[49]

It is often difficult to distinguish between communication that is informative and communication that is persuasive. Editorial judgments are always being made as to which stories should be covered and which should be omitted, which picture of a politician should be published, or what kind of headline should be written. Thus it is useful to view surveillance and correlation as two functions that can be shared by a particular message.

**socialization**

The process of educating young people and new members about the values, social norms, and knowledge of a group or society.

**entertainment**

Media communication intended primarily to amuse the audience.

*Socialization and Transmission of Culture.* **Socialization** is the process of integrating people within society through the transmission of values, social norms, and knowledge to new members of the group. It is through the media, along with our friends, family, school, and church, that we learn the values of our society. Socialization is important not only to young people as they are growing up but also to immigrants learning about and assimilating into their new country, high school students heading off to college, and new graduates going to work.[50]

The media provide socialization in a variety of ways:

- Through role models in entertainment programming

- Through goals and desires as presented in media content

- Through the citizenship values portrayed in the news

- Through advertisements for products that may be useful to us in different stages of our lives

*Entertainment.* **Entertainment** is communication designed primarily to amuse, even if it serves other functions as well, which it almost always does.

A television medical drama would be considered entertainment, even though it might educate a person about life in a hospital or the symptoms of a major illness. In fact, a major characteristic of all television programming, including entertainment programming, is to let people know what life outside their own world is like.[51]

## Agenda Setting

Although explanations of powerful direct effects did not hold up under research scrutiny, people still had a hard time accepting that the news media and political campaigns had little or no effect on the public. **Agenda-setting theory** provided an alternative explanation that did not minimize the influence of the media on society.[52] This theory holds that issues that are portrayed as important in the news media become important to the public—that is, that the media set the agenda for public debate. If the media are not able to tell people what to think, as the direct effects model proposed, perhaps they can tell people what to think *about.* Agenda-setting theorists seek to determine whether the issues that are important to the media are also important to the public.[53] For example, health care issues received much more discussion and attention in the United States following extensive coverage of health care reform legislation before Congress in the summer of 2009. The Pew Research Center found that, over a five-week period, health care was the top topic for news coverage, overwhelming discussion of the economic crisis and two wars.[54]

The initial study of agenda setting was conducted in Chapel Hill, North Carolina, by Donald Shaw and Maxwell McCombs. The researchers found, among uncommitted voters in the 1968 presidential election, a strong relationship between the issues the press considered important and the issues the voters considered important. Since these voters had not already made up their minds about the upcoming election, their most likely source of cues, the researchers concluded, was the mass media. The study compared the content of the press and the attitudes of voters and found a strong correlation. Even though the researchers did not find evidence that the press persuaded people to change their opinions, they did find that the issues featured in the campaign and in the press were also the issues that voters felt were important.[55]

There are, however, some limits on the usefulness of the agenda-setting concept. If a story does not resonate with the public, neither the media nor the candidates will be able to make people care. For example, reports that Ronald and Nancy Reagan had conceived a child before they were married did not seem to do any damage to Reagan's image; nor was the Rev. Pat Robertson's campaign damaged by reports that the candidate and his wife had lied about the date of their wedding anniversary to hide the fact that their first child was conceived premaritally.

**agenda-setting theory**
A theory of media effects that says that the media don't tell the public what to think but rather what to think about—thus the terms of public discourse are set by what is covered in the media.

# Uses and Gratifications Theory

**Uses and gratifications theory** turns the traditional way of looking at media effects on its head. Instead of looking at the audience as a sheep-like mass of receivers of messages, uses and gratifications theory views audience members as active receivers of information of their own choosing. Uses and gratifications theory is based on the following assumptions:

- Audience members are active receivers who have wants and needs. They then make decisions about media use based on those wants and needs. For example, in this approach, television doesn't *do things* to children, children *make use* of television.

- Media compete with many sources of gratification. I might watch television in the evening to relax. Television would be competing with reading a magazine, going for a walk, or playing with my son as alternative ways of relaxing.

- Audience members are aware of these choices and make them consciously.

- Our judgments about the value of various media uses must come from the audience's perspective.[56]

The idea behind uses and gratification theory is that individuals are constantly seeking gratifications, and the media compete to provide them. Media scholar Arthur Asa Berger says that among the gratifications that audience members might seek are to be amused, to experience the beautiful, to have shared experiences with others, to find models to imitate, and to believe in romantic love.[57] So someone who doesn't care about football might still watch a game on television and enjoy it because he wants to spend time with friends. Although he is consuming media, that's not the real point of his interaction with the television set.

# Social Learning

At some point in your life you've been told that experience is the best teacher. While experience may be a good teacher, it is also a harsh one, forcing us to suffer from our mistakes. Fortunately, we don't have to make all these mistakes ourselves, according to social psychologist Albert Bandura's **social learning theory**. Bandura writes, "If knowledge and skills could be acquired only by direct experience, the process of human development would be greatly retarded, not to mention exceedingly tedious and hazardous."[58] Instead, he says that we are able to learn by observing what others do and the consequences they face. Bandura says humans go through three steps to engage in social learning:

- We extract key information from situations we observe.

- We integrate these observations to create rules about how the world operates.

- We put these rules into practice to regulate our own behavior and predict the behaviors of others.

The media, by widening the information about the world that we are exposed to, plays an important role in social learning. Think about a child who watches Batman defeat evil bad guys (EBGs) by physically fighting with them. Fighting with the EBGs proves to be a successful strategy and generally earns the super-hero praise and the keys to Gotham City. So while watching the animated show may not lead directly to the child engaging in violence, it could teach him that fighting is an effective way of solving problems that leads to social approval. He may then try out the practice by fighting with his sister, at which point he discovers it does not lead to social approval from his parents, and he stops the behavior. Or he might try it out by fighting with his friends and discover that it leads to his receiving respect. From this simplistic example we can see how social learning theory can be applied to analyzing media. The content of the media can provide a large-scale source of content from which social learning can take place.[59] If the behavior being modeled is successful in achieving the person's goals, it may continue to be used. Think of the *Batman*-watching child who gains respect among his friends by fighting. If the behavior is unsuccessful in achieving results, the person may try other strategies. Think of the *Batman*-watching child who earns parental disapproval by fighting with his sister. He may sharpen his verbal or negotiating skills to gain the upper hand in conflicts with his sister.

## Symbolic Interactionism

George Herbert Mead wrote back in 1934 that what holds us together as a culture is our common creation of society through our interactions based on language, or **symbolic interactionism**. We engage in symbolic interactions in which we continually attempt to arouse in others the feeling we have in ourselves by telling others how we feel. If our language is understood, we are able to communicate; if, on the other hand, we do not share common meanings, we will not be understood.[60] The mass media are by far the biggest source of shared meanings in our world. (Truth One—The media are essential components of our lives.) If you think back to our discussion of the meaning of the yellow ribbon in Chapter 1, you can see how this works. We start with an arbitrary symbol—the yellow ribbon. We assign it meaning and then propagate that meaning through portrayal through the media. Eventually nearly everyone comes to have the same shared meaning of the looped ribbon, and the ribbon

**symbolic interactionism**

The process by which individuals produce meaning through interaction based on socially agreed-upon symbols.

becomes a universal symbol of support—support for the troops, for disease sufferers, and for all kinds of social causes.

Sociologist W. I. Thomas provides us with one of the most quoted and understandable statements of symbolic interactionism: "If men define situations as real, they are real in their consequences."[61] If we ignore the outdated gender bias of the quote, there's a lot to analyze there. What Thomas is saying is that if people view a problem as being real, and behave as though a problem is real, it will have real consequences, even if the problem does not truly exist. Back in 1938, Orson Welles had a famous radio adaptation of H. G. Wells's *War of the Worlds*. The radio play was misinterpreted by some to be an actual news story, and there were many accounts at the time of people panicking and even committing suicide out of fear of the Martians invading New Jersey. Ever since then, broadcasters have been very careful to run extensive disclaimers on the air every time they run a *War of the Worlds*–style story, to make sure they don't panic their audience. There is also a widespread fear of powerful effects that the mass media can have on susceptible audience members. The only problem is that the research conducted at the time on the *War of the Worlds* panic was seriously flawed, and criticism of the research, dating back to the 1940s, has largely been ignored, in part because the belief in the *War of the Worlds* effect is so strong. The truth is that there was far more perception of panic than actual panic at the time. In summary, it doesn't matter much now whether the panic actually took place. What matters is that people believe that it did.[62]

## Spiral of Silence

**spiral of silence**

A theory that suggests that people want to see themselves as holding a majority opinion and will therefore remain silent if they perceive that they hold a minority opinion. This tends to make the minority opinion appear to be less prevalent than it is.

German media scholar Elisabeth Noelle-Neumann, with her **spiral of silence**, has raised the question of why people become unwilling to express what they perceive to be a minority opinion. Noelle-Neumann became interested in these questions in part by trying to find out why the Germans supported political positions that led to national defeat, humiliation, and ruin in the 1930s–1940s or why the French under German occupation were seemingly complacent as Jewish friends and neighbors were sent off to concentration camps. Noelle-Neumann says that societies function on the basis of perceived consensus. We want to view ourselves as part of a majority, and holding the consensus opinion. Thus people will refrain from expressing opinions that they think will be at odds with those of their friends and neighbors, even though their neighbors might actually agree with them.[63]

So how do people receive the cues that indicate what popular public opinion is, so that they might agree with it? The media are important public institutions because they are often our best source of public opinion. Central to Noelle-Neumann's argument is that when people believe they are in the minority with their opinion, they will tend to stay quiet on the topic, thus feeding the sense that a particular opinion is held by a minority. Thus it becomes a death spiral of diversity of ideas, as more and more people come to believe that they hold a minority opinion.[64]

While the spiral of silence is a fascinating explanation of how public opinion functions, it is difficult to independently verify and prove whether it, in fact, works that way. Radicals will oftentimes speak up with unpopular opinions precisely because they are unpopular. And people who care deeply about an issue will speak out simply because they feel they are correct. As an example, think about the willingness of the country crossover group the Dixie Chicks to put themselves and their careers at risk by criticizing President George W. Bush in the early days of the Iraq war at a time when they knew their views would be unpopular. One recent study suggests that the spiral of silence will be much stronger in cultures that value conformity of opinion, such as Taiwan, and will be much weaker in individualistic cultures, such as the United States.[65]

## Media Logic

**Media logic** is an approach to analyzing the effects of mass media developed by David Altheide and Robert Snow. They argue that we live in a media world in which the dominant cultural forms are those defined by the media.[66] The media provide major types of content—news, sports, action, drama, comedy, and advertising—that follow standardized formats. When we turn on a television set, long before we can say what specific program is on, we can use format cues to tell what type of program it is, even if we've never seen it before. These standard formats become a lens through which we view our everyday life. For example, we may use the format of a sports broadcast to describe our presidential races and apply soap opera formats to describe ongoing political scandals. We also use these formats to shape our behaviors, especially when we want to get media attention. So when an organization has something important happening, its officials plan the event around the needs and schedules of the media they want to cover them.[67] Thus the event that the media covers is constructed especially to facilitate its being covered. Think about a group of protesters protesting the construction of a new power plant on a cold, rainy day. They huddle under their shelters with their signs until a news crew from a local television station shows up. Then the protesters come to life, marching and chanting for the benefit of the cameras. The mere fact that the cameras are there changes what's happening.

## Cultivation Analysis

George Gerbner (1919–2005), the best-known researcher of television violence, did not believe televised violence has direct effects on people's behavior, but he was deeply concerned about its effect on society as a whole.[68] Gerbner developed an alternative to traditional message effects research called **cultivation**

**media logic**
An approach to studying the mass media that says the forms the media use to present the world become the forms we use to perceive the world and to create media messages.

**cultivation analysis**
An approach to analyzing the effects of television viewing that argues that watching significant amounts of television alters the way an individual views the nature of the surrounding world.

*Filmmaker Eli Roth has drawn extensive criticism for the extreme torture violence in his* Hostel *horror film series.*

**mean world syndrome**

The perception of many heavy television watchers of violent programs that the world is a more dangerous and violent place than facts and statistics bear out.

**analysis**. His argument was that watching large amounts of television cultivates a distinct view of the world that is sharply at odds with reality.[69]

Over the years, Gerbner and his colleagues analyzed thousands of network television programs for the themes they present and the level of violence they include. In a series of studies beginning in 1967, Gerbner's team found high levels of violence on television. They defined violence as "the overt expression of force intended to hurt or kill."[70]

Network officials have been openly critical of Gerbner, saying that his studies weren't representative of television as a whole and that his definition of violence was not useful because it does not discriminate between the fantasy violence of a *Roadrunner* cartoon and the more graphic gore of a *Saw* or *Hostel* movie.

Gerbner compared the rate of violence on television to the rate occurring in the real world. He concluded that television cultivates a view of the world that is much more violent than the world we live in. The nature of the violence is different as well, with most television violence occurring between strangers rather than between family members, as does real-life violence. Gerbner said that, because of this, people who watch a great deal of television perceive the world differently than do light viewers. Heavy television viewing cultivates a response that Gerbner calls the **mean world syndrome**. In an appearance before Congress, Gerbner testified:

> The most general and prevalent association with television viewing is a heightened sense of living in a "mean world" of violence and danger. Fearful people are more dependent, more easily manipulated and controlled, more susceptible to deceptively simple, strong, tough measures and hard-line postures. . . . They may accept and even welcome repression if it promises to relieve their insecurities. That is the deeper problem of violence-laden television.[71]

## TEST YOUR MEDIA LITERACY

### Effects of Television Violence

**MOREonline**

You can find links to two additional articles by George Gerbner on televised violence along with more background on him at **http:// ralphehanson.com.**

As you read in the section on cultivation analysis, one of the biggest areas of concern about media effects is how violence on television affects viewers, especially children. George Gerbner was one of the nation's leading researchers on televised violence. Gerbner explained what he considered to be major misconceptions about the effects of televised violence and what his research suggested the real effects were. He argued that watching large amounts of television cultivates a distinct view of the world that is at odds with reality.

• • • • • • • • • • • • • • • • • • •

**Who is the source?**
Who was George Gerbner? What was he best known for? Whom did he work with?

**What is he saying?**
According to Gerbner, what are the effects of television violence? What did Gerbner say are the consequences of televised violence?

**What do you and your classmates think about Gerbner's arguments?**
What did you believe the effects of televised violence to be? How did reading about Gerbner's research change your understanding of media violence? Do you think that televised violence has an effect on you? How about on other people? Why do you feel that way?

Gerbner argued that, because of televised violence, heavy television viewers are more likely to

- Overestimate their chances of experiencing violence
- Believe that their neighborhoods are unsafe
- State that fear of crime is a very serious personal problem
- Assume that the crime rate is rising, regardless of the actual crime rate[72]

The effect of violent television, Gerbner argued, is not that it will program children to be violent; instead, the real harm is more complex:

- Violent programming pushes aside other ways of portraying conflict.
- Violent programming deprives viewers of other choices.
- Violent programming facilitates the victim mentality.
- Violent programming discourages production of alternative programming.[73]

# MEDIA, POLITICS, AND SOCIETY

Our understanding of the media and the campaign process has evolved over the past 100 years. In the early decades of the twentieth century, scholars and critics worried that voters might be manipulated and controlled by campaign messages sent through the media, especially those that might be sent subliminally. This understanding changed in the 1940s and 1950s as scholars came to suspect that media effects might in fact be selective and indirect. Currently it is believed that an interactional relationship exists among politicians, the press, and the public in which each influences the others.

## How Do Political Campaigns Affect Voters?

If, as *The People's Choice* study indicates, campaigns do not have strong, direct effects on voters, what are candidates trying to accomplish with their campaigns? They may be trying to directly persuade voters with the content of the messages, but more likely they are trying to shape the campaign in more subtle ways. These are interactional models that say that the interaction among voters, the media, and the campaigns triggered by the ads are more important than any direct persuasion of voters. Here are two examples:

The **resonance model** says that the candidate's success depends in part on how well his or her basic message resonates with voters' preexisting political feelings. Thus the candidate who does the best job of sending out messages that connect with target voters is the one most likely to win. The communication goal for the campaign is not so much to get people to change their minds as it is to get voters to believe that they share viewpoints with the candidate.[74] The resonance model was clearly used in the 2008 campaign with ads by both Democratic candidate Barack Obama and Republican candidate John McCain. Obama got strong resonance out of a commercial that claimed McCain was out of touch with ordinary people because he didn't know how many houses he owned. McCain got a similar resonance by charging Obama with being more of a celebrity than a serious politician. (You can see both of these commercials online at http://ralphehanson.com.)

The **competitive model** looks at the campaign not in isolation but as a competition between two or more candidates for the hearts and minds of voters. Hence the success of a campaign message, such as a speech that criticizes the candidate's opponent, depends as much on the opponent's reaction as it does on the message itself. Voter response can also depend on how the media react to the message. If the message attracts media attention, it may be played repeatedly on news broadcasts, as well as on political talk shows.[75] During the 2008 Democratic presidential primary, then-candidate Hillary Clinton leveled charges against Obama that he had lifted political rhetoric from Massachusetts governor Deval Patrick. Similar charges that Sen. Joe Biden had lifted a speech from the

**resonance model**
A model of political campaign effects that attributes a candidate's success to how well his or her basic message resonates with and reinforces voters' preexisting political feelings.

**competitive model**
A model of the effects of a political campaign that looks at the campaign as a competition for the hearts and minds of voters.

British Labor Party leader helped sink his campaign for the presidency back in 1988.[76]

But Obama did not suffer the same sort of damage that Biden did. Why? First, Obama and Governor Patrick are friends, they share the same political adviser, and they have long shared a similar message. Second, Patrick did not object to the use of his words. Finally, Obama did not react particularly defensively to the charges of plagiarism. So, according to the competitive model, the public's direct reaction to the charges didn't matter as much as how the public reacted to Obama's reaction to the charges.

*Democratic Internet consultant Phil de Vellis grabbed the political world's attention in March 2007 with his Hillary Clinton–bashing parody of Apple's "1984" Super Bowl commercial.*

## Media and Political Bias

One of the main reasons the direct effects model still has some support is that many critics believe the media affect the public's political opinions by presenting reports that are biased toward a particular candidate or political party. But, as we discuss in Chapter 6, in holding up detached, factual, objective journalism as an ideal for reporting, the press was making a commercial decision, not a moral one. During the penny press era of the 1830s to 1860s, newspapers tried to appeal to the broadest possible audience. The best way to attract a large number of people, publishers felt, was not to take an identifiable political point of view, as had newspapers of the colonial era. The alternative to this supposedly objective style is a more opinionated form of reporting that takes on an explicit point of view, such as that found in *Time, Newsweek,* or many British or European newspapers, such as London's liberal *Guardian* or conservative (Tory) *Telegraph.* These publications have a clearly understood political viewpoint that is designed to appeal to a specific audience.[77]

This opinionated style has also been adopted by the brash cable channel Fox News, which rejects the traditional neutral style of CNN and the major broadcast networks.[78] Fox News commentator Bill O'Reilly says that part of his network's popularity comes from its willingness to think about what audience members want. "Unless your package is meaningful to the viewer, they're gone," he says. "The networks—and I include CNN in this—haven't figured that one out yet."[79] Erik Sorenson, former president of the MSNBC cable news channel, suggests that there is nothing wrong with taking a particular point of view. "I think a lot of people are beginning to ask, 'Is there something phony about pretending to be objective and reading off a teleprompter in the twenty-first century?'"[80] There can be no question that airing partisan news and commentary is a successful business strategy. Since 2002, Fox News has been the top-rated twenty-four-hour news network, and MSNBC's prime-time audience grew by 57 percent in 2008, in part because of the network's expanded use of liberal commentators such as Keith Olbermann and Rachel Maddow in the evening. (The audiences for all three of the major cable news networks grew in 2008, due to people tuning in for election news. But MSNBC saw the largest percentage growth in audience size even though it was still the third largest in terms of total audience.[81])

*Liberal Versus Conservative Bias.*   Leaving aside the news media that take an explicit political viewpoint, is there a predictable bias in the American news media? Critics on both the right and the left maintain that there is either a liberal or a conservative bias in the media's coverage of the news. Journalist and author Richard Reeves notes that, for each example of a bias in one direction, there is an example of bias in the opposite direction. For instance, Cokie Roberts at ABC News is the daughter of two Democratic members of Congress, but Diane Sawyer of the same network was on Republican president Richard Nixon's staff.[82] Although individuals and individual programs in the media clearly hold differing views about the news, does the argument of an overall bias within the news media hold up to scrutiny?

Liberals and conservatives trade arguments about media bias. Conservatives point out that there are disproportionate numbers of liberals working as reporters. Liberals argue that large corporations own the media and that they slant the news in favor of industry and business. The argument that there is a liberal bias in the news media often focuses on charges that reporters are more liberal than the public at large. According to a study of more than 1,000 journalists conducted by David Weaver and G. Cleveland Wilhoit, journalists are somewhat more likely to label themselves as Democrats than the public as a whole and somewhat less likely to consider themselves Republican, and the percentage who consider themselves independent is close to the national average.[83] Overall, 34 percent of the journalists in the study were female. Only 8.4 percent of journalists in America are non-white, compared to 29 percent of the population as a whole, but the percentage of non-whites in the media is growing.[84]

On the one hand, a 1985 study found that journalists were more likely to hold a range of liberal views than the public at large. The explanation for this finding may be that people who go into journalism tend to be concerned about injustices within society, a personality type that could tend toward liberal or progressive political views. Some observers argue that journalists have a "liberal and cosmopolitan" approach to the world, and this shapes journalistic views of good and bad.[85] A widely reported study in 2007 said that journalists who made political contributions were more likely to give to Democrats than Republicans. What wasn't reported nearly as often was that very few journalists made political

# TEST YOUR MEDIA LITERACY

## Bias in the News

You can read the news story about the experiments, along with a reader chat with the author of the article, at **http://ralphehanson.com**.

No matter what the news media do, they are likely to be charged with being biased. How do critics know this bias exists? They just have to look at the news. It's perfectly obvious, "they" say. But two recent research studies found that if you take a news story about a partisan issue, readers or viewers from both sides will claim that it is biased against their point of view. The studies showed that as long as the story tried to present a nuanced view that presented multiple sides of an issue—that is, what journalists would call an unbiased view—partisans on either side of the issue viewed the story as hopelessly biased. On the other hand, if the story had a strong point of view—that is, it *was* biased—people tended to perceive it as less biased.[1]

**Who are the sources?**
Who conducted the two studies written about in the story? Where do they work? What are their fields of study?

**What are they saying?**
How do partisans react to stories that are supposedly neutral (or unbiased)? How do neutral observers react? How do they react to stories that have an explicit point of view? How would you categorize their research in terms of being message, medium, ownership, or audience based? Can you categorize the type of theory base the researchers were using?

**What evidence is there?**
How did the two researchers reach their conclusions? How did they conduct their research?

**What do you and your classmates think about media bias?**
What stories do you or your classmates see as being biased? Do you ever think that stories are biased in your favor? How do you feel when a story is trying to be balanced by presenting information you disagree with? In light of these studies, how do you think the news media should respond to charges of being biased? Do you prefer neutral-style reporting or news with an explicit point of view? Why?

[1] Shankar Vedantam, "Two Views of the Same News Find Opposite Biases," *Washington Post*, July 24, 2006, A02.

contributions. In fact, the study found that fewer than two-tenths of one percent of all journalists made political contributions.[86]

On the other hand, if one looks at the editorial pages of the major newspapers, a somewhat different bias might appear. Between 1948 and 1990, 78 percent of newspaper presidential endorsements were for Republicans, but Republican candidates for president received 51 percent of the popular vote, which would tend to suggest that the editorial pages of newspapers are somewhat more conservative than the public at large.[87] So when you hear charges of media bias being thrown about, remember Truth Six—Activism and analysis are not the same thing.

Karl Rove, former top adviser to President George W. Bush, in a speech to college students, summed up the issue by saying that while he thinks the press is generally liberal: "I think it's less liberal than it is oppositional. . . . Reporters now see their role less as discovering facts and fair-mindedly reporting the truth and more as being put on earth to afflict the comfortable, to be a constant thorn of those in power, whether they are Republican or Democrat."[88]

You can read an extended debate on the issue of media bias online at http://ralphehanson.com.

*Gans's Basic Journalistic Values.*　　There is more to the bias argument than the liberal-versus-conservative issue. For example, some observers charge that the media have a bias toward attractiveness or charisma. There can also be a bias toward making money or attracting an audience. Political scientist and media scholar Doris Graber argues that when it comes to selecting stories for coverage, the strongest bias is for those that will have the greatest appeal to the publication's or program's audience.[89]

Rather than looking for examples of bias in the news, media sociologist Herbert Gans set out to find the actual values exhibited within the stories themselves. He asked what the values, the biases, of journalism were. To find the answer, he studied the content of the CBS and NBC news programs, *Time* magazine, and *Newsweek*.

Gans found eight enduring values in the stories he studied: ethnocentrism, altruistic democracy, responsible capitalism, small-town pastoralism, individualism, moderatism, social order, and leadership. These values were not stated explicitly; rather, they emerged from what was presented as being good and normal and what was presented as bad.[90] Let's look briefly at each of Gans's values:

1. *Ethnocentrism* is the idea that your own country and culture are better than all others. This shows up in the U.S. media in stories that compare other countries' values to American values. To the degree that other countries live up to American ideals, they are good; if they are different, they are bad. Therefore, enemies of the United States are presented as evil because they don't conform to our values. Stories can be critical of the United States, but they are criticizing deviance from basic American values, not those values themselves.

2. *Altruistic democracy* is the idea that politicians should serve the public good, not their own interests. This leads to stories that are critical of corrupt politicians. By the same token, citizens, as voters, have the same obligation to work for the public good and not for selfish interests. Special-interest groups and lobbyists are suspect because they are not working for the common good. This was perhaps best illustrated by the Watergate hearings in the 1970s, which revealed the corrupt behavior that

occurred in the White House so that President Richard Nixon could stay in power. President Bill Clinton was criticized for his affair with Monica Lewinsky in part because he was serving his own interests rather than working for the good of the American public.

*Financial products companies such as AIG received lots of negative press in 2008 and 2009, in part because of the media's value of responsible capitalism.*

3. *Responsible capitalism* is the idea that open competition among businesses will create a better, more prosperous world for everyone. But by the same token, businesses must be responsible and not seek excess profits. The same is true of labor unions. Hence the news media tend to be harsh in their coverage of greed and deception by big businesses, yet they still tend to praise people who develop and grow companies. This is why there has been so much negative coverage of banking and investment companies such as AIG following the stock market crash in 2008.

4. *Small-town pastoralism* is nostalgia for the old-fashioned rural community. The agricultural community is where all goodness is rooted, while big cities are dangerous places that suffer from numerous social problems. Suburbs, where many people live, tend to be overlooked entirely.

5. *Individualism* is the constant quest to identify the one person who makes a difference. People like the notion that one person can make a difference, that we are not all cogs in a giant machine. Reporters like to use a single person as a symbol. That explains in part why journalists focused on the murder of Neda Agha-Soltan during protests about the contested 2009 Iranian elections. Instead of trying to talk about the wide range of people involved in the protests, they used Agha-Soltan as a symbol to represent all the protestors.[91]

6. *Moderatism* is the value of moderation in all things. Extremists on both the left and the right are criticized. Although the media attempt to present a balance of opinions, they tend to report on views that are mildly to the left and right of center. One of the strongest criticisms the media can make is referring to an individual as an extremist.

7. The value of *social order* is seen primarily in the coverage of disorder. When journalists cover stories that involve disorder, such as protests, floods, disasters, or riots, the focus of the story tends to be on the restoration of order. This was one of the biggest issues in the media's coverage of the floods following Hurricane Katrina. The social order was in question

for months following the storm, and the press focused heavily on how that order might be restored.[92]

8. Finally, the media value *leadership*. The media tend to look at the actions of leaders, whereas the actions of lower-level bureaucrats—which may well be more important—are ignored. This is in some ways an extension of the bias toward individualism, the difference one person can make.

Overall, Gans argues that there is reformist bias to the media, which tend to advocate "honest, meritocratic, and anti-bureaucratic government."[93] Journalists like to argue that since both sides criticize the press, they must be doing a good, balanced job.[94] Perhaps a better explanation for why both conservatives and liberals charge the media with bias is that the eight values Gans found within the media reflect a combination of both liberal and conservative values—again illustrating why people holding a particular viewpoint will see bias in the media's attempt to be neutral and balanced.

## CHAPTER Summary

With the rise of mass society and the rapid growth of the mass media starting in the nineteenth century, the public, media critics, and scholars have raised questions about the effects various media might have on society and individuals. These effects were viewed initially as being strong, direct, and relatively uniform on the population as a whole. After World War I, critics were concerned that media-oriented political campaigns could have powerful, direct effects on voters. This view, though still widespread, was largely discredited by voter studies conducted in the 1940s and 1950s. These studies found that the voters with the strongest political opinions were those most likely to pay attention to the campaign and hence were least likely to be affected by the campaign. More recently, research has expanded to move beyond looking just at the effects that media and media content have on individuals and society to examinations of how living in a world with all-pervasive media changes the nature of our interactions and culture.

Understanding the effects of media on individuals and society requires that we examine the messages being sent, the medium transmitting them, the owners of the media, and the audience members themselves. The effects can be cognitive, attitudinal, behavioral, and psychological.

Media effects can also be examined in terms of a number of theoretical approaches, including functional analysis, agenda setting, uses and gratifications, social learning, symbolic interactionism, spiral of silence, media logic, and cultivation analysis.

Our understanding of the relationship among politicians, the press, and the public has evolved over the past half-century. Recent studies have supported interactional approaches to understanding campaign effects, including the resonance and competitive models.

Many people claim that the media are biased toward one political view or another. Conservative critics argue that there is a liberal bias arising from the tendency of reporters to be more liberal than the public at large. The liberals' counterargument is that the press has a conservative bias because most media outlets are owned by giant corporations that hold pro-business views. Finally, some critics argue that the media hold a combination of values that straddle the boundary between slightly left and right of center. The press in the United States began as partisan during the colonial period but adopted a detached, factual, objective style in the 1830s to appeal to a broader audience.

# KEYTerms

opinion leaders   48
geographics   55
demographics   55
psychographics   55
surveillance   57
status conferral   57
correlation   57
socialization   58
entertainment   58
agenda-setting theory   59

uses and gratifications theory   60
social learning theory   60
symbolic interactionism   61
spiral of silence   62
media logic   63
cultivation analysis   63
mean world syndrome   64
resonance model   66
competitive model   66

# CONCEPTReview

Rise of mass society and mass communication
Message effects
Medium effects
Ownership effects
Active audience effects
Conceptions of media bias

# The Media Business

## Consolidation, Globalization, and the Long Tail

**CHAPTER 3**

**When you think** major media moguls, names such as News Corporation's Rupert Murdoch, Viacom's Sumner Redstone, or the late Walt Disney generally come to mind. If you are talking about music, perhaps producers David Geffen or Rick Rubin might get suggested. But when it comes to analyzing who the most powerful people in media are, one name that ought to jump to the front is that of Steve Jobs. Steve Jobs? Isn't he the Apple computer guy? Certainly. But he is also emphatically in the media business. A quick check of Apple's balance sheet shows that the California computer company did $18.2 billion in the media business, selling iPod media players, music, movies, TV shows, audio books, and accessories in 2008. Apple's computer sales over the same time period? $14.3 billion.[1] That's why these days the company's name is Apple, not Apple Computer.

Jobs co-founded Apple back in 1976 with his friend Steve Wozniak. "The Woz" was the inventor, and Jobs was the business man and visionary. Wozniak left the company in 1983, and Jobs was forced out by Apple's board of directors in 1985.[2] After leaving Apple, Jobs founded NeXT Inc., which built an innovative UNIX-based computer that was used by Tim Berners-Lee to create the World Wide Web.[3] (You can read more about Berners-Lee in Chapter 10.)

Then in 1997 Apple had a change of heart, bought out NeXT Inc., and brought Jobs back as its interim CEO. The NeXTSTEP software morphed into OS X, Apple's radical and successful remake of its computer operating system. By 2001, Jobs had dropped *interim* from his title and started Apple on the path to its current success, where the Mac was not just a computer but rather a "digital hub" for all types of media and entertainment content. It was also the year that Apple introduced its iconic media player, the iPod.[4]

**Steve Jobs**

With the iPod, and its accompanying iTunes software, Jobs solidified his company as a player in the new media business. Jobs did numerous things people told him he couldn't do. He persuaded the major recording labels to offer their music through Apple's iTunes store. He persuaded the major broadcast and cable networks to sell their television shows through the iTunes store. He persuaded major movie studios to sell and rent their movies through. . . . Oh, you get the picture.[5]

Apple has not been Jobs's only company, however. In addition to being the founder of Apple, he also took Pixar, a $10 million computer graphics company bought from *Star Wars* director George Lucas, and turned it into America's leading animation studio, valued in excess of $7 billion when he sold it to Disney in 2006.[6] Pixar has, as of 2009, produced ten animated movies, each of them a number-one hit, including the *Toy Story* movies, *Finding Nemo*, *The Incredibles*, *WALL-E*, and *Up*. Upon the sale of Pixar, Jobs became Disney's biggest stockholder and a member of the company's board of directors.[7] Disney's purchase of Pixar was seen as more than just the acquisition of a successful animation house; it also brought in talent that truly understood digital media convergence. Media consultant Richard Doherty says that Jobs is unique in Hollywood, "with one foot on Tomorrowland, and the other on Main Street USA. He has a canny ability to know what the consumer wants."[8]

Jobs is a notorious perfectionist. That has made him both difficult to work with and highly admired. As an example, Jobs's seemingly informal product announcements, with him dressed in his trademark jeans and black mock turtleneck, are heavily rehearsed to come off just so.[9]

In 2004 Jobs faced his biggest battle, not with stockholders or management, but with cancer. Jobs suffers from a rare form of pancreatic cancer that has left him looking painfully thin and raised questions about his long-term health. Then in 2009 Jobs took a six-month leave-of-absence from Apple, supposedly because of a hormone

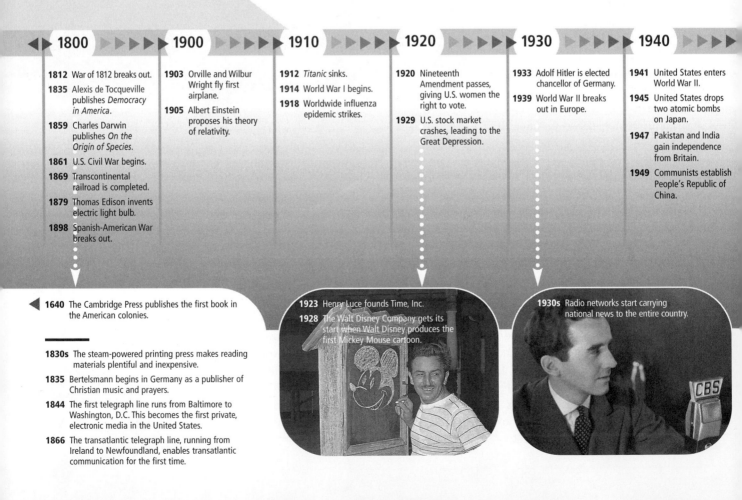

**◀▶ 1800 ▶▶▶▶ 1900 ▶▶▶▶ 1910 ▶▶▶▶ 1920 ▶▶▶▶▶ 1930 ▶▶▶▶ 1940 ▶▶▶▶**

**1812** War of 1812 breaks out.

**1835** Alexis de Tocqueville publishes *Democracy in America*.

**1859** Charles Darwin publishes *On the Origin of Species*.

**1861** U.S. Civil War begins.

**1869** Transcontinental railroad is completed.

**1879** Thomas Edison invents electric light bulb.

**1898** Spanish-American War breaks out.

**1903** Orville and Wilbur Wright fly first airplane.

**1905** Albert Einstein proposes his theory of relativity.

**1912** *Titanic* sinks.

**1914** World War I begins.

**1918** Worldwide influenza epidemic strikes.

**1920** Nineteenth Amendment passes, giving U.S. women the right to vote.

**1929** U.S. stock market crashes, leading to the Great Depression.

**1933** Adolf Hitler is elected chancellor of Germany.

**1939** World War II breaks out in Europe.

**1941** United States enters World War II.

**1945** United States drops two atomic bombs on Japan.

**1947** Pakistan and India gain independence from Britain.

**1949** Communists establish People's Republic of China.

**◀ 1640** The Cambridge Press publishes the first book in the American colonies.

**1830s** The steam-powered printing press makes reading materials plentiful and inexpensive.

**1835** Bertelsmann begins in Germany as a publisher of Christian music and prayers.

**1844** The first telegraph line runs from Baltimore to Washington, D.C. This becomes the first private, electronic media in the United States.

**1866** The transatlantic telegraph line, running from Ireland to Newfoundland, enables transatlantic communication for the first time.

**1923** Henry Luce founds Time, Inc.

**1928** The Walt Disney Company gets its start when Walt Disney produces the first Mickey Mouse cartoon.

**1930s** Radio networks start carrying national news to the entire country.

imbalance that turned out to be "more complex than he had thought." As was revealed at the end of his leave, Jobs was actually getting a liver transplant necessitated by complications from his cancer.[10]

When Jobs was diagnosed with cancer back in 2004, doctors told him he did not have long to live. Later diagnostic work showed that Jobs had a treatable form of the usually fatal cancer. But the news that he could be dying had a big impact on Jobs. In a commencement address he gave at Stanford University not long after his initial cancer surgery, he told students:

> Remembering that I'll be dead soon is the most important tool I've ever encountered to help me make the big choices in life. Because almost everything—all external expectations, all pride, all fear of embarrassment or failure—these things just fall away in the face of death, leaving only what is truly important. . . . There is no reason not to follow your heart.[11]

Although Jobs is not a traditional media mogul, he does share similarities with other media pioneers. Consider the example of Black Entertainment Television (BET) founder Robert Johnson. The great-grandson of a freed slave, Johnson started one of cable television's most profitable channels with only $15,000 in borrowed money and an

---

## 1950 ▶▶▶▶▶ 1960 ▶▶▶▶▶ 1970 ▶▶▶▶▶ 1980 ▶▶▶▶▶ 1990 ▶▶▶▶▶ 2000 ▶▶▶▶▶

**1950** Korean War begins.

**1953** Francis Crick and James Watson discover structure of DNA.

**1957** Soviet Union launches spacecraft *Sputnik I*.

**1963** Martin Luther King Jr. delivers "I Have a Dream" speech during Washington, D.C., civil-rights march.

**1969** Neil Armstrong walks on the moon.

**1974** U.S. president Richard Nixon resigns due to Watergate scandal.

**1975** Vietnam War ends.

**1977** Apple II personal computer is introduced.

**1978** First test-tube baby is born.

**1983** First HIV/AIDS cases are documented.

**1985** Ozone hole is discovered over Antarctica.

**1986** Space shuttle *Challenger* explodes.

**1989** The Berlin Wall falls.

**1991** Soviet Union disbands.

**1993** European Union is formed.

**1994** Nelson Mandela is elected president of South Africa.

**1997** Diana, Princess of Wales, dies in car accident.

**2001** Al Qaida attacks World Trade Center and Pentagon.

**2003** United States invades Iraq.

**2003** Human genome project is completed.

**2005** Terrorists bomb London's transport system.

**2005** Hurricane Katrina hits the U.S. Gulf Coast.

**2008** Barack Obama is elected U.S. president.

**1952** Rupert Murdoch takes over the Australian newspaper the *Adelaide News* and begins to build his News Corporation empire.

**1983** Fifty companies dominate the American media industry.

**1985** All three of the original television broadcast networks are sold by their original owners.

**2000** Six companies control a majority of the American media industry.

**2004** GE buys Vivendi Universal to form NBC Universal.

**2005** CBS and Viacom split.

**2006** Google buys YouTube for $1.65 billion.

**2006** Disney buys Pixar for $7.4 billion.

**2009** Time Warner starts downsizing, separating from AOL and Time Warner Cable.

investment of $500,000 from cable mogul John Malone. Like Jobs's sale of Pixar to Disney, Johnson sold his channel and many of its connected media properties to media giant Viacom in 2000 for $3 billion.[12] It was the same story in 1996 when CNN founder Ted Turner sold all his cable channels to Time Warner, including the various CNN networks, superstation WTBS, TNT, Turner Classic Movies, and the Cartoon Network.[13]

In recent years, ownership of newspapers, book and magazine publishers, recording labels, movie companies, and Internet companies has been increasingly concentrated, going from the hands of the families that started them into the hands of a small number of very large corporations. On the other hand, entrepreneurs like Jobs are able to use digital technologies to create new media that can turn upside-down Big Media's focus on using traditional tools to deliver media using the same techniques they have for years.

In this chapter we look at who owns the media, what the trends in media ownership are, and what these ownership patterns may mean for the future of mass communication. That means we will be spending a lot of time with Truth Two—There are no mainstream media—and Truth Seven—There is no "they." Instead of looking at "the media" as a unified whole, we look at who owns and controls the varied mass media and how new channels are emerging rapidly.

# THE DEVELOPMENT OF THE MEDIA BUSINESS IN THE UNITED STATES

The U.S. media are unique in the world in that they are almost entirely privately owned and operated for profit. Even the broadcasting industry, which in most countries is tightly controlled by the government, is run by private businesses.[14]

## A Tradition of Private Ownership

The media in the United States have a long tradition of private ownership, dating back to the 1640s. The media industry was among the first in the American colonies: The first printing press came to the Massachusetts Bay Colony in 1638. It was used to establish the Cambridge Press, publisher of the *Whole Book of Psalmes*, better known as the *Bay Psalm Book*. This became the colonies' first best seller and was even exported back to Great Britain and Europe. Most of the early published works consisted of religious tracts, such as sermons, and were printed under license of the colonial government.[15]

Newspapers were published throughout the colonial and revolutionary period, but they were not the large, general-appeal publications we are familiar with today. Instead, they provided commentary and gossip that would appeal to members of a particular political group. Benjamin Harris, who published the first newspaper in the colonies in 1690, also ran a coffeehouse, and the content of his paper, *Publick Occurrences both Foreign and Domestic*, resembled the talk in his coffeehouse. Only one issue of the paper appeared, in part because Harris had failed to obtain a license to publish.

Although the newspapers of the colonial period were much smaller than those to come during the 1800s, they could nevertheless be quite profitable. Publisher and statesman Benjamin Franklin became relatively wealthy publishing his *Pennsylvania Gazette*—but his success was due at least in part to his ability, as postmaster general, to prevent competing newspapers from being distributed through the mail.[16] Franklin, along with several other successful publishers, was able to use the paper's profitability to improve his publications and thus increase his success. He was an intense competitor, vying with other publishers for the top writers and editors in the book, newspaper, and magazine businesses.[17] In many ways, he established the pattern that media moguls would follow for the next two and a half centuries.

Even though print media were widespread in America in the 1700s, subscription prices were high and publications were subsidized by political parties. It wasn't until the development of **penny press** newspapers in the 1830s that the news industry really got started. These inexpensive, widely circulated papers were published in large numbers and were the first American newspapers to be supported primarily through advertising revenue and read by large numbers of people.[18] The same model of advertising-supported media guided the development of the magazine industry in the 1800s.

In the United States, unlike most other countries, the electronic media have always been privately owned, beginning with the telegraph line between Washington, D.C., and Baltimore in 1844. By 1849 the telegraph was being used to transmit news on a regular basis. Although it was replaced by newer technology in the twentieth century, the telegraph set the stage for private ownership of electronic media.[19] Today the broadcasting industry is primarily a private business in the United States, although it is regulated by the government. In contrast, while Britain has a thriving commercial broadcasting industry, the publicly funded British Broadcasting Company has a much bigger presence than the United States' Public Broadcasting System (PBS). And while the Internet, the most recent of the electronic media, began as a partnership between the military and universities in the 1960s and 1970s, it was fully opened up to business and the public in the 1990s.

**penny press**
Inexpensive, widely circulated papers that became popular in the nineteenth century. They were the first American media to be supported primarily through advertising revenue.

## The Growth of National News

Magazines had national circulation with news and entertainment in the nineteenth and early twentieth centuries, and radio networks carried national news from the 1930s on, but it was the growing popularity of television networks in the 1950s that gave the United States a true national media culture. For the first time, people routinely depended on nationally available media for their news. The CBS and NBC television networks started carrying a half-hour nightly news broadcast in 1963; ABC followed suit in 1967, and CBS added its weekly newsmagazine *60 Minutes* in 1968. In 1979 ABC started running a late-night news update called *America Held Hostage* when American embassy employees in Iran were taken hostage. As the hostage crisis dragged on for 444 days, the update evolved into the program now known as *Nightline.*

Public affairs network C-SPAN began broadcasting on cable in 1979. It carried full coverage of the U.S. House of Representatives live and unedited; coverage of the Senate was added in 1986. CNN went on cable in 1980, promising not to go off the air until "the end of the world." CNN subsequently went worldwide with CNN International and CNN en Español. National talk radio also grew in popularity during this time, beginning in 1978 with Larry King, who interviewed guests and then let callers ask questions as well.

Newspapers have found it easier to reach a national audience with the development of satellite communication. Nationally distributed newspapers use satellite links to deliver pages to remote printing plants. For example, *USA Today*, which started publication in 1982, has thirty-two printing plants around the country that receive pages by satellite every night. The *New York Times* is available for home delivery throughout much of the country, and the New York Times Company reaches a global audience through its *International Herald Tribune*, which has both a European and Asian edition.

All this means that, even though a relatively limited number of companies own the media outlets, Americans have access to a wide range of competing news sources. The absolute number of independent sources has declined, but their availability is vastly improved.[20] In addition to these giants, several slightly smaller companies are extraordinarily influential on how our media operate. While the focus in this chapter is on the media in the United States, we take a much broader look at global media in Chapter 15.

# BIG MEDIA

Media journalist Ken Auletta notes that massive changes have taken place in the media industry during the past thirty years. In 1980 the videocassette recorder (VCR) was a scarce luxury, cable television was just starting to become popular, the personal computer was for hobbyists, the Internet was available only to academics and the military, *USA Today* had yet to be published, MTV and CNN were not yet on cable, there were only three broadcast television networks, you couldn't buy a compact disc (CD), and mobile phones were connected to large boxes and used only by the wealthy and people with mobile offices.

Today video recorders in one form or another are found in 90 percent of all U.S. homes, basic cable is in more than 52 percent and is available to over 95 percent, direct broadcast satellite television is in 24 percent, radio is universally available, over 90 percent of American teens have access to the Internet at home, *USA Today* sells more than 2.1 million copies a day, there are at least six national broadcast networks, and over 85 percent of Americans have mobile telephones.[21] In Europe, there are approximately 4,000 television channels available; and in Western Europe, approximately 86 percent of all adults have a mobile phone.[22]

What's going to happen to the media business? Will there still be broadcast networks? Will cable be rendered obsolete by direct broadcast satellites and broadband video sites? Is print dead? Is there still such a thing as mass communication? Auletta warns consumers to be skeptical of predictions that a particular medium will die out: "Not too many decades ago, the kind of people who transform fads into social trends predicted that movies would kill radio, then predicted that television would kill movies, and then announced that the PC would kill television. But we do know this: Changes in the way we communicate will transform the way we live."[23]

Although consumers have vastly more media choices than they did in the past, the number of companies providing those choices has declined substantially. Media critic and Pulitzer Prize–winning journalist Ben Bagdikian writes that in 1983 the media business was dominated by fifty corporations that controlled more than half the newspaper, magazine, television, radio, and music output in the United States. By 1987 this number had shrunk to twenty-nine companies, and as of 2004 five companies controlled a majority of the media output in the United States: Time Warner, Disney, Viacom, Bertelsmann, and News Corporation. A sixth company can be added to this list—General Electric. GE is the major owner of NBC Universal and is larger than any of Bagdikian's big five, but it receives only a small portion of its income from its media holdings. It is, however, still substantially larger than the remaining top media firms.[24]

These six companies control five of the top six broadcast networks in the United States; they have the largest cable television holdings in the United States; they own the majority of the direct broadcast satellite operations in the world; and they own the largest book publishing houses in the world, the largest newspaper companies in the world, and the largest music providers in the world. Although there are companies in India and Nigeria that produce more movies than the studios listed here, they are not as profitable. In short, these six media companies are dominant, not only in the United States, but in the entire world.

Bagdikian says that these companies exercise their power through **vertical integration**, defined with respect to the media business as controlling every aspect of a media product from production through delivery to consumers. A vertically integrated company creates content, delivers it into the home through communication networks, and even owns the phone and cable wiring that brings the media into the home. Bagdikian says:

> The new actors are bigger than ever before and have subsumed some of the old actors. What we have now is a small number of companies. Each has far more

**vertical integration**
Controlling all aspects of a media project, including production, delivery to consumers in multiple formats, and the promotion of the product through other media.

communications power than anything in the past. You have Disney/ABC, which has major newspapers, a regular television network, movies, studios, books. It controls every step in the process: the creation of content, control of the delivery system nationally, and the wire into the home. It's a closed circuit. Nobody gets on that circuit that you don't want.[25]

Since these corporations control so much of what is available to the public, it is worth examining who they are and what they control as well as how they are having to change to react to the new media environment of the twenty-first century. Companies that had counted on consolidation to bring in profits from synergy were likely to be disappointed as often as they were pleased. In general, the word **synergy** refers to a combination of effects that is greater than the sum of the individual effects. For example, two medications given together may do more than twice as much good as the two medicines given separately. In the media business, synergy means that a combined company can offer more value, cost savings, or strength than the two companies could separately.

But there is more to our media world than just the giants of Big Media. There are the major companies that are more limited in the scope of their media ownership, such as Clear Channel with its 850+ radio stations; and Gannett with approximately 85 daily newspapers (including *USA Today*), 850 nondaily publications, and 23 television stations.[26] There are also the growing number of companies that dominate new media, such as Google, Apple, and Yahoo. So after we talk about Big Media, we'll get to several other smaller, but still significant, media companies.

## Time Warner: The Biggest of the Big

In the world of Big Media, Time Warner stands a head taller than all of its competitors. With 2008 sales of $46.98 billion, it brought in $9 billion more than Disney. Although Disney is still a long ways from catching up to Time Warner, it has closed the gap between the two by 25 percent since 2005. Time Warner is a major player in film, television, cable TV, publishing, and online content and is the home to iconic media characters including Scooby Doo, Harry Potter, and Batman (see Table 3.1).[27]

**synergy**
Where the combined strength of two items is greater than the sum of their individual strengths. In the media business, synergy means that a large company can use the strengths of its various divisions to successfully market its content.

---

| TABLE 3.1 | WHAT DOES TIME WARNER OWN? |
| --- | --- |

**Magazines**

More than 30 magazines, including

- *Time* (8 different editions, including *Time for Kids*)
- *People* (4 editions, including *Teen People*)
- *Sports Illustrated* (3 editions, including *SI for Kids*)
- *DC Comics* (including *Batman*)

**Cable Networks**

- HBO networks (at least 16 channels)
- CNN networks (at least 6 channels)
- WTBS
- TNT
- Cartoon Network (at least 4 channels)

**Broadcast Television Network**

- The CW Television Network (co-owned with CBS)

**Movie and TV Studios**

- Warner Brothers
- New Line Cinema
- Castle Rock Entertainment
- Hanna-Barbera Cartoons

*Sources:* "Who Owns What," *Columbia Journalism Review,* www.cjr.org/resources/index.php; *Hoover's Company Profile Database: Time Warner Inc.* (Austin, Texas: Hoover's Inc., 2009).

*Note:* This table lists only a sample of Time Warner's holdings. The company also owns multiple television and movie production companies.

# TEST YOUR MEDIA LITERACY

## Synergy

Media reporter Ken Auletta argues that synergy is the reason given for much of the media merger activity that has occurred in the past twenty years. Synergy can take many forms.[1] Synergy can also be used to cross-promote a company's products; for example, when NBC Universal acquired the Weather Channel, it started featuring NBC morning weather personality Al Roker on the channel, along with light morning news. In return, NBC's local affiliate stations around the country get access to extreme weather footage collected by the Weather Channel.[2]

*Advertising Age* noted that a giant media company like Time Warner or Viacom can be compared to an advertising supermarket: "its shelves abundantly stocked with competing TV stations, radio channels, print publications, websites, content providers, and even syndicators, all under one roof."[3]

News Corporation, which owns the 20th Century Fox movie studio, the Fox Broadcasting network, and the Fox News Channel, used synergy to build profits surrounding the release of 2007's *The Simpsons Movie*. The movie, based on the long-running Fox Broadcasting series, grossed $183 million in the United States and $527 million globally. According to *Variety* magazine, the movie's success can be attributed at least in part to year-long plans for cross-media promotion by News Corporation officials. (It didn't hurt, of course, that both critics and audiences loved the movie. You can find out just how much critics loved it at the review Web site Rotten Tomatoes, owned, interestingly enough, by News Corporation.)[4]

Nicolas Johnson, former commissioner of the U.S. Federal Communications Commission, has been highly critical of the ways in which media corporations have used synergy:

> When you contract with an author to write a book and sell it in the stores you own, produce the movie in the studio you own and run it in the theaters you own, make it into a video and distribute it through the stores you own, then put it on the cable system you own and the broadcast stations you own, promote it on the TV network you own, and write it up in the entertainment magazine you own, that's pretty tough to compete with.[5]

**MORE online**

You can read more about Ken Auletta and media synergy at **http://ralphehanson.com**.

### Who is the source?
Ken Auletta has written about the media business for the *New Yorker* and is the author of several books about the media business, including *Three Blind Mice, The Highwaymen: Warriors of the Information Super Highway,* and *Backstory.* How do you think Auletta's background has shaped his view of media synergy?

### What is he saying?
What is media synergy? What effect does it have on the decisions made by Big Media? Does synergy help or hurt consumers? Why? How would Big Media companies respond to what Auletta has said?

**What kind of evidence does he provide?**

Think about examples of synergy for each of the Big Media companies. Do you think that these attempts at synergy support the arguments that Auletta is making? Is there evidence that disputes Auletta's claims about synergy?

**How do you or your classmates react to Auletta's arguments?**

How do efforts at synergy affect your media consumption? How do you see recent synergy efforts among books, music, movies, and television shows? Do you question the honesty and fairness of coverage that news outlets give to their corporate owners?

[1] Ken Auletta, *Three Blind Mice: How the TV Networks Lost Their Way* (New York: Random House, 1991); John Wicklein, "More Print/TV Partnerships," *Columbia Journalism Review* (March/April 2001).

[2] Michael Malone, "Weather Channel to Share With NBC Affiliates," *Broadcasting & Cable,* September 22, 2009, www.broadcastingcable.com/article/354878-Weather_Channel_To_Share_With_NBC_Affiliates.php.

[3] Richard Linnett and Wayne Friedman, "Crossroads for Cross-platform Deals," *Advertising Age,* January 22, 2001, 10.

[4] Cynthia Littleton and Pamela McClintock, " 'Simpsons' Success Lifts Fox; Box Office Hit a Victory for Synergy," *Variety,* July 30, 2007; Box Office Mojo, "Movies—The Simpsons Movie," boxofficemojo.com/movies/?id=simpsons.htm.

[5] Dean Alger, *Megamedia: How Giant Corporations Dominate Mass Media, Distort Competition, and Endanger Democracy* (Lanham, Md.: Rowman & Littlefield Publishers, 1998).

*Time, Warner Brothers, TBS, and AOL.*    The media giant Time Warner started out as the publisher of *Time* magazine, founded in 1922 by Henry Luce and his prep-school friend Briton Hadden. *Time* quickly prospered; by 1930 Luce had started the business magazine *Fortune,* which was followed by the photo magazine *Life* in 1936. By the 1980s Time Inc. had added multiple magazines, book publishers, local cable companies, and the HBO cable movie channel to its holdings. In 1989 Time merged with Warner Communications, which had grown out of the Warner Brothers movie studio. This merger combined a major movie studio with the nation's largest magazine publisher.

Among Time Warner's businesses were a large number of **local cable television systems**, which deliver programming to individual homes, and Home Box Office (HBO), one of the first premium cable networks. In 1996 Time Warner vastly expanded its stable by purchasing cable pioneer Ted Turner's group of channels, which included the CNN networks, WTBS, TNT, Turner Classic Movies, and the Cartoon Network. Along with his cable properties, Turner also sold his Internet operations and movie studio. When Time Warner took over Turner Broadcasting System (TBS), Turner became a vice president of the new company and its largest stockholder. More significantly, the Turner networks had passed from the control of a single individual to that of a publicly owned company, in much the same way that Robert Johnson's BET would later be bought by Viacom.[28]

All these mergers were seen as fairly straightforward moves toward consolidated ownership at the end of the twentieth century. What was not expected was an offer by upstart new media company AOL to buy Time Warner in a deal valued

**local cable television systems**

The companies that provide cable television service directly to consumers' homes.

at $106 billion.[29] At the time of the offer, the transaction seemed to make sense. It would bring together the largest Internet service provider with the nation's second largest cable provider so the new company could offer high-speed Internet access through its cable television lines. The combination of AOL and Time Warner would give the new company a huge pool of material to offer customers and multiple methods of delivering it—from printed magazines to television networks to online services.[30] But the marriage of the two companies did not turn out well. The new company soon cut more than 4,000 jobs and sold off numerous properties including its sports teams, its book division, and the Warner Music Group.[31]

*The Twenty-first Century at Time Warner.* Although Time Warner is the biggest of the Big Media, that bigness has been a mixed blessing for the company since 2000:

- The problem with synergy—When Time Warner and AOL merged, there was widespread discussion of possible synergies from the combined resources of the two companies. But as AOL founder and former Time Warner board member Steve Case points out, those synergies never really took off: "Unfortunately, that 'one company' strategy never got off the ground. Instead, each division 'did its own thing. . . . ' "[32] The worst example of synergy problems occurred shortly after CNN was acquired by Time Warner. CNN started a series of nightly newsmagazine programs called *NewsStand: CNN & Time*. The show was launched on June 7, 1998, with a sensational program charging that the U.S. military had used nerve gas during the Vietnam War. The story ran both on television and on *Time*'s cover. Within a month after airing and printing the story, however, Time Warner retracted it, saying that it was "unsupportable."[33] The company also apologized to the military and fired the producers responsible for the story. The reputations of both news organizations were damaged as a result of the episode.

- Advantages of synergy—There are examples, however, of synergy working for Time Warner. Owning multiple channels allows a company to repackage media content for different audiences. Warner Brothers can first show a movie in theaters, then sell it through Time Warner cable's pay-per-view division, then market DVDs of it through the company's home video division, air it on the HBO premium movie channel, and broadcast it on WTBS or TNT basic cable channels. Having first access to new movies drives up the value of WTBS and TNT by raising their ratings, bringing in more advertising revenue, and encouraging more cable systems to carry the channels.

- The role of AOL—When Time Warner merged with AOL in 2001, it was portrayed widely as AOL buying out Time Warner, and the name of the company became AOL Time Warner. But the corporate importance of AOL has been declining ever since the merger, and AOL has had to reinvent itself as an advertising-supported content provider rather than as an Internet access point.[34] As of 2009, Time Warner was in the process of spinning off AOL to be its own, publicly traded company, thus ending the era of the merged company. Former AOL chairman Steve Case severed his ties with the company in 2005.[35]

- Bigger isn't always better—After years of bringing more and more media outlets together, Time Warner has started cutting some loose. The company has shut down unsuccessful cable channels like CNN/Sports Illustrated and CNN/Money and, as mentioned above, sold off multiple properties. In addition to spinning off AOL as its own company, Time Warner has also cut loose Time Warner Cable, the nation's second largest provider of residential cable television services. Despite all these changes, the company still lost $13 billion in 2008, raising the question of whether bigger media companies are more effective.[36]

## Disney: The Mouse That Grew

The Walt Disney Company, popularly known as the Mouse, may be the world's most famous media company, with its wealth of recognizable characters such as Mickey Mouse and Donald Duck (see Table 3.2). In 2008, it had revenue of $37.84 billion, an increase of nearly $6 billion since 2005. Although still significantly smaller than Time Warner, the company is solidly in second place among Big Media, and it has been reliably turning annual profits in the range of $3–$4 billion over the past several years.[37]

*From Mickey Mouse to Media Giant.*    The Disney Company got its start in 1928, when Walt Disney started producing Mickey Mouse cartoons. The first two silent Mickey cartoons came and went with little fanfare, but the third, which featured synchronized music and sound effects, was a huge hit. Walt Disney produced more than 100 short animated cartoons featuring Mickey and his friends. In 1937 he took animation to the next level by releasing the first feature-length cartoon, *Snow White and the Seven Dwarfs*. A major success for the studio, the film held the box-office record of $8 million until *Gone With the Wind* was released in 1939.

In the 1950s the Disney Company started producing live-action feature films and wildlife documentaries.[38] It was also in the 1950s that Disney opened its first theme park, in California.

Walt Disney was among the first Hollywood movie producers to see the potential of television, for which he produced and hosted a weekly program for more than a decade.[39] He understood synergy very early, using his television show to promote his movies and theme park. The Disney Company has also been licensing merchandise longer than almost any other media company. In 1930 the company signed its first international licensing contract for Mickey Mouse products, and the famous Mickey Mouse watch went on sale in 1933. By 1954 the company was selling more than 3,000 Disney items, ranging from pajamas to school supplies.[40]

After Walt Disney's death in 1966, the company lost much of its direction.[41] But in 1984 Michael Eisner, formerly of ABC television and Paramount Pictures,

**WHAT DOES DISNEY OWN?**

**Book Publishing**

- Hyperion Books
- Disney Publishing Worldwide

**Magazine Publishing**

Numerous magazines, including

- *Biography*
- *Discover*
- *US Weekly* (partial)
- *ESPN Magazine*
- *Marvel Comics*

**Broadcast Network**

- ABC

**Broadcast Television Stations**

Disney owns stations in at least 10 cities, including Chicago, Los Angeles, San Francisco, New York City, and Houston.

**Radio**

70 stations, including

- ABC Radio
- Radio Disney
- ESPN Radio

*(NOTE: As of this writing, Disney was selling some of its radio stations.)*

**Cable Networks**

Many cable networks (either partially or in full), including

- The Disney Channel (plus 8 international versions)
- ESPN Networks (at least 5 versions)
- A&E Television Networks
- ABC Family
- Lifetime Television (at least 3 versions)

**Movie Studios and Distributors**

- Walt Disney Pictures
- Touchstone Pictures
- Buena Vista Productions
- Pixar
- Miramax Films

**Other Properties**

- Theme parks in China, Japan, France, and the United States
- A cruise line business
- More than 700 Disney stores
- Numerous international television broadcasting and production companies

*Sources:* "Who Owns What," *Columbia Journalism Review,* www.cjr.org/resources/index.php; *Hoover's Company Profile Database: Time Warner Inc.* (Austin, Texas: Hoover's Inc., 2009).

took over as head of the studio, a job he held until 2005. Under Eisner's leadership the Disney Company produced a series of popular animated films, formed new movie companies like Touchstone Pictures—which produced films such as *Pretty Woman* for adults—and moved into television.[42]

In addition to being a significant force in American media, the Disney Company has also been developing a presence throughout Europe and Asia. As of 2008, approximately 25 percent of Disney's earnings came from outside North America, but the quest for an international audience has not always gone smoothly.[43] For example, Disneyland Paris, which opened in 1992, went through four name changes and numerous cultural changes before it became profitable. For example, the park had to serve wine to please its French visitors. Tokyo Disneyland, which opened in 1983, started off slowly but was soon busier than the

*The Walt Disney Company has worked extensively in recent years to expand its offerings in China, including a theme park in Shanghai.*

California Disneyland. But the market Disney is most interested in is China, with its 1.3 billion potential consumers.[44]

Disney had been doing business in China for several years before the communists came to power in 1949. But for the next thirty-five or so years, Disney and other Western businesses were barred from the country. By the mid-1980s China was becoming more open to Western business and culture, so in 1985 Disney began negotiations with Chinese broadcast media to bring Mickey Mouse and Donald Duck cartoons to Chinese television. Said former Disney president Frank Wells, "There are at least three generations of children in China who don't know who Mickey and Donald were."[45]

Disney agreed to let Chinese television show the company's cartoons for free, and the Chinese broadcasters would be allowed to dub the cartoons into Chinese with whatever "ideological content" changes they deemed necessary. What was Disney getting out of the deal? Access to the Chinese public. Although the potential audience for the cartoons was relatively small, the company hoped that children who watched them would want the officially licensed Mickey and Donald toys. Unfortunately for Disney, most of the toys sold in China were unlicensed "pirate" editions. Piracy has also been a problem for sales of movies in the world's most populous country. Estimates suggest that as many as 90 percent of all movies sold in China are pirated editions that sell for between 70¢ and $1.10.[46]

In 1996 Disney's relationship with China hit a rough period when Touchstone released the movie *Kundun*. The film, which deals with Tibet and the Dalai Lama, outraged the Chinese government. (China controls Tibet and has attempted to suppress the teachings of the Dalai Lama.) After *Kundun*'s release, Disney programming was banned briefly in China.[47]

By 2002 Disney had successfully distanced itself from *Kundun* and was airing its cartoons on *The Dragon Club*, which reaches 60 million Chinese households, and by 2005, Disney had twenty-three programming blocks on Chinese television. The company also had more than 1,800 Disney Corners in Chinese department stores.[48]

Disney opened Hong Kong Disneyland in 2005. Despite having early problems, including overcrowding and cultural misunderstandings, the park has been growing and Disney invested $800 million into expanding the park in 2009.[49] Chinese visitors don't seem to be bothered by the fact that rides have English soundtracks. One Chinese guest told the *Washington Post*, "I don't expect to see many Chinese things in Disneyland. I came to see different things, fresh things."[50] Despite the global economic problems, Disney has continued to work on plans to open a theme park in Shanghai. Media analyst David Miller told the *Los Angeles Times* that the parks "will serve as a platform to promote all things Disney in China—whether it's movies, DVDs, or TV shows in syndication."[51]

Disney's reach extends far beyond its children's programming and theme park operations. Central to the Disney Company today is the ABC broadcast network and the ESPN cable networks. ABC had been an independent company until 1985, when it was bought by Capital Cities. Ten years later, Disney bought Capital Cities and acquired ABC as part of the deal.[52] Unlike Viacom and Time Warner, Disney is primarily a content company—a producer of programming. Although it owns ten television stations and a number of radio stations, it has not (as of this writing) invested heavily in local cable companies, theaters, or an Internet service provider. It also has invested in retail stores and theme parks.[53]

*The Twenty-first Century at Disney.*    Disney has had a series of ups and downs over the past several years, sometimes in the same areas of the company. These include

- Animation—Disney's animation studio suffered a string of failures starting in 2000 with traditional, hand-drawn animation, but the company revitalized its cartoon offerings by acquiring Pixar, the studio responsible for *Toy Story* 1 and 2, *WALL-E*, and *Up*. The acquisition made Pixar (and Apple) CEO Steve Jobs Disney's largest shareholder and a member of its board of directors.[54] (For more on the connections between Steve Jobs and Disney, see the beginning of the chapter.)

- Synergy at Disney—Synergy isn't just a good idea at Disney, it's a corporate passion. Two or three times a year the company runs a "boot camp" for executives called Disney Dimensions. For eight days executives play a costumed character at a theme park and learn how meals are cooked and beds are made, how movies are animated, how the finance and legal departments are run, and how the television networks do business.[55] While Disney still uses synergy to cross-market consumer products, theme parks, and media content, the company has also taken synergy much farther than that. In 2009 Disney announced that it was buying Marvel Comics for $4 billion, bringing Iron Man, Spider-Man, X-Men, and 5,000 additional characters into the Disney fold. This could give Disney billions of dollars more in toy revenue each year, a potential Marvel-based theme park, video games, and, of course, movies.[56]

- Media convergence at Disney—Just as Disney saw the potential for bringing together movie and television properties back in the 1950s and 1960s, so has it understood how it can move into using online media to promote its brands. The company is partial owner of the online streaming video service Hulu and uses it to provide viewers with additional opportunities to watch shows from ABC, ABC Family, the Disney Channel, and SOAPnet. Disney was also among the first of the Big Media companies to make its movies and television shows available through Apple's online iTunes store.[57]

## News Corporation: A Worldwide Giant

News Corporation is Australian Rupert Murdoch's media giant. It controls 20th Century Fox movie studios, the Fox Broadcasting network, the top-rated Fox News Channel, and the *Wall Street Journal*. Murdoch has a worldwide presence in nine different media: newspapers, magazines, books, broadcasting, direct-broadcast satellite television, cable networks, a movie studio, home video, and the Internet (see Table 3.3). In fact, the only continent on which Murdoch doesn't own media properties is Antarctica.[58] In fiscal year 2009, News Corporation had sales of $30.42 billion, placing it right between Disney and the combined sales of Viacom and its former network CBS.[59]

---

 **TABLE 3.3**

# WHAT DOES NEWS CORPORATION OWN?

**Newspapers**

More than 275 newspapers worldwide, including

- *Wall Street Journal*
- *New York Post*
- *Times of London*
- *The Sun* (London tabloid)
- *The Australian* (national daily)

**Magazines**

All or part of 6 magazines, including

- *Big League*
- *The Weekly Standard*

**Book Publishing**

Multiple book-publishing houses, including

- HarperMorrow Publishers (along with divisions in England, Australia, and Canada)
- Avon
- Ecco

**Broadcast Television Networks**

- Fox Broadcasting
- MyNetworkTV (a broadcast network launched in 2006)

**Broadcast Television Stations**

News Corporation owns more than 25 television stations in at least 17 cities, including New York City; Los Angeles; Minneapolis; Washington, D.C.; and Phoenix.

**Cable Networks**

Numerous cable networks, including

- Fox News Channel
- Fox Sports Net
- Fox Sports International (including coverage of Latin America and the Middle East)
- Speed Channel
- FX

**Direct Broadcast Satellite Companies**

- British Sky Broadcasting (BSkyB)
- Star Group
- Sky Italia

**Movie Studios**

- 20th Century Fox (including at least 7 spin-off studios)
- Interactive
- Fox Interactive
- MySpace.com

*Sources:* "Who Owns What," *Columbia Journalism Review,* www.cjr.org/resources/index.php; *Hoover's Company Profile Database: News Corporation* (Austin, Texas: Hoover's Inc., 2009).

*From Australia to the World.*
Rupert Murdoch's father
owned two Australian newspapers. But when the elder Murdoch died in 1952, the younger
Murdoch had to sell one of the
papers to cover inheritance
taxes. So Murdoch's News Corporation empire grew out of a
single newspaper with a circulation under 100,000, the *Adelaide News.*[60]

By 1964 Murdoch had put
together a major newspaper
chain and had begun publishing *The Australian,* a national
newspaper. In 1969 he moved
to Britain, taking over the Sunday tabloid *News of the World* and

*Australian Rupert Murdoch, shown
here in 1985, heads News
Corporation, which owns, among
many other media properties, the
New York Post.*

eventually acquiring four more tabloids. In 1977 he moved to the
United States, where he acquired the *New York Post* and transformed
it into a lively, politically conservative paper.

In the 1980s Murdoch bought the 20th Century Fox movie studio and
a number of U.S. television stations, and used them to create the Fox television network. He also became an American citizen at this time because the
United States does not permit foreign ownership of a television network. The
Fox News cable network was launched in 1996, and as of 2009, it was by far the
most popular of the cable news operations.[61] In addition to its more than
twenty-five broadcast television stations, book publishing operations, and
broadcast and cable networks, News Corporation is also the world's dominant
player in the direct broadcast satellite business, owning a large portion of BSkyB
(Britain), Sky Italia (Italy), and the Star Group (Asia). It also owns a stake in
China's state-owned telecommunications company.[62] Until 2008 News Corporation also owned about a third of DirectTV (which serves the United States),
but it traded its interest in the company to reclaim its stock from investor Liberty Media.[63] The Murdoch family owns approximately 40 percent of News
Corporation, and Murdoch runs his business using the same hands-on style he
used when it was a small, family-owned company.

By far the biggest news surrounding News Corporation in recent years was its
2007 purchase of the *Wall Street Journal* and its parent company, Dow Jones Inc.
Murdoch paid a substantial premium for the paper to buy it from its long-time
controlling owners, the Bancroft family. Although the *Journal* has always had a
politically conservative editorial page, the paper's news coverage has generally
been considered even handed. When Murdoch first expressed interest in the

*Journal*, there were concerns in the news industry that he would apply the same partisan style to the paper that he used with the Fox News Channel. To date, that doesn't seem to have happened. Murdoch has been active in the paper's management, but he has not made substantial change in the paper's style or approach to news.[64]

**The Twenty-first Century at News Corporation.**    News Corporation seems to have figured out the rapidly changing media world of the new century. It is the fastest growing of the Big Media companies, going from annual sales of $16 billion in 2002 to more than $30 billion in 2009.[65] How has it managed to be so successful?

- Giving consumers what they want—Although News Corporation is known for its politically conservative newspapers and cable news channel, the company is generally pragmatic about delivering what audiences want. Fox Broadcasting carries shows like *The Simpsons*, *Family Guy*, and *American Dad*, which frequently make the lists of the most objectionable shows on television; and News Corporation's British tabloids can get quite racy—the London *Sun* includes a photo of a topless woman as a regular feature.

- Wise use of multiple platforms—News Corporation produces a wide range of content that can be distributed through multiple platforms. For example, a movie produced by 20th Century Fox can be shown in theaters, sold on a disc by 20th Century Fox Home Entertainment, aired on Fox Broadcasting, shown again on the FX cable channel, and finally used as an afternoon or late-night program on a News Corporation–owned television station.[66] This multiplatform approach then leads to. . . .

- Global synergy at News Corporation—News Corporation's direct broadcast satellite systems currently cover much of the globe. With his various studios, Murdoch also owns the means to producing content to flow out over these channels. He has, in the words of media journalist Ken Auletta, both content and the pipeline. Owning every step of the process is important, Murdoch says: "We'd like to be vertically integrated from the moment of creation through to the moment of delivery into the home."[67] Although News Corporation owns media properties around the world, Murdoch does not take a one-size-fits-all approach in providing content to these varied channels. "You would be very wrong to forget that what people want to watch in their own country is basically local programming, local language, local culture," Murdoch says. "I learned that many, many years ago in Australia, when I was loading up [News Corporation's network] with good American programs and we'd get beat with second-rate Australian ones."[68]

## Viacom and CBS: Bringing Together Cable and Broadcasting

The relationship between media conglomerate Viacom and established broadcast network CBS has been a long-term on-again, off-again one. Although they are currently two separate corporations with separate stocks, ownership and management of the two companies heavily overlap. The companies had a combined 2008 income of approximately $28.5 billion, with $14.6 billion coming from Viacom and $13.9 billion from CBS. The two companies together are slightly smaller than News Corporation. CBS owns the CBS broadcast network, half of the CW broadcast network, a number of television production companies, approximately thirty broadcast television stations, and the Simon & Shuster publishing group. Viacom owns the movie studio Paramount and numerous cable channels, including Comedy Central, BET, and the various MTV and Nickelodeon channels (see Table 3.4).[69]

## TABLE 3.4　WHAT DO VIACOM AND CBS OWN?

Viacom and CBS split into separate corporations in 2005, though they are still largely owned and managed by the same people. In general, CBS owns broadcasting and publishing properties while Viacom owns cable and movie properties.

**Broadcast Television Networks (CBS)**
- CBS television network
- The CW Television Network (co-owned with Time Warner)

**Broadcast Television Stations**
CBS owns approximately 30 television stations in at least 27 cities, including New York City, Los Angeles, Chicago, Philadelphia, and San Francisco.

**Radio Properties**
- CBS Radio operates 147 radio stations, most of which are in the top 50 U.S. markets.

- CBS is a partial owner of the Westwood One radio syndicator.

**Cable Networks**
Viacom and CBS own many cable channels, including
- MTV Networks (17 channels, including MTV, VH1, and Nickelodeon)
- BET (four channels)
- Country Music Television
- Showtime Networks
- Comedy Central (partial owner)

**Movie Studios**
- Paramount Pictures
- MTV Films
- Nickelodeon Movies

**Book Publishing**
- Simon & Shuster

*Sources:* "Who Owns What," *Columbia Journalism Review,* www.cjr.org/resources/index.php; *Hoover's Company Profile Database: Viacom* (Austin, Texas: Hoover's Inc., 2009); *Hoover's Company Profile Database: CBS Inc.* (Austin, Texas: Hoover's Inc., 2009).

*Sumner Redstone, speaking here to guests at television studios in Istanbul, Turkey, turned the small content-production company Viacom into a media industry giant.*

***The Child Buys the Parent.*** CBS became a force in broadcasting when William S. Paley and his father bought United Independent Broadcasters and turned it into the Columbia Broadcasting System (CBS). In the mid-1980s, when all three of the original broadcast networks changed ownership, CBS was bought by investor Laurence Tisch and his Loews Corporation. Westinghouse bought Tisch's company in 1995, and by 1997 it had sold all its nonmedia business and was simply CBS, Inc.

Then, in one of the strangest twists in media history, CBS was bought by Viacom in 1999. What made this transaction so unusual was that Viacom had begun as a small film production unit within CBS. Later, in 1971, the federal government became concerned that the broadcast networks were becoming too powerful, so it forced them to sell their content production units. As an independent company, Viacom grew into a major producer of cable television programming; its products included MTV and Nickelodeon.

In 1987 theater owner Sumner Redstone bought Viacom. Under Redstone's leadership the company became a dominant media corporation in the 1990s. It acquired the Blockbuster video store chain, the Paramount movie studio, and the start-up television network United Paramount Network (UPN). Finally, Viacom bought CBS, the television network that had given birth to it decades before.[70] Most recently, in 2005, Viacom and CBS split back into two separate corporations with separate stocks being traded. So, they are no longer a single Big Media company, right? Well, sort of. Sumner Redstone and his daughter Shari were, as of 2009, still the number-one and number-two executives of both companies.[71]

***The Twenty-first Century at Viacom and CBS.*** The split of Viacom and CBS into separately traded companies is the most visible change at Redstone's companies, but other, more significant changes have happened there as well:

■ Indecency—CBS and Viacom have been at the center of the debate of broadcast indecency that came out of Janet Jackson's infamous "wardrobe malfunction" during the 2004 Super Bowl broadcast. (For more on the issue of broadcast indecency, see Chapter 13.) Radio stations owned by CBS had also drawn fire from critics and the Federal Communications Commission for sexually explicit broadcasts by shock-jocks Howard Stern and Opie and Anthony, all of whom have since left CBS. Viacom has paid more than $3.5 million in fines and promised to suspend and possibly fire anyone who makes an indecent broadcast over the company's properties.[72]

- Music videos—Viacom continues to be the dominant force in music videos, owning BET (rap and hip-hop), MTV (music appealing to teens and twenty-somethings), VH1 (music appealing to people who were teens a long time ago), and Country Music Television.

- Bigger isn't always better—Common wisdom held that making media companies bigger makes them better. But since 2005, Viacom has been moving in the opposite direction. There was, of course, the splitting of Viacom and CBS. Then in 2008, Viacom sold its ownership of the DreamWorks movie studio that it had purchased in 2006 to Indian movie studio Reliance Entertainment. Prior to being purchased by Viacom, DreamWorks was one of the last remaining large-scale independent movie studios.[73]

*Singer Janet Jackson, performing with Justin Timberlake, flashes her bare breast nationwide during the 2004 Super Bowl. CBS was fined a record $550,000 for violating broadcast indecency regulations.*

## Bertelsmann: The World's Largest Publisher

The media companies we have discussed so far are widely diversified, with their fingers in almost every medium imaginable. In contrast, the German media corporation Bertelsmann is more focused on the book and music publishing business, although it also owns magazines, newspapers, and Internet and broadcast properties (see Table 3.5). Bertelsmann is both the world's largest publisher and the largest publisher of English-language books. In 2008 it had sales of $22.7 billion.[74]

*Books Still Matter.*    Bertelsmann started out in 1835 as a publisher of Christian music and prayers. It was also the original publisher of the fairy tales of the

## TABLE 3.5 | WHAT DOES BERTELSMANN OWN?

**Book Publishing**
- Random House (including Bantam, Doubleday, Dell, and Ballantine)
- Waterbrook Press
- Knopf
- Fodor's Travel Publications

**Magazines**
- Numerous trade magazines
- More than two dozen European magazines, including the German publication *Stern*
- Multiple North American magazines (partially or in full), including *Family Circle* and *National Geographic*

**Television**
- Numerous European television stations (partially or in full), including RTL, Europe's largest television company
- Multiple television production companies

*Sources:* "Who Owns What," *Columbia Journalism Review*, www.cjr.org/resources/index.php; *Hoover's Company Profile Database: Bertelsmann* (Austin, Texas: Hoover's Inc., 2009).

Brothers Grimm in the nineteenth century. After World War II the company was run by Reinhard Mohn, a former German Luftwaffe officer who learned to speak English while in a prisoner-of-war camp in Kansas.[75]

Unlike most of the other media giants, Bertelsmann is a privately held company—it is owned by a German foundation that mandates that the company not only earn a profit but also operate for the benefit of its employees and various social causes.[76] Bertelsmann sees book publishing as one of the key media of the twenty-first century and, having purchased the major American publisher Random House for $1.4 billion in 1998, has a much stronger presence in this area than the other media giants. Bertelsmann obtains a major portion of its revenue from books and controls 15 percent of the U.S. book market.

It published Dan Brown's enormous bestsellers *The Da Vinci Code* and *The Lost Symbol*. It also owns the RTL Group, Europe's largest television broadcaster, and a large number of magazines through its Gruner + Jahr division, including *Family Circle*, *Parents*, and *YM*.[77]

**The Twenty-first Century at Bertelsmann.** As a publisher and European broadcaster, Bertelsmann is not in the public eye the way Time Warner, Viacom, and Disney are. It does not have Scooby-Doo, SpongeBob, or Mickey Mouse as mascots, but it has quietly made its presence felt:[78]

- Returning to core strengths—Up until 2002, Bertelsmann looked like it was preparing to become a generalized media giant on the scale of Time Warner or Disney under the leadership of CEO Thomas Middelhoff. But members of the Mohn family forced Middelhoff out and returned the company to its core business of book and magazine publishing. Ever since, the company has been gradually selling off peripheral businesses and buying back its stock.[79]

- Broadcasting in Europe—Bertelsmann is big in European television, owning 90 percent of the RTL Group, Europe's largest broadcaster. In addition to operating more than forty-five television channels in a dozen countries, it also produces the wildly popular *American Idol* and a wide range of other *Idol* programs around the world.[80]

■ Adapting to the changing music business—Bertelsmann has long been in the music business, first with the Bertelsmann Music Group (BMG) and later with its partnership with Sony, Sony BMG Music Entertainment.[81] But with the massive changes that file sharing and digital downloads have brought to the music industry, Bertelsmann has taken a new approach. It sold out its interest in Sony BMG to Sony, and it's now involved with pressing CDs for other publishers and managing the song catalogs of more than 200 artists without being their publisher. So Bertelsmann has gotten out of the business of selling music and is now in the business of assisting companies that do sell it.[82]

*Publishing giant Bertelsmann is known for best-selling books such as* The Lost Symbol, *the latest from* Da Vinci Code *author Dan Brown.*

## General Electric/NBC Universal: Embracing the Digital Age

The Radio Corporation of America (RCA) was the original monopoly in the broadcast business. Initially the federal government established RCA to consolidate all the patents required to start the radio business. In 1926 RCA formed the National Broadcasting Company (NBC) to provide radio programming across the country. As is described in more detail in Chapter 9, NBC had two networks, the Red and the Blue. In the 1940s it sold the Blue network, which became ABC.[83] In the 1930s RCA began developing television technology and was the first network with regularly scheduled television broadcasts.

In 1985 General Electric bought both NBC and RCA. The purchase was controversial from the very beginning because GE differs from the rest of the top media firms in that its primary business is not media but manufacturing and financial services. GE makes consumer electronics, electric generating plants, and aircraft engines. Critics questioned whether a major defense contractor ought to be allowed to own a broadcast network.[84]

In 2004 GE purchased the media holdings of French company Vivendi Universal, which included movie and television production studios, cable channels, and theme parks. The deal gave GE 80 percent of the new NBC Universal, and Vivendi 20 percent.[85]

Although GE/NBC Universal is one of the world's largest corporations, it is only sixth on the list of the largest media companies; NBC Universal is the only one of the Big Four broadcast networks that is not part of a major media conglomerate (see Table 3.6). GE is a global conglomerate whose sales in 2007 reached $172.7 billion. During that time, NBC Universal had $15.4 billion in sales, which makes it about one-third the size of industry leader Time Warner.[86]

*The Twenty-first Century at NBC Universal.*  NBC has been trying for several years to recover from the loss of its popular comedies *Friends* and *Seinfeld* that made it the number-one network in the 1990s. It has been the fourth-rated broadcast network for several years and has tried several approaches to both cutting costs and attracting viewers, including personnel cuts at NBC News, emphasizing game shows and reality programming early in the evening, and giving long-time *Tonight Show* host Jay Leno a five-day-a-week prime-time talk show. Leno's new show was perhaps the most radical move by the network, cutting the number of prime-time hours produced per night from three to two.[87] But the move lasted only seven months before Leno switched back to late night. NBC Universal's cable channels have been more successful; the USA network is one of the most popular basic cable channels. In 2008 NBC Universal, along with other investors, acquired the Weather Channel and its Web site, Weather.com.[88]

**TABLE 3.6 | WHAT DOES NBC UNIVERSAL (GENERAL ELECTRIC) OWN?**

NBC Universal is owned primarily by GE. This list does not include the many industrial and financial services that make up the majority of GE's business.

**Broadcast Television Networks**
- NBC broadcast network
- Telemundo Spanish-language broadcast network

**Broadcast Television Stations**
GE owns 28 television stations, some of which are NBC affiliates and some of which broadcast the Spanish-language Telemundo network.

**Cable Networks**
Numerous cable networks (partially or in full), including
- CNBC (financial news)
- MSNBC (news)
- Bravo
- Syfy
- USA
- The Weather Channel

**Movie Studios**
- Universal Pictures
- Focus Features

**Online Properties**
- Weather.com
- Hulu (streaming video)

*Sources:* "Who Owns What," *Columbia Journalism Review,* www.cjr.org/resources/index.php; *Hoover's Company Profile Database: NBC Universal* (Austin, Texas: Hoover's Inc., 2009).

## TEST YOUR MEDIA LITERACY

### Making Money With *American Idol*

*American Idol,* produced by a division of Bertelsmann and airing on Fox Broadcasting, might be the most profitable multimedia property of all time, with a total value of $2.5 billion. That's more than the gross domestic product of the European nation Moldova, according to news site MSNBC.[1] Mike Brunker, who leads a special projects reporting team for the news channel and Web site, writes that *American Idol* draws that astronomical amount of revenue from a wide range of sources:

Advertising—For 2007 *American Idol* was expected to bring in approximately $500 million a year in advertising revenue from traditional commercials. *Idol* was charging $620,000 per thirty-second spot for the 2007 season.

Product Placement—During the 2006 season, *Idol* had 4,086 paid product placements during the show. This involves a sponsor paying to have its product featured during the show itself rather than during a commercial slot, when viewers can tune out. *The Amazing Race* was a distant second in the number of product placements, with only 2,790.

Licensing—Bertelsmann's Freemantle Media division, which produces *Idol*, has licensed *Idol* merchandise to more than forty companies and was looking to add an *Idol* ice cream, an *Idol* Monopoly game, and an *Idol* theme park ride.

Online Advertising—Freemantle sold online advertising to go with the streaming version of the program that airs on the Internet after the broadcast version is over.

International Broadcasting—*Idol* programs air in more than 150 countries.

Concerts—After the series is over, *Idol* stars go on national tours.

Text Messages—During the 2006 season, viewers voted more than 64 million times by sending text messages. The cell phone company that partnered with *Idol* to provide the voting shared the revenue produced by the text messages.

CD Sales—Even in the depressed CD market, *Idol* stars such as Carrie Underwood, Kelly Clarkson, and Chris Daughtry have each sold more than a million copies of their CDs.

Publications—Winners such as Taylor Hicks have written books about their lives, and there is always *American Idol: The Magazine* for those looking for something shorter.

**MORE online**

You can read more about how *American Idol* makes money and view an interactive graphic on *Idol* revenue at **http:// ralphehanson.com.**

• • • • • • • • • • • • • • •

### Who is the source?

The report on *American Idol*'s success comes from MSNBC's Web site, a division of NBC Universal. The story is based, in part, on a story published in *Advertising Age,* a major advertising industry trade magazine. What do you know about MSNBC and NBC Universal? How credible is the company's report on *American Idol*? Who are they trying to reach with this story? How do you think MSNBC makes money?

**What does the report say?**

What are the sources of income for *American Idol*? In addition to broadcasting on Fox, on what other media does *American Idol* content appear? Who are the companies involved with producing and distributing *American Idol*? Why do you think these particular companies produce the program? Who is the audience for *American Idol*?

**What kind of evidence do they provide?**

What kinds of data does the report present? Do those data support the assumption that *American Idol* is a big success? What doesn't the report say about the show and its audience?

**How do you or your classmates react to this report?**

Do you watch *American Idol*? Why do you think people watch the program? Have you bought any of the tie-in products related to the show? Do you know people who have? How do you feel about the product placement on the program? Do you think the program is too commercialized?

[1] Mike Brunker, " 'Idol' Empire Conquers New Multimedia Worlds; Hit Show's Creators Find New Ways to Squeeze Out Financial High Notes," January 15, 2007, www.msnbc.msn.com/id/16580677.

In fall 2009 the news broke that Comcast was in negotiations to purchase 51 percent of NBC Universal from General Electric, which would give the cable television giant controlling ownership of the network/movie studio. What complicates the transaction is that French media company Vivendi SA owns 20 percent of NBC Universal. Vivendi could play the role of a spoiler, or at least complicate the deal, if it refuses to sell its shares in NBC Universal. Even if all the parties involved agree to the sale, the deal will have to pass approval by federal regulators, a process that could reportedly take six months to a year. This isn't the first time Comcast has made a play for one of the Big Media companies. Back in 2004 Comcast tried unsuccessfully to buy the Disney Company. Should Comcast succeed in purchasing NBC Universal, you can find an update to this section of the chapter at http://ralphehanson.com.[89]

## Other Major Players

Although they do not challenge any of the cross-media giants for size and scope, there are at least fifty more major players in the American media market. A complete list of these companies can be found at the "Who Owns What" page at *Columbia Journalism Review*'s Web site (www.cjr.org/resources/index.php).

Let's take a brief look at two of these companies that illustrate the strong concentration of ownership in individual media.

*Gannett Co. Inc.*    Gannett is the biggest newspaper publisher in the United States, owning both the largest number of daily newspapers of any company and the largest single paper, *USA Today*. Gannett also owns the Army Times Publishing Company, British newspaper publisher Newsquest, television stations in sixteen U.S. states, nine printing plants, and a direct marketing division.

*USA Today* has a daily circulation of 2.1 million, and the rest of the company's approximately ninety American daily papers deliver a total of 6.5 million copies a day. In addition, Gannett owns approximately 850 nondaily publications.[90] Gannett started out with a single newspaper in 1906, the *Elmira Star-Gazette* in New York state. Gannett then bought out the competing paper in town, the *Evening Star*, and merged it in with the *Gazette*, thus eliminating the competition. The company repeated this pattern—buying up the competition and shutting it down—across the country.[91] The Gannett newspaper chain grew steadily through the 1970s and early 1980s, but it gained the most attention in 1982 when it launched *USA Today* as a national newspaper. Starting a new national paper was an expensive, long-term project; the paper didn't turn a profit until 1993. There is widespread concern that the newspaper industry as a whole is in a major circulation and advertising sales decline, and Gannett is no exception. It has had a steady decline in revenue, and in 2008 the company suffered major losses.[92]

*Clear Channel Communications, Inc.*    No company illustrates better the rapid move to consolidation of ownership than Clear Channel Communications. Up until 1996, Clear Channel was a significant, though not large, player in the radio business, owning thirty-five radio stations and nine television stations. But in 1996 the Federal Communications Commission lifted most of the restrictions on the number of stations a single company could own. By 2005 Clear Channel owned, operated, or programmed more than 1,200 radio stations in the United States. Since that peak, the owners took the company private and sold off a number of stations, so that, as of 2009, Clear Channel owned 850 stations reaching more than 90 million people.[93] The company also owns more than 900,000 outdoor advertising billboards. Although it is by far the dominant radio company in the United States, it does face substantial competition from the new satellite radio services.[94]

# MEDIA ECONOMICS AND THE LONG TAIL

Lists of major media companies generally include companies like cable television company Comcast, magazine publisher Meredith, or the movie and music divisions of Sony. What don't show up as often are the new media publishers such as Yahoo, Google, and Apple. Yahoo publishes content in fifteen different languages, Google is working at digitizing and making available online every book ever written, and Apple is the world's largest provider of legal music downloads. They also specialize in providing a wide range of media content that appeal to a relatively small group of consumers. But when those many small groups are added together, they become an audience big enough to rival those being attracted by Big Media.

The world of Big Media is the world of blockbusters—selling a lot of copies of a limited number of products. Blockbusters include the big summer movies that cost more than $100 million to produce and require the sale of millions of tickets to be a financial success. They are novels by Nicholas Sparks and Stephanie Meyer. They are records by Jay-Z, Taylor Swift, or the Black Eyed Peas. They are the common media products, the common culture we all share.

Despite the consolidation of the media business and the ever-growing emphasis on the importance of blockbusters to Big Media, a strange phenomenon has been taking place. The annual box office has been falling for movies, broadcast television has lost one-third of its audience, sales of CDs are plummeting, and yet, people seem to be consuming more media content than ever.

## The Short Head Versus the Long Tail

Chris Anderson, in his book *The Long Tail*, argues that we are leaving the era of mass culture and entering one that is vastly more individualistic and much less mass oriented. He writes that, when he was growing up, the only alternatives to Big Media were at the library and the comic book store. But today there are vastly more choices at both the commercial and noncommercial levels. Take Apple's iTunes music and video store. Through it, you can buy current blockbuster songs, movies, and television shows, but you can also find rather obscure materials, like new grass band Crooked Still or an EP by the Arizona-based band Calexico. Or you can follow the ongoing saga of Lonelygirl15 over at YouTube. Or you could take a look the obscure horror film *The Mutant Chronicles* from mail-order DVD rental company Netflix.

This is how Anderson describes the shift that has taken place as consumers turn from the mass content produced by broadcasters and publishers to the more focused content provided by broadband connections to the Internet:

> The great thing about broadcast is that it can bring one show to millions of people with unmatchable efficiency. But it can't do the opposite—bring a million shows to one person each. Yet that is exactly what the Internet does so well. The economics of the broadcast era required hit shows—big buckets—to catch huge audiences. The economics of the broadband era are reversed. Serving the same stream to millions of people at the same time is hugely expensive and wasteful for a distribution network optimized for point-to-point communication.[95]

In short, our mass communication is becoming less mass, and we have new media companies that specialize in providing narrowly focused content. Anderson uses the statistical term the **long tail** to refer to this phenomenon.

Figure 3.1 depicts this phenomenon as a distribution curve showing that a relatively limited number of media products—books, songs, DVDs—sell the most copies. This area of a limited number of products and high sales on the left—the "**short head**"—is where Big Media companies like to live. When a movie comes to a local theater, it needs to attract about 1,500 people over a two-week period for the run to be a success. That means that you won't see a lot of the more obscure movies in your local theater. A CD has to sell at least four copies a year to justify the shelf space it takes up—that is, to pay the rent on its shelf space. Even if it will sell 5,000 copies nationwide, if it can't sell four copies in your local store, your local store can't pay the rent on the half-inch of shelf space the CD takes up. So Big Media are all about finding the limited number of hits that will appeal to the most people. As Anderson observes, that's what they have to do to survive.[96]

To see the short head portion of the demand curve, look at Wal-Mart, the United States' biggest music retailer. The discount giant carries about 4,500 different CDs in its stores. Of those, 200 CDs account for more than 90 percent of their sales. But what about the remaining thousands and thousands of songs that a limited number of people are interested in buying? They constitute the long tail portion of the graph that extends off to the right. This is where

**long tail**
The portion of a distribution curve where a limited number of people are interested in buying a lot of different products.

**short head**
The portion of a distribution curve where a large number of people are interested in buying a limited number of products.

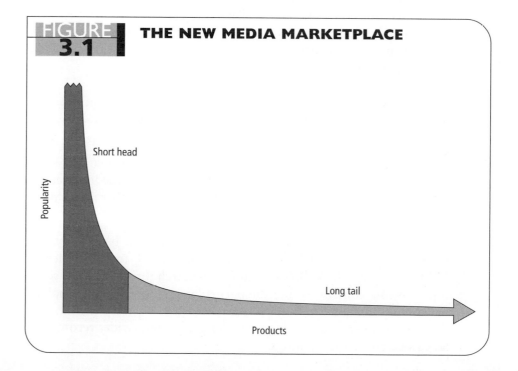

**FIGURE 3.1**    **THE NEW MEDIA MARKETPLACE**

Short head

Long tail

Popularity

Products

a limited number of people are interested in buying a lot of different products (as opposed to the short head, where a lot of people are interested in buying a limited number of products).

In contrast to Wal-Mart, Anderson uses online music service Rhapsody as an illustration of the long tail portion of the demand curve. As of 2005, Rhapsody offered approximately 1.5 million different music tracks to download. Not surprisingly, the big hits sell a lot of copies. But if you move beyond the big hits—the top 25,000 tracks—you find that Rhapsody still sells a lot of music. From the 25,000 best-selling tracks to the 100,000th best-selling track, sales of each song are at least 250 copies a month and make up nearly a quarter of Rhapsody's downloads. From the 100,000th to the 800,000th most popular songs—and that's a long way down the popularity chart—Rhapsody is still selling enough to make up 16 percent of its business. How can Rhapsody afford to do this? Two factors come into play: 1) Its cost of inventory is minimal—it just has to store the songs on a big array of hard drives; it doesn't have to physically stock the music. 2) It does business over the entire country with a single store, so it doesn't need a lot of consumers in a single location who want to buy something. If they live anywhere in the United States, that's good enough.[97]

## Characteristics of the Long Tail

Anderson writes that the biggest players in the long tail include Rhapsody, which lets subscribers download songs; Apple, the largest seller of legal music downloads; Netflix, which offers hundreds of thousands of different DVDs by mail; and Amazon, the dominant online seller of books, movies, and CDs. These companies can offer selection far beyond the current hits. Anderson argues that there are six principles that drive the success of the long-tail portion of the media marketplace:

- High number of goods—There are far more niche goods than hits. This means that if you can sell enough different niche goods, you can get as many sales as if you were selling a limited number of hits.

- Low cost of reaching markets—The cost of reaching niche markets is falling dramatically, thanks to the ease of reach provided by the Internet and the ability to—in many cases—sell a digital download rather than a physical product.

- Ease of finding niche products—Consumers need to be able to find these niche products. This means there need to be tools—Anderson calls them filters—that allow consumers to search through a huge selection of media content to find the particular material they are looking for. This is something Internet movie rental store Netflix excels at. Netflix has consumers rate a series of movies and then provides recommendations based on those ratings.

- Flattening of the demand curve for mainstream hits—Once consumers can find their niche products, the demand curve tends to flatten. Now that consumers can find the full range of products available, there will be relatively less demand for the hits and more demand for the niche products. This will make the long tail longer, and lower the demand for the hits.

- Size of collective market—There are so many niche products that they collectively can have as big a market as the hits do. In other words, you can sell as much focusing on the long tail as on the short head if you can offer enough choices.

- Tailoring to personal tastes—Once niche products become available, findable, and affordable, consumers will choose to go with media content that fits their personal wants and needs rather than consuming the hits that hold a mild appeal to so many. Media hits will become less important because consumers can get what they want rather than what happens to be available locally.[98]

## Consequences of the Long Tail

Anderson says that a number of consequences arise out of a shift to the long tail from traditional mass media:

- Democratization of the means of production—It used to be that to record a CD you needed a big, expensive recording studio. Now anyone with a laptop computer and some inexpensive software can put together a multi-track recording or edit a short video. You can publish a professional-looking book without the benefit of a major publisher using a laser printer and a local copy shop. The development of the powerful home computer made it possible for anyone to be a media producer.

- Democratization of the means of distribution—Through the Internet and sites like eBay and Amazon, anyone can open a national, or even international, sales channel. YouTube gives ordinary people a place to distribute their home-produced video. I even run a tiny media-oriented bookstore using an Amazon partnership. As Anderson puts it, "The PC made everyone a producer or publisher, but it was the Internet that made everyone a distributor."[99]

- Greatly reduced cost of connecting suppliers and consumers—Sellers and consumers can now find each other through tools such as Google search, iTunes, YouTube, and blogs.

Our twenty-first-century media world has room for a wide range of distribution channels. For the hits, there is nothing like Big Media for distribution. Movie theaters, book stores, big box retailers (like Wal-Mart), broadcast network television, and magazines do a great job of selling or distributing media

*Steven Chen (left) and Chad Hurley launched the video-sharing Web site YouTube in 2004. It has since become one of the top locations on the Internet for user-generated video.*

content that appeals to a large group of people. Second are the hybrid retailers—companies like Amazon or Netflix, who have no bricks-and-mortar retail stores but have to send out a physical product such as books, CDs, or DVDs. The hybrid retailers can have national distribution and serve niches, but they still deliver a physical product. Finally, the digital retailers, like Apple iTunes or Rhapsody, sell downloads with no physical product. Any store that sells a virtual rather than a physical product handles the farthest end of the long tail.[100]

One of the most successful providers of long-tail content has been Google's video service YouTube. While YouTube started as a way to make video easy to share, it quickly grew into a major alternative source of video entertainment. "We are providing a stage where everyone can be seen. We see ourselves as a combination of *America's Funniest Home Videos* and *Entertainment Tonight*," co-founder Chad Hurley told Associated Press reporter Michael Liedtke.[101]

Unlike the infamous music file-sharing site Napster, YouTube has not been confrontational with Big Media. They've always promptly removed any content at the request of corporate copyright owners, but they've also pursued extensive revenue-sharing projects with those same companies. They also limit clips by users to ten minutes, which helps prevent large-scale copyright infringement from posting entire movies or television shows.[102] (YouTube has entered into contracts with Big Media companies to stream longer videos of professionally produced content.)[103]

With 100 million video downloads available and 70 million unique visitors per month, YouTube has a bigger audience than many cable channels.[104] But YouTube differs significantly from cable television. A television channel decides to put up a limited amount of programming each day and hopes that an audience will look at it, whereas YouTube puts up lots of content produced by both professionals and amateurs, and then sees what the audience decides to look at. Unlike traditional television, YouTube is capable of delivering programming that reaches audiences that range in size from dozens to millions.

"We accept everyone that uploads video to our site, and it's the community that decides what's entertaining," Hurley says.[105] YouTube's expansive approach is a prime example of Truth One—The media are essential components of our lives. YouTube combines the roles of creator, program manager, and viewer into a single person. YouTube is an expression of the audience's interests with almost unlimited levels of choice.

Diane Mermigas of the *Hollywood Reporter* sees the merger of Google and YouTube as "the first viable new-media successor to broadcast and cable television." She says the combination provides the tools needed to post, view, find, and place advertising on both amateur and professional video programming over broadband channels. She sees the pair leading the charge to have the "eyeballs, ad dollars and creative content that have sustained traditional television" move over to Internet video.[106] This is also why Steve Jobs has succeeded in making Apple a success in the online media world. Apple understood that consumers needed an easy way to find and then use digital content, providing both the online iTunes Music Store and the various iPods to play back the downloads. Using Apple's products, a consumer could download, transport, and access content anywhere and at any time.[107] The new media companies that are becoming significant and growing players understand the nature of the long tail and will deliver what consumers want.

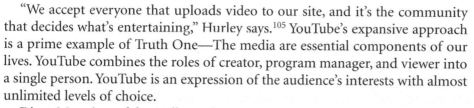

## WHO CONTROLS THE MEDIA?

Despite the growing presence of the long tail, the news and entertainment business is still dominated by a small number of highly profitable big businesses. This is clearly a source of concern for those who worry that only a limited number of interests control what is being presented to the public at large. But media scholar Michael Schudson argues that, even though the media are run by profit-seeking capitalists, the media do a good job of providing responsible journalism. The *New York Times* still views its primary responsibility as providing readers with an accurate reporting of the day's news. Furthermore, the media present a variety of viewpoints, even if they tend to focus on the middle ground rather than the extreme left or right.[108]

It is easy to view the media giants as powerful forces (the "they" of Truth Seven—There is no "they") that control the lives of their audiences. While it is true that there is no "they," reality is far more complex than that. Numerous pressures on the media influence what they deliver: from owners, to stockholders, to advertisers, to the audiences themselves. Companies seek profits, but they must also seek credibility, largely because their credibility gives value to the product they are selling. As long as a wide range of audiences exist, the media will strive to carry a diversity of content.

**broadband networks**
High-speed channels for transmitting multimedia content into the home via cable or wireless connections.

Bob Herbold of Microsoft told *Advertising Age* that the media landscape is being changed radically by the rise of **broadband networks**, which are high-speed channels for sending data and video into the home via cable or wireless connections. No longer can the networks dictate what people will view: "One of the things that will be dramatically different than the past is that your ability to capture the individual for a period of time and almost force them to watch something will be greatly diminished."[109]

Consumers now have the option of going to traditional Big Media companies or viewing events directly. Those with the time and inclination can watch the actions of the U.S. government on three separate C-SPAN networks. Anyone who can afford a high-speed Internet connection can receive virtually an unlimited array of media choices.

Critics often ask whether Big Media control society. This is a worthy question, but it is overly simplistic because it assumes that a single force runs these powerful institutions. The media-literate consumer remembers Truth One—The media are essential components of our lives—and asks a somewhat different question: "Who controls the media and their content?" It's not an easy question to answer. The influence of media owners is limited. If people don't want to watch a certain movie, no amount of promotion can get them to go see it. If a television show is offensive, few major companies will want to advertise on it. So the list of those who control the media needs to include advertisers, governments, pressure groups, news sources, and audience members themselves.

## Owners

Owners of the media have ultimate control over the content their newspapers, Web sites, or television stations carry. Critics charge that corporate owners may attempt to control the news that is reported by the news organizations they own. There is rarely a direct order from headquarters to kill a story, but that doesn't mean the owners don't exercise control over content, directly or indirectly. In the late nineteenth and early twentieth centuries, financiers such as J. P. Morgan and the Rockefeller family bought controlling ownership of magazines that had been harassing them, such as *Harper's*, *Scribners*, and *Century*, and simply stopped the unflattering exposés. It wasn't so much censorship as new owners taking the magazines in safer directions.[110]

Perhaps the biggest issue is how news organizations cover stories involving their owners. In the case of ABC News, the owner is the Walt Disney Company. Former Disney president Michael Eisner told National Public Radio, "I would prefer ABC not to cover Disney. . . . I think it's inappropriate for Disney to be covered by Disney. . . . ABC News knows that I would prefer them not to cover [Disney]."[111] But sometimes ABC News does try to cover its parent corporation. In October 1998 ABC News investigative reporter Brian Ross had been working on a story about the hiring of a convicted pedophile at a Disney resort. The story claimed that several children had been sexually assaulted at Disney properties, and that Disney did not do as much as it could to check potential employees for possible criminal backgrounds. After it had been in development for several months, the story was killed by the president of ABC News. How accurate was the story? According to the media criticism magazine *Brill's Content*, the story passed review by ABC's lawyers but was likely to have been fairly sensationalistic. *Brill's Content* also found no evidence that the Disney Corporation made any effort to stop the story. The management at ABC News simply did not want to broadcast the story.[112]

As media companies grow, the possibilities for conflicts of interest increase as well. Media scholar Mark Crispin Miller says, "There are a lot more boats that a reporter runs the risk of rocking if he or she tries to do investigative journalism. Journalistic enterprises live or die by their credibility, and if consumers are suspicious, that can be bad for business."[113]

But the potential for conflicts of interest may be more potential than real. General Electric, owner of the NBC broadcast network, is frequently cited as an example of a company that might try to control how its news operation would cover its parent company. In a story about consumer boycotts, NBC made no mention of boycotts against its parent company, GE. Nor did it mention GE in a story about defective bolts in nuclear reactors. But media critic Todd Gitlin writes that since 1990 NBC News has "routinely" covered scandals involving General Electric.[114]

## Advertisers

With the exception of books, CDs, and movies, American commercial media are supported largely by advertising revenue. As a result, advertisers have a major influence on the types of news and entertainment presented in the media. They can threaten to withdraw their advertising if they don't like a story; they might even suggest that a particular topic should be covered or not covered. Some companies simply don't want to have their ads next to controversial material, whereas others may be trying to stop the media from running stories that would be directly damaging to the company.[115] Tobacco companies have long punished magazines that run antismoking stories by withholding ads from those publications. But the influence of advertisers can be more subtle. For a while in the 1990s automaker Chrysler asked magazines to alert the company if controversial articles would be appearing near its ads.[116]

There is no question that television programming is produced to attract the specific audiences that advertisers want to reach. A group of advertisers has even established a fund to promote the development of "family-friendly" television programs—that is, programs designed to attract the kind of audience the advertisers want to target.[117] For further discussion, see Chapter 11.

## Government

Governments around the world influence how media companies operate. When AOL and Time Warner merged, they faced eleven months of review by the U.S. Federal Trade Commission, which feared that the resulting giant firm would dominate the broadband communication market.[118] The companies had to deal with a similar review by government regulators in Europe as well.

Rupert Murdoch's News Corporation, whose satellite services provide television to much of Europe and Asia, has had to make compromises in the content it provides. For example, objections by the Chinese government led Murdoch to drop the British Broadcasting Corporation (BBC) from his Star satellite system in China. Although he wasn't happy with the decision, he says it was the only way he could sell television services in China.[119] Murdoch also stopped the HarperCollins publishing division of News Corporation from publishing a book written by Hong Kong's last British governor that was critical of the Beijing government.[120] When Murdoch's News Corporation bought the *Wall Street Journal*, some critics were concerned that the paper would lighten up its criticism of the Chinese government.[121]

While the United States has a relatively unregulated media marketplace, the government still places numerous controls on the broadcast industry. These are discussed in depth in Chapter 13.

## Special Interest Groups

Special interest groups often put pressure on the media either to avoid dealing with particular topics in what they consider to be an offensive manner or to stay away from certain topics altogether. For example, when the *Philadelphia Inquirer* made the decision to reprint controversial Danish cartoons that portrayed the prophet Muhammad in an offensive way, Muslims in the Philadelphia area responded by picketing the paper. The cartoons also ran in the University of Illinois student paper, the *Daily Illini*. Publishing the cartoons sparked a debate about the issue on campus, prompted peace protests, and started a public dispute by the staff of the paper as to whether the cartoons should have run.[122] For more on the Danish cartoons, see Chapter 15.

## News Sources

Among the strongest influences on the news media are the people who provide stories. Those who are available to provide information or be interviewed will determine what kinds of stories are reported. In general, the views that are most likely to be reported come from people who are in positions of authority or have institutional connections. These people are often government officials, business executives, or experts in a specialized field. They can choose with whom they will speak, and they are able to negotiate ground rules for interviews.

In contrast, ordinary people, poor people, and the disadvantaged typically have little influence on the media or how stories are covered.[123] For example, in 1992 Zoë Baird was nominated to be attorney general of the United States. It soon became known, however, that she had hired two Hispanic domestic workers to take care of her children and had not paid Social Security taxes for them. Baird eventually had to withdraw her name from nomination. The story received extensive coverage

both because of the political implications and because of the likelihood that other professional women
would run into similar problems.
But most of the news media ignored
the plight of Latino domestic workers who weren't receiving Social
Security benefits. Because they were
not in positions of power, domestic
workers such as those Baird had
employed weren't seen as sources
and hence had no influence. The
one exception was the Spanish-
language television network Univision, which reported the story
from the point of view of low-paid
immigrant workers.[124]

Actress Lindsay Lohan at one
point required journalists to promise in advance not to ask questions
about her father's legal problems, a requirement that prompted
numerous news organizations to simply pass on interviewing the
young star. Model Heidi Klum released pictures of her newborn
daughter to the press in an attempt to keep photographers at bay.
"They always want to shoot the baby," Klum told *USA Today*. "Everyone
wants to know what the baby looks like. They run after me, like they've
never seen anyone with a stroller before!"[125] When a magazine is planning
to run a story about a major celebrity, it must negotiate who the photographer
will be, who the writer will be, and how much control the source will have over
photo selection and article content. The negotiations involve not just the particular story being run but also whether the celebrity will be available for future articles for that magazine and other publications handled by the same company. Since
many magazines depend on newsstand sales, and having a top celebrity on the
cover can make the difference in an issue's success, the magazines are often willing
to negotiate. Not all magazine editors are satisfied with the practice, however. Bob
Guccione Jr., founder of *Spin*, says, "Access to stars today is so controlled. In the
'60s and '70s, there was a fresh reporting that was honest and frank. Today, readers
can sense this is propaganda, just a stage in a marketing campaign."[126]

In 2007 the magazine *GQ* killed a lengthy unflattering story about the Hillary
Clinton presidential primary campaign. At about the same time, the magazine
was also working on a story about the charitable work being done by former
president Bill Clinton, a story scheduled to run on the cover. According to the
Washington, D.C., news Web site Politico.com, the Clinton campaign "pulled a
page from the book of Hollywood publicists and offered *GQ* a stark choice: Kill
the piece, or lose access to . . . Bill Clinton."[127] Why would the magazine agree to
do this? Primarily because the former president's face "is viewed within the

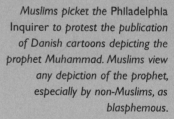

*Muslims picket the Philadelphia Inquirer to protest the publication of Danish cartoons depicting the prophet Muhammad. Muslims view any depiction of the prophet, especially by non-Muslims, as blasphemous.*

magazine industry as one that can move product."[128] *GQ* editor Jim Nelson denies that there was a connection between the killing of one story and the former president's willingness to pose for the magazine's cover.

## Audiences

The power of audiences comes primarily from their willingness to read a particular book, watch a particular movie, or listen to a particular CD. Nothing can make audience members pay attention to media content. If the audience is not there, the media are not likely to carry the programming.

In an attempt to gauge their audiences' interests, the major media companies conduct continual research. *Sports Illustrated* has surveyed readers on several occasions to decide which story should be featured on the cover. *National Geographic Traveler* routinely uses a 200-person online focus group to help guide its cover choices, and *Teen People* regularly contacts as many as 9,000 readers to see what interests them.[129]

The women's cable television channel Oxygen started off with a strong self-help format but switched to a lighter style after its focus group research showed that women wanted entertainment more than advice. As reporter Alessandra Stanley wrote in the *New York Times*, researchers told Oxygen that "smart, sensitive women want to watch dumb TV."[130] Movie producers and directors routinely make changes in their films on the basis of test audience research. The 2006 independent film *Little Miss Sunshine* grossed eight times its cost of production after incorporating edits to the movie based on the results of a small test screening. Audience members had liked the movie but had been confused about where the family was traveling in the road trip at the center of the film.[131]

Focus group research sometimes affirms what the director already wanted to do. When Warner Brothers questioned whether young people would sit still for a two-and-a-half-hour version of the movie *Harry Potter and the Sorcerer's Stone*, producers showed it to a children's focus group. Members of the test audience reported that the length was not a problem; in fact, they wanted to see more details from the book in the film.[132]

## CHAPTER Summary

The American media industry, the largest in the world, is run by private business with only minor government control. Having gotten its start in the 1640s, it was among the first industries in the American colonies. However, media business did not become big until the 1830s, when high levels of literacy and the development of the steam-powered printing press allowed for the mass production of newspapers, books, and magazines. The growth of the electronic media in the second half of the twentieth century helped create a national media culture as the same content became available simultaneously throughout the country.

Six large companies have come to dominate the American and much of the global media. They own the major television networks, broadcast stations, cable channels and providers, newspapers, magazines, record labels, movie studios, and Internet services. These companies tend to be vertically integrated—producing, promoting, and delivering content to the consuming audience. These diversified companies hope to make use of synergy to enhance the value of their various media outlets. The Big Six media companies operating in the United States are Time Warner, Disney, News Corporation, Viacom/CBS, Bertelsmann, and General Electric.

Widespread access to the Internet has brought about the rise of smaller-scale new media companies that specialize in providing a wide range of media content that appeal to relatively small numbers of consumers. These niche markets, known as the long tail of media, when combined can rival the size of the markets for blockbuster media content.

While the media industry is dominated by a limited number of companies, these companies have to please a wide range of groups in order to operate successfully. Those groups include the companies' owners, advertisers, government, special interest groups, news sources, and audience members.

## KEY Terms

penny press   79
vertical integration   81
synergy   82
local cable television systems   84

long tail   103
short head   103
broadband networks   108

## CONCEPT Review

American tradition of private ownership of media
Growth of Big Media
Revenue sources for the media
Media synergy
Long-tail media
Forces that control the mass media (owners, advertisers, government, special
    interest groups, news sources, and audiences)

# Books
## The Birth of the Mass Media

**James Frey's book** *A Million Little Pieces* was published in 2003 as a memoir of crime, violence, drugs, alcohol, and redemption. Despite some questions raised early on about its essential truthfulness, it was a wildly popular best seller, and many readers deeply identified with Frey. Two years later, he reemerged on the best-seller list after being featured on Oprah Winfrey's television book club. In fact, his book was a top seller for 2005, coming in second only to *Harry Potter and the Half-Blood Prince*, with 1.77 million copies.[1] The book was originally marketed as a novel but was rejected by seventeen publishers. Frey then reworked the manuscript into a memoir for a division of Doubleday, supposedly removing all of the made-up material. Frey was featured on *The Oprah Winfrey Show* in October 2005, with Winfrey raving that it was "like nothing you've ever read before. Everybody at Harpo is reading it. When we were staying up late at night reading it, we'd come in the next morning

James Frey

Margaret Seltzer,
aka Margaret B. Jones

saying, 'What page are you on?' "[2]

But in January 2006, the muckraking investigative Web site The Smoking Gun (TSG) reported that the book was filled with exaggerations and "a million little lies."[3] TSG investigated Frey when the site had trouble finding a mug shot from one of Frey's numerous arrests portrayed in the book. (TSG has a big section devoted to celebrity mug shots.) What the site's researchers found in their investigation was that Frey either fabricated or grossly embellished the accounts of his involvement in a train accident that killed a girl, the time he spent in jail, and the details of a friend's suicide.[4]

Winfrey subsequently had Frey back on her show following the revelation to confront him about his fabrication. She told Frey and her audience, "I feel duped. But more importantly, I feel that you betrayed millions of readers."[5]

*New York Sun* book critic Adam Kirsch says that the willingness of the public and publishing business to embrace Frey's fictive memoir is not surprising: "Once, young writers aspired to write novels, and many first novels ended up reading like thinly disguised memoirs. Now, young writers aim to break into the marketplace with quirky or pitiful memoirs, hoping to follow in the footsteps of best sellers like David Sedaris and Haven Kimmel."[6]

Kirsch notes that it isn't hard to see that *Pieces* is a work of fiction, with Frey making use of standard fictional devices and stock characters throughout the book, including the prostitute with a heart of gold, the "avuncular mobster" who treats the author like a son, the abusive priest, and the evil dentist.[7]

Memoirs are the hot literary property of the twenty-first century. In February 2006, right after the Frey scandal, more than half of the books on the *New York Times* best-selling nonfiction list were memoirs.

Charles Adams, an editor at Algonquin Books, says that publishers know that memoirs are more a version of the truth rather than some absolute truth: "As an editor, I've always known that memoirs are selective truth. I don't know that I've ever known anybody who created things, made them up, so much as I know that people edit their memories. We all do this." But he goes on to say that what Frey did went way beyond selective memory. "Look, he flat-out lied to his agent, he lied to his publisher, he lied to his readers. This was not misremembering, or changing things to protect anybody."[8]

This blurring of the lines between truth and fiction is an example of Truth Four—Nothing's new: Everything that happened in the past will happen again. In February 2008, two years after the Frey incident, the Holocaust memoir *Misha: A Memoire of the Holocaust Years* by Misha Defonseca was discovered to be a fabrication. A week

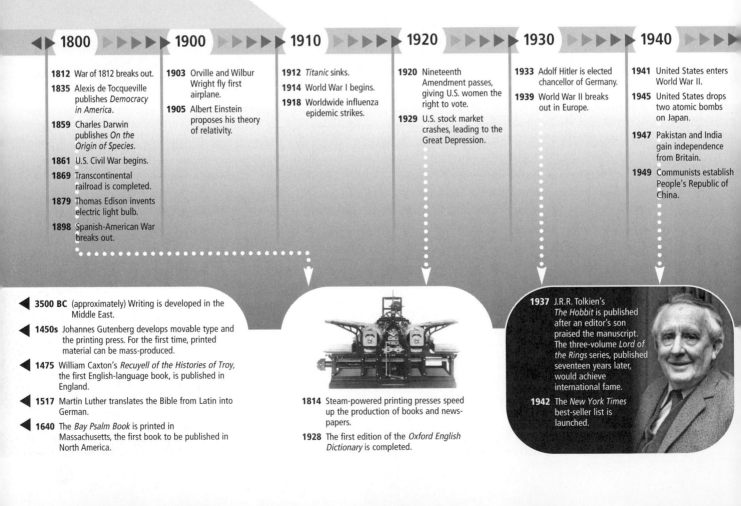

**1800**

**1812** War of 1812 breaks out.
**1835** Alexis de Tocqueville publishes *Democracy in America*.
**1859** Charles Darwin publishes *On the Origin of Species*.
**1861** U.S. Civil War begins.
**1869** Transcontinental railroad is completed.
**1879** Thomas Edison invents electric light bulb.
**1898** Spanish-American War breaks out.

**1900**

**1903** Orville and Wilbur Wright fly first airplane.
**1905** Albert Einstein proposes his theory of relativity.

**1910**

**1912** *Titanic* sinks.
**1914** World War I begins.
**1918** Worldwide influenza epidemic strikes.

**1920**

**1920** Nineteenth Amendment passes, giving U.S. women the right to vote.
**1929** U.S. stock market crashes, leading to the Great Depression.

**1930**

**1933** Adolf Hitler is elected chancellor of Germany.
**1939** World War II breaks out in Europe.

**1940**

**1941** United States enters World War II.
**1945** United States drops two atomic bombs on Japan.
**1947** Pakistan and India gain independence from Britain.
**1949** Communists establish People's Republic of China.

**3500 BC** (approximately) Writing is developed in the Middle East.
**1450s** Johannes Gutenberg develops movable type and the printing press. For the first time, printed material can be mass-produced.
**1475** William Caxton's *Recuyell of the Histories of Troy*, the first English-language book, is published in England.
**1517** Martin Luther translates the Bible from Latin into German.
**1640** The *Bay Psalm Book* is printed in Massachusetts, the first book to be published in North America.

**1814** Steam-powered printing presses speed up the production of books and newspapers.
**1928** The first edition of the *Oxford English Dictionary* is completed.

**1937** J.R.R. Tolkien's *The Hobbit* is published after an editor's son praised the manuscript. The three-volume *Lord of the Rings* series, published seventeen years later, would achieve international fame.
**1942** The *New York Times* best-seller list is launched.

later, Margaret Seltzer, whose pen name is Margaret B. Jones, was outed for fabricating her gang-life memoir *Love and Consequences* about growing up as a half-white, half–Native American foster child in Los Angeles. In reality, Seltzer is all white and grew up in an upper-middle-class Los Angeles neighborhood where she attended private school.[9] Seltzer's book was a clear fabrication. Geoffrey Kloske, publisher of Seltzer's book, told the *New York Times*, "The fact is that the author went to extraordinary lengths: she provided people who acted as her foster siblings. There was a professor who vouched for her work, and a writer who had written about her that seemed to corroborate her story."[10]

Books are a source of entertainment, culture, and ideas in society and have given rise to more lasting controversies than almost any other medium. Book publishing is also a major business supported by the people who buy books. In this chapter we look at how books developed from a hand-copied medium for elites into a popular medium consumed by millions, how society was revolutionized by the development of printing, how the publishing business operates, the conflict between literary and popular writing, and efforts to censor writers.

## Timeline

### 1950
- **1950** Korean War begins.
- **1953** Francis Crick and James Watson discover structure of DNA.
- **1957** Soviet Union launches spacecraft *Sputnik I*.

### 1960
- **1963** Martin Luther King Jr. delivers "I Have a Dream" speech during Washington, D.C., civil-rights march.
- **1969** Neil Armstrong walks on the moon.

### 1970
- **1974** U.S. president Richard Nixon resigns due to Watergate scandal.
- **1975** Vietnam War ends.
- **1977** Apple II personal computer is introduced.
- **1978** First test-tube baby is born.

### 1980
- **1983** First HIV/AIDS cases are documented.
- **1985** Ozone hole is discovered over Antarctica.
- **1986** Space shuttle *Challenger* explodes.
- **1989** The Berlin Wall falls.

### 1990
- **1991** Soviet Union disbands.
- **1993** European Union is formed.
- **1994** Nelson Mandela is elected president of South Africa.
- **1997** Diana, Princess of Wales, dies in car accident.

### 2000
- **2001** Al Qaida attacks World Trade Center and Pentagon.
- **2003** United States invades Iraq.
- **2003** Human genome project is completed.
- **2005** Terrorists bomb London's transport system.
- **2005** Hurricane Katrina hits the U.S. Gulf Coast.
- **2008** Barack Obama is elected U.S. president.

- **1973** English teacher and laundry worker Stephen King sells his first novel, *Carrie*, for an advance of $2,500.

- **1995** Online bookseller Amazon.com first appears on the Internet.

- **2000** Three of J.K. Rowling's *Harry Potter* books appear on the *New York Times* best-seller list, leading to the creation of a separate children's best-seller list.
- **2007** Amazon.com launches the Kindle e-book reader.

# THE DEVELOPMENT OF THE BOOK AND MASS COMMUNICATION

Books, consisting of words printed on paper, were the original medium of mass communication (although the Roman Catholic Church had achieved a degree of mass communication through sermons, as discussed in Chapter 1). Books allowed ideas to spread, encouraged the standardization of language and spelling, and created mass culture. Books and other printed materials also helped bring about such major social changes as the Protestant Reformation.

## Early Books and Writing

Before there could be books, there had to be writing. Writing is thought to have originated around 3500 BC in the Middle East, in either Egypt or Mesopotamia. This means that written language is around 5,500 years old; spoken language, in comparison, is thought to be at least 40,000 years old. The great advantage offered by writing was that information could be stored. No longer did people have to memorize enormous amounts of information to maintain it. Stories could be written down and preserved for generations. However, writing was not yet a form of mass communication. Reading and writing were elite skills held by people called scribes; their rare abilities gave them power within religious institutions and government (which were often one and the same).[11]

*The Origins of Writing.*   The earliest form of writing was the **pictograph**, which consisted of pictures of objects painted on rock walls. The next major development was the **ideograph**—an abstract symbol that stands for an object or an idea. An ideograph is more formalized than a pictograph, with one symbol for each object or idea. Languages such as Chinese, Korean, and Japanese still make use of ideographs. The major challenge created by having one symbol for each word is that people have to learn thousands of individual symbols. For example, literary Chinese has 50,000 or more symbols, and everyday written Chinese has between 5,000 and 8,000 symbols.

Ideographs are often used as international symbols, such as those seen on street signs. They are particularly useful in areas where many languages are spoken. Imagine a traveler in Europe looking for a place to take a bath. With an ideograph, a single symbol can stand for *bain* in French, *bad* in Danish, or *baño* in Spanish.

Sometime after 2000 BC phonographs (not to be confused with record players) were first used. **Phonography** is a system of writing in which symbols stand for spoken sounds rather than for objects or ideas. **Alphabets**, in which letters represent individual sounds, were developed between 1700 BC and 1500 BC. Sound-based alphabet writing, with only a few dozen symbols, was relatively easy to learn compared to the earlier systems of ideographs. Being a scribe thus became less of an elite position. Among the earliest surviving written works are

**pictograph**
A prehistoric form of writing made up of paintings on rock or cave walls.

**ideograph**
An abstract symbol that stands for a word or phrase. The written forms of the Chinese, Korean, and Japanese languages make use of ideographs.

**phonography**
A system of writing in which symbols stand for spoken sounds rather than objects or ideas. Among the most widely used phonographic alphabets are the Latin/Roman used in English and the Cyrillic used for writing Russian.

**alphabets**
A form of writing in which letters represent individual sounds. Sound-based alphabet writing allows any word to be written using only a few dozen unique symbols.

the Greek poet Homer's *Iliad* and *Odyssey*.[12]

*The Development of Paper.* Once people had a way to record ideas in writing, they needed something to write on. The earliest documents were written on cave walls, rocks, and clay tablets, but these media had limited usefulness. Imagine taking notes on slabs of wet clay that had to be taken back to your dorm room to dry. Something light, portable, and relatively inexpensive was needed. **Papyrus**, a primitive form of paper made from the papyrus reed, was developed by the Egyptians around 3100 BC. Papyrus was placed on 20- to 30-foot-long rolls known as scrolls. Although it was more useful and portable than stone or clay tablets, papyrus had a tendency to crumble or be eaten by bugs. **Parchment**, which was made from the skin of goats or sheep, eventually replaced papyrus because it was much less fragile.

Pictographs, such as these from Canyonlands National Park in Utah, are among the earliest forms of writing. These ancient images can be seen on remote rock walls throughout the park.

**Paper**, made from cotton rags or wood pulp, was invented by the Chinese between 240 BC and 105 BC.[13] Knowledge of papermaking was brought from China to Baghdad by the Muslims in the late 700s, and then to Europe by way of Spain in the mid-eleventh century. Papermaking spread throughout Europe during the 1300s, but it didn't replace parchment until printing became common in the 1500s.

*Books Before the Era of Printing.*   Throughout the early medieval period (AD 400–800), most books in Europe were religious texts hand-copied by monks in the **scriptoria**, or copying rooms, of monasteries. Because of the difficulty of preparing parchment, monks sometimes scraped the writing off old parchments to create new books. This led to the loss of many Greek and Latin texts. Books that had lasted hundreds of years and survived the fall of Rome were lost simply because they were erased!

With the rise of literacy in the thirteenth century, the demand for books increased. It soon exceeded the output of the monks, and the production of books shifted to licensed publishers, or stationers. Books were still hand-copied one at a time from a supposedly perfect original (or *exemplar*). One title from this era was Geoffrey Chaucer's *The Canterbury Tales*, which is still in print today.

By the fourteenth century, books were becoming relatively common. Religious texts known as illuminated manuscripts were embellished with pictures

**papyrus**
An early form of paper made from the papyrus reed, developed by the Egyptians around 3100 BC.

**parchment**
An early form of paper made from the skin of goats or sheep, which was more durable than papyrus.

**paper**
A writing material made from cotton rags or wood pulp; invented by the Chinese between 240 BC and 105 BC.

**scriptoria**
Copying rooms in monasteries where monks prepared early hand-copied books.

and elaborately decorated calligraphy, in part to help transmit the message to nonliterate audiences.[14]

## The Development of the Printing Press

Printing was invented in China toward the end of the second century. Images were carved into blocks of wood, which were inked and placed on sheets of paper, thereby reproducing the image. However, woodcuts saw limited usage because materials could not be reproduced rapidly. Between 1050 and 1200 both the Chinese and the Koreans developed the idea of movable type, but with thousands of separate ideographs, printing was not practical.

*Gutenberg and Early Typesetting.*   Johannes Gutenberg (1394–1468), a metal worker living in Mainz, Germany, in the mid-1400s, became the first European to develop movable type. Although he developed the first practical printing press (using a modified winepress), Gutenberg's most significant invention was the **typemold**, which enabled printers to make multiple, identical copies of a single letter without hand-carving each.

The most famous of Gutenberg's printed books was his edition of the Bible published in 1455. Approximately 120 copies of this Bible were printed, of which 46 are known to survive. In the 1980s one of Gutenberg's Bibles sold for $5.39 million at Christie's auction house.[15]

Typesetting was a difficult task in Gutenberg's day. The printer selected a type case containing all the characters of a typeface in a particular size and style known as a **font**—from a font or fountain of type. (Today the word *font* has become largely synonymous with *typeface* and is no longer restricted to mean a particular size and style—for example, bold or italic.) The printer then took from the case the letters needed to spell the words in a line of type and placed them on a type stick, which looked something like the rack used to hold letters in a Scrabble game. Once an entire line had been set, he placed it in a printer's frame, which held the type down.

Italics were invented in 1501 by the Italian printer Aldus Manutius (1450–1515), from whom the early desktop publishing firm Aldus took its name. By the 1600s printers could purchase mass-produced type rather than making their own typemolds. Many popular typefaces originated in the seventeenth and eighteenth centuries and are named after the printers who devised them: Claude Garamond, William Caslon, John Baskerville, and Giambattista Bodoni. A quick check of a computer's font menu will show how many of them are still in use.[16]

## The Invention of Mass Culture

Gutenberg's development of the typemold and printing press signaled the invention of mass communication and massive cultural changes. Culture was moving from something that was produced in the local community to

**typemold**
A mold in which a printer would pour molten lead to produce multiple, identical copies of a single letter without hand-carving each.

**font**
All the characters of a typeface in a particular size and style. The term *font* is typically used interchangeably today with the word *typeface*.

something that would have a regional, national, or even international scope by being transmitted through the new mass media.

*Standardized Books and Language.* The first of the changes wrought by movable type was the printing of standardized books. The printing press allowed text to be stored in multiple "perfect" copies. No longer could copyists insert mistakes when they reproduced a book. Printing thus gave students identical copies of books to study. The printing press also made books available in greater numbers and at lower cost. Although printing did not make books inexpensive, it did make them affordable to people besides priests and the wealthy, especially through the growth of libraries. The printing press also made new types of books available, particularly those written in a country's common language, such as German, instead of Latin, which was spoken only by the highly educated.

*German metal worker Johannes Gutenberg, depicted here, developed the typemold and printing press that led to the first mass-produced books.*

English printer William Caxton (c. 1422–1491) helped establish the rules for English, standardizing word usage, grammar, punctuation, and spelling, accomplishing much of this simply by publishing books in English rather than in the more scholarly Latin.[17] The standardization of the English language came about gradually, though. For example, in his journals written in the early 1800s, explorer William Clark notes that he and Meriwether Lewis set out "under a jentle brease."[18] It's not so much that Clark didn't know how to spell these words; at the time, there was still no single "correct" spelling. (See box, "Test Your Media Literacy: How Do Words Get into the Dictionary?")

*Dissemination of Ideas and the Reformation.* By far the most important effect of the printing press was that it allowed ideas—such as the Protestant Reformation—to spread easily beyond the communities where they originated. Although the printing press did not cause the Protestant Reformation, it certainly helped it take root.

Martin Luther, the German monk who founded the Lutheran Church, clearly understood how the printing press could be used to spread his ideas throughout Europe. In 1522, Luther translated the New Testament of the Bible into German so that ordinary people might be able to read it. The advent of the printing press

## How Do Words Get into the Dictionary?

Putting together the definitive English dictionary was a big job, and one that never really ended. The first edition of the *Oxford English Dictionary* (*OED*) began in 1857 with the goal of finding the origin of every word in the English language. When the authors started the project, they thought it might take ten years. Instead, the first edition, all ten volumes of it, was not completed until April 1928.

Today the *OED* has been through two editions and several supplements. In the 1990s work began on an electronic version of the dictionary. The next fully revised edition of the dictionary is slated to appear in 2010, but in the meantime the online version is being updated four times a year.[1] Each month contributors to the *OED* submit more than 18,000 new words to be considered for inclusion. The following words are among those added to the electronic edition in 2008:[2]

- *Podcasting*—A means of making audio material available.

- *Ew*—A word of disgust.

- *Subprime*—Loans made on unfavorable terms to borrowers unable to qualify for conventional loans.

**MOREonline**

You can read more about the history of the *Oxford English Dictionary* at **http://ralphehanson.com.**

• • • • • • • • • • • • • • • • • •

### What is the source?
What makes the *OED* different from the dictionary you have on your desk? Why would hundreds of lexicographers contribute entries to its first edition? Is there a need for so many sources? How might their background(s) influence the inclusion of new words?

### What is the purpose of this work?
Why do the precise meanings of words matter? If the first edition of the *OED* took more than seventy years to create, and the process of updating it is ongoing, is having an accurate and complete dictionary worth all this effort?

### How do you and your classmates use the dictionary?
When was the last time you looked up the meaning of a word in the dictionary? Did it mean what you thought it did? What new words would you or your friends add to the dictionary? Does anyone worry about whether a word is being used correctly anymore? Do the uses or meanings of words change too fast for a dictionary to keep up with them? Does the dictionary have a purpose other than to record definitions?

[1] Margalit Fox, "The O.E.D. Adds the Web to Its Lexicon," *New York Times,* November 5, 1998, G1.

[2] Quarterly update commentaries, www.oed.com/news, August 18, 2009.

and the publication of books in the language of everyday life helped doom Latin as a spoken language and put literacy—and the ability to interpret religious texts—within the reach of common people for the first time in history.

The creation of a literate mass society also helped spread scientific ideas such as Copernicus's claim that the earth was not the center of the universe. Books made it possible for people to learn individually, thus allowing new ideas to break into an otherwise closed community. This is also why every government since Gutenberg's time has wanted at least some control over the mass media.[19] So with the mass media barely started, we see the first examples of Truth One— The media are essential components of our lives—and Truth Five—New media are always scary.

## Books in the New World

The first printing press in the New World was set up by the Spanish in Mexico City in 1539; by 1560 the press had issued more than thirty-seven titles. This was a full century before the British in the Massachusetts Bay Colony would start printing. Unfortunately, none of the books from the Spanish press survive today.[20]

Printing in North America began in 1640 with the publication of *The Whole Booke of Psalmes*, known familiarly as the **Bay Psalm Book**. Put together by Puritans who were unhappy with existing translations of the psalms, the first edition sold 1,700 copies, a spectacular accomplishment when one considers that only 3,500 families lived in New England at the time. (Book historian James D. Hart suggests that some of these copies were being exported back to England.)[21] Over the next 125 years the *Bay Psalm Book* went through at least fifty-one editions in the colonies and Europe.

In 1731 Benjamin Franklin established one of the colonies' early circulating (or subscription) libraries in Philadelphia. Patrons had to pay forty shillings initially, then ten shillings a year to continue borrowing volumes. Franklin's patrons were businessmen and tradesmen. Franklin's name occurs repeatedly in discussions of the media of the colonial era. He was an important book, magazine, and newspaper publisher—the Ted Turner or Rupert Murdoch of his day.

What did people in the American colonies read? Among the best-known authors was Franklin himself, whose *Poor Richard's Almanack* sold nearly 10,000 copies per year, far more to date than any other books at the time in North America.[22] Nonreligious books that sold well in New England included those on agriculture and animal husbandry, science, surveying, and the military.

But not everything was of serious interest. In the 1680s Boston's leading bookseller attempted to order two copies of the book *The London Jilt, or, the Politick Whore; shewing all the artifices and stratagems which the Ladies of Pleasure make use of, for the intreaguing and decoying of men; interwoven with several pleasant stories of the Misses' ingenious performances*, a title not that different from what might be ordered today.[23]

**Bay Psalm Book**
The first book published in North America by the Puritans in the Massachusetts Bay Colony. The book went through more than fifty editions and stayed in print for 125 years.

Samuel Richardson's *Pamela*, published in 1740, was the first English novel. It was a book for the middle class, with characters and situations that ordinary people could identify with. Franklin published a colonial edition of the novel in 1744, but it would be forty-five years until the first American novel would be published.

## The Development of Large-Scale, Mass-Produced Books

The industrial prosperity of the mid-1800s spurred the growth of cities and the emergence of the middle class. During this time, the number of people who attended public schools grew as well. Education up to the high school level, although still not universal, was becoming common.[24] It was also a period of growth for libraries; the number of subscription libraries tripled between 1825 and 1850. American industrialist Andrew Carnegie financed the construction of nearly 1,700 public libraries from 1900 to 1917; since then, the number of public libraries has continued to grow and is estimated at 10,000 today.[25] Mass culture in the United States expanded throughout the nineteenth century, disseminated widely through penny press newspapers, magazines, Sunday School tracts, and inexpensively produced books.

**Serial novels**, which were published in installments, were popular in the 1830s and 1840s. Charles Dickens published the *Pickwick Papers* as a serial novel. Serial publication made each section of the book less expensive than a whole book, which appealed to readers, and brought in a steady flow of income, which appealed to publishers.[26] Serial novels got a boost again in the 1990s when Stephen King published his novel *The Green Mile* in paperback serial form. The first paperbacks, the so-called **dime novels** (which, despite their name, often sold for as little as a nickel), were heroic action stories, popularized by authors such as Bret Harte, that celebrated democratic ideals. The Civil War was a big time for sales of dime novels, with copies being shipped to Union soldiers as a morale booster.

The 1800s saw massive changes on the business side of publishing, too. Hand-powered flat-bed presses could print no more than 350 pages a day, but the new steam-powered **rotary press** (invented in 1814) could print as many as 16,000 sections (not just pages) in the same amount of time. Through all this, type still had to be set by hand, much as it was in Gutenberg's day. But 1885 saw the introduction of the Mergenthaler **Linotype** typesetting machine, which let a compositor type at a keyboard rather than pick each letter out by hand, thus speeding up the printing process once again. The Linotype was the standard for typesetting until the age of computer composition.

The nineteenth century thus brought the first real mass media that could be recognized today, with books, newspapers, and magazines being printed and distributed in forms that anyone could afford. With the growth of democracy and mass-produced reading materials came the growth of mass literacy.

**serial novels**
Novels published and sold in single-chapter installments.

**dime novels**
Inexpensive paperback books that sold (despite their name) for as little as five cents and were especially popular during the Civil War era.

**rotary press**
A steam-powered press invented in 1814 that could print many times faster than the older, hand-powered flat-bed presses.

**Linotype**
A typesetting machine that let an operator type at a keyboard rather than pick each letter out by hand. The Linotype was the standard for typesetting until phototypesetting became common in the 1970s.

# BUYING AND SELLING BOOKS

In the twentieth century the writing and selling of books became big business, with a huge variety of books being published. The numbers have continued to grow in the early twenty-first century. In 1995, 1.2 million separate books were available; and by 2005, Amazon.com claimed to have more than 3.7 million titles available. Of course, most bookstores don't carry anywhere near that number; still, the giant superstores typically carry 50,000 to 150,000 titles.[27]

Getting all those books from the author's computer or typewriter into the hands of readers is what the publishing business is all about. It involves three major players: publishers, writers, and booksellers.

## Publishers

**Publishers** are the companies that buy manuscripts from authors and turn them into books. Although there are thousands of publishers worldwide, just twenty companies publish nearly 80 percent of all books today. This proportion has grown substantially since the 1920s, when the twenty largest publishers were responsible for only 50 percent of all books published.[28] This transformation has taken place because regional publishers are buying up small, independent publishing houses, and international conglomerates are buying up major national publishing companies. As a result, the range of ownership of the publishing business is increasingly limited, and fewer people are making more of the decisions that determine what people will be able to read.[29]

The process of consolidation in the publishing industry can be seen in the story of American publisher Random House. Random House was founded in 1925. After years of growth, in 1960 the company acquired another major American publishing house, Alfred A. Knopf. In 1965 Random House was bought by media conglomerate RCA, and throughout the 1970s and 1980s, Random House continued to grow, buying up a host of publishers. Finally, in 1998, German media giant Bertelsmann bought Random House and combined it with its existing publishing holdings.[30]

Random House has continued to grow by acquiring smaller publishers. In 2009 Random House acquired Ten Speed Press, an independent alternative publisher of titles like *What Color Is Your Parachute?* and *The Moosewood*

*Kit Carson on the War-path, published by Munro's Ten Cent Novels, was one of the many dime novels read by the newly literate public in the nineteenth century.*

**publishers**
The companies that buy manuscripts from authors, turn them into books, and market them to the public.

*Cookbook.* This acquisition brings to mind another, when News Corp., through its HarperCollins division, bought out literary publisher Ecco Press. Daniel Halpern, founder of the press, told the *Washington Post,* "People will say, 'There goes another independent press, isn't it too bad.' The short answer is, 'Yes, it's too bad.' But that's the reality. Let's not be sentimental about this stuff. This is not a time when the small press can survive."[31]

*The World's Top Publishers.*    The publishing business is a global industry, with owners in the United States, Germany, Britain, Canada, and the Netherlands. These companies publish a variety of books, ranging from best-selling fiction to textbooks to technical references. The following figures report the companies' revenue only from book publishing.[32] The top five global publishers are:

| | | |
|---|---|---|
| 1. *Pearson*—Major education publisher | $7.4 billion | United Kingdom |
| 2. *Reed Elsevier*—Professional publications | $6.7 billion | United Kingdom/ Netherlands/ United States |
| 3. *Thomson Reuters*—Financial publications | $5.1 billion | Canada |
| 4. *Wolters Kluwer*—Financial publications | $4.9 billion | Netherlands |
| 5. *Bertelsmann*—*Random House* | $4.3 billion | Germany |

For U.S. publishers, the top five are:

| | |
|---|---|
| 1. *McGraw-Hill*—Textbook giant | $2.7 billion |
| 2. *Scholastic*—Harry Potter's American publisher | $2.2 billion |
| 3. *John Wiley*—Technical publisher | $1.7 billion |
| 4. *HarperCollins*—Popular **trade books** | $1.4 billion |
| 5. *Reader's Digest*—Special interest books | $1.1 billion |

**trade books**
General-interest fiction and nonfiction books that are sold in hardback or large-format paperback editions.

**university and small presses**
Small-scale publishers that issue a limited number of books covering specialized topics. They are often subsidized by a university or an organization.

*University and Small Presses.*    Not all publishing is done by large corporations; a substantial number of **university and small presses** issue a limited number of books and may not be in the business for profit. Among their titles are books that serve a limited geographic or subject area or an academic discipline, mostly scholarly books or textbooks. An example of a small press is Interweave Press, which publishes books about knitting, weaving, and crafting. But academic presses occasionally print breakout books. The late Norman Maclean, an English professor at the University of Chicago, had his memoir about growing up in Montana and fly-fishing published by the University of Chicago Press. The book, *A River Runs Through It*, was an enormous success (and was made into a movie directed by Robert Redford and starring Brad Pitt).[33]

No small publisher has had more surprising success than the Naval Institute Press (NIP). It's a nonprofit publisher that produces, for the most part, books about naval history and strategy. Typical titles include *Destroyer Captain*, *Stealth Boat*, and *Combat Fleets of the World*. But it has also published military fiction titles, two of which became major best sellers. The first of these was Tom Clancy's *The Hunt for Red October*. Clancy, who was working as an insurance agent at the time, had peddled his manuscript about a Russian submarine captain to just about every major publisher in the United States, but none expressed any interest in the book. Finally he submitted it to the NIP. Although the publisher had never handled a work of fiction before, it eagerly put Clancy's book into print. During the months following publication, the book's sales increased gradually as people talked about this great novel from an obscure little publisher. Finally, six months after it was published, *The Hunt for Red October* was at the top of the best-seller lists, just through word of mouth.

The NIP's second big success was Stephen Coonts's *Flight of the Intruder*. Coonts had queried thirty-six publishers about his Vietnam War novel; thirty of them refused to even look at the manuscript and four rejected it. He was waiting to hear from the last two when Clancy's success encouraged him to submit it to the NIP. *Flight of the Intruder* made it onto the *New York Times* best-seller list seven weeks after publication, helped in part by a blurb from Clancy and by the fact that book reviewers were now familiar with the NIP. *Flight of the Intruder* spent six months on the best-seller list and sold 230,000 copies in hardback.[34]

*Vanity Presses and Self-Published Books.* **Vanity presses** are publishers that print books with the author paying all the costs of publication and distribution (a process known as self-publishing). Many authors believe that contracting with a vanity press means that they'll see their book in bookstores, but this is rarely the case. Most authors who self-publish see little or no return on their investment. Yet those who take all the risk on the book also make all the profit—should there be any.

Yet every now and then a self-published book comes along that surprises everyone. *The Celestine Prophecy*, by James Redfield, has sold 6 million copies and spent more than two and a half years on the *New York Times* best-seller list. The book can be described as a New Age self-help novel of adventure; it deals with an ancient Peruvian manuscript that lists nine insights leading to spiritual awareness. After spending two years writing it, Redfield sent his manuscript to numerous publishers, who showed little interest in the offbeat book. So he used his life savings to have the book privately published. Selling books from the trunk of his car, he managed to move 100,000 copies. At that point, Redfield was able to sell the hardback rights to Warner Books for $850,000. In 1995 the book was the best-selling title by an American author. It also spawned a host of sequels written by Redfield, his wife, and various collaborators.[35]

The world of self-published books has changed dramatically in recent years, with authors contracting with publish-on-demand and electronic

**vanity presses**
Companies that print books and distribute books with the author paying all the costs (a process known as self-publishing).

printing services to deliver their books to consumers without having to have a large number of physical books in inventory. At a time when traditional publishers are facing cutbacks, *New York Times* reporter Motoko Rich found that self-publishing companies are growing rapidly.[36] Print-on-demand publishers such as AuthorHouse, Wordclay, and Xlibris are releasing thousands of titles. These get printed when a customer orders a copy through either the publisher's Web site or through an online bookseller such as Amazon.com or BarnesandNoble.com.

People self-publish for a variety of reasons. Some, like Redfield, do so because he couldn't find a traditional publisher; others do so because they feel a published book gives them credibility; while still others just want a nice gift for family or friends. In other cases, hobbyists may publish specialized books primarily to disseminate information about the hobby, not to make a profit.

*The Government Printing Office.*    Surprisingly, the federal government is one of the nation's biggest publishers. You've probably seen ads on late-night television telling you that you can get a booklet about almost anything from an address in Pueblo, Colorado. Most of its titles are government reports, but the U.S. Government Printing Office has published an occasional best seller, including the *9/11 Commission Report*, the Warren Commission's report on the Kennedy assassination, and the so-called Pentagon Papers (discussed in Chapter 13). The Government Printing Office is moving rapidly into putting federal publications into electronic form, with approximately 300,000 available online. Up to 50 percent of federal documents now are published only in electronic form, with no paper equivalent.[37]

## Authors

The next group of players in the publishing business are the authors, the people who write the books. Most media attention goes to blockbuster authors like J. K. Rowling and Stephen King or literary authors like John Updike and Anne Tyler; less is written about the vast majority of authors who write without a multimillion-dollar contract, a book tour, or television commercials during *Oprah*. But what is the publishing experience like for the average author?

Consider the story of a typical book, a science fiction romance titled *Moon of Desire*. Pam Hanson (a first-time author and the wife of this book's author) and her mother, Barbara Andrews (who had written several romance novels in the 1980s), wrote a proposal for the novel along with a sample chapter and submitted them to a publisher in March 1992 (see Figure 4.1).

Then they waited.

In June the publisher agreed to acquire the manuscript. The authors received a contract for the book, which called for the manuscript to be

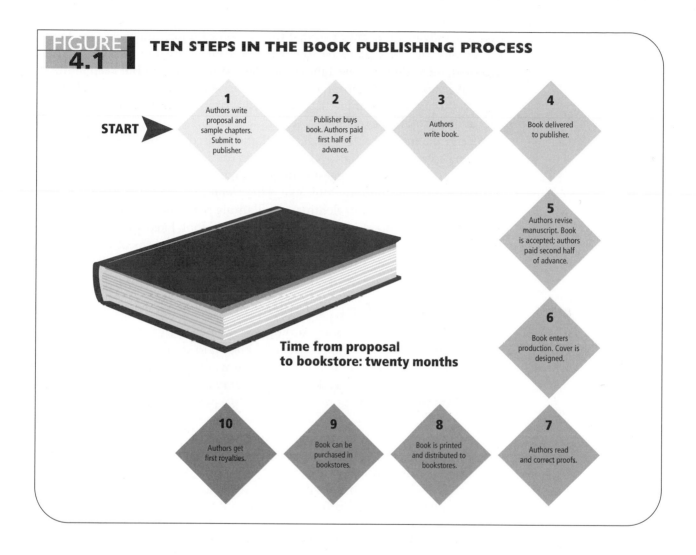

**FIGURE 4.1**

# TEN STEPS IN THE BOOK PUBLISHING PROCESS

**START**

**1** Authors write proposal and sample chapters. Submit to publisher.

**2** Publisher buys book. Authors paid first half of advance.

**3** Authors write book.

**4** Book delivered to publisher.

**5** Authors revise manuscript. Book is accepted; authors paid second half of advance.

**6** Book enters production. Cover is designed.

**Time from proposal to bookstore: twenty months**

**10** Authors get first royalties.

**9** Book can be purchased in bookstores.

**8** Book is printed and distributed to bookstores.

**7** Authors read and correct proofs.

delivered on December 1. With the contract signed, the authors were paid the first half of their advance. This did not mean, however, that they got rich. Advances for first novels are typically between $1,000 and $5,000, and this advance was typical.

Then came the work of writing the book—90,000 words, or about 360 typed, double-spaced pages. The mother and daughter traded drafts back and forth, working on computers with identical word-processing programs. A week before the deadline, they sent the finished book to their editor at the publishing company. If the authors had missed their deadline, the publisher would have had the right to reject the book and cancel the contract.

A few weeks later, in early January 1993, the editor sent revisions to the authors. Manuscript revisions may consist of anything from trivial changes in punctuation or grammar to major changes in characterization or plot. In this case, the only major change was that the mutant cannibals menacing the heroine in one chapter had to be toned down a bit. Once the manuscript was accepted, the authors received the second half of the advance. But keep in mind that advances are against royalties (a percentage of the selling price of each book paid to the author), meaning that the advance payments will be deducted from the author's royalty payments.

After a manuscript has been accepted and revised, the book goes into production. An artist creates a cover illustration on the basis of information from an "art fact sheet" that suggests possible scenes for the cover and describes what the hero and heroine look like. The *Moon of Desire* cover featured the hero and heroine on a raft floating on a flaming sea. A book designer lays out the rest of the book, deciding what the pages will look like, what typeface will be used, and how big the book will be. (These can be serious considerations. Stephen King was required to cut 50,000 words, the length of a short novel, from the original edition of *The Stand* so that it could fit on the printing press.)

Once the book is set in type, a copy of the ready-to-print pages—known as **proofs**—is sent to the authors. Authors are supposed to correct only blatant errors in proofs, although some have been known to start rewriting the book at this point. As is usual in popular fiction, Hanson and Andrews had about a week to read the proofs of their book and send them back to the publisher; after the corrections were made, the proofs were sent to a printer to produce the finished book.

At this point it's time to start marketing the book. This may include placing advertisements in newspapers, fan magazines, or even on television and scheduling a book tour and media appearances. But Andrews and Hanson, like most first-time novelists, had to make do with virtually no marketing support. Twenty months after the original proposal was submitted, the book was available in bookstores.

Book publishing can be lucrative for some, but the majority of writers make very little money. Tom Clancy's multimillion-dollar advances are exciting but not typical. David Lamb, who wrote *Stolen Season*, a book about minor-league baseball, notes that the average annual income for someone who lists "book writer" as an occupation on his or her income tax form is about $6,500. Hanson and Andrews, who wrote their book under a single pseudonym, Pam Rock, saw their first royalties beyond the initial advance in December 1994, more than two and a half years after the initial proposal was sent in.

## Booksellers

The last major players in the book business are the book wholesalers and retailers, the companies that take the book from the publisher to the book-buying public.

**proofs**
The ready-to-print typeset pages sent to book authors for final corrections.

*Bookseller and Distributor Consolidation.* The Ingram Book Group, the nation's largest book wholesaler, distributes millions of books and audiobooks from more than 43,000 publishers to more than 30,000 retail outlets, including Amazon.com. In essence, Ingram and its smaller competitors are the sources from which bookstores buy their books.[38]

The buyers at Ingram are among the most important in the book business; they determine how many copies of a book will be stocked in the company's warehouses. This can, in turn, determine the size of a book's press run. Ingram's buyers are respected not only by bookstore owners but also by scholarly presses.[39]

Among booksellers, Barnes & Noble is a proverbial 800-pound gorilla. The company's revenues total more than $5 billion a year, and it operates nearly 800 stores throughout the United States under the Barnes & Noble and B. Dalton names, along with its online bookstore, BarnesandNoble.com. Overall, Barnes & Noble controls about 20 percent of the consumer book business in the United States.[40] The Borders Group, which includes the mall-based Waldenbooks, is the nation's second largest **bricks-and-mortar** book retailing chain, with $3.8 billion in sales for 2008.[41]

The alternative to these big stores—which frequently offer book clubs, live music, and book events, and often have in-store cafes—are the independent bookstores, which are represented by the American Booksellers Association (ABA). The ABA currently represents 1,200 independent bookstores, down from 5,200 in 1991.[42] The independent stores are gradually losing market share to the chain outlets.

A major alternative to both the chain and the independent bookstores are online bookstores, most notably Amazon.com, discussed later in the "Future of Books" section.

Another type of bookseller is the mail-order book club. The Book-of-the-Month Club is the nation's oldest and largest book club. Its books were originally selected by an elite group of readers, but they are now chosen by the club's marketing directors. The judges were eliminated in mid-1994, when their role had become essentially ceremonial. The club focuses on marketing best sellers rather than bringing out books by new authors whom readers may not appreciate. A former book club judge argued in the *New York Times* that the placing of a marketing manager in the number-two position at the club has transformed it from a literary organization into a mail-order store that could just as easily sell kitchen supplies or clothes.[43]

In recent years book clubs have faced increased competition from book superstores and online bookstores. But in addition to sales, book clubs generate mailing lists that can be used to market other products. Book clubs are also important because, when they are operated by the publisher, they produce a high level of revenue by cutting out the intermediate bookstore. For example, romance publisher Harlequin has a book club for each of its major imprints. Recently book clubs have started operating online, believing that this will help them attract young readers.

**bricks-and-mortar stores**
Bricks-and-mortar stores are those that have a physical presence at which you can shop.

## The Textbook Business

Textbooks are different from other books in one major respect—the people who select the books aren't the same as the end-users, the people who have to buy and pay for them. Students charge that, because of this disconnect, faculty don't take price sufficiently into account when picking books for their courses.

Estimates on how much students spend per year on textbooks vary widely, but a Government Accountability Office study estimated costs at $900 per year. The same report showed that textbook prices have increased at more than twice the overall rate of inflation between 1986 and 2004.[44] Retail bookseller giant Barnes & Noble also has a separate division devoted to selling textbooks, which did more than $1.9 billion in business in 2007 through its 625 campus bookstores. Along with making money for the company itself, the stores also give the school they're associated with a cut of the sales.[45]

John Frederick, provost of the University of Nevada at Reno, attributes some of the high costs to the bundling of CDs and Web site passwords with new textbooks. When students buy the books used, however, they often do not get access to the Web site or have the CDs. "The publishers engage in a lot of tactics to limit the used-book market," Frederick said. "It is a real problem, but until universities band together to create policies that would control the price of textbooks or exert some kind of market pressure to reduce the cost, there won't be any easy solutions."[46] To be fair to the publishers, they have high fixed costs compared to the booksellers, including development, permissions, royalties, marketing, design, typesetting, and printing, which they must incur to put out even one copy of a new or revised edition. Figure 4.2 compares the profits and costs of publishers and authors from new editions to the profits of booksellers from new and used editions.

Schools have tried a variety of approaches to control costs. Minnesota State University in Mankato tries to purchase several copies of expensive textbooks to put on reserve in the library, while other universities have worked at setting up textbook rental programs.[47]

Other schools are trying out electronic textbooks, delivered using portable devices called **e-book readers**. Arizona State University is experimenting with using electronic textbooks delivered to students through the Amazon Kindle DX e-book reader. The thirty required books for a yearlong history of human culture class would typically cost $475. Students will pay half that amount for Kindle editions. Of course, in this pilot program, students don't have to pay the $498 the Kindle DX would normally cost. As of 2009, e-books make up approximately 2–3 percent of textbook sales. Although electronic textbooks typically cost less than paper books, students are not able to sell back their electronic copies at the end of the semester.[48] (There is more on e-books in the "Future of Books" section at the end of this chapter.)

Bookstore manager Marie Stewart noted that publishers often put out plainer, black-and-white edition textbooks in other countries at half the price of the fancier editions published in the United States and wondered "why we can't

**e-book reader**
A portable device for viewing, and sometimes selling, electronic books and other texts. Among the most popular are the Amazon Kindle and the Sony eReader.

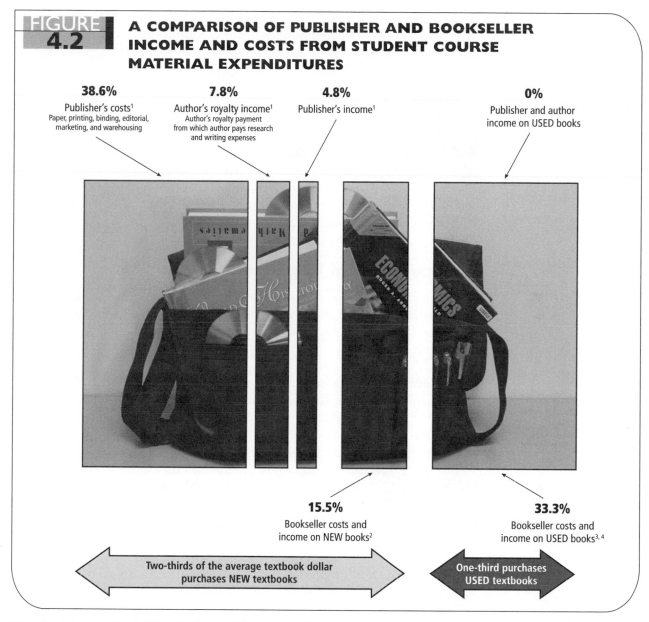

**FIGURE 4.2**

## A COMPARISON OF PUBLISHER AND BOOKSELLER INCOME AND COSTS FROM STUDENT COURSE MATERIAL EXPENDITURES

**38.6%**

Publisher's costs[1]
Paper, printing, binding, editorial, marketing, and warehousing

**7.8%**

Author's royalty income[1]
Author's royalty payment from which author pays research and writing expenses

**4.8%**

Publisher's income[1]

**0%**

Publisher and author income on USED books

**15.5%**

Bookseller costs and income on NEW books[2]

**33.3%**

Bookseller costs and income on USED books[3, 4]

Two-thirds of the average textbook dollar purchases NEW textbooks

One-third purchases USED textbooks

*Source:* Association of American Publishers, http://www.publishers.org/main/HigherEducation/attachments/Graphic.pdf.

*Note:* This graphic is reflective of the costs of course material expenditures when it was created in 2004 and may not fully represent the cost of similar materials today.

[1] Data from the Association of American Publishers.

[2] Data from the National Association of College Stores.

[3] Data from the *Student Monitor*, LLC.

[4] A portion of these costs represents money paid to students to acquire used books.

get that price."[49] (You might note that this book was designed to be substantially less expensive than many of the competing texts on the market.)

Students also try to cut their textbook costs, by buying used books. The manager of the Oregon State University bookstore notes that more than 40 percent of the textbooks sold at the store are used.[50] Of course, with used textbooks, neither the publisher nor the author gets a cut of the sales, only the bookstore.

# BOOKS AND CULTURE

For all the attention that movies, television, CDs, and video games get from social critics, books continue to be a major source of excitement, controversy, money, and even violence.

## The Importance of Blockbuster Books

A continual tension exists between blockbuster books that make large amounts of money for publishers and so-called important books that have lasting literary value. But this tension is nothing new; it dates back at least to the middle of the nineteenth century.

*Great Books Versus Popular Books.*   As noted earlier in this chapter, the mid-1800s were a period of strong growth for the publishing business, with the number of serious novels and popular fiction titles increasing rapidly. Americans wrote almost 1,000 novels from 1840 to 1850, up from the 109 books of American fiction published between 1820 and 1830.[51]

The 1850s saw the publication of Nathaniel Hawthorne's *The Scarlet Letter*, Herman Melville's *Moby-Dick*, and Walt Whitman's *Leaves of Grass*, but none of these "great books" sold nearly as well as popular novels written by and for women. Hawthorne resented losing sales to popular women authors. He once became so frustrated that he commented, "America is now wholly given over to a d——d mob of scribbling women, and I should have no chance of success while the public taste is occupied with their trash—and should be ashamed of myself if I did succeed."[52]

The **domestic novels** that Hawthorne was complaining about told of women who overcame tremendous problems through their Christian strength, virtue, and faith, ending up in prosperous middle-class homes. One of the best known of Hawthorne's "scribblers," at least today, is Sarah Josepha Hale. She was well known not only as a novelist but also as a writer of children's books (she was the author of "Mary Had a Little Lamb") and the editor of *Godey's Lady's Book*, a popular women's magazine of the day (see Chapter 5).[53]

Women authors of popular fiction continue to sell well today. According to the Romance Writers of America, approximately 8,000 romance titles were released in 2007, most of which were written and edited by women. Annual

**domestic novels**
Novels written in the nineteenth century by and for women that told the story of women who overcame tremendous problems to end up in prosperous middle-class homes.

revenues from sales of romances totaled $1.375 billion in 2007.[54]

Hawthorne's complaints about popular fiction outselling serious writing are often echoed today. Major publishers work hard to promote a limited number of blockbuster books—in part because only a small percentage of books make a profit. For example, in 2000 romance publisher Harlequin recorded a dramatic increase in profits primarily because of two best-selling titles.[55] Typical among the best-selling authors who publishers love is mystery writer Janet Evanovich. She started writing romance novels for Bantam, then branched out into the wildly successful Stephanie Plum bounty hunter novels. Evanovich's novels mix together humor, adventure, mystery, and romance: "I wanted to write the book that made people feel good. If you are having a bad day, you could read my book and I might make you smile."[56] Why did Evanovich choose to write about a somewhat inept female bounty hunter? She saw a space for it in the marketplace. "So I took what I loved about the romance genre and squashed it into a mystery format."[57] The first printing of her 2009 novel *Finger Lickin' Fifteen* was 2 million, and 30 million copies of her books are in print.[58] In contrast, books by modern literary writers such as John Updike will do well to sell more than 100,000 copies.

Not every best-selling book is popular fiction, however. J. D. Salinger's *The Catcher in the Rye*, considered to be one of the most popular books of all time, continues to sell about 250,000 copies a year.[59]

These blockbuster authors illustrate the main thrust of the publishing business today—finding writers who can turn out one big hit after another. Harry Hoffman, retired chief executive of Waldenbooks, points out that books have to compete with Nintendo and television. In essence, publishing no longer views itself as being in the literature business; instead, it considers itself to be in the entertainment business.[60]

Of course, popular fiction and literature can sometimes intersect. Among the most influential best sellers of the past fifty years is John Ronald Reuel (J. R. R.) Tolkien's epic-length fantasy trilogy, *The Lord of the Rings*. Initially published in England in 1954 and 1955, the story has remained continuously in print and has now sold more than 100 million copies—11 million during 2002 alone. (The sales boost in 2001 and following years can be attributed in part to the popularity of the movie series based on the books.)

Tolkien, an English professor at Oxford, was a colleague of C. S. Lewis, author of the popular *Chronicles of Narnia*, which also formed the basis for a popular movie series. A veteran of World War I, Tolkien specialized in the history of language and literature, and his passion was European myths and sagas. He started

*Famed photographer Mathew Brady took this portrait of celebrated American author Nathaniel Hawthorne in the mid-nineteenth century. Brady's role in the development of photojournalism is discussed in Chapter 5.*

work on *The Hobbit*, his first book set in the fictional Middle Earth, in 1930, telling the story of Bilbo Baggins and his adventures. *The Hobbit* was written initially to entertain Tolkien's four children, but the book was published in 1937 after the 10-year-old son of an editor read the manuscript and liked it. The book was a success, and the publisher asked for a sequel. Seventeen years later, the first part of *The Lord of the Rings* was published.

Tolkien wrote the story as a single book, but the publisher divided it into three volumes to make it more practical to print and sell. In fact, the story was so long that even Tolkien didn't know what to do with it. In a letter to his publisher, Tolkien wrote, "My work has escaped from my control, and I have produced a monster: an immensely long, complex, rather bitter, and rather terrifying romance, quite unfit for children (if fit for anybody)."[61]

Although Tolkien died in 1973, his books have had a lasting influence on American popular culture. *The Lord of the Rings* strongly influenced rock groups such as Yes and Led Zeppelin, and it inspired Gary Gygax to quit his job as an insurance salesperson and devote himself to developing his role-playing game "Dungeons and Dragons." The online game "EverQuest," which is based on fantasy themes created in *The Lord of the Rings*, receives more than $5 million a month in subscription revenue from its fans. There is even an academic journal devoted to Tolkien's Middle Earth and its linguistics. Most important, the entire genre of contemporary fantasy literature owes its existence to Tolkien. The fantasy sections in bookstores and the whole genre of swords-and-sorcery movies would not exist but for the inspired writings of a British professor.[62]

*Magical Teen Series Break the Best-Seller Lists.* The biggest publishing phenomena in recent years have been J. K. Rowling's magical *Harry Potter* books and the *Twilight* vampire series by Stephenie Meyer. Both series deal with supernatural worlds inhabited by young people who suffer from normal teen angst along with all the supernatural conflicts brought about by vampires, werewolves, and wizards. Rowling's seven-volume *Harry Potter* series has 143 million copies in print in the United States. Meyer's teen-vampire romance series has had four volumes published to date and has sold 40 million copies.[63]

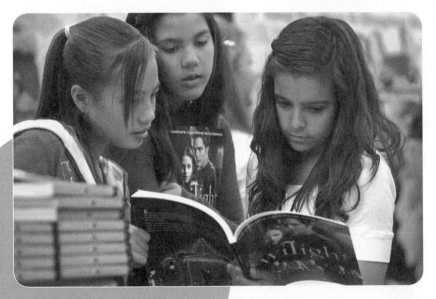

Teen and tween girls have made Stephenie Meyer's Twilight *books massive best sellers on the same scale as J. K. Rowling's* Harry Potter *novels.*

In addition to bringing the joy of reading to millions of young people (and adults, for that matter), the two authors have also upset the major

## TEST YOUR MEDIA LITERACY

### The Literary Equivalent of a Big Mac and a Large Fries

A reader survey sponsored by the publishing industry showed that if people found themselves stranded on a desert island, their first choice in books would be the Bible. Their second choice? A Stephen King novel. King has had more than twenty books on the *New York Times* best-seller list, making him one of the most popular living authors. King's works are often criticized for being nothing more than popular fiction, a charge that King cheerfully accepts: "I'm a salami writer," King told *USA Today*. "I try to write good salami, but salami is salami. You can't sell it as caviar." He has also said that his work is "the literary equivalent of a Big Mac and a large fries."[1]

King dismisses the separation between serious literature and popular fiction, saying that there must be a good story to go with good writing: "So-called literary critics who praise gorgeous writing without a story are like some guy dating a model, saying she's dumb as a stone boat but is great to look at."[2]

Despite making no claims to being a literary writer, King was honored in 2003 when he was given the National Book Award for his contribution to American writing. The award was controversial because King has been considered a popular writer rather than a serious one. In his acceptance speech, King said he hoped his being honored would help bridge the gap between the two. "For far too long the so-called popular writers of this country and the so-called literary writers have stared at each other with animosity and a willful lack of understanding. . . . But giving an award like this to a guy like me suggests that in the future things don't have to be the way they've always been. Bridges can be built between the so-called popular fiction and the so-called literary fiction."[3]

King's selection for the National Book Award didn't end up being an isolated incident. Popular children's writer Judy Blume (discussed in the next section of this chapter) won the following year.

**MORE online**

You can find links to a commentary on writing by Stephen King and hear his National Book Award acceptance speech at **http://ralphehanson .com**.

### Who is the source?

Stephen King is a popular American horror writer who has written dozens of novels, screenplays, collections of short fiction, and two books on the craft of writing. He is also the winner of the 2003 National Book Award. How do you think King's background has shaped the kinds of stories he writes? Has King written any novels that could be considered literature? Which ones? Why?

### What is he saying?

What does King mean when he says he is the "literary equivalent of a Big Mac and a large fries"? Is he being hard on himself, or is that a fair statement? Do authors choose their audience, or does the audience choose them?

best-selling book lists. Prior to the publication of *Harry Potter and the Goblet of Fire*, the fourth book in the series, the *New York Times* had been ranking books by sales in four categories: fiction and nonfiction, paperback and hardback.

But in February 2000, *Harry Potter* was threatening to take up four spots on the *Times* hardback fiction list.[64] This dominance spurred complaints by publishers who felt that the children's books were keeping their authors who wrote for adults from being recognized.[65] So before *Goblet of Fire* was released, the *New York Times* created a separate best-seller list for children's books. Some people in the industry praised the new list, saying that it gave children's books the attention they deserved, whereas others claimed that it had been created just to keep the young wizard from taking up four slots on the fiction list.

According to Caron Chapman of the Association of Booksellers for Children, the top books on the children's best-seller list will not change as often as those on the adult list:

> Adults constantly want the newest and the latest. But in children's bookselling it's not the newest or the latest, but the best that teachers and parents are looking for. Adult bestseller lists have nothing to do with the best book, but which title has the most marketing support that week.[66]

By 2009, Meyer's *Twilight* books were occupying four of the top ten spots on the *USA Today* best-seller list, which combines all books (hardback, paperback, fiction, and nonfiction) into a single list. But *Breaking Dawn*, the fourth book in the series, does not appear on any of the *New York Times* best-seller lists. Instead, the story of Bella and Edward, along with that of Harry, Hermione, and Ron, inhabits the Children's Series Books list. This list treats the entire series as essentially a single entity rather than individual titles.

Children's books can appeal to adults as well. Carl Davies, who works in educational publishing, says, "There seems to be a big crossover between what children like and what adults like, and Harry Potter is the best example of that. But it's not just adults reading the modern favorites, because what's clear is that children are also reading the classics of the past that their parents read."[67]

## Books and Censorship

Books are capable of exciting great passion in readers, those who love them and those who hate them. Wherever there are books, there are people who will want to ban or control them for one reason or another. Attempts at control can range from removing the book from a school library to threatening to kill the author.

*Book Banning.*   In the United States most book censorship efforts are local rather than national in scope. Book banning is generally limited to removing specific titles from school libraries or reading lists. Typically such efforts involve books thought to contain offensive language, racial bias or stereotypes, sexual material, or offensive treatments of religion.[68] Occasionally, though, a book's publisher will instigate the censorship. Ray Bradbury's novel *Fahrenheit 451* tells the story of a "fireman" whose job is to burn books rather than put out fires. (Fahrenheit 451° is the temperature at which book paper starts to burn.) The book was originally published in 1953, but in 1967 Ballantine Books brought out an edition for high schools that modified seventy-five passages in the text to eliminate such words as "hell," "damn," and "abortion." This was done without Bradbury's knowledge or consent. When he found out about it thirteen years later, he demanded that the edited version be withdrawn.[69]

Different titles show up on various lists of banned or challenged books, but a few appear repeatedly. Maya Angelou's *I Know Why the Caged Bird Sings* has had its position on many schools' reading lists challenged because of its description of the rape of the author as a child. Other frequently challenged books include the Goosebumps series by R. L. Stine, J. D. Salinger's coming-of-age novel *The Catcher in the Rye*, and Kurt Vonnegut's account of the firebombing of Dresden, *Slaughterhouse Five*.[70]

Not all banned books are contemporary. A number of classics have been banned as well. According to the American Library Association, the following books are frequently challenged:[71]

- *The Scarlet Letter*, by Nathaniel Hawthorne, because a book about adultery conflicts with a community's values.
- *Of Mice and Men*, by John Steinbeck, because it contains profanity.
- *Twelfth Night*, by William Shakespeare, because the comedy is perceived as promoting homosexuality.

## MOST CHALLENGED BOOKS OF 2008

The American Library Association has been tracking the most challenged books for several years. There have been substantial changes in the titles that have been challenged in recent years, with none of the titles on 2008's list having appeared on the 2001 list. Challenged books are those that some individual or group has attempted to remove or restrict. They do not need to have been successful in getting the title banned.

1.   *And Tango Makes Three,* by Justin Richardson and Peter Parnell

2.   *His Dark Materials* trilogy, by Philip Pullman

3.   *TTYL, TTFN, L8R, G8R* (series), by Lauren Myracle

4.   *Scary Stories* (series), by Alvin Schwartz

5.   *Bless Me, Ultima,* by Rudolfo Anaya

6.   *The Perks of Being a Wallflower,* by Stephen Chbosky

7.   *Gossip Girl* (series), by Cecily von Ziegesar

8.   *Uncle Bobby's Wedding,* by Sarah S. Brannen

9.   *The Kite Runner,* by Khaled Hosseini

10.  *Flashcards of My Life,* by Charise Mericle Harper

*Source:* The American Library Association, www.ala.org/ala/issuesadvocacy/banned/frequentlychallenged/21stcenturychallenged/index.cfm.

*The Adventures of Huckleberry Finn*, Mark Twain's classic, has, for a range of reasons, been in trouble ever since its publication in 1885. *Little Women* author Louisa May Alcott said of *Huck Finn*, "If Mr. Clemens cannot think of something better to tell our pure-minded lads and lasses, he had best stop writing for them." Mark Twain was not bothered by Alcott's comments in the least, responding, "That will sell 25,000 copies for us, sure."[72] The town library of Concord, Massachusetts, banned the book as unfit, while others described it as "rough, coarse, and inelegant."[73] The basic complaint was that the novel was disrespectful and contained profanity. More recently, *Huck Finn* has been criticized as being racist. While Pulitzer Prize–winning novelist Jane Smiley does not want to see *Huck Finn* banned, she suggests that it does not deserve its position in the canon of great American literature.[74]

*Judy Blume.*   American writer Judy Blume is a perennial member of the lists of banned authors because of her novel *Forever*, a story about a teenager's discovery of her sexuality. What does Blume write about that is so upsetting? Wet dreams, wanting to belong, death, divorce, cruelty by kids, masturbation, and menstruation.[75]

Blume was a New Jersey housewife when she wrote her first picture book in 1969. Ten of her books are on *Publishers Weekly*'s list of the top 200 children's paperbacks of all times, and two are in the top ten. More than 65 million copies of her novels have been sold, and her books have been translated into twenty languages.[76]

While Judy Blume is upset that her books are banned, she is more upset about what the banning does to her readers:

> It upsets me much more for the message that it sends to young people, which is, there is something in these books that we do not want you to know. And if you do not read about it, you never know about it. And that something, for the most part, is puberty, anything to do with sexuality. And, you know, they are all going to go through puberty whether their parents want them to or not.[77]

Most attempts at censoring books in the United States result in at most a book's being removed from a school library, but that is not always the case in the rest of the world. Few cases of censorship have been quite as spectacular as the efforts to suppress Indian-born novelist Salman Rushdie's intensely controversial novel, *The Satanic Verses*, a religious satire/allegory that is extremely offensive to Muslims. Rushdie's book was first banned in India in the fall of 1988. It also caused rioting in Pakistan in 1989. At that time Iran's Ayatollah Khomeini placed a death sentence, or *fatwa*, on Rushdie for the book's blasphemous content.

In the early days of the *fatwa*, Rushdie went into hiding and moved from house to house daily. According to some sources, the *fatwa* played a role in eventually breaking up his marriage.[78] Khomeini died several months after issuing the *fatwa*, making it difficult to remove the death sentence and leaving Rushdie in a kind of lifelong limbo. Among the reasons why the book offended Muslims was that it contains a dream sequence in which prostitutes pretend to be wives of the prophet Muhammad in order to increase their business, and it refers to Muhammad as Mahound, a Christian demon.[79] The text also contains trilingual puns that require an understanding of Hindu, Muslim, and British culture.

After the death threat, several major chain bookstores did not carry *The Satanic Verses*, but most independent booksellers continued to sell it. The chain stores eventually relented, and *The Satanic Verses* ended up at the top of the *New York Times* best-seller list.

In the fall of 1998 the Iranian government, through its foreign minister Kamal Kharrazi, said that it would give no reward or assistance for killing Rushdie. However, as of this writing, militant Islamic organizations are still allegedly offering bounties of as much as $3 million on the author's life.[80] Despite the lifting of the official government death threat, Rushdie is not allowed to fly on British Airways planes.[81] Rushdie was fifty-one when the nine-year-old *fatwa* was lifted, and although he still sees a continued need for caution, he views the threat as ended. Rushdie had this to say to the *New York Times* about what it was like living under the *fatwa*:

> It's an extraordinary thing to see people walking down the streets of foreign cities, carrying your picture with the eyes poked out and calling for your death. It's as if somebody were to break your picture of the world, and everything you think about somehow ceases to be true.[82]

Although Rushdie himself was never attacked, several other individuals with connections to his book were killed or injured. Hitoshi Igarashi, the Japanese translator of *The Satanic Verses*, was stabbed to death in Tokyo in July 1991; Italian translator Ettore Capriolo was beaten and stabbed by a man demanding Rushdie's address; and William Nygaard, Rushdie's Norwegian publisher, was shot and wounded in October 1993.

Rushdie is not the only author to face threats. In 2008 Britain's Scotland Yard stopped an attempt to firebomb the publisher of *The Jewel of Medina*, a controversial book about the prophet Muhammad and his child bride by American author Sherry Jones. The attack targeted Jones's Dutch publisher

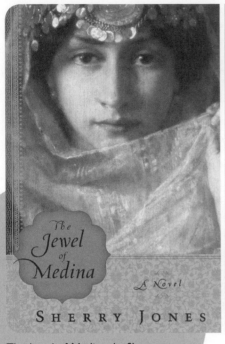

*The Jewel of Medina, by Sherry Jones (right), generated international controversy when extremists attempted to firebomb the offices of its British publisher.*

Martin Rynja. The American publisher of *Jewel*, Random House, cancelled its publication because the company feared it might incite violence. (Random House is the largest English-language publisher and is owned by German publishing giant Bertelsmann.) Random House has been accused of canceling publication of the book after having the manuscript criticized by an associate professor of Islamic history at the University of Texas. Jones was able to replace Random House with Beaufort Books as her American publisher.[83]

Other authors who have received death threats include Bangladeshi doctor, poet, and novelist Taslima Nasreen; Nigerian poet Ken Saro-Wiwa; and Nobel Prize–winning Nigerian author Wole Soyinka.[84]

## THE FUTURE OF BOOKS

As we discussed in Chapter 3, the digital media and the Internet are bringing big changes to the media business, providing consumers with alternatives to blockbuster books. Instead, a limited number of consumers spread out across the country can access far more specialized content than they could find in even the biggest brick-and-mortar bookstore. This phenomenon is known as the long tail. The long tail recognizes that we are no longer limited by geography as to what media we will buy and whom we will talk to. As Chris Anderson, the author of *The Long Tail*, explains, "We are turning from a mass market back into a niche nation, defined now not by our geography but by our interests."[85]

### Books and the Long Tail

The Internet launched the long-tail segment of the media by allowing a company to produce a catalog that is available to everyone with very little marginal cost for each additional viewer. Amazon.com founder Jeff Bezos started selling books on the Internet because the Web was the only practical way to offer the variety that he sought:

> It . . . turns out that you can't have a big book catalog on paper; it's totally impractical. There are more than 100,000 new books published every year, and even a superstore can't carry them all. The biggest superstores have 175,000 titles and there are only about three that big. So that became the idea: let Amazon.com be the first place where you can easily find and buy a million different books.[86]

And this was the radical notion—instead of offering a selection of books, why not offer every book, all 5.6 million or so English-language books in print. Amazon can keep the most popular books in stock in their warehouses, and seamlessly order books from publishers if they are in smaller demand. They can even offer out-of-print books from private stores that partner with Amazon, or custom-publish them through arrangements they've made with publishers. (This is a prime example of Truth Two—There are no mainstream media. With long-tail retailers like Amazon, consumers are no longer limited to just the biggest books from the biggest publishers.)

The online bookstore began operations in July 1995, and by December 1998 it had served more than 4.5 million customers. Why is it called Amazon? Because it begins with an A and therefore will appear first on alphabetical lists. In 1998 Amazon started selling videos and CDs, and since 1999 it has added toys, clothing, kitchen equipment, and other merchandise.

A key feature of Amazon is that it tracks customers' interests by recording what they've already bought on Amazon.com. Each time a buyer enters the site, a personalized home page shows related books that the customer might not have known about otherwise. Shoppers looking at the description of Jimmy Buffett's autobiography, *A Pirate Looks at Fifty*, for example, also see a recommendation for Herman Wouk's *Don't Stop the Carnival*, which tells the tale of a man running a hotel on a tropical island and is one of Buffett's favorite books.

Online bookstores are among the most successful businesses in electronic commerce. One reason for their initial success was that in the early days of the commercialized Internet, people who owned computers were also likely to read books. Also, well-educated people, who tend to read for pleasure and entertainment, are likely to work in offices where they have Internet connections and thus can buy books online. Finding books online can be easier than finding them in a bookstore, especially if the title is obscure. A former Random House executive notes that the online bookstores provide instant gratification.

Marketing partnerships are an important element of online bookstores. Anyone who wants to can set up an online bookstore on his or her Web site in partnership with Amazon and will receive a small commission for every book sold. In the past, BarnesandNoble.com had partnerships with the *New York Times* and *USA Today*'s Web sites that let readers purchase the books being written about in the papers. Of course, such partnerships raise questions about objectivity: Can a book review be objective when the newspaper that's reviewing the book is also selling the book?[87]

## Electronic Publishing and Print-on-Demand

In the past few years a new form of publishing has emerged: electronic books. These can be classic books that have been placed on the Internet, best sellers designed to be read on an electronic viewer, or new books published only in electronic format. Electronic distribution has become a popular format for self-publishing, as well. Although some electronic titles are designed to be read on a computer, the most exciting development is the e-book reader, a small handheld device with a screen that can hold hundreds of separate titles. Whereas many people are reluctant to give up paper and ink, others think that being able to carry an entire library in a device the size of a single paperback sounds pretty good.[88]

We've been hearing about e-books replacing standard books, or at least becoming commonplace for several years now. Franklin offered one, Sony has had a variety of them, books have been sold that can be read on PDAs and smart-phones, Project Gutenberg has been putting public domain books up online, and there are multiple publishers out there pushing their online book wares.

At least one alternative e-book format has been successful for many years, and that's the audio book, for which a voice actor, famous or not, reads books (or even magazine articles) aloud so that they can be listened to on a cassette player, a CD player, or (more recently) an MP3 player. In 2008, audio books accounted for $331 million in sales, according to the Audio Publishers Association.[89]

Unlike electronic print books, audio books have found a market among the commuting and exercising class. They provide a distinct value to consumers in that they allow readers to consume books and the like in environments where they couldn't easily read. Audio books also have the advantage of being readily under-standable—everyone knows what "books on tape" are, even if most people buy them on CDs or as digital downloads. Finally, even though special equipment is required to use them, you likely already own the equipment or can buy it for very little money. This means there's very little risk in adopting this new technology.

When most people talk about e-books, however, they're referring to books in the form of a text file that can be read on a computer screen or some other media device.

A big barrier to the widespread adoption of e-books is that consumers are hesitant to buy an expensive device that could be left orphaned with no new content. Other people are concerned that the devices are just too complicated to use: How do you get the books downloaded? Where do you find them? How do you operate the thing?

Finally, there's the whole question of whether e-books provide a compelling advantage to readers. What do they get out of the device that they don't get out of a traditional paper book?[90] For those of us who are big readers, we generally like books and see no reason to go to one more gizmo.[91]

*Slate* writer Jacob Weisberg is typical among fans of Amazon's Kindle, which has become the dominant e-book reader on the market for a variety of reasons, not the least of which is that you can buy the books from Amazon.com and have them downloaded directly to your e-book reader without any connection to a computer.[92]

Amazon founder Jeff Bezos, in an interview on *The Charlie Rose Show,* said that a successful e-book reader should be cheap enough that everyone can own one and that every book in the world should be available on it.[93] But he might have added that e-books need to guarantee users that once they buy a book for their reader, they'll be able to keep it.

That's the problem faced by readers who purchased George Orwell's *1984* or *Animal Farm.*[94] During the summer of 2009, people who purchased copies of the two classic novels discovered that Amazon had erased the books from their Kindles and refunded the purchase price. It turned out that the publisher offering the two books through Amazon did not have the legal right to sell them in the United States. So Amazon used its electronic connection to take the text off the e-book readers.

To its credit, Amazon realized that erasing the titles was a bad mistake. As consumers pointed out, if you bought an illegal paperback copy of a book, Amazon wouldn't be able to take it back. And it should be no different for e-books.

Amazon founder Jeff Bezos posted an unambiguous apology on the company's Web site shortly afterward:

> This is an apology for the way we previously handled illegally sold copies of *1984* and other novels on Kindle. Our "solution" to the problem was stupid, thoughtless, and painfully out of line with our principles. It is wholly self-inflicted, and we deserve the criticism we've received. We will use the scar tissue from this painful mistake to help make better decisions going forward, ones that match our mission.[95]

*Print-on-Demand.* The other side of electronic publishing is **print-on-demand**, in which the physical book is not printed until it's ordered, or when the distributor of the book prints additional copies in small batches. This is how Amazon supplies some of its smallest-selling titles. The company has banks of

*E-book readers, such as Amazon's Kindle, allow consumers to download books, magazines, and newspapers to take with them anywhere.*

**print-on-demand**
A form of publishing in which the physical book is not printed until it's ordered, or when the distributor of the book prints additional copies in small batches.

## TEST YOUR MEDIA LITERACY

### My Kindle Ate My Homework!

When you buy a book at the bookstore, you expect to be able to do whatever you want with it. As long as you don't misplace it, it's yours. You can read it, mark it up, or even resell it. But with e-books, especially those with digital rights management that limits their use to your reader, the rules are different.

How different?

That's what Michigan high school senior Justin Gawronski discovered in 2009. He had been assigned George Orwell's novel *1984* as summer reading for his Advanced Placement English class. He bought and downloaded a copy of the book using his Amazon Kindle. He made full use of the Kindle's note-taking function, electronically highlighting passages and keying his notes in the device to pages in the book. But when Amazon discovered it was selling an unlicensed copy of Orwell's classic (see previous page), the company reached into his Kindle and zapped *1984* out of existence.

Now, finding a free copy of *1984* online to replace the copy he lost is not difficult. (The Web site www.george-orwell.org has all of Orwell's works for free.) What was a problem for Gawronski was that he lost all the connections between what he had read and what he had written, along with all the highlighting. It was as though all the notes he had taken in the margin of the book had been stripped out and run together without any context.[1]

Gawronski is suing Amazon for deleting the book without his permission, rendering his notes "useless." This has led some commentators to call this the "Kindle ate my homework case."[2] Gawronski is suing Amazon for removing the book from his Kindle and, more important, for interfering with his note-taking. He is seeking at least $5,000 in damages. Gawronski's attorney told the press, "Amazon.com had no more right to hack into people's Kindles than its customers have the right to hack into Amazon's bank account to recover a mistaken overpayment."[3]

Brad Stone, writing in the *New York Times,* points out:

> A growing number of civil libertarians and customer advocates wants Amazon to fundamentally alter its method for selling Kindle books, lest it be forced to one day change or recall books, perhaps by a judge ruling in a defamation case—or by a government deciding a particular work is politically damaging or embarrassing.[4]

Stone quotes a law professor who says that deleting the illegal copy of *1984* was the right thing to do, given all the problems associated with online copyright. Especially since Amazon refunded everyone's money.

**MORE online**

You can find a link to articles about the Justin Gawronski case and e-books in general at **http://ralphehanson.com.**

**Who is the source?**

What kinds of people are using e-books? How are they using them?

### What are they saying?

What are the complaints that users have against e-books in general? Why was Justin Gawronski unhappy with what happened with his copy of *1984?*

### What is the difference between a printed book and an e-book?

What advantages does an e-book have over a printed book? Should e-book sellers have the right to delete books from your e-book reader if they were improperly sold? Should a court be allowed to order that a defamatory book be deleted from an e-book reader? Do you really own the books you have on an e-book reader? Or is it more like renting a book? Do printed books still have any advantage in the twenty-first century?

### How do you and your classmates feel about electronic books?

Think about why you might buy a Kindle or another e-book reader. Would you prefer to get your textbooks and college readings in that format? Would you choose to use an e-book reader if it saved you money on textbooks? Would it bother you that you would no longer be able to sell back your books? Would you trust an e-book reader to store your books and notes?

[1] Mark Millian, "Kindle Teen Tattles on Amazon for Losing His Homework," *Los Angeles Times,* July 31, 2009, www.thisisbrandx.com/2009/07/kindle-teen-tattles-on-amazon-.html.

[2] David Sarno, "Highlights From the '1984' Lawsuit Against Amazon," *Los Angeles Times,* July 31, 2009, latimesblogs.latimes.com/technology/2009/07/highlights-from-the-1984-lawsuit-against-amazon.html.

[3] Christopher Null, "Amazon Ate My Homework: Kindle Kid Sues Over Deleted Notes," August 4, 2009, tech.yahoo.com/blogs/null/146875.

[4] Brad Stone, "Amazon Faces a Fight Over Its E-Books," *New York Times,* July 27, 2009.

large-capacity laser printers that can turn out fresh copies of books from digital copies stored on a computer. This allows the company to stock books at a cost that approaches zero until the book is ordered.[96] Book wholesaler Ingram also does print-on-demand through its subsidiary Lightning Source, which can print 100,000 different titles from more than 2,300 publishers.[97]

## CHAPTERSummary

Early forms of writing first appeared in the Middle East about 3500 BC. Over the next 2,000 years, writing evolved from simple pictographs to highly developed ideograms and the sound-based alphabet system. Modern rag-based paper was developed in China between 240 BC and 105 BC. In medieval Western Europe early hand-copied books were created primarily by monks and other religious figures. Because they were difficult to produce, these books were expensive and rare.

In the mid-fifteenth century Johannes Gutenberg developed the typemold. Printing presses using Gutenberg's movable type allowed books and other publications to be mass produced for the first time, leading to numerous cultural changes, including the Protestant Reformation, the rise of literacy, and standardization of grammar and spelling.

In the New World, publishing began soon after European settlement, first in Mexico City by Spanish settlers and later by British colonists in the Massachusetts Bay area. As literacy and education spread throughout the growing middle class during the nineteenth century, improvements in printing technology made inexpensive popular reading materials such as dime novels and serials readily available. The first comprehensive dictionary of the English language also was produced during the nineteenth century.

The modern book business has three major participants: publishers, authors, and booksellers. The book business, like the rest of the media industry, has been characterized by rapid consolidation, with a limited number of companies controlling a substantial portion of the publishing, distribution, and retail business.

Publishers produce a wide range of books, but most of the industry's profits come from a limited number of best-selling titles from authors like Stephen King, Tom Clancy, and Janet Evanovich. Young-adult authors such as J. K. Rowling and Stephenie Meyer have been extremely popular and dominated the best-seller lists in recent years. The textbook industry has come under increased scrutiny by both legislators and consumers for high costs. Responses have included textbook rental, electronic editions, and lowered costs of production.

Although books rarely attract the degree of controversy that movies, television, or video games do, they are occasionally banned in the United States, typically by an individual library or school district. The most common reason for restricting books is that they contain offensive language, racial bias or stereotypes, sexual material, or offensive comments about religion. Outside of the United States, some controversial authors have faced threats of violence or even death, most notably Salman Rushdie, author of *The Satanic Verses*. Such bans and threats almost never prevent the books from being sold, however.

The Internet has become an important marketplace for books, especially those for which demand is limited. Online bookstores such as Amazon.com can keep books available by selling them as digital downloads or as print-on-demand titles. E-book readers are becoming increasingly popular as a means of distributing books, especially textbooks.

## KEYTerms

## CONCEPTReview

Development of paper and writing
Impact of standardized books
The publishing business
Censorship
Book-banning
*Fatwa*
Memoir
Popular fiction/literature
Mass market/trade publications
Long-tail book sales

# Magazines

## The Power of Words and Images

**CHAPTER 5**

**Few magazine** photographers are as recognizable as Annie Leibovitz. Best known for her sometimes controversial covers for *Vanity Fair* and *Rolling Stone*, Leibovitz has been documenting popular culture for more than forty years.

Leibovitz started out wanting to be a painter, but she dropped out of art school to live on a kibbutz, a collective farm, in Israel. When she returned to the United States, she submitted a photo she had taken of beat poet Allen Ginsberg to *Rolling Stone* magazine. Her photo was accepted, and she went to work for the publication full time at age twenty. She became the premiere rock-and-roll magazine photographer of the 1970s, shooting the Rolling Stones, Grace Slick and Jefferson Airplane, and Rod Stewart. But the photo that put her on the map was a cover portrait for *Rolling Stone* of a naked John Lennon clinging to Yoko Ono taken just hours before he was murdered.[1]

It was during her time at *Rolling Stone* that Leibovitz learned the practical details of shooting successful magazine covers: The subject of the photo has to be recognizable, there has to be something worthy of notice in the picture, and there has to be room for the magazine's name and a few lines of type.

Leibovitz went on to shoot for *Vanity Fair*, doing many of its best-known covers, including the infamous nude Demi Moore, eight months pregnant. The Moore cover sold an extra 500,000 copies of the magazine, and former editor Tina Brown notes that *Vanity Fair* picked up about 75,000 new subscriptions as a result. The Moore cover led to 95 separate television stories, 64 radio shows, and 1,500 newspaper articles.[2] It has even been credited with spearheading a trend toward using pregnant women as a subject in art.[3]

Brown told *Inside Media*, "When we did the Demi Moore cover, I felt it was an enormously positive pushing of the envelope, because it was really about liberating women from a stereotype, allowing women to realize that this was a time when they were beautiful, and not succumb to the whole myth of glamour."[4] Of course, other women pointed out that now they were expected to be toned, tan, and glamorous even in the late stages of pregnancy.[5]

How does Leibovitz get her startling images, such as the one of tennis star Martina Navratilova down on all fours, screaming? "The big mystery is no mystery," Leibovitz told *Folio* magazine. "You just have to ask if the person is willing to do something.

**Annie Leibovitz poses with her iconic photograph of a pregnant Demi Moore.**

And usually, if you believe in your ideas strongly enough, you'll find that most people are willing to go along with you."[6]

In recent years Leibovitz has been best known for celebrity portraiture, including the "Got Milk?" mustache, Gap, and Dove's "Campaign for Real Beauty" ads, but she still takes magazine photography seriously. Her Lennon and Moore covers took the top two positions in the American Society of Magazine Editors' top forty magazine covers of the past forty years. And her *Vogue* cover featuring actress Kirsten Dunst dressed as Marie Antoinette made *Advertising Age*'s Top Ten of 2006.[7]

Looking at Leibovitz's long career in magazine journalism, you can see a prime example of Truth Three—Everything from the margin moves to the center. She started shooting counterculture figures for the upstart magazine *Rolling Stone* and progressed to shooting A-list celebrities for *Vanity Fair* and *Vogue* in the 1990s and 2000s.[8] But even as she has moved to the center of mainstream culture, Leibovitz continues to

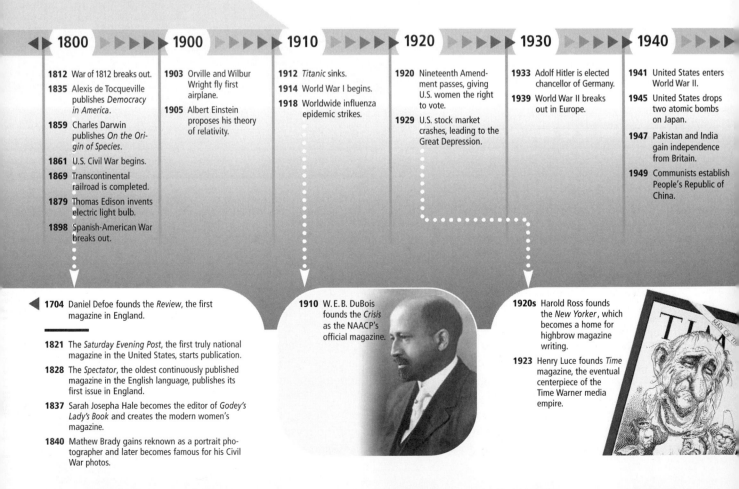

**1800** ▶▶▶▶ **1900** ▶▶▶▶ **1910** ▶▶▶▶ **1920** ▶▶▶▶ **1930** ▶▶▶▶ **1940** ▶▶▶

**1812** War of 1812 breaks out.

**1835** Alexis de Tocqueville publishes *Democracy in America*.

**1859** Charles Darwin publishes *On the Origin of Species*.

**1861** U.S. Civil War begins.

**1869** Transcontinental railroad is completed.

**1879** Thomas Edison invents electric light bulb.

**1898** Spanish-American War breaks out.

**1903** Orville and Wilbur Wright fly first airplane.

**1905** Albert Einstein proposes his theory of relativity.

**1912** *Titanic* sinks.

**1914** World War I begins.

**1918** Worldwide influenza epidemic strikes.

**1920** Nineteenth Amendment passes, giving U.S. women the right to vote.

**1929** U.S. stock market crashes, leading to the Great Depression.

**1933** Adolf Hitler is elected chancellor of Germany.

**1939** World War II breaks out in Europe.

**1941** United States enters World War II.

**1945** United States drops two atomic bombs on Japan.

**1947** Pakistan and India gain independence from Britain.

**1949** Communists establish People's Republic of China.

**1704** Daniel Defoe founds the *Review*, the first magazine in England.

**1821** The *Saturday Evening Post*, the first truly national magazine in the United States, starts publication.

**1828** The *Spectator*, the oldest continuously published magazine in the English language, publishes its first issue in England.

**1837** Sarah Josepha Hale becomes the editor of *Godey's Lady's Book* and creates the modern women's magazine.

**1840** Mathew Brady gains reknown as a portrait photographer and later becomes famous for his Civil War photos.

**1910** W. E. B. DuBois founds the *Crisis* as the NAACP's official magazine.

**1920s** Harold Ross founds the *New Yorker*, which becomes a home for highbrow magazine writing.

**1923** Henry Luce founds *Time* magazine, the eventual centerpiece of the Time Warner media empire.

court controversy. Her portrait of fifteen-year-old Disney star Miley Cyrus for *Vanity Fair* drew outraged complaints from both Cyrus and parents of her young fans. The photo showed Cyrus in a provocative pose with her back uncovered and her front draped in a satin sheet. Leibovitz eventually apologized for the photo, saying, "I'm sorry that my portrait of Miley has been misinterpreted. . . . The photograph is a simple, classic portrait, shot with very little makeup, and I think it is very beautiful."[9]

Provocative covers by photographers such as Annie Leibovitz help draw readers into magazines that cover every imaginable topic, from fashion, to sports, to news. In this chapter we look at how the magazine industry grew from a general national medium into one that serves a wide range of narrow interests. We look at the types of magazines published today, some controversies that surround magazine articles and advertisements, how the magazine industry operates, and what the future of the magazine industry holds.

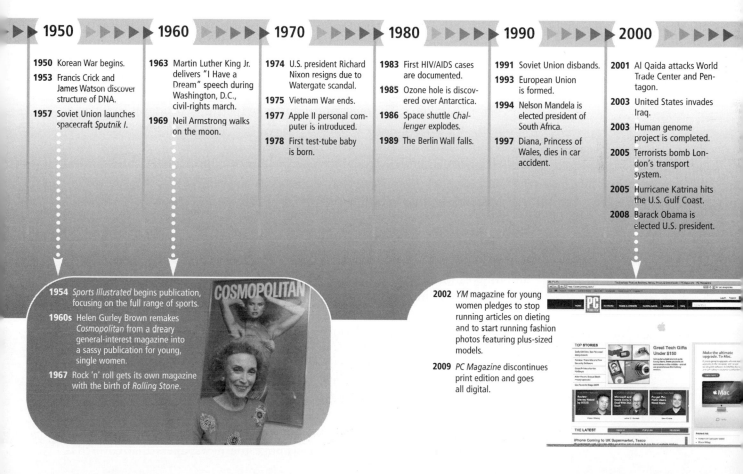

**1950** ▶▶▶▶▶ **1960** ▶▶▶▶▶ **1970** ▶▶▶▶▶ **1980** ▶▶▶▶▶ **1990** ▶▶▶▶▶ **2000** ▶▶▶▶▶

**1950** Korean War begins.

**1953** Francis Crick and James Watson discover structure of DNA.

**1957** Soviet Union launches spacecraft *Sputnik I.*

**1963** Martin Luther King Jr. delivers "I Have a Dream" speech during Washington, D.C., civil-rights march.

**1969** Neil Armstrong walks on the moon.

**1974** U.S. president Richard Nixon resigns due to Watergate scandal.

**1975** Vietnam War ends.

**1977** Apple II personal computer is introduced.

**1978** First test-tube baby is born.

**1983** First HIV/AIDS cases are documented.

**1985** Ozone hole is discovered over Antarctica.

**1986** Space shuttle *Challenger* explodes.

**1989** The Berlin Wall falls.

**1991** Soviet Union disbands.

**1993** European Union is formed.

**1994** Nelson Mandela is elected president of South Africa.

**1997** Diana, Princess of Wales, dies in car accident.

**2001** Al Qaida attacks World Trade Center and Pentagon.

**2003** United States invades Iraq.

**2003** Human genome project is completed.

**2005** Terrorists bomb London's transport system.

**2005** Hurricane Katrina hits the U.S. Gulf Coast.

**2008** Barack Obama is elected U.S. president.

**1954** *Sports Illustrated* begins publication, focusing on the full range of sports.

**1960s** Helen Gurley Brown remakes *Cosmopolitan* from a dreary general-interest magazine into a sassy publication for young, single women.

**1967** Rock 'n' roll gets its own magazine with the birth of *Rolling Stone.*

**2002** *YM* magazine for young women pledges to stop running articles on dieting and to start running fashion photos featuring plus-sized models.

**2009** *PC Magazine* discontinues print edition and goes all digital.

# THE DEVELOPMENT OF A NATIONAL CULTURE

Before radio and television, magazines were people's primary sources for in-depth news, ideas, and pictures. In 1704 Daniel Defoe, later famous for writing *Robinson Crusoe*, founded the first real magazine in England—a weekly periodical called the *Review*. Physically, the *Review* looked just like the newspapers of the era. But newspapers focused exclusively on news, whereas Defoe's magazine covered public policy, literature, and morals. Edward Cave's *Gentleman's Magazine* was the first publication to use the word *magazine*, derived from the original meaning of the word as a place where goods or supplies are stored.[10]

What is a **magazine**? It's a periodical that contains articles of lasting interest. Typically magazines are targeted at a specific audience and derive income from advertising, subscriptions, and newsstand sales. Magazines are also intended for a broader geographic area than newspapers, and in the nineteenth century they increased in both number and circulation as the demand for nationwide advertising grew. (For more about the connection between the growth of advertising and magazines, see Chapter 11.)

**magazine**
A periodical that contains articles of lasting interest. Typically magazines are targeted at a specific audience and derive income from advertising, subscriptions, and newsstand sales.

## Early Magazines

In 1740 Benjamin Franklin announced his plan to publish *The General Magazine*, with lawyer John Webbe as editor. But in a story that could rival any of today's headlines, Webbe was stolen away by publisher Andrew Bradford to edit his *American Magazine*. As a result, Bradford's magazine was published three days before Franklin's. The magazine industry in the New World was less than a week old, and it had already had its first battle.[11]

The 100 magazines published prior to 1800 contained many reprints from newspapers around the colonies as well as items from British magazines. Magazines were free to reprint whatever they wanted because at the time there were no copyright laws or copyright protections.

## The *Saturday Evening Post*

Just as television and the Internet do today, the magazines of the eighteenth and nineteenth centuries provided news, education, and entertainment. Their collections of humor, verse, and stories were designed for the small amounts of leisure time people had in the early 1800s. Because libraries were in short supply, magazines often were the only regular source of high-quality written entertainment.

The most significant of the early magazines was the *Saturday Evening Post*, first published on August 4, 1821. It looked like a four-page newspaper, and a year's subscription cost two dollars, half payable in advance.[12] It contained essays, poetry, obituaries, stories, and a column called "The Ladies' Friend." It had advertising, and by the 1830s it was illustrated as well. The *Post* was in many ways the first truly national medium—unlike the newspapers that covered a single city, it was read in every American state from Maine to Florida. For at least forty years, the *Post* was *the* voice of the United States. It published the writings of Edgar Allan Poe, Harriet Beecher Stowe, James Fenimore Cooper, and Nathaniel Hawthorne. The *Post* appealed to a broad, general audience, rather than the more exclusive audience of literary magazines. By 1848 it was the leading weekly in the United States, and even as late as 1937 it had a circulation of more than 3 million.

In 1928 Leon Chipple described the *Post* as follows:

> This is a magic mirror; it not only reflects, it creates us. What the [*Saturday Evening Post*] is we are. Its advertising helps standardize our physical life; its text stencils patterns on our minds. It is a main factor in raising the luxury-level by teaching us new wants. . . . But it does more than whet our hunger; by blunt or subtle devices it molds our ideas on crime, prohibition, Russia, oil, preparedness, immigration, the World Court. . . . This bulky nickel's worth of print and pictures is a kind of social and emotional common denominator of American life.[13]

For more than a century the *Saturday Evening Post* was one of the dominant magazines in the United States.

This is an early statement, though not a unique one, that speaks to Truth One—The media are essential components of our lives. It does not imply that magazines are the creators of our world. Rather, it claims that the magazine is an integral, inseparable part of who we are in the media world.

With the coming of television, the *Post* found its preeminent position in American culture fading. The world was changing, but the *Post* did not change with it. It was stuck in the middle-class America of the pre–World War II era that it depicted in its Norman Rockwell covers. Following a series of editorial and advertising missteps, the *Post* gradually became a monthly publication, and as of 2001 it was being published only bimonthly as a nostalgia and health magazine. The coming of television would also force magazines in general to change from appealing to broad audiences to focusing on narrower, more specific audiences.

## The Birth of Photojournalism

In addition to providing the first national source of news and commentary, magazines were the first source of **photojournalism**—the use of photographs to portray the news in print. At first, pictures were printed in periodicals by using hand-engraved plates copied from photographs. Then in the 1880s came the invention of the **halftone**, an image produced by a process in which

**photojournalism**
The use of photographs to portray the news in print.

**halftone**
An image produced by a process in which photographs are broken down into a series of dots that appear in shades of gray on the printed page.

*War photography hasn't changed that much since its beginnings in the American Civil War. This image of the battle of Gettysburg (left) was taken in 1863 by photographer Timothy H. O'Sullivan, who initially trained under Mathew Brady. The photo on the right was taken in 2006 by Abdul Khaleq and is of Afghan dead following a suicide bombing in Lashkar Gah in southern Afghanistan.*

photographs are broken down into a series of dots that appear in shades of gray on the printed page. The halftone allowed the photograph to be reproduced directly in the publication rather than being copied into a drawing.

The photographer Mathew Brady is often credited with inventing photojournalism in the mid-nineteenth century. Beginning in 1845, Brady became famous for making portraits of noted Americans. He attempted to sell printed reproductions of his photographs, and though the effort failed because the costs were too high, he set the stage for later celebrity photographers like Annie Leibovitz. Brady also realized that much of the value of his photographic portraits came from their being reproduced as engravings, woodcuts, lithographs, and the like. The original was valuable, but so were the reproductions. Today Brady is best remembered for his pictures of the American Civil War, the first war to be photographed from beginning to end.

During the war Brady was as much a studio operator as a photographer. He supervised the work of a number of talented photographers, and he made sure that the photos found their way into magazines and newspapers. By 1863 *Harper's Weekly* was reproducing Brady's Civil War photos, which horrified American audiences. The photographers followed the Union Army in wagons filled with their equipment and portable darkrooms. Many of the photos credited to Brady, whose eyesight was failing, were likely shot by his assistants. Photographers working for Brady often got extremely close to the line of fire. Thomas C. Roche, who often worked for Brady, got so close that he was seen shaking dirt off himself and his camera after shells hit nearby. In fact, some of Brady's best photographers left his employ so that they might get the credit they thought they deserved for making pictures under such dangerous conditions. Brady's greatest contribution was not so much the individual war photographs that he may or may not have taken as what evolved from the photographs: the idea that photographs are published documents preserving history.[14]

# THE MAGAZINE BUSINESS

After the American Civil War, the number of magazines and their circulation grew rapidly. This growth was fueled by a number of factors, such as the emergence of a new middle class, whose members had learned to read in public schools and were now starting to read magazines. Also, a growing number of national advertisers saw the magazine as an efficient means by which to reach their target audiences. Magazine distribution was aided by the **Postal Act of 1879**, which allowed periodicals to be mailed across the nation easily and inexpensively. Improvements in printing, typesetting, and illustration engraving also contributed to the growth of magazines.

## The Economics of Magazine Publishing

The post–Civil War era saw the introduction of several magazines—including *Popular Science, Good Housekeeping, National Geographic, Vogue,* and *Outdoor Life*—that are still in existence. From the start, these magazines provided news, ideas, advice for the home, and entertainment. They are all examples of **consumer magazines**—publications targeting an audience of like-minded consumers. As of 2008, there were approximately 7,300 consumer magazines, the largest title count since 2000, when there were more than 8,000 titles.[15] Of those, 195 were new magazines launched in 2008.

Consumer magazines cover a wide range of topics, but if it seems to you that the most popular subject is celebrities, you wouldn't be far off. An analysis of the content of 160 magazines found that the largest number of pages (15.8 percent) were devoted to entertainment and celebrity coverage. This was followed by apparel and accessories with 12.1 percent of the pages, and travel/transportation with 8.4 percent of the pages. You can see the full analysis in Table 5.1.[16]

Deriving their revenue from subscriptions, newsstand sales, and advertising, consumer magazines tend to be the most visible and profitable segment of the industry. Their continued success is due to their focus on specific audiences; they stand in contrast to the many general-interest magazines that have failed as new media took their places. Top magazine advertisers include pharmaceuticals, apparel and accessories, home furnishings and supplies, toiletries and cosmetics, and automotive. Among other subjects mentioned previously, the major categories of consumer magazines are journals of opinion and commentary, newsmagazines, and women's and men's magazines.

## Trade Magazines

The second major category of periodicals consists of **trade magazines** (also known as business-to-business magazines), which are published for people who work in a particular industry or business. Trade magazines tend to be smaller, less colorful, and more specialized than consumer magazines. While

**Postal Act of 1879**
Legislation that allowed magazines to be mailed nationally at a low cost. It was a key factor in the growth of magazine circulation in the late nineteenth century.

**consumer magazines**
Publications targeting an audience of like-minded consumers.

**trade magazines**
Magazines published for people who work in a particular industry or business.

| TABLE 5.1 | TOP MAGAZINE TOPICS BY PAGE COUNT, 2009 | |
|---|---|---|
| **Type of content** | **Pages** | **Percent** |
| Entertainment/celebrity | 28,496 | 15.8% |
| Wearing apparel/accessories | 21,836 | 12.1% |
| Travel/transportation | 15,178 | 8.4% |
| Home furnishings/management | 14,998 | 8.3% |
| Food and nutrition | 12,943 | 7.2% |
| Culture | 11,279 | 6.3% |
| Business and industry | 10,281 | 5.7% |
| Sports/recreation/hobby | 8,368 | 4.6% |
| Health/medical science | 7,934 | 4.4% |
| Beauty and grooming | 7,350 | 4.1% |
| National affairs | 7,031 | 3.9% |
| General interest | 6,825 | 3.8% |
| Self-help/relationships | 5,257 | 2.9% |
| Building | 4,642 | 2.6% |
| Personal finance | 4,484 | 2.5% |
| Global/foreign affairs | 2,409 | 1.3% |
| Gardening and farming | 2,380 | 1.3% |
| Children | 2,288 | 1.3% |
| Consumer electronics | 1,744 | 1.0% |
| Fiction | 618 | 0.3% |

*Source:* Adapted by the author from *Magazines: The Medium of Action: Handbook 2009/2010* (New York: Magazine Publishers of America, 2009).

*Note:* You can read more about the latest magazine publishing statistics at http://ralphehanson.com.

there are about twice as many trade magazines as consumer magazines, they account for about 17 percent of the industry's revenue.[17] Trade magazines vary radically in circulation, scope, and the degree to which people outside of the industry know about them. For example, *Women's Wear Daily* is routinely quoted in the mainstream press and talked about by anyone interested in fashion. On the other hand, *Practical Accountant,* which covers all aspects of public accounting, is unlikely to be heard of outside of its very specialized field. The biggest topics for trade magazines are the computer industry, agriculture, medicine, and manufacturing.[18] Whereas some trade magazines are available by subscription, many have *controlled* circulation, meaning that people have to qualify in order to subscribe. For example, the grocery trade magazine *Frozen Food Marketing* is sent free of charge to people who work as frozen food producers, processors, and marketers. Subscribers have to fill out a survey form once or twice a year to continue qualifying for their free subscription. Advertisers know that most of the people who receive the magazine actually buy the products being advertised.[19] Trade magazines have suffered during the recent recession, with ad revenues down more than 30 percent in 2009.[20]

## Literary and Commentary Magazines

Although today in the United States there are relatively few **literary magazines**—publications that focus on serious essays and short fiction—they were part and parcel of the magazine market of the 1800s. Two that still survive are *Harper's* (not to be confused with *Harper's Bazaar*) and the *Atlantic*.

**literary magazines**
Publications that focus on serious essays and short fiction.

The literary magazines helped to establish authors such as American writers Edgar Allan Poe and Mark Twain, along with British writers such as Joseph Conrad and Thomas Hardy. *Harper's* magazine was founded in 1850 and was known for its illustrations, especially during the American Civil War. By 1863 *Harper's Weekly* was reproducing Mathew Brady's portraits and Civil War photos. *Harper's* continues today as an influential publication, best known for its monthly "Index" of loosely connected facts and statistics.

In recent years the *Atlantic* (known until recently as *Atlantic Monthly*) has had a reputation for publishing provocative nonfiction by authors such as Tracy Kidder, and it is one of the few magazines that still publish poetry and short fiction. (Take a look back at Table 5.1 to see how small a role fiction plays in magazine content these days.) Despite the overall trend toward specialization, the *Atlantic* has been doing well in the twenty-first century. It has cut back to ten issues a year from twelve in 2007 but has had a 12 percent increase in circulation.[21]

Political journals also flourished in the late nineteenth and early twentieth centuries. The *Nation* and the *New Republic* are examples of progressive political opinion still being published today. The *Nation*, founded in 1865, discussed current affairs, improving the lot of the working class, and civil rights. The *New Republic*, founded in 1914, promoted labor, civil rights, and antifascism. Both magazines featured letters from readers as an interactive forum for discussion. More than just filler, these letters were central to the magazines' content. The idea of reader feedback as a central component of a publication has reached its full potential on Internet magazines that feature elaborate discussion boards.

The *Nation* and the *New Republic* depend on subsidies from the capitalist system they often criticize. Although the *Nation* claims to be the oldest continuously published American weekly, it loses money every year.[22] According to publisher Victor Navasky, the magazine's poor financial showing is due to a combination of factors, including small circulation and the fact that the magazine is not "advertiser friendly":

William F. Buckley Jr. founded the *National Review* *as a conservative response to magazines like the* New Republic *and the* Nation.

At the *Nation,* we're in the business of attacking the companies that more financially successful magazines are in the business of soliciting for advertising, most notably tobacco. But these titles of opinion are at the core of what journalism should be about, and at their best, they can set the standard for the profession.[23]

William F. Buckley's *National Review* was founded in 1955 as a conservative response to these magazines. In terms of circulation, it is the largest of the three discussed here (more than 178,000 copies per month). Although it is technically a for-profit venture, which means it can endorse candidates and legislation, its leading source of income remains donations from readers. As is typical for opinion magazines, the conservative *National Review* gains readership when Democrats are in power and loses readership when Republicans win elections. (That pattern is reversed for the liberal *New Republic* and *Nation,* which lose circulation when Democrats win elections.)[24] Founder Buckley died in 2008, and his son Christopher left the board of directors of the magazine after endorsing Barack Obama for president. You can read more about both William and Christopher Buckley at http://ralphehanson.com.

*The* Crisis: *Giving African Americans a Voice.*   One of the most important functions of a magazine of ideas is to offer a voice to those who otherwise would be kept silent. That was the purpose of W. E. B. DuBois's journal, the *Crisis.* DuBois, a Harvard-educated civil rights leader, started the *Crisis* as the official voice of the National Association for the Advancement of Colored People (NAACP) in 1910. At first the magazine had only 1,000 subscribers, but by 1920 it had a monthly circulation of 100,000. The *Crisis* became as successful as other political journals, such as the *Nation* and the *New Republic,* with almost as many white readers as black readers.

At its inception, the journal was one of a very few outlets for black writers. "Up until [1910] there were only five black writers who'd been published. The NAACP saw a need for art and literature," says Manie Barron, who has edited an anthology of writings from the *Crisis.*[25] The *Crisis* was the leading voice against segregation in the South. It featured debates between DuBois and African American educator and leader Booker T. Washington over the proper role of black education, and the first appearance of many of Langston Hughes's poems.[26]

DuBois edited the *Crisis* until 1934. After he stepped down, the journal gradually became more of an African American consumer magazine than an independent journal of black intellectual writing. To address the problem, the NAACP suspended publication of the magazine for about a year in the mid-1990s to work on giving it a new focus. According to civil rights leader Julian Bond, who oversaw the remake of the magazine, "[The *Crisis*] was once the place where you read about race, and the new board wanted to make it that again."[27]

*The Muckrakers.* Investigative reporting was made famous by the Watergate political scandal of the early 1970s, but it began in the late 1800s at several newspapers and magazines. The most lasting examples came from the so-called muckraking magazines. The term **muckrakers** was coined by President Theodore Roosevelt to describe socially activist investigative journalists publishing in progressive-minded magazines in the early years of the twentieth century. Although Roosevelt favored the social and political reforms that the exposés clearly indicated were necessary, he suggested that the investigative reporters who published such stories were "muckraking"—that is, they were digging up dirt without stopping to see the good things in the world.

**muckrakers**
Progressive investigative journalists typically publishing in magazines in the early years of the twentieth century.

The most famous of the muckrakers was Samuel S. McClure, who led the fight at the beginning of the twentieth century for "business, social and political reform."[28] Although McClure was a reformer, he also sought to make a profit through the investigative articles he published in his magazine, *McClure's*. Although the writing in *McClure's* was sensationalistic, it was based on fact. Circulation skyrocketed, and it was hard to find copies of the magazine on newsstands. Advertisers liked the magazine for the attention it attracted and its high readership.

*McClure's* took on the insurance industry, the railroads, and urban problems. Two of the most prominent writers at *McClure's* were Lincoln Steffens and Ida Tarbell. Steffens started work at *McClure's* in 1902 and was quickly sent out into the field to report on municipal government corruption. Over the next two years his reporting on the misdeeds of officials in St. Louis, Minneapolis, Pittsburgh, Philadelphia, Chicago, and New York led to indictments and reform. The resulting six articles were eventually collected in the classic book *The Shame of the Cities*.[29] But the magazine's most famous target was Standard Oil. Tarbell had been assigned to write a series of stories that would showcase the oil giant's achievements. Working with the full cooperation of company officials, Tarbell spent five years writing the fifteen-article series, which revealed that the company had achieved its incredible success through the use of bribes, fraud, and violence.[30]

By 1908 the muckraking movement had played itself out. The original talented and committed muckrakers had moved on to other pursuits, and they were replaced by people who were more concerned with sensationalism than with accuracy.

## Newsmagazines

Henry Luce, through the now enormous Time Warner media empire, has probably done more to shape the American media environment than virtually anyone

*Margaret Bourke-White rests her camera on a steel gargoyle at the top of New York's Chrysler Building in 1934.*

else. Luce was born in China, the son of a Christian missionary, and he graduated from Yale in 1920. He conceived the idea of *Time* magazine while in prep school with his friend Briton Hadden.

The two founded the magazine in 1923 as a reaction against the journalism of the time. They wanted a magazine that would keep readers up-to-date on current events in a single weekly magazine. Organized around news departments, *Time* was written in a style that put the news in context and told the reader how to think about the issues, a style that the magazine maintains to this day. While *Time* presents multiple sides of a story, it also indicates which side the magazine thinks is correct, rejecting the notion of objectivity as impossible.

Luce later took on the world of business with *Fortune*, a glossy magazine featuring the photography of Margaret Bourke-White. The magazine's purpose was to "reflect industrial life as faithfully in ink and paper and word as the finest skyscraper reflects it in stone, steel, and architecture."[31] Luce also was convinced that Americans wanted to get their news through pictures, so he started *Life* magazine in 1936. A success from the start, *Life* had 230,000 subscribers for its first issue and a print order for 466,000 copies. Within four months the print order was for more than 1 million copies.[32]

When *Life* was launched, the big star at the magazine was neither the editor nor a writer; it was photographer Margaret Bourke-White. Bourke-White was more than just a photographer—she became a cultural icon. Bourke-White's greatest love was industrial photography. Smokestacks, trains, steampipes, bursts of flame—these were the subjects she most wanted to shoot. In 1929 Henry Luce, the founder of *Time*, saw Bourke-White's photos of the Otis Steel mill and foundry and decided that she was the photographer he wanted to make pictures for his new magazine, *Fortune*. Bourke-White went on to shoot photos by hanging off the stone gargoyles at the tops of skyscrapers, and to photograph in Russia at a time when most foreigners were not allowed to take pictures of Soviet industry.[33]

In 1936 she journeyed across the South with writer Erskine Caldwell, who had written the controversial novels *God's Little Acre* and *Tobacco Road*. At the time, Caldwell was America's most banned writer because of his sexually explicit (for the time) descriptions of relationships between men and women. Together

Caldwell and Bourke-White documented the poverty of the South in the book *Have You Seen Their Faces?*

Following Bourke-White's work at *Fortune*, Luce put her to work on *Life* two months before it started publication. Her first assignment for the new magazine was photographing the dams of the Columbia River Basin. But she also shot pictures of people living in Montana—the taxi dancers in the bars, the prostitutes, the customers bowling. The cover photo was typical of Bourke-White's industrial photography: the monumental Fort Peck Dam with a couple of tiny figures included to indicate scale. But her photo essay about the people in the bar, which included a picture of a four-year-old who sat there at night while her mother waited tables, created an uproar among *Life*'s readers and brought the magazine a tremendous amount of attention.[34]

During World War II, Bourke-White became the first woman photographer accredited by the U.S. Army. The army even designed a uniform for her that became the model for those worn by all women correspondents. During the war she was on an American ship in the Mediterranean Sea that was torpedoed by a German U-boat. As she left the ship on a lifeboat in the middle of the night, Bourke-White's biggest frustration was that the darkness prevented her from taking photographs:

> I could think of nothing but the magnificent pictures unfolding before me, which I longed to take and could not. I suppose for all photographers their greatest pictures are their untaken ones, and I am no exception. For me the indelible untaken photograph is the picture of our sinking ship viewed from our dangling lifeboat.[35]

Luce went on to create *Sports Illustrated*, which debuted on August 12, 1954. Critics suggested that the magazine would face an early demise because no one would be interested in it. After all, football fans wouldn't want to read about basketball or hockey. But by 1968 *Sports Illustrated* had a circulation of 1.5 million; it currently sells more than 3.2 million copies a week.[36]

## Women's Magazines

One of the biggest categories of consumer magazines are those targeted at women. Women's magazines got their start in 1830, when Louis Godey began publishing *Godey's Lady's Book*. Edited by Sarah Josepha Hale from 1837 to 1877, *Godey's* was one of the most influential magazines dealing with American life, even though it was much more lowbrow than *Harper's* or the *Atlantic Monthly*. Magazine historian James Wood writes:

> *Godey's* became an American institution in the nineteenth century. It affected the manners, morals, tastes, fashions in the clothes, homes, and diet of generations of American readers. It did much to form the American woman's idea of what she was like, how she should act, and how she should insist that she be treated.[37]

*Fashions for December 1842*

Godey's Lady's Book, *under editor Sarah Josepha Hale, featured hand-colored fashion plates of the latest styles from Europe, such as those pictured here from 1842.*

**service magazines**
Magazines that primarily contain articles about how to do things in a better way; such articles include health advice, cooking tips, employment help, or fashion guides.

*Godey's* also was a place were women writers could be published alongside established male authors. Hale took responsibility for openly promoting women writers. Previously, women writers had to use initials or male pseudonyms, or publish in unsigned columns. Hale, however, boldly printed the names of women authors. In the same way that the *Crisis* gave voice to African American writers, *Godey's* gave women a forum. (Black women's magazines existed then as well. For example, *Ringwood's Afro-American Journal of Fashion* was being published in Cleveland in the 1890s.)

Hale also campaigned for education and exercise for women, so it isn't surprising that illustrations in *Godey's* frequently showed women carrying books, magazines, and letters. Hale argued that women needed to receive an education for their own sakes, not just to make them better wives and mothers. The fiction Hale published in *Godey's* even portrayed single women leading satisfying lives.

Hale wrote a column for fourteen years, and her last editorial appeared in *Godey's* in December 1877. She was eighty-nine years old. Hale died in 1879, and though the magazine lived on without her for a while, it was never the same.

Why does Hale still matter to us today? It is because women's magazines continue to follow in her footsteps. They provide a place for women to come together apart from men and provide material that is of specific interest to women, such as articles about women's health. They also celebrate women artists and writers.[38]

*The Seven Sisters.* Following in the tradition of *Godey's Lady's Book* were the mainstream women's **service magazines**—magazines that primarily contain articles about how to do things in a better way; such articles include health advice, cooking tips, employment help, or fashion guides. The top ones were once known as the seven sisters: *Good Housekeeping, McCall's, Redbook, Ladies' Home Journal, Woman's Day, Better Homes and Gardens,* and *Family Circle.* Each is distinctive, but they all deal with a concern for home, family, and quality of life from a traditional woman's perspective.

Cyrus H. K. Curtis founded the *Ladies' Home Journal* in 1883, and in many ways it was essentially the same magazine then that it is today. It promoted a traditional view of a woman's role in the home; it told her how to dress, what to cook, how to raise children, and how to decorate the house. But it also dealt with issues that were controversial at the time, such as venereal disease and premarital sex. In 1906 the magazine argued against the so-called double standard, in which young men were allowed to sow their wild oats while women were expected to remain virgins. Women and children were paying the price, the magazine argued, because parents would not discuss the implications of sexual promiscuity with their sons, and the young men who were most promiscuous and likely to carry disease were those most likely to appeal to women. Similar concerns about AIDS and other sexually transmitted diseases appear in magazines today.[39]

The seven sisters were reduced to six in 2001 when *McCall's*, founded in 1876, ceased publication. It was reformulated and renamed *Rosie*, after the television talk show host and movie star Rosie O'Donnell. The new magazine was successful, with a growing circulation and ad pages, until O'Donnell quit her talk show and publicly came out as a lesbian, at which point she started having trouble with her publisher. The feud over editorial direction and the choice of editor led to the magazine's folding in December 2002. *Rosie* was the first major women's service magazine to cease publication since 1957.[40]

Since the demise of *Rosie*, there has been some speculation about what will happen to the remaining six sisters. *Better Homes and Gardens*, which features home design and garden care ideas along with articles on parenting, is somewhat different from the rest, and *Redbook* has evolved into something closer to the various women's fashion/beauty/lifestyle publications than to its fellow service magazines.[41] But a market clearly remains for magazines targeted at a traditional female audience. Five of the remaining six magazines are among the top twenty in terms of annual gross revenue, bringing in more money than such high-profile titles as *Vanity Fair*, *Entertainment Weekly*, or *Rolling Stone*.[42]

*Fashion/Beauty/Lifestyle Magazines.*   The fashion/beauty/lifestyle (FBL) magazines are read by about 40 million women every month. This number includes readers of the women's service magazines, along with more youth-oriented magazines such as *Glamour* and *Cosmopolitan*.

Compared to service magazines, the fashion books (magazines are often called books in the trade) focus more on clothes and style and less on lifestyle. Prominent among them are *Vogue* and *Harper's Bazaar*. *Vogue*, established in 1892, has long been the leading fashion magazine. Edna Woolman Chase started working for *Vogue* in the 1890s, became its editor in 1914, and remained there until 1952, thus becoming one of the longest-tenured voices in fashion. *Vogue* has some editorial content about people, culture, and ideas, but it is devoted primarily to fashion, both in its editorial content and in its advertising. *Vogue* has long been an international presence, with Paris, Milan, and London editions, and it started publishing a Russian edition in 1998.

Each of the FBLs claims that it has a unique editorial focus. Such protestations aside, the magazines may be more alike than they are different. Paula Span of the *Washington Post*, a former freelance writer for *Glamour*, says:

> [These magazines] take a remarkably narrow view of women's interests. The proverbial visitor from space would conclude that earthling women in their twenties and thirties care only about their bodies and what to put in them and on them, their relationships with men and, to a far lesser extent, their jobs; the rest of the world is largely absent.[43]

**Cosmopolitan.**    If the seven sisters were the most venerable members of the women's magazine family, *Cosmopolitan* is the naughty cousin. Until 1996 *Cosmo* spoke with the voice of its long-time editor, Helen Gurley Brown. Brown took over at *Cosmo* in 1965 and turned the "insipid, faintly intellectual" magazine into *the* magazine for young women, with a peak circulation of 3 million in 1985. (As of 2008, *Cosmo* had a monthly circulation of 2.9 million.)[44] Brown coined the term *mouseburger* to describe the quiet, introverted "girl" *Cosmo* was out to help. Under Brown, readers were "*Cosmo* girls," though more recently the magazine has updated its image to "fun, fearless, and female."

*Cosmo* has always focused on practical advice about relationships, work, fashion, health, beauty, and sex. But when acclaimed women's magazine editor Bonnie Fuller took over the helm, the magazine started dealing with issues like AIDS and sexual harassment. Fuller told the *New York Times*, "I wanted to make it more seductive, not so much in a sexual sense, but in a sense that the reader just couldn't wait to get it and then just couldn't possibly put it down."[45] Fuller also eliminated the occasional male pinups that have appeared in *Cosmo* over the years. (The most famous pinup was the one of Burt Reynolds published in 1972. His nude photo in *Cosmo* may have cost him the Oscar for the movie *Deliverance*.)

*Cosmopolitan* has a presence that extends far beyond the United States, with fifty-six international editions published from Britain to Thailand, from Poland to Indonesia, to Malaysia. Its British edition has a circulation in excess of 400,000 copies a month. Critics charge that *Cosmo* is exporting American culture and values to the rest of the world. Helen Gurley Brown, who remained as editor of the international editions after stepping down as editor of the U.S. edition, had this to say to the *South China Morning Post*:

> People have very flatteringly said that *Cosmo* is like Coca-Cola or McDonald's, and I say "Glory Hallelujah!" There is nothing bad about Coca-Cola—unless you drink too much of it—and McDonald's makes delicious hamburgers. We are exporting what people want. . . . We're not trying to change Asian culture. . . . It's a magazine for women who love men, who love children and motherhood and who have a choice of doing work. Now, that doesn't sound so heinous or reprehensible, does it?[46]

## Men's Magazines

Many men's magazines, such as *Field and Stream* or *Motor Trend*, appeal to men through their hobbies. Women might read them, but the target audience is male. There are also men's magazines featuring provocative photos of women, such as *Playboy* and (originally) *Esquire*. The most recent trend in men's magazines is toward lifestyle magazines that resemble women's magazines but are intended for men; they include *Maxim* and *FHM*.

### Esquire: A Morale Booster for the Troops.

*Esquire* was founded in 1933, and though it published original work by writers such as Ernest Hemingway and F. Scott Fitzgerald, it was also known for its risqué pinups by artists Alberto Vargas and George Petty. These airbrushed drawings of impossibly perfect women frequently got the magazine into legal trouble for violating obscenity laws, but the pictures would be considered extremely mild by today's standards. (The University of Kansas houses the *Esquire* archives of pinup art, some of which is quite valuable. The collection's estimated value is between $10 and $20 million.) *Esquire*, and especially its pinups, was considered an important morale booster during World War II and the Korean conflict, with comedian Bob Hope quoted as saying, "Our American troops are ready to fight at the drop of an *Esquire*."[47]

In recent years *Esquire* has suffered from an identity crisis, with declining circulation and advertising revenue. It has changed ownership at least twice in the past twenty-five years, and it has changed its look and formula several times. Despite its problems, *Esquire* always has room for fine writing. Jim Harrison's *Legends of the Fall* first appeared there, as did many of Tom Wolfe's most influential nonfiction articles in the 1960s. But in the early 2000s *Esquire* returned to its roots and started placing greater emphasis on good writing and, as a result, picked up advertisers who want to reach a more upscale audience.[48]

### Playboy: A Magazine and a Lifestyle.

*Playboy* first appeared in 1953 as a competitor to *Esquire*, and it made no pretense about what it was really about— pictures of nude women—though, like *Esquire*, it publishes articles by many noted writers. But in addition to the photos and the articles, *Playboy* promoted a lifestyle: the sexually free good life.

Founder Hugh Hefner started out doing circulation promotion for *Esquire* at $60 a week. He wanted to create a magazine that would appeal to

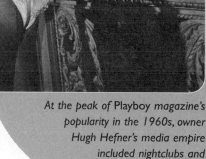

*At the peak of Playboy magazine's popularity in the 1960s, owner Hugh Hefner's media empire included nightclubs and merchandise as well.*

young urban males much like himself. He started by paying $200 for color printing plates and the rights to publish a nude photo of Marilyn Monroe. He obtained permission to reprint stories and articles by well-known writers, as well as cartoons and dirty jokes. After collecting subscriptions from around the country, he started *Playboy* for less than $7,000.[49] Hefner says that he would like to be remembered for changing attitudes toward sex: "I would like to be remembered as someone who has had a significant impact in changing sexual values, in changing the repressive attitudes toward sexuality."[50]

Although *Playboy* still goes out to 2.6 million readers every month (it sold 7 million copies a month at its peak of popularity in 1972), it gets very little attention compared to newcomers like *Maxim*. In September 2002 *Playboy* hired away *Maxim*'s executive editor in an attempt to bring a more modern attitude to the aging magazine.[51]

**Maxim: *The Rebirth of Men's Magazines.*** One of the most successful of the new men's magazines is *Maxim*, which offers a blend of sex, sports, and humor. Launched in April 1997 as a spin-off of the British version, it has been influential, with *Details*, *GQ*, and *Esquire* all mimicking its style. As of 2008, *Maxim* had a monthly circulation of 2.5 million copies, enough to make it the twenty-second largest circulation magazine in the United States (see Table 5.2 for a list of the top ten magazines). As recently as 1998, it wasn't even in the top 200.[52]

Former editor Mark Golin, one of the few men to have been on the staff at *Cosmopolitan*, says that *Maxim* stands out among men's magazines because it is not about a single topic, such as cars, clothes, or computers. Instead, it tries to meet the needs of the "inner guy." "There's a guy inside all men," Golin told the *New York Times*, "and whether you're pumping gas in Iowa or you're working on Wall Street, you can't ignore your inner guy."[53] (The "guy" is an interesting media concept widely used in whiskey billboard advertising ["Wine coolers, for the guys?"], radio ["This isn't sports radio, it's guy radio"],[54] and television [*Movies for Guys* on TNT], as well as in magazines.)

The *Times* has referred to *Maxim* as "the *Playboy* of the 1990s," and its cleavage-laden covers and sexy humor would seem to support that label. Why the adolescent focus on women? Golin explained it this way: "I think if you are going to have a general-interest magazine for men, well—surprise, surprise, one of men's general interests is women."[55]

One reason magazines like *Maxim* are so profitable is that they attract a great deal of fashion and gadget advertising. They feature scantily clad women, reviews of electronics, entertainment, fashion, and humor. Moreover, they tend to feature "quick tidbits" of information rather than full-fledged articles.[56]

In Britain, *Maxim* and competitors *FHM* and *Loaded* have seen sharp declines in circulation in recent years, as have the weekly magazines for men, *Zoo* and *Nuts*. The weeklies feature the same raunchy sexual content but more up-to-date humor and sports gossip.[57] What has taken their place as the most popular men's magazine? *Men's Health*, with its articles on improving your diet, drinking less, and exercising more.[58]

## TABLE 5.2 | WHAT ARE THE TOP TEN MAGAZINES?

| Magazine | Circulation**, *** |
|---|---|
| 1. *AARP The Magazine* | 24,349,637* |
| 2. *Reader's Digest* | 8,168,667 |
| 3. *Better Homes and Gardens* | 7,659,823 |
| 4. *National Geographic* | 5,060,377 |
| 5. *Good Housekeeping* | 4,684,811 |
| 6. *Woman's Day* | 3,920,867 |
| 7. *Family Circle* | 3,914,927 |
| 8. *AAA Westways* | 3,842,577 |
| 9. *Ladies' Home Journal* | 3,840,645 |
| 10. *People* | 3,823,604 |

*Source:* "Magazines by Circulation for Six Months, Ended December 31, 2008," *Advertising Age.* Available from http://adage .com/datacenter/article?article id=106355. Reprinted with permission from *Advertising Age/American Demographics.* Copyright Crain Communications Inc., 2008.

*\*AARP The Magazine* may be a bit of a surprise as the top magazine in the country, but as the magazine of the American Association of Retired Persons, it goes out to every member.

*\*\*Time,* ranked seventh in 2006, had fallen to twelfth for the second half of 2008.

*\*\*\*Sports Illustrated* comes in at fifteenth (3.2 million), *Cosmopolitan* at seventeenth (2.9 million), *Playboy* at twenty-first (2.7 million), *Maxim* at twenty-second (2.5 million), *O, The Oprah Magazine* at twenty-fourth (2.4 million), and *Rolling Stone* at fifty-fourth (1.5 million).

Adventuring is another important area for men's magazines. Some men like to go looking for danger, and magazine articles give readers a chance to do so—but safely. For example, a 1998 issue of *Men's Journal* contained an article entitled "Climb Mount Rainier: A Serious Mountaineering Challenge With Minimal Risk of Headline-Making Deaths. Call It Everest for Everyman."[59]

The magazine industry has recently tapped men as a major new audience for service magazines like *Men's Health* and *Men's Journal*. The editors of these magazines have been featured in gossip columns and are getting the kind of high-profile media attention that was formerly limited to the editors of leading women's magazines like *Vogue* or *Harper's Bazaar*.[60]

## MAGAZINES AND MODERN SOCIETY

Magazines may not have the dominant place in the media market today that they had in the late nineteenth and early twentieth centuries, but they are still a critical component of our culture. One reason magazines remain important is that they are able to reach narrow, specific communities with a slickly produced message. Among the major controversies surrounding magazines today are the images of women they present, the blurring of editorial and advertising content, the level of reality in editorial content, and the appropriateness of material aimed at teenagers.

## Magazines and Body Image

It's no secret that a significant number of girls and young women suffer from eating disorders as a result of their quest to find beauty through thinness. The trend toward excessive thinness as a standard of beauty has become more prominent in recent decades. In 1972, 23 percent of U.S. women said that they were dissatisfied with their overall appearance. By 1996 that figure had grown to 48 percent. Critics frequently charge that the thin models in fashion magazines (both in ads and in editorial content) are at least partially responsible for promoting extreme thinness as attractive. In 1953, when Marilyn Monroe was featured in the debut issue of *Playboy*, she was a size twelve with measurements close to the then-ideal of 36-22-35, which by today's standard would make her a **plus-sized model**. Today, the much-photographed Jennifer Aniston is an impossible (for most women) size zero.[61]

**plus-sized model**
A female fashion model who wears average or larger clothing size.

British Calvin Klein model Kate Moss was known in the 1990s for her waif-like look that was coined "heroin chic," because of the resemblance to an emaciated heroin addict. After Moss admitted she had been drunk on the job for the last ten years, Calvin Klein ended his long-running contract with the super-thin model, though the designer claimed the separation had nothing to do with her confession.[62] The controversy surrounding Moss went beyond her drinking and alleged drug usage, heroin-chic look, and posing nude in slick magazine advertisements for jeans and underwear. The big source of criticism was that she presented an unrealistic and unobtainable image of what an attractive woman should look like. A teenage girl who runs track, weighs ninety-five pounds, and is five feet tall told *People* magazine: "I'm not happy if I think I look fat in what I'm wearing. Kate Moss looks so cool in a bathing suit. I don't know if I'm conditioned [to think this way] or if it's just me, but I don't think anything could make me abandon my desire to be thin."[63]

Advertisers of products other than clothing have become concerned about the thin image being presented in fashion magazines. When photos of model Trish Goff appeared in the British edition of *Vogue* in 1996, Omega Watches pulled its ads from the magazine, saying that the magazine was portraying skeletal anorexic-looking models.[64]

By 2006 criticism of overly thin models was coming from no less than former Victoria's Secret model Frederique van der Wal. The Madrid, Spain, Fashion Week shows banned models whose body mass index was too low.[65] In 2007 Madrid's Fashion Week shows again banned super-thin models, as did the Milan shows.

Remember Truth Three—Everything from the margin moves to the center? It's possible that the women's magazines' willingness to use models of differing sizes is becoming more commonplace than it was several years ago. In 2005 Dove shook up the world of cosmetic and beauty product advertising with its "Campaign for Real Beauty" featuring attractive ladies of a variety of sizes posing in their underwear, photographed by Annie Leibovitz. Around the same time, Nike ran ads portraying athletic women with "big butts" and "thunder thighs," leading some observers to ask whether the era of the waif and heroin chic was over. Were we going to see more images of "realistic-looking" women in magazine features and advertisements?[66] (That, of course, begs the question as to what constitutes real women. Are size-two women not real? Or is it more that average-sized women are ignored by the media?) Dove followed up this campaign with one celebrating how women look as they age in support of a line of "Pro-Age" products. These ads again were controversial for featuring nude (nonexplicit) photos of women over the age of fifty. (Once again, they were shot by Leibovitz.)

This nearly nude image of Lizzi Miller became a subject of national debate because it showed the plus-sized model's small belly pooch.

Now, five years after Dove's launch of the "Campaign for Real Beauty" in the United States, the question is—have alternative images of beauty made it into the mainstream?

*Glamour* magazine set off somewhat of an Internet phenomenon with a small photo it ran in its September 2009 issue. It's a nearly nude image of model Lizzi Miller sitting on a bench with a big smile on her face. As FBL magazine photos go, it's not a shocker. Certainly other photos in the magazine, either editorial or advertising, showed more skin. So why did this photo garner so much attention? Ms. Miller has a small belly pooch.

*Glamour* editor-in-chief Cindi Leive writes on her blog:

> It's a photo that measures all of three by three inches in our September issue, but the letters about it started to flood my inbox literally the day *Glamour* hit newsstands. . . . "I am gasping with delight . . . I love the woman on p 194!" said one . . . then another, and another, andanotherandanotherandanother. So . . . who is she? And what on earth is so special about her?
>
> Here's the deal: The picture wasn't of a celebrity. It wasn't of a supermodel. It was of a woman sitting in her underwear with a smile on her face and a belly that looks . . . wait for it . . . *normal*.[67]

The photo goes with a story by Akiba Solomon about women feeling comfortable in their own skin. The photo has no caption, no mention of who

# TEST YOUR MEDIA LITERACY

## Should Magazine Covers Be True-to-Life?

*Self*, a health and fitness magazine for women, found itself in the middle of a controversy in the fall of 2009 over its portrayal of how women look—specifically, singer Kelly Clarkson. The *American Idol* star was featured on the September 2009 cover of the magazine. Her image went through the usual digital retouching for color correction and the like, but the photo editor also added in a few digital hair extensions and, while he or she was at it, slimmed down Clarkson considerably. Usually accusations of "photoshopping" are met with denials or statements that only minimal changes were made. But *Self* editor-in-chief Lucy Danziger said that when it comes to magazine cover shoots, editors should do whatever it takes to make the cover model look her best. Even if that means changing her body digitally.[1] Read Danziger's blog entry about the Clarkson cover at http://www.self.com/magazine/blogs/lucysblog/2009/08/pictures-that-please-us.html.

You can read and watch more about Kelly Clarkson's *Self* cover at http://ralphehanson.com.

Although Kelly Clarkson, pictured here in June 2009, says she is happy with her fluctuating weight, *Self* magazine used a photoshopped image of her on its September 2009 cover that made the singer look thinner than she was.

### Who is the source?

Who is Lucy Danziger? What does she do?

### What was done to the Clarkson photograph featured on the cover of *Self*?

Look at the Kelly Clarkson *Self* cover on Danziger's blog. How does Clarkson's appearance differ on the cover from the unretouched photograph above? Is the image on the cover an authentic portrait of Clarkson? Why or why not?

**What does Danziger say about the cover?**

How does Danziger defend the cover? According to Danziger, how does a magazine cover differ from a conventional photograph? What does Danziger say the changes to Clarkson accomplished?

**How do you and your classmates react to the Clarkson cover?**

What do you and your friends think about the Clarkson magazine cover? Why do you think the changes were controversial? How far should digital artists go with changing a cover model's appearance? The Clarkson story was about "Total Body Confidence." Do the changes to her photograph undermine the message of the headline? Why or why not?

[1] Lucy Danziger, "Pictures That Please Us," *Self*, August 2009, www.self.com/magazine/blogs/lucysblog/2009/08/pictures-that-please-us.html.

the model is, no mention of the fact that she wears a size 12/14 and weighs 180 pounds.

The response to this small photo has been big. In less than two weeks, more than 770 comments were posted to Leive's blog about the photo, not to mention the many e-mails. Most of the comments were laudatory. One woman called it "the most amazing photograph I've ever seen in any women's magazine," while another wrote, "Thank you Lizzi, for showing us your beauty and confidence, and giving women a chance to hopefully recognize a little of their own also."

Not everyone loved the photo and what it stood for, however. One commenter wrote, "I must say I have to agree that the normalization of obesity is a disturbing trend today." Another commented, "We have enough problems with obesity in the US and don't need your magazine promoting anymore of it. Shame on *Glamour* for thinking this was sexy!"[68]

Mary Pipher, author of *Reviving Ophelia*, a book about teen girls and body image, says the new emphasis on diverse images of beauty in fashion magazines is a good, if limited, step. "Presenting a broader range of beauty, even if it's under the guise of selling cosmetics, gives girls more permission to think they too are attractive."[69]

## Who's in Control? Advertising Versus Editorial

One of the biggest conflicts in the magazine business is the separation between the editorial and advertising departments. Articles attract readers, but advertisements pay many of the bills. So a continual struggle exists between editors and advertisers to keep the content separate from advertisements, to please advertisers, and to make money for the publishers.

*Synergy and Magazines.* We're used to seeing massive synergy in the movie and television business with product placement and product-themed shows.

But *Shape* magazine seems to have hit a new high—or low—with the practice. The September 2005 issue of the women's fitness magazine featured the coverline, "Win Liz Hurley's Cover Look." Hurley is on the cover wearing a bikini from her own line of clothing, and she's wearing makeup credited to Estée Lauder, for whom Hurley is a paid endorser. This all goes with a two-page ad inside the cover from the cosmetic maker. So Hurley is promoting her clothing line and the cosmetics she endorses, and *Shape* is getting a major ad from the cosmetics manufacturer. Hurley and *Shape* magazine said that there is no connection between the ad and the editorial feature. Magazine expert Samir A. Husni told the *New York Times* that what *Shape* did was nothing new. "It's more a reflection of the entire industry."[70]

*The Blurring of Advertising and Editorial Content.* When is a magazine article not an article? When it's an advertisement, of course. One women's magazine featured a "senior merchandising editor" wearing a beautiful new coat in a feature called "Hot Shot of the Month." However, the "editor" was really an advertising staffer, and the "hot shot" was really a free promotion for a favored advertiser.[71] Such **advertorials**—defined as advertising material in magazines designed to look like editorial content rather than paid advertising—are nothing new, but they have generally been accompanied by a disclaimer saying that the item is an advertisement or a special advertising section.

For example, an ad by software company CrossWorlds featured a photo of a woman in a dress with a plunging neckline (she was the company's president) taken by noted photographer Richard Avedon. Although the photo ran in many magazines, only one identified it as an advertisement for CrossWorlds.[72]

## Censorship and Teen Magazines

Sometimes the truth can get magazines into as much trouble as faked letters or digitally altered photos. In 1998 a New York school district removed *Seventeen*, *Teen*, and *YM* from the middle school library in response to complaints by parents that the magazines contained inappropriate sexual material.[73] The superintendent said that he took the magazines out of the middle school library—but not the high school library—because the sex and health columns were not appropriate for children ages ten to fourteen.[74] According to the *New York Times*, the complaints focused on material about "having sex, using at-home pregnancy tests, taking the birth-control pill, vaginal discomfort, using a condom, masturbation, tampons, stretch marks, and worries about various body fluids and HIV."[75]

Such incidents are rare, however. What is more common is for school districts to control the contents of student-produced publications. Such was the case in Grand Ledge, Michigan, where school officials removed information about Planned Parenthood and changed information about the state's abortion law from a story about teen pregnancy scheduled to run in the high school magazine *The Comets' Tale*.[76]

**advertorials**
Advertising materials in magazines designed to look like editorial content rather than paid advertising.

## The Importance of Magazine Covers

As Annie Leibovitz demonstrated with her photo of a pregnant Demi Moore for the cover of *Vanity Fair*, what appears on a magazine's cover can make or break its newsstand sales. Despite the dramatic overall rise in the annual circulation of magazines, single copy sales have been falling steadily since 1975, so publishers have been eager to find ways to make their publications stand out from the crowd.[77] For example, *Family Circle* magazine decided that it would try to stand out in the displays near supermarket checkout lines by using soothing, homey images rather than celebrity covers.

Dick Stolley, one of the founding editors of *People* magazine, established the following rules for covers:

- Young is better than old.
- Pretty is better than ugly.
- Rich is better than poor.
- Music is better than movies.
- Movies are better than television.
- Nothing is better than a dead celebrity.[78]

Janet Chan, editorial director of parenting publications for Time, Inc., says, "You'll follow a lot of rules and you could say that's the science, but I think a lot of it is gut. For me, thinking of designing a cover is looking for the image that says, 'You want to take this puppy home.'"[79]

*Covers and Race.*    The fear of losing sales can make editors reluctant to take chances, and one result of editorial caution is that relatively few non-whites appear on the covers of men's, women's, teen, and entertainment magazines. *New York Times* reporter David Carr notes that in 2002 less than 20 percent of American magazine covers featured people of color and that five years earlier only 12.7 percent of people appearing on magazine covers were non-white.[80] (This survey did not include fashion magazines such as *Vogue*.) (You can learn more about the *New York Times* magazine cover study at http://ralphehanson.com.)

When actress Halle Berry appeared on the cover of *Cosmopolitan* in December 2002 after starring in the James Bond movie *Die Another Day*, she was only the fifth black person to be portrayed on the magazine's cover since 1964, when *Cosmo* became a women's magazine. And Berry was the first minority on *Cosmo*'s cover since 1990, when Naomi Campbell appeared. Editor Kate White says that Berry was chosen because she is typical of the magazine's cover models: "She is beautiful, powerful, successful, and she can open a movie."[81]

One of the clearest examples of the segregation of magazine covers can be seen with the ever-controversial *Sports Illustrated* swimsuit issue. As of 2009, the magazine has featured only two women of color on the cover—Tyra Banks in 1997 and Beyoncé in 2007. Even in 2006, when the cover featured eight models wearing

Despite the problems that women of color have had getting placed on magazine covers, first lady Michelle Obama has been featured on numerous publications, and People magazine editor Larry Hackett says she is a "solid seller."

**coverlines**
Teaser headlines on magazine covers used to shock, intrigue, or titillate potential buyers.

swimsuit bottoms, all of them were white, and most were blond. (It is worth noting that *Sports Illustrated* has had at least one Hispanic model on the cover.)[82]

According to Carr, editors at the top consumer magazines believe that, all things being equal, covers with white models sell better than those with a minority model. However, *O*, which always features Oprah Winfrey on the cover, has a largely white readership. And singer-actress Jennifer Lopez, golfer Tiger Woods, and tennis-playing sisters Venus and Serena Williams have increasingly appeared on magazine covers. Teen magazines, which often focus on the multiracial music business, are also quite likely to show people of color on their covers. Of course, since Barack Obama was elected president, first lady Michelle Obama has been on numerous magazine covers, including *Vogue, O, US Weekly, Ladies' Home Journal, People,* and *Glamour.*

*Coverlines.* Along with the cover image, coverlines have to draw readers into the publication. **Coverlines** are teaser headlines used to shock, intrigue, or titillate potential buyers. Keep in mind that coverlines are important for subscribers as well as newsstand sales. If a subscriber is going to renew a magazine, he or she must want to read it, preferably as soon as it arrives. The goal is for coverlines to appeal to as many readers of the magazine as possible. "I would say 85 percent of your cover has to appeal to 100 percent of the audience," says magazine editor Susan Kane.[83] Numbers are often used in coverlines because they suggest value ("79 beat-stress ideas. Rush less, work smarter, find happiness and balance now!")—in other words, they imply that a great deal of good material is to be found inside the magazine.[84]

One thing that makes FBL magazines stand out in the checkout line are their distinctive coverlines. The first issue of *Glamour* under editor Bonnie Fuller had the coverline "Doing it! . . . 100 women's secret sexual agendas—Who wants what, how bad and how often." The same month, *Cosmopolitan* had the coverline "Sex Rules! 10 Make-Him-Throb Moves So Hot You'll Need a Fire Hose to Cool Down the Bed." Even *Redbook*, a service magazine targeted at mothers approaching middle age, proclaims "Sex every night: can it deepen your love? Yes! Yes! Yes!" "Put 'orgasm' on the cover and it will sell," said former *Glamour* editor Ruth Whitney.[85] Of course, some of these covers are *too* hot for grocery stores, which may place blinders over them to avoid offending their customers.[86]

# TEST YOUR MEDIA LITERACY

## Race, Beauty, and Magazine Covers

Trisha Goddard is a black British talk show host who's been described as a cross between Jerry Springer and Oprah Winfrey. American audiences may know her from the horror-comedy film *Shaun of the Dead*. She's also the mother of two girls. In a commentary in London's *Daily Mail*, she writes that she was startled in the summer of 2006 to see a black face (of R&B singer Jamelia) staring back at her from the cover of the British edition of *Cosmopolitan* magazine. "It took me a moment to realize why a simple photo of this beautiful girl had pulled me up short," she writes. "Then I realized it was because I'm so unused to seeing a non-white face on the cover of a mainstream magazine."[1]

The implication of rarely seeing a woman of color on the cover of a magazine hit home to Goddard when her twelve-year-old daughter Madison said that she thought she looked ugly. What did Madison think a pretty girl looked like? "Well, she's got a little upturned nose, and blonde or light brown hair, and blue eyes." Goddard quickly realized that her daughter was describing a white girl.

Were editors being racist in using primarily white models on magazine covers? Goddard says no. Instead, she writes that magazine editors pick as cover models personalities who are well liked by readers. When the editors find black women who are popular with readers, the magazines sell well. The problem, according to the editor of British *Cosmo*, is that there are only a few black women who resonate with readers.

### MOREonline

You can read Trisha Goddard's entire commentary and learn more about the singer Jamelia at **http://ralphehanson.com.**

### Who is the source?

How do you think Trisha Goddard's background has shaped her view of magazine covers? Is she qualified to comment on diversity of magazine covers? Would it make a difference if she were white? Asian?

### What is she saying?

What is Goddard's complaint about magazine covers? What made her start being critical of them? What does she blame the problem on? What does she see as the solution to the problem?

### What kind of evidence is there for a lack of diversity on magazine covers?

What kind of evidence is there that magazine covers do not represent diversity? Is there evidence that disputes this claim? Are there more kinds of diversity to be concerned about other than race? If so, what are they?

### How do you and your classmates react to Goddard's arguments?

Look at ten issues of the magazines you read. Who is on the cover? What race are they? How do your findings correspond with those of the *New York Times* study discussed earlier in this chapter? How do you feel about the covers of the magazines you receive? Do you see anything that disturbs you? (You don't have to limit these questions to those of race.)

[1] Trisha Goddard, "Why These Pictures Shock Me," *Daily Mail*, November 9, 2006, 48.

# THE FUTURE OF MAGAZINES

Although the magazine industry has gone through massive changes, in many ways it is still the same as the industry founded in 1741. (Providing another example of Truth Four—Nothing's new: Everything that happened in the past will happen again.)

## Magazines for the Twenty-first Century

According to media scholar Leara D. Rhodes, the American magazine industry has been a series of "launches and failures, new magazines, and revitalization of old ones."[87] Rhodes says that successful magazines have traditionally shared a number of characteristics, including the following:

- Building a relationship between the magazine and its readers

- Providing information readers can't easily find other places

- Adapting to social changes

- Being supported by advertisers

- Adjusting to economic changes and limitations

- Shaping public discourse by defining the major issues of society[88]

Just as *McClure's* led to reform of the oil industry at the turn of the previous century, Seymour Hersh's *New Yorker* articles about the abuses at Abu Ghraib prison in Iraq led to investigations of the way prisoners were being treated.

The total circulation of magazines in the United States has risen as the population's overall level of education has increased, thus raising the level of literacy. From 1970 to 2005, the annual paid circulation of all magazines measured by the Audit Bureau of Circulation grew by 67 percent. (The Audit Bureau of Circulation certifies to advertisers how many copies of the largest consumer magazines are actually sold.)[89] Rhodes says that, as educational availability and literacy rise in Asia and Latin America, it seems likely that they will also see a substantial growth in magazine circulation.

We can identify several current trends in magazine publishing:

- Magazines are targeting narrower audiences—Unlike the general-interest magazines of the nineteenth and first half of the twentieth century, contemporary magazines are targeted at specific audiences. *Maxim* has successfully targeted young men, a group the magazine industry ignored previously; *Lucky* magazine is devoted to shopping; and Oprah Winfrey's *O* magazine deals with empowering women. Says magazine executive Kevin Coyne, "It's the Me Generation saying, 'I have tastes and preferences, and now I can seek them out in various forms.' It's all about the consumer exercising his choices."[90]

- Presentation is important—The layout and graphics of magazines are critical in determining how people will respond to them. Journalist Michael Scherer writes that magazines today "are filled with color, over-sized headlines, graphics, photos, and pull quotes."[91]

- Articles are short—Magazines like *Maxim, Blender, InStyle,* and *US Weekly* have replaced many of their full-fledged articles with text boxes that look like extended captions. Keith Blanchard of *Maxim* says, "If you are trying to reach cranky retirees, maybe six-thousand-word rants are appropriate. [*Maxim*] readers are busier today than they will ever be in their lives; they have shorter attention spans than any previous generation; they are chronically over-stimulated and easily bored."[92]

## Cross-media Synergy

Media scholar Rhodes says that magazine publishers view Internet publishing as a complement to their paper publications rather than as competition. This has been especially true for the business-to-business (or trade) magazines: "Television is fueling magazines. ESPN produces a show and if the viewer wants more information about the sport, they get a magazine. Net sites are . . . gathering readers on-line, then launching physical editions of their magazines. Individual television programs, from *Seinfeld* to *Star Trek,* are spawning their own magazines."[93]

Few online only magazines have been successful—*Salon* and *Slate* are the major exceptions—but magazine-based Web sites have been much more successful. In 2009 Ziff Davis Media's flagship publication *PC Magazine* went all digital, discontinuing its paper (or "dead-tree") edition.[94]

Magazine scholar Samir Husni notes that his professors back in the late 1970s and early 1980s told him that "print was dead." But now in the twenty-first century, "We have now three times the number of magazines that were offered for sale back then and the numbers continue to grow. . . . [I]nk on paper will be with us as long as we have trees."[95] In fact, it is the portable, paper format that readers say they like about magazines. Nina Link, president of the Magazine Publishers of America, says, "The physical attributes of a magazine are very much part of the experience of reading a magazine—the size, the portability, the quality of the graphics and the ease of use."[96]

One thing that is changing is how we store old issues of magazines. In the past, the only option was to keep them in boxes in a damp basement or garage, where they would start to mildew. Today there are electronic archives, either for free or for pay. The *New Yorker* offers many of its previous stories and reviews online, or for $179 you can buy a complete archive of every issue of the magazine that comes on its own 80-megabyte portable hard drive.

Just about every source talking about the future of magazines notes that magazines and their readers have a strong relationship. The magazine is not just a source of information; it is a statement of identity. The magazine was the original narrowcasting vehicle, and it is still going strong in the twenty-first century.

## CHAPTER Summary

Magazines were the first media to become national in scope rather than appealing to a limited geographic area. They also contained articles designed to be of lasting appeal. Although there were magazines during the colonial period, the first significant American magazine was the *Saturday Evening Post*. Espousing conservative, middle-class values, the *Post* was seen as a reflection of American society. Literary and commentary magazines flourished in the nineteenth century, and several of them survive today. These magazines provided a forum for important authors and were among the first to feature the work of pioneering photojournalists such as Mathew Brady.

W. E. B. DuBois expanded the range of commentary magazines with the founding of the *Crisis* as the official magazine of the NAACP. The *Crisis* became the first magazine to provide a forum for black writers. The early twentieth century saw a trend in investigative magazine reporting known as muckraking. The work of the muckrakers set the stage for much of the investigative reporting done today by newspapers and television news.

Henry Luce founded *Time* magazine in 1923, creating what would become one of the nation's largest media companies—Time Warner. Luce's publishing empire grew to include not just the news in *Time* but also photojournalism in *Life,* sports journalism in *Sports Illustrated,* and personality and celebrity journalism in *People.*

Women's magazines got their start with *Godey's Lady's Book* under the editorship of Sarah Josepha Hale. In addition to editing the magazine, Hale established many of the principles of modern magazines: copyrighting the stories, running original material, and paying authors for their work. The seven sisters women's service magazines followed in much the same tradition as *Godey's*, being concerned mainly with the home, family, and quality of life. An alternative to the traditional values of service magazines is offered by the more youth-oriented fashion/beauty/lifestyle magazines, such as *Glamour* and *Cosmopolitan*.

Many magazines targeted at men appeal to them through their hobbies, but the two most influential men's magazines are *Esquire* and *Playboy.* Although *Playboy* was initially more explicit with its pinup photography, both it and *Esquire* now feature men's fashion, lifestyle coverage, and articles by well-known writers. In recent years a new type of men's magazine focusing on adventure, fashion, health, and sex has appeared; the most popular of these magazines is *Maxim.*

Trade publications are magazines that cover a particular industry rather than being designed for consumers. Although they often are more serious and have less photography and color than the consumer magazines, they make up a substantial portion of the magazine market.

Fashion magazines have been criticized in recent years for featuring extremely thin models in both ads and editorial content. Critics argue that the unrealistic image promoted by these models can contribute to the development of eating disorders in young women. Several magazines and advertisers have bucked this trend and feature plus-sized models and even ordinary people. Other conflicts in the magazine industry include the blurring of editorial content and advertising, and the photos and headlines used on covers.

Magazines in the twenty-first century are continuing many of the trends that made them successful throughout their history, including building relationships with readers, adapting to change, being supported by advertisers, and defining major issues in society. Magazines continue to be successful in their print formats but are expanding their content with Web sites and other electronic offerings.

## KEY Terms

magazine   154
photojournalism   155
halftone   155
Postal Act of 1879   157
consumer magazines   157
trade magazines   157

literary magazines   159
muckrakers   161
service magazines   164
plus-sized model   170
advertorials   174
coverlines   176

## CONCEPT Review

Development of the magazine industry
The influence of magazines on national culture
The development of photojournalism
The difference between consumer and trade magazines
The role magazines play in giving voice to groups
The controversy over the influence of magazine content on body image
The battle between advertising and editorial content
Function and controversy of magazine covers and coverlines
Relationship between magazines and their readers

# Newspapers and the News

## Reflection of a Democratic Society

**CHAPTER 6**

**Reporters generally** work under the ideal that they are supposed to be detached, objective observers of the news, no matter what happens. But when Hurricane Katrina unleashed the flooding of New Orleans in August 2005, the staff of the *Times-Picayune* could not and would not hold back their feelings.

On Monday, August 29, after the storm hit, James O'Byrne, features editor for the *Times-Picayune*, was covering Katrina with Doug MacCash, the paper's art critic. Unlike the national reporters located in the higher areas of the city who were saying that New Orleans had "dodged a bullet," the pair were on their bicycles on a railroad bridge looking over Lake Pontchartrain. The two could see what the others could not—that a huge flood of water was heading into the city not from the sea but from the lake.

O'Byrne said everyone at the paper knew things would be bad when the meteorologist they used as a source asked, "How far above sea level is the third floor of your building?"[1]

On Tuesday morning, the eighty-or-so staff members who had stayed behind were forced to evacuate, riding in the back of newspaper delivery trucks. The paper initially planned to publish a blog when possible, but the staff couldn't stand the thought of not covering such a big story in their own hometown. Sports editor David Meeks made the suggestion to management: "Give me a delivery truck and a small group of writers. We'll go back."[2]

The staff never stopped publishing online, and by Thursday they were printing a paper edition again. The challenges facing them were enormous. There were questions of how to eat, where to stay, how to submit stories. The paper set up new headquarters in Baton Rouge, about an hour away. The head of IT had to charge $22,000 worth of software and computers on his corporate card with the hope that he would somehow get reimbursed.[3]

Photographer Ted Jackson didn't quite follow instructions when the order to evacuate came. While on his way to the circulation trucks, the photographer saw an abandoned flatboat at the *Times-Picayune*'s back steps with a broken broom to use as a paddle. So, Jackson said, with "two cameras, my cell phone, my laptop and a small backpack of food and water, I shoved off and paddled away over coworkers' flooded cars."[4]

*Times-Picayune* employees are evacuated in delivery trucks in the wake of Hurricane Katrina.

183

Jackson quickly saw that he was going to be personally involved with the story whether he wanted to be or not. "I suddenly realized the moral and ethical dilemma I was facing. Everyone stranded by the flood would want my small boat and would do anything to take it. . . . Would I let people drown when I had the only boat in sight?" He decided he would rescue people in the water but not those who were on land or in a house.

The first person he rescued was a fellow *Times-Picayune* photographer who held a plastic bag full of photo data cards in his teeth.

After hours of rowing around and taking pictures, Jackson collapsed for a while and then started hitchhiking rides in Blackhawk helicopters to get out to make more pictures. There was no way Jackson could stay detached following his odyssey. He writes, "I've covered tragedies all over the world, but it's different when it's your own town. Cataclysmic annihilation is starting to feel normal. This story is ours to cover, but it's more than that. This is now our life."[5]

O'Byrne says, as all the reporters at the paper do, that this was their story, a part of their lives. (Even for reporters, or perhaps especially for them, Truth One is

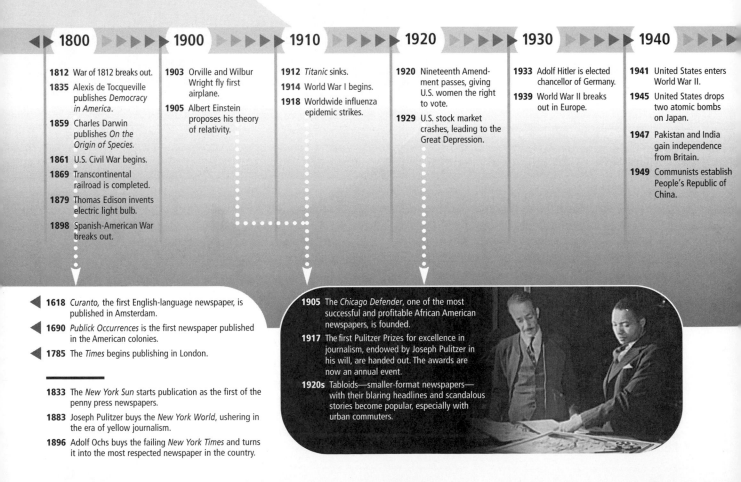

## 1800

**1812** War of 1812 breaks out.
**1835** Alexis de Tocqueville publishes *Democracy in America*.
**1859** Charles Darwin publishes *On the Origin of Species*.
**1861** U.S. Civil War begins.
**1869** Transcontinental railroad is completed.
**1879** Thomas Edison invents electric light bulb.
**1898** Spanish-American War breaks out.

## 1900

**1903** Orville and Wilbur Wright fly first airplane.
**1905** Albert Einstein proposes his theory of relativity.

## 1910

**1912** *Titanic* sinks.
**1914** World War I begins.
**1918** Worldwide influenza epidemic strikes.

## 1920

**1920** Nineteenth Amendment passes, giving U.S. women the right to vote.
**1929** U.S. stock market crashes, leading to the Great Depression.

## 1930

**1933** Adolf Hitler is elected chancellor of Germany.
**1939** World War II breaks out in Europe.

## 1940

**1941** United States enters World War II.
**1945** United States drops two atomic bombs on Japan.
**1947** Pakistan and India gain independence from Britain.
**1949** Communists establish People's Republic of China.

**1618** *Curanto*, the first English-language newspaper, is published in Amsterdam.
**1690** *Publick Occurrences* is the first newspaper published in the American colonies.
**1785** The *Times* begins publishing in London.

**1833** The *New York Sun* starts publication as the first of the penny press newspapers.
**1883** Joseph Pulitzer buys the *New York World*, ushering in the era of yellow journalism.
**1896** Adolf Ochs buys the failing *New York Times* and turns it into the most respected newspaper in the country.

**1905** The *Chicago Defender*, one of the most successful and profitable African American newspapers, is founded.
**1917** The first Pulitzer Prizes for excellence in journalism, endowed by Joseph Pulitzer in his will, are handed out. The awards are now an annual event.
**1920s** Tabloids—smaller-format newspapers—with their blaring headlines and scandalous stories become popular, especially with urban commuters.

vital—The media are essential components of our lives.) "We are narrator and subject of the story of New Orleans, a quandary that, pre-Katrina, we were usually able to avoid." He notes that more than one-third of his department's staff lost their homes from Katrina. "They, like dozens of *Times-Picayune* employees, understand the stress, the despair, the frustration and the struggle that is life in New Orleans still today."[6]

The fact that they could not remain detached did not excuse the reporters from their responsibility to be accurate observers, something that was difficult in all the confusion of the storm and flood. Reporter Brian Thevenot said that some stories were reported as fact with only partial support. The story of a single mentally ill man shooting at a single rescue helicopter got turned into snipers at the Superdome shooting at the rescue helicopters. And widespread stories about the rape of children, again at the Superdome, were undocumented, though some rapes certainly could have occurred.[7] Thevenot and the staff of the *Times-Picayune* took the accuracy responsibility seriously enough to run their corrections as a major front-page story about a month after the storm.[8]

**1950**  **1960**  **1970**  **1980**  **1990**  **2000**

**1950** Korean War begins.
**1953** Francis Crick and James Watson discover structure of DNA.
**1957** Soviet Union launches spacecraft *Sputnik I.*

**1963** Martin Luther King Jr. delivers "I Have a Dream" speech during Washington, D.C., civil-rights march.
**1969** Neil Armstrong walks on the moon.

**1974** U.S. president Richard Nixon resigns due to Watergate scandal.
**1975** Vietnam War ends.
**1977** Apple II personal computer is introduced.
**1978** First test-tube baby is born.

**1983** First HIV/AIDS cases are documented.
**1985** Ozone hole is discovered over Antarctica.
**1986** Space shuttle *Challenger* explodes.
**1989** The Berlin Wall falls.

**1991** Soviet Union disbands.
**1993** European Union is formed.
**1994** Nelson Mandela is elected president of South Africa.
**1997** Diana, Princess of Wales, dies in car accident.

**2001** Al Qaida attacks World Trade Center and Pentagon.
**2003** United States invades Iraq.
**2003** Human genome project is completed.
**2005** Terrorists bomb London's transport system.
**2005** Hurricane Katrina hits the U.S. Gulf Coast.
**2008** Barack Obama is elected U.S. president.

**1955** The *Village Voice*, one of the oldest and most respected of the alternative weeklies, is founded in the Greenwich Village section of New York City.
**1969** The *Washington Blade*, the oldest and largest of the gay newspapers, is founded.

**1972–1973** *Washington Post* reporters Bob Woodward and Carl Bernstein run a series of investigative stories about the burglary of the Democratic National Committee headquarters at the Watergate hotel. The resulting scandal implicates President Richard Nixon and his staff, and leads ultimately to Nixon's resignation.
**1982** The Gannett newspaper chain starts publishing the colorful national newspaper *USA Today.*

**1997** *Dallas Morning News* becomes the first newspaper to break a major story—Timothy McVeigh's confession to the Oklahoma City bombings—on its Web page.
**2002** *Wall Street Journal* reporter Daniel Pearl is murdered while covering Middle East terrorism.
**2006** The New Orleans *Times-Picayune* wins Pulitzer Prizes for its Hurricane Katrina reporting.
**2009** The *Christian Science Monitor* and the *Seattle Post-Intelligencer* go Web only.
**2009** The *Washington Blade* shuts down.

## TEST YOUR MEDIA LITERACY

### Reporting on Katrina

**MOREonline**

You can read more about the *Times-Picayune* coverage of Hurricane Katrina at **http:// ralphehanson.com.**

Covering Hurricane Katrina and its aftermath was a life-changing experience for the staff at the New Orleans *Times-Picayune*. Not only were their homes destroyed and lives turned upside down, but they were also forced to confront some of their long-held beliefs on how journalism ought to be done.

**Who is the source?**

Brian Thevenot and James O'Byrne were reporters for the New Orleans *Times-Picayune*, and Ted Jackson was a photographer for the paper. How do you think their backgrounds shaped how they covered Hurricane Katrina? Does it make a difference that they were residents of New Orleans?

The key issue to Thevenot is that the *Times-Picayune* (and other news organizations) went back after the storm and made a real effort to find out how much of the atrocity stories was true and what was myth. As Keith Woods, of the journalistic think tank the Poynter Institute, told Thevenot, "Don't forget, the journalists kept reporting—the reason you know that things were reported badly is because the journalists told you."[9]

In 2006 the *Times-Picayune* shared the 2006 Pulitzer Prize for public service, along with the Biloxi-Gulfport, Mississippi, *Sun-Herald*, and received a second prize for breaking news reporting. What explains the Pulitzers and the great reporting? Features editor James O'Byrne says it was the paper's local staff that made the difference. "As veterans of the hometown paper, our team's knowledge of the city, their ability to go everywhere and to understand the scope, impact and context of what was happening, was why the *Times-Picayune* owned this story. It was but one of the many moments that defined what it means to be a newspaper."[10]

Thanks to the efforts of reporters and photographers like those at the New Orleans *Times-Picayune*, newspapers provide reports about current events both close at hand and around the world. Some media observers have questioned whether this oldest of news media has any future, suggesting that words and pictures on paper will be replaced by news and images on broadcast television, cable television, and the Internet. The newspaper industry is clearly going through a period of change, but it is far from dying. In this chapter we look at how journalism and the press developed in the United States, how newspapers operate today, whom newspapers large and small are now serving (that is, their audiences), and how newspapers are responding to the changes taking place around them.

**What are they saying?**

Go online and read at least one of the narratives written by the New Orleans reporters who covered the storm and flooding. What problems did the staff of the *Times-Picayune* face in covering Hurricane Katrina? How well did they feel they lived up to journalistic standards in their reporting?

**What do others say about their reporting?**

What kinds of criticism have been leveled against the journalists for their coverage of Hurricane Katrina? How have they been praised? How did their lack of detachment and objectivity affect how they were perceived?

**How do you and your classmates react to the *Times-Picayune* reporting?**

Do you and your classmates think that the staff of the *Times-Picayune* were more or less honest in their reporting because they got so involved in the story? What problems did their involvement lead to? Should reporters get personally involved with stories that are smaller than the flooding of a city?

# INVENTING THE MODERN PRESS

Newspapers first appeared soon after Gutenberg's invention of movable type. The first English-language newspaper was *Curanto,* published in Amsterdam in June 1618. This was not a newspaper as we would recognize it today, but rather a single broadsheet filled with both British and foreign news. By 1622, similar papers (or newsbooks, as they were called) were being published in Britain. The government attempted to control these papers, which were empowering the new capitalist class at the expense of the aristocracy, but the papers still got distributed through places such as coffeehouses.[11] (And if you look ahead to the 1960s and 1970s in the United States, this is not all that different from how the early gay and alternative newspapers were distributed, thus illustrating Truth Four—Nothing's new: Everything that happened in the past will happen again.) Among those publishing broadsheets were church reformers Martin Luther and John Calvin, and their religious writings helped bring about some of the earliest attempts at censorship as well.[12]

## Colonial Publishing: A Tradition of Independence

*Publick Occurrences* is frequently cited as the first newspaper in the American colonies; its first and only issue was published in 1690. As happened with many papers of the era, the government promptly shut it down; in this case the government objected to the paper's disparaging remarks about the King of France. The first paper to publish multiple issues was the *Boston News Letter,* founded in 1704.

*Benjamin and James Franklin.* Just as media dynasties exist today, they existed in the American colonies, with Benjamin and James Franklin having their hands in just about every medium available at the time. Starting in 1721, James, the elder of the two brothers, published the *New England Courant,* the first newspaper to be published without the explicit approval of the British crown. When James was thrown into prison for irritating the authorities, the sixteen-year-old Benjamin, who had been working as a printer's apprentice, took over the paper. By 1729 he had purchased the *Pennsylvania Gazette* and began turning it into the most influential paper in the colonies. Franklin published the colonies' first political cartoon, the oft-reprinted "Join or Die" cartoon, and he introduced the weather report as a regular feature.[13]

## The Penny Press: Newspapers for the People

The newspapers of the American colonies had little in common with newspapers today. Before the 1830s, daily papers contained shipping news and political essays. Designed primarily for the wealthy elite, these papers were often underwritten by political parties, and their content was determined by the editors' opinions. Although we might consider this biased coverage, these early papers made no pretense of objectivity. Why should they? Each political party had its own paper, and the small number of subscribers (2,000 at most) tended to share similar viewpoints. Battles between rival newspapers could get quite heated, even extending to physical violence.

Colonial newspapers were quite expensive, costing as much as six cents a day at a time when a worker might make eighty-five cents a day. Papers were typically available only by annual subscription, which had to be paid in advance. These papers showed their business bias with names like the *Advertiser* or the *Commercial.* They typically consisted of four pages, with the front and back filled primarily with advertising and the inside pages with news and editorial content.[14]

*Benjamin Day and the* New York Sun. In the 1830s Benjamin Day conceived a new type of newspaper, one that would sell large numbers of copies to the emerging literate public. On September 3, 1833, he started publishing the *New York Sun.* The paper's motto was "It shines for all." The newly developed steam engine made the *Sun* possible. Hand-powered presses, which hadn't changed much since Gutenberg's time, could print no more than 350 pages a day, but a steam-powered rotary press could print as many as 16,000 sections (not just pages) in the same amount of time (see Chapter 4).[15]

The *Sun* emphasized facts over opinion. Papers that followed in its wake had names like *Critic*, *Herald*, or *Star*. These inexpensive papers sold for a penny or two on the street, so they soon earned the name penny press. Instead of being subsidized by political parties, the penny papers were supported by circulation and advertising revenues. They also didn't have to worry about subscribers who wouldn't pay their bills, since they were all sold on the street for cash.[16]

Now that publishers could economically print large numbers of papers, they could command a big enough circulation to attract advertising. As a result, their profits came primarily from advertising revenues, not from subscriptions or subsidies. The makers of patent medicines, which often consisted largely of alcohol or narcotics, were the biggest advertisers. Want ads (today's classifieds) also became a prominent feature of the papers.

Penny papers were typically independent rather than being the voice of a particular political party. In fact, they tended to ignore politics altogether because their readers weren't interested in political issues. As an example, one day the *Sun*'s congressional news column reported: "The proceedings of Congress thus far, would not interest our readers."[17]

The concept of "news" was invented by the penny press: These papers emphasized news—the newest developments from the police, courts, and the streets. The traditional papers called the penny papers sensationalistic, not because they ran big headlines or photos—neither existed at the time—but because they were printing "news" instead of political arguments or debates. The penny press also moved toward egalitarianism in the press. The affairs of ordinary people were as much news as accounts of rich aristocrats.[18]

The British press went through a similar period of change, going from the highly partisan press of the 1700s to the more "objective" focus on news by the end of the nineteenth century—again a change largely in response to the rise of a literate working class and the desire to reach a large audience for the paper's advertising.[19]

*A Modern Democratic Society.* The 1830s were a period of intense growth for the United States—in industry, in the economy, and in political participation. The penny newspaper was a vital part of this growth, providing the information the public needed to make democracy work. In 1830 there were 650 weeklies and 65 dailies in the United States, but in just ten years those numbers had doubled: to 1,241 weeklies and 138 dailies.[20] It was a period when more

*Newsboys sold newspapers on the streets of New York and other major cities for one or two cents a copy during the penny press era of the nineteenth century.*

people were working for wages outside the home and were starting to use consumer goods purchased with cash. The penny press provided a means for advertising these goods, which in turn expanded the market for them.

The United States was being transformed from a rural community to an urban society, from an agricultural nation to an industrial one, from self-sufficient families to a market-based economy. Michael Schudson argues that the penny papers were a strong force in this change:

> These papers, whatever their political preferences, were spokesmen for egalitarian ideals in politics, economic life, and social life through their organization of sales, their solicitation of advertising, their emphasis on news, their catering to large audiences, their decreasing concern with the editorial.
> The penny papers expressed and built the culture of a democratic market society, a culture which had no place for social or intellectual deference.[21]

During the Civil War era, the press continued its move toward independence of political parties. The press was providing people with news about the war and whether the nation would continue to exist. Following the war, newspapers continued to grow and began to be an important part of people's everday life. This was the establishment of Truth One—The media are essential components of our lives. Hazel Dicken-Garcia, in her history of the nineteenth-century press, writes:

> The press became a "habit" as Americans, perhaps for the first time, recognized a vital need for it and established it as [a] part of lives in a way that was unprecedented. Families sought news of relatives fighting in the war, and national leaders needed information about events as a basis for making decisions and forming policies for conducting the war. . . . Since everyone had a stake in the war and thus a driving need to know about events, the newspaper became primary reading material as never before.[22]

## Pulitzer, Hearst, and the Battle for New York City

If the penny papers of the first half of the nineteenth century gave birth to modern journalism, the battles between New York publishers Joseph Pulitzer and William Randolph Hearst in the 1880s and 1890s provided journalism's turbulent adolescence.

*Pulitzer and the* New York World.   Joseph Pulitzer came to the United States from Austria in 1864 at the age of seventeen to fight in the Civil War. He survived the war, studied law, and went on to become a reporter for a German-language newspaper. In 1878 he bought the *St. Louis Post and Dispatch* and became its publisher, editor, and business manager.

In 1883 Pulitzer bought the failing *New York World*, and in just three years he boosted its circulation from 15,000 to more than 250,000. High circulation was critical because large readership numbers attracted advertisers who were willing to pay premium prices. Twelve years after Pulitzer bought the paper, it had a daily circulation of 540,000.[23]

Pulitzer changed the appearance of the paper's front page, replacing dense type with huge multicolumn pictures and big headlines. He brought to journalism a sense of drama and style that appealed immensely to his turn-of-the-century audience. Author and press critic Paul Weaver credits Pulitzer with the invention of the modern newspaper's front page. Before Pulitzer, the front page was no different from any other page in the paper. Pulitzer started the practice of giving the most important story the biggest and widest headline and running that story above the fold of the paper, where it would be immediately visible to anyone looking at the paper on a newsstand. Thus, **above the fold** came to refer to a prominent story.

Pulitzer made many other innovations. He changed headlines so that they said something about the story. For example, a pre-Pulitzer New York paper ran the story about President Lincoln's assassination under the headline, "Awful Event." Pulitzer required his editors to use headlines containing a subject and an active verb, so that the Lincoln assassination might have run under the headline, "Lincoln Shot." Pre-Pulitzer stories told readers what they needed to know in a formal, structured way. Pulitzer presented the news as a story that people wanted to read; journalists went from just being reporters to being storytellers as well.[24]

*New Readers: Immigrants and Women.* The New York City of the 1880s and 1890s was a city of immigrants—people who wanted to learn to speak and read English—and the city's newspapers were important teachers. Pulitzer's *New York World* used big headlines, easy words, and many illustrations, all of which helped the paper appeal to the immigrant community. This was also the period when the modern Sunday paper got its start. In 1889 half of all New Yorkers bought Sunday papers. To make his Sunday editions more appealing, Pulitzer started trying out illustrations, comic strips, and color Sunday comics.

Pulitzer also tailored his newspaper to women readers by publishing women's pages and romantic fiction. He had a difficult time balancing the interests of women against those of male readers. He didn't want to offend male working-class readers by making the paper too feminist in content, but he couldn't ignore the independent women who were now reading papers. Women were the primary purchasers of household items, and advertisers wanted to reach them. So the newspaper needed to tailor its content to reach these "new women" while still appealing to its male working-class readers.

No one epitomized the journalism of Pulitzer's *New York World* better than "stunt journalist" Nellie Bly, who proved that women could go to the same extremes as men when trying to get a story. From her first act at the *World*

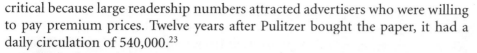

**above the fold**
A term used to refer to a prominent story; it comes from placement of a news story in a broadsheet newspaper above the fold in the middle of the front page.

Pioneering woman journalist Nellie Bly created a sensation in the late 1800s with her "stunt journalism" written for Joseph Pulitzer's New York World.

(pretending to be insane in order to get an insider's report on a women's lunatic asylum) to her most famous stunt (traveling around the world in under eighty days), she always did things more extravagantly than anyone else.[25]

Bly, who lived from 1864 to 1922, wrote hundreds of newspaper articles, generally long and in the first person, for the *Pittsburg Dispatch*, the *New York World*, and the *New York Evening Journal*. She was born Elizabeth Jane Cochran but went by the nickname Pink (probably for the pink dresses she wore). It was at the *Dispatch* that she started using the pen name Nellie Bly. In addition to covering women's stories for the *Dispatch*, Bly wrote a travelogue of a journey to Mexico under the headline "NELLIE IN MEXICO." She also made a name for herself covering the plight of young women working in factories.

In 1887 Bly moved to New York in the hope of finding a job at one of the city's vibrant daily papers. First on her list was Pulitzer's *New York World*. She eventually was able to see John Cockerill, managing editor of the *World*. It was Cockerill who suggested that Bly go undercover to write a story about the women's lunatic asylum. If her story was good, he told her, she would get the job.

The asylum had been charged with abusing inmates, but none of the stories written about it had the power of Bly's insider account. To gain access, Bly moved into a rooming house and proceeded to act erratically so as to be committed to the asylum. Once inside, she wrote articles describing patients being fed rotten food and being choked and beaten by nurses. After ten days an attorney for Pulitzer came to rescue her. The series of stories she produced was a masterpiece.

With this series Bly proved that a woman could find success in sensationalistic journalism and that she could tell a great story under dangerous circumstances. Today many people would consider it unethical for reporters to pretend to be someone they aren't, and many major papers would reject their work. But in the New York of Hearst and Pulitzer, Bly's stunts were wildly successful and were imitated by other reporters.[26]

**The Era of Yellow Journalism.**   William Randolph Hearst came from a wealthy family and began his newspaper career as editor of the *San Francisco Examiner*, which was owned by his father. Having dominated the San Francisco newspaper market, Hearst followed Pulitzer into the New York market by purchasing the *New York Journal*. Soon he was using Pulitzer's own techniques to compete against him. Hearst and Pulitzer became fierce rivals, each trying to outdo the other with outlandish stories and stunts. This style of shocking, sensationalistic reporting came to be known as **yellow journalism**. Why yellow? At one point the two papers fought over which one would publish the popular comic strip "The Yellow Kid," which featured a smart-aleck character and could be considered the "Doonesbury" of its day. Eventually both papers featured their own "Yellow Kid" drawn by different artists.

Nowhere was yellow journalism more exaggerated than in the *World*'s and *Journal*'s attempts to drum up fury over the events taking place in Cuba, which led to the Spanish-American War. War, then as now, sold a lot of newspapers, and Hearst did his best to sensationalize the conflict in Cuba. Hearst sent reporter Richard Harding Davis and artist Frederic Remington to Havana, Cuba, to cover the possible hostilities between the Spaniards and the Cubans. But there was little to report, and Davis and Remington were kept away from the fighting. According to a popular story, Remington became so discouraged that he telegraphed Hearst asking permission to return to New York: "Everything is quiet. There is no trouble here. There will be no war. Wish to return." Hearst's supposed reply? "Please remain. You furnish the pictures and I'll furnish the war."[27] It's uncertain whether this story is true, but there is no doubt that Hearst used the power of the press to sway public opinion.

Pulitzer eventually repented for his excesses during the yellow journalism era by endowing a school of journalism at Columbia University. He also endowed the Pulitzer Prizes that every year honor the best reporting, photography, and commentary in journalism.

## The Tabloids

Reading newspapers isn't the sort of thing people ever feel a need to apologize for—unless they are reading one of the tabloids. These include not only weekly supermarket tabloids, such as the *Star* and the *National Enquirer*, but also a substantial number of daily tabloids, such as the *Daily News* and the *Chicago*

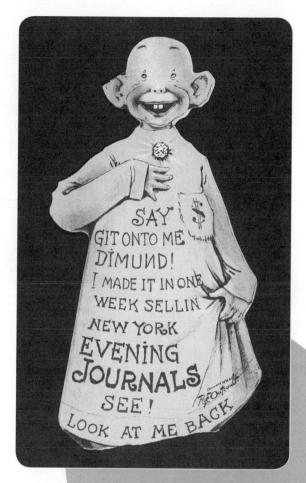

*The Yellow Kid was such a popular early comic strip character that both the* New York Journal *and the* New York World *had separate versions of the feature drawn by two different artists.*

**yellow journalism**

A style of sensationalistic journalism that grew out of the newspaper circulation battle between Joseph Pulitzer and William Randolph Hearst.

*The* Daily News *and the* New York Post *are fierce rivals in the highly competitive New York tabloid market.*

**tabloid newspapers**

Newspapers with a half-page (11-by-14-inch) format that usually have a cover rather than a traditional front page like the larger broadsheet papers.

**broadsheet newspapers**

Standard-sized newspapers, which are generally 17 by 22 inches.

**jazz journalism**

A lively, illustrated style of newspapering popularized by the tabloid papers in the 1920s.

*Sun-Times,* that present the news in a lively style that makes people want to read them.

*The* New York Daily News. Tabloids first became popular during the 1920s. **Tabloid newspapers** are printed in a half-page (11-by-14-inch) format and usually have a cover rather than a traditional front page. They stand in contrast to **broadsheet newspapers**, which are the standard size of 17 by 22 inches. With a resurgence of sensationalism that hadn't been seen since the yellow journalism of the Hearst and Pulitzer era, the papers of the 1920s became known for a lively, illustrated style known as **jazz journalism**.

One of the great early tabloids was the *New York Daily News,* which is still popular today.[28] The paper features big photos, huge headlines, and sensationalistic stories. Its most famous cover ran on January 13, 1928. Ruth Snyder had been convicted of murdering her husband and had been sentenced to electrocution. Then, as now, executions of women were rare. Although photographers were excluded from the execution, the *Daily News* sent in a Chicago photographer (because he wouldn't be recognized by anyone present) who had strapped a camera to his ankle. At the moment of the execution, he pulled up his pant leg and took the picture. The photo ran the next day under the headline "DEAD!"[29]

Today's tabloids are no less cutthroat and competitive than Hearst's and Pulitzer's papers in the late 1800s or the tabloids in the 1920s. The *Daily News* continues to do battle on the streets of New York with its rival, the *New York Post.* They compete not only to be the primary paper of working-class New Yorkers but also to be the tabloid that readers of the more serious *Times* pick up for their gossip stories, sometimes referred to as "twinkies."[30]

How fierce is the competition between these two papers? On one occasion the *New York Post* ran an Associated Press photo of a girl competing in a spelling bee. But because she was sponsored by the *Daily News,* the *Post*'s biggest rival, the *Post* used a computer to edit out the *Daily News* logo from the sign she was wearing.[31] Of course, competition among the American tabloids is nothing compared to that of the British working-class papers. The tabloids such as the *Sun* or the *Daily Mirror* are intensely sensationalistic, and the *Sun* even features a daily topless pinup on its page 3. The tabs also substantially outsell the more responsible papers.

## Broadcast News

In the 1920s, newspapers started having competition from new outlets. Broadcast media began to provide up-to-the-minute news delivered with a speed and immediacy that newspapers could not match.

*Radio News.*   News was a part of radio programming from the very start. KDKA demonstrated the power of radio news with its 1920 nighttime broadcast of the Harding-Cox presidential election results—before the newspaper stories appeared the next morning. The newspapers, understandably, were upset by radio's apparent poaching on their territory. In fact, in the 1930s they threatened to cut off radio stations' access to Associated Press news and even threatened to stop running radio program listings. The newspapers insisted that unless the news was of "transcendent importance," radio shouldn't broadcast it until the newspapers were available. Not surprisingly, the radio networks didn't think much of this idea. Although various restrictions were tested for a short while, in the end radio news could not be stopped. As we will see again and again, old media usually try unsuccessfully to hold back the development of new media, providing yet another example of Truth Four—Nothing's new: Everything that happened in the past will happen again. Yet the old media do not go away. Instead, after a period of resistance, they change and adapt to the new environment.[32] Radio eliminated the extra editions of newspapers that used to be published whenever dramatic news occurred, but newspapers as a whole suffered only a slight decline in circulation.[33]

One place where radio held clear superiority over newspapers was in the realm of live news. Radio could, for the first time, bring news from around the world to people "as it happened." At no time was this more apparent than during World War II. When Adolf Hitler's army marched into Austria in 1938, CBS was on the air from Europe with immediate news and up-to-the-minute commentary. No radio correspondent of the era stood out more than CBS's European director, Edward R. Murrow. When Germany declared war on England in 1939, Murrow reported it from London in a voice that was to become familiar to all Americans. During the bombing of London, Americans listened to his live reports, which contained not just the news but also the sounds of everyday life: the air raid sirens, the anti-aircraft guns, and the explosions of bombs. Murrow spoke directly to listeners from London rooftops and made them feel as if they were there with him.[34]

*Television News Goes 24/7.*   Television news started with brief coverage of the 1940 Republican national convention on an experimental NBC television station in New York City. By 1948, both the Democratic and Republican conventions were covered extensively for the still-tiny television audience. Documentary programs such as *See It Now*, hosted by former CBS radio newsman

Edward R. Murrow, took on lightweight topics as well as intensely controversial issues such as Wisconsin senator Joseph McCarthy, who had accused numerous people of being communists. The program also aired notable segments on the Korean War. In 1947, NBC started TV's longest-running news and commentary program, *Meet the Press*, which is still on today.

In August 1948 the *CBS-TV News* started airing for fifteen minutes every weeknight, setting the standard length for network news until the 1960s. When the ocean liner *Andrea Doria* sank in 1956, a CBS camera crew on a seaplane got footage of the ship going down, which was broadcast promptly. Journalist and broadcast professor Edward Bliss Jr. notes that with the film of the *Andrea Doria*, "[t]elevision had demonstrated that it could take the public to the scene of a major story more effectively than any other news medium."[35]

Television started playing a major role in presidential elections starting in 1960, with the famous Kennedy-Nixon debates.

In 1963, CBS expanded its nightly news show to half an hour, with Walter Cronkite at the anchor desk. Along with the news, the program featured commentary from veteran newsman Eric Sevareid. NBC soon followed the new format, joined four years later by ABC. During this time videotape, satellite communication, and color started coming into common use, giving television news more immediacy and impact than ever before. With correspondents bringing into American homes graphic news from the war in Vietnam, along with spectacular coverage of the moon landing in 1969, television news rose in importance as the way to see what was happening in the world.

On November 3, 1979, the staff of the American Embassy in Tehran was taken hostage by Iranian militants, and ABC started a nightly news update at 11:30 p.m. eastern time. That news update eventually turned into *Nightline* with anchor Ted Koppel, and it became one of the most respected news shows on television. The following year, Ted Turner's CNN went on the air with news twenty-four hours a day and the promise that the station would not sign off until the end of the world.[36] By the time the Gulf War began in January 1991, viewers were turning to CNN, not the networks, for news.[37] But CNN's dominance was not to last. By 2003 and the war in Iraq, CNN was facing competition in the twenty-four-hour news business from Fox News and, to a lesser extent, MSNBC. As early as 2002, the year after the September 11 terrorist attacks, Fox News was getting consistently higher ratings than the more established CNN. Fox did a number of things to distinguish itself from its rival. Most significantly, it was willing to take a point of view. While CNN and the broadcast networks followed the traditional objective, or neutral, style of reporting, Fox took an opinionated view in the manner of the major newsmagazines and European newspapers.[38] According to the Nielsen ratings, Fox News has fewer unique viewers than does CNN, but they watch the channel for a longer period of time.[39]

# THE NEWS BUSINESS

The newspapers of the yellow journalism era were the primary source of news at the time. They faced competition from magazines, but heavyweights like *Time* or *Newsweek* had yet to weigh in. Radio news was a decade or two away, television news would have to wait half a century, and CNN was nearly 100 years in the future. Although newspapers today owe a huge debt to the great papers of the past, they are operating in a substantially different media environment, one that is saturated with fast, up-to-the-minute competition.

## Newspaper Conglomerates—Consolidation and Profitability

Unlike those of Hearst and Pulitzer, today's newspapers typically face little competition from other newspapers. There are 1,422 daily newspapers currently being published, down about 25 percent from 100 years ago. This doesn't mean that cities are going without newspapers, however, only that there are relatively few (less than 1 percent) that have competing papers.[40] Also, most newspapers today are owned by large **chains**, corporations that control a significant number of newspapers or other media outlets. Former journalist Ben Bagdikian notes in his book *The Media Monopoly* that before World War II more than 80 percent of all American newspapers were independently owned. Today that picture has reversed, with chains owning more than 80 percent of all papers. The British press has had a longer tradition of concentration of ownership, with three lords owning 67 percent of the daily circulation as early as 1910.[41]

**chains**
Corporations that control a significant number of newspapers and other media outlets.

Why is the consolidation in the publishing business taking place? Sometimes family owners just want to get out of the newspaper business. In many cases inheritance laws virtually force the sale of family-owned papers after they have been passed down through three generations. The chain with the largest circulation is Gannett, the publisher of *USA Today*, which owns approximately eighty-five daily newspapers that have a combined circulation of more than 6.5 million.[42] In addition to Gannett, major publishers include Thomson Newspapers, Cox Newspapers, the New York Times Company, Advance Publications (formerly Newhouse), the Tribune Company, and Dow Jones & Company. In Britain, the largest single owner of newspapers is Rupert Murdoch's News Corporation, which publishes the tabloids the *Sun* and the *News of the World* as well as the more respected broadsheets the *Times* and the *Sunday Times*. News Corporation publishes more than 175 newspapers in five countries and is the largest publisher of English-language newspapers.

Until recently, newspaper publishing was one of the most profitable businesses in the United States. The Gannett newspaper chain had earnings as high as 30 to 40 percent profits from its papers.[43] The average profit for publicly owned newspaper chains in 2005 was nearly 20 percent, noticeably higher than that for companies in the Fortune 500.[44] But all that changed in the late 2000s. Annual newspaper advertising revenue fell by 23 percent between 2006 and 2008, dropping from $49.3 billion to $38 billion.[45] The drops in income were the worst at metropolitan dailies, whereas national newspapers like *USA Today* and the *Wall Street Journal* performed relatively well. The decline in stock prices of newspaper companies was even more dramatic, falling by 83 percent during 2008. For more on what these economic changes mean to the newspaper industry, see the section "The Future of Newspapers" at the end of this chapter.

## National Newspapers

Until 2009 the United States had three national newspapers: *USA Today,* the *Wall Street Journal,* and the much smaller *Christian Science Monitor.* But in April 2009, the *Monitor* suspended its daily publication as a newspaper and became an all-electronic Web-based news channel.[46] Both *USA Today* and the *Journal* rely on satellite distribution of newspaper pages to printing plants across the country. In other respects the two papers could not be more different: The *Journal* has the look of an old-fashioned nineteenth-century paper, and *USA Today* originated the multicolored format. The *New York Times,* although it is a major metropolitan newspaper, is also generally considered to be a national newspaper. We discuss the *Monitor*'s switch to the Web at the end of this chapter.

### USA Today: *News McNuggets*.
When the Gannett newspaper chain founded *USA Today,* journalists made fun of the new national paper, calling it McPaper. They claimed that the brightly colored paper full of short stories was serving up "News McNuggets" to an audience raised on television news. John Quinn, a former editor of the paper, once joked that *USA Today* was "the newspaper that brought new depth to the meaning of the word shallow."[47] Critics of the paper warned that starting a national newspaper was a good way for Gannett to lose a lot of money in a hurry, and the critics were right. In its first decade *USA Today* reportedly lost more than $800 million. But by 1993 the paper started turning a profit, and in 2008 it had an average daily circulation of $2.1 million.[48]

The paper now has strengthened its national news section, increased its international news section, and begun running in-depth stories. The paper also tries to get stories other papers don't have rather than just providing an easy-to-understand product. In addition, it has beefed up its foreign staff and hired outside reporters from prestigious newspapers and magazines.

One reason *USA Today* has become more influential is that it is found everywhere. A traveler is much more likely to find *USA Today* in a hotel than the *Washington Post* or the *New York Times.* Even the critics have started coming around in recent years. Ben Bagdikian, who once described the paper as "a mediocre piece of journalism," recently said, "It has become a much more serious newspaper. They have abandoned the idea that every person who picks up the paper has an attention span of 30 seconds. . . . I don't think it's a joke anymore."[49]

What influence has *USA Today* had on the newspaper industry as a whole? First and foremost, *USA Today* changed the look of newspapers. It drove color onto the front page and made black-and-white papers look drab in comparison. Second, it was organized clearly by section, thus initiating a trend in which papers began imposing more structure on the news. Finally, and most controversially, *USA Today* has led the trend toward shorter stories.[50]

The most important effect of *USA Today* is that it has forced the industry to reconsider what a newspaper should be. *USA Today* is a national provider of Web news as well as a newspaper. Its site provides content that is in many ways quite different from that contained in the paper. The best-seller list in its Thursday print edition includes 50 books, but the list on its Web site includes 150 books. Former editor Karen Jurgensen says, "The challenge we face is that technological changes, the alternatives to newspaper reading . . . especially in recent years with the growth of the Internet, pale in comparison to the changes we're going to see in the next decade."[51]

### *The* Wall Street Journal.

The major competition to *USA Today* for national readership comes from the *Wall Street Journal*. The *Journal* was the last major paper to start using color, and it has still not fully embraced photography. Instead, it uses pen-and-ink drawings for the "mug shots" that accompany its stories. The *Journal* has cultivated an old-fashioned look with its long, single-column stories and multi-line headlines that deliberately evoke the newspaper layouts of the pre-Pulitzer era.[52] It did undergo a substantial redesign in 2006, primarily to make the paper narrower so that it didn't use as much newsprint. The *Journal*'s circulation is similar to *USA Today*'s (the *Journal* has a circulation of 2.0 million compared to *USA Today*'s 2.1 million),[53] but it does not attempt to be a comprehensive newspaper. It is the definitive source of financial news, it is highly regarded for its national and international news from reporters like the late Daniel Pearl, and its editorial page is one of the nation's leading conservative voices. As was discussed in Chapter 3, the *Wall Street Journal*, along with its parent Dow Jones Inc., was acquired by

*At a time when many newspapers are facing financial problems, national newspapers like the* Wall Street Journal *are doing relatively well.*

Rupert Murdoch's News Corporation. To date this has not resulted in substantial changes to the paper.[54]

*English-Language International Newspapers.* There are three major English-language international newspapers. The best known of these is the *International Herald Tribune*, which is published in Paris and distributed in 180 countries. Formerly owned in partnership by the *Washington Post* and the *New York Times*, it is now owned exclusively by the *New York Times*.[55] The paper was founded in 1887 as a European edition of the now-defunct *New York Herald*. Traditionally the *Tribune* reprinted articles from a variety of papers, but it is now based more directly on the *New York Times* content.[56]

*Financial Times*, owned by British media conglomerate Pearson, is primarily a business newspaper. Its one-time editor, Gordon Willoughby, told *Ad Age Global* magazine, "We see ourselves as an international window on the business world. There is a global business engine, and it is becoming increasingly outward looking, and that plays to what we're good at."[57]

Although the *Wall Street Journal* is thought of primarily as a U.S. paper, it also publishes European and Asian editions. "We aspired to be the global newspaper of business and the newspaper of business globally. We don't aspire to overtake local newspapers in the U.K., Germany, or Japan," says Richard Tofel of the *Journal*.[58]

None of these papers has a large circulation, with the *Tribune* selling approximately 264,000 copies a day, the international editions of the *Journal* selling 186,000, and the *Financial Times* 269,000.[59]

## The Metropolitan Press

The metropolitan newspapers are the big-city papers that most people think of when they talk about the power of the press.

*The* New York Times. If there is a debate over whether *USA Today* or the *Wall Street Journal* is the nation's biggest paper, there is no question about which paper is most influential. When people in the United States refer to the *Times* without naming a city, they are almost certainly referring to the *New York Times*. According to at least one definition, news is what is "printed on the front page of the *New York Times*." News stories in the United States often don't become significant until they have been covered in the *New York Times*. The front page of the *New York Times* has as much news on it as an entire half-hour network newscast. The Sunday *New York Times* is huge: In September 1998 the paper published an "Arts and Leisure" section with 124 pages, a record for the *New York Times*—and that was just one section![60]

According to *Time* magazine, "A *Times* morning-after analysis of a presidential debate can set the agenda for days of campaign coverage and punditry. Its

| TABLE 6.1 | TOP TEN DAILY NEWSPAPERS IN TERMS OF WEEKDAY CIRCULATION, SEPTEMBER 2009 |
| --- | --- |

| Paper | Weekday circulation |
| --- | --- |
| 1. *USA Today* | 2,113,725 |
| 2. *Wall Street Journal* | 2,082,189 |
| 3. *New York Times* | 1,039,031 |
| 4. *Los Angeles Times* | 723,181 |
| 5. *Washington Post* | 665,383 |
| 6. (New York) *Daily News* | 602,857 |
| 7. *New York Post* | 558,140 |
| 8. *Chicago Tribune* | 501,202 |
| 9. *Houston Chronicle* | 425,138 |
| 10. *Arizona Republic* | 389,701 |

*Source:* "Newspaper Circulation Ranking Index," *Advertising Age,* March 31, 2009. Available from www.adage.com/datacenter. Reprinted with permission from *Advertising Age/American Demographics.* Copyright, Crain Communications Inc. 2009.

decision to feature, say, a murder in Texas on Page One can prompt hordes of reporters to hop a plane south. Its critics can make or break a Broadway play or turn an obscure foreign film into tomorrow's hot ticket."[61]

While the *Times* is only third in circulation behind the two biggest national newspapers, it does have about 1 million subscribers. While the *Times* is classified here as a metropolitan paper, it has as much in common with the major national papers as with the city papers. More than one-third of its readership is outside New York City. For a list of the top ten newspapers in the United States, see Table 6.1.

The *New York Times* has been a respected newspaper ever since Adolf Ochs bought the failing penny press paper in 1896 and gave it an emphasis on serious national and international news. Its stodgy look, with long columns of type, earned it the nickname "Gray Lady." However, on October 16, 1997, the *Times* started running color photos on its front page, joining virtually every other paper in the country in this practice. Yet even with color the paper doesn't look like *USA Today.* As the *American Journalism Review* put it, "Don't expect the Gray Lady to step out in any gauche dress just to show off."[62] The *Times* is basically a black-and-white paper with color used as accents, according to newspaper design expert Mario Garcia.[63]

Watergate reporters Carl Bernstein (left) and Bob Woodward talk with reporters after attending a memorial service for W. Mark Felt, their source who was known as "Deep Throat."

**Watergate scandal**

A burglary authorized by rogue White House staffers of the Democratic National Committee headquarters in the Watergate office and apartment building and its subsequent cover-up led to the resignation of President Richard Nixon in 1974. Bob Woodward and Carl Bernstein, two reporters from the *Washington Post,* covered the Watergate scandal.

*The* Washington Post. The *New York Times* set the standard for newspaper journalism in the twentieth century and continues to do so today, but in the 1970s the *Washington Post* inspired a generation of young journalists with its coverage of the **Watergate scandal**, the subsequent cover-up, and the downfall of President Richard Nixon. Watergate was a story that shook the nation and transformed the *Post* from a big-city paper to one with a national reputation.

The scandal started with a "third-rate burglary" of the Democratic National Committee headquarters in the Watergate office and apartment complex on June 16, 1972. When the five Spanish-speaking burglars were arrested, one was found carrying an address book that contained the number for a phone located in the White House.

Among those assigned to cover the story were two young reporters, Bob Woodward and Carl Bernstein. They soon realized that this was no ordinary burglary. As weeks and then months went by, their painstaking reporting connected the burglars to the White House and eventually to the president himself. They further discovered that the White House had been systematically sabotaging the Democratic presidential candidates and attempting to cover up these actions.

During the summer of 1973, Americans were spellbound by the Senate hearings into the Watergate scandal. Finally, with impeachment seeming a certainty, Nixon resigned as president on August 8, 1974.[64]

Watergate was no doubt a high point for the *Post*, but the Janet Cooke story was likely one of its lowest. Cooke was hired by the *Washington Post* to improve its coverage of the African American community. She was a young African American woman who claimed to have a degree from Vassar, and she was a fantastic writer. On Sunday, September 28, 1980, Cooke delivered just the kind of story she had been hired to write—a compelling account of an eight-year-old boy named Jimmy who was a heroin addict being shot up by his mother's boyfriend. Although the story was compelling, it wasn't true—something that was not discovered until the story was awarded the Pulitzer Prize in 1981. Days after Cooke won the award, reporters learned that her college credentials had been fabricated, and soon she confessed that Jimmy's story had been made up as well.[65]

Cooke obviously had not behaved ethically in fabricating the story and her credentials. But Bob Woodward, who was one of Cooke's editors, also accepts responsibility for printing the story. Woodward explains the journalistic and moral lapse in an interview with *Washingtonian* magazine:

> When we found [the story] was a fraud, we exposed it ourselves, putting all the information, very painfully, in the paper. We acknowledged a lapse of journalism.
>
> It took me a while to understand the moral lapse, which was the more unforgivable one. I should have tried to save the kid and then do the story. . . . If it happened now, I'd say, "Okay, where's this kid who's being tortured to death?"
>
> My journalistic failure was immense, but the moral failure was worse. And if I had worried about the kid, I would have learned that the story was a fraud. There would have been no journalistic failure.[66]

Fourteen years after Cooke's story was written, retired *Post* editor Ben Bradlee was still haunted by the story and by the blow it delivered to the paper's credibility: "That was a terrible blot on our reputation. I'd give anything to wipe that one off."[67]

*The* Los Angeles Times.    When people talk about the press in general, they are usually speaking of the major East Coast papers like the *Washington Post* and the *New York Times*. In the early 2000s the *Los Angeles Times* established a national presence as well. While it may not have "push[ed] the *New York Times* off its perch,"[68] it has been one of the most respected papers on the West Coast, winning three Pulitzer Prizes in 2003, five in 2004, two in 2005, and one each in 2007 and 2009.

Lately, however, the *Los Angeles Times* has been in the news more often for the controversy surrounding cost-cutting by its owner, the Tribune Company, which also owns the *Chicago Tribune* and superstation WGN.

Since 2003 the paper has cut more than 500 people from its newsroom, taking the number of journalists working for the paper from more than 1,100 to slightly more than 500. In addition, two respected editors and a publisher either quit or were fired.[69]

The paper had previously attracted controversy over its requirement in the late 1990s that reporters attempt to include quotes from women and minorities in their stories. This wasn't so much political correctness as it was marketing correctness. Just as the penny papers started running less politically biased stories to attract the largest possible audience, so today the *Los Angeles Times* is reaching out by quoting more women and Latinos to boost that segment of the paper's readership.[70] Publisher Mark Willes, who ran the paper from 1995 to 2000, set goals for increasing the number of quotes from women and minorities, and made them a factor in determining editors' raises.[71]

Reporters at the paper raised several questions about the new requirement: 1) Should they always identify people by race and/or sex to make sure each source gets counted as a woman or minority? What if the race or sex of a person isn't relevant to the story? 2) What if the reporter is interviewing someone over the phone and doesn't know the race of the interviewee? Does he or she have to ask? 3) What categories constitute diversity: women, blacks, Native Americans, gays and lesbians, Hispanics? Certainly. But what about a Russian immigrant, a Jew, or a Muslim? 4) Does interviewing one African American guarantee that all black viewpoints have been covered? Some reporters questioned whether specific minority groups even have a unified point of view.[72]

Editors refer to building diversity by quoting minorities and women in stories that aren't about minority issues as **mainstreaming**. Mainstreaming has extended far beyond the *Los Angeles Times*. The *San Jose Mercury News* uses the process in its food section to include material on Eastern Europeans, Southeast Asians, and African Americans and how they are cooking. Keith Woods, former diversity coordinator for the Poynter Institute, writes that mainstreaming is a problem when "people with little expertise and less to say have been forced into stories simply because they fit a demographic quota."[73] Yet when the process brings in a wider range of sources and gets journalists to know more about their community, then it is successful. Quotas for mainstreaming by quotes are currently in a decline, but the principle—making newspapers more inclusive—is still very much alive.[74]

**mainstreaming**
The effort by newspapers such as the *Los Angeles Times* to include quotations by minorities and women in stories that aren't about minority issues.

**community press**
Weekly and daily newspapers serving individual communities or suburbs instead of an entire metropolitan area.

## Community and Suburban Papers

The **community press** consists of weekly and daily newspapers serving individual communities or suburbs instead of an entire metropolitan area. These papers are making extensive use of the Web. *American Journalism Review* lists approximately 1,100 daily newspapers on its Web site, but it also lists close to 1,200 nondaily community papers.

One of the reasons community papers are important is that they publish news that readers can't get anywhere else. Journalism professor Eric K. Meyer points out that community newspapers "have the most loyal audiences and the news that you can't get elsewhere. A local newspaper won't get scooped by CNN."[75]

Readers often go to a local newspaper, either in the paper format or on the Web, when they feel that the national press isn't covering a story in enough detail. According to the Pew Research Center's Project for Excellence in Journalism, for the past twenty years about 90 percent of newspaper readers have gone to the local paper for news about where they live. During Hurricane Katrina, the New Orleans *Times-Picayune* went from 80,000 page hits a day to 30 million as people around the world tried to find out what was happening in the Crescent City. While the *Times-Picayune* is generally considered a metropolitan paper, in the days, weeks, and months following Hurricane Katrina it was functioning very much as a community paper.[76]

## NEWS AND SOCIETY

What is news? Ask ten different journalists and you'll come up with ten different definitions. One way of defining news is to list its characteristics, the values journalists use when they select which stories to report. These include the following:

- Timeliness—An earthquake that happened last night is more newsworthy than one that happened two months ago.

- Proximity—An auto accident in your town in which two people are injured is more likely to make it into the paper than an auto accident 300 miles away in which two people are killed.

- Prominence—When two movie stars have lunch together, it's news. When you have lunch with your mother, it's not.

- Consequence—A $50 billion tax cut is more newsworthy than a $5,000 one.

- Rarity—The birth of an albino tiger is news.

- Human interest—Events that touch our hearts, such as the birth of octuplets, often make the news.

Another way to define news is to look at the wide range of ways newspaper editors think of it. Charles Dana, editor of the *New York Sun* in the late 1800s, defined news as "anything that will make people talk."[77] John B. Bogart, a city editor of the *Sun*, gave us a classic definition: "When a dog bites a man, that is not news. But when a man bites a dog, that *is* news." As mentioned earlier in the chapter, news is often defined as "that which is printed on the front page of the *New York Times*."[78] Noted journalist Walter Lippmann defined news as a "picture of reality on which men can act."[79] And there are cynics who say that the perfect news story is one that deals with "pets, tits, or tots."[80]

### Sources, Advertisers, and Readers—Whom Do You Please?

Traditionally, newspapers have maintained a figurative wall between the business department and the newsroom, sometimes jokingly called the "separation of church and state." Reporters and editors are supposed to be concerned not with profits but rather with reporting the news as best they can. But the barrier is coming down, and editors are increasingly looking at their newspaper as a product that should appeal to advertisers as well as readers.

John Oppedahl, who has been editor and publisher of the *Arizona Republic* as well as publisher of the *San Francisco Examiner*, says that editors must be concerned about the business health of their papers: "Editors have to become more interested and more involved in how their enterprises make money. . . . If you take the view that editors really have been marketers all along, and maybe never wanted to say it, now I think they need to admit that they are."[81]

However, sometimes publishers go from printing news that *readers* want to publishing news that *advertisers* want. For example, many newspapers now publish advice and news about personal investing in addition to the traditional stock reports. While these features are undoubtedly popular with readers, they are even more popular with advertisers, who want their ads for financial services surrounded by stories telling readers that they ought to be investing.

The Project for Excellence in Journalism annual report for 2006 stated the situation fairly baldly: "At many old-media companies, though not all, the decades-long battle at the top between idealists and accountants is now over. The idealists have lost."[82]

## Patriotism and the Press—Reporters Risk Their Lives to Report the News

Covering the news, especially from a war zone, can be a dangerous occupation. Journalists' deaths in Iraq peaked in 2006 and 2007, with thirty-two dying each of those years. Since then, the death rate has dropped dramatically, falling to eleven for 2008 and three for the first nine months of 2009. As of October 2009, 139 journalists had died in Iraq since the U.S. invasion began in March 2003. Well over half of the journalists who died during the Iraq war were deliberately murdered as opposed to dying in battles.[83]

"The deaths in Iraq reflect the utter deterioration in reporters' traditional status as neutral observers in wartime," said Committee to Protect Journalists executive director Joel Simon. "When this conflict began . . . , most journalists died in combat-related incidents. Now, insurgents routinely target journalists."[84] This continues a trend that started with the murder of popular *Wall Street Journal* reporter Daniel Pearl back in 2002. The videotape discovered on February 25, 2002, showed Pearl being stabbed to death and then decapitated. Pearl had been kidnapped in Pakistan on January 23 while attempting to reach a radical Islamic cleric for an interview.[85] But the story he was chasing was apparently a trap designed by a group calling itself the National Movement of Pakistani Sovereignty.[86] Four men were eventually captured and convicted in Pakistani courts for his kidnapping and murder. Pearl and his wife, Mariane, a freelance broadcast journalist, had arrived in Pakistan shortly after the September 11, 2001, attacks. He was covering the country as part of his job as the *Journal*'s South Asia bureau chief.

Mariane Pearl says that her husband's kidnapping was not a typical one in which the goal is ransom or exchange. "My feeling is that the killing of Danny was more of a declaration of war."[87] Why Pearl was murdered is not clear. His widow speculates that it could have been for a story he had written or something he was working on. He may have simply been a symbol of the West.

Terry Anderson, an Associated Press reporter who was kidnapped in Lebanon in 1985 and held hostage for seven years, asks, "Why would anyone undertake this kind of work?" He finds the answer within Pearl's life. At the time of his kidnapping, Pearl was determined to try to understand why a man would pack his shoes with explosives before boarding an airplane. Anderson says that correspondents like Pearl put themselves at risk because they believe in reporting the truth:

*A portrait of Daniel Pearl rendered in the distinctive style of the* Wall Street Journal *is displayed along with a candle prior to a memorial service for the murdered journalist.*

> They believe it is better for you to know that such things happen than not to know. They believe it is better for you to see the faces of the victims, almost always innocent children and women, and to hear their voices than to let them die ignored and unrecognized. They believe that if they can just make you pay attention, your horror and anger and outrage will match theirs, and you will demand that such things stop. And sometimes, they are right.[88]

For more on the dangers reporters face on the job, visit http://ralphehanson.com.

## The Alternative Press

Throughout this chapter we have emphasized mainstream, corporate-run, big-city newspapers. But there are also a wide range of **alternative papers** that serve specialized audiences ranging from racial and ethnic minorities, to gays and lesbians, to young people.

*Contemporary Minority/Ethnic Papers.* The African American press has had a significant presence in the United States since at least 1827. Nearly 4,000 black newspapers have been published in the United States at one time or another.[89]

*Freedom's Journal* was among the first black newspapers; it was founded in 1827 to show all readers, white and black, that "black citizens were humans who were being treated unjustly."[90] Many black editors of the era faced great danger when they printed articles that contained fact-based accusations against whites. Mobs would destroy the newspaper's offices, and editors who had not left town might be murdered.

**alternative papers**
Weekly newspapers that serve specialized audiences ranging from racial minorities, to gays and lesbians, to young people.

Editors of black papers faced further difficulties because much of the intended audience for the papers was illiterate. Moreover, because the majority of the audience was poor, relatively little advertising was available. These editors put their lives and livelihoods at risk publishing a paper that few might read and that probably would lose money.

A variety of emancipation papers followed in the footsteps of *Freedom's Journal*, but none had as great an impact as the *North Star*, which published its first issue in Rochester, New York, on December 3, 1847. Its editor, Frederick Douglass, was known as a gifted writer, and his new paper let readers know that it would be fighting for an end to slavery and the recognition of the rights of blacks. The *North Star* was read and noticed, but it faced the same problems as earlier black papers, including anti-black violence, a shortage of qualified staff, and a chronic lack of money. What it did have was a clear mission and a distinctive journalistic style. The *North Star* was published from 1847 until 1860.[91]

Another important African American paper is the *Chicago Defender*. Founded in 1905, the *Defender* was considerably less serious than the *North Star*, modeling its style on the yellow journalism of William Randolph Hearst. It was designed to be a black paper with a mass following rather than a publication for black intellectuals and white elites. It was also designed to appeal to advertisers and even make money for its publisher.

Clearly, the *Defender*'s goals included profit as well as advocacy. The paper was sensational, with large red headlines trumpeting stories of crime. By 1920 the *Defender* had a circulation of more than 280,000, a spectacular number at the time. It reached far beyond Chicago, with two-thirds of its readers outside the city.[92]

The *Defender* encouraged southern blacks to move north to find jobs in Chicago and, not coincidentally, become loyal subscribers to the paper. In retaliation, it was banned throughout the South, and at least two of the paper's distributors were murdered. *Defender* editor Robert Abbott fought for civil rights and an end to lynchings. Abbott, born in 1868, has been credited with founding "the modern Negro press."[93] He demonstrated that black papers could be profit-making institutions as well as activist publications.

In the 1950s the *Defender* became a daily tabloid. For a while it provided extensive, day-by-day coverage of the civil rights movement. In 2003 the *Defender* and three other papers owned by relatives of Abbott were sold to Real Times, Inc., following the death of long-time publisher and editor John H. Sengstacke in 1997.[94]

What makes a black paper authentically black? In his book *The Black Press, U.S.A.*, Roland Wolseley suggests several qualifications: The paper must be owned and managed by blacks, it must be intended for black readers, and it must be an activist for the black community.[95]

Spanish-language newspapers are also doing well. While their circulation is declining—as is the case with newspapers across the board—their advertising revenue is growing, most of which is from local advertising.[96] *El Nuevo Herald*, published as a companion to the *Miami Herald*, is the United States' largest Spanish-language paper, with a circulation in excess of 80,000. But the two papers are different in much more than just the language. Journalist Dan Grech, speaking on the NPR radio show *On the Media*, said, "The *Miami Herald*, like most U.S. newspapers, prizes objectivity. *El Nuevo Herald* is more like papers in Latin America and Europe that push for social change."[97]

For more about the *Defender*, *El Nuevo Herald*, and other ethnic newspapers, visit http://ralphehan son.com.

John Sengstacke, part owner and manager of the Chicago Defender, *a leading African American newspaper with a national circulation in the middle of the twentieth century, reviews layouts with an assistant.*

***The Gay Press.*** The question of authenticity is a difficult one for the entire alternative press, not just for ethnic papers. How can a paper represent the interests and concerns of a particular group yet still operate as a profitable commercial venture? This question has been particularly problematic for the gay press.

The *Washington Blade* was the oldest and biggest gay weekly paper in the country.[98] It was started in 1969 as a one-page mimeograph that was distributed in several gay bars at a time when such establishments were routinely raided by police. More recently, a typical edition of the *Blade* ran to more than 100 pages, with news about health as well as legal and political issues. In the early 1990s one of the key features of the *Blade* was the large number of obituaries of men who had died of AIDS; these have become much less numerous in recent years. The *Blade* became such a success that it expanded outside the District of Columbia in 1997 with the *New York Blade News*.

But in 2009 the recession hit the media industry hard, including the lesbian/gay/bisexual/transgender (LGBT) press. The most prominent of the gay papers to be affected was the *Washington Blade*. Just weeks after the *Blade*'s fortieth anniversary party, the paper's parent company, Window Media, shut down after investors were unable to meet financial requirements from their Small Business Administration financing. With the closing of Window Media, a number of gay papers across the country were shuttered, along with the *Blade*. The *New York Blade News* also ceased publication in 2009, when its parent company, HX Media, closed.[99]

Why did these previously successful publications fail? There are several likely reasons:

- Like many media companies in the late 2000s, the owners of LGBT newspapers were facing severe financial problems. Even though the *Washington Blade* was reportedly turning a profit up until the time it closed, its parent company was not.

- The audiences for LGBT media were early adopters of online social media and Web-based publications.

- Gay culture has moved into the mainstream. Remember Truth Three—Everything from the margin moves to the center. When gay and lesbian papers were founded in the 1960s and 1970s, reporters at the papers feared for their personal safety. Reporter Lou Chibbaro Jr., who had been with the *Blade* since 1976, told the *Washington Post* that, over the course of his career there, he had gone from writing under an assumed name in the 1970s to sitting in the front row at a presidential press conference in 2009. With gay and lesbian issues increasingly being covered by Big Media, there may not be the same demand for gay-specific newspapers now.[100]

The trend of gay publications moving to the mainstream has been an ongoing one. In the 2000s, there was an extensive debate in New York over whether straight-owned papers could adequately cover the LGBT community. In a 1997 interview with *Editor & Publisher* magazine, Troy Masters, the former publisher of a gay-owned New York newspaper, laid out the issue clearly in a way that could apply equally well to culture- or community-specific alternative papers outside the gay community:

> There needs to be a hard look at whether or not a publication that serves a specific group of people—whether they're of a certain race, nationality, sexual orientation, or whatever—can be owned and run by people who are not from that place. Do they truly understand the culture they're getting involved with, to treat the business the way it needs to be treated and to be sensitive to those they're trying to reach? It's very important, I think, for those kinds of publications to be treated first as a culture, and lastly as a marketplace.[101]

*"Underground Papers."*    A third kind of alternative paper is the so-called alternative weekly. When these papers got started in the 1960s and 1970s, they were known first as underground newspapers, then as alternative weeklies. Today some prefer to be called just weeklies.[102] Among the popular weeklies now are the Chicago *Reader*, the Boston *Phoenix*, and the New Times chain.

Alternative weeklies present a stark contrast to the traditional urban newspapers in that they continue to grow in circulation. Among the Association of Alternative Weeklies, average circulation reached 7.64 million in 2005.[103]

Although much of the content of these papers is relatively mainstream, the advertising often includes messages for phone sex, personals, and massage parlors. Many of these papers, depending solely on ad revenues, are distributed free. They attract young people who have left behind daily newspapers and network news in favor of CNN, MSNBC, Fox News, and the Internet.

Just as mainstream newspapers are bought up by corporate newspaper chains, so are alternative papers consolidated in alternative chains. This trend raises the question of whether these feisty papers will retain their independence and unique voice after becoming part of corporate America, or if they will lose the qualities that made them popular in the first place. For example, in some cases new owners have blocked potentially offensive cartoons and April Fool's Day editions. However, advertisers like the young, affluent readership these weekly papers can deliver, and they have expressed concern that watered-down content will lead to reduced reader interest.[104]

When the first edition of this book came out, there were two major alternative chains: New Times, based in Phoenix, Arizona, publishes at least ten papers, and Stern Publishing of New York, which produces the most established alternative newspaper, the *Village Voice*, publishes at least seven papers. The *Village Voice*, founded in 1955, has a weekly circulation of 247,502, by far the largest of all the alternative weeklies in the country. *Phoenix New Times*, established in 1970, has a weekly circulation of 132,000. In 2005 New Times merged with the *Village Voice* chain. The new combined company controls about 14 percent of the circulation of alternative weekly papers.[105]

# THE FUTURE OF NEWSPAPERS

Trying to make sense of what is happening to the newspaper business is difficult, in part because of Truth Two—There are no mainstream media. Some of the most visible segments of the newspaper business are facing major challenges, which critics are fond of pointing out. But other portions of the business, especially the more rural community papers, are thriving. So to understand the changing newspaper market we have to look at it as several media, not just one.

## Are Newspapers a Dying Medium?

There can be no doubt that the business of the major urban newspapers is changing. They are losing circulation, cutting back on staff, and facing pressure from stockholders to give a better return on investment. On the other hand, the newspapers that can be seen as national in scope (the *Wall Street Journal,* the

New York Times, and USA Today) are holding tight in terms of paid circulation and readership. And smaller newspapers in more rural areas are also doing well. The big problem is with the major urban papers.

The afternoon dailies were the first to feel the effects of the changing media landscape. Afternoon papers, especially the giant papers published by Hearst and Pulitzer, were enormously popular in the early 1900s. These papers were bought by factory workers who started their jobs too early to read a paper in the morning and preferred to buy papers on their way home. Today, however, afternoon papers don't fit neatly into most people's schedules. Morning papers are still convenient and valued, but afternoon papers have to compete with the evening television news. Also, it is easier for morning papers to provide up-to-date coverage. Not much happens overnight as the morning paper is being put together, but the afternoon paper's news is already old. Distribution is also difficult because of heavy traffic during the day, something that morning papers, which go out between midnight and four in the morning, don't have to worry about.[106]

Most of the job losses have been at the major urban papers. According to the 2006 Project for Excellence in Journalism report, the top three newspapers lost no circulation, and the loss at the smaller newspapers was "modest." The big-city papers that have to cover a large metro area and host of suburbs are the ones in trouble. The problem is that these big papers can serve "as watchdogs over state, regional and urban institutions, to identify trends, and to define the larger community public square."[107] A good example of a paper undertaking this watchdog function is the Washington Post's stories about the substandard conditions and care for injured Iraq war veterans at Walter Reed military hospital. In addition to being an important national story, it was also an important local story for the Washington, D.C., area. (You can find links to these stories at http://ralphehanson.com.)

A few of these papers have suspended their paper editions and become exclusively Web-based publications. Among the most prominent of these was the Christian Science Monitor in April 2009.[108] It's hard to imagine a newspaper without paper, but it's a trend that's been going on for some time. For close to ten years, Arthur Sulzberger of the New York Times has been saying that the Times is no longer in the business of

The Christian Science Monitor suspended its paper publication in April 2009 and became a Web-only news outlet.

putting black ink on white paper and then selling it to people. Instead, the *New York Times* is in the news business and the ad sales business, and they are going to be delivering news and advertising in whatever forms make it profitable for them to do so.[109] (This issue is discussed further in Chapter 10.) Another paper to go Web-only was the *Seattle Post-Intelligencer*, which stopped publication in March 2009 but retained a reduced Web presence dominated by commentary.[110]

The change at the *Monitor* to all-electronic distribution is not as radical as some observers are claiming. Although the *Monitor* has had a substantial presence on the Web, its daily circulation of approximately 50,000 copies was relatively small compared to either *USA Today* or the *Wall Street Journal*, both of whom measure their circulation with the word *million* attached. The *Monitor's* importance comes not from its size but rather from its overall reputation as one of the country's best papers. Its Web site attracts about 1.5 million page views per month.[111]

Other papers have shut down completely. Colorado's oldest newspaper, the *Rocky Mountain News*, closed on February 27, 2009, when owner E. W. Scripps Co. was unable to find a buyer. The *Rocky* had a reputation as a lively tabloid that was still a solid, respectable paper, having won four Pulitzer Prizes since 2000. The paper had operated under a joint operating agreement with the *Denver Post*, under which the two papers shared business and publication facilities but had rival news operations.[112]

## Newspapers and the Web

When television news started to become popular in the 1950s, newspapers were gradually forced away from a reliance on **breaking news**—an ongoing news story that requires frequent updating. With only one or two editions a day, there was no way a newspaper could compete with television, which can update ongoing news continuously. But the Web has changed the picture dramatically. Now morning newspapers like the *Washington Post* can publish updates throughout the day not subject to the disadvantages of a traditional afternoon paper.[113] And when a breaking story calls for continual updating, a paper's Web site can provide those updates as well.

**breaking news**
An ongoing news story that requires frequent updating.

*Breaking News Online.*   The *Dallas Morning News* is one of the papers that pioneered the use of the Web to break news. Two stories brought the *Morning News* and its Web site to national attention. The first was a breaking story revealing that Oklahoma City bombing suspect Timothy McVeigh had confessed to a private investigator about the bombing of the Alfred P. Murrah federal building. The story was controversial. Some felt that it would prejudice McVeigh's chances of obtaining a fair trial, but the editors at the *Morning News* believed that they had an obligation to publish it.[114] Rather than waiting for the next day's edition, editors ran the story on the paper's Web site at 3:15 p.m. on February 28, 1997. This was history in the making because it was the first time a newspaper broke

## TEST YOUR MEDIA LITERACY

### Can Journalists Be on Social Media?

Everyone needs to be careful about revealing too much through social media like Twitter or Facebook, but journalists see this as a particularly difficult issue because of fears of alienating sources and readers.

*Wall Street Journal* reporters are not supposed to post about how a story was reported. The paper's code of conduct says: "Let our coverage speak for itself, and don't detail how an article was reported, written or edited." Reporters are also required to get their editor's permission before friending a confidential source.[1]

The BBC has fairly elaborate guidelines on using social media, especially when they identify themselves as BBC employees. One rule suggests that BBC employees should not include a political identification online, even if they don't indicate that they work for the BBC.[2]

Even tweets intended for a limited, private audience can be problematic. Raju Narisetti, one of two managing editors for the *Washington Post*, discontinued his personal Twitter account after questions about his tweets were raised by *Post* staff members. One of the tweets in question read, "We can incur all sorts of federal deficits for wars and what not, but we have to promise not to increase it by $1 for healthcare reform? Sad." Another read, "Sen Byrd (91) in hospital after he falls from 'standing up too quickly.' How about term limits. Or retirement age. Or commonsense to prevail."[3]

The *Washington Post* issued guidelines in fall 2009 about what editorial employees ought to be posting online. The guidelines read, in part:

> When using [social networks], nothing we do must call into question the impartiality of our news judgment. We never abandon the guidelines that govern the separation of news from opinion, the importance of fact and objectivity, the appropriate use of language and tone, and other hallmarks of our brand of journalism.
>
> What you do on social networks should be presumed to be publicly available to anyone, even if you have created a private account. It is possible to use privacy controls online to limit access to sensitive information. But such controls are only a deterrent, not an absolute insulator. Reality is simple: If you don't want something to be found online, don't put it there.
>
> *Post* journalists must refrain from writing, tweeting or posting anything—including photographs or video—that could be perceived as reflecting political, racial, sexist, religious or other bias or favoritism that could be used to tarnish our journalistic credibility.[4]

*Washington Post* media reporter Howard Kurtz joked on his Twitter account that "Under new WP guidelines on tweeting, I will now hold forth only on the

**MORE online**

You can read more about these social media policies at **http://ralphehanson .com**.

weather and dessert recipes." In a blog post about the Twitter guidelines, Kurtz listed his own, informal rules for his Twitter account:[5]

> Don't say something that makes you look like a blithering idiot.
>
> Don't appear to be in the pocket of Democrats or Republicans....
>
> Stick to subjects on which you actually have a clue.
>
> Refrain from boring people with the minutiae of your daily life.
>
> Don't say anything you couldn't defend as fair analysis in print or on the air.

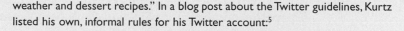

### Who are the sources?

You have looked at codes of conduct for journalists' use of social media at several major news organizations from around the world. What are these news organizations? How do they differ from each other?

### What are they saying?

These codes of conduct tell reporters under what circumstances they can make posts on social media such as Twitter and Facebook. What kinds of rules do they expect reporters to follow? What happens to journalists who violate these standards?

### What kind of evidence indicates that journalists misuse social media?

What examples do the news organizations give to illustrate the problem of journalists misusing social media? What harm do they say this will bring to the news organization?

### How do you and your classmates react to journalists using social media?

Do you or your classmates follow the social media feeds of any journalists? What do you discover about them from their tweets or Facebook posts? Do you think that journalists risk appearing biased by what they post to their social media feeds? Do you think it is right for news organizations to restrict how journalists use their social media accounts?

[1] Diane Brady, "What's the Right Corporate Policy for Twitter, Facebook and Blogs?" *Business Week*, May 14, 2009, www.businessweek.com/careers/managementiq/archives/2009/05/whats_the_right.html.

[2] BBC, "Editorial Guidelines," www.bbc.co.uk/guidelines/editorialguidelines/advice/personalweb.

[3] Andrew Alexander, "*Post* Editor Ends Tweets as New Guidelines Are Issued," *Washington Post*, September 25, 2009, voices.washingtonpost.com/ombudsman-blog/2009/09/post_editor_ends_tweets_as_new.html?wprss=ombudsman-blog.

[4] Ibid.

[5] Howard Kurtz, "To Tweet or Not to Tweet," WashingtonPost.com, October 1, 2009, www.washingtonpost.com/wp-dyn/content/article/2009/10/01/AR2009100101537.html.

a major story on its Web site rather than on the front page of the paper itself. That evening the story was headline news on CNN, and each time the story ran, it was attributed to the *Dallas Morning News*.

Why was the story published initially on the Web site rather than in the paper? A number of explanations have been suggested. Publishing the story on the Web eliminated the possibility of a broadcast organization or another paper achieving a **scoop**—a news story that a news organization reports well ahead of its competitors. The editors figured that as long as they had the story, they should publish it as quickly as possible. Others argued that as long as the story had the *Morning News* brand on it, it didn't matter where the paper published it. What mattered was that the paper received credit for it. Finally, it has been suggested that the paper chose the Web so that McVeigh's attorneys would be unable to obtain a restraining order against the paper that would stop it from publishing the story.[115]

The second major story to draw attention to the *Morning News* Web site was not one that the paper was proud of. The paper published the story that a witness had seen President Bill Clinton and White House intern Monica Lewinsky in a "compromising" situation; the story appeared in the first edition of the paper and on its Web site. But then the source retracted the story. In running the story, the paper broke its own rule that stories from unnamed sources must be confirmed by a second, separate source. Because of a communication mix-up, the Dallas office mistakenly believed that the Washington office had that confirmation.[116] The *Morning News* pulled the story, but the damage had already been done because the story was picked up from the paper's Web site and swept across the country. It was then broadcast on radio, television, and cable. This was a major embarrassment for the paper and a prime example of a modern difficulty: When stories are posted on the Web, errors may be reproduced nationwide instead of being confined to a single city.[117]

These two stories illustrate both the advantage and the danger of newspapers going online—the Web puts them back in the breaking-news business, but it also makes them more vulnerable to the types of errors broadcast news operations face in trying to be first. (For more on how news organizations can run into trouble under deadline, see Chapter 14's discussion of the media coverage of the Sago Mine Disaster.)

*What the Web Offers Newspapers.* What do people look for in online news? First, they want national and international news, followed by business, sports, and entertainment. They are also looking for credibility, something that can be in short supply on the Web.

Newspaper Web sites are particularly good at presenting interactive features on breaking news. Readers of the *Chicago Tribune* can type in their address and see what their ballot will look like before going to the polls. And the *Denver Post* offers video, photos, and podcasts through its Web site. The paper's library of

**scoop**
A news story that a news organization reports well ahead of its competitors.

podcasts—downloadable audio programs that can be listened to on an iPod or other MP3 player—is wide ranging, including local, national, business, and sports news, as well as original arts programming.

Will the Web replace newspapers in the near future, as some writers suggest? Daniel Rosensweig, president of the online computer news site ZDNet, doubts it: "I think history has shown that one medium doesn't necessarily replace another medium. It actually expands the number of people who come in and use information."[118] According to the Pew Research Center for the People and the Press, roughly 30 percent of people go to the Internet for news on a regular basis. Who are these people? It's not primarily teens who ignore the old media; instead the people who are going online for news generally seek multiple news sources and they use the Web to supplement their news diet. Some do go to newspaper Web sites for news, but more go to MSNBC, Yahoo, and CNN. Of course, when they go to Yahoo for news, they are getting a range of news sources that Yahoo brings together on a single page.[119]

New sources of news are the little electronic devices so many of us carry—cell phones, personal digital assistants (PDAs; for example, Blackberry or Palm Pilot), and iPods. An iPod as a news channel? Lots of news programs, such as those mentioned earlier from the *Denver Post*, are now available as download-able podcasts that can be listened to on portable music players. Many papers, such as the *Washington Post* and *USA Today*, have special editions of their Web sites designed for mobile device accessibility. So far, blogs have had more of an influence on the press than on the public at large, with only 4 percent of adults reporting reading blogs on a regular basis in 2006. It is clear, however, that blog use will grow rapidly in the coming years.[120]

Throughout all this growth, the amount of time adults spend with the news has stayed relatively stable—about sixty-seven minutes a day. What has changed is the number of sources consumers have to turn to for that consumption.

## CHAPTERSummary

The first newspapers were published in Europe in the seventeenth century. Numerous papers were published in the American colonies, but they faced extensive censorship from the British government. Newspapers printed before the nineteenth century tended to be partisan publications that were supported through high subscription fees and political subsidies. This changed with the rise of the penny press in the 1830s. The penny papers were mass produced on steam-powered printing presses and contained news of interest to ordinary people. The papers cost one or two cents and were supported by advertisers who wanted to reach the papers' large numbers of readers.

The late nineteenth and early twentieth centuries were characterized by the yellow journalism of the New York newspapers published by Joseph Pulitzer and William Randolph Hearst. The two publishers tried to attract circulation and attention by running comic strips, advice columns, and sensational stories about sex, crime, and scandal. This was also the time when newspapers started running extensive headlines and illustrations.

The major classes of newspapers today include the following:

- National papers that attempt to cover issues of interest to the entire country, such as *USA Today* and the *Wall Street Journal.*
- Metropolitan papers that cover a particular city, such as the *New York Times* and the *Washington Post.*
- Community papers that serve a particular town or suburb and provide news that readers cannot get elsewhere.
- Alternative newspapers that serve specialized populations rather than a broad, general audience. These can serve ethnic populations within a community, groups such as gays and lesbians, or even young people who are not interested in traditional newspapers.

Evolving technology has brought changes to the newspaper business. The rise of television news resulted in a decline in the number of afternoon newspapers, and changes in news consumption patterns have drawn audiences and advertisers away from both newspapers and broadcast television news. The Web has given newspapers new opportunities to update the news rapidly and new ways to deliver the news. Whatever the method of delivery, reporters struggle with the issue of objectivity, especially when the story is close to home and when they are risking their lives to report the news.

## KEY Terms

## CONCEPT Review

Reporter objectivity and detachment
Tradition of journalistic independence
Advertising-supported media
Changing newspaper market
Consequences of corporate ownership of newspapers
Determining the proper role for the alternative press
Balancing serving investors, advertisers, and readers
Risks of reporting from a war zone
New media versus old sources of news

# Audio
## Music and Talk Across Media

**CHAPTER 7**

**This is the story** of two artists: the band Erik Goes to Germany and singer Katrina Leskanich. They couldn't be more different. One is a group you've likely never heard of. The other fronted a hugely popular band back in the 1980s. Neither of them currently has a recording contract. Both are distributing and promoting their music using the same tools in the long-tail part of the audio industry.

Erik Goes to Germany is a pop punk band made up of a group of friends who recently completed high school. "The band got started the summer of our junior year when my best friend Erik went to Germany for the year," says band founder Cody Cheesebrough. "I thought, I'm going to get really bored, so I got a MacBook so I could record music."[1] Cheesebrough and his friends started writing songs and recording them using

Erik Goes
to Germany

Katrina Leskanich

Apple's Garage Band software. The band has since become more sophisticated in their recording, using industry-standard software Pro Tools 8 and Reason 4.

In addition to recording, the band has played a number of shows in the Morgantown, West Virginia, area.

Erik Goes to Germany is a prime example of a major new part of the audio industry—the bands inhabiting the long tail of the music industry. Remember, the long tail is a statistical term that refers to the portion of a distribution curve in which a limited number of people are interested in buying a lot of different products. This is opposed to the short-head portion of the curve, in which a large number of people are interested in buying a limited number of products.

In the past, unsigned bands with little to no money would have few opportunities to get their music before a larger audience. Perhaps, if they were lucky, they might get a local radio station to play one of their songs, but that would be about it. But no matter where you are, you could be listening to Erik Goes to Germany's music in a matter of minutes or buying a copy of their latest CD. A quick search on Google will point you to the band's pages on social networking sites MySpace, Facebook, and Pure Volume. Distribution of the band's music is handled by CD Baby, which sells the music through its own Web site as well as iTunes, Amazon.com, Napster, and other online music stores.

If you think back to Chapter 3—The Media Business—you'll remember that the long tail has some key characteristics:

- Democratization of the means of production—Erik Goes to Germany records its music, and enhances it, using readily available software on Cheesebrough's Mac-Book computer. His computer is a bottom-of-the-line Apple laptop computer that he uses to do homework, surf the Internet, and record music by his band.

- Democratization of the means of distribution—The band distributes its music using the music player on its MySpace page. Musicians of a lot of different levels use this tool. It has the advantage of being completely free. This is important because Cheesebrough's main source of income is from a local summer job he's working before heading off to college. So far, the band's most popular song has had more than 6,000 plays.

- Lowering the cost of connecting suppliers and consumers to near zero—Erik Goes to Germany is promoting itself through MySpace, a Facebook group, and iTunes, none of which costs band members anything.

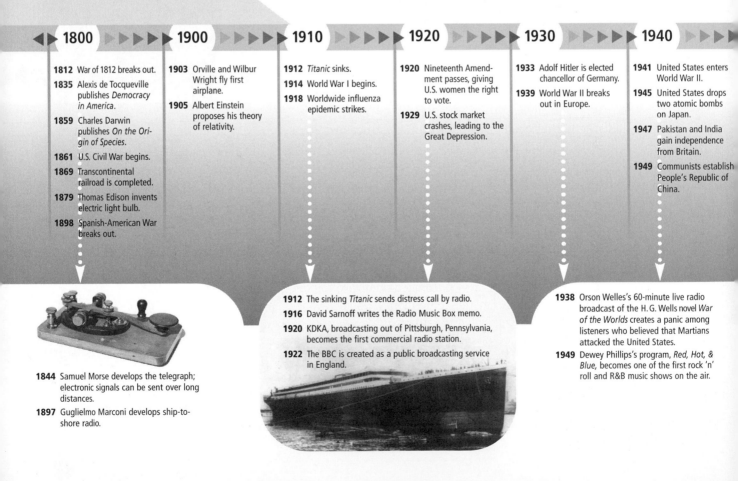

**1800** ▶▶▶▶ **1900** ▶▶▶▶ **1910** ▶▶▶▶ **1920** ▶▶▶▶ **1930** ▶▶▶▶ **1940** ▶▶▶

**1812** War of 1812 breaks out.
**1835** Alexis de Tocqueville publishes *Democracy in America*.
**1859** Charles Darwin publishes *On the Origin of Species*.
**1861** U.S. Civil War begins.
**1869** Transcontinental railroad is completed.
**1879** Thomas Edison invents electric light bulb.
**1898** Spanish-American War breaks out.

**1903** Orville and Wilbur Wright fly first airplane.
**1905** Albert Einstein proposes his theory of relativity.

**1912** *Titanic* sinks.
**1914** World War I begins.
**1918** Worldwide influenza epidemic strikes.

**1920** Nineteenth Amendment passes, giving U.S. women the right to vote.
**1929** U.S. stock market crashes, leading to the Great Depression.

**1933** Adolf Hitler is elected chancellor of Germany.
**1939** World War II breaks out in Europe.

**1941** United States enters World War II.
**1945** United States drops two atomic bombs on Japan.
**1947** Pakistan and India gain independence from Britain.
**1949** Communists establish People's Republic of China.

**1844** Samuel Morse develops the telegraph; electronic signals can be sent over long distances.
**1897** Guglielmo Marconi develops ship-to-shore radio.

**1912** The sinking *Titanic* sends distress call by radio.
**1916** David Sarnoff writes the Radio Music Box memo.
**1920** KDKA, broadcasting out of Pittsburgh, Pennsylvania, becomes the first commercial radio station.
**1922** The BBC is created as a public broadcasting service in England.

**1938** Orson Welles's 60-minute live radio broadcast of the H. G. Wells novel *War of the Worlds* creates a panic among listeners who believed that Martians attacked the United States.
**1949** Dewey Phillips's program, *Red, Hot, & Blue*, becomes one of the first rock 'n' roll and R&B music shows on the air.

Although Erik Goes to Germany's members can't quit their day jobs, it is, Cheeseborough says, "always a nice surprise when I check the band's CD Baby account and there's money there."[2]

Now for Katrina Leskanich. If you lived through the 1980s, you likely remember the Katrina and the Waves summer anthem "Walking on Sunshine." And even those too young to have noticed it the first time around have probably heard it in movie sound-tracks and on TV shows. The band had several other modest hits in the United States and the United Kingdom.

But now Ms. Leskanich, the band's lead singer, is fifty-plus years old. And fresh-faced stars of the 1980s aren't going to get a lot of attention from the music industry twenty-five years later. Her latest album, *Walking on Sunshine*, was released independently in February 2009. It's received little, if any, radio airplay, but it was featured on the popular podcast *Coverville*. You won't find a copy of the CD at your local music retailer, but you can find it on Amazon.com as either a download or a burn-to-order CD, or you can buy a download from iTunes.[3] An alternative version of the album was released through CD Baby, the same company that distributes Erik Goes to Germany's music.

## Timeline

**1950**

- **1950** Korean War begins.
- **1953** Francis Crick and James Watson discover structure of DNA.
- **1957** Soviet Union launches spacecraft *Sputnik I*.

**1960**

- **1963** Martin Luther King Jr. delivers "I Have a Dream" speech during Washington, D.C., civil-rights march.
- **1969** Neil Armstrong walks on the moon.

**1970**

- **1974** U.S. president Richard Nixon resigns due to Watergate scandal.
- **1975** Vietnam War ends.
- **1977** Apple II personal computer is introduced.
- **1978** First test-tube baby is born.

**1980**

- **1983** First HIV/AIDS cases are documented.
- **1985** Ozone hole is discovered over Antarctica.
- **1986** Space shuttle *Challenger* explodes.
- **1989** The Berlin Wall falls.

**1990**

- **1991** Soviet Union disbands.
- **1993** European Union is formed.
- **1994** Nelson Mandela is elected president of South Africa.
- **1997** Diana, Princess of Wales, dies in car accident.

**2000**

- **2001** Al Qaida attacks World Trade Center and Pentagon.
- **2003** United States invades Iraq.
- **2003** Human genome project is completed.
- **2005** Terrorists bomb London's transport system.
- **2005** Hurricane Katrina hits the U.S. Gulf Coast.
- **2008** Barack Obama is elected U.S. president.

- **1959** DJ Alan Freed, among others, called to testify before a congressional committee about payola in the radio business.
- **1964** The "British Invasion," exemplified by the Beatles, the Rolling Stones, and the Who, transforms rock 'n' roll music.

- **1971** National Public Radio starts broadcasting with the evening news show *All Things Considered*.
- **1979** Sony introduces the Walkman portable cassette player.
- **1982** The compact disc launches in Europe.
- **1987** WFAN becomes the country's first all-sports radio station.

- **1995** The first MP3s are available on the Internet.
- **1996** The Telecommunications Act of 1996 leads to increased concentration of radio ownership.
- **2005** iTunes software begins to support podcasting.
- **2006** Shock jock Howard Stern leaves terrestrial radio for satellite broadcasting.
- **2007** Talk show host Don Imus is fired from CBS and MSNBC for making racist comments on the air.
- **2008** Sirius and XM merge, creating a single satellite radio service in the United States.

Katrina Leskanich, like Erik Goes to Germany, is a long-tail artist. She started out as a performer who had a good short-head career, making hit records for major labels. But now Leskanich is much more a niche artist, distributing her music through digital downloads and promoting her music through online tools. Both artists are prime examples of what's happening in the audio industry today. Programming is no longer the exclusive product of Big Media.

In this chapter we look at how the recording industry and radio developed together as our first electronic media. We then examine how society has changed, how cultures have grown and merged, and how audience members have responded to the production of shared music and talk. Finally, we look at where the industries are headed in the twenty-first century.

# HISTORY OF SOUND RECORDING AND TRANSMISSION

Before there could be mass consumption of popular music, there had to be a means of recording and distributing it. The means evolved from Thomas Edison's early efforts with the phonograph, through the development of the gramophone, and later the LP and the compact disc. The recording industry changed the way people consumed music. Before the phonograph and gramophone, the only way to experience music was to perform it yourself or go to a concert. The invention of the record meant that recordings of professional musicians became the standard way to hear music.

## Storing Musical Performances: The Development of the Recording Industry

A variety of stories have been told about Thomas Edison and his invention of an early sound recording machine, the **phonograph**, in 1877. One version has Edison giving a sketch of the phonograph to employee John Kruesi with the instruction, "the machine must talk."[4] Another has Edison sketching the phonograph, with a note at the bottom telling his assistant to "build this."[5]

*Edison's First Recordings.* These stories do not do justice to Edison's true genius or to the difficulties of creating a machine that would record and play back the voice. Running through these myths is the mistaken notion that Edison came up with an idea for sound recording that worked perfectly the first time it was tried. In reality, Edison and his assistants probably worked as long as ten months on the problem of the phonograph before they finally succeeded in

**phonograph**
An early sound-recording machine invented by Thomas Edison; the recorded material was played back on a cylinder.

recording Sarah Josepha Hale's children's rhyme, "Mary Had a Little Lamb." This famous first recording lasted no more than ten seconds.[6]

*Emile Berliner: Mass-Produced Music.*    As with so many media inventions, no one was quite sure what to do with Edison's phonograph. Edison envisioned it as a dictation machine. Reproducing music was only number four on his list of uses.[7] The biggest flaw with his invention was that Edison's foil cylinders did not hold up to repeated playing and could not be reproduced. It took the work of a young German immigrant to make the phonograph a truly practical device.

Emile Berliner arrived in the United States in 1870 at the age of nineteen. By 1888 he had developed a method for recording sound on flat discs rather than on cylinders. Berliner's disc recordings (or records) were louder and more lifelike than the cylinder recordings of Edison or Bell. He called his device the **gramophone**. Eventually, however, all record players were called phonographs.

Berliner also helped develop the idea of the recording industry. With Edison's phonograph, every recording was an original. Berliner viewed his invention not as a business dictating machine but as an entertainment device. His discs could be reproduced from the original etched-zinc master, allowing publishers to mass produce high-quality—at least for the time—musical recordings almost as easily as printers could reproduce books. Because of this, Berliner saw that "prominent singers, speakers, or performers may derive an income from royalties on the sale of their phonautograms."[8]

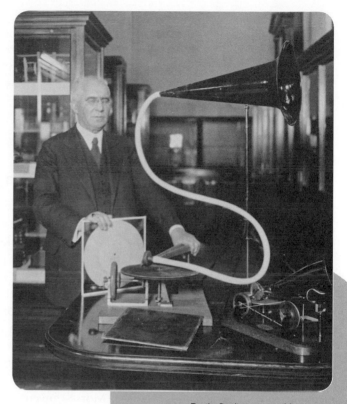

Emile Berliner was able to turn Thomas Edison's idea for a phonograph into a commercially viable product that lasted in one form or another for more than 100 years.

**gramophone**

A machine invented by Emile Berliner that could play prerecorded sound on flat discs rather than cylinders.

**high fidelity (hi-fi)**

A combination of technologies that allowed recordings to reproduce music more accurately with higher high notes and deeper bass than was possible with previous recording technologies.

*A New Way of Publishing Music.*    By 1935 the term **high fidelity (hi-fi)** was being used to refer to a combination of technologies that allowed recordings that reproduced music more accurately, with higher high notes and deeper bass, than previous forms of recording had allowed. One of the developments that helped pave the way for hi-fi was the electric phonograph (along with the amplifier and loudspeakers), which was replacing the all-mechanical gramophone. By 1949 magnetic tape recorders were commonplace in recording studios. Musicians no longer had to record directly onto discs.

The phonograph changed the face of music. Previously, there were only two ways to store music. The first, and oldest, was for parents to teach their children

**non-notated music**
Music such as a folk song or jazz solo that does not exist in written form.

**telegraph**
The first system for using wires to send messages at a distance; invented by Samuel Morse in 1844.

**wireless telegraph**
Guglielmo Marconi's name for his point-to-point communication tool that used radio waves to transmit messages.

the traditional songs of their culture. The alternative was written music, or musical scores, that contained symbols for the musical notes to be played. The phonograph provided a revolutionary way of storing the actual music, not just the symbols written down by the composer. It also made possible the storage of **non-notated music**, such as folk songs or jazz solos, which did not necessarily exist in written form. Music scholar Charles Hamm compares the phonograph to a musical time machine that allows listeners to go back and hear the actual sounds.[9]

## Transmitting Music and Talk: The Birth of Radio

Around the time the recording industry was getting started, radio was under development as one of the first media to break through the barrier of space. With print media like books, magazines, and newspapers, the message being transmitted was always on a piece of paper that had to be carried from one place to another. Thus, the fastest form of transportation at the time was also the fastest channel of communication. This meant that it could take weeks for a message to cross the Atlantic or Pacific Ocean, or even to get from New York to California or from London to Moscow. But in the nineteenth century, several inventions would separate communication and transportation, starting with the wired media of the telegraph and telephone and moving on to the wireless technology of radio.

Samuel Morse's invention of the **telegraph** in 1844 allowed messages to be sent electrically, so that they didn't have to be carried from place to place. No longer did transportation set limits on communication. Messages could travel at the same speed as electrons traveling along a wire.[10] By 1866 a telegraph cable extended across the Atlantic Ocean, so that even that giant barrier had been conquered.

But the wire itself was a serious limitation. Telegraph wires could break (or be cut, as they frequently were during the American Civil War). To communicate with ships at sea, a *wireless* telegraph would be necessary.

In 1888 the German physicist Heinrich Hertz found that he could detect the signal created by an electrical spark on one side of a room with a small loop antenna on the other side. What he had created was essentially the simplest possible radio transmitter and receiver. In 1894 Guglielmo Marconi read about Hertz's work and concluded that he could create a **wireless telegraph**, a point-to-point communication tool that used radio waves to transmit messages. Over a period of several years he developed a system to send and receive radio signals, with the distance traveled by his signals expanding from the length of his attic to the width of the Atlantic Ocean.[11]

*Radio as Mass Communication.*    In 1901 physicist Reginald Fessenden started sending voice signals over a radio in his laboratory. On Christmas Eve in 1905, he broadcast poetry and Christmas carols. Since his continuously modulated voice signals could be received by the same equipment that received Morse code, wireless operators up and down the Atlantic coast heard Fessenden's amazing broadcast. Though it would be years before regularly scheduled commercial broadcasts would begin, Fessenden had set the stage for broadcasting something more than just Morse code.

Up to 1905, it was the scientists who were driving the radio business with their new technologies, but it was a young American Marconi employee who saw that radio could be much more than a way to send messages from one person to another. David Sarnoff, born in 1891, was a good student, but the need to help support his Russian-immigrant family led him to leave school after the eighth grade to work full time. In a story that seems almost too good to be true, the fifteen-year-old Sarnoff went to the *New York Herald* to try to get a job as a journalist. As luck would have it, the first person he met at the *Herald* building worked for a telegraph company. Sarnoff went to work for the Commercial Cable Company, and from that point on, he never left electronic media.[12]

*The Radio Music Box Memo.*   In 1915 Sarnoff addressed a document to the director of American Marconi that he considered the most important of his career, the so-called **Radio Music Box memo**, which outlined radio's potential as a popular mass medium. While Sarnoff did not invent the technology of radio and was not the first person to send out entertainment over the radio, he did summarize what radio could, and indeed did, become. Sarnoff's insight was that radio could be more than a point-to-point medium, a one-on-one form of communication. As Sarnoff saw it, what was then perceived as the great disadvantage of radio as a telegraph tool—that everyone who listened could hear the message—could be turned into an enormous advantage if one wanted to send out messages that everyone was *supposed* to listen to. In his memo, Sarnoff wrote:

> I have in mind a plan of development which would make radio a household utility in the same sense as the piano or phonograph. The idea is to bring music into the houses by wireless.
>
> While this has been tried in the past by wires, it has been a failure because wires do not lend themselves to this scheme. With radio, however, it would be entirely feasible. For example, a radio telephone transmitter having a range of, say, 25 to 50 miles can be installed at a fixed point where instrumental or vocal music or both are produced. . . . The receiver can be designed in the form of a simple "Radio Music Box" and arranged for several different wave lengths, which should be changeable with the throwing of a single switch or pressing of a single button.[13]

With this memo Sarnoff essentially invented radio as a social institution. But this new medium would have to wait, because on the eve of U.S. involvement in World War I, the navy was buying all of Marconi's transmitters. Although American Marconi did not act on Sarnoff's memo, the young immigrant did

**Radio Music Box memo**
David Sarnoff's 1915 plan, outlining how radio could be used as a popular mass medium.

*Listening to music over headphones is nothing new, but in the 1920s this farmer needed a wheelbarrow to move the radio set (left) from place to place.*

not forget the ideas for radio's potential that he had laid out so clearly.

### More Receivers Than Transmitters.

One of the biggest surprises of the radio business was that so many more receivers were sold than transmitters. Manufacturers had assumed at the start that there would be almost as many people sending as receiving messages.[14] In reality, however, electronic communication was following in the footsteps of print. The earliest books had been hand-copied and passed from one person to another. But just as the printing press sent books, magazines, and newspapers to the masses, radio was now becoming a mass medium.

### The RCA Radio Monopoly.

During World War I the navy had taken control of all radio technology, including the patents, and it wanted to maintain control after the war. But civilian government officials in the United States, in keeping with the U.S. tradition of independent media, rejected the idea of all-government control. In an attempt to avoid anarchy in the new medium, the navy advocated creating a private monopoly to control radio development.

The Radio Corporation of America (RCA) was formed as a consortium of four major companies: General Electric, AT&T, Westinghouse, and United Fruit Company. General Electric was included because it made radio transmitters and owned what had formerly been American Marconi. AT&T was the world leader in wired communication, and Westinghouse owned many critical patents. But why was United Fruit Company a part of RCA? United Fruit had used radios to connect its boats to banana plantations in South America and while doing so had developed improved technology that the monopoly needed. These four companies brought together the 2,000 or so patents that were needed to make the radio business work. RCA would not only become a major producer of radio equipment but also founded NBC, the first of the major broadcasting networks.[15]

Westinghouse employee and self-educated engineer Frank Conrad started making Sarnoff's dream of the Radio Music Box come true. In 1920, with Westinghouse's support, Conrad started broadcasting music on Sunday afternoons.

Westinghouse then built Conrad a more powerful transmitter and put together a broadcast schedule. Pittsburgh's radio station KDKA was licensed for broadcast on October 27, 1920. Others soon followed. Over in Britain, the British Broadcasting Company was created in 1922. It was initially a privately run company owned by the manufacturers of broadcasting equipment, and its first station was licensed in 1923. In 1927 the company became the British Broadcasting Corporation, a public, noncommercial monopoly for broadcasting in the United Kingdom.[16]

*Radio Advertising.*    Although KDKA was the first commercial radio station, it was not the first station to run a commercial. KDKA existed to provide programming, with the goal of getting people to buy radio sets. But WEAF, broadcasting in New York City, was the first station to sell airtime to advertisers. The modest success of these commercials soon led to radio advertising by oil companies, department stores, and American Express.

The radio industry considered several possibilities for making money. One possibility was to support radio broadcasting with a "tithe" (a specified percentage) of revenues from sales of radios by all manufacturers; another possibility was to support it with a substantial public endowment. The problem was that neither of these schemes would provide enough money to pay for the high-priced entertainers that listeners wanted to hear. This meant that radio stations were going to need advertising revenue. Ultimately the rest of the media industry would accept advertising as the main source of income for broadcasting. In Britain, by contrast, the original BBC was supported by revenue from selling radio receivers and radio-receiving licenses, and it was prohibited from selling commercials.[17]

*Radio Networks.*    By 1923 more than 600 radio transmitters were broadcasting in the United States. These stations were limited to the programming they could produce locally. How would these stations fill their broadcast day? In big cities this was no problem because there were plenty of concerts, lectures, and sporting events to put on the air, but rural areas or small towns were limited in their selection of locally produced culture and entertainment. In another of his famous memos, Sarnoff suggested that RCA form a new company, a **network**, to provide programming to a large group of broadcast stations, thus making a wider selection of programming available to smaller stations.

RCA established the National Broadcasting Company (NBC) on July 22, 1926. It was the United States' first major broadcasting network, and it survives today in the form of the NBC television network. NBC was actually two networks, the "Red" and the "Blue." (Due to an antitrust ruling, RCA was eventually forced to sell the Blue network, which then became ABC.)

*William Paley and the Power of Radio Advertising.*    With the growing demand for radio programming, the two NBC networks soon faced new competition,

**network**
A company that provides common programming to a large group of broadcast stations.

## FIGURE 7.1  THE EARLY RED AND BLUE NBC RADIO NETWORKS

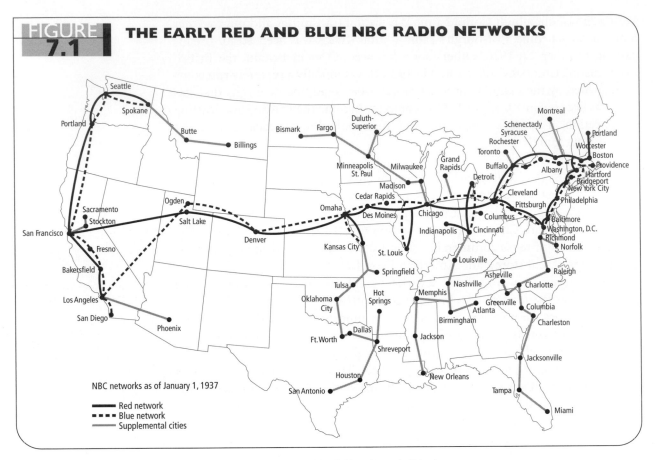

*Source:* "Bob Hope and American Variety," July 24, 2002, http://www.loc.gov/exhibits/bobhope/images/vc85.jpg.

none more significant than William Paley's Columbia Broadcasting System (CBS). Although Paley was born in the United States, his parents were Russian immigrants. He grew up in a wealthy household, and his family owned a successful cigar company. William Paley's father, Sam, had been approached about advertising his cigars on the fledgling United Independent Broadcasters (UIB) network. Sam Paley was not interested, but William was.

William Paley bought his first radio ads while his father was away on business, and although Sam initially chastised his son for wasting money, he soon heard people talking about the wonderful show his company sponsored. That was enough to convince him. William then developed a program called *La Palina Smoker* that featured an orchestra, a singer, and a comedian. It also resulted in increased cigar sales. Before long William, who was not quite twenty-seven years old, had the opportunity to buy UIB, which he did with help from his father. Once he became president of the network, he promptly renamed it the Columbia Broadcasting System.[18]

Better than anyone else, Paley understood that broadcasting was a business that had to make a profit on its own. NBC believed that its mission was to develop programs for the benefit of its listeners, but CBS realized that its real clients were the advertisers who sponsored the programs. Its programs were designed and produced specifically to attract the kind of audience a particular advertiser was looking for. For CBS, the "product" was the audience its programs attracted.

## From the Golden Age to the Television Age

The 1920s, 1930s, and 1940s came to be known as the **golden age of radio**, an era in which radio played the same role that television does today. Radio was the mass medium that served as the primary form of entertainment in the household. This was a big change. It meant that people were getting most of their entertainment from outside the home rather than from within. Instead of being entertained by Aunt Martha's and Cousin Sue's piano duets, they were listening to Bing Crosby's crooning or Bob Hope's comedy on the radio.

**golden age of radio**
A period from the late 1920s until the 1940s, during which radio was the dominant medium for home entertainment.

**soap operas**
Serialized daytime dramas targeted primarily at women.

*Golden Age Radio Programming.*    A wide range of programming was available on the radio during the golden age. Live music, both popular and classical, was a staple. NBC even had its own orchestra performing on a regular basis. There were also dramas and action programs, including *Little Orphan Annie*, *The Lone Ranger*, and *The Shadow*.

Some radio programs from the golden age survive today as television programs, most notably **soap operas**. The soaps, as they are called for short, are daytime dramas targeted primarily at women; they got their name from the commercials for soap and other cleaning products that ran during the shows. For better or worse, soaps were the first programs targeted specifically at women, a key audience for advertisers. It wasn't until the advent of television in the 1950s that soaps ceased to be a major part of radio programming.[19] CBS's *The Guiding Light* started on the radio in 1937, moved over to television in 1952, and finished its seventy-two-year run on September 18, 2009.

*Amos 'n' Andy.*    Despite the popularity of soap operas, no radio show attracted a bigger audience than *Amos 'n' Andy*, the first nationally broadcast daily drama.[20] *Amos 'n' Andy* began in January 1926 on Chicago radio station WGN as *Sam 'n' Henry*. The show would be a fixture on the radio, in one form or another, for nearly thirty-five years. Starring on the show were two white actors—Charles Correll and Freeman Gosden—who played the roles of two African Americans, Sam and Henry, who owned the Fresh Air Taxi Company. Correll and Gosden wrote all the scripts themselves and furnished the voices for

# TEST YOUR MEDIA LITERACY

## When Is a Radio Show Racist?

*Amos 'n' Andy* has been both praised and criticized. It was condemned as racist by many groups, including the NAACP, that saw the humor in the show as demeaning and the characters as uneducated and ignorant of city life. The most lasting criticism of the show, however, was that it was produced by whites predominantly for the entertainment of whites. One of my African American students summed up the issue clearly: "So what you are telling me is that the most popular show in the country was about white people making fun of black people?" Clearly a show created under these parameters wouldn't be acceptable today.

But *Amos 'n' Andy* may not have been as racist as it seemed. Freeman Gosden and Charles Correll were guests of honor at an annual picnic hosted by the *Defender*, Chicago's leading weekly black newspaper in 1931. In addition, several members of the black press had good things to say about the show in its early days. It was also one of the few programs that showed African Americans (even if played by whites) in everyday life. The supporting characters in the fictional Lodge were middle-class blacks, a social phenomenon many whites at that time didn't even know existed.[1]

### Who is the source?
Who wrote, acted, and produced the show? Who were critics of the program?

### What are they saying?
What are the central criticisms of the program? What are the arguments in support of the program?

### What kind of evidence is provided?
What evidence is provided that the show had support at the time it was aired in the African American community? What is the evidence that the program was racist? How did these views change over time?

### How do you and your classmates react to *Amos 'n' Andy*?
Was it the fact that the stars were white and the characters were black that made the show racist? Why do you think so? Is it possible for a program to make jokes about racial issues without being racist? How could it do this?

[1] Melvin Patrick Ely, *The Adventures of Amos 'n' Andy* (New York: Free Press, 1991).

the title characters and the members of their fraternal lodge, the Mystic Knights of the Sea. Their names were later changed to Amos and Andy when Correll and Gosden syndicated the show nationally, since WGN owned the characters of Sam and Henry. At the peak of its popularity, *Amos 'n' Andy* was played in restaurants and in movie theaters between shows so that people wouldn't have to stay home to listen.

For the history of radio news, see Chapter 6—Newspapers and the News.

*The BBC: Voice of the Old Empire.*    Although in the United States radio is generally seen as an entertainment medium, the British Broadcasting Corporation (BBC) has been broadcasting news and culture worldwide for more than seventy years.

As mentioned earlier, the BBC was created as a public service in the 1920s. In the 1930s it started broadcasting on the shortwave radio band, which allowed its signals to extend around the world. During World War II the BBC was the international voice of opposition to the Nazis, broadcasting in more than forty languages, including French, Danish, and Hindi.[21] Listening to BBC broadcasts in Nazi-occupied Europe was a punishable offense.

Today the BBC's World Service radio network has an audience of approximately 150 million people. According to the BBC's Caroline Thomson, the goal of the World Service is to reach approximately 95 percent of the world's population.[22] The logistics of doing this become complicated when the BBC is broadcasting in a dozen or more different time zones. When do you broadcast a morning show on a network heard around the world?

BBC's international reach can be seen with the program *Focus on Africa.* For a continent that depends on radio as its primary medium of mass communication (for more on media in Africa, see Chapter 15), the BBC provides a reliable source of news that is not censored by local governments. To avoid charges of being a colonial voice of white Britain in black Africa, most of the reporting on the show is done by African journalists. *Focus on Africa* is such an important source of news that it is often rebroadcast on local African stations, sometimes just by taking a shortwave radio and holding it up to the station's microphone.[23]

While the BBC has long been known for its shortwave broadcasts, it has been changing in recent years. It still broadcasts by shortwave in Asia and Africa, but it now relies on webcasting, FM stations, and satellite services to reach the United States, Canada, Australia, New Zealand, and the Pacific Islands.[24] Also, since the collapse of communism in Eastern Europe and the rising conflict in the Middle East, the BBC has closed a number of its Eastern European–language radio services and has been working on launching an Arabic-language television service.[25]

*Becoming a Companion Medium.*    As television claimed more and more of the broadcast audience, radio was forced to change. No longer were people sitting down in their living rooms to listen to programs on the radio. Instead, they turned on the radio while they did other things: working, washing dishes, driving. Yet radio did not fade away; instead, it reinvented itself as companion radio, a medium that would always be there to keep listeners company. Radio host Julius Lester put it this way: "Radio is so integral a part of us now that we do not consciously notice its presence; it is a member of the family, a companion, and the voices issuing through its speakers are those not of strangers but of friends."[26]

## Changing the Musical Experience: From Social Music to Personal Soundtracks

Being able to store and transmit musical performances was extremely important, but that may not have been the biggest change brought about by the invention of the phonograph and radio. Rock historian James Miller writes that the phonograph (and eventually radio) represented a vast expansion of people's access to music: "Symphonies that a person living in the nineteenth century would have been lucky to hear once were available for repeated listening on home phonographs."[27] Before the invention of the phonograph or radio, people had to go to a concert hall, theater, or club to hear music if they didn't play it themselves.

**social music**
Music that people play and sing for one another in the home or other social settings. In the absence of radio, recordings, and later, television, this was the means of hearing music most readily available to the largest number of people.

*The Death of "Social Music."*    The phonograph and radio brought a wider range of music into the household, but it also led to the loss of so-called **social music**, music that people play and sing for one another in the home or in other social settings. Prior to the new technology, people had to play an instrument or sing to have music in the home. Sheet music was a popular feature in magazines like *Godey's Lady's Book*, along with recipes and sewing patterns. For most people there was little social distance between the performer and the audience, and musical instruction played a greater role in the education of the upper and middle classes. With advances in technology over the years, however, the social connections available through a shared musical experience would change profoundly.

*Akio Morita's "Personal Soundtrack."*    Akio Morita is not a household name, but the Japanese engineer who invented the Sony Walkman has influenced how people listen to music as much as anyone since Thomas Edison and Emile Berliner.

When the Walkman was introduced in 1979, it was available in two versions— either as a tiny tape player or as a stereo FM radio. They were relatively expensive, with the tape player version costing upward of $200, but they allowed each person to live in his or her own "personal musical cocoon."[28]

Until 1979 the only way to take music away from home was with either a poor-quality pocket AM radio or a giant boom box. Writer RiShawn Biddle points out that the Walkman was more than just a way to protect your fellow bus passengers from your choice of music: "It's also been a coach, concert hall, and personal reader for millions of workout warriors, housewives, and retirees. For travelers, it is a trusty companion, something to ward off talkative salesmen and grandmothers loaded with wallet-size photos."[29]

Media scholar Michael Marsden notes that the Walkman gives people privacy in public areas: "It's your personal space that you've created, in a world in which we don't have a lot of personal space. It's a totally private world."[30]

Not everyone is so enthralled with the effects of the Walkman, however. Critic John Zerzan argues that the Walkman is one of a number of technologies that lead to a "sort of withdrawal from social connections."[31] One thing the Walkman has clearly done, however, is contribute greatly to the trend of personalized media use characterized by iPods, MP3 players, music downloads, and podcasts.

# MUSIC, YOUTH CULTURE, AND SOCIETY

Though recorded music was on the market long before there was **rock 'n' roll**, rock 'n' roll was born alongside modern recording technology and flourished on the radio. It was amplified from the start, featured new instruments like the solid-body electric guitar, and brought together a host of traditions from white hillbilly music to black rhythm and blues. World War II spurred the development of rock 'n' roll as a cross-cultural phenomenon because blacks and whites mixed socially during the war more often than they had before and because the Armed Forces Radio played a range of white and black musical styles.

## "Rock 'n' Roll" and the Integration of Music

Before 1948, recordings by popular black musicians were referred to as **race records** and included everything from blues, to gospel, to jazz. But in 1949 the editors of *Billboard* magazine, which ranks sales of all types of records, started calling the genre rhythm and blues (R&B).[32] It was at the same time that "folk" records came to be called "country and western."[33]

**rock 'n' roll**
A style of music popularized on radio that combined elements of white hillbilly music and black rhythm and blues.

**race records**
A term used by the recording industry prior to 1949 to refer to recordings by popular black artists. It was later replaced by more racially neutral terms such as R&B, soul, or urban contemporary.

Rhythm and blues records produced by African American artists were more likely to be played on jukeboxes in clubs than on the radio in the 1940s.

Why did R&B emerge when it did? There are a number of reasons. One is that the big bands that played jazz and swing (popular in the 1930s and 1940s) were expensive because there were so many musicians. An amplified blues band with a singer, an electric guitar, an electric bass, and a drummer could make a lot of sound, and great dance music could be built around the strong bass beat.[34] Also, African American musicians gained respect when white artists recorded cover versions of black songs.[35]

On December 28, 1947, a black R&B singer named Wynonie Harris recorded "Good Rockin' Tonight" in a studio in Cincinnati, Ohio. The song would become a big hit on black jukeboxes and radio stations. Was this the first rock 'n' roll song? Entire books have been devoted to answering that question, but "Good Rockin' " is as likely a candidate as any. It was a jukebox hit for Harris, and later a radio hit when **covered** by young Elvis Presley. It certainly helped give this new kind of music its name. The following year brought a series of songs with the word *rock* in the title, including "We're Gonna Rock, We're Gonna Roll," "Rockin' at Midnight," "Rock the Joint," and "Rock and Roll."

By and large, these songs were not played on white radio stations. The problem wasn't the color of the musicians; it was the meaning of the word *rock*. As record promoter Henry Glover put it, "We were restricted with our possibilities of promoting this song because it was considered filth. . . . They had a definition in those days of the word 'rock,' meaning the sex act, rather than having it known as 'a good time,' as they did later."[36]

**covers**
Songs recorded (or covered) by someone other than the original artist. In the 1950s it was common for white musicians to cover songs originally played by black artists, but now artists commonly cover all genres of music.

*Elvis Presley and Chuck Berry: Blending Black and White Musical Traditions.* While Harris and numerous other R&B singers were performing rock 'n' roll in the late 1940s and early 1950s, two stars—one white, the other black—would put rock 'n' roll on the national and international map. Elvis Presley and Chuck Berry demonstrated what could be done with the blending of hillbilly (or country) and R&B.[37]

Elvis Presley made his first recording in 1953, although no one knows the exact date. Marion Keisker, the woman behind the desk at Memphis Recording

Service, remembered a young man who recorded a couple of songs on a ten-inch acetate disc for his mother. When she asked Presley whom he sounded like, his response was, "I don't sound like nobody."[38] Keisker had the good sense to make an extra copy of Presley's recording and file it under the heading "Good ballad singer." "The reason I taped Elvis," she explained, "was this: Over and over I remember Sam [Phillips, Keisker's boss] saying, 'If I could find a white man who had the Negro sound and the Negro feel, I could make a billion dollars,' this is what I heard in Elvis."[39]

The man who would become known as "the king" soon started performing hillbilly music in Memphis and recording for Phillips, starting with "Good Rockin' Tonight." To Presley, performing was almost a religious experience: "It's like your whole body gets goose bumps," Presley said. "It's like a surge of electricity going through you. It's almost like making love, but it's even stronger than that."[40]

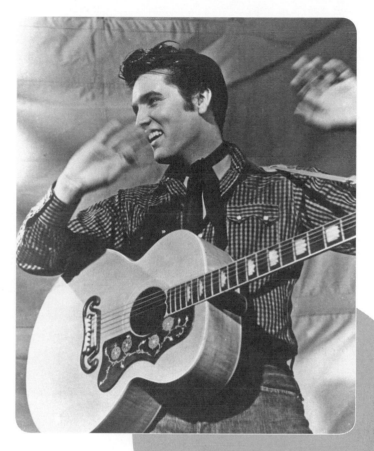

*Elvis Presley became the "king" of rock 'n' roll by combining elements of hillbilly and R&B music.*

Just as hillbilly singer Elvis Presley borrowed from R&B, so blues guitarist Chuck Berry borrowed from the white hillbilly singers. The song "Maybelline" was based on an old fiddle tune called "Ida Red" and supposedly got its name from a mascara box. Others claim that Maybelline was the name of a cow in a third-grade reading book. Either way, the song combined a hot guitar, a hot car, and a hot woman.

Berry wanted to break out of some of the restrictions of traditional blues. While his audience at the clubs wouldn't stand for any change in the basic blues style, they had no problem with Berry's original rendition of an old white fiddle tune. Berry's unconventional style made people sit up and take notice. Berry recalls people talking about his music at an African American club: "Some of the clubgoers started whispering, 'Who is that black hillbilly at the Cosmo?' After they laughed at me a few times, they began requesting the hillbilly stuff and enjoyed trying to dance to it. If you ever want to see something that is far out, watch a crowd of colored folk, half high, wholeheartedly doing the hoedown barefooted."[41]

Presley started playing "Maybelline" in Louisiana while Berry was playing it in New York. This illustrates a key feature of the birth of rock 'n' roll: Two previously segregated types of music were coming together and becoming a new musical form—one that teens couldn't get enough of.

*Rock Radio.* Another reason for rock 'n' roll's growing popularity was that disc jockeys like Alan Freed and Dewey Phillips were playing rock 'n' roll and R&B records on their radio shows.

On October 29, 1949, Dewey Phillips started a show on WHBQ in Memphis called *Red, Hot & Blue* that played R&B records. The show became an instant hit and quickly went from forty-five minutes in length to three hours. WHBQ's program director remembered it this way: "He got something like seven requests his first night. Well, the next night, I don't know the exact amount, but it was more like seventy requests. Then, even more incredible, the next night, it was closer to seven hundred."[42] Although Phillips was white, he played music by black artists and had a substantial audience from black radio listeners in Memphis. This was unusual at a time when most stations appealed either to the white or the black community, but not to both.

*Chuck Berry's music, played on rock 'n' roll stations in the 1950s and early 1960s, appealed to African American and white listeners alike.*

**girl groups**

A musical group composed of several women singers who harmonize together. Groups such as the Shirelles, the Ronettes, and the Shangri-Las, featuring female harmonies and high production values, were especially popular in the late 1950s and early 1960s.

## The Changing Face of Popular Music

The 1950s were a period of transition for popular music, with tastes shifting from the Tin Pan Alley songs of an Irving Berlin or Cole Porter to the songs of a Chuck Berry or Buddy Holly that were rooted in R&B. Already firmly established through concerts and radio airplay, rock 'n' roll would now take center stage with records produced by artists ranging from **girl groups** to the Rolling Stones.

*Motown: The Sound of Young America.* No record label was more important in bringing R&B to the masses than Detroit's Motown Records. Motown, founded by Berry Gordy Jr., was the most successful of the independent record labels, and one of the most successful black-owned businesses.

Popular culture scholar Gerald Early says that the real importance of Motown was that it took black music and sensibilities and made them important for the public at large. He also credits Motown with establishing a black popular culture at a time when jazz—especially the improvisational work of Miles Davis and John Coltrane—was becoming highbrow culture. One of the big accomplishments of Motown was that it no longer published songs by black artists for white artists to cover, as was common practice in the 1950s and early 1960s. Instead, the African American Motown artists themselves turned out the hits. Motown moved black music into the mainstream and out of the world of race records, thus illustrating Truth Three—Everything from the margin moves to the center.[43]

The move of African American music and artists into the mainstream mirrored larger changes in society. In May 1961 African American Freedom Riders staged sit-ins to desegregate restrooms and lunch counters in bus stations in the South. In October 1962 the Motown Revue was doing its part to promote desegregation with such established acts as the Marvelettes, Marvin Gaye, and the Supremes. While the Motown artists were not Freedom Riders, they broke some of the same ground on their tour. Mary Wilson of the Supremes put it this way:

> Our tours made breakthroughs and helped weaken racial barriers. When it came to music, segregation didn't mean a thing in some of those towns, and if it did, black and white fans would ignore the local customs to attend the shows. To see crowds that were integrated—sometimes for the first time in a community—made me realize that Motown truly was the sound of young America.[44]

Motown's years as an independent company came to an end in 1988, when Gordy sold the label to Boston Ventures for $61 million. Motown was subsequently sold to Polygram in 1993 for $301 million. It still exists, but it is now a small unit within a media giant.

The lasting effect of Motown artists can be seen with the huge outpouring of affection for Michael Jackson following his death in 2009. (For more on media coverage of Michael Jackson's death, see Chapter 1—Living in a Media World.)

*The British Invasion: A Rougher Rock.*    In the 1960s rock underwent a number of changes. The most significant of these were brought about by groups that came to the United States from England. The so-called **British invasion** began in 1964 and brought a rougher edge to white rock 'n' roll with the music of the Beatles, Dusty Springfield, the Hollies, the Who, and of course, the Rolling Stones. To appreciate the influence of these British bands, one need only look at the charts. In 1963 only one British band had made it onto *Billboard*'s charts; in 1964, thirty-four had done so.[45]

**British invasion**
The British take on classic American rock 'n' roll, blues, and R&B transformed rock 'n' roll and became internationally popular in the 1960s with groups such as the Beatles and, later, the Rolling Stones and the Who.

**concept album**
An album by a solo artist or group that contains related songs on a common theme or even a story, rather than a collection of unrelated hits or covers.

**producer**
The person who puts together the right mix of songs, songwriters, technicians, and performers to create an album; some observers argue that the producer is the key catalyst for a hit album.

Traditionally, recorded music by popular groups was a means of promoting their live shows. But by 1966 it had become almost impossible for the Beatles to perform live because their screaming fans drowned them out. In fact, Beatles scholar Allan Moore notes that by 1966 the band had ceased touring because they couldn't hear themselves play. Instead, they became a studio band whose music was heard primarily on records and the radio.[46] In 1967 the Beatles recorded an album, *Sgt. Pepper's Lonely Hearts Club Band,* that transformed rock in a number of ways: It was one of rock's first **concept albums**—an album that brought together a group of related songs on common themes. It was also one of the first rock albums that was more than a collection of hit singles and their flip sides.[47]

What exactly was the concept of this album? Many of the songs had autobiographical themes derived from John Lennon's and Paul McCartney's childhood memories of Liverpool, England. Also, the songs were supposedly being played by the fictional band of the title.[48]

Interpretations of the songs on this album have varied. Some claim that "Lucy in the Sky With Diamonds" was about the drug LSD. Lennon said that the song was based on a picture his son Julian drew when he was four years old. Others have said that McCartney's song "Fixing a Hole" was about injecting himself with heroin, though McCartney's own account was that it was about renovating an old farmhouse he had recently purchased. In 2004 McCartney acknowledged publicly that there were, indeed, drug references in many Beatles songs, including "Lucy in the Sky With Diamonds."[49] For a link to articles in which McCartney discusses this, visit http://ralphehanson .com. Part of what made *Sgt. Pepper* so successful, however, was that it didn't matter which interpretation the listener supplied. They all worked. The members of the band were more concerned about how the songs sounded than what they meant.

*Sgt. Pepper* gave rise to albums that were designed to be played from beginning to end, though these two-sided vinyl records had to be turned over at the twenty-three-minute mark. The seamless presentation of seventy minutes of music would have to wait for the 1980s and the advent of the CD.

*Sgt. Pepper* highlights a change that was starting to take place in the music business: The long-playing record (LP) was replacing the single as rock music's main format. Moore notes that in 1967 bands still relied primarily on singles to promote themselves and albums were secondary. But that was changing with groups such as Cream and Led Zeppelin focusing on albums. Led Zeppelin's greatest hit, "Stairway to Heaven," was never released as a single, probably because it wouldn't fit the short format of the 45.[50]

*The Growing Importance of Producers.*    As popular music increasingly became a studio creation, the albums' **producers** became as important as the artists themselves. The main job of a producer is to put together the right songs, songwriters, technicians, and performers in the creation of an album.

Rock historian Charlie Gillett argues that the producer is the person who is responsible for making hit records. Producer Rick Rubin revitalized Johnny Cash's career near the end of his life with a series of albums that included songs by U2, Nine Inch Nails, and Tom Petty, among others; and producer Kenneth "Babyface" Edmonds has created or revived the careers of such artists as Aretha Franklin, Toni Braxton, Whitney Houston, Boyz II Men, and TLC. Unlike the producers and writers of the Motown era, Edmonds occasionally goes into the studio himself. Although he has produced at least fifty-seven top hits, Edmonds is quick to give praise to the artists who perform his songs.[51]

With rock, the producer shapes the sound and becomes an integral part of the musical process. Few albums demonstrate this as clearly as Pink Floyd's *Dark Side of the Moon*. Starting in 1973, *Dark Side of the Moon* spent 741 weeks on the *Billboard* Top 200 album chart, far longer than any competitor (though other albums have sold more copies). Alan Parsons produced the album, released in 1973, which painted a bleak picture of "alienation, paranoia, schizophrenia." But more than any message of the songs, *Dark Side of the Moon* painted an incredible sonic picture. It used stereo to its fullest extent, sending sounds swirling around the listener's head. Parsons recorded a wide variety of voices talking, laughing, and screaming, which were mixed in at various times and speeds.[52] Pink Floyd continued the direction of the Beatles' *Sgt. Pepper* album, in which rock was music made to be recorded and constructed as much as performed.

The role of the producer continued to grow throughout the 1970s with **disco** and a range of heavily produced club music, including rap, house, and techno. Disco was primarily a means of getting people to dance. It came out of the gay male subculture in New York City and was popularized in the 1977 hit movie *Saturday Night Fever*. Disco was in many ways the ultimate producer music, in

Rick Rubin has been one of the leading producers of the twenty-first century, working with acts ranging from the Red Hot Chili Peppers to the Dixie Chicks.

**disco**
The name of the heavily produced techno club dance music of the 1970s, which grew out of the urban gay male subculture, with significant black and Latino influences. In many ways, disco defined the look and feel of 1970s pop culture, fashion, and film.

which the beat and the overall sound created by the producer mattered more than the vocals or talents of the instrumentalists.

Why does disco matter today? First and foremost, it was an entire genre of music that depended on technology and the producer, building on trends started by bands like Pink Floyd and the Beatles. It also made black and Latino music more important commercially and led the movement toward the splintering of pop music into a range of genres.[53]

## Country: Pop Music for Adults

**Country music** was born in the late nineteenth century, evolving out of a range of musical forms including Irish and Scottish folk music, Mississippi blues, and Christian gospel music.[54] It was originally called "old-timey" or hillbilly music. Country grew in the 1950s and 1960s with the so-called Nashville sound popularized by musicians such as Jim Reeves, Eddy Arnold, and Patsy Cline. It was at about this time that Elvis Presley took the hillbilly sound in another direction with early rock 'n' roll, but country never disappeared.

In 1980 many Americans rediscovered country music with the hit film *Urban Cowboy*, starring John Travolta, and the 1990s and 2000s saw the growth of country music by artists such as Rascal Flatts, the late Johnny Cash, and Carrie Underwood, as well as movies such as *O Brother Where Art Thou?* and *Walk the Line*. In 2008 country singer Taylor Swift was America's best-selling album artist, with more than 4 million copies sold.[55]

Why does country music continue to be so popular? "Country music is about lyric-oriented songs with adult themes," according to Lon Helton, a music journalist. "You've probably got to be 24 or 25 to even understand a country song. Life has to slap you around a little bit, and then you go, 'Now I get what they're singing about.'" Unlike the sex and drugs of rock 'n' roll, country deals with suburban issues like "love, heartache, family ties, and middle-aged renewal."[56]

*Country artist Taylor Swift was America's best-selling album artist in 2008.*

## Concerns About Effects of Music on Young People

Some of the biggest controversies surrounding rock have involved not the music but the words—from 1950s lyrics dealing with "rocking and rolling," to references to drugs in the 1970s, to derogatory comments about women in

**country music**
Originally referred to as hillbilly or "old-timey" music, this genre evolved out of Irish and Scottish folk music, Mississippi blues, and Christian gospel music, and grew in the 1950s and 1960s with the so-called Nashville sound.

contemporary rap. Since rock's inception, parents and other concerned adults have wondered about the effects of its lyrics on impressionable listeners, thus illustrating Truth Five—New media are always scary. This questioning has led to product liability trials, congressional hearings, and movements to label and/or ban certain albums for objectionable content.

It is difficult to know what the influence of a song's words will be. Adults often read metaphorical meanings into a song while young people see only the literal meaning of the lyrics. Understanding music also goes beyond the content of the lyrics. Listeners pay as much attention to the melody, rhythm, and style of music as they do to the lyrics. Finally, songs are often as much about feelings as they are about rational thought. They set a mood rather than transmit a specific message.[57] (For some examples of misinterpreted lyrics, listen to Brian Ibbott's "Lyrics Undercover" podcast. You can find links to these podcasts at http://ralphehanson.com.)

Few music formats have engendered as much controversy as rap and hip-hop. **Rap music** came to prominence in the United States in 1979, arising from the hip-hop culture in New York City. It emerged in clubs with DJs playing and remixing different records and sounds and then speaking (or rapping) over the top. Blondie's rap hit "Rapture," which came out in 1980, was among the first rap songs to receive mainstream radio airplay.[58]

Rap was really an outgrowth of several trends dating back to the Beatles' *Sgt. Pepper* and Pink Floyd's *Dark Side of the Moon*. With the advent of multi-track recording, producers were adding layers of talk and ambient sound to the music created by band members. Rap simply extended this process, making the DJ part of the music and sampling from a range of already completed musical recordings. There was no longer a single "correct" mix of the various tracks; instead, the final version would be constructed by whoever wanted to work with it.

Among the controversies surrounding rap is the complaint that rap is misogynistic and violent. Rappers defend the violence in their recordings by noting that we live in a violent world; the violence in the recordings is simply "keeping it real." Michael Fuchs, a former executive of media giant Time Warner, says that he sees some of the criticism of rap as racist: "It's a fact that white kids are buying black music and are being influenced by it, and that frightens their parents. It's not very different than the feeling my parents had thirty years ago when rock and roll came out—about the influence of black music."[59]

### The Importance of Pop Music.
Popular music today goes well beyond just the composition; it is an entire social statement. Besides the music, there are the photos on the cover of the CD, the text within the booklet inside the CD, the music video, the interviews on *Entertainment Tonight*, the posters, the Web site, and the fashion. It is through popular music that young people often make their first contact with much of our culture. It provides young people not just with music but with an entire identity.[60] Our identification with the music

**rap music**
This genre arose out of the hip-hop culture in New York City in 1979. It emerged in clubs with DJs playing and remixing different records and sounds and then speaking (or rapping) over the top.

of our youth is something that sticks with us throughout adulthood. Alternative rocker Liz Phair points out, "There's something that happens to people as they reach adulthood. They spend a lot of time trying to figure out what first hit them about rock 'n' roll. It's like the first time you took a drug. You want that first time back."[61]

# FROM SINGLES TO DIGITAL DOWNLOADS: MAKING MONEY IN THE RECORDING INDUSTRY

For as long as there have been methods for recording and playing back sounds, there have been debates over how to make money selling music. Berliner's 78-rpm discs were fragile, held only three and a half minutes of music, and had only marginal sound quality by today's standards. So while there was no question that 78s needed to be replaced, there was no consensus on what the new format should be.

## LPs Versus 45s

**long-playing record (LP)**

A record format introduced by Columbia Records in 1948. The more durable LP could reproduce twenty-three minutes of high-quality music on each of two sides and was a technological improvement over the 78-rpm.

**45-rpm disc**

The record format was developed in the late 1940s by RCA. It had high-quality sound but held only about four minutes of music on a side. It was the ideal format for marketing popular hit songs to teenagers, though.

**compact disc (CD)**

A digital recording medium that came into common use in the early 1980s. CDs can hold approximately seventy minutes of digitally recorded music.

The **long-playing record (LP)** was developed by Columbia Records and revealed in 1948. The discs were labeled unbreakable; this was not quite true, but the vinyl LPs were much less delicate than the 78-rpm discs. More important, an LP could reproduce twenty-three minutes of high-quality music on each side. CBS demonstrated the system to RCA president David Sarnoff and offered to let RCA, its competitor, use the system. But RCA declined the offer and put out its own format, the **45-rpm disc**. It had high-quality sound, but the 45 could play only about four minutes of music at a time.[62] Eventually record players were sold that would play both 45s and LPs, and both formats existed side by side, with the LP used for longer compositions and the 45 for single popular songs.

## Compact Discs and Digital Recording

Work on the **compact disc (CD)** was started by Philips Electronics physicist Klaas Compaan as early as 1969. Compaan had the idea of photographically recording music or video on discs that could be read with a laser. Not wanting to get into the kind of format war that raged between the 45 and the LP in the 1940s, Philips joined with Sony to create a standard for the compact disc. The CD was launched in Europe in 1982 and in the United States in 1983.

While we have generally talked about new media being scary to consumers (Truth Five), **digital recording** (a method of recording sound that involves storing it as a series of numbers) has been the scariest of the new media to people in the music industry. With **analog recording** (the original method of recording that involved cutting a groove on a record or placing a magnetic signal on a tape that was an image of the sound wave being recorded), copies were not as good as the originals, and copies of copies showed further degradation in quality. Thus the prospect of home digital recordings, which are exactly the same as the originals without loss of quality, upset companies whose livelihood depended on the sales of original recordings.

For several years home digital copying was held up by the recording industry, which wanted CD players to include security chips that would stop people from making copies. Of course, as soon as the industry came up with a way to stop people from copying digital music, hackers responded with ways of breaking the system. Ultimately, home CD copying emerged from the computer industry rather than the music industry. People wanted to be able to "burn" CDs with their own data, programs, and music.[63]

## Music on the Internet

The most recent format for music is the compressed music file known as **MP3** (short for Moving Picture Experts Group audio layer 3). MP3s can be played on a computer or a portable MP3 player such as an iPod, or they can be burned onto a recordable CD. The files can be easily shared over the Internet by e-mail, on Web sites, or by music-sharing services like Limewire.

Aside from allowing people to share music files, one of the biggest effects of this new distribution channel has been to allow new groups to publicize their music by delivering it directly to the consumer through the Internet, either through their own Web site or social networking sites like MySpace. Remember that Erik Goes to Germany and Katrina Leskanich, the examples we discussed in the opening vignette, are recording and distributing their music without using traditional music labels. Similarly, after a dispute with one of his record labels, the eccentric rock and soul musician Prince started selling music directly to consumers through his New Power Generation Web site.[64]

Some independent or maverick musicians and bands might applaud the increased exposure they get from the Internet, but the music industry is intensely concerned about music file "sharing," preferring to call it theft, piracy, or copyright violation. What worries publishers is that no one is paying for these files.[65] Publishers have tried various copy protection schemes to stop consumers from making digital copies, some going so far as to put software on their CDs that spies on consumers and reports back to the publisher how the music is being used.[66] And, as is discussed in Chapter 10—The Internet, the recording industry for the past several years has been filing suit against consumers who have been downloading unlicensed copies of music from the Internet.[67]

**digital recording**

A method of recording sound—for example, that used to create CDs—that involves storing music in a computer-readable format known as binary information.

**analog recording**

An electromechanical method of recording in which a sound is translated into analogous electrical signals that are then applied to a recording medium. Early analog recording media included acetate or vinyl discs and magnetic tape.

**MP3**

Short for Moving Picture Experts Group audio layer 3; a standard for compressing music from CDs or other digital recordings into computer files that can be easily exchanged on the Internet.

# TEST YOUR MEDIA LITERACY

## How Will the Recording Industry Survive?

The recording industry has gone through nearly a decade of declining sales. In 2000, American music fans bought 785.1 million albums. By 2006, that had dropped to 588.2 million (including both CDs and digital downloads). And in 2008, that number had reached 428.4 million.[1] That's a 45 percent drop in sales over eight years. The industry has blamed consumers for the decline, thanks to file sharing, piracy, and easy home duplication of CDs. What the industry has not done is come up with a coherent response to the massive change that's taking place in the music business, whether it likes it or not.

One person who seems to have some kind of idea about what modern music consumers want is *uber*-producer Rick Rubin, who has been responsible for the success of the Dixie Chicks, Metallica, Neil Diamond, the Beastie Boys, and the Red Hot Chili Peppers. Columbia Records hired Rubin in 2007 to co-head the label, hoping the producer could revitalize the music business. Although it is not clear that Rubin will be able to turn around Columbia Records as a manager, he clearly understands how to produce records people want to listen to and buy.[2]

In an interview with *New York Times Magazine*, Rubin says that he is focused more on finding music that he, and other people, will like rather than looking for another star:

> And you wonder why people don't buy CDs anymore. One song is great and the other is . . . Everything I do, whether it's producing, or signing an artist, always starts with the songs. When I'm listening, I'm looking for a balance that you could see in anything. Whether it's a great painting or a building or a sunset. There's just a natural human element to a great song that feels immediately satisfying. I like the song to create a mood.[3]

**MORE online**

You can find a link to the complete text of the *New York Times Magazine* article about Rick Rubin at **http://ralphehanson.com** along with examples of music he's produced.

### Who is the source?

Who is Rick Rubin? What has he done in the music industry?

### What are they saying?

What does Rubin think is wrong with the music industry? What does he think should be done to revitalize it?

### What kind of evidence is there?

What evidence does the *New York Magazine* reporter present that shows Rubin has the ability to help turn around the music industry? What has he done in the past to make artists successful? Does he have the ability to help a music label as well as individual artists? Why do you think so?

### How do you and your classmates feel about the music industry?

How often do you and your friends pay for music compared to "sharing" it over the Internet? Why do you pay for music? What could record labels do that would make you more willing to buy CDs or legal downloads?

[1] James Callan, "U.S. Album Sales Decline 14% While Online Track Sales Surge," Bloomberg.com, January 1, 2009, www.bloomberg.com/apps/news?pid=20601103&sid=aC7ekniUw9Fs&refer=us; Brian Hiatt and Serpick Evan, "The Record Industry's Decline," *Rolling Stone*, June 28, 2007.

[2] Tim Arango, "Producer's Track Record as a Label Executive Is Raising Questions," *New York Times*, February 7, 2009.

[3] Lynn Hirschberg, "The Music Man," *New York Times Magazine*, September 2, 2007.

## The Problem of Payola

With radio airplay so important to the success of records in the pre-MTV/pre-Internet era, record promoters were willing to do almost anything to get their records played on the major radio stations. This included payoffs to disc jockeys in the form of money or gifts, known as **payola**, to get them to play a particular record. In 1959 this common practice gained notoriety when an internal fight between the two major music-licensing companies went public. The fight was between the old guard of the **American Society of Composers, Authors and Publishers (ASCAP)**, which represented the older Tin Pan Alley style of music, and **Broadcast Music, Inc. (BMI)**, which represented rock 'n' roll, R&B, and country artists and composers.

On November 21, 1959, early rock 'n' roll disc jockey Alan Freed was fired from radio station WABC for refusing to sign a statement that he had never been paid to play a record. Freed, along with Dick Clark and other prominent disc jockeys, was called to testify at congressional hearings on the payola scandal. Freed had taken a variety of payments, including cash, gifts, and even publishing credits, in return for playing particular records, and he viewed this practice as acceptable. Giving in to the demands of the ABC network that carried his *American Bandstand*, Clark gave up all his connections to the music publishing business to concentrate on his music shows, but Freed never recovered from the scandal and died from complications of alcoholism in 1965.[68]

Concerns about payola in various forms have resurfaced over the years, most recently in 2004 when major record companies were accused of attempting to keep music by independent artists off the air in favor of their own performers by making payments to stations owned by major media companies.[69]

# THE BUSINESS OF RADIO

The payola scandals underscored the problems radio faced in the late 1950s and early 1960s. With the coming of television, radio was forced to change and no longer tried to be all things to all people. Instead, each station appealed to a particular audience. Teenagers didn't have to listen to the same programs as store clerks; stockbrokers didn't have to listen to the same programs as college students. Want rock 'n' roll? There's a station for it. Oldies? Another choice or two. News? Talk? Classical music? Soul? If you live in an urban area, chances are you can find stations serving all these different radio formats. Over the past decade, radio has continued to change, undergoing a massive change of ownership and seeing the growth of numerous new competitors.

**payola**
Payoffs to disc jockeys in the form of money or gifts to get them to play a particular record.

**American Society of Composers, Authors and Publishers (ASCAP)**
The original organization that collected royalties on musical recordings, performances, publications, and airplay.

**Broadcast Music, Inc. (BMI)**
A competitor of ASCAP that has generally licensed new composers and artists who had not been represented by ASCAP, including a lot of what was known as "minority music"—including blues, country, Latin, and unpublished jazz compositions.

**format radio**
A style of radio programming designed to appeal to a narrow, specific audience. Popular formats include country, contemporary hits, all talk, all sports, and oldies.

## Finding a Niche: Popular Radio Formats

The most popular radio format in 2008 in the United States was country, with 12.7 percent of stations carrying it (see Table 7.1), followed closely by news/talk, which commands 10.7 percent of the national audience. Adult contemporary **format radio** consists of light rock and is designed to appeal to listeners aged twenty-five to forty, especially women; it draws about 7.2 percent of the audience. Pop contemporary hit radio (CHR) is what used to be known as Top 40; while it would seem to be primarily a teen format, more than half of its audience is older than twenty-five. Classic rock draws 4.5 percent of the audience and is the most popular among listeners aged thirty-five to fifty-four. Rhythmic CHR

## POPULAR RADIO FORMATS

Although the ratings of various radio formats vary from month to month, here is an overall picture of the audience percentage of the various top formats.

| Format | Audience portion | # of stations |
|---|---|---|
| Country | 12.7% | 1,683 |
| News/talk/information | 10.7% | 1,553 |
| Adult contemporary (AC) | 7.2% | 798 |
| Pop contemporary hit radio (Top 40) | 5.6% | 381 |
| Classic rock | 4.5% | 514 |
| Rhythmic CHR | 4.0% | 156 |
| Urban adult contemporary | 3.7% | 170 |
| Urban contemporary | 3.7% | 154 |
| Mexican regional | 3.4% | 302 |
| Hot AC | 3.2% | 451 |
| Classic hits | 2.8% | 288 |
| Oldies | 2.6% | 750 |
| All sports | 2.3% | 560 |
| Contemporary Christian | 2.2% | 724 |
| Alternative | 2.1% | 315 |
| Talk/personality | 1.8% | 202 |

*Source:* "Radio Today: How America Listens to Radio," 2008 edition (Arbitron, 2008).

*Note:* Other formats include album-oriented rock, adult hits, classical, active rock, new AC/smooth jazz, and Spanish contemporary. For a complete discussion of the many flavors of radio formats, go to http://ralphehanson.com.

was a format developed to appeal to the United States' changing ethnic makeup, with listeners spread fairly evenly among black, Hispanic, and "other."[70]

*Spanish-Language Broadcasting.* As the Hispanic population in the United States, especially in the Southwest and Florida, continues its rapid growth, Spanish-language stations are increasing in popularity and drawing high ratings. As of spring 2007, more than 870 Spanish-language stations were broadcasting in a variety of formats. This is a huge growth from the 533 Spanish-language stations broadcasting in 1998. These include multiple styles of music, news/talk/information, and religious programming.[71] The top-rated stations in Los Angeles frequently broadcast in Spanish and play either Mexican or adult contemporary music. The Los Angeles Dodgers baseball team has two sets of play-by-play announcers, one for English broadcasts, and the other for the team's Spanish-language network. And ESPN has a Spanish-language all-sports radio network based out of Miami that focuses heavily on soccer games and news.[72]

ESPN Deportes is a popular Spanish-language sports radio network headquartered in Miami.

Spanish-language stations are getting strong support from advertisers who want to reach the Hispanic community, and evidence indicates that Spanish-speaking consumers respond better to advertisements in their own language than to those in English.[73]

## Talk Radio: Politics, News, Shock Jocks, and Sports

As mentioned earlier, news/talk is one of the top radio formats. Talk radio has exploded during the past twenty-five years. In 1985, only 200 stations carried the format; by 1995, that number had grown to more than 1,000 stations. Marvin Kalb, formerly with CBS News, credits talk radio with providing a sense of community that people don't find anywhere else: "If we still gathered at town meetings, if our churches were still community centers, we wouldn't need talk radio. People feel increasingly disconnected, and talk radio gives them a sense of connection."[74] Talk radio is also important to the radio industry as more and more young people turn away from broadcasting to digital sources of music.[75]

*Conservative Rush Limbaugh hosts the most popular political talk show on radio.*

*Political Talk.* Talk radio is a major source of political information for 44 percent of Americans, and the political information they are getting from talk radio is largely conservative.[76] Although journalism generally values balanced coverage, New York radio host Brian Leher notes that such coverage doesn't mesh well with the nature of talk radio: "Some people's views don't fit neatly into traditional conservative or liberal labels. But that's not what's wanted in the media these days, especially in talk radio. They want you to be 100 percent confident that you have the truth and 100 percent predictable in your views."[77] Carl Anderson, senior vice president for programming and distribution for ABC Radio Networks, says that radio stations are looking for entertaining hosts who have a strong point of view and the ability to "connect with an audience."[78] Overall, talk radio leans strongly conservative, with Rush Limbaugh and Sean Hannity being the two most popular hosts. According to *Talkers* magazine, you have to get down to number 12, moderate-to-independent host Jim Bhannon, to get to a political talk host who isn't conservative. The most successful liberal talk radio host as of 2008 was Ed Schultz, who has less than a quarter of Limbaugh's audience and was number 16 on the *Talkers* list of top talk show hosts.[79] For a complete list of the top talk radio hosts, visit http://ralphehanson.com.

*Shock Jocks.* Not all talk radio is political; some is just plain rude. The **shock jocks**, including Opie and Anthony (whose real names are Gregg Hughes and Anthony Cumia), and Todd Clemm (known as "Bubba the Love Sponge"), have been described by critics as "disgusting," "racist," and "repulsive."[80] Nationally syndicated Opie and Anthony were fired after airing the sounds of two people having sex in a New York cathedral, but Clemm was kept on the air after slaughtering and barbecuing a wild boar during his show. Opie and Anthony have returned to the airwaves with a slightly toned-down show. Howard Stern, the most controversial of the shock jocks, left terrestrial radio in 2006 for satellite broadcasting, where he has a multiyear contract worth $500 million.[81]

*All-Sports Radio.* Sports occupies a growing segment of the talk format. The cable television network ESPN now provides sports radio programming and even has its own station in Chicago.[82] Some stations have gone so far as to adopt what has been called a guy radio format. "This isn't sports radio, it's guy radio," says 40-something radio host Glenn Ordway of Boston's WEEI. "It's what guys our age talk about in bars and on golf courses. . . . This is not broadcasting we're doing, it's narrowcasting."[83]

Although it's a narrow segment of the radio-listening public, the dedicated, loyal, and fanatic fans are very attractive to advertisers. "What separates sports radio from other radio is the passion of its listeners, and that makes it fertile hunting ground for us," says one major guy radio advertiser. "These are men who scream at their radios instead of punching the dial looking for the next cool song."[84]

## Radio Consolidates and Goes High Tech

Prior to 1985, broadcast owners were restricted nationally to seven AM radio, seven FM radio, and seven television stations.[85] During the 1980s, with the growth of cable and satellite television, the **Federal Communications Commission (FCC)** relaxed some ownership rules, which resulted in greater consolidation of ownership through media mergers. The trend toward broadcast deregulation was accelerated greatly with the Telecommunications Act of 1996. Although most of the law dealt with the cable television and telephone industries, the law lifted the restrictions on overall broadcast ownership. A single company could now own unlimited numbers of radio stations, with up to eight stations in a single market.[86]

The impact on radio was almost immediate. Within a year and a half, radio ownership had become far more concentrated and far less diverse. By 2003 the number of radio stations on the air had grown by 5.9 percent, but the number of station owners had fallen by 35 percent.[87] Clear Channel used the rule change to buy up $30 billion worth of radio stations nationwide, going from owning 42 stations in 1995 to more than 1,200 stations by 2003.[88] As of 2008, Clear Channel was the largest station owner in the United States, with 833 stations. Though it is down from its peak in 2006, Clear Channel still owns more than twice as many stations as its nearest competitor, Cumulus, with 346 stations. Spanish-language broadcaster Univision owns 69 stations.[89]

Many stations now operate with virtually no staff other than a few people to sell and produce advertising. The music, news, weather, and talk all come from either a satellite service or a computer hard drive, with automation software serving up the local commercials, announcements, and programming. If it sounds like programming is the same on radio from one side of the country to the other, it could be because the stations you are listening to all get their programs from the same centralized source.[90]

**Federal Communications Commission (FCC)**

The federal agency charged with regulating telecommunications, including radio and television broadcasting.

## Public Radio

With approximately 11,000 commercial stations, radio is a big business in the United States. But for all the power and reach of the commercial radio business, public radio provides a significant alternative.

*National Public Radio.* Public radio was authorized by the 1967 Public Broadcasting Act, which was designed primarily to create educational television. The act allocated stations at the lower end of the FM dial for noncommercial broadcasting, and most of the station licenses went to colleges and universities. In 1971 National Public Radio (NPR) went on the air with its first program, the evening newsmagazine *All Things Considered.*[91]

One thing *All Things Considered* could do that other broadcasters couldn't was present the news in depth. Eight-minute-long stories are not unusual, and twenty-minute stories are broadcast when the topic merits the length. This occurs in a medium in which thirty seconds is considered a long story.

The public radio network remained relatively small until two major developments occurred. The first was the growth of satellite delivery of network programming. The satellite let good signals go out to all stations no matter how remote they were. The second development was the installation of FM radios in most private cars. Since public radio was almost exclusively on the FM band, the advent of FM car radios made it possible to reach interested people with enough time to pay attention. Not surprisingly, NPR's biggest audiences are in cities whose workers have long commutes. By 1997 there were 560 NPR stations, and they could reach 90 percent of the U.S. population.[92] As of 2009 NPR had a weekly audience of 20.9 million, an increase of 9 percent over the year before.[93]

*National Public Radio's morning news program attracts a larger audience than any of the television morning news shows.*

NPR launched the two-hour news program *Morning Edition* in 1979, and since then it has become the most-listened-to morning news show in the country, with 7.6 million listeners tuning in daily. This is about one-third larger than the *Today* show's audience and 60 percent higher than that of ABC's *Good Morning America.*[94] Of course, this isn't a completely fair comparison because *Morning Edition* is on radio and the other two shows are on television. Americans also view NPR as being a particularly credible source of news, with people rating the radio network as having a higher level of believability than CBS, NBC, ABC, MSNBC, and Fox News.[95]

One of the major challenges facing public radio is the continual problem of funding. NPR's news division has a yearly budget of about $24 million and a staff of about 200 people, not counting the reporters working for all the affiliated stations. Only 16 percent of the public radio budget comes from the federal government. The biggest chunk comes from the listeners, or friends, of public radio, who contribute approximately 60 percent of the stations' budgets. The rest comes from states and universities that host the stations, and corporate underwriters, which are named during the programs they help support. These underwriting announcements began as brief mentions, but today they often include a message promoting the company, and some have come to resemble ten-second commercials. While most of these underwriting announcements promote the companies themselves as institutions, there are also announcements promoting particular books or television programs.[96] NPR has been hit hard by the 2008–2009 recession and had to cut more than seventy employees because of revenue shortfalls, though not all of these cuts were from the news division.[97]

National Public Radio has long had a Web site archive of its stories broadcast on *Morning Edition* and *All Things Considered*, but it is now treating its Web site as a news destination rather than just a support site for the network's broadcasts.

You can find links to NPR stories and Web sites at http://ralphehanson.com.

*Live Music on the Radio.*    Not all music broadcast on the radio today is prerecorded on CDs. One of public radio's most popular shows is Garrison Keillor's *A Prairie Home Companion*, which features a range of live music, skits, guests, and the centerpiece of the show, Keillor's monologue delivery of the news from Lake Wobegon, a mythical town in Minnesota that represents the stereotypical small Midwestern town, "where the women are strong, the men are good looking, and all the children are above average." *Mountain Stage,* produced by West Virginia Public Radio, has been broadcasting live performances by a variety of artists since 1984. In addition to country, bluegrass, and folk artists, the show has featured performers such as Crash Test Dummies, Sheryl Crow, Sarah McLachlan, Counting Crows, and They Might Be Giants. Although *Mountain Stage* does not generally carry stadium show headliners, R.E.M. did do an acoustic segment on the show.[98]

Producer Andy Ridenour told *Billboard* magazine that the show's greatest strength is that it exposes audience members to different artists and types of music: "One of the most common complaints we hear is that people don't get to hear anything new on the radio. Here, they get a chance to hear an artist they like and maybe two artists they never heard of."[99]

# THE FUTURE OF SOUND

For the past 100 years or so, the recording industry has been making money off the sale of little packages, either discs or cartridges of some sort. The coming of radio created a first blip in the market, with sellers wondering why people would buy records when they could get the music for free on the radio. The record companies soon learned that they could get revenue from licensing the music to the radio stations, and from promoting their records by having them played on the radio. Then came computers and the Internet, which allowed people to burn copies of CDs on blank media or transmit them to other people as MP3 files over the Internet. Now radio—the recording industry's old nemesis—is facing new competition of its own, from satellite radio, podcasts, and other technologies. There is no question of whether the entire sound industry is going through a massive change. The only real question is what will emerge.

## Radio's New Look: HD and Satellite

Radio is a medium that has gone through periods of intense change throughout its history as technology and use patterns have changed. It started with AM radio as the primary medium for news and entertainment. Then, in the late 1940s and early 1950s, television displaced radio and transformed it into a companion medium that people listened to in the background rather than something that dominated their attention. A third round of change came when FM broadcasting became popular in the 1970s, bringing stereo and high fidelity to broadcasting. FM eventually surpassed AM in popularity, especially in music, leaving AM radio to be dominated by sports, talk, and news—radio formats that don't suffer from low fidelity and the lack of stereo.[100]

And now conventional analog broadcasting on the AM and FM bands is facing competition from new digital options—HD and satellite radio.

People used to listen to radio predominantly in their cars and at home. Now people are listening in the office using radio stations' Web streams. They also download audio podcasts or go to pay satellite services.

Despite the new options, analog broadcasting remains by far the most popular choice—90 percent of Americans still listen to **terrestrial radio** every week. According to Arbitron, the leading radio rating service, terrestrial radio reached 235 million listeners in 2008, up slightly from the year before. Among those listeners,

**terrestrial radio**
AM and FM broadcast radio stations.

- 39 percent are at home

- 35 percent are in the car

- 23 percent are at work[101]

*HD Radio.*    Terrestrial radio isn't just sitting still as digital technology takes over the sound business. In many markets **HD radio** provides listeners with CD-quality sound and the choice of multiple channels of programming. But HD radio has not really taken off as a new medium. As of July 2008, only 500,000 HD radios had been sold in the United States and only 29 percent of American consumers were aware that HD radio exists.[102] Another problem is that car makers aren't putting HD radios in cars as standard equipment, though Audi is planning to start doing so in 2010.[103]

*Satellite Radio.*    In 2008 the two competing **satellite radio** services, Sirius and XM, merged to become Sirius XM. The two services still offer separate programming but have spillover between them. They've also united their efforts to promote the idea of subscription radio. Sirius XM ended 2008 with close to 19 million subscribers. Although the number of subscribers grew in 2008, the number of people who said they were aware of it did not grow, nor was there growth in the number of people who said they were at least somewhat likely to subscribe.[104] Neither of the two companies turned a profit as independents, and the newly merged company came close to filing for bankruptcy in February 2009, saved only by an infusion of cash provided by Liberty Media, the owner of satellite television service DIRECTV.[105]

The biggest name on satellite radio is former broadcast shock jock Howard Stern, who moved over to Sirius after his protracted and very public battle with Viacom, which syndicated him, and the FCC, which fined his stations more than

**HD radio**
Sometimes also referred to as high-definition radio, this technology provides listeners with CD-quality sound and the choice of multiple channels of programming but is not yet commonly available in mass-market outlets nor as standard equipment in cars.

**satellite radio**
The radio service provided by digital signal broadcast from a communications satellite. This service covers a wider area than terrestrial radio, is supported by subscribers, offers programming that is different from corporate-owned terrestrial stations, but is costly and doesn't provide local coverage, such as traffic and weather reports.

| TABLE 7.2 | DIGITAL AUDIO AUDIENCES, 2009 |
|---|---|

According to Arbitron, the leading radio rating service, the use of digital audio sources varies considerably by age. Below are several examples.

| Digital audio users | Percentage |
|---|---|
| Listen weekly to online radio (ages 12+) | 17 |
| Listen weekly to online radio (ages 18–34) | 19 |
| Own an iPod or other MP3 player (ages 12–17) | 71 |
| Own an iPod or other MP3 player (ages 18–24) | 64 |
| Own an iPod or other MP3 player (ages 25–34) | 55 |
| Cell phone users who say it has a "big impact" on their lives (ages 12+) | 47 |
| AM/FM radio users who say it has a "big impact" on their lives (ages 12+) | 21 |

*Source:* "The Infinite Dial 2009: Radio's Digital Platforms" (Arbitron, Edison Media Research, 2009), http://www.arbitron.com.

$2.5 million over a ten-year period.[106] Stern seems to be thriving on satellite radio, with no corporate or FCC censors to put limits on him. In an interview with the *New York Times,* Stern said, "We're talking about the stuff you can't talk about. The show on terrestrial radio in the last ten years had been so watered down."[107]

Satellite radio also provides news and public affairs channels such as CNN, Fox News, BBC World Service, and National Public Radio. One advantage of satellite radio over regular radio is that travelers will be able to tune in to a channel in New York and listen to it all the way to California. The disadvantage, other than the cost, is that these services provide no local content such as traffic reports, local news, or weather forecasts—the staples of car radio.[108]

## Music and the Long Tail: Alternatives to Broadcasting

Terrestrial radio is also facing competition from the new audio media that are redefining how we view radio. The Project for Excellence in Journalism (PEJ), which has been discussing the state of American media for more than six years, has stopped reporting about "radio" and moved to talking about "audio." PEJ suggests that radio can handle the transition to the digital world better than other media because "Voice and music are mobile and move easily among new platforms. And audio has done better as a medium of holding its audience than some other sectors."[109]

It would be a mistake, though, to just look at the Big Media alternatives, such as HD radio and satellite radio. Individual audience members can now become message providers by setting up their own Webcasts or podcasts with nothing more than a computer, a microphone, and a connection to the Internet. With these technologies, even programming that extends deep into the long tail of media content can be distributed easily.

*Webcasting.* The original online alternative to radio was Webcasting, or Internet radio. This can take a wide range of forms. Some Internet radio is tied to a terrestrial station; others are Internet only. Internet users can go to the station's Web site, or they can go to a "metasite" that has links to hundreds of different stations. Apple's iTunes music player offers hundreds of channels; XM's and Sirius's Web sites offer a selection of the satellite programs. Looking for Portuguese music from Brazil? It's there. A favorite radio station in New York when you head off to college in West Virginia? It's there.

Webcasting greatly extends the reach of stations, especially small ones with low-powered transmitters. A 6,000-watt station that can barely cover fifteen miles over the air can reach an entire city, not to mention the world, over the Internet. In essence, Webcasting can do for a small radio station what cable did for Ted Turner's local Atlanta television station, WTBS—turn it into a radio superstation that anyone in the world can receive.

A recent study by Arbitron found that an estimated 42 million Americans listen to online radio on a weekly basis.[110]

*Podcasting.*    One of the most exciting long-tail alternatives to terrestrial radio and prerecorded music is the **podcast**. Podcasts are audio programs distributed over the Internet as MP3 compressed music files that can be listened to online or downloaded to a computer or an MP3 player, and they open up distribution of audio programming to anyone with a basic computer and an online connection.

It is difficult to say exactly when podcasting got started, but summer 2004 is the commonly held period because that's when RSS 2.0, which could handle enclosures (essentially attachments) along with straight text, was released. It's also when former MTV VJ Adam Curry and software developer Dave Winer wrote the program iPodder. It was one of the first programs available that could download a podcast off the Internet and transfer it to an iPod. It's much easier to say when podcasting became widely known—February 9, 2005, when *USA Today* ran two articles about the new medium and phenomenon in the paper.[111]

In May 2005 podcasting became easier when Apple's iTunes software started supporting subscriptions to podcasts. You don't need an iPod to listen to a podcast (any computer or MP3 player will do), but iPods have a huge portion of the market, and iTunes support meant that even those with low levels of technical sophistication were able to listen to podcasts.[112]

Ownership of iPods and other MP3 players has grown dramatically. A survey in April 2006 showed that 20 percent of American adults owned iPods or other MP3 players. By January 2009, 51 percent owned iPods or other MP3 players. Despite the name *podcast*, ratings service Arbitron found that 69 percent of podcast listeners used their computers to play the programs; only 28 percent loaded them onto their iPods or other mobile players.[113]

That's not to say that podcasting is anywhere nearly as popular as radio. As of January 2009, 43 percent of Americans said they were aware of podcasts, nearly twice the proportion aware of them in 2006. Podcast audiences are growing but still not huge, with 22 percent of all Americans having ever listened to an audio podcast, and 11 percent listening to them on a monthly basis. But podcasts have a long way to go to come even close to terrestrial broadcasting in popularity, with 92 percent of Americans aged 12 and older reporting using AM/FM radio at least once a week.[114]

**podcast**
An audio program produced as an MP3 compressed music file that can be listened to online at the listener's convenience or downloaded to a computer or an MP3 player. Podcasts sometimes contain video content as well.

*The* Coverville *podcast generally airs three times a week and can feature such unusual songs as the Norwegian version of "Time Warp" from the* Rocky Horror Picture Show.

## TEST YOUR MEDIA LITERACY

### Podcasts: The Long Tail of Audio

You can find links to these and many other podcasts at **http://ralphehanson.com**.

The variety of programming available from podcasts is truly mind-boggling. There are, of course, podcasts produced by Big Media in support of their broadcast programs. Fox, CBS, NBC, and ABC all produce podcasts (some of which include video as well) in support of their programs; and National Public Radio and its member stations podcast all or part of many of their programs. Then there are professionally produced podcasts from smaller media, such as motorcycle racing news and features from SuperbikePlanet.com's *SoupKast.* Finally, there are independent, long-tail media podcasts. There is the *Dawn and Drew Show,* which is one of the earliest podcasts that's still going out; *MuggleCast* and *Imprint,* two podcasts that deal with the popular *Harry Potter* and *Twilight* book and movie series; and, of course, there is *Coverville.*

**Who are the sources?**

Who are the people producing podcasts? Are they different from those producing programming for radio?

**What are they saying?**

What kind of programming is played on these podcasts? How does podcast content differ from programming on terrestrial radio? How does it differ from satellite radio (if you've listened to it)?

**What evidence is there that podcasting will be a long-lasting phenomenon?**

Listen to a podcast, if you haven't done so already. What evidence is there that podcasting is an alternative to broadcasting? How significant a force in the industry is podcasting?

**Do you and your classmates listen to podcasts?**

Which ones? Why do you listen to them? What makes you go to the trouble of downloading them? Or, if you don't listen to them, why don't you? Are there any barriers to your listening to them?

Brian Ibbott has been at the heart of this new medium for almost as long as it has existed with his popular podcast *Coverville.* Ibbott posted his first episode in September 2004. As of this writing, he was approaching his 600th show.

Ibbott says he got into podcasting because he'd always wanted to be a DJ. "I knew if I did my own show, I wanted it to have something unique and not just a sampling of my favorite music. I wanted it to be something that had a theme to it. And one of the types of music I collect are cover songs."[115]

*Coverville* is notable for being one of the first podcasts to play music that's been licensed by ASCAP and BMI, the two major organizations that collect royalties for songwriters every time a published song is performed. But reaching the agreement took some doing because no one had ever tried to negotiate the rights for a podcast before. In fact, Ibbott had to explain to the ASCAP representative what a podcast was. They finally set up an agreement similar to that for Webcasts—streaming audio content transmitted over the Internet.

Ibbott has successfully licensed the rights to the compositions, but he's still working on the rights to the recorded performances. For independent artists not signed to a major recording label, it's easy. He just gets a note from the artist saying it's okay to include the song on *Coverville.* But for artists with a major label, it gets complicated. Ibbott has talked with the Recording Industry Association of America (RIAA), the industry group that goes after people who share copyrighted songs over the Internet, and he is following their recommendations. The RIAA licensing was a bigger issue in the early days of the show, when 90 to 100 percent of the music played on *Coverville* was registered with the RIAA. But now independent artists "hear about the show and send me music," Ibbott says. "It's getting easier and easier for me to put together a show that's all independent artists."

After producing so many episodes, Ibbott has a good handle on what makes for a great cover song: "It has to be unique. It has to sound like the band covering it and not try to be a note-by-note reproduction of the original. It has to be a good song. It has to stand on its own even if it weren't a cover. It doesn't have to be recognized, but it helps."

Ibbott will play some highly unusual covers, such as William Shatner's version of Pulp's "Common People," but he does have limits. He has a few that he sets aside for a worst-cover-ever show and others that he just doesn't play. "I stay away from covers done by current pop stars who get enough airplay. There's nothing clever about the cover. It's like their agent said 'I really like this song, why don't you do a cover of this.'"

It's hard to measure accurately the audience size for podcasts, but Ibbott's best estimate is that each episode of *Coverville* has about 40,000 listeners. Could a new independent podcaster attract an audience that large? It would be tough, Ibbott admits. "If I started *Coverville* today, would I have gotten the same size of audience? I don't think I would have. Getting in early was definitely key."

You can find more about *Coverville,* and links to several popular episodes of the program, at http://ralphehanson.com.

## New Economic Models for the Music Industry

There can be no question that the many sectors of the sound industry are currently facing a heavy dose of Truth Five—New media are always scary. The issues of file sharing, user-generated content, and music videos (topics also covered in Chapter 9—Television and Chapter 10—The Internet) are forcing changes to how radio and the recording industries are going to make money.

Computer technology has made it easy to manufacture pirate editions of CDs that can be sold on the street at a deep discount. (For that matter, it has made it easy for consumers to "burn" copies of their CDs for their friends for free.) The industry charges that this is stealing from artists and that the new media for distributing music is going to destroy the recording industry. These new technologies are certainly changing the music business, but they probably aren't destroying it.

*USA Today*'s technology writer Kevin Maney points to the example of China, where the music business is thriving even in the face of rampant piracy. Maney argues that in China, most CDs on the market are pirate editions, so artists have no choice but to make an income through live performances, sale of merchandise, and commercial endorsements.[116]

It can be argued that piracy and file sharing hurt the record labels more than they do the musicians. File sharing may even help musicians. Roger McGuinn, former front man of the 1960s band The Byrds, says that he received only a fraction of a cent per record on the early Byrds albums and never saw any royalties at all on a solo album that sold 500,000 copies. How did he make his money? Touring. Now McGuinn gives away tracks on his Web site and sells CDs that he's recorded at a home studio straight to fans at concerts and online. He tells *USA Today* that these home-produced CDs are the only ones that have made him money.[117] Classical and jazz banjo player Bela Fleck, of Bela Fleck and the Flecktones, makes the majority of his income touring across the United States in the summer. Fleck says his band makes 70 percent of its income from concerts, 20 percent from album sales, and 10 percent from merchandise. The CDs are mostly made to help fans discover his music.[118]

It is true that CD sales have been falling steadily over the past several years, but that doesn't mean that music sales are declining. For 2008 the overall sales of music rose 11 percent to 1.51 billion units (including albums, singles, videos, and digital downloads), with the growth driven by online sales. But sales of albums dropped from 500.5 million to 428.4 million. Media consultant Ted Cohen told Bloomberg News, "We're moving towards the inevitable digital environment. Whether it's on a cell phone or a computer, people now want instant access to music."[119] Oddly enough, 2008 saw a significant growth in the number of analog vinyl records sold. In fact, 2008 was the best year for LP sales since Nielsen SoundScan started tracking their sales in 1991, with 1.88 million vinyl albums purchased. Steve Sheldon, president of Rainbo Records, says that young people value the cover art, liner notes, and sound that come with LPs. "There's nothing like a vinyl record," Sheldon says. "It's analog. It sounds as close as you're going to get to the artist."[120]

Media technology journalist Mark Glaser writes that record labels and artists don't have a "god-given right" to sell CDs for $13 to $18 apiece. He outlines the wide range of choices consumers have now:

> As music lovers, we now have many more choices for how we can get our music fix. We can listen to the radio, to satellite radio, to Internet radio, or hear new music on TV shows like *American Idol* or on commercials. We can download free music from file-sharing networks [though that can be illegal]. We can hear music straight from the Web site of artists, and even get their tracks from MySpace pages. We can buy physical albums from the dwindling number of retail music stores or Wal-Mart and Target, or buy digital tracks or albums from iTunes or other online outlets.[121]

# CHAPTERSummary

The ability to record sounds began in 1877 with Thomas Edison's invention of the phonograph. Though Edison's machine could record and play back sound, it was relatively fragile and the foil-covered cylinders could not be reproduced nor did they stand up to repeated playing. Emile Berliner's gramophone, however, played music on flat discs that were stronger than Edison's cylinders and could be mass produced. This technology allowed musical performances to be stored and replayed. As prerecorded music became widely available, the nature of music consumption changed. People's major contact with music became recordings by professional musicians rather than live performances by amateurs.

Radio was an outgrowth of work done on the telegraph by Samuel Morse. Physicists such as Heinrich Hertz conducted early experiments on the detection of radio waves, but Guglielmo Marconi developed the commercially viable wireless telegraph.

Radio was used initially as a tool for sending messages from one person to another. David Sarnoff was among the first to see radio's potential as a tool for mass communication; CBS founder William Paley saw its potential as an advertising medium that incidentally provided entertainment. KDKA, the first commercial radio station, went on the air in 1920, ushering in the golden age of radio, in which radio was the dominant medium for home entertainment. Radio was also a major source of news, offering an intimacy and immediacy that newspapers couldn't match.

The organizations ASCAP and BMI were established to ensure that musicians and composers would be paid for the music they wrote and performed on stage, on records, and on the radio, as well as songs published in written form.

A wide range of recording formats has been used over the years, including the 78-rpm disc, the 45-rpm single, the LP, the compact disc, and the MP3 computer file. Each has given rise to concerns about changes in the purchasing and use of music.

Rock 'n' roll was a hybrid style of music that grew out of white hillbilly music and black rhythm and blues in the late 1940s and early 1950s. Because rock 'n' roll crossed racial lines, it became part of the integration of American society in the 1950s and 1960s. Rock 'n' roll became popular largely through recordings sold in record stores and played on the radio rather than through live performances. It evolved into an art form that existed primarily for recorded playback rather than live performance.

In the 1960s and 1970s rock music became more heavily produced, and there was a shift from hit singles to albums. Music by groups like the Beatles and Pink Floyd brought the role of the producer to the forefront, a move that accelerated with the development of disco and rap.

Parents and other adults have expressed concern about lyrics that include profanity, references to suicide and violence, and sentiments that are derogatory toward women.

As television displaced radio as the dominant broadcast medium, radio was transformed into a companion medium with a wide range of formats designed to appeal to narrow, specific audiences. These formats include many types of music, Spanish-language broadcasting, talk, news, and sports.

FM has gradually replaced AM as the dominant radio band. Although FM has a shorter broadcast range, it has much higher quality sound (higher fidelity).

Although the majority of radio stations are commercial, public radio—a staple of FM radio programming—provides an important alternative. Terrestrial radio is still the dominant sound medium; however, it faces growing competition from Webcasting, podcasting, and satellite radio.

## KEYTerms

# CONCEPT Review

Creation of recording industry
Changing ways of experiencing music
Popular music and social change
Role of music producers
Technology and the transformation of the music business
Radio and the transformation of the news business
The changing role of radio

# Movies
## Mass Producing Entertainment

**CHAPTER 8**

**Anyone who's gone** to the movies in the past twenty years could have told you that George Lucas and Steven Spielberg are the two highest-paid men in Hollywood, with annual paychecks of $170 million and $150 million, respectively. But Tyler Perry, coming in at number six with an annual income of $75 million, may come as a bit of a surprise.[1]

The Atlanta-based filmmaker has built a successful career producing Christian-themed comedies outside of the Hollywood system. Perry is typically writer, director, actor, and producer, and he's had an enviable box office track record built on low-budget, African-American-cast films that reliably bring in $40–$90 million apiece.

Perry made his breakout in 2005 with his surprise hit *Diary of a Mad Black Woman*. In it, Perry plays the cranky, aging, gun-carrying granny Madea, who has become his signature character. *Diary*, along with

Tyler Perry

Perry's next four mov-
ies, was ranked num-
ber one the weekend it
was released. His first five
movies brought in more than
$20 million on their opening
weekends. Considering that these
movies cost less than $20 million each to pro-
duce (*Diary* reportedly cost only $6 million), Perry's had a great record.[2]

According to Miki Turner, writing at the movie Web site Fandango, Perry has been successful because he's been serving an underserved audience—black churchgoers. Reuben Cannon, Perry's producing partner, told Turner: "The thing [Perry] cares most about is his audience and they know that. That's why they support him. He's giving them what they want. He's giving them these portraits of themselves or people they know that they've never seen on screen before."[3] As Turner points out, "Conventional Hollywood wisdom suggests there's no market for films . . . with strong, positive messages about the power of forgiveness, or those featuring a tall black man in drag."

Perry is outside of the Hollywood mainstream in more ways than just the themes of his movies. He works independently out of Atlanta, he ignores the critical disdain for his movies, and he finances his own films. As African American film critic Wesley Morris points out, "Perry is not August Wilson, Charles Burnett, or Spike Lee, nor does he want to be. But he is well on his way to being America's most important black entertainer."[4]

Lionsgate, the studio that distributes Perry's films, does not go the conventional route in promoting his films. The studio rarely has screenings for the critics, who are uniformly harsh on Perry's films. His movie *Tyler Perry's Madea Goes to Jail* scored a 28 percent fresh on the *Rotten Tomatoes* movie review site as of this writing, but it brought in more than $90 million and opened as number one against the animated film *Coraline* and the thriller *Taken*.[5] Instead, Lionsgate, which does mostly low-budget horror films, promotes Perry's movies among the black community. Morris says that to properly understand a Tyler Perry movie, you need to watch it with an enthusiastic group of Perry fans: "That's half the fun: hearing a partisan crowd crack up, break down, suck its teeth, scream at the abusers, tsk-tsk the nincompoops, and inevitably, go awww."[6] Morris attributes a lot of the appeal of Perry's films to the fact that he has great parts for women and gives them opportunities to make use of their talent in a way that more mainstream directors don't.

Perry first found fame as a playwright, and many of his early films started out as plays. But success did not come to Perry overnight. Before finding an audience for his plays and movies, Perry had been homeless for three months.[7]

Perry had the opportunity to shoot a pilot for a sitcom with CBS television in 2002, but he turned them down over the issue of creative control. When he started work on his first movie, *Diary of a Mad Black Woman*, he was close to a deal with Fox but again walked away over the issue of creative control. That's why he ended up with Lionsgate, one of the few truly independent film studios.[8]

After working out of older facilities in downtown Atlanta, Perry has built his own multimillion-dollar studios in Atlanta. The facility includes five sound studios used for his movie and television projects.[9]

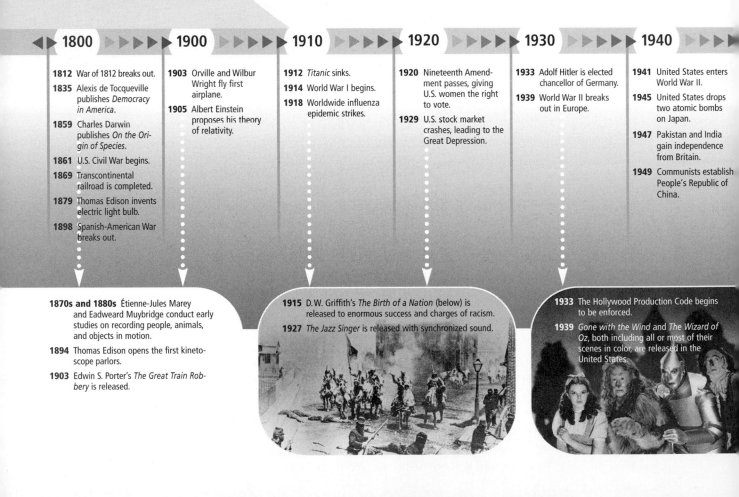

**1800**  ▶▶▶▶  **1900**  ▶▶▶▶  **1910**  ▶▶▶▶  **1920**  ▶▶▶▶  **1930**  ▶▶▶▶  **1940**  ▶▶▶

**1812** War of 1812 breaks out.
**1835** Alexis de Tocqueville publishes *Democracy in America*.
**1859** Charles Darwin publishes *On the Origin of Species*.
**1861** U.S. Civil War begins.
**1869** Transcontinental railroad is completed.
**1879** Thomas Edison invents electric light bulb.
**1898** Spanish-American War breaks out.

**1903** Orville and Wilbur Wright fly first airplane.
**1905** Albert Einstein proposes his theory of relativity.

**1912** *Titanic* sinks.
**1914** World War I begins.
**1918** Worldwide influenza epidemic strikes.

**1920** Nineteenth Amendment passes, giving U.S. women the right to vote.
**1929** U.S. stock market crashes, leading to the Great Depression.

**1933** Adolf Hitler is elected chancellor of Germany.
**1939** World War II breaks out in Europe.

**1941** United States enters World War II.
**1945** United States drops two atomic bombs on Japan.
**1947** Pakistan and India gain independence from Britain.
**1949** Communists establish People's Republic of China.

**1870s and 1880s** Étienne-Jules Marey and Eadweard Muybridge conduct early studies on recording people, animals, and objects in motion.
**1894** Thomas Edison opens the first kinetoscope parlors.
**1903** Edwin S. Porter's *The Great Train Robbery* is released.

**1915** D. W. Griffith's *The Birth of a Nation* (below) is released to enormous success and charges of racism.
**1927** *The Jazz Singer* is released with synchronized sound.

**1933** The Hollywood Production Code begins to be enforced.
**1939** *Gone with the Wind* and *The Wizard of Oz*, both including all or most of their scenes in color, are released in the United States.

Even though Perry goes the independent route, he has major talent in his films, including Janet Jackson, Alfre Woodard (ABC's *Desperate Housewives*), and Kathy Bates (Stephen King's *Misery*).[10]

As Perry continues to find success, Lionsgate is working at moving beyond his core audience of black churchgoers. "We want a crossover from African-American audiences to general audiences, and we're seeing that," says Tom Ortenberg of Lionsgate. "People are responding to movies about family, faith and redemption. That's a universal appeal Tyler is tapping into."[11]

You can look at reviews and the box office performance of Tyler Perry films by following the link at http://ralphehanson.com.

Regardless of the size of a movie's budget or profits, we still go to the movies for the same basic reason: to escape from the world around us. We spend a couple of hours in a darkened room with a group of people and share a created experience—a bit of excitement, sentiment, or romance. In this chapter we look at how the movie industry developed from peepshow kinetoscopes to today's large-screen theaters. We examine the roles of movies in society, public concerns about movies, and efforts by government and industry to regulate their content.

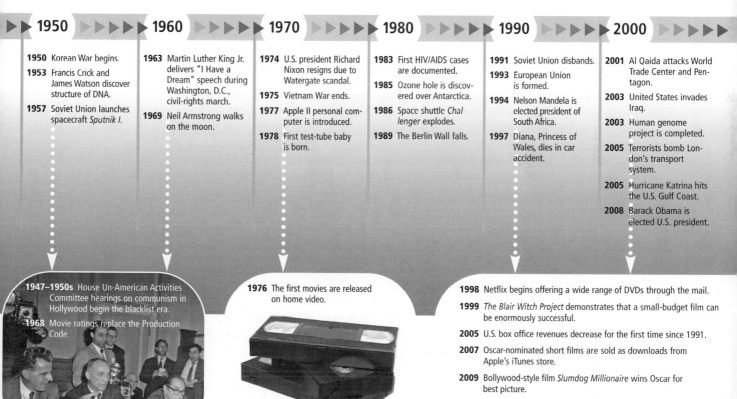

▶▶ **1950** ▶▶▶▶ **1960** ▶▶▶▶ **1970** ▶▶▶▶ **1980** ▶▶▶▶ **1990** ▶▶▶▶ **2000** ▶▶▶▶

**1950** Korean War begins.

**1953** Francis Crick and James Watson discover structure of DNA.

**1957** Soviet Union launches spacecraft *Sputnik I.*

**1963** Martin Luther King Jr. delivers "I Have a Dream" speech during Washington, D.C., civil-rights march.

**1969** Neil Armstrong walks on the moon.

**1974** U.S. president Richard Nixon resigns due to Watergate scandal.

**1975** Vietnam War ends.

**1977** Apple II personal computer is introduced.

**1978** First test-tube baby is born.

**1983** First HIV/AIDS cases are documented.

**1985** Ozone hole is discovered over Antarctica.

**1986** Space shuttle *Challenger* explodes.

**1989** The Berlin Wall falls.

**1991** Soviet Union disbands.

**1993** European Union is formed.

**1994** Nelson Mandela is elected president of South Africa.

**1997** Diana, Princess of Wales, dies in car accident.

**2001** Al Qaida attacks World Trade Center and Pentagon.

**2003** United States invades Iraq.

**2003** Human genome project is completed.

**2005** Terrorists bomb London's transport system.

**2005** Hurricane Katrina hits the U.S. Gulf Coast.

**2008** Barack Obama is elected U.S. president.

**1947–1950s** House Un-American Activities Committee hearings on communism in Hollywood begin the blacklist era.

**1968** Movie ratings replace the Production Code.

**1976** The first movies are released on home video.

**1998** Netflix begins offering a wide range of DVDs through the mail.

**1999** *The Blair Witch Project* demonstrates that a small-budget film can be enormously successful.

**2005** U.S. box office revenues decrease for the first time since 1991.

**2007** Oscar-nominated short films are sold as downloads from Apple's iTunes store.

**2009** Bollywood-style film *Slumdog Millionaire* wins Oscar for best picture.

**2010** James Cameron's *Avatar* replaces *Titanic* as movie box office champion.

# THE DEVELOPMENT OF MOVIES

The movie industry has its roots in the 1880s, but it wasn't until the early twentieth century that movies became a major public entertainment. In the late 1920s and early 1930s, movies gradually grew from ten-minute silent films into talking films up to two hours long. Although movie attendance peaked in the 1940s, viewing movies in theaters remains popular today despite competition from television and home video.

## The First Moviemakers

Thomas Edison is generally credited with developing the American motion picture industry, but like other media, movies came into being because of the work of many people; Edison was just one of several scientists and engineers who created the new medium of film.

*Young people in the 1940s dressed a little more formally when they went to the movies than do today's movie audiences, but Chicago moviegoers were still looking to have fun away from parental supervision for an afternoon or evening.*

*Edison, Marey, and Muybridge.* In the 1870s and 1880s, at least two people were working on the problem of capturing and portraying motion. The first was Étienne-Jules Marey. Trained in medicine, Marey sought to measure and transcribe motion, starting with blood and the heart and then moving on to how animals move. While Marey was never able to project moving pictures, he did help develop systems for taking repeated photos of people and animals in motion.[12]

British photographer Eadweard Muybridge was the second major influence on Edison. Muybridge, like Marey, wanted to capture the motion of animals on film. To settle a bet, the governor of California hired him to establish whether all four hooves of a horse leave the ground when it is galloping.[13] Muybridge set up twenty-four cameras at evenly spaced locations around a racetrack. Tripwires allowed the passing horse to trigger the cameras. (Muybridge established that all four hooves do leave the ground during a gallop.) Muybridge then projected the images using a type of zoetrope, a child's toy that put a series of images on a spinning cylinder.

THE HORSE IN MOTION.

Illustrated by

MUYBRIDGE.

ht, 1878, by MUYBRIDGE.                    MORSE'S Gallery, 417 Montgomery St., San Franci

Patent for apparatus applied for.                                        AUTOMATIC ELECTRO-PHOTOGRAPH.

OMET," owned by LELAND STANFORD; ridden by G. DOMM, cantering at an 8 minute gait over the Palo Alto track, 17th June,

The negatives of these photographs were made at intervals of twenty-one inches of distance, ; they illustrate consecutive positions assumed during a single stride of the horse. The vertical lines were twenty-one inches apart; the horizontal lines represent elevations of four inches each. The negatives were each exposed during the two-thousandth part of a second, and are absolutely "untouched."

*Photographer Eadweard Muybridge demonstrated in 1878 how a series of photos could depict a horse in motion. These photos were taken by a row of cameras activated when the horse ran past and broke a string running from the track to the camera.*

Muybridge eventually photographed both animals and humans moving against a black-and-white grid; his photos were published in 1887 in a book titled *Animal Locomotion*. He became a celebrity, touring the country to lecture and display his photographs.

At about the same time, Edison assigned an employee to work on the motion picture project. The first movies were not projected on a screen; instead, they were viewed by an individual viewer on a peepshow-like device that Edison called the **kinetoscope**. The moving picture was first demonstrated to the public on May 9, 1893, at the Brooklyn Institute of Arts and Sciences in the form of a thirty-second film called "Blacksmith Scene." Other early films showed a man sneezing, "Sandow the Strong Man" displaying his muscles, and Annie Oakley riding her horse. You can view a number of these early films online by following the link at http://ralphehanson.com.

The kinetoscope was soon replaced by a system in which films were projected on a screen, and the viewing of projected movies was transformed from a solitary activity to a group experience. The first American theaters grew out of the penny arcades where kinetoscopes had been located. These early theaters came

**kinetoscope**

An early peepshow-like movie projection system developed by Thomas Edison that could be seen only by an individual viewer.

to be known as "nickelodeons" because tickets cost five cents. By 1900 the nick-elodeon theaters were a popular entertainment throughout American cities.

*Early French Filmmakers.*   In France two brothers, Auguste-Marie and Louis-Jean Lumière, started working with Edison's motion picture ideas in 1894. They created what they called a *cinématographe,* a portable movie camera that could also be used as a projector. The brothers also set the standards for the speed at which film would be shot and the format of the film, details that Edison would eventually adopt. On December 28, 1895, they opened their first theater, where they showed short movies portraying everyday life in families, at factories, and on the street.

One of the earliest films to tell a story rather than record everyday life was created by another Frenchman, Georges Méliès. His most famous film was the 1902 *A Trip to the Moon,* which featured special effects such as a spaceship hitting the man in the moon in the eye. But although it told a story, it was essentially a stage show captured on film.[14]

*Edwin S. Porter: Telling a Story With Film.*   Edwin S. Porter expanded on Méliès's ideas to create one of the first hit movies in the United States. While working as a projectionist for Edison, Porter saw Méliès's *A Trip to the Moon* many times. He soon started making movies for Edison, most notably the 1903 film *The Great Train Robbery.* Porter laid out almost every element of the action movie in this film, telling the story of a group of outlaws who get on a train, rob the strongbox and the passengers, kill everyone who gets in their way, and eventually get shot and killed by the posse hunting them down. The movie, containing twelve separate scenes shot in a variety of locations, tells a realistic story. *The Great Train Robbery* helped establish how stories could be told through film. It is also an early example of Truth Five—New media are always scary. After all, Porter's film showed audiences exactly how to go about robbing a train.[15]

*D. W. Griffith: The Birth of the Blockbuster.*   Director D. W. Griffith was the George Lucas or Steven Spielberg of the silent movie era, creating epic movies that captured the entire nation's imagination. At a time when most directors were making movies that ran for twenty-five minutes at most, Griffith produced films that ran for an hour or more. In essence, Griffith created the first modern **feature-length film**. Griffith's most significant film—*The Birth of a Nation,* released in 1915—told the story of the rise of the Ku Klux Klan in the years following the Civil War. The film ran for over three hours and, at a cost of more than $110,000, was the most expensive movie to date. It also cost audiences more to see it; tickets were $2 in the big cities at a time when admission to most pictures was less than a dollar.

Based on Thomas Dixon's book *The Clansman,* Griffith's film was blatantly racist. At the time of its release, the film was criticized for a range of reasons, including its portrayal of African Americans as "nothing but beasts" and its

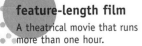
**feature-length film**
A theatrical movie that runs more than one hour.

attack on the North. One critic, referring to the three miles of film used in making the movie, called it "three miles of filth."[16]

Griffith soon outdid himself with another movie, *Intolerance*, which ran even longer than *The Birth of a Nation*. It cost nearly $500,000 to make and told four separate stories spread out over a period of 2,500 years. It was a bold, dramatic film but a financial failure, costing Griffith the fortune he had made with *The Birth of a Nation*.

*Intolerance* marked the point at which outside financial backing became necessary for a movie to get produced. Today the only exceptions are low-budget movies like *The Blair Witch Project* and movies made by very wealthy directors such as George Lucas. (Lucas financed the *Star Wars* prequel series, Episodes I, II, and III, in part with profits from *Star Wars* merchandise and his special-effects house, Industrial Light and Magic.)

Outside financing means that directors are accountable to the people who control the purse strings. Few directors today have the right to a "final cut," or final version, of the movie. That right is generally reserved by the people who control the money.[17]

*Movie Stars.*   In the early days of the movie industry, studios were reluctant to give actors screen credit for fear that this would encourage them to ask for more money. But the studios soon discovered that the public liked some actors and actresses better than others and were more likely to go to a movie featuring one of their favorites.

Directors like D. W. Griffith employed a group of regular players in all their films. Florence Lawrence was one of the first to break out of this anonymous group; Griffith's studio, Biograph, paid her a stunning (for the time) $25 a week. Linda Griffith, D. W.'s wife, wrote in a memoir, "[Florence's] pictures became tremendously popular, and soon all over the country Miss Lawrence was known as 'The Biograph Girl.' "[18] After Lawrence left Biograph for a rival studio, Independent Motion Picture, she became one of the first actresses to receive a screen credit.[19]

## The Studio System

Why are so many movies made in Hollywood? Although the earliest movies were filmed in New Jersey and New York, the appeal of Southern California soon became apparent. One argument for going west was to get away from Thomas Edison's "patent police," who tried to control the use of movie technology. But California also offered almost constant sunlight as well as the varied settings of ocean, desert, and mountains. In addition, the new movie studios needed a great deal of space, and at the beginning of the twentieth century, land in California was still relatively cheap.

At about the same time, the movie studios figured out that the most effective way to produce movies was with a factory-like process known as the

**studio system**

A factory-like way of producing films that involved having all of the talent, including the actors and directors, working directly for the movie studios. The studios also had almost total control of the distribution system.

**block bookings**

Requiring a theater owner to take a whole series of movies in order to get a few desirable, headliner films. This system was eventually found to violate antitrust laws.

**studio system**, in which all of the talent worked directly for the movie studios. Paramount Pictures, MGM, Warner Brothers, and other major studios controlled every aspect of the production process, from writing to editing. They employed a number of writers, directors, and actors ("stars"), who were under contract to work for a weekly salary. The movies were put together in assembly-line fashion. The studios also had almost absolute control of the distribution system.

Distribution was carried out in two ways. The first way was **block bookings**, in which theater owners were required to book a whole series of movies in order to get a few desirable films. The studio package might offer four headliner movies with big-name stars; ten mid-range pictures; ten at a lower level; and twelve no-star, bottom-of-the-line pictures. Sometimes salespeople insisted that theaters take the studio's entire package of fifty-two films, one for each week of the year. The second, and even more effective, way for studios to guarantee that their movies would be shown was to buy up theaters.[20]

The silent movie stars "sweet" Mary Pickford and "swashbuckling" Douglas Fairbanks were one of the first Hollywood power couples and were two of the founders of the United Artists movie studio.

*United Artists.* Actors and directors soon rebelled against the controls placed on them by the studio system. Despite being pampered and well paid, they had to make the movies the studios told them to make. By 1919 several of the most popular performers and directors, including D. W. Griffith, Charlie Chaplin, Mary Pickford, and Douglas Fairbanks, joined forces to create their own company, United Artists.

Instead of producing movies as the other major studios did, United Artists acquired and distributed movies after independent film producers had completed them. United Artists was essentially a model for the modern film studio—not a maker of films but a distributor and a source of financing.

United Artists remained a significant independent force in the movies until 1981, when one of its movies, Michael Cimino's *Heaven's Gate*, managed to lose almost its entire cost of production—$44 million—forcing the nearly bankrupt studio to merge with MGM. (*Heaven's Gate* was a dusty, confusing, and depressing western that was relatively expensive for the time it came out.[21])

*Talking Pictures.* In terms of technological developments in the movies, color and black-and-white movies coexisted for many years, but movies with sound replaced silent films almost immediately. Once people had both seen and heard their favorite stars, there was no turning back.[22]

Although many people point to *The Jazz Singer*, released in 1927, as the first talking film, it was actually a silent film with two talking (and singing) segments. The first successful demonstration of the talking picture was a series of short films that accompanied the feature *Don Juan* in 1926. *Don Juan* was a silent film, but it had a **synchronized soundtrack** (movie sound that synchronized voices with the pictures) with musical accompaniment, and the accompanying films demonstrated the equipment that would make talking films possible. This set of short films included performances by opera singers and a talk by Will H. Hays, president of the Motion Picture Producers and Distributors of America.

*The Jazz Singer* was called a **talkie**—a movie with synchronized sound—but it was the singing as much as the talking that impressed most people. In the movie, Al Jolson, talking to his mother, delivered one of the cinema's most prophetic lines, "Come on, Ma. Listen to this."[23] The public loved it. It was talking pictures like *The Jazz Singer* that helped build Warner Brothers into one of the nation's premier movie studios. Until then, Warner Brothers had been a relatively small player. The studio's breakthrough came with the realization that talkies were about more than talk. As Harry Warner put it, "If it can talk, it can sing."[24]

The movie industry as a whole was leery of talking pictures for a couple of reasons. On the simplest level, talking pictures in the early days required that stars be able to speak well while acting, something that wasn't necessarily easy to do. (In the contemporary movie industry, much of the dialogue is rerecorded after the photography is finished.) A bigger problem was that talking pictures were expensive. Not only did theaters have to upgrade their equipment, but the noisy movie cameras had to be muffled in soundproof booths, and noisy equipment that allowed cameras to swoop around the actors couldn't be used. These noise problems restricted the camera's mobility in the early talkies, and kept them from being as visually interesting as the best of the silent films such as *Metropolis* or *Nosferatu*. There was also the problem of noise in the vicinity of the studios (such as the roar of passing trains). Even the bright arc lights used to light the sets made a sizzling sound that had to be eliminated. As one industry observer noted, "It was easy to make pictures, easy to make records; but another matter to make them together."[25]

The influence of talking films soon gave rise to concerns like those familiar to us today. One newspaper columnist complained, "The talkies will make Hollywood the slang center of the United States. . . . A wisecrack recorded in Hollywood will be heard in all corners of the country months before the same quip could travel from town to town across the continent with a road show or a vaudeville troupe."[26]

**synchronized soundtrack**

Sound effects, music, and voices synchronized with the moving images in a movie.

**talkie**

A movie with synchronized sound; these quickly replaced silent films.

It took a while for the talking movies to find their way. As one critic pointed out in *Harper's* in 1929, the talkies were neither plays nor silent movies. They were something new, and Hollywood had to determine what that was. Writers, directors, and actors had to figure out what could be done with the new medium. Animation pioneer Walt Disney, for example, saw sound more as a way to add music and sound effects to his cartoons than as a way to make them talk.[27] In recent years the quality of sound has become increasingly important, both in theaters and at home. George Lucas's *Star Wars*, released in 1977, broke new ground not only with its visual effects but also with its sound effects. It was among the first movies to fully exploit the Dolby sound system, and the Lucas-developed THX theater sound system has become a standard for high-quality movie sound.

*The End of the Studio System.*   By 1938 the U.S. Department of Justice was starting to look at the movie studio system as a monopoly that needed to be brought under control. It decided to make a test case with Paramount Pictures. Paramount and the other major studios were charged with conspiring to set the terms for theaters renting their films—requiring them to charge certain minimum prices and to accept block booking—and discriminating in favor of certain theaters. The studios also worked to keep independent films out of theaters they owned.

An early portion of the settlement of what became known as the "Hollywood Antitrust Case"[28] required studios to show theater owners films before booking them, limit block bookings to five movies at a time, and no longer force theaters to book short films. But the power of the studios was not truly dismantled until 1948, when the U.S. Supreme Court ruled that the studios must sell their theaters. This final portion of the case's settlement led to the system in use today, in which the studios primarily finance and distribute films produced by independent companies rather than make movies themselves with their own staff.[29]

## The Blacklist

The years following World War II were a dark time for the movie industry. The studios' power was diminished by the Supreme Court's rulings in the antitrust case, and some politicians had an overwhelming fear that Hollywood and its movies might be playing a role in spreading communism. In 1947 a congressional committee, known as the **House Un-American Activities Committee**, under the leadership of Parnell Thomas, held hearings on possible communist influences in Hollywood.

In his introductory remarks, Thomas laid out the fears quite clearly:

> We all recognize, certainly, the tremendous effect which moving pictures have on their mass audiences, far removed from the Hollywood sets. We all recognize that what the citizen sees and hears in his neighborhood movie house carries a powerful impact on his thoughts and behavior.

**House Un-American Activities Committee**

The congressional committee, chaired by Parnell Thomas, that held hearings on the influence of communism on Hollywood in 1947. These activities mirrored a wider effort to root out suspected communists in all walks of American life.

With such vast influence over the lives of American citizens as the motion-picture industry exerts, it is not unnatural—in fact, it is very logical—that subversive and undemocratic forces should attempt to use this medium for un-American purposes.[30]

It is this legacy of fear—fear that the movies and other media would have undesirable effects on unsuspecting audience members (remember Truth Five—New media are always scary)—that led to the research and controls on the movie industry. (This topic is discussed in depth later in this chapter.)

There were two weeks of committee hearings, the most divisive of which involved ten "unfriendly witnesses" who questioned the right of the committee to ask them about their associations and beliefs. The committee repeatedly asked the question, "Are you now, or have you ever been, a Communist?" Instead of answering, the witnesses, known as the **Hollywood Ten**, challenged the constitutionality of the hearings. They were jailed for contempt of Congress, and the movie industry instituted a **blacklist**, which banned anyone from working in Hollywood who was a known communist, a suspected communist, or a communist sympathizer.[31]

In December 1949 Parnell Thomas was convicted of padding his payroll and went to jail himself. But hearings continued under new leadership in the early 1950s, and by 1953 the blacklist contained the names of as many as 324 suspected communists. The contracts of those who were blacklisted could be cancelled; if they were freelancers, the studios simply wouldn't buy their work.[32]

The hearings tore Hollywood apart. Some of the unfriendly witnesses had to move. The uncooperative witnesses lost their jobs and were ostracized, and those who had provided names were viewed as informers.

While the blacklist was in place, several writers continued to sell screenplays under assumed names or wrote screenplays without any credit at all. In 1956 Dalton Trumbo, writing under the name Robert Rich, won an unclaimed Academy Award for his screenplay for *The Brave One*. In 1957 David Lean's epic movie *The Bridge on the River Kwai* won an Oscar for best screenplay. The script, written by Carl Foreman and Michael Wilson, was based on a novel by the French author Pierre Boulle. But since the scriptwriters were blacklisted, the credit went to Boulle, who could not write or speak English.[33] The blacklist was finally broken in 1960, when Trumbo received screenwriting credits for the films *Spartacus* and *Exodus*.

## Television and the Movies

In the 1950s people began turning to television rather than movies for routine entertainment. The exodus of families to the suburbs also contributed to a decline in movie audiences, especially in the old urban Art Deco movie palaces. Sports, both professional and collegiate, started drawing audiences away from the movies as well.[34]

**Hollywood Ten**
A group of ten writers and directors who refused to testify before the House Un-American Activities Committee about their political activities. They were among the first people in Hollywood to be blacklisted.

**blacklist**
A group of people banned from working in the movie industry in the late 1940s and 1950s because they were suspected of being communists or communist sympathizers. Some of them, such as a few screenwriters, were able to work under assumed names, but others never worked again in the industry.

*Visitors at the 2009 Comic-Con convention in San Diego watch a preview of James Cameron's 3-D movie Avatar.*

In 1946 movie audiences reached their peak, with 80 million tickets sold every week. But by 1953 ticket sales had dropped by almost half, to 46 million a week. It was clear that Hollywood would have to do something to reverse this trend.

*Larger-Than-Life Movies.* One thing Hollywood did to entice viewers away from television was to make the movies shown in theaters bigger and better than before. Hollywood tried three-dimensional (3-D) movies, but they required special projection equipment and 3-D glasses. The gimmick started out successfully, but people soon became bored with the novelty, which ultimately added little to the movie experience. Almost the only serious movie to be released in the 3-D format was Alfred Hitchcock's *Dial M for Murder.* The 3-D format found a revival in the 2000s, especially with movies targeted at children such as Pixar's *Up* or Brendan Fraser's *Journey to the Center of the Earth.*[35] Theaters using 3-D digital projectors have also found success with 3-D concert films, such as those featuring Disney star Miley Cyrus and her alter ego, Hannah Montana, as well as the Jonas Brothers.[36] And, of course, there was the phenomenal success of James Cameron's 3-D presentation of *Avatar.*

More successful were attempts to project a larger picture on the screen. The most extreme of these was the Cinerama process, in which each scene was filmed from three slightly different angles and projected on a huge curved screen using three projectors. The purpose was to create the feeling of realism through the use of peripheral vision. The Cinerama theaters could also handle smaller wide-screen systems such as CinemaScope.

Along with the larger screens came larger movies, including epics like *The Ten Commandments* and the gladiator movie *Spartacus.* Today wide-screen technology is starting to find its way into television through the use of digital video discs and high-definition digital broadcasts.

*The Advent of Color.* Television also helped bring about the conversion to color movies. During the 1950s television was almost exclusively black and white. Color was first used in Hollywood in the 1920s at about the same time that sound came in, but it was expensive, the studios were focusing on the conversion to sound, and black-and-white film was easier to work with. Still, there are some important color movies from this era: *Gone With the*

*Wind* and *The Wizard of Oz* made effective use of color—think of the vivid images of Dorothy's ruby red slippers—silver in the original L. Frank Baum books—and Scarlett O'Hara's green velvet dress made from the parlor drapes.

One factor that delayed the conversion to color movies was that they initially required a complex camera that shot simultaneously on three separate reels of film (one for each of the three additive colors—cyan, magenta, and yellow). After World War II, American studios adopted a process used in Germany to shoot in color using a single reel of film, which made color filming much easier. Competition from television forced Hollywood to start using color in virtually every film from the 1950s on.[37]

Occasionally period-piece movies will be released in black and white for effect—think of the 2005 Oscar-nominated *Good Night, and Good Luck* or *Schindler's List,* which won the Oscar for best picture in 1993. Other movies are shot predominantly in black and white with brief spots of color, such as the live-action/computer-animation blend of *Sin City.*

*The Growth of Multiplex Theaters.*    In recent decades movie theaters themselves have been changing to meet the needs of a changing audience. As large numbers of people moved from cities to suburbs, the vast Art Deco movie palaces that seated as many as 2,000 people were no longer being filled. Gradually these megatheaters have been replaced by smaller theaters grouped together in what is known as a **multiplex.** These have a single box office and concession stand but anywhere from three to twenty screens. Each of the auditoriums is relatively small, but when a major movie is released, it can be shown in several of the theaters.[38] The number of theater screens has grown in recent years to almost 39,000, after declining in 2000 and 2001 to approximately 25,000. Many of these new theaters feature stadium seating, improved sound systems, and premium refreshments, like real butter on the gourmet popcorn.[39]

**multiplex**
A group of movie theaters with anywhere from three to twenty screens that share a common box office and concession stand. Largely a suburban phenomenon at first, they replaced the old urban Art Deco movie palaces.

*Going to the Movies Today.*    Even in the age of DVD and Blu-ray players, pay-per-view cable, and home theater systems, going to the movies is something special. People go for a variety of reasons—to learn things, to escape from everyday life, to enjoy a pleasant activity, to pass the time, to avoid feeling lonely, to fit in with others, or to learn about themselves.[40] Young people who are dating may go to the movies for no other reason than to be alone in the dark away from parental supervision.

But there are other things that make going to the movies unique. Movies are typically "edgier" than what is shown on television, although cable and home video have changed this substantially. There is also the larger-than-life aspect of movies like the *Harry Potter* or *Pirates of the Caribbean* series, *Avatar,* or *The Dark Knight,* which bring people into theaters for an overwhelming visual and sound experience. While the giant screen Cinerama system has died out, large-format IMAX theaters that were traditionally used for science and nature films at museums are now screening popular releases on their multi-story-tall screens. Action and science fiction movies such as *Star Trek* or *Transformers* can take in a substantial amount of their opening weekend revenue from IMAX theaters, in part because IMAX theaters can charge as much as $15 a person for tickets.[41]

Movies can also be a group experience. People watching the *Saw* horror movies at home may not have the overwhelming sense of dread that comes from being in a theater full of terrified people.

Movie scholar Garth Jowett writes, "Teenagers and young adults will probably always want to escape the confines of the home, and others will more than likely continue to be motivated to seek out an experience which allows intense individual involvement with little risk within an appealing social context."[42]

# THE MOVIE BUSINESS

**blockbuster era**
A period from the late 1970s to the present day when movie studios make relatively expensive movies that have a large, predefined audience. These movies, usually chock full of special effects, are packaged with cable deals and marketing tie-ins, and can be extremely lucrative if they are able to attract large, repeat audiences.

If the early 1900s were the silent film era and the 1930s and 1940s were the studio era, then the period from the late 1970s to the present day is the **blockbuster era**, in which studios try to make relatively expensive movies with a large, predefined audience. These movies are packaged with cable deals and marketing tie-ins, such as McDonald's Happy Meal toys.

## The Blockbuster Era

Steven Spielberg is generally credited with creating the blockbuster era with the release of his 1975 summer hit *Jaws*. It was the first movie to gross more than $200 million, and it set the stage for the big summer movies. Prior to *Jaws*, it was believed that a movie had to be released during the Christmas season to be a major success. *Jaws* had a number of things going for it: It was directed by one of the most popular directors of the late twentieth century, it featured a compelling musical score by John Williams, and it was based on a best-selling novel by Peter Benchley.

*Jaws* was accompanied by a giant television advertising campaign that began three days before the movie's release. But the marketing of the movie had started two years earlier with an announcement that the movie rights had been acquired and speculation about who the stars might be. Journalists were taken to the production site in record numbers to keep the stories flowing. The movie's release was scheduled to occur within six months of the publication of the paperback book, and the book's cover included a tie-in to the movie. As the release date for the movie approached, copies of the paperback were sent out to waiters, cab drivers, and other ordinary people to build word of mouth. Finally, the movie was given a summer release date to capitalize on the beach and swimming season.

The *Jaws* campaign was designed to get people to the movie and talk about it. If the talk had been negative, all the advertising in the world couldn't have saved the movie. But with everyone talking up the movie, *Jaws* took off.[43]

Its success started a tradition of larger-than-life summer movies that would continue with the *Star Wars* trilogies, the *Indiana Jones* series, the *Spider-Man* series, and the *Pirates of the Caribbean* series. Some observers have gone so far as to describe the summer blockbuster movie as "a wide-screen, color, stereophonic *ride*."[44] The description is apt, because by the 1990s, many of the studios had followed Disney's lead and produced theme parks with rides based on movies where the ride sometimes cost more to produce than the movie itself.

With the growing size of the home video market and the problem of movie piracy, moviemakers are working to maximize their initial audience. In July 2008, *The Dark Knight* set a record of opening in 4,366 theaters. It brought in more than $158 million on its opening weekend in the United States and made more than $203 million in its first five days.[45] You can read more about the economics of *The Dark Knight* with a link at http://ralphehanson.com.

*Avatar* may be the most commercially successful movie in history (see Table 8.1), but it didn't have the biggest audience. That honor belongs to the Civil War epic *Gone With the Wind,* which sold more than 100 million tickets in 1939 and countless more for multiple rereleases over a thirty-year period (see Table 8.2).[46] One reason the 2009 *Avatar* is at the top of the box office charts is that tickets for it cost much more than the Depression-era tickets for *Gone With the Wind.* Adjusted for inflation, *GWTW* ticket prices would have brought in a total of $1.51 billion, considerably more than the domestic box office receipts of *Avatar.*

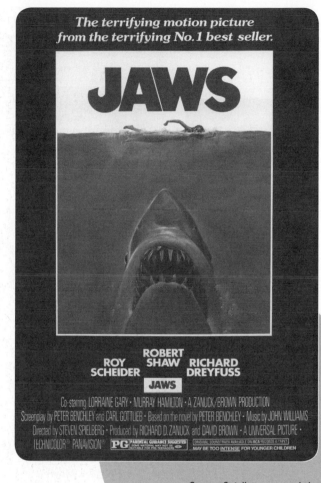

Steven Spielberg created the summer blockbuster film with Jaws. The 1975 film was the first movie to gross more than $200 million.

## BOX OFFICE RECEIPTS OF TOP MOVIES (ACTUAL DOMESTIC REVENUE)

| Rank | Movie | Year of release | Box office receipts |
|------|-------|-----------------|---------------------|
| 1 | Avatar | 2009 | > $601 million* |
| 2 | Titanic | 1997 | $601 million |
| 3 | The Dark Knight | 2008 | $533 million |
| 4 | Star Wars | 1977 | $461 million |
| 5 | Shrek 2 | 2004 | $441 million |
| 6 | E.T.–The Extra-Terrestrial | 1982 | $435 million |
| 7 | Star Wars–Phantom Menace | 1999 | $431 million |
| 8 | Pirates of the Caribbean: Dead Man's Chest | 2006 | $423 million |
| 9 | Spider-Man | 2002 | $404 million |
| 10 | Transformers: Revenge of the Fallen | 2009 | $402 million |
| 99 | Gone With the Wind | 1939 | $199 million |

*Source:* "Domestic Grosses," Box Office Mojo, February 2, 2010. Available from http://boxofficemojo.com/alltime/domestic.htm. Used with permission.

*Estimated. *Avatar* was still in wide release at the time this was written; actual earnings will be signficantly higher.

## BOX OFFICE RECEIPTS OF TOP MOVIES (ADJUSTED FOR INFLATION)

| Rank | Movie | Year of release | Box office receipts |
|------|-------|-----------------|---------------------|
| 1 | Gone With the Wind | 1939 | $1.51 billion |
| 2 | Star Wars | 1977 | $1.33 billion |
| 3 | The Sound of Music | 1965 | $1.06 billion |
| 4 | E.T.–The Extra-Terrestrial | 1982 | $1.06 billion |
| 5 | The Ten Commandments | 1956 | $977 million |
| 6 | Titanic | 1997 | $957 million |
| 7 | Jaws | 1975 | $955 million |
| 8 | Doctor Zhivago | 1965 | $926 million |
| 9 | The Exorcist | 1973 | $824 million |
| 10 | Snow White and the Seven Dwarfs | 1937 | $813 million |

*Source:* "Domestic Grosses; Adjusted for Inflation," Box Office Mojo, February 2, 2010. Available from http://boxofficemojo.com/alltime/adjusted.htm. Used with permission.

*Note:* Although not currently listed, *Avatar* would come in at number 21 as of February 2010, falling between *Fantasia* (1941) and *The Godfather* (1972).

## Home Video

Home videocassette recorders (VCRs) started becoming an important movie venue in the 1980s, and by 1994 over 85 percent of all U.S. homes had a VCR. Today digital video discs (DVDs) and high-definition Blu-ray discs have largely displaced the VCR. As of 2006 nearly 81 percent of all households had a DVD player, whereas 79 percent had VCRs. This is a big change from 1999, when 89 percent of households had VCRs, and fewer than 7 percent had DVD players.[47] DVDs provide a higher-quality image and dramatically better sound than videocassettes, and they have popularized the letterbox (or wide-screen) format. Pixar's *The Incredibles* brought in $261 million in theaters, making it one of the most successful films of 2004. When it was released on DVD, it made an additional $368 million.[48]

In addition to making more money for the studios, home video opened up a world of older movies and foreign movies to today's audiences. Previously, movie lovers could see a film only when it first came out or was rereleased, when it was shown in 16-mm format on a college campus or in a revival house, and then on late-night television. With videos and now DVDs, people can watch movies again and again, whenever they want.

## Digital Production and Projection

The revolution that started with desktop publishing—which enabled people to produce books, newspapers, and magazines on their computers and laser printers—has begun transforming the production of movies. Using an inexpensive digital video camera and a computer with video-editing capabilities, anyone can make a movie. Such movies can be transferred to 35-mm film for projection, converted to videotape, or "streamed" on the Internet.[49] (For more about movies on the Internet, see Chapter 10.)

Computers first came to Hollywood in a big way with *Star Wars* (Episode IV for the purists). Director George Lucas used a computer-controlled camera to shoot the space battle scenes. He was able to create multiple layers of images more easily because he could make the camera move exactly the same way on each shot. More recently, Lucas's *Star Wars Episode II* was the first big-budget feature to be shot entirely using high-definition video.

*Sky Captain and the World of Tomorrow*, released in 2004, was the first mainstream American movie to computer animate all the backgrounds and sets in an otherwise live-action movie.[50] Director Kerry Conran wrote his own software to create computer-generated backgrounds that would meld with the live-action footage of the actors shot before a blue screen, in much the same way that computer special effects are added into movies. In this case, though, without the computer-generated backdrops, there would be nothing other than the actors. There were no "sets" to speak of. The only "real" things in the film were the actors, their costumes, and the props they were holding.

Conran told the *Washington Post* back in 2004 that he believed his technology would allow filmmakers more freedom to pursue their visions:

> The studios today are in this awkward and horrible position where films cost so much money to make, they have to be cautious so they can appeal to the broadest possible audience, so that is half the point of this experiment, to see if independent filmmakers and studios can both take chances again, to think differently.[51]

While the technology might have allowed filmmaker Conran to make a movie he couldn't have otherwise, the film did not come cheap, costing a reported $70 million. But Conran saw that $70 million price tag as a bargain compared to the much more expensive action thrillers such as the *Spider-Man* franchise.

At the time the film came out, no one had seen anything quite like it, and veteran movie producer Jon Avnet proclaimed the process "a version of the virtual studio" and "unquestionably the wave of the future."[52]

Unfortunately for the film's creators, audiences in neither the United States nor anywhere else in the world were particularly interested in the film. With a domestic gross of only about $38 million and a worldwide gross of $58 million, the film did not make back its production costs through ticket sales.[53]

Conran predicted correctly back in 2004 that his techniques would find their way into action, fantasy, and science fiction movies. "In a romantic comedy, where you have the people walking through a park, it makes less sense to go to the effort to completely create this park than go outside and shoot it," he told the *Pittsburgh Post-Gazette*. "It's probably not suited for everything, but it could be used for anything."[54]

The surprise hit *300,* based on a graphic novel, would likely never have been made if not for the budget economies of digital production. The movie, which gave an over-the-top re-creation of the Battle of Thermopylae with all digital sets and backgrounds, cost only $65 million to produce, cheap compared to the recent sword-and-sandal epics *Troy*—which cost $175 million—and *Gladiator*—which cost $103 million. With that low cost of production, *300* was able to earn back its basic budget the first weekend of release, and it eventually earned more than $210 million domestically and $456 million worldwide.[55] What made the film so cheap? First, it was shot in Canada, where production and labor costs are lower. Second, it was shot completely on high-definition video on a blank sound-stage using the technology pioneered in *Sky Captain*. With the success of *300,* we see avant-garde techniques becoming mainstream, providing yet another instance of Truth Three—Everything from the margin moves to the center.[56]

For a look at how the movie *300* was adapted from Frank Miller's graphic novel, visit http://ralphehanson.com.

*Star Wars* creator George Lucas wrote in 1999 that he believed that film and projectors would soon be replaced by digital computer projection. *Variety* magazine, which covers the movie industry, expects half of the world's movie screens to have digital projectors by 2013. Aside from questions about the quality of the images, digital projectors give a better 3-D image than do conventional projectors, and they drastically lower the cost of distributing prints to theaters.[57] The six major movie studios of the Motion Picture Association of America (MPAA) have written standards, known as the Digital Cinema Initiative, so that theaters have a consistent set of rules for how digital projection will be handled. The biggest challenge for the conversion to digital projection is expected to be cost—with estimates varying from $20,000 to close to $100,000 per screen, depending on the theater's size and the desired quality.[58]

## What Makes a Movie Profitable?

Although a blockbuster movie can be enormously profitable, a relatively low percentage (20–30 percent) of movies actually make money. Movies can be financial failures even if they make $40 million and can be successful even if they make only $2 million—it all depends on how much the movie cost to produce and promote.[59]

The best known way to make money in the movies is to produce a big-budget blockbuster with big stars and a name director, have a giant domestic and international box office, sell lots of licensed products, sell millions of DVDs, and generally turn the movie into a Fortune 500 corporation. Sometimes this process even produces a pretty good film. Look at the Batman movie *The Dark Knight* as an example. It took in more than $530 million domestically and $468 million from the foreign box office on a budget of $185 million.[60] When you spend that much money making a movie, it has to be a success. Of course, with talent like director Christopher Nolan, actor Heath Ledger, and the screenwriting team of Christopher and Jonathon Nolan, it was bound to do well. Another example would be Robert Downey Jr.'s *Iron Man,* which ended up as a bit of a surprise summer hit with a box office north of $300 million.[61]

Sometimes the international box office can help redeem a domestic stinker. That was the case with Eddie Murphy's *Meet Dave.* It had a $60 million budget and a domestic box office of $11.8 million. But it redeemed itself slightly with a foreign box office of $38 million.[62] It wasn't even close to being a hit, but it wasn't a total disaster.

The alternative approach is to make a movie with a tiny-to-small budget with a clear target audience, have a modest box office, and make a great return on investment. A good example of this would be 2008's *High School Musical 3: Senior Year.* The *High School Musical* franchise took an unusual route to popularity. The first two movies in the series aired initially on Disney's basic cable channel. Only the third outing got a theatrical release. It cost $11 million to make and brought in $42 million its opening weekend. Like a summer event movie, it brought big levels of product tie-ins and video sales. And the movie's global box office topped out at an amazing $252 million.

Disney's *High School Musical 3* *turned big profits on a small production budget.*

On a smaller scale was the Christian-themed *Fireproof.* Produced for a budget of $500,000, it was promoted through churches and grossed more than $33 million. Now *Fireproof* did not make a large amount of money, but any movie that can bring in 66 times its cost of production has to be seen as a success.[63]

(For lists of top movies, by revenue, refer back to Tables 8.1 and 8.2.)

The problem for studio executives, of course, is figuring out in advance which movie can support a large budget, and which one can't. It's easy to figure out the big-budget movies that are likely to be blockbusters (well, maybe, at least those that ought to be blockbusters, if they are done right . . . ). But why do little movies like *Little Miss Sunshine, The Blair Witch Project,* or *Slumdog Millionaire* break out to become hits?

According to *USA Today* movie critic Susan Wloszczyna, these movies, and others like them, are ones that "grab the people who actually part with money to see movies."[64] The basics are pretty straightforward: Make an interesting film that doesn't fit a big-budget mold, keep the costs under control, and be savvy about how you promote it. If it does well, the upside is almost unlimited. If you miss, the movie is still likely to make back its cost through video, cable, and broadcast rights.

Take, for example, two movies starring Natalie Portman: *V for Vendetta* and *Garden State.* Neither movie had a large box office; both were quirky, idiosyncratic films; and both turned a profit. *V for Vendetta* was a dark, worrisome movie in which the main character, V, is a terrorist. While he is fighting fascism, he's also killing innocent people. What gave the filmmakers the freedom to make such an interesting film? The budget. *Vendetta* had a production budget of $54 million and brought in a domestic box office of $70 million and an international box office of $62 million. Not a big success, but not a big budget either, especially for a sci-fi action flick. Or let's get a little more personal in scale, with Zach Braff's *Garden State.* This story of a young man coming home to New Jersey for a funeral after trying to make it in Hollywood brought in more than ten times its production budget of $2.5 million. It had a charming script, good actors working for low salaries, and a great alternative pop sound-track, with tracks by Coldplay, Zero 7, and Thievery Corporation.[65]

Noted director Spike Lee says that he has maintained his independence as a moviemaker largely by keeping costs under control: "I've been very comfortable, for the most part, in that I view myself as an independent filmmaker—as one of the few directors that has final cut. And the deal's always been this: 'Spike, we're not willing to give you so much money, so make do with what you've got.' You can't argue with that."[66]

# MOVIES AND SOCIETY

The possible negative effects of movies have long been a source of concern. Although movies are attended by people of all ages, they appeal most strongly to adolescents and young adults, who are perceived as particularly vulnerable to media influences. But as film critic Glenn Kenny points out:

> [S]ince film is by and large a popular (and terribly expensive) art, the vast majority of moviemakers want to give the audience the pictures they think the audience wants to see, or the pictures that preview cards and focus groups tell moviemakers the audience wants to see. This kind of give-and-take makes it difficult to tell the dancer from the dance, as it were; add to that the fact that certain movies affect the way we look at other movies, and the puzzle of how we're changed by them becomes more complex.[67]

## How Much Influence Do Movies Have?

The debate over how movies affect people is contentious, even today. Movie-makers claim that they don't shape society, they just reflect it. But this ignores the fact that movies are a central part of society, and even mirrors have effects. Movie historian Gerald Mast notes that "movies have . . . been an immensely powerful social and cultural force. . . . They have produced social changes—in ways of dress, patterns of speech, methods of courting. And they have mirrored social changes—in fashion, sexual mores, political principles."[68]

A well-known example of the purported effects of the movies comes from the 1934 Clark Gable and Claudette Colbert movie *It Happened One Night*. Counter to the standard of dress for men at the time, Gable's character took off his shirt and exposed a bare chest; he wore no undershirt. After the movie was released, sales of undershirts reportedly plummeted because of Gable's example,[69] though whether the fall-off in sales of undershirts ever happened is a matter of some debate.[70]

*Research Results.* As movies grew in popularity in the 1920s, people became concerned about their effects on viewers, especially young people. The Payne Fund, a private foundation, sponsored a series of thirteen studies, several of which analyzed the content of movies, who was going to the movies, and what, if any, effects the movies were having on the audiences. The researchers found that a small number of basic themes appeared in movies over and over again: crime, sex, love, mystery, war, children, history, travel, comedy, and social propaganda. More than three-fourths of all movies dealt with crime, sex, or love.

A second major finding was that people could remember a surprising amount of what they had seen in movies, even six months after seeing them. Why such a high level of recall? Perhaps it was because movies were novel at the time, but another explanation was that movies gave people something to talk about, thus stimulating recall.

Some critics suggested that movies might be responsible for moral decay, and one of the studies looked at whether the morals portrayed in movies were at odds with those of the viewing public. Not surprisingly, the moral standards of characters in movies tended to be lower than those of viewers. After all, people who behave differently from us are the most interesting to watch.

Herbert Blumer, a noted social psychologist, conducted a major study that examined the diaries of young people who recorded how they thought they had been influenced by movies. He found that participants reported imitating the behaviors they saw in movies and copying the actions of their favorite stars in their games and play. Young people reported that they saw movies as a source of ideas about action, romance, and standards of beauty. In essence, they were using the movies to learn how to behave as an adult.[71]

**The Program.**    The controversy over the effects of movies on young people didn't end in the 1930s. One of the more controversial cases in recent years was that of the 1993 movie *The Program.* In the film, the hero, a college quarterback, performs a variety of extreme stunts, often while intoxicated. He rides a motorcycle recklessly through a rock quarry; lies down in the middle of a busy highway, flipping through a magazine as cars and trucks swerve to avoid him; and plays chicken with an oncoming freight train. The movie was popular among college students, and it is, by many accounts, a good film with lessons about the importance of sobriety and depending on friends.

But the movie became notorious after an eighteen-year-old was killed in Pennsylvania. According to *Time* magazine, the young man and three carloads of friends saw the movie at a drive-in theater not far from the young man's home. The next weekend he recreated the "lying-down-in-the-highway" stunt from the movie. While doing so, he was hit and killed by a pickup truck.

The reaction to the Pennsylvanian's death was immediate. In Hollywood, Disney's Touchstone Pictures division announced that it was shipping new prints of *The Program* without the highway scene, though the many other depictions of self-destructive behavior—like the "jumping-in-front-of-the-train" scene—were left in. U.S. Attorney General Janet Reno used the death as part of her argument that the entertainment industry should reduce its focus on violence.

The young man's death seemed to be a clear-cut case of cause and effect. He watched a scene in a movie, copied the behavior being portrayed, and was killed. The problem with that explanation is that high school students in his community had been lying down in the middle of the street for at least two years, long before the movie was released. According to one young woman from the area, she and twenty other students took turns "arranging themselves like sardines across a road." According to the student, who was in the seventh grade at the time, "All my friends were doing it, so I did it. I wasn't even thinking of getting hit."[72]

This case raises some important questions about the effects of movies. Clearly, if the students had been lying in the street for two years before *The Program* came out, the movie could not have been the direct cause of their behavior. But was there no relationship between the movie and the death? On the one hand, the young man who was killed was imitating something he had seen. On the other hand, why weren't young people imitating the "jumping-in-front-of-the-train" scene?

What is clear is that the relationship between movies and behavior is difficult to analyze. Hollywood would like people to believe that it does nothing more than reflect conditions prevailing in society. But movies quite often display extreme situations that are designed to shock audiences, not to reflect the real world. Critics argue that the movies lead to deviant behavior. And yet much of the criticism often arises when a single example of deviant behavior is copied from a scene in a movie.[73] This is an example of Truth Six—activism and analysis are not the same thing.

*Hooray for Bollywood: India's Movie Industry.*    The biggest source of movies in the world is not California or even the United States as a whole. That honor belongs to Bollywood—the filmmakers of India, especially the city of Mumbai (formerly Bombay). Although Bollywood films are popular worldwide, they are not seen frequently in the United States. But 2009's Oscar winner for best picture may help change that. *Slumdog Millionaire*, a British movie set in India that makes use of a lot of the stylistic conventions of Bollywood, won eight Oscars and made more than $140 million in the United States.[74]

Each year Bollywood produces more than 1,000 films that are distributed throughout Africa, China, and the rest of Asia. A BBC News Online poll found that the world's most popular movie star was not Harrison Ford or Julia Roberts; it was Indian actor Amitabh Bachchan, who has starred in more than 100 Bollywood movies.[75] (And as a little bit of movie trivia, in *Slumdog Millionaire* the young Jamal escapes from a locked room by jumping into an outhouse pit in order to get an autograph from Bachchan.)

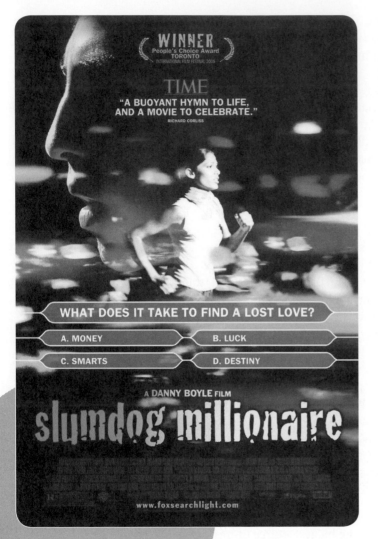

WINNER
People's Choice Award
TORONTO
INTERNATIONAL FILM FESTIVAL 2008

TIME

"A BUOYANT HYMN TO LIFE,
AND A MOVIE TO CELEBRATE."
RICHARD CORLISS

WHAT DOES IT TAKE TO FIND A LOST LOVE?

A. MONEY    B. LUCK

C. SMARTS    D. DESTINY

A DANNY BOYLE FILM

slumdog millionaire

www.foxsearchlight.com

*Director Danny Boyle's Oscar-winning* Slumdog Millionaire *exposed many Americans to the vibrant style of India's Bollywood films.*

Typical of India's films are the *masala*, or spice, movies. They feature several musical numbers, a strong male hero, a coy heroine, and an obvious villain.[76] The movies have as many as ten separate storylines—in contrast to American movies, which typically tell one or two stories.

One reason for the musical numbers in Indian films is that they help break through language barriers. India alone has more than twenty-five languages. Anupam Sharma, who works in the Indian movie industry, says that Bollywood movies touch people throughout the world: "Because of the distances and different dialects in India, music is the universal language."[77] When it comes to romance and sex, Bollywood films tend to be far more conservative than American films. "India is still clinging on to its social values, which explains Bollywood's success everywhere but in America," said Priya Joshi, an Indian cinema scholar. "Bollywood films don't have any kissing in them or tend not to. Warner Bros. used to make movies like this in the past. . . . If it's ready to return to its roots, then it's ready for Bollywood."[78]

Movie critic Roger Ebert writes that American audiences could enjoy these films: "It is like nothing [Americans] have seen before, with its startling landscapes, architecture and locations, its exuberant colors, its sudden and joyous musical numbers right in the middle of dramatic scenes, and its melodramatic acting (teeth gnash, tears well, lips tremble, bosoms heave, fists clench)."[79] If that sounds similar to the musical movie *Moulin Rouge*, that's no accident. Director Baz Luhrmann acknowledges he was inspired in part by the Bollywood moviemaking style.[80]

## The Production Code: Protecting the Movies From Censorship

Movies are somewhat different from other media in that their producers have always been conscious of the need for limits on what they can portray. In 1909 theater owners formed the National Board of Censorship to establish a national standard for movies. The idea was that the board would ban offensive films, with the implication that approved films were suitable to be shown. Ironically the board was formed primarily to protect the theater owners from trouble rather than to protect their audiences from offensive films.[81]

What was considered objectionable content in movies of this era? Prostitution, childbirth, and masturbation were all decried in the 1920s, as was drug use.[82] One critic argued that there was no question that censorship was necessary. The only question was whether the censors should be controlled by the industry or by the government.[83]

*Hollywood and Morality.*    One of the factors prompting censorship efforts was that the behavior of stars offscreen was considered as immoral as some of the movies themselves. When Mary Pickford, a silent-movie star who made a specialty of heroines with ringlets, like Rebecca of Sunnybrook Farm, quietly divorced her husband to marry her costar Douglas Fairbanks, her behavior became the talk of the nation. Actor Fatty Arbuckle became entangled in scandal after it appeared that he had bribed a district attorney to cover up the presence of a dozen "party girls" at one of his parties. He was later accused of murdering one of his guests—a young aspiring actress—at another party. Although he was eventually acquitted after three trials, the public never fully forgave him and he didn't appear onscreen for over a decade.[84] A 1922 pamphlet charged that Hollywood was a mass of "wild orgies," "dope parties," "kept men," and "kept women."[85]

*The Birth of the Production Code.*    The motion picture industry began formalizing its morality rules with "The Don'ts and Be Carefuls," a set of guidelines passed in 1927. The impetus for this action was a series of hearings by the Federal Trade Commission and the threat of government regulation.[86] As has generally been the case with the movie industry, censorship of the movies came from within the industry for economic reasons. Movie historian Gerald Mast describes the moral dilemma in which the moviemakers found themselves:

> Because the movies have sold sex and violence from the beginning (what extremely popular and public art ever sold anything else?), and because they were created within and supported by a society that condoned neither the doing nor the display of sex and violence, the motion picture industry has been in the paradoxical position of trying to set limits on how much it would let itself sell.[87]

Facing a range of accusations of immorality, the studios looked for someone who could improve the industry's image. They found that person in Will H. Hays, who had been U.S. Postmaster General in 1921–1922. Hays was named president of the Motion Picture Producers and Distributors of America and

**Production Code**
The industry-imposed rules that controlled the content of movies from the 1930s until the current movie ratings system came into use in 1968.

became famous for his development of the **Production Code**, which controlled the content of movies from the 1930s until movie ratings came into use in 1968.[88] The purpose of the code, in its early days, was primarily to convince people that Hollywood was doing something about morality in the movies. But by 1933 Hollywood was forced to start living up to the standards it professed to support.[89]

Among other things, the code required that evil not be made to look alluring and that villains and law breakers not go unpunished: "Crime shall never be presented in a way that might inspire others with a desire for imitation. Brutal killings are not to be presented in detail." Also, there could be no profanity or blasphemy in the movies. The code was also fairly strict about sex, noting that scenes of passion needed to be handled carefully: "Excessive and lustful kissing, lustful embraces, suggestive postures and gestures, are not to be shown." Interracial romance was also forbidden.[90]

Only occasionally could anything "immoral" get past the code, and big-budget movies from major studios were more likely to get away with pushing the edge of acceptability. Rhett Butler's closing line in *Gone With the Wind,* "Frankly, my dear, I don't give a damn," was shocking to audiences in 1939 because nothing so raw had previously been allowed by the censors.[91]

## The Ratings System

By the 1960s many movies were violating provisions of the Production Code, and some were even released without the code's approval. This forced a reevaluation of how movies were judged. Otto Preminger's 1953 movie *The Moon Is Blue* was the first major American movie to be released without code approval. Although it was controversial at the time, it would be considered mild today—imagine a movie causing a stir for including the words *virgin* and *mistress.*

In 1968, under the direction of its new president, Jack Valenti, the MPAA scrapped the increasingly outdated Production Code. The code was replaced with a system of voluntary ratings indicating the audience for which the movie was most appropriate.

*How Are Movies Rated?*    Movie ratings are assigned by a panel of ten to thirteen parents who live in the Los Angeles area. In 1999 the panel consisted of seven women and five men ranging in age from twenty-eight to fifty-four. It included homemakers, carpenters, a teacher, a food and beverage manager, and a manicurist. On a typical workday the raters screen and discuss three movies. They then assign each movie one of the following ratings:

- G: General audiences. All ages admitted.

- PG: Parental guidance suggested. Some material may not be suitable for children.

- PG-13: Parents strongly cautioned. Some material may be inappropriate for children under age 13.

- R: Restricted. Persons under age 17 will not be admitted unless accompanied by a parent or adult guardian.

- NC-17: No one under age 17 will be admitted.

This system evolved from the original system of four ratings: G, M, R, and X. The rating of M (mature audiences) was soon changed to GP (general audiences, parental guidance suggested) and then to PG (parental guidance).

Certain kinds of content usually prompt particular ratings. Drug use generally requires at least a PG-13 rating. Sexually oriented nudity results in an R rating. (*Titanic* got by with a PG-13 rating because its nudity occurred when an artist sketched his model, and not in a later love scene.) Violence that is rough and persistent requires an R. A single use of the "F-word" requires a PG-13. If that word is used more than once, or used in a sexual sense, the movie is supposed to be rated R, though the board may override that rule by a two-thirds vote. (As an example, the Julia Roberts movie *My Best Friend's Wedding* used the "F-word" in a sexual sense and still received a rating of PG-13.)

Some critics charge that gay sex is more likely than heterosexual sex to receive a severe rating. It appears likely that the 1969 Oscar-winning movie *Midnight Cowboy* was given an X rating primarily because actor Jon Voight portrayed a male prostitute who serviced male clients. Others have charged that female sexuality is more likely to receive restrictive ratings than is male sexuality; interracial sex is also considered inflammatory.

Some movies get submitted for ratings in early versions to see how far directors can go and still get the desired R rating. *Bruno*, a mockumentary by the creator of *Borat*, got a rating of NC-17 the first time it was submitted. Several scenes implying gay sex were removed before the

*Writer, director, and actor Sacha Baron Cohen deliberately pushes the limits of the MPAA ratings system with his raunchy movies, such as* Bruno *and* Borat.

film was granted an R. Sacha Baron Cohen, the film's writer and star, was required to deliver an R-rated version of the movie for theatrical release, though an unrated version will likely be released on home video. One movie executive told the Hollywood blog *The Wrap*, "A guy like Sacha shoots what he wants, and then he negotiates."[92] (Editing the movie down to an R rating didn't end up making the movie a success. As of this writing, *Bruno* was on track to make substantially less than *Borat*.[93])

**Indiana Jones *and PG-13.*** In the mid-1980s it became clear that the rating system had a weakness. Movies were being released with a PG rating that did not merit an R but nevertheless included content that went beyond a PG rating. A new rating was proposed, PG-13, which would inform parents of the content of the film but not set limits on who could be admitted.

The rating change was supported strongly by director Steven Spielberg, who forced the issue with *Indiana Jones and the Temple of Doom* and *Gremlins.* Both movies were attacked for being too violent and intense for preteens, although they did not include content that would require an R rating. Spielberg observed ironically, "I've never made an R movie and hope never to make one, so I've been one of the first to appeal for a ratings change that would take the onus off the filmmaker as parent to America. That's not our role."[94] (This was back when Spielberg was making youth-oriented summer blockbuster action films rather than his more serious films dealing with World War II, the Holocaust, and terrorism.)

Media mogul Barry Diller, head of Paramount Studios in the 1980s, summed up the problem with the rating system, which at the time contained four ratings, even though only two could be used on a regular basis:

> It became apparent some time ago that only the PG and R ratings mattered much anymore. Nobody anticipated it, but both the G and X acquired negative associations—one for being innocuous, the other for being pornographic. There was a growing difference between what seemed appropriate content for teens and preteens.[95]

Today PG-13 is seen as the most desirable rating because teenagers see these movies as more sophisticated than those rated G or PG.[96] Between 1995 and 2009, PG-13 movies had the highest average gross box office, with 1,711 movies earning an average gross of just under $40 million. Movies with G and PG ratings were close at $35 million. But the average box office for R-rated movies was only $14.5 million, and NC-17 movies grossed an average of $3.4 million.[97]

**The X Problem.** A second major problem with the rating system had to do with the X rating. The trouble began when the MPAA did not trademark the X rating and therefore could not control its use. The pornography industry began labeling its unrated films XXX on the theory that if X was adult, XXX would be *really* adult. Because the X rating became associated with pornography, many newspapers and television stations refused to carry advertisements for X-rated movies, and many theaters pledged not to show such movies, despite the artistic merit that some movies receiving the rating may have.

In 1990 the MPAA threatened to assign an X rating to *Henry & June*, which portrayed the relationship between writer Henry Miller, his wife, and writer Anaïs Nin. The producers protested, and the MPAA responded by creating a new rating, NC-17, which supposedly was less prejudicial than X. In reality, little changed; theaters and media outlets treat the new rating as equivalent to X.

Movies that receive the dreaded NC-17 rating often must be reedited to qualify for the more commercially viable R rating. But the producers of *Midnight Cowboy*, the first and only X- or NC-17-rated movie to win an Oscar for best picture, decided against reediting the film. Producer Jerome Hellman notes that after the movie won the Oscar, the film board offered to give the film an R rating if the producers would cut one frame from the movie so that it could be advertised as a "re-cut" version. The producers refused, but the board relented and changed the movie's rating to R.[98]

Some people in the movie industry have speculated that Steven Spielberg's World War II film *Saving Private Ryan* should have received an NC-17 for the violence in the opening scene about the D-Day invasion of France but avoided it because of Spielberg's reputation. Filmmaker Spike Lee, speaking at the Cannes Film Festival, said:

> The MPAA has two different standards: one for violence, one for sex. I mean, I like *Saving Private Ryan* very much, especially the first hour. But if that's not an NC-17 film, I don't know what is. That's the way war should be depicted. But when people walk around picking up their severed arms and stuff like that, that's an R?[99]

Former MPAA president Jack Valenti defended *Private Ryan*'s R rating: "*Saving Private Ryan* was a reenactment of one of the most crucial days in American history. I think every 13-year-old in the country ought to see it, even though it was rated R, to understand that the freedom you take for granted was paid for in blood."[100]

In 2007 the MPAA made some slight revisions to the rating scheme. These include a new warning to discourage parents from bringing young children to more intense R-rated movies. The ratings board now reveals the demographics of the people who do the ratings. There have also been calls to expand the acceptability of the NC-17 rating so that the R rating is not applied to movies that children shouldn't be allowed to see. But the updates to the rating system did not go so far as to create an official "hard R" rating that would ban all viewers under the age of 17 from attending the movies.[101]

Regardless of the criticisms, parents appreciate the rating system. A 1999 survey showed that three-fourths of U.S. parents find the ratings useful in deciding what their children should be allowed to see.[102]

# TEST YOUR MEDIA LITERACY

## Movie Ratings

As we already discussed, the movie rating scheme is controversial for a number of reasons. Dan Glickman, the chairman of the MPAA, discussed the state of the movie industry and the ratings process in a 2008 speech on the fortieth anniversary of the movie rating system. Glickman, a former congressman and U.S. secretary of agriculture, says that the rating scheme exists to help parents pick appropriate movies for their children rather than to limit what adults can see:

> Ratings do not exist to cast judgment on whether a movie is "good" or "bad." The system is not a gatekeeper of society's morality and values. It does not require artists to promote behavior and beliefs deemed socially or morally upright. Some, from time to time, try to pressure the system into taking on these inappropriate roles in a free society. But the primary mission is transparency for parents—clear information about the content of films.
>
> Raters themselves are parents. They have no prior industry affiliation. Their job is to reflect what they believe would be the majority view of their fellow parents. So in rating a film, they ask questions any parent would ask: Would I let my kids watch this? At what age? With or without an adult? What would I want to know about this film to make my decision?[1]

Glickman notes that different topics upset parents at different times. In the 1960s and 1970s, drugs were not the hot issues that they are today. And in the past several years, a number of objections have been raised against smoking in movies, with some groups arguing that smoking in movies should lead to a mandatory R rating. He goes on to say that despite criticisms of the ratings system, 80 percent of parents with children under the age of thirteen "thought of the ratings system as useful."

### MORE online

You can read Dan Glickman's speech from a link at **http://ralphehanson.com.**

. . . . . . . . . . . . . . . . . .

### Who is the source?
Who is Dan Glickman? What is the MPAA? How does Glickman represent the movie industry? What are his interests in doing so?

### What is he saying?
What does Glickman say is the function of the movie rating system? What do critics say is wrong with it? How does he respond to parents?

### What evidence is there?
What evidence does Glickman present that the rating system is working? How does the movie industry respond to criticism? And why would the movie industry respond (or why wouldn't it)?

### What do you and your classmates think?
How well do you and your friends think the rating system is working? Did it keep you out of R-rated movies when you were younger? Do you believe parents use the rating system as intended? What do you think constitutes a G rating? PG-13? R or NC-17?

[1] Dan Glickman, *40 Years of Freedom: A Progress Report on the Modern Movie Ratings System* (Washington, D.C.: Media Institute, 2008), www.motionpictureassociation.org/press_releases/glickman%20speech%20--%20media%20institute%20--%20sept%2010%202009.pdf.

# THE FUTURE OF MOVIES

The movie business is facing an uncertain future. In 2005 the U.S. box office was down by 6 percent from the year before.[103] There were a lot of explanations for what caused the downturn. Conservative critics claimed that Hollywood was too liberal and was making movies that didn't appeal to the American public.[104] Others have claimed that the problems were too many sequels and remakes. While sequels, remakes, and raunchy movies have continued to draw big audiences, the total size of the movie audience has stayed below the 1.58 billion ticket level it hit in 2002. (Keep in mind that audience size peaked back in the 1940s, with sales of just over 4 billion tickets a year.[105]) Since 2005, movie ticket sales have hovered in the area of 1.3–1.4 billion tickets per year.[106] Although the Hollywood box office has continued its climb in dollar amount, that has been driven more by increased ticket prices than by an increase in audience size.

Why are movie audiences declining, or staying the same? The sharp decline of movie audience size back in the 1940s and 1950s was clearly a function of the rise of television as a new medium.[107] Currently movie audiences have many more alternatives than they did in the 1950s, with cable/satellite television, home video, pay-per-view, and Internet sources.

Regardless of the reasons, the movie industry has to react to this changing economic reality. The studios are doing so by building up their big-release summer movies as major brands, using the Internet to promote their products, and finding new ways to distribute small movies to a dispersed audience.

## Movies as a Brand

In the 1980s, domestic box office receipts accounted for more than 50 percent of movie income for studios; by 1995 this figure had fallen below 15 percent. Today studios earn as much or more from **ancillary, or secondary, markets** as they do from domestic ticket sales. These are movie revenue sources other than the domestic box office. For example, home video rights may be worth twice the theatrical box office total.[108] Ancillary markets include the following:

■ International distribution rights

■ Pay-per-view rights

■ Premium cable channel rights

■ Network television

■ Home video

■ Book rights

■ Toys and clothes

■ Product placement

**ancillary, or secondary, markets**

Movie revenue sources other than the domestic box office. These include foreign box office, video rights, and television rights, as well as tie-ins and product placements.

Summer and holiday blockbuster movies have evolved into more than just films. They've become entire cottage industries—brands if you will—in and of themselves. Take the 2009 hit movie *Transformers: Revenge of the Fallen.* It will be one of the highest-grossing movies for the year, producing $369 million in domestic box office over its first four weeks of release. It also did $404 million in international ticket sales over the same time period.[109] Electronics company LG created a limited-edition *Transformers* phone. *Transformers* director Michael Bay then directed a thirty-second television commercial for the phone, using the talents of Digital Domain, the same special-effects company that brought the robots to life in the movie. Digital Domain also did the effects for *Transformer*-themed commercials for fast food company Burger King.[110] Prior to the movie's release, Kmart had a promotional tie-in giving away free tickets to the movie to people who bought at least $50 in menswear, along with a promotion of *Transformer* toys, video games, and clothing. The 7-Eleven convenience store chain offered *Transformer* Slurpee cups, character straws, and movie-themed flavors.[111] On a much larger scale, the 2010 Chevy Camaro was featured in the movie as the *Transformer* Bumblebee. Bumblebee served as a major character in video games developed for the Sony Playstation 3, Microsoft X-Box 36, and the Nintendo Wii. And if the toy version wasn't enough, Chevrolet built a special-edition Camaro with Bumblebee paint and a *Transformers* badge.[112]

The *Transformers: Revenge of the Fallen* brand example illustrates how important marketing tie-ins can be for a big-name movie and how the brand can become as important—and lucrative—as the movie itself. For links to examples of these products, visit http://ralphehanson.com.

## Movie Promotion on the Internet

When Daniel Myrick and Eduardo Sanchez headed out into the Maryland woods in October 1997 to film *The Blair Witch Project*, they had no idea they were creating what would become one of the big hits of 1999 or that they would change how movies are promoted.

*Blair Witch* purports to be a documentary filmed by three students investigating the legend of a murderous witch who lived in the woods near Burkittsville, Maryland. The movie did not even have a script; instead, the actors started with only a thirty-five-page plot outline. The actors were also the film crew, using an old 16-mm film camera and a $500 High-8 video camera. The total cost of filming the movie was between $35,000 and $60,000, although some critics wonder how it could have cost even that much.[113] The movie eventually grossed more than $250 million worldwide.

The performers shot twenty hours of film and tape over an eight-day period while wandering about in the woods. The directors left notes for the actors each day, but the performers were given a lot of latitude. "We let [them] do what they wanted to do," Myrick says. "We gave them little clues as to where we wanted the scenes to go, but most of it was improvised."[114]

Myrick and Sanchez, along with Artisan, promoted *Blair Witch* in the same low-budget way in which it had been filmed, making use of cable television and the Internet rather than mainstream media. The pair created a mock documentary about the making of the movie, *The Curse of the Blair Witch*, which aired on the Sci-Fi Channel, and many viewers took this as evidence that the events recorded in the film had actually occurred. The promotional campaign capitalized on the confusion over whether the movie was fact or fiction, and many people who saw the film during the first week or two after its release thought that it might be real.[115]

Ten years after the movie was scaring movie fans and producers alike, *Los Angeles Times* blogger Glenn Whipp argues that the biggest impact of *The Blair Witch Project* was in the effectiveness of the Web-based viral marketing campaign put together for the movie. The movie had good buzz coming out of showings at the Sundance and Cannes film festivals, and marketing materials made it sound like the footage for the film had been found. Horror film director Scott Derrickson told Whipp, "The blurb on the poster said this was 'found footage,' and there was nothing in the marketing to lead you to believe it was anything but that."[116]

The 1999 surprise hit, The Blair Witch Project, *was made to look like a student documentary film, and its low-budget promotion scheme using a Web site, homemade flyers, and word-of-mouth channels made many people think that it was a true story.*

Web sites are now being used to court fans months or even years before a movie comes out. In many cases, the Web site is designed to maintain awareness of the movie even after the advertising is done, and to build awareness once again when the movie is released on video. Independent film producer Mark Duplass (*The Puffy Chair*) says that in addition to changing how movies are promoted, *Blair Witch* has also changed how movies look, with "[t]he semi-improvised nature, the hand-held digital camera work, the naturalistic acting inside a genre piece, the idea of 'We don't have a [lot] of money, so let's build a budget that's appropriate, so we can execute it correctly.'"[117]

## MOVIES AND THE LONG TAIL

The long tail is going to have a bigger and bigger effect on the movie industry in the years to come. But 2007 marked the point at which it jumped to the forefront. Before then, unless you lived in New York or Los Angeles, you were not

# TEST YOUR MEDIA LITERACY

## The Long Tail of the Movies

When *Long Tail* author Chris Anderson tries to explain the central concepts of his book, he often points to the online DVD rental store Netflix as a prime example. In 2009 Netflix carried 100,000 different DVD and Blu-ray titles. It also has more than 12,000 titles available for immediate viewing over either a computer or a streaming video box that connects the subscriber's television set to the Internet. Netflix has, of course, Sofia Coppola's 2006 version of *Marie Antoinette* starring Kirsten Dunst. But it also has the 1938 version of the film starring Norma Shearer in the title role, with John Barrymore as King Louis XV and Tyrone Power as Marie Antoinette's lover. For those who really want to delve deeply into the topic, Netflix also offers at least three documentaries on the ill-fated queen: *Marie Antoinette*; *Marie Antoinette: The Scapegoat Queen*; and *Marie Antoinette: Queen of Versailles*. Anderson found that audiences aren't just interested in a few big hits; they are interested in a deep pool of choices. The problem has always been distribution. Movie theaters are great for showing a limited number of movies to a lot of people. That's why theater owners love the summer blockbusters. But when you can draw from audiences nationwide, even movies with a limited appeal can be successful. As you can imagine, the tiny and dedicated cadre of Marie Antoinette fans is spread out all over the country.

Netflix reports that about 30 percent of its business comes from new releases, and 70 percent comes from older films. Why? Netflix provides the tools on its Web site to help its customers find these older movies. Netflix tracks the movies you've rented previously and how you've rated them. It then uses that information to recommend other movies you'd like. Anderson says that if Netflix can use consumer data to recommend films, the cost of marketing small movies to consumers is lowered to almost zero:

> Advertising and other marketing can represent more than half of the costs of the average Hollywood blockbuster, and smaller films can't play in that game. Netflix recommendations level the playing field, offering free marketing for films that can't otherwise afford it, and thus spreading demand more evenly between hits and niches."[1]

How do you go about predicting what people who are renting movies from Netflix will want to watch next? That's the question Netflix is desperately trying to answer. If Netflix wants to stay in business, the company needs to convince its customers to keep paying their monthly subscription fees, even when they've watched all the recent popular hits. So Netflix developed its Cinematch software to predict what movies customers will like based on what movies they've liked previously. To keep improving its recommendations, Netflix is offering a $1 million prize to a programmer who can improve the predictive quality of its software by 10 percent. The key difficulty for Netflix is the quirky

### MORE online

You can read more about Chris Anderson and the long tail in Chapter 2 and online at **http://ralphehanson.com.**

independent film, like *Napoleon Dynamite*. People tend to have very strong, and very unpredictable, reactions to the movie, which makes it difficult to predict what other movies they will like. If anyone can crack the "why we like/don't like quirky indy movie" problem, they'll be a long way toward winning the Netflix prize.[2]

Four years after its initial release, *Hotel Rwanda*, a serious drama about the Rwandan genocide, was still number fourteen on the Netflix Top 100 list, although it grossed only $25 million in its original theatrical release. Netflix has allowed an audience to find this movie through its customer recommendation system, even though it hasn't had a giant advertising budget and a potato chip tie-in.

**Who is the source?**

Who is Chris Anderson? What is his background? What has he done?

**What is he saying?**

What is the long tail? How do hit movies differ from more ordinary films? How do Netflix DVD rental patterns differ from those at Blockbuster neighborhood stores? How does the long-tail effect change marketing strategies?

**What evidence does Anderson provide?**

What evidence does Anderson provide of the popularity of movies in the long tail? What does he say drives the popularity of long-tail films? How do long-tail effects change audience expectations?

**What do you and your classmates think?**

Do you or your friends have an account with Netflix? If you do, how often do you rent a recent hit movie? How often do you rent an older or more obscure film? Are you more likely to rent an obscure or non-mainstream film if it comes recommended? Has this expanded your interests into a variety of film genres?

[1] Chris Anderson, *The Long Tail* (New York: Hyperion, 2006), 110.

[2] Brooke Gladstone, "Knowing Me, Knowing You," On the Media, http://ralphehanson.com/blog/archive_08_12.html.

likely to have seen the Oscar winners for best animated short film and best live-action short. But in 2007, the films were available as digital downloads from Apple's iTunes store at $1.99 each. This means that for less than the price of a movie ticket in an urban market, you could download and view all five nominated films in either category, even if you live in Kearney, Nebraska. What you are seeing here is nothing less than the full impact of the long tail hitting the mainstream movie industry. (For more on how the long tail is affecting the distribution of short films, visit http://ralphehanson.com.)

Also, Netflix provides distribution for foreign films that might not be shown all that often in the United States—like the films of Hungarian director Bela Tarr or the avant-garde art films of artist Stan Brakhage.

Famed film critic Roger Ebert has found that on his review Web site, www .rogerebert.com, no one review accounts for more than 1 percent of the page views. Instead of the blockbusters dominating the traffic, most of the more than 10,000 reviews on the site are attracting some level of attention.[118]

## CHAPTER Summary

Ways of recording motion on film were first developed by photographers Étienne-Jules Marey and Eadweard Muybridge in the 1880s. Inventor and entrepreneur Thomas Edison applied their ideas in building the first practical motion picture display system, the kinetoscope. In France the Lumière brothers invented the first portable movie camera and the first projector that could be used to display movies to a crowd.

Early directors such as Edwin S. Porter developed movie storytelling techniques that were expanded eventually into the feature-length film by D. W. Griffith. Griffith demonstrated that the public was interested in and willing to pay for larger-than-life films with longer running times. Griffith was also one of the first directors to seek outside financing for his movies.

From the 1920s through the 1940s, the studio system dominated moviemaking in the United States. Under the studio system, all the talent—from writers to directors to actors—was under contract to the studios. The major studios, such as Paramount and Warner Brothers, ran the movie industry like a factory assembly line, controlling which movies were made and how they were distributed. The studio system ended when the U.S. Supreme Court broke up the studios' monopoly in 1948.

A troubled time followed for the movie industry. The 1950s brought new competition from television and a controversial blacklist of writers, directors, and actors who were suspected of being communists. Hollywood responded by producing bigger, more spectacular movies; making almost all movies in color; and breaking up giant theaters into smaller, multi-theater complexes known as multiplexes.

The movie industry is currently dominated by high-budget blockbuster movies with a large, predefined audience and marketing tie-ins. Although the initial domestic box office receipts are still important, movies often make more income from ancillary, or secondary, markets such as foreign rights, video rights, and cable television rights. Blockbuster movies are now seen as a brand of interrelated products rather than just a movie. Yet smaller, low-budget movies often carry less risk of failure because they don't have to make nearly as much money to be profitable. Movies targeted at niche audiences can also be profitable if they have a controlled budget.

Moviemakers are increasingly relying on digital technology to make and promote movies. In addition to being used for special effects, digital technology makes it possible to shoot and edit low-budget movies using digital video rather than more expensive film. Directors can even shoot the movie on a blank soundstage and insert the sets and backgrounds digitally. Digital technology in the form of the Internet is also being used to promote movies directly to consumers.

Since the 1920s there have been concerns about the effects that movies may have on young viewers. Hollywood has attempted to protect itself from criticism, initially by limiting the content of movies through its Production Code and more recently with age-based ratings.

Theatrical movies are facing increased competition from home video. While the total box office has risen in recent years, the number of people attending the movies has declined. Moviemakers are responding with innovative new ways of promotion, and by finding audiences for movies of more limited interest.

## KEYTerms

kinetoscope   269
feature-length film   270
studio system   272
block bookings   272
synchronized soundtrack   273
talkie   273
House Un-American Activities Committee   274

Hollywood Ten   275
blacklist   275
multiplex   277
blockbuster era   278
Production Code   290
ancillary, or secondary,
   markets   295

## CONCEPTReview

Digital filmmaking
The idea of moving pictures
The rise and fall of the studio system
The blacklisting of suspected communists in the 1940s and 1950s
The changes television forced on the movie industry
How movies can make profits from being big or being small
The effects of movies on society
How Hollywood has responded to threats of censorship
How Hollywood has responded to the changing nature of the movie market

# Television

## Broadcast and Beyond

**The most prominent** television news critic in America is not a journalist, academic or even a politician. He's comedian Jon Stewart. Stewart's primary job is as host of Comedy Central's *The Daily Show*, a program featuring satire and fake news. Stewart is also known as one of the most popular sources of news among college students.[1]

Stewart started getting kudos as a press critic when he appeared as a guest on CNN's program *Crossfire* in October 2004, supposedly to promote his fake history book, *America*. But during his appearance, Stewart refused to play the part of the obedient talk show guest. He not only questioned the quality of cable political talk shows but also questioned whether they should exist at all.

Along with fake news segments, Stewart's *Daily Show* also has guests, including

Democratic presidential candidate Barack Obama, Republican presidential candidate John McCain, and Pakistani leader Pervez Musharraf.

*Crossfire*, in contrast, was a daily debate show on current political issues that featured hosts and guests from the left and right. As Paul Begala, one of *Crossfire*'s liberal hosts, put it, "Our show is about all left vs. right, black vs. white, paper vs. plastic, Red Sox against the Yankees."[2]

And it's that polarizing debate that Stewart objected to during his appearance. "I made a special effort to come on the show today because I have privately, amongst my friends and also in occasional newspaper and television shows, mentioned this show as being bad . . . ," Stewart said on the program. "It's not so much that it's bad as it's hurting America."

**Jon Stewart**

When conservative host Tucker Carlson tried to compare the questions Stewart asked 2004 presidential candidate John Kerry on his show with those *Crossfire* would have asked, Stewart's response was, "If you want to compare your show to a comedy show, you're more than welcome to."

That was Stewart's point: A show supposedly about serious political debate is no different than a satirical comedy show. Political talk shows are staged with props and costumes to generate the highest possible level of conflict. In essence, they are the professional wrestling rings of journalism. Stewart's central objection was that programs such as *Crossfire* and Fox News's *O'Reilly Factor* are all about shouting and scoring points, not about transmitting the basic information needed to cast informed ballots on Election Day.

In his book *Amusing Ourselves to Death*, the late Neil Postman wrote that television, by its very nature, turns everything into entertainment. Postman argued that no matter what we watch on television, "the overarching presumption is that it is there for our amusement and pleasure."[3] So it should not be surprising that Stewart, as a television comedian, has been acclaimed as the most important voice of political news for the younger generation.

Fox's Bill O'Reilly claims that Stewart's audience is nothing but "stoned slackers." Maybe so, but according to Nielsen Media Research, viewers of Stewart's *Daily Show* are more likely to have four years of college than viewers of *The O'Reilly Factor*.[4] Stewart's viewers also scored better on a political knowledge test than did non–*Daily Show* viewers.

So how important is Stewart? In 2007 a Pew Research Center survey found that Stewart was tied with Dan Rather, Tom Brokaw, Brian Williams, and Anderson Cooper as the fourth most admired news person in the country. (Katie Couric was the most admired.) Among respondents under the age of thirty, Stewart tied O'Reilly for the top spot as most admired journalist.[5] Why would Americans, especially young Americans,

**◄► 1800 ►►►► 1900 ►►►► 1910 ►►►► 1920 ►►►► 1930 ►►►► 1940 ►►►►**

**1812** War of 1812 breaks out.

**1835** Alexis de Tocqueville publishes *Democracy in America*.

**1859** Charles Darwin publishes *On the Origin of Species*.

**1861** U.S. Civil War begins.

**1869** Transcontinental railroad is completed.

**1879** Thomas Edison invents electric light bulb.

**1898** Spanish-American War breaks out.

**1903** Orville and Wilbur Wright fly first airplane.

**1905** Albert Einstein proposes his theory of relativity.

**1912** *Titanic* sinks.

**1914** World War I begins.

**1918** Worldwide influenza epidemic strikes.

**1920** Nineteenth Amendment passes, giving U.S. women the right to vote.

**1929** U.S. stock market crashes, leading to the Great Depression.

**1933** Adolf Hitler is elected chancellor of Germany.

**1939** World War II breaks out in Europe.

**1941** United States enters World War II.

**1945** United States drops two atomic bombs on Japan.

**1947** Pakistan and India gain independence from Britain.

**1949** Communists establish People's Republic of China.

**1927** Inventor Philo T. Farnsworth demonstrates his all-electronic television system.

**1939** NBC starts regular television broadcasts from New York City; these are suspended with the advent of World War II.

**1948** Milton Berle (right) and Ed Sullivan go on the air with variety shows, initiating the golden age of television; the first community antenna television (CATV) systems are established.

consider the comedian a journalist? A year-long study of *The Daily Show* by the Pew Foundation's Project for Excellence in Journalism found the following:[6]

- Stewart covers roughly the same range of national political issues that other political talk/commentary shows do.

- The show carries twice as much press news as conventional news media do.

- Stewart tends to avoid stories that couldn't be joked about, such as the collapse of the Minneapolis interstate bridge or the Virginia Tech shootings.

- Stewart's humor requires a well-informed audience to "get" his jokes.

- *The Daily Show* draws an audience similar in size to that of Fox's *Hannity & Colmes* or CNN's *Election Center*.

Even with his long history of being confrontational with established members of the press, celebrity journalists still seem to be surprised when Stewart attacks. In 2007 MSNBC *Hardball* host Chris Matthews appeared on *The Daily Show* to promote a new

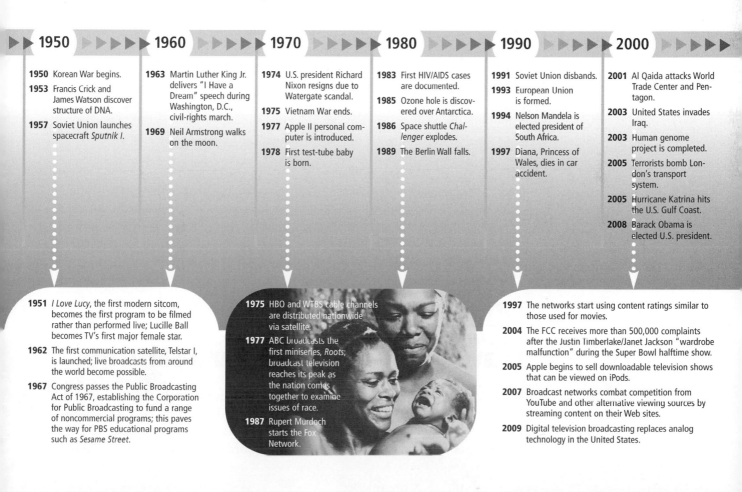

## 1950   1960   1970   1980   1990   2000

**1950** Korean War begins.

**1953** Francis Crick and James Watson discover structure of DNA.

**1957** Soviet Union launches spacecraft *Sputnik I*.

**1963** Martin Luther King Jr. delivers "I Have a Dream" speech during Washington, D.C., civil-rights march.

**1969** Neil Armstrong walks on the moon.

**1974** U.S. president Richard Nixon resigns due to Watergate scandal.

**1975** Vietnam War ends.

**1977** Apple II personal computer is introduced.

**1978** First test-tube baby is born.

**1983** First HIV/AIDS cases are documented.

**1985** Ozone hole is discovered over Antarctica.

**1986** Space shuttle *Challenger* explodes.

**1989** The Berlin Wall falls.

**1991** Soviet Union disbands.

**1993** European Union is formed.

**1994** Nelson Mandela is elected president of South Africa.

**1997** Diana, Princess of Wales, dies in car accident.

**2001** Al Qaida attacks World Trade Center and Pentagon.

**2003** United States invades Iraq.

**2003** Human genome project is completed.

**2005** Terrorists bomb London's transport system.

**2005** Hurricane Katrina hits the U.S. Gulf Coast.

**2008** Barack Obama is elected U.S. president.

**1951** *I Love Lucy*, the first modern sitcom, becomes the first program to be filmed rather than performed live; Lucille Ball becomes TV's first major female star.

**1962** The first communication satellite, Telstar I, is launched; live broadcasts from around the world become possible.

**1967** Congress passes the Public Broadcasting Act of 1967, establishing the Corporation for Public Broadcasting to fund a range of noncommercial programs; this paves the way for PBS educational programs such as *Sesame Street*.

**1975** HBO and WTBS cable channels are distributed nationwide via satellite.

**1977** ABC broadcasts the first miniseries, *Roots*; broadcast television reaches its peak as the nation comes together to examine issues of race.

**1987** Rupert Murdoch starts the Fox Network.

**1997** The networks start using content ratings similar to those used for movies.

**2004** The FCC receives more than 500,000 complaints after the Justin Timberlake/Janet Jackson "wardrobe malfunction" during the Super Bowl halftime show.

**2005** Apple begins to sell downloadable television shows that can be viewed on iPods.

**2007** Broadcast networks combat competition from YouTube and other alternative viewing sources by streaming content on their Web sites.

**2009** Digital television broadcasting replaces analog technology in the United States.

book he had written. At the close of the interview, Matthews invited Stewart to come on his show in return. Stewart's response? "You know what? Can I say this? I don't troll." Matthews responded furiously, "You are unbelievable! You . . . This is a book interview from hell. This is the worst interview I've had in my life! . . . You are the worst!"[7] In March 2009 Stewart started criticizing financial reporting by CNBC's star analyst Jim Cramer for failing to properly warn the public about the risks associated with the stock market. Stewart eventually had Cramer on *The Daily Show* for an interview in which he confronted Cramer with all his wrong predictions.[8]

Aside from being funny, what does Stewart do that other broadcast journalists don't? Blogger and newspaper columnist Dan Froomkin says that Stewart and his colleague Stephen Colbert are willing to call out their guests for lying and dissembling. That's something regular journalists aren't willing to do, Froomkin says, because they don't want to lose access to sources, rock the corporate boat, or be charged with being partisan.[9] Michigan State University journalism professor Steve Lacy told the Project for Excellence staff, "My students tell me they read the news for facts, but they watch Jon Stewart for the truth."[10]

There's even some evidence that Stewart is becoming a source of breaking news. There's a pretty good argument to be made that the first news report of Secretary of Defense Donald Rumsfeld's resignation following the 2006 midterm election came from *The Daily Show*'s "Indecider" blog at least twelve hours before ABC News had it on the air. For more on the details of how the Rumsfeld story broke and video of several of Stewart's most famous interviews, visit http://ralphehanson.com.

The television environment today is radically changed from the time when CBS news anchor Walter Cronkite was the most respected broadcaster in America. We've gone from three nationwide broadcast networks to at least six, and from no cable-only stations to hundreds, and we've gained multiple formats for viewing prerecorded movies and shows at home. In this chapter we look at how this new television world came about and how it has influenced society. We start with the development of broadcast television and then cable/satellite television. We then consider who controls the television industry, how the world portrayed on television compares to the "real" world, and how television is becoming more interactive. We look at the roles television plays within society as a major recreational activity, a view of the world, and an influence on young people. And, finally, we look at where television is headed.

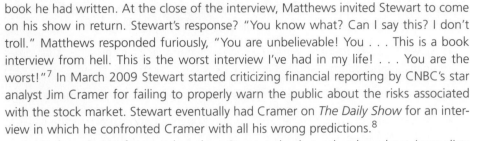

# TELEVISION: BROADCAST AND CABLE/SATELLITE

Television has seen massive changes since its birth in the 1930s. Initially it provided a limited number of options that were broadcast at no cost to viewers. Viewers could watch only the programs offered by the major networks, and only at the times when those programs were being broadcast. But in the 1980s the balance of power between audience and broadcasters began to change. Not only did videocassette recorders (VCRs) allow viewers to choose when they would watch programs, but a range of broadcast, cable, and satellite channels allowed viewers a wider choice of what programs to watch. Television has in effect become two media: broadcast and cable/satellite.

## Broadcast Television

Broadcast television in the United States is based on the idea that programming should be available to all viewers and should be paid for through advertising. Although today broadcast television is just one part of our TV diet, for many years it was the only item on the menu.

*The Invention of Television.*    The story of Philo T. Farnsworth, the man who invented electronic television, is almost too good to be true. He was born in a log cabin, he rode a horse to school, and he developed the central concepts of television at the age of fourteen. Unlike Edison or even Samuel Morse, Farnsworth did not become a household name, yet he invented one of the most significant devices of the twentieth century.

Farnsworth was born in Utah in 1906. When he was twelve, his family settled in Idaho, and in their new house were magazines about radio and science, which fueled Farnsworth's creativity and imagination.[11] Farnsworth's heroes were Edison and Bell, but he wanted to do them one better. He wanted to send out moving pictures as well as sound, and he wanted to do it all electronically, without any moving parts.

Farnsworth came up with the idea of breaking a picture into lines of light and dark that would scan across a phosphor-coated screen like words on a page. The electrons that would paint the picture on the screen would be manipulated by an electromagnetic field. According to television scholar Neil Postman, legend has it that Farnsworth's great idea came to him "while he was tilling a potato field back and forth with a horse-drawn harrow and realized that an electron beam could scan images the same way, line by line, just as you read a book."[12]

By age twenty-one Farnsworth had developed an all-electronic system for transmitting an image using radio waves. On September 7, 1927, he successfully transmitted an image of a straight line. "There you are, electronic television," he commented.[13]

*Philo T. Farnsworth developed the central principles of television broadcasting at age fourteen, and by the age of twenty-one he had produced a working television transmission system.*

Farnsworth, however, was not the only person working on the concept of television. Vladimir Zworykin, a Russian immigrant with a doctorate in engineering, was trying to develop television for David Sarnoff at RCA. Although he had made progress on electronic television and had filed for a patent on it in 1923, the U.S. Patent Office eventually ruled that Farnsworth had been the first to make a working television transmitter. The ruling was based in part on testimony from Farnsworth's high school chemistry teacher, who presented drawings that Farnsworth had made when he was sixteen showing almost exactly how to build a television transmitter. RCA kept fighting Farnsworth and promoting Zworykin and Sarnoff as the inventors of television, but Farnsworth eventually prevailed. For the first time, RCA had to pay royalties to an outside inventor.[14]

Just when all looked rosy for Farnsworth, World War II broke out, and for four years nothing was done with commercial television. Farnsworth's patents expired in 1947, right before television took off. Yet it was not missing out on the chance to cash in on his invention that Farnsworth came to regret. Farnsworth's son Kent later noted that his father was rather bitter about his invention in general: "I suppose you could say that he felt he had created kind of a monster, a way for people to waste a lot of their lives. Throughout my childhood his reaction to television was 'There's nothing on it worthwhile, and we're not going to watch it in this household, and I don't want it in your intellectual diet.'"[15]

*The Beginning of Broadcasting.* The first significant television broadcasts using all-electronic systems occurred in 1939, when NBC started sending out television broadcasts from the New York World's Fair. But American involvement in World War II halted the manufacture of television sets in 1942, and most stations went off the air. Peace came in 1945, and by 1946 RCA had television sets back on the market.

From 1948 to 1952, the licensing of new television stations was frozen to give the Federal Communications Commission (FCC) and television producers time to figure out how the technology should be used and controlled. Because of the freeze, only some cities had television. The television cities saw drastic drops in attendance at movies and sporting events. Restaurant owners hated the popular variety program *Your Show of Shows*, which aired on Saturday nights, because customers rushed home to watch television instead of staying out to eat and drink.[16] During the same period, the Supreme Court issued its ruling in *United States v. Paramount*, breaking the studios' control over the movie industry (see Chapter 8). Television was ready to take over the entertainment industry.

A number of shows characterized this early period of television. Milton Berle, host of the *Texaco Star Theater*, came to be known as "Mr. Television" with his funny costumes and physical humor. The *Ed Sullivan Show* (originally called

*Toast of the Town*) became the place to see new and innovative talent. In later years Sullivan would feature the Beatles and Elvis Presley. The 1950s also saw a number of anthology dramas, essentially short plays or movies, with a new cast and story each week. One show that made a successful leap from radio to television was Edward R. Murrow's CBS news documentary series *Hear It Now*, which became *See It Now* on the new visual medium.

*Lucy, Desi, and the End of Live Television.*   No other entertainment program of the 1950s would have a longer, more lasting impact than one produced by a brash redheaded actress and her Cuban American husband.

When Lucille Ball and Desi Arnaz created their groundbreaking sitcom *I Love Lucy* in 1951, they had to overcome two major obstacles. The first was persuading CBS to let Arnaz play Lucy's television husband. At that time, this was controversial because Ball was white and Arnaz Hispanic. The second challenge was that most television shows at the time were being broadcast live from New York City studios. But Lucy and Desi wanted to continue to live in California. Their solution was to film the show before a studio audience, edit the program like a movie, and ship it to New York to be broadcast. Within a year, *I Love Lucy* was the most popular show on television.

Lucille Ball and her husband, Desi Arnaz, created the modern situation comedy in 1951 with their show I Love Lucy, which was filmed rather than performed live.

Being filmed rather than performed live meant that there were high-quality copies of *I Love Lucy* that could be shown again and again. Arnaz held the rerun rights to the show, which gave the couple the money to build their own television production company, Desilu Studios. More than fifty years after *Lucy* first went on the air, audiences are still laughing at the show.

The format Ball and Arnaz created, a half-hour comedy filmed with three cameras before a live studio audience, became a mainstay of television programming. Today the situation comedy remains one of the most popular program formats.[17]

*The Arrival of Color Television.*   The networks started experimenting with color television as early as 1954, but by 1959 only three shows were regularly being shown in color. (The familiar NBC peacock logo was initially created to show black-and-white viewers that they were missing programs in color.) It wasn't until 1965 that all three of the original television networks were broadcasting in color. One reason for the slow acceptance of color was the price of the television sets. The *Boston Globe* notes that in 1965 color televisions cost the equivalent of what a midline HDTV set cost in 2000 (between $2,500 and $5,000).[18] The switch to color was not completed until the early 1970s.[19]

## Cable and Satellite Television

Today cable and satellite television constitutes almost a separate medium from broadcast television, but initially cable was designed as nothing more than a delivery system for broadcast channels.

*Local cable television companies bring in a variety of programming choices via satellite.*

*Community Antenna Television.* In the early days of television, people in remote areas or in communities sheltered by mountains frequently could not receive the new signals. Among these was Mrs. L. E. Parsons of Astoria, Oregon. Parsons wanted to have television, but the nearest station was 125 miles away. Her husband solved the problem by placing an antenna on top of a local hotel and running a cable into their apartment. Once word got out that the Parsons family had television, the hotel, local bars, and even the neighbors started asking for connections to their antenna. This early form of cable television, which simply retransmitted broadcast channels, came to be known as **community antenna television (CATV)**.[20]

Connecting to these early cable systems was expensive; the cost ranged from $100 to $200. Although there were isolated experiments with subscription channels, for the most part cable remained a way to serve areas with poor reception, and the FCC devised restrictive rules to keep it that way. Until the 1970s cable was primarily a way to get a good TV signal, not additional programming.[21]

*Satellite Distribution and the Rebirth of Cable.* By 1975 the face of cable television was beginning to change. The FCC began loosening the rules on cable companies, and new channels were distributed via satellite.[22]

Home Box Office (HBO) was the first service to make the leap from merely providing access to providing programming. In 1975 it requested permission from the FCC to start sending out its programming nationwide via satellite.

**community antenna television (CATV)**

An early form of cable television used to distribute broadcast channels in communities with poor television reception.

Surprisingly, not one of the **Big Three networks** (NBC, CBS, and ABC) objected to the upstart service as it gained access to their viewers across the country. After all, HBO was just an office, some videotape machines, and a satellite uplink. It had no affiliates, no stations, and could reach only people who were on cable, a small fraction of the viewing market. But the satellite system had a key advantage. Five hundred cable systems could obtain the programming as cheaply as one. They just had to put up a dish to bring in the signal.

Although HBO was the first to go nationwide, no one has done more than Ted Turner to create modern cable television. After his father's suicide in 1963, the twenty-four-year-old Turner inherited a billboard company that was in financial trouble.[23] Turner was not content with running one of the nation's largest billboard companies, so in 1970 he bought Channel 17 in Atlanta. The UHF station was in serious financial trouble, largely because it was located on a part of the broadcast band that many television sets couldn't receive and many people didn't bother to look at. Turner promptly renamed the station WTCG, which stood for Turner Communication Group.

Turner's next big step was buying the last-place Atlanta Braves baseball team and the Atlanta Hawks basketball franchise, thus guaranteeing him exclusive rights to a pair of shows that would run more than 200 episodes a year. It was also programming that would motivate Atlantans to make the effort to find Channel 17.

When RCA launched a television satellite in 1976, Turner saw his next big opportunity. He realized that he could use the satellite to send his station nationwide and provide programming to the growing number of cable systems. On December 27, 1976, WTCG became Superstation WTBS (Turner Broadcasting System). With that step, Turner became one of the first of a new breed of television entrepreneurs who were turning local stations into national powerhouses.

At this point, Turner made the riskiest move of his career: He created Cable News Network (CNN), the first twenty-four-hour news channel. In its early years, CNN had many technical problems and no reputation to speak of. Critics, in fact, referred to CNN as the "Chicken Noodle Network" because it paid its employees poorly and was run amateurishly.[24] Despite the network's problems, however, viewers soon discovered that if they wanted breaking news, they could find it immediately on CNN. Unlike ABC, NBC, and CBS, CNN did not have to interrupt soap operas or sitcoms to put news on the air.

When ABC and Westinghouse tried to start a competing cable news service in 1982, Turner launched his second news network, CNN Headline

*Cable television pioneer and CNN founder Ted Turner created a media empire with global reach that goes a long way to fulfilling the ideal of the global village.*

News, which featured round-the-clock half-hour newscasts. Since then, CNN has grown into CNN Radio, CNN International, CNN Airport Network, and CNN en Español.

Turner took his idea of repackaging material a step further by buying up the MGM movie library and the Hanna-Barbera cartoon library, giving him control of the Flintstones, the Jetsons, and Scooby Doo. He used these, along with additional sports broadcasting rights, to program WTBS, along with Turner Network Television (TNT), the Cartoon Network, and Turner Classic Movies.

In 1996 Turner Broadcasting was acquired by media giant Time Warner, and although Turner lost direct control of his networks, he did get access to the Warner Brothers library of movies and classic cartoons.

When *Time* magazine's editors declared him their Man of the Year in 1991, they wrote that Turner had fulfilled Marshall McLuhan's ideal of the global village. CNN has not made all people brothers and sisters, but *Time* said that the network has given people a window on the world:

> In 1991, one of the most eventful years of this century, the world witnessed the dramatic and transforming impact of those events of live television by satellite. The very definition of news was rewritten—from something that *has happened* to something that is *happening* at the very moment you are hearing of it. A war involving the fiercest air bombardment in history unfolded in real time—before the cameras.[25]

Before long, numerous channels were available to cable companies via satellite, including Black Entertainment Television and the children's network Nickelodeon. In 1978, amid much ridicule, the Entertainment and Sports Programming Network (ESPN) was launched as a twenty-four-hour-a-day sports channel carrying such little-known sports as Australian Rules football and curling. But ESPN quickly grew into one of the most popular channels on cable.[26]

During this period, nine out of ten viewers were watching prime-time programs on the networks, which were still controlled by the people who had started the first radio networks: William Paley at CBS, David Sarnoff at NBC, and Leonard Goldenson at ABC.[27] However, the 1980s saw the growth of a new kind of cable—a service that brought new channels into the household along with the original networks. Cable television viewers have access to a wide range of programming, most of which can be grouped into a few major categories:

- Affiliates of the Big Four broadcast networks (ABC, NBC, CBS, and Fox)

- Independent stations and smaller network affiliates

- Superstations—local independent stations that broadcast nationwide via satellite (WTBS, WGN, etc.)

- Local-access channels—channels offering local government programming and community-produced shows

- Cable networks—advertiser-supported networks that may also receive small fees for each subscriber on a particular cable system (MTV, CNN, BET, etc.)

- Premium channels—extra-cost channels that don't carry advertising (HBO, Showtime, etc.)

- Pay-per-view channels—channels showing special events, concerts, and movies that subscribers pay for on an individual basis

- Audio services—high-quality music services[28]

Cable services offered massive competition to the broadcasters and created a new television landscape. Approximately 52 percent of all American households (about 64.5 million) subscribe to cable service.[29] By way of comparison, in the United Kingdom cable was in 12.9 percent of all homes by the end of 2004.[30]

*Hollywood and the VCR.*    Although videotape has been used in television studios since the 1950s, it was not until the late 1970s that the **videocassette recorder (VCR)** became a household appliance that allowed viewers to make permanent copies of television shows. VCRs took time to catch on. Initially there were two incompatible formats (VHS and Beta), and the machines themselves were expensive, costing $800 or more. In 1985 only two out of ten U.S. homes had VCRs, but by 1991 they could be found in seven out of ten homes.

Consumers loved the fact that they could record programs and watch them later, but movie and television producers were upset that people were recording—and keeping—programs without paying for them. They were also concerned that movies and programs would be duplicated and resold around the world. Universal and Disney sued Sony over its promotion of the VCR for recording movies, but in 1984 the U.S. Supreme Court ruled that television viewers had the right to record copyrighted programs for their own personal use. Piracy of the programming was clearly illegal, but this was not the fault of the equipment manufacturers.[31]

VCR ownership peaked in 1999, with nearly 89 percent of households owning a VCR. By the end of 2006, that proportion had fallen ten points to 79 percent. VCRs were replaced predominantly by DVD players, which are now in 79 percent of all homes.[32] VCRs are also facing competition from the new digital video recorders (DVRs), such as TiVo, that record television programs on a computer hard disk. The DVR lets a viewer jump in to start watching a recorded show fifteen minutes after it came on the air. The viewer can then fast forward through the commercials, and by the time the show is over

**videocassette recorder (VCR)**

A home videotape machine that allows viewers to make permanent copies of television shows and, thus, choose when they want to watch programs.

*Although cable television remains the largest alternative to broadcast programming in the United States, satellite delivery is much more common throughout much of the world, as is illustrated by this block of apartments in the Turkmen city of Turkmenabat.*

**direct broadcast satellite (DBS)**

A low-earth-orbit satellite that provides television programming via a small, pizza-sized satellite antenna; DBS is a competitor to cable TV.

the viewer has caught up with the "live" broadcast. DVRs are seen as easier to use than VCRs but typically require a monthly subscription fee to use. As of May 2009, DVRs were in 32 percent of American households, approximately double the percentage of households from 2006.[33] (This gives us another example of Truth Four—Nothing's new: Everything that happened in the past will happen again.)

*Direct Broadcast Satellites.* Satellite programming providers have been competing with cable since the 1980s, but their success was limited initially because of the rapid growth of cable, the large dish antennas required, and the limited number of channels consumers could receive. All this changed in the 1990s with the advent of the low-earth-orbit **direct broadcast satellite (DBS).** Several DBSs were launched to deliver programming through a new kind of antenna about the size of a pizza.

As of December 2008, approximately 24 percent of all U.S. households had satellite television. Satellite service in the United States grew rapidly from the mid 1990s until about 2007, when adoption of the new delivery system stabilized at current levels.[34] In Europe, which has less of a tradition of cable television than in the United States, DBS services are very popular. News Corporation's Sky Italia has 4 million subscribers in Italy, and BSkyB serves almost one-third of the households in the United Kingdom and Ireland.[35]

DBS is now competing head-to-head with cable. A problem the satellite services face in this competition is that their subscribers still have to put up an old-fashioned antenna to get local broadcast stations. To address this drawback, in major markets DBS companies provide local stations via satellite as well.[36]

Some people subscribe to both cable and satellite. For them, cable serves the house as a whole and satellite is used on just one or two televisions to provide specialized programming. Among the choices DBS systems provide is the possibility of "buying" every Sunday NFL football game. The viewer can then pick the game he or she wants, not the one that the biggest audience wants.[37]

## Digital Television

Just as sound recording has moved to digital formats with CDs and MP3 files (see Chapter 7), so is television shifting from the analog technology of Farnsworth and Zworykin to computerized digital technology. All television broadcasting in the United States was scheduled to be digital by February 17, 2009, but in January 2009 the federal government decided that people weren't ready for the transition, despite several years of warnings that the change would be taking place. Critics of the move to digital broadcasting pointed out that many of the households that rely on broadcast signals for television have incomes under $30,000 and may have trouble affording the set-top box that converts digital broadcast signals into analog signals that old-fashioned television sets can display. To help solve this problem, the government issued coupons to help poor families buy the converters. In fact, a shortage of the coupons was among the reasons that the conversion was delayed.

On Friday, June 12, 2009, the last of the analog television broadcast stations was shut off. That doesn't mean that everyone started using new digital sets, however. Instead, many people will continue to get their television from a digital cable or satellite box, or get a converter box. On the two days following the shutdown of analog broadcasting, the FCC received approximately 400,000 calls to its hotline, considerably below the 600,000 to 3 million calls they were expecting.[38]

There are two distinct digital formats. **High-definition television (HDTV)** is in a wide-screen format (like a theater movie) and features an ultra-clear high-resolution picture with superior sound. The other digital format is **standard digital television**, which will make it possible to broadcast up to six channels on the same frequency space that now carries one channel. However, the picture is no better than that produced by existing signals.[39] Using standard digital, a PBS station could choose to put out a single HDTV program or four digital programs at the current resolution, giving children a choice at any given time between *Arthur*, *Barney*, *Sesame Street*, and *Wishbone*.

The development of HDTV began in the 1980s, and on November 1, 1998, the launch of the space shuttle *Discovery* was the first event to be covered in a nationwide broadcast using a digital television signal. The broadcast was viewed by a tiny audience of just a few hundred people in twenty cities, with forty-two stations carrying digital signals.[40] HDTV-capable sets were in about 32 percent

*Following the conversion to digital broadcasting in 2009, you couldn't even give away old-fashioned analog television sets. These analog sets were packaged up for recycling.*

**high-definition television (HDTV)**

A standard for high-quality digital broadcasting that features a high-resolution picture, wide-screen format, and enhanced sound.

**standard digital television**

A standard for digital broadcasting that allows six channels to fit in the broadcast frequency space occupied by a single analog signal.

of all TV households by the end of 2008 and were projected to hit 67 percent by the end of 2010. Some people will use these for over-the-air HDTV, some will use them for DVD and high-definition DVD programming, some for video games, and some just to watch regular TV.[41]

# FROM BROADCASTING TO NARROWCASTING: THE CHANGING BUSINESS OF TELEVISION

Television got its start with the three networks that dominated the radio industry in the 1940s: NBC, CBS, and ABC. There were some independent stations as well, such as WGN in Chicago and WOR in New York, which had grown out of major independent radio stations, but for the most part, everyone in the country was watching NBC, CBS, or ABC. This would remain the status quo until cable and VCRs exploded in popularity in the 1980s.

## Networks and Affiliates

**television network**

A company that provides programs to local stations around the country; the local affiliate stations choose which programs to carry.

**Public Broadcasting System (PBS)**

A nonprofit broadcast network that provides a wide range of public service and educational programs, which is funded by government appropriations, private industry underwriting, and viewer support.

The Big Three **television networks** are the companies that have provided programs to local stations around the country since the start of the television industry. These affiliate stations require a license from the FCC, equipment, and a local staff. The choice of what shows to carry is up to the local station. If a station carries a particular program, the station receives a fee from the network, along with the revenue from selling local commercials during the show. The network makes its money from the national commercials that run during the program. If an individual station decides that it could make more money running a locally produced program, such as a college basketball game, or a program from an independent producer, it can do so. In that case, the station pays for the program but keeps all the advertising revenue. The only exceptions are the dozen or so stations that each network owns and operates; although they have a certain amount of independence, these stations must please their network owners.[42]

## Educational Broadcasting Becomes Public Broadcasting

Noncommercial broadcasting in the United States was conceived as a way of delivering educational programming. Then Congress passed the Public Broadcasting Act of 1967, which established the Corporation for Public Broadcasting to provide funds for a wide range of noncommercial programs, including public service as well as educational programs. The noncommercial, or public, stations came to share programming through a new network, the **Public Broadcasting System (PBS).** This nonprofit broadcast network is funded by government appropriations, underwriting by private industry, and support from viewers.[43]

While PBS stations eventually became widely available, they tended to have small audiences except for their daytime children's programming, which included the ground-breaking *Sesame Street*.[44] *Sesame Street*'s creator, Joan Ganz Cooney, says that the goal of the show was to give disadvantaged inner-city children a head start on school: "We argued that it would make all the psychological difference in their success in school if [disadvantaged children] came in with the same kind of skills as a middle-class child."[45] *Sesame Street* was also designed to have a slick, fast-paced, commercial look. It even had "sponsors," such as the number 5 and the letters "Q" and "U."

When the show premiered on November 8, 1969, it immediately grabbed a significant audience, and even now it is among the most watched of all children's shows. But was it a success at helping disadvantaged children develop reading and math readiness? That question is difficult to answer. At least one major study found that *Sesame Street* was successful in preparing children for school, but that "advantaged" children gained fully as much from it as disadvantaged students; thus, the show was not closing the gap between the haves and the have-nots.

*Big Bird has been helping children learn to read and count on* Sesame Street *since the show first went on the air in 1969.*

In the 1990s PBS started attracting a significant audience with programming like the Ken Burns documentaries *The Civil War* and *Baseball*. Those larger audiences, in turn, led to support from a number of large corporations that hoped their brief underwriting announcements would reach the upscale audiences who watch PBS. These announcements are not quite commercials, but they do allow corporations to present a brief message to viewers. Among recent PBS underwriters are oil giant BP, GMC Trucks, AT&T, and State Farm Insurance.

## The Fox Network

The 1980s brought numerous changes to the broadcasting market. Not only were VCRs and cable becoming popular, but there was also a new broadcast network. Australian newspaper publisher Rupert Murdoch started the Fox

Network after buying Twentieth Century Fox and incorporating it into his mammoth News Corporation (see Chapter 3). He put the new network on the air in 1986 by buying stations in six of the top ten television markets. Although companies had tried to set up alternative broadcast networks before, none had really succeeded. Murdoch had an advantage in that during the 1980s people were becoming accustomed to watching cable channels, which meant they were no longer wed to regular network programming.

Fox was able to attract independent stations because it was offering them free programming rather than making them rely on syndicated material, most of which consisted of network reruns. The offerings were initially limited, with a late-night talk show starring Joan Rivers followed by Sunday-evening programming beginning in 1987.

While Fox managed to attract viewers with shows like *The Simpsons* and *Married With Children,* what put it on the map was stealing NFL football away from the Big Three. NFL football was a show that people were accustomed to watching; now they just had to watch it on a new network. Fox also brought in the under-thirty viewers coveted by advertisers with hit programs like *The X-Files* and *Melrose Place.*[46] The Big Three broadcast networks were becoming the **Big Four networks.**

More recently, Fox has been attracting large audiences with hit shows such as *American Idol, 24,* and *House.*

**Big Four networks**
The broadcast landscape we know today: the Big Three networks plus the Fox Network.

## Defining Ratings

One of the biggest concerns for television networks, whether broadcast or cable, is the size of their audiences. Rates for commercials, which provide all the income for broadcast networks and a substantial portion of the income for cable services, are determined by how many people are viewing a show at a given time.

Measuring television audiences used to be pretty simple, at least in principle. You found out how many people watched a given show at a given time on one of three major networks, and you had your answer. The fact that you depended on a limited sample of people who had to fill out complex diaries or use a set-top "people meter" may have complicated things a bit, but basically, it was simple. But now we have four major broadcast networks, PBS, several minor broadcast networks (including Univision, which has been growing), dozens of major cable networks, and hundreds of specialized cable networks. There is also the issue of measuring the alternative methods for viewing these programs, the most important of which is delayed viewing on DVR.

With the expansion of choices, the ratings required for a show to be a success have gotten smaller. In 2006 the top-rated drama *CSI* brought in fewer than 20 million viewers per week. In 1996 *ER* was the top-rated drama, and it drew an audience of more than 30 million viewers per week.[47]

Now that DVRs are in more than 30 percent of all homes, the number of people watching shows on a delayed basis has become more important. Nielsen, which measures television audiences, now looks at the three-day delayed audience who actually watch the commercials on the DVR.

The major provider of viewership data, known as *ratings*, is Nielsen Media Research. The company keeps track of the shows watched in 9,000 homes located across the United States. Although the Nielsen families receive a token payment for their participation, they are essentially volunteering to keep track of all their television viewing. Nielsen uses a combination of methods to measure audience size. In the largest urban markets, the company uses a device called the **PeopleMeter.** Viewers push buttons on the machine to record who is watching programs at specific times. In smaller markets, viewers fill out daily diaries, listing what they watched.

While Nielsen tracks overall network viewership throughout the year, the company looks at the audience size of individual stations four times a year (November, February, May, and July) during periods known as **sweeps**. Networks and individual stations often schedule their best—or at least most popular— programming during sweeps periods to attract the highest possible ratings. These higher ratings allow them to charge more for commercials. Nielsen also tracks the ages and sex of audience members, and advertisers are oftentimes as concerned about the demographics of their audience as they are about the absolute size of it.

Nielsen provides networks and stations with several different measurements. The most important of these is the **rating point**, the percentage of the total potential television audience actually watching the show. For example, Nielsen estimated that there were 114.5 million households with televisions in use in 2008. If 1,145,000 homes viewed a particular program, that would produce a rating of 1 (1,145,000 / 114,500,000 = .01, or 1 percent of the total potential audience). A program viewed in 15 million households would have a rating of 13.1.[48]

The second major measurement Nielsen provides is the **share**, the percentage of television sets in use that are tuned to a particular show. Instead of telling producers how many households were watching the show, the share measures how popular a particular show is compared to everything else that is broadcast at the time. Although a show that airs at 1:00 in the morning might have a relatively low rating (say, 3 or 4), it could have a high share (30 or 40) because a large portion of a small audience is watching it.[49]

## An Earthquake in Slow Motion

Fox, cable, and the VCR changed everything for the television industry, a set of changes that media writer Ken Auletta called "an earthquake in slow motion." In 1976 the prime-time viewing audience belonged to the Big Three, with nine out of ten viewers watching network programming. By 1991 the Big Three had lost a third of their viewers. These viewers hadn't stopped watching television; they had just moved to other channels. In 1976 the typical home had a

**PeopleMeter**

An electronic box used by the ratings company Nielsen Media Research to record which television shows people watch.

**sweeps**

The four times during the year that Nielsen Media Research measures the size of individual television station audiences.

**rating point**

The percentage of the total potential television audience actually watching a particular show. One rating point indicates an audience of approximately 1.14 million viewers.

**share**

The percentage of television sets in use that are tuned to a particular show.

choice of 7 broadcast channels; by 1991 it had a choice of 33 cable channels.[50] Today, homes with digital cable programming can have access to more than 100 channels.

Another part of the earthquake was that the original Big Three networks were sold to new owners in 1985. NBC was taken over by General Electric, CBS was purchased by investor Larry Tisch, and ABC was purchased by Capital Cities Communications. Since that time, ABC has been acquired by Disney, CBS has been purchased by Viacom, and Comcast was attempting to buy NBC. The networks are now units within large conglomerates and no longer controlled by the people who started them.[51]

The earthquake also affected profits. Revenues for the broadcast networks plummeted in the 1990s, whereas cable network revenues grew. The music channel VH1, generally considered a second-tier cable channel, made $42.5 million in profits in 1998, outdoing three of the Big Four broadcast networks. MTV, one of the biggest cable networks, made about $250 million in the same period.[52]

Despite their lower profitability, the broadcast networks generally have much bigger audiences than cable services, attracting about 60 percent of the viewers. Popular cable shows like professional wrestling typically attract an audience of about 5 million viewers, whereas the top-rated network shows like *24* typically attract three times as many viewers.[53]

Why, then, are cable channels making more money than the broadcast networks? There are multiple reasons. Cable programs are typically cheaper to produce than network programs. For example, most of the core programming for MTV is provided by recording companies in the form of music videos. MTV doesn't have to bid against other networks for top talent and top-rated shows. In addition, broadcasters have a single source of revenue—advertising—whereas most cable channels have both a subscription fee and advertising revenue. With cable and satellite programming, consumers are increasingly paying for their programming, just as they pay for utilities such as electricity, gas, and water.[54]

This difference is critical. The original Big Three networks have to pay their affiliates hefty fees to carry their programs. In the 1980s ABC was paying affiliates $120 million a year to carry its programs; in contrast, ESPN collected $120 million in fees in 1987 from cable companies that carried its programming. Instead of relying entirely on advertising revenue, ESPN was getting half of its income from subscriber fees.[55]

## Diversity on Television

Broadcast television and the major cable networks have been roundly criticized for presenting a distorted view of reality. Aside from the issue that people on television comedies and dramas are not only attractive and funny but also resolve problems in less than an hour, there are complaints that television presents a world that is overwhelmingly white, male, and middle class.

In 1999 the Big Four networks introduced twenty-six new shows; not one of them featured a non-white lead character. This led to protests and threats of boycotts by African American and Latino groups. Ralph Farquhar, an African American television producer, told the *Arizona Republic*, "I don't believe they're intentionally [excluding minority talent]. But people have to pay attention, you know? The makeup of America . . . has changed radically over the past 20 or 30 years, and yet TV doesn't necessarily reflect the diversity and the composition of the American population."[56]

Scott Sassa, a Japanese American network television executive, recalls being upset as a child when he saw an Anglo playing an Asian character. "I've got to tell you, growing up, seeing David Carradine as a Chinese guy [ticked] you off," Sassa said, referring to the martial arts series *Kung Fu*. Sassa says that the networks will have to reach out to non-whites in a meaningful way if they want to hold on to their audiences: "You not only want to see someone that looks like you on TV—you want to see someone that is a role model, someone that you want to aspire to be. That's what we need to do—create role models that are diverse, that make people in these minority groups feel good."[57] Calls to add diversity to program-ming and pressure on program sponsors have even crossed over to PBS, despite public television's better reputation on diversity issues. Documentary filmmaker Ken Burns's latest film on World War II was the subject of protests by Hispanic activist groups, such as the Hispanic Association of Corporate Responsibility, for not including the oral histories of Hispanic veterans. Burns agreed to recut the 14.5-hour film and include interview footage of Hispanics.[58]

There were signs that things were changing in 2006–2007 when thirty-two of the forty-three new scripted shows featured Hispanic, African American, and Asian American actors.[59] But none of the new shows in the 2008–2009 season featured an African American lead.[60] For the 2009–2010 season, one of the few new broadcast network shows featuring an African American lead character was the animated series *The Cleveland Show* (a spinoff of *Family Guy*). In a controversial twist, *The Cleveland Show*'s lead character is African American, but he is voiced by white actor and show creator Mike Henry. Henry calls any comparison between his show and the old radio series *Amos 'n' Andy* "reckless." "[T]hey've said we're taking food out of the mouths of African-American actors. . . . It's the opposite of that. Most of our cast is African-American and we have tons of friends in the community."[61] (You may remember from Chapter 7 that *Amos 'n' Andy* told the story of two African American friends who were voiced by white actors.[62])

A study by *Entertainment Weekly* magazine found that the 2008 television season was considerably whiter than the American population as a whole. Among the most prominent shows featuring diverse casts are the medical drama/soap opera *Grey's Anatomy*, the mysterious serial drama *Lost*, and the superhero series *Heroes*. Shonda Rhimes, creator of *Grey's Anatomy*, told *Enter-tainment Weekly* that although she has seen progress in casting diversity, she thinks there is room for improvement. "Do I want to see any more shows where

# TEST YOUR MEDIA LITERACY

## Diversity on Television

Broadcast television has long been criticized for lacking racial and ethnic diversity. As executive producer and creator of ABC's hit series *Grey's Anatomy*, Shonda Rhimes is changing television. In an interview with PBS talk show host Tavis Smiley, Rhimes shares her experiences in creating and producing *Grey's Anatomy*:[1]

**Rhimes:** . . . Being a woman of color, I wanted to have a diverse cast. But what was interesting was I never specified a race for any of the actors, for any of the characters or any of the roles. So I just said, we're going to audition people, actors of every race for every single role. . . . And we did and it worked. I mean, I think television has a responsibility to create a diverse world, period. . . .

**Smiley:** But I say that not to cast aspersions, but only because it seems to me that if more people in this—I mean, I'm ranting about this all the time, as our viewers know, and I will continue to rant about it until this business gets better at this, but it seems to me that if more people used that philosophy, if they wrote a good piece of work and auditioned everybody, or as we like to say eer'body, if eer'body got a chance to audition for the role and the best person stepped forward and received the role, that this business might change much more rapidly than it is now.

**Rhimes:** This business would change exponentially and go forward in leaps and bounds. What was interesting about it was we sent out the script and they only sent us white actors.

**Smiley:** So even when you didn't specify that the actor had to be white, they still sent you white actors.

**Rhimes:** Yes. And we had to call back and say, excuse me, where are all the actors of color? Where are the Hispanics, where are the Asians, where are the African Americans, where are the actors of color? And they went, oh, so this is a diverse role. And I said, they're all diverse roles. All of the roles in the show are. And now we're at a point where when our casting director sends out something for a guest-starring role, everybody knows. If you have an actor who you think is great, we don't care what they look like. We don't care what color they are. Send them over, because they might get the part.

### MORE online

You can find links to several other stories about multicultural television casts at **http:// ralphehanson.com**.

### Who is the source?
Who is Shonda Rhimes? What is her background? What does she do?

### What is she saying?
What does Rhimes have to say about how she cast the show *Grey's Anatomy*? Why did she choose the cast members she did? Was she trying to accomplish something or make a point?

someone has a sassy black friend? No, because I'm nobody's sassy black friend. I just want to see shows in which people get to be people and that look like the world we live in. The world is changing, and television will have to follow."[63]

If you want to make some comparisons on your own, 2008 U.S. Census estimates break down the current population as follows:

ABC's hit series Grey's Anatomy was one of the earliest shows to feature "colorblind" casting, where none of the characters had a specified race until after actors had auditioned for the parts.

> White, not Hispanic—66%
>
> Hispanic—15%
>
> African American—14%
>
> Asian—5%
>
> American Indian—2%
>
> Pacific Islander—0.37%

(These values add up to more than 100 percent because some people overlap in categories.)[64]

In addition to having a reputation for being the most confusing show on television, *Lost* was also known for its diverse cast. There was the middle-aged interracial couple Rose and Bernard who played a prominent role in the show's second season. Todd Boyd, of USC's School of Cinema-Television, says that interracial couples are no longer "a big deal" on television. "In the past, in movies and television, introducing an interracial couple assumed that the narrative had to revolve around the difficulties and complications they encountered. That's not the case anymore. . . . Couples have all kinds of problems that have nothing to do with race." For Bernard and Rose, those problems involve being stranded on a tropical island with a polar bear and a monster and no chance of escape.[65]

Along with being known for tropical polar bears and a smoke monster that can read character's souls, *Lost* also featured the first leading character who doesn't speak English. Korean American actor Daniel Dae Kim played Jin Kwon, who spoke only Korean his first season on the show. Kim told the *Washington Post*, "I think it's really doing a lot for what we deem acceptable on television and what we can expect the viewer to follow." Although Kim was born in South Korea, he did have to relearn Korean to play the part.[66]

Kim's character started something of a trend, with Hispanic characters now routinely speaking lines in Spanish, sometimes with English subtitles. The idea, producers say, is to have shows that sound like America, not just look like it.[67] This process of adding non-English-speaking characters provides an illustration of Truth Three—Everything from the margin moves to the center. What once was unusual gradually becomes mainstream.

*Univision and Spanish-Language Broadcasting.*   Although Latinos are seriously underrepresented on the Big Four English-language networks, there has been substantial growth in Spanish-language television. Univision, a Spanish-language broadcast network, is actually the fifth largest network, something Univision trumpeted in a 2005 full-page ad in the *New York Times*. Univision tends to do particularly well among the highly prized eighteen- to thirty-four-year-old demographic. The network's popular *telenovela* "Mañana Es Para Siempre" ("Tomorrow Is Forever") routinely took second place in its timeslot among the younger demographics. Univision could also beat the weakest of the Big Four in overall viewers during prime time on many nights.[68]

In addition to Univision, the Spanish television market includes the much smaller Telemundo network, along with a host of independent stations. Most markets offer no more than two Spanish-language television stations, but Phoenix, Arizona, has at least five.

The most popular programs on Spanish television are the **telenovelas**, or soap operas, which make up fifteen of the top twenty Spanish programs and are popular in both Latin America and the United States. Produced primarily in Mexico and Brazil, the *telenovelas* are exceedingly detailed and involved miniseries, with each story lasting about a year.[69]

The *telenovelas* are at the heart of the criticism of Spanish-language networks. Latino critics say that the networks need to do more than just rerun Latin American programs; they need to make programs about Hispanics living in the United States. (Approximately half of Univision's programming comes from outside the United States.) There have also been complaints that the U.S. networks do not show dark-skinned Hispanics.

*telenovelas*
Spanish-language soap operas popular in both Latin America and the United States.

In an interesting twist, *telenovelas* have started making the jump over to English-language television. In the 2006–2007 season, ABC had a big hit with *Ugly Betty*, which is based on the hit Colombian *telenovela, Yo Soy Betty, la Fea*, though its ratings faded during the 2009–2010 season.[70]

To address the criticisms, Univision has started producing its own American-based sitcom, and it scored major hits by airing live broadcasts of the 2002 and 2006 FIFA World Cup soccer tournaments.[71] It has taken cues from other American networks, with a game show called *A Million* that follows the same basic format as *Who Wants to Be a Millionaire?* The network has also followed the lead of VH1's *Behind the Music*, with a series highlighting the downfalls of popular music stars.[72]

In 2005 ABC became the first network to start offering its prime-time programs either dubbed or closed-captioned in Spanish. The translation takes considerable effort to make sure that the jokes still work. Ruben Veloso, who heads the company that translates *Desperate Housewives* and *Lost* for ABC, says that sometimes they have to massage the script to keep it true to the storyline and to keep the innuendo and double entendres in the dialog.[73]

*Black Entertainment Television.*   Cable television also has networks that attempt to appeal to non-white audiences. The most significant is Black Entertainment Television (BET). The twenty-four-hour network reaches 60 million households, including 12.5 million black households.[74] When BET was acquired by media giant Viacom, it was already a $2 billion corporation that included restaurants, magazines, books, music, and cable networks.[75]

Started in 1980 as a local Washington, D.C., channel, BET was the nation's first black-owned cable network.[76] Although BET carries primarily talk shows and music videos, the network has also produced a series of made-for-television movies based on the Arabesque line of African American romance novels.[77]

Aside from the network's success in attracting viewers, BET became profitable

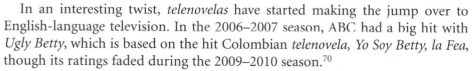

*In addition to running lots of talk shows and music videos, Black Entertainment Television features an annual* Celebration of Gospel *concert.*

because major advertisers such as General Motors are looking for media to reach non-white consumers. The *New York Times* says that this is part of an ongoing trend of multicultural marketing aimed at African American, Hispanic, and Asian American consumers, which account for increasing segments of the U.S. population. BET's Louis Carr says that non-white consumers "have to be taken much more seriously, not as a secondary target but as a primary target. In places like New York, Chicago,

Los Angeles, Detroit, Philly, if you add up the African American population, the Hispanic population and the Asian population, they're not minorities anymore. They're majorities."[78] (Another example of Truth Three—Everything from the margin moves to the center.)

*Audience Members as Programmers: Public Access Cable.* Among the greatest voices for diversity on television are the **public access channels** carried on many cable systems. These channels air public affairs programming and other locally produced shows; they include community bulletin boards, educational programming, coverage of government meetings, and programs created by members of the community. Public access channels allow people to deliver their ideas directly to the public without going through a gatekeeper such as a journalist or another third party. At its best, public access is a soapbox that goes beyond the town square and all the way into a majority of homes in the community.[79]

> **public access channels**
> Local cable television channels that air public affairs programming and other locally produced shows.

More than 15,000 hours of public access programming are produced each year at more than 2,000 locations. Following are some examples of public access programming:

- In Greensboro, North Carolina, several African American churches use the public access channel to bring sermons to house-bound people.
- A public access station in Massachusetts carries a weekly show, *Haiti Tele-Magazine Network*, for Haitian immigrants.
- In Dallas, Texas, a weekly program focuses on the local Iranian community.[80]

But public access television doesn't always live up to the standard of the public good. Unsuccessful experimental films, exhibitionism, and racist hate speech can also find their way onto public access channels.

According to Laura Linder, who has studied public access television extensively, most programming on these channels is fairly conventional, but some of it is controversial. Viewers in one community complained about an animated film that they believed promoted drug use. On another controversial program, the host—eventually arrested for cruelty to animals—butchered and cooked iguanas. Controversial programs often lead to calls for eliminating public access channels, but the courts have generally ruled that public access cable is a free speech forum and therefore is protected as long as nothing illegal is broadcast.

How important are local access cable channels? It depends in large part on local activists. According to independent public access television producer Chris Hill, "If there's good public access, it's a result of grassroots organizing by people who see this as an important public resource."[81]

Linder says that public access programming differs from other forms because it is produced by audience members, not by media professionals. Public access cable is part of the trend toward more interactive media like the Internet and local talk radio. It transforms viewers into media producers rather than just audience members.

# TELEVISION AND SOCIETY

Few new social institutions have become an integral part of society faster than television did in the late 1940s and early 1950s. In 1948 there were fewer than 100,000 televisions in use; a year later that number was more than 1 million, and by 1959 there were 50 million sets in use. In less than ten years television had become a part of everyday life in the United States. Television viewership tended to grow more slowly in the highly regulated European market, something we talk about in depth in Chapter 15.

As television became commonplace, people started to worry about its effects on viewers: How much time were people spending viewing television? What activities would it replace? Why were people watching television? Most important, what effect, if any, would the content of television programs have on viewers? Would it lead to violence and juvenile delinquency? Would it take children into the world of adults too early? Would it transform society?

## Television as a Major Social Force

In *Tube of Plenty*, Erik Barnouw argues that television had a revolutionary impact on society:

> The advent of television was widely compared, in its impact, with that of the Gutenberg printing press centuries earlier. Television was beginning to be seen as the more revolutionary innovation. The reasons were so obvious that they had seldom been discussed. Television viewing required no skill beyond normal human functions. Reading, on the other hand, was a skill acquired over years via effort and drilling—and not acquired by everyone. It generally involved the mediation of father, mother, grandfather, grandmother, teacher, priest, and others, a factor favoring social continuity, a transmittal of values. Television short-circuited all this. It could begin in cradle or playpen, and often did. It could bypass father, mother, grandfather, grandmother. It reached the child long before teacher and priest. Their role in the acculturation process had been sharply reduced. They had sporadically, fitfully, sought to recapture a more decisive role by seeking to control the images on the tube—but that control had slipped elsewhere, to the world of business. In a development of historical significance, the television's messages had become dominant social doctrine.[82]

Barnouw is arguing that although television audiences have fragmented with the growth of cable, satellite, and home video, television is still the dominant shared experience in the modern world, reaching more people than schools, families, and churches.

*Time Spent Watching Television.*    One reason social critics have been so concerned about the influence of television is that Americans spend a lot of time watching television. Estimates of the amount vary. Nielsen Media Research says that the average person watches about four hours of television a day.[83] According to another estimate, Americans spend fifteen hours a week actively watching

*According to Nielsen Media Research, the average American has the television on about four hours a day.*

television and have the TV turned on for an additional twenty-one hours a week while doing other things.

Television viewing can also be looked at in terms of how it dominates our free time. A study of the functions of television in everyday life notes that on average Americans spend half of their leisure time watching television. The same study showed that at any given moment in the evening more than one-third of the U.S. population is watching television; in the winter that proportion rises to over 50 percent.[84]

A study by the Kaiser Family Foundation found that children spend an average of nearly four hours a day watching television or videos.[85] (For more on these figures, turn back to Chapter 1.)

***Television as Competition for Other Activities.***    Although television viewing is often reported in terms of average amounts of time spent viewing, such figures don't always give a complete picture. The differences between heavy and light television viewers can be significant. A 1990 study found that people who watch a lot of television tend to spend more time home alone than light viewers. The study also showed that light viewers spend more time walking than heavy viewers.

Unfortunately, these studies usually cannot determine why people behave in these ways. Do heavy viewers stay home specifically to watch television, or are they unable to get out of the house for one reason or another? Perhaps busy people who like to walk don't have time to watch television. One finding that is not difficult to interpret was that people who watch sports on television also tend to participate in sports. The study also found that the amount of time people spend reading does not seem to be affected by how much television they watch.[86]

## How Do Viewers Use Television?

In addition to examining how much television people are watching, researchers have studied how and why people watch television. These uses and gratifications studies seek to determine what uses people make of television viewing and what gratifications (or benefits) they gain from it. The central premise of these studies is that television (like other media) is not an actor that does things to viewers. Instead, audience members are active participants who select programming to meet particular needs.

What might these needs be? The study *Television in the Lives of Our Children* found that children watch television for many of the same reasons that adults do:

- To be entertained.

- To learn things or gain information. In many cases this information relates to socialization: how to act like an adult, how to be a better athlete, how other people live.

- For social reasons. The content of TV doesn't matter so much as the fact that they watch it with friends or talk about it at school the next day.

The researchers also found that different children watched the same program for different reasons. One child might watch a cartoon show because he was lonely and the show provided company, another might watch it because it made her laugh, and a third might watch it because his friends were watching it.[87]

*When Mary Tyler Moore and Dick Van Dyke played a married couple on* The Dick Van Dyke Show *in the 1960s, they had to sleep in separate beds to keep the network standards department happy.*

## Standards for Television

In the 1950s and 1960s, networks and advertisers imposed strict controls on what could be shown on television. For example, Mary Tyler Moore and Dick Van Dyke played the married couple Laura and Rob Petrie on *The Dick Van Dyke Show*, which aired from 1961 to 1966. Although married, the Petries had to sleep in separate twin beds. Sponsors also raised their eyebrows when Moore wore jeans and capri pants on the show because these garments might be considered suggestive. Moore fought the sponsors and won, saying, "I'll dress on the show the way I dress in real life."[88] This was the era when comedian Lucille Ball had to use the word *expecting* rather than *pregnant* on her show when she was obviously carrying a child.[89]

What could be shown was determined by each network's own standards and practices department. The goal of these departments, which at one time had as many as sixty people working in them, was to make sure the network did not lose viewers or sponsors because of offensive content. Since the 1980s they have decreased in size by 50 percent or more. This change is due partly to a loosening

## TEST YOUR MEDIA LITERACY

### No Sense of Place

Media scholar Joshua Meyrowitz, in his book *No Sense of Place,* argues that the very existence of television is an influence on society because it breaks down the physical barriers that separate people. In the past, he says, people were limited to interacting with those whom they could see and hear face-to-face. Meyrowitz describes how the coming of electronic media, and television in particular, changed this:

> The boundaries marked by walls, doors, and barbed wire, and enforced by laws, guards, and trained dogs, continue to define situations by including and excluding participants. But today such boundaries function to define social situations only to the extent that information can still be restricted by restricting physical access.[1]

These boundaries can be broken at many levels. A child watching television can see people talking about adult topics such as infidelity, pregnancy, or cross-dressing. A teenager in New York City can see the impact of drought on people in Iowa. Young men can listen in on what women say on a "girls' night out." In each of these cases, in the pre-television era the viewer would have been isolated because of his or her "place," whether it be geographic location, age, sex, or socioeconomic status. But television gives everyone an equal view into these formerly separate worlds.

This breakdown of place has occurred not just within the United States but throughout the industrialized world. As we discussed in Chapter 3, the United States is the world's largest supplier of entertainment programming; it is also the largest supplier of imagery to the world. The most important effect of CNN and other satellite-based television news services is that they give people everywhere in the world access to the same information at the same time, whether they are heads of state, diplomats, soldiers, or citizens. The late Don Hewitt, long-time producer of the CBS newsmagazine *60 Minutes,* said that this global sharing of information is changing the world:

> When there was a disaster, it used to be that people went to church and all held hands. Then television came along, and there was this wonderful feeling that while you were watching Walter Cronkite, millions of other Americans were sharing the emotional experience with you. Now the minute anything happens they all run to CNN and think, "The whole world is sharing this experience with me."[2]

### MORE online

You can find a link to an interview with Joshua Meyrowitz, in which he talks further about the consequences of television breaking down the barriers of place, at **http://ralphehanson.com.**

• • • • • • • • • • • • • • •

### Who is the source?

Who is Joshua Meyrowitz? What book has he written?

**What is he saying?**

According to Meyrowitz, how has television transformed society? What does Meyrowitz mean when he says television and other electronic media break down the barriers of place? What kind of barriers does Meyrowitz suggest are being broken by television?

**What evidence is there?**

What examples of this process does Meyrowitz provide? When and where does it take place?

**What do you and your classmates think about Meyrowitz's arguments?**

List some examples of how television has let you see aspects of everyday life that would normally remain hidden from you. Does television take you "places" you couldn't go to otherwise? List some examples. Do you ever use television to deliberately watch worlds you wouldn't be able to see otherwise?

[1] Joshua Meyrowitz, *No Sense of Place* (New York: Oxford University Press, 1985).

[2] William A. Henry III, "History as It Happens; Linking Leaders as Never Before, CNN Has Changed the Way the World Does Its Business," *Time,* January 6, 1992, 24–27.

---

of societal standards throughout the 1970s, but it is also a response to the more explicit content of cable television programming.[90]

Alfred Schneider, who served as a censor for ABC television for more than thirty years, observes that the networks feel freer to deal with difficult topics today than in earlier decades:

> Sometimes the quality of a particular program allows you to do things that you would not permit in other programs. I once said that in my lifetime there would never be full frontal nudity on network television. I was wrong. I lived to see *War and Remembrance*, where I permitted full frontal nudity in the concentration camp scenes. I finally justified it by saying that this was not nudity, this was death.
>
> As we see the growth of more distribution systems, the growth of independents, my position will have to change. As the populace becomes more educated, more inquisitive, more concerned about issues, I will be more comfortable taking greater risks knowing that people will seek out their choices.[91]

In 1997 broadcasters fundamentally changed their programming controls; instead of placing an occasional warning before programs considered inappropriate for children, they implemented a two-part rating system modeled after the one used for movies. There is an age-appropriateness rating that closely matches the movie system, with ratings of G, PG, TV-14 (for 14-year-olds and older), and TV-MA (for mature audiences). Many networks also provide a content rating of S (sexual content), V (violence), L (crude language), and/or D (adult dialogue).[92] It was also in 1997 that the so-called V-chip, an electronic device allowing parents to block programs with certain content ratings, began to be included in television sets.

Television producers were initially concerned that shows with ratings for violence or sexual content might be harder to market. But rather than restricting television content, broadcasters have used the ratings to warn viewers that material on a program will be explicit. Robert Thompson, director of Syracuse University's Center for the Study of Popular Television, says,

> The people who wanted ratings to put the brakes on this new explosion of raunchy television saw just the opposite happen. Anybody should have seen this coming. If you give producers the opportunity to use a TV-MA rating, it's an invitation to make TV-MA programs.[93]

For the most part, the R-equivalent TV-MA rating has been confined to cable television shows like Comedy Central's raunchy cartoon *South Park*. The Big Four broadcast networks have rarely aired programs with the TV-MA rating, the most notable being uncut broadcasts of serious R-rated movies such as *Schindler's List* and *Saving Private Ryan*.

## The Problem of Decency

The line of what was acceptable on broadcast television was redrawn following the 2004 Super Bowl halftime show when Justin Timberlake exposed Janet Jackson's breast. The FCC received more than 500,000 complaints.[94] Immediately following the broadcast, the FCC started talking about the problem of indecency on television. References to sexual or bodily functions are considered to be indecent. FCC rules say that broadcast radio and television stations can't air indecent material between 6:00 a.m. and 10:00 p.m., when children are most likely to be watching. This differs from obscene programming (discussed further in Chapter 13), which "describes or shows sexual conduct in a lewd and offensive way" and has no "literary, artistic, political, or scientific value."[95] Obscene material is not protected by the First Amendment. Rules about indecency apply to broadcast materials but not to cable or satellite material.

There is no single standard for what constitutes broadcast indecency, and this standard clearly changes over time. During the 1990s and early 2000s, bare bottoms became common on shows such as *NYPD Blue*. But following the Janet Jackson fuss, even this minimal nudity has been digitally blurred when shown on broadcast television.

The consequences of the Janet Jackson stunt have been widespread. Not only have reality programs such as *Survivor* become careful to digitally blur any hint of nudity that occurs during the programs' competitions, but there has been some serious fallout as well. Several CBS affiliates hesitated to rebroadcast the documentary *9/11* because of the rough language used by firefighters in the film.[96] In 2004, sixty-six ABC affiliate stations refused to air the R-rated movie

*Saving Private Ryan* for fear they would be fined for the movie's graphic violence and extensive profanity.[97] (Congress raised the fines from \$32,500 to \$325,000 per "incident" following the Jackson case, which is why smaller stations are cautious about any program that might trigger an FCC response.) Broadcast standards in Europe are far more likely to regulate hate speech, advertising, and materials that are harmful to children than to control nudity.[98]

Gene Policinski, executive director of the First Amendment Center, questions whether television can really tell the story of events such as the 9/11 attacks or the invasion of Normandy during World War II within the limits of decency rules:

> War is a bloody hell, and *Private Ryan* brought home the terror and anguish, as well as the heroics and sacrifices, of the heralds of the "greatest generation" who stormed ashore at Normandy in a manner no sanitized depiction had done previously. Who can view any veteran of that invasion in the same manner after seeing that film?[99]

# THE FUTURE OF TELEVISION

Whether it is delivered by broadcast, cable, or satellite, television is changing so quickly that it might be unrecognizable to Philo T. Farnsworth. The cable industry, for example, is in the process of replacing copper wire with fiber-optic cable that uses light rather than electricity to send out video and other types of signals. Fiber-optic cable has the advantage of being able to carry much more information than copper wire can, but more important, it has the capacity to allow audience members to send signals back to the program providers.[100]

## Interactive Television

This new control of television by consumers is available at a number of levels. As the number of available channels increases, cable providers can offer multiple versions of single channels. Cable movie provider HBO offers multiple channels, each of which has movies starting at different times. The same is happening with pay-per-view channels, on which movies start at fifteen-minute intervals.

Consumers themselves can add to their degree of control. As mentioned earlier in the chapter, with DVRs viewers are able to not only record programs and view them whenever they wish but also pause a program to take a phone call or get a snack and restart it when they return. In essence, the digital recorders give viewers the same control over "live" television that they have over prerecorded programs.

*Video-on-Demand.* One service that has really taken off in the past several years and has the potential to change the entire industry is **video-on-demand**. This consists of television channels that allow viewers to order movies, news, or other programs that are digitally delivered at any time over fiber-optic lines. Time Warner began experimenting with such a system in 1993 and made its Full Service Network available to subscribers in Orlando, Florida. During the experiment, the company found that people like having more choices, that they want to be able to pause a show and continue it later, and that young people adapt better to new technology than do older people. But the technology Time Warner used in Orlando could not keep up with demand as the number of subscribers increased.[101]

Video-on-demand has now moved into the mainstream, with cable providers making it available in at least 30 million homes. These systems allow consumers not only to pick the program they want to watch but also to pause, rewind, and fast-forward through the content. The ability to fast-forward scares traditional broadcasters, because subscribers will be able to skip past the commercials that pay the networks' bills.[102] Cable and satellite companies are also seeing competition from online services such as Amazon.com and Netflix. Whereas Amazon provides pay-per-view streaming movies over the Internet to consumers, rental service Netflix has a large library of streaming movies available on an "all you can watch" basis to anyone who subscribes to their DVD rental service and has a broadband Internet connection.[103]

*Interacting With Programs.* Interactive television goes beyond giving viewers a chance to select their own programming. It involves making them active participants in the programming. Among the most famous (or infamous) interactive television episodes was one that appeared on *Saturday Night Live.* Comedian Eddie Murphy played a cook who was about to boil Larry the Lobster. Viewers could call in on special phone lines to vote on whether Larry should or should not get cooked at the end of the show. (Compassionate viewers ended up saving Larry that night, though the lobster's final fate remains unknown.) It is not that much of a reach to go from voting on whether to save Larry the Lobster to calling in to vote on which singer to eliminate from the current season of *American Idol.* Brian Garden of MTV says, "You are growing up with a generation that is almost overly empowered. They aren't satisfied with anything less than full control."[104] John Pavlik of the Center for New Media at Columbia University sees interactivity as becoming a standard part of television:

> When you transform people from couch potatoes into active participants, you turn TV programs into something like a sticky website. They want to keep playing along. Every program can have an interactive component. I think it will become the main way we connect to our televisions.[105]

# The Earthquake in Slow Motion Continues

Earlier in this chapter, we discussed Ken Auletta's "earthquake in slow motion"—how the cable and satellite revolution brought about massive changes to the television business in the 1980s and 1990s. This earthquake has continued to shake up television into the twenty-first century with the growing importance of broadband video and alternative viewing devices.

*Convergence of Television and the Internet.*  Media analysts have been talking for years about convergence in the media industry with audio, video, still images, and text coming together in a single medium. It hasn't happened yet, but computers and television are definitely starting to converge, though not always in the ways that people were expecting. Mike Bloxham, of Ball State University, tells *Media Post*,

> The difference between the TV and the PC is getting less almost by the month. They're kind of morphing, and the only real difference is the size of the screen, where I'm using it, my need state or mind state, and, at the moment, the amount of interactivity.[106]

On Wednesday, October 12, 2005, Apple set off perhaps one of the biggest tremors in this ongoing quake, when it announced a new version of the iPod music player that would handle video files as well as music. All well and good, you say. We've had cool digital video players before. But the big news was that Apple was partnering with Disney to sell ABC's top-rated television shows through the iTunes music store. These programs, including *Lost* and *Desperate Housewives*, are available the day after they air on the network, at a cost of $1.99. They come without commercials. So, for $1.99 you can download a legal copy of your favorite show to watch on either your computer or your iPod.

What makes this so revolutionary is that it is changing the entire economic framework for television programming. Instead of selling audiences to advertisers, Apple is selling programs to consumers, who will pay directly for the programming.[107] All mass media have both a hardware and a software component. There's been portable video hardware before, but there has not been a truly revolutionary new source of programming for these devices that can be used by ordinary people. The fact that Disney was willing to sell its top television titles the day after they air on broadcast in a form that people can keep and replay as often as they want is truly a major change in the media world. As of spring 2007, all of the Big Four networks were selling episodes through iTunes, as were cable powerhouses, such as Cartoon Network, Bravo, BET, Comedy Central, The CW, ESPN, MTV, PBS, and the SyFy Channel, to name just a few.

Since then, there have been a significant number of new opportunities to watch current television programs online. Netflix, through its streaming service, offers current-season episodes of several shows. ESPN broadcasts a wide

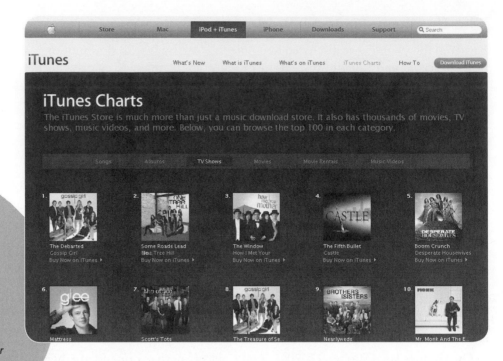

When Apple launched its iTunes TV store in 2005, the company made it easy for people to buy individual television show episodes to view on their computer, iPod, or television set.

range of sporting events through its ESPN360 Web site, for which Internet providers have to pay a premium. The biggest source of current programming is the Web site Hulu, a joint project of NBC Universal, Fox, and Disney, which offers current episodes of many, though not all, shows aired by the partnering networks. The problem for the media companies is that making the shows available for free on the Web may decrease the likelihood that people will pay to receive them via cable. As of fall 2009, cable provider Comcast was attempting to purchase NBC Universal, along with a major stake in Hulu. Were Comcast to do so, media industry analysts speculate that the company would start charging for access to Hulu.[108]

If you want to make sense out of how much television is changing, take a look at your author's favorite television show, *Lost*. Here's how I can and do consume the show:

- *As a broadcast program*—Actually, that's not completely true. I often watch it an hour or so after it airs using my DVR and skipping through the commercials.

- *As a paid download from the iTunes store*—I've purchased several episodes at $1.99 each. Once when I was traveling, I downloaded it using the wireless Internet connection (WiFi) in my hotel room. On another occasion, I wanted to watch an episode for a second time, and I'd already erased it from the DVR.

■ *As a free, commercial-supported, streaming Webcast from ABC.com*—As long as I have a broadband connection to the Internet, I can watch the most recent reruns from ABC's Web site.

■ *As a rented DVD on my DVD player*—I've rented several episodes on DVD using my Netflix mail order video rental account. I don't need to purchase the disks when I can have them in my mailbox within a couple of days of requesting them.

■ *As a stream from Netflix*—As a subscriber to Netflix, I am able to view episodes of *Lost* instantly using my television set that's hooked up to a streaming box.

As you can see, television is no longer something that gets broadcast on a single channel at a specific time. It's something about which we can make choices. Downloads are also available from Amazon.com, as well as from the broadcast networks themselves. Direct sales to consumers are a big part of it, but so are advertising-supported Webcasts.[109]

The question facing the industry now is how broadcast networks go about compensating their affiliate stations for their share of the revenue on these digital downloads. After all, many of the people who are watching the shows online are skipping it on their local station. Yet the show could never have become so popular without local affiliates carrying it. (Or at least that's the argument the affiliates are making.) Both Fox and CBS have reached agreements with their affiliates to share the revenue from their Internet video—anywhere from 12.5 to 25 percent of the advertising and transaction revenue from the online programming.[110] NBC Universal has an agreement with YouTube to use the video-sharing service to promote its new shows and to run clips of its recent programs.

Why are the networks going online? Certainly making money is a reason, but it may not be the primary one. The recording industry may have lost the battle to convince the public that sharing music over the Internet is wrong, but the television business doesn't intend to make the same mistake. The best option they see for stopping piracy is selling the public what they want—TV shows on their computers and iPods. Anne Sweeney of ABC's Media Networks says the streaming and downloads of the network's popular shows are essential. She notes that before the network put *Lost* up on its Web site, there were as many as 25,000 illegal downloads of the show the day following the broadcast.[111]

# CHAPTERSummary

Television was developed in the 1920s and 1930s by independent inventor Philo T. Farnsworth and RCA engineer Vladimir Zworykin. Commercial broadcasting began in the United States in 1939, but its development was put on hold by the outbreak of World War II. By the early 1950s, television was established as the dominant broadcast medium. Color television broadcasts came into widespread use in the 1960s.

Although primitive forms of cable television existed in 1948, cable did not become a significant medium until the early 1980s, when satellite distribution of channels became common. Among the early cable channels were a number of networks created by Ted Turner. Viewers gained access to additional choices in the form of VCRs and direct broadcast satellite service. Television broadcasting is currently in the process of switching from analog signals to multiple digital formats, and VCRs are being replaced by DVRs, DVDs, and video-on-demand technology.

Television networks have been criticized for failing to include women and minorities in their programming, but cable channels have delivered more programming that addresses diverse interests. Networks have also been criticized for carrying too much violent and sexually explicit programming. But television has been praised for breaking down geographic and social barriers. Broadcast television is currently going through a cycle in which "indecent" content is being suppressed by the government.

Television is changing rapidly, with audience members getting many new options to control how and when they receive programming. With VCRs, DVRs, interactive television, and broadband video, viewers can choose what they watch and when they watch it. They are also able to interact with the programming through telephone and Internet resources.

# KEYTerms

community antenna television (CATV)   310
Big Three networks   311
videocassette recorder (VCR)   313
direct broadcast satellite (DBS)   314
high-definition television (HDTV)   315
standard digital television   315
television networks   316
Public Broadcasting System (PBS)   316

Big Four networks   318
PeopleMeter   319
sweeps   319
rating point   319
share   319
*telenovelas*   324
public access channels   326
video-on-demand   334

## CONCEPT Review

The differences between broadcast television and cable/satellite television

Ted Turner's ideas for repackaging programming for cable and distributing it nationwide

How Hollywood and other content providers have resisted changes in television technology

The impact that digital broadcasting will have on the television industry

Ken Auletta's "earthquake in slow motion"

The changing face of diversity on television

How standards of decency change on television

How audience members are taking control of how they interact with television

# The Internet

## Mass Communication Gets Personal

**One of the central** principles of contemporary computer culture is that you have to surf the edges—that is, the only way to keep up is to stay ahead of the technology curve. So back in the 1980s all you needed to be at the forefront of interactive communication was the hot new technology of e-mail. By the 1990s e-mail was becoming passé as folks started sending instant messages using online services and the Internet. By the early 2000s communication had gone wireless and text messaging was becoming dominant, with teens spending more time texting than talking on their mobile phones.[1]

Then in 2006 three college dropouts developed Twitter, a new medium that combines elements of mobile text messaging, online instant messaging, and a good dose of blogging. It has more than 5 million people regularly answering the question, "What are you doing?" in 140 characters or less.[2]

Evan Williams, Jack Dorsey, and Biz Stone started the microblogging Twitter service as a project while they were working for the podcasting company Odeo. Despite their lack of college degrees (something they share with Microsoft co-founder Bill Gates and Apple co-founder Steve Jobs), the three had substantial high-tech business experience. Williams was a co-founder of Blogger, an early blogging tool, which was acquired by Google in 2003; Stone was one of the founders of the early social networking site Xanga; and Jack Dorsey ran a courier dispatch software company.[3]

Twitter is designed to let people communicate with their friends, family, and coworkers using messages no longer than 140 characters. The little messages, known as "tweets," can be delivered to your friends, your acquaintances, or anyone in the world who can be bothered to read them. You can send and receive tweets on your cell phone as text messages, as e-mails, on Facebook, or through a widget on a Web page.

Social networking expert Clay Shirky told NPR's *On the Media* that the 140-character limit of Twitter is essential to its success. "There's a certain relief . . . in being forced to write in short form. When you're writing an email . . . you can end up agonizing over it and so forth. But if you can only say one thing, if you can only, you know, manage a sentence or even a sentence fragment, it really makes you concentrate on what it is you're wanting to say."[4]

Although much of Twitter's content is made up of reports of ordinary daily activities, it can move beyond the mundane. During the 2008 terror attacks in Mumbai, India, much of the news coming out of the country was through social networking tools such

Jack Dorsey's original sketch of what would become Twitter. In this version he called it stat.us.

as Twitter. For many people, this was their first exposure to Twitter.[5] (For more on how news about the attacks travelled, see the beginning of Chapter 15.) Politicians are tweeting as well: President Barack Obama has an official Twitter feed, as does Sen. John McCain. And you really can't be a celebrity these days without a Twitter. Ashton Kutcher has 3.7 million people following his tweets, Ellen DeGeneres has 3.4 million followers, and Britney Spears has 3.4 million.[6] NASA even has the Mars Phoenix probe sending out first-person tweets, allegedly from the surface of Mars. (Why do I suspect that they are being written by a public relations person at the Jet Propulsion Lab? It's clever, in any event.)

*St. Paul Pioneer Press* technology reporter Julio Ojeda-Zapata uses Twitter as a reporting tool. For example, he found out about an earthquake in the Los Angeles area via Twitter, and he used a Twitter question to find people who obsessively stay on their laptops during vacations.[7] Bloggers covering live events (such as the Republican National Convention) use Twitter to make blog posts from their smartphones. In fact, the busiest outside link to this author's blog in August 2008 came from a tweet posted by journalist Patrick Gavin during the RNC.

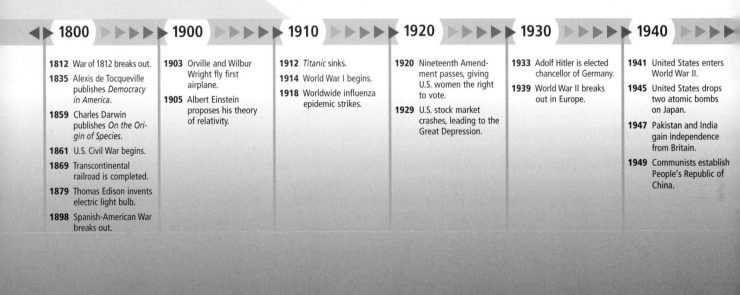

**1800**

**1812** War of 1812 breaks out.
**1835** Alexis de Tocqueville publishes *Democracy in America*.
**1859** Charles Darwin publishes *On the Origin of Species*.
**1861** U.S. Civil War begins.
**1869** Transcontinental railroad is completed.
**1879** Thomas Edison invents electric light bulb.
**1898** Spanish-American War breaks out.

**1900**

**1903** Orville and Wilbur Wright fly first airplane.
**1905** Albert Einstein proposes his theory of relativity.

**1910**

**1912** *Titanic* sinks.
**1914** World War I begins.
**1918** Worldwide influenza epidemic strikes.

**1920**

**1920** Nineteenth Amendment passes, giving U.S. women the right to vote.
**1929** U.S. stock market crashes, leading to the Great Depression.

**1930**

**1933** Adolf Hitler is elected chancellor of Germany.
**1939** World War II breaks out in Europe.

**1940**

**1941** United States enters World War II.
**1945** United States drops two atomic bombs on Japan.
**1947** Pakistan and India gain independence from Britain.
**1949** Communists establish People's Republic of China.

Technology consultant Charlene Li told the *Sunday Times* of London that Twitter will be valuable to businesses because they can use it to set up a two-way relationship with their customers, creating a sense of interaction. At a time when many consumers decide not to watch television commercials by fast-forwarding through them using their DVRs, they are still willing to receive messages such as electronic coupons. "Twitter is a great platform to push out those messages," Li said. "I don't mind Starbucks making an announcement on my Twitter page but I don't want them in my inbox."[8]

As of 2009 Twitter had an estimated value of approximately $1 billion, even though it has no income source other than venture capital. Co-founder Jack Dorsey says he's not concerned. "It took Google four to five years for revenue. We will be patient, too."[9] Like many new media, Twitter may evolve into something that is a hybrid: free to consumers and paid for by businesses. The company is reportedly looking to bring out premium features for corporate clients, such as analytical tools for tracking how fans of a business use the service. Twitter is looking at a second pay-tool that would allow tweeters to add to their posts GPS data from their phones.[10]

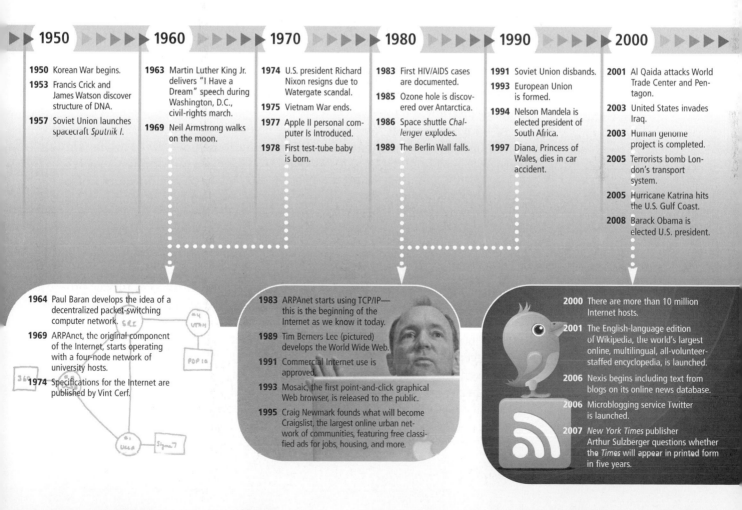

**1950**

**1950** Korean War begins.

**1953** Francis Crick and James Watson discover structure of DNA.

**1957** Soviet Union launches spacecraft *Sputnik I*.

**1960**

**1963** Martin Luther King Jr. delivers "I Have a Dream" speech during Washington, D.C., civil-rights march.

**1969** Neil Armstrong walks on the moon.

**1970**

**1974** U.S. president Richard Nixon resigns due to Watergate scandal.

**1975** Vietnam War ends.

**1977** Apple II personal computer is introduced.

**1978** First test-tube baby is born.

**1980**

**1983** First HIV/AIDS cases are documented.

**1985** Ozone hole is discovered over Antarctica.

**1986** Space shuttle *Challenger* explodes.

**1989** The Berlin Wall falls.

**1990**

**1991** Soviet Union disbands.

**1993** European Union is formed.

**1994** Nelson Mandela is elected president of South Africa.

**1997** Diana, Princess of Wales, dies in car accident.

**2000**

**2001** Al Qaida attacks World Trade Center and Pentagon.

**2003** United States invades Iraq.

**2003** Human genome project is completed.

**2005** Terrorists bomb London's transport system.

**2005** Hurricane Katrina hits the U.S. Gulf Coast.

**2008** Barack Obama is elected U.S. president.

**1964** Paul Baran develops the idea of a decentralized packet-switching computer network.

**1969** ARPAnet, the original component of the Internet, starts operating with a four-node network of university hosts.

**1974** Specifications for the Internet are published by Vint Cerf.

**1983** ARPAnet starts using TCP/IP—this is the beginning of the Internet as we know it today.

**1989** Tim Berners-Lee (pictured) develops the World Wide Web.

**1991** Commercial Internet use is approved.

**1993** Mosaic, the first point-and-click graphical Web browser, is released to the public.

**1995** Craig Newmark founds what will become Craigslist, the largest online urban network of communities, featuring free classified ads for jobs, housing, and more.

**2000** There are more than 10 million Internet hosts.

**2001** The English-language edition of Wikipedia, the world's largest online, multilingual, all-volunteer-staffed encyclopedia, is launched.

**2006** Nexis begins including text from blogs on its online news database.

**2006** Microblogging service Twitter is launched.

**2007** *New York Times* publisher Arthur Sulzberger questions whether the *Times* will appear in printed form in five years.

Twitter is a key new communication technology because it bridges the gap between mobile phones, mobile Internet, and traditional computer-based Internet access. The Internet is in the process of establishing itself not just as a new medium of mass communication but also as one where established media companies, new companies, and individuals can make a profit delivering content to widely distributed and varied audiences. In this chapter we look at the origins of the Internet, how it has changed from its original government roots, how it has evolved from a tool for computer sharing into a major new mass medium, and how it has caused social change everywhere from the corporate boardroom to the Middle East.

# THE DEVELOPMENT OF THE INTERNET

The Internet is the most recent of the mass media. It is still rapidly evolving and changing, just as radio did in the 1920s and television in the 1950s. (Truth Four—Nothing's new: Everything that happened in the past will happen again.) Like radio, the Internet was not conceived initially as a mass medium. Instead, the first wide-area computer networks were designed to enable academics and military researchers to share data. But these early users soon found that the most useful benefit of the network was being able to send electronic mail to one another instantly.

Although the earliest components of the Internet were in use by 1969, the Net was limited largely to interpersonal communication until 1991, when Tim Berners-Lee released the World Wide Web as an easy and uniform way to access material on the Internet. Since then the Internet has become a medium unlike any other because it is the only one that incorporates elements of interpersonal, group, and mass communications.

So what is the **Internet**? A national panel on the future of the Internet defines it this way: "The Internet is a diverse set of independent networks, interlinked to provide its users with the appearance of a single, uniform network."

The Net starts with the link from your computer to an Internet service provider (ISP). For an ISP, you might choose America Online, a cable company, your telephone company, or possibly a small local company that sells Internet service in one or two counties. The messages then flow from the smaller links into bigger and bigger digital pipelines (the Internet's "backbone") that carry millions of messages across the country.

The backbone was initially a set of high-speed data lines controlled by the National Science Foundation as part of a replacement of its original network, but these lines have since been replaced by high-speed fiber-optic lines run by about a dozen major communication companies.

**Internet**
"A diverse set of independent networks, interlinked to provide its users with the appearance of a single, uniform network"; the Internet is a mass medium like no other, incorporating elements of interpersonal, group, and mass communications.

## Packet Switching: Letting Computers Talk to Each Other

Today people use the Internet to communicate with other people, but the technology was developed to let computers talk to one another. In the early 1960s researchers on both sides of the Atlantic Ocean were working on the problem of how to transfer information stored on one computer to another.

In 1964 engineer Paul Baran was designing a military communication network that could survive a nuclear strike. Baran was unhappy with the existing telephone network because it depended on central switching hubs that could be destroyed by a single bomb. He wanted to create a decentralized network in which every element was equal, one that would continue to function even if substantial portions of it were destroyed. He sought to design a network in which every computer was connected to several other computers so that if one computer failed, an alternative route using different computers could be established. Baran's second insight was that computers could break large messages into a number of smaller message blocks, or packets, that could be sent independently across the network. **Packet switching**, as Baran's scheme came to be known, cuts messages into little pieces and sends them along the easiest route to their final destination (see Figure 10.1). The receiving computer starts reassembling the messages and asks for any missing packets to be resent.[11]

The U.S. Air Force was initially willing to implement Baran's network, but AT&T, which had a monopoly on long-distance phone service at the time,

**packet switching**
A method for breaking up long messages into small pieces, or packets, and transmitting them independently across a computer network. Once the packets arrive at their destination, the receiving computer reassembles the message into its original form.

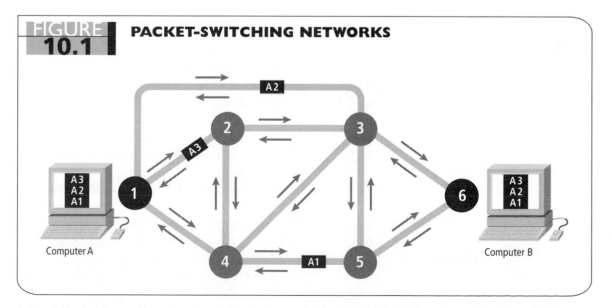

**FIGURE 10.1 | PACKET-SWITCHING NETWORKS**

Packet switching is at the core of how wide-area computer networks operate. The sending computer breaks down the message into a number of smaller pieces, or packets, that can be sent separately across the network. These packets each follow their own routes to the destination computer, where they are reassembled into the original message.

refused to cooperate, so Baran put his idea on hold.[12] Meanwhile, in England, researcher Donald Davies was working on a proposed public communication network. Davies and Baran, working independently, came up with remarkably similar notions for packet switching. The major difference is that Davies was not designing a network for military use. He was attempting to facilitate interactive computing over long distances. Davies gave packet switching its name.[13]

## ARPAnet

Eventually the U.S. military built the first nationwide packet-switching network. However, the network that was built was intended to serve the needs of academic researchers, not to survive nuclear war.

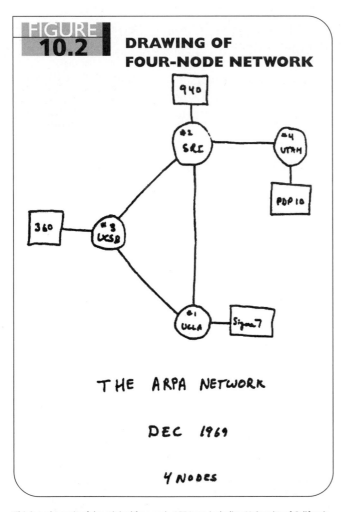

**FIGURE 10.2**

**DRAWING OF FOUR-NODE NETWORK**

This is a schematic of the original four-node ARPAnet, including University of California–Los Angeles, Stanford Research Institute, University of California–Santa Barbara, and University of Utah.

*Source:* http://personalpages.manchester.ac.uk/staff/m.dodge/cybergeography//atlas/historical.html.

The network was built by a farsighted division of the Pentagon called the Advanced Research Projects Agency (ARPA). ARPA's Information Processing Techniques Office was headed by psychologist J. C. R. Licklider, who was interested in how people could use computers to improve communication. Licklider imagined a computer network hooked up to home computer consoles and televisions that could create a "giant teleconference" in which people could argue and debate political and other issues. Individuals, political action groups, and journalists could all come together in a single space.[14]

One of the things ARPA did was to supply universities and research organizations with large, expensive computers. As a way of controlling costs, ARPA started considering the possibility of sharing these computers by means of a network. Licklider suggested the creation of what he called the Intergalactic Computer Network. He envisioned a network of computers sharing files and power, regardless of where the users or the computers were located. Colleague Larry Roberts says, "[Licklider] saw this vision in the early sixties. He didn't have a clue as to how to build it. He didn't have any idea how to make this happen. But he knew it was important."[15]

In 1968 the contract to build the network was given to a Boston-based consulting firm on the condition that it be built in under one year. By the fall of 1969 **ARPAnet** connected four different institutions (see Figure 10.2), and the first component of the Internet was running. The initial nodes would be University of California–Los Angeles (UCLA), Stanford Research Institute, University of California–Santa Barbara, and University of Utah. ARPAnet came online at about the same time as the first moon landing. Neil Armstrong took his "one small step" on the moon on July 16, 1969, and the first tests on ARPAnet were done on Labor Day weekend the same year. On October 1 the first message was sent from one node to another—from UCLA to Stanford Research Institute. Whereas the moon landing was noted throughout the world as one of the great achievements of humanity, no one outside of ARPA was aware that a new, world-changing medium had just been born.[16]

*From 1968 to 1969 Boston-based consulting firm BBN developed ARPAnet, the predecessor of today's Internet.*

## Connecting Incompatible Networks

As ARPAnet expanded to more and more universities, other networks were formed. Hawaii had the radio-based Alohanet; SatNet connected computers via satellite; and the Mobile Radio Network in San Francisco connected computers mounted in trucks. Each of these small networks worked well in its own limited and defined sphere, but they couldn't communicate with one another. How could they be linked together?

*Creating the Internet's Protocols.* The answer came from work done by Bob Kahn and Vint Cerf. The pair envisioned a box, or gateway, that would serve as a translator for all the various incompatible networks. The individual networks would talk to the gateways using a common set of rules or "protocols." Their protocol was known as **TCP/IP**. TCP stands for Transmission Control Protocol, which controls how data are sent out on the Internet. IP stands for Internet Protocol, which provides the address for each computer on the Internet. The term *Internet* was coined in 1973 as an abbreviation for "internetworking of networks." TCP/IP let packets from one network be repackaged for transmission and then converted into a form that the receiving (incompatible) computer from another network could understand.

The specifications for the Internet were published in 1974—before there were personal computers, before the development of the World Wide Web, and before

**TCP/IP**

TCP stands for Transmission Control Protocol, which controls how data are sent out on the Internet; IP stands for Internet Protocol, which provides the address for each computer on the Internet. These protocols provided common rules and translations so that incompatible computers could communicate with each other.

local-area networks were commonplace. But Kahn and Cerf's basic standard survived all these changes and is still in use today. In 1983 ARPAnet itself started using TCP/IP internally instead of the original protocol put together in the 1960s.

*Commercial Networks.* As academics started making personal use of the Internet, nonacademics became interested in computer communication and started buying access to network services through companies like CompuServe, Prodigy, and Quantum. Quantum made an online service for the Commodore 64, the most popular personal computer in 1983, which later expanded to numerous other computers. In 1989 Quantum became America Online (AOL). AOL became a success for a variety of reasons: It was set up as a consumer communication network from the start, it had an easy-to-use graphical interface, and it was inexpensive. Between 1993 and 1998 the number of AOL subscribers grew from 200,000 to 8 million.[17]

*The Next-Generation Internet.* With all the public and commercial traffic flowing on the Internet, next-generation networks are now under construction to serve the same purpose as ARPAnet—to provide academics and other researchers with high-speed links to computers around the world, especially the limited number of supercomputers. These new and improved networks have the potential to move data ten to twenty times faster than the conventional Internet, given ideal conditions. Their primary advantage is that they make possible much-higher-quality video and interactive applications. For example, students at medical schools in different parts of the country can view an interactive medical simulation simultaneously using the new network, something that would have been impossible with the older, slower lines. As of 2009, more than 200 U.S. universities, 70 corporations, 45 government agencies, and 50 international organizations belonged to the Internet2 consortium, one of the leading next-generation networks, with an estimated 10 million users.[18]

## COMPUTERS AS COMMUNICATION TOOLS

With the coming of networks, and especially the internetworking standards, computers were transformed. Bob Taylor, who helped oversee the creation of ARPAnet, says, "Computers were first born as arithmetic engines, but my own view . . . is that they're much more interesting and powerful as communication devices because they mediate human-to-human communication."[19] The thing that makes computer-based communication so powerful is that it includes virtually every level of communication, from the interpersonal communication of e-mail and instant messaging to the mass communication of the World Wide Web.

# Interpersonal Communication: E-mail and Instant Messaging

Although its original purpose was the sharing of resources, the most important factor in the development of the Internet was **electronic mail** (**e-mail**), defined simply as a message sent from one computer user to another across a network. Primitive e-mail existed prior to the Internet, but people could send messages only to other users on the same physical computer. There was no way to send a message from one computer to another.

In 1972 ARPAnet's Ray Tomlinson wrote a simple file-transfer program that would send a message from one system to another. Says Tomlinson, "It seemed like an interesting hack to tie those two together to use the file-transfer program to send the mail to the other machine. So that's what I did. I spent not a whole lot of time, maybe two or three weeks, putting that together and it worked."[20] When the software that operated ARPAnet was updated, Tomlinson's e-mail application was sent out over the Net so that everyone would have the same materials. ARPAnet was not developed with e-mail in mind, nor would ARPA have funded its network for that purpose. But once e-mail was there, everyone on the Net started using it. They could send messages to multiple people at once, they could cross time zones, they could include data files, or they could just exchange friendly greetings.

Tomlinson also created the form of address using the @ symbol. It was a way of saying, "This is a message for a person 'at' a particular computer." The other reason was that the @ symbol did not appear in users' names or locations. It was the one symbol that meant what Tomlinson wanted it to mean and that was not already in use. Len Klienrock, who worked on ARPAnet, says that Tomlinson's early e-mail program illustrated the power of the Net: "People-to-people communications was what excited people. You know, machine-to-machine or human-to-machine was not all that exciting. At that point, we perhaps should have been able to predict the kind of phenomena we see today."[21] Even since the growth of the World Wide Web in the 1990s, e-mail continues to be the most important Internet application for the largest number of people, even if it isn't as trendy as newer technologies.

Interpersonal communication on the Internet has expanded beyond e-mail through a variety of "chat" services, most notably **instant messaging (IM)** programs, which are e-mail systems that allow users to chat with one another in real time, hold virtual meetings that span multiple cities or even countries, and keep track of which of their "buddies" are currently logged on to the system. Although most IM services are free, they do not adhere to a common standard, so users of Microsoft's IM program can't communicate with AOL's subscribers. This violates a generally accepted standard for the Net (discussed later in the chapter) that every user ought to be able to communicate with every other user, regardless of the computer or program he or she is using.[22]

**electronic mail (e-mail)**
A message sent from one computer user to another across a network.

**instant messaging (IM)**
E-mail systems that allow two or more users to chat with one another in real time, hold virtual meetings that span multiple cities or even countries, and keep track of which of their "buddies" are currently logged on to the system.

## Group Communication: Listservs and Newsgroups

E-mail and instant messaging can act as a vehicle for group as well as individual communication. This occurs through listservs and newsgroups.

**Listservs** are Internet discussion groups that use e-mail to exchange messages between as few as a dozen people or as many as several thousand. A listserv subscriber sends a message to a central address, where it is duplicated and sent out to all the members of the group. Replies to the message are similarly received by everyone in the group. This can prove to be embarrassing when someone replies to a message, thinking that the response will go to a single person, and it is instead broadcast to the entire membership.[23] The distinguishing characteristic of a listserv is that users must subscribe to the group. In some cases, it is limited to people who work in a particular office; in other cases, anyone who is interested in the topic may join.

Newsgroup bulletin boards are the next step. Newsgroups allow people to post and reply to messages from anywhere in the world. They may have a definite list of subscribers or be open to anyone who wants to stop by for a look. **Usenet**, the original Internet discussion forum, is the Users Network, a "worldwide distributed bulletin-board system."[24] It contains literally thousands of specialized topics, ranging from computer technology to old television sitcoms to ways to kill Barney the Dinosaur. It was through Usenet groups that many of the early developments on the Internet were publicized, including the World Wide Web and the first Web browser.

Since the birth of the World Wide Web (discussed in the next section), a huge number of Web-based discussion groups have arisen. Frequently associated with media Web sites, these groups often blur the lines between newsgroups and listservs, allowing subscribers to choose between viewing the messages on a central Web site or receiving them via e-mail.

## Mass Communication: The World Wide Web

Until 1990 using the Internet for anything more than e-mail was a challenge. Information was scattered about in various places, with no easy way to access it. All that was to change with the invention of the World Wide Web by British physicist Tim Berners-Lee. Berners-Lee, who built on the ideas of several Internet pioneers, created the software that allows the Internet to work as a medium of mass communication. He developed a system that is easy to use, allows users to access any type of information, and has a simplified single addressing system for accessing any document located on the Web anywhere in the world.

*Predecessors of the Web.*    The idea of the Web dates back to the 1960s. In 1968 Stanford researcher Doug Englebart staged a demonstration of his vision of an interactive computer at the Fall Joint Computer Conference in San Francisco. Englebart, who also invented the computer mouse, showed a pair of computer

**listservs**
Internet discussion groups made up of subscribers that use e-mail to exchange messages between as few as a dozen people to as many as several thousand.

**Usenet**
The Users Network is the original Internet discussion forum that covers thousands of specialized topics. It is a worldwide bulletin-board system that predates the World Wide Web.

terminals in an "online" session that included word-processing documents, hypertext documents, and live video images (sent over closed-circuit analog lines). Englebart was ahead of his time and largely ignored, but his work was the first expression of what would come with the Macintosh, Microsoft Windows, and video conferencing.[25]

Another early vision of the Web, more philosophical than technical, came from Ted Nelson. Nelson described a form of "nonsequential writing" that he called **hypertext**—material formatted to contain links that allow the reader to move easily from one section to another and from document to document. The most commonly used hypertext documents are Web pages. Nelson's ideal was for all the world's literature to be made available in hypertext form to empower the reader and eliminate the distinction between the teacher and the student. In effect, he was promoting the idea of the hypertext library, anticipating by several years Project Gutenberg, a Web site featuring public-domain literature that has been scanned and uploaded by volunteers.

**hypertext**

Material in a format containing links that allow the reader to move easily from one section to another and from document to document. The most commonly used hypertext documents are Web pages.

### *Tim Berners-Lee and the Birth of the World Wide Web.*   When Tim Berners-Lee was a child, his parents owned a Victorian-era advice book called *Enquire Within Upon Everything.* What would it be like, Berners-Lee wondered, if there really was a book that contained everything you might want to know? In 1980 he made his first attempt to create such a resource by writing a program called Enquire to organize documents, lists of people, and projects on his computer. The hypertext program would let him find and connect any of his documents. Although Enquire was limited to Berners-Lee's computer, the young British physicist thought about the possibilities of the program extending beyond his own computer to every computer in the world:

*For inventing the World Wide Web, Tim Berners-Lee was honored with a Lifetime Achievement Award at the 2009 Webby Awards.*

> Suppose all the information stored on computers everywhere were linked. . . . Suppose I could program my computer to create a space in which anything could be linked to anything? All the bits of information in every computer . . . on the planet would be available to me and to anyone else. There would be a single, global information space.[26]

Berners-Lee was never asked to create the Web; he simply thought it would be a good idea for researchers to be able to find documents they needed

**World Wide Web**

A system developed by Tim Berners-Lee that allows users to view and link documents located anywhere in the world using standard software.

**uniform resource locator (URL)**

One of the three major components of the Web; the address of content placed on the Web.

**hypertext transfer protocol (http)**

A method of sending text, graphics, or anything else over the Internet from a server to a Web browser.

**hypertext markup language (HTML)**

The programming language used to create and format Web pages.

regardless of which computer those documents resided on. In 1989 he returned to his Enquire idea and started writing the software for a system he called the **World Wide Web**, which allows users to view and link documents located anywhere in the world using standard software.

By 1990 the European Organization for Nuclear Research (CERN), where Berners-Lee was working at the time, had the first Web server and a simple browser. (A Web server is a program that makes Web pages available on the Internet. A browser is a program for viewing Web pages.)

The World Wide Web has three major components:

1. The **uniform resource locator** (**URL**)—the address of content placed on the Web. An example is www.mysite.com.

2. The **hypertext transfer protocol** (**http**)—the standard set of rules used by Web servers and browsers for sending and receiving text, graphics, or anything else on a Web site. When you type http://, you are telling your Web browser to use this protocol, or set of rules.

3. The **hypertext markup language** (**HTML**)—the programming language used to create Web pages. It consists of all the tags (brief computer commands) that say how text ought to be presented, where graphics should be placed, and what links should be included.

Although the Web has grown immensely in complexity since it was invented, these three basic elements remain central to how it operates.

Berners-Lee released the Web software in summer 1991 on several Internet newsgroups. These early users helped him test and debug the program and made suggestions for improvement. The Web started spreading around the world, and although it wasn't quite the intergalactic network that Licklider had envisioned with ARPAnet, it was a start.

Whereas Berners-Lee developed the Web on a NeXT computer system, the development of browsers for a wide range of computers was done on a volunteer basis by people around the world. These individuals were willing to share their work, but language barriers sometimes posed a problem. One of the early browsers had documentation only in Finnish. (You can read more about Steve Jobs and the NeXT computers at the beginning of Chapter 3.)

The most surprising thing about the World Wide Web may be that it was developed almost entirely as a collaborative, nonprofit venture. "What amazed me during the early days was the enormous amount of free energy that went into developing that technology," says Michael Folk, one of the early Web developers. "People from all over the world contributed huge amounts of time and ideas in a surprisingly noncompetitive, collaborative way."[27]

You can find links to Berners-Lee's Web site, along with the first-ever Web address, at http://ralphehanson.com.

*A Vision for the Web.* Although the World Wide Web has grown far beyond what anyone could have imagined, and has changed immeasurably, it is still shaped by the basic vision of Tim Berners-Lee. His goal was to create a completely decentralized system for sharing information that would have no central hub. With no central control, the whole system could *scale*—that is, grow almost indefinitely—yet still work properly. Berners-Lee was looking for a system in which any computer could link to any other computer: "The power of a hypertext link is that it can link to absolutely anything. That's the fundamental concept."[28]

The success of the World Wide Web illustrates one of the major strengths of the Internet: Although users can buy a Web browser or Web server, the basic technology is free. Says Dave Walden, who worked on the original ARPAnet software, "[Berners-Lee] brought out something, he gave it to a few of his friends, they tried it, they saw that it was good, and he gave it away. It went all over the world. That's how the World Wide Web standard came on the world."[29]

The next time you go surfing on the Web, look for evidence of the principles—openness and accessibility—on which it is based:

- Information of all kinds should be available through the same window, or information space. This means that you don't have to use one program to look up phone numbers and another to find the news.

- All documents on the Web must be equally accessible.

- There must be a single address that will take users to a document.

- Users should be able to link to any document at any space.

- Users should be able to access any type of material from any type of computer.

- Users should be able to create whatever types of relationships between information that they want to. It should be possible to link a document to any other document.

- The Web should be a tool not just for information but also for collaboration. It is designed for interaction as well as publication.

- There is no central control of the Web.

- The Web software should be available free to anyone who wants to use it.

## Bringing the Net to the Public

Before 1993 the Internet and the World Wide Web belonged primarily to university and military personnel who had used ARPAnet. But in his history of the Internet, *Nerds 2.0.1*, Stephen Segaller notes that three things happened during the early 1990s to turn the Internet into a significant social force: The

World Wide Web code was posted to the Internet, commercial users were allowed onto the Net for the first time, and the first easy-to-use graphical Web browser was written and posted to the Net. With these changes, the Internet outgrew its military and research origins and became a public medium.

*Mosaic.*    Although Berners-Lee had created a browser as part of the original World Wide Web, it was limited in terms of the computers it would run on, and it could not display anything other than text. **Mosaic**, the first easy-to-use graphical Web browser, was created by a group of student programmers led by Marc Andreessen at the University of Illinois at Champaign-Urbana. The developers wanted to create a tool that would make it easier to find things on the Internet and would provide an incentive to put information on the Web. As with the original Web software, Mosaic was posted on the Internet, free for users to download. More than 1 million users downloaded Mosaic in 1993 (the year it was released), and Andreessen, then twenty-one and graduated, decided that he should go into business.

Netscape Communications was cofounded by Andreessen and computer entrepreneur Jim Clark. Their product, Netscape Navigator, was the first commercial Web browser and became the standard for the industry. The company gave away the product to private users but required commercial companies to license it for use. Within two years 65 million people were using Navigator. In the mid-1990s Microsoft developed the Internet Explorer browser, which soon became a centerpiece of the Windows operating system.[30]

*The Last 100 Yards.*    Thanks to the private development of high-speed communication networks, the text, graphics, sound, and video of the World Wide Web can travel from remote servers to cities and towns around the world.[31] The stream of data flows as bursts of laser light down hair-thin fiber-optic cables. But the most difficult part of the process is getting the material across the last 100 yards, from utility poles along the street into businesses, schools, and homes.

As of April 2009, 63 percent of adult Americans were using high-speed broadband connections to the Internet at home, compared to 42 percent in March 2006. Dial-up **narrowband service** using modems on conventional copper phone lines is largely dying out, with only 7 percent of Americans using it at home.[32] **Broadband service**, such as a cable modem from a cable television provider or a digital subscriber line (DSL) from a phone company, offers connections that are at least ten times faster than dial-up service. But broadband offers more than just increased connection speed. With a broadband connection, subscribers are connected to the Net whenever their computer is turned on. This means that they don't have to download their e-mail; it's always there. It means that things like online radio, instant messaging, and streaming video are easily accessible. Using the Web to do ordinary things like look up a phone number or a dictionary definition is as easy as turning on a television set.[33]

**Mosaic**
The first easy-to-use graphical Web browser, developed by a group of student programmers at the University of Illinois at Champaign-Urbana.

**narrowband service**
A relatively slow Internet connection using a modem and conventional copper phone lines. Although it is acceptable for viewing text and graphics, it is generally considered too slow for video and audio service.

**broadband service**
A high-speed continuous connection to the Internet using a cable modem from a cable television provider or a digital subscriber line from a phone company. Broadband service is also available in many offices through ethernet lines. Broadband connections are typically ten or more times faster than dial-up services using a modem.

Users are also increasingly cutting the cable and using wireless connections to hook up their computer, PDA, or mobile phone to the Internet. The Pew Internet and American Life Project found that 56 percent of Americans have accessed the Internet by wireless technology, including 39 percent of Americans who have accessed wireless Internet using a laptop computer and 32 percent of Americans who have ever gone online using a mobile device such as a cell phone or some other handheld device.[34] Mobile Internet use is especially prevalent in the African American community, where 29 percent of the population use mobile devices to access the Internet on an average day, compared to 19 percent of the American population as a whole. If you look at Twitter traffic, of the estimated 5 million people who have Twitter accounts, more than 800,000 of them have sent or received tweets using an AT&T or a Verizon phone.[35]

You can read much more about how broadband subscribers are using the Internet by following the link to the Pew Internet and American Life study on home broadband adoption at http://ralphehanson.com.

# NEW MEDIA AND ONLINE ENTERTAINMENT

The Internet is evolving rapidly as a mass medium, and the path that it will follow is still uncertain. But it will incorporate a range of players. These include traditional publications and companies such as the *Washington Post*, CNN, National Public Radio, and the major movie studios. Then there are new media publications and companies like *Slate* or *Salon*: professionally produced online media that don't have a traditional broadcast or print component. These are often referred to as dot-coms. Most significant are the independent sites—zines, Weblogs, user-generated video, Webcams, and gossip pages—that are operated by anyone who wants to be a publisher and has a Web site, such as the movie gossip site Ain't It Cool News or motorcycle racing news Superbike Planet. Finally, there are aggregator sites, such as Google, YouTube, and Yahoo, which attempt to bring order to the inherently unorganized Web.

## Traditional Versus New Media

Traditional media companies that publish news online are sometimes called *click and mortars.* They have larger economic and journalistic resources than do the dot-coms. These are existing media companies such as Gannett (publisher of *USA Today*), NBC, and Disney.[36] MSNBC, frequently cited as the most visited news site on the Web, is owned jointly by Microsoft and General Electric (which partially owns the NBC broadcast network).

Along with reprinting news that is printed or broadcast by traditional media, these sites may include supplementary material that cannot appear in the original publication. For example, the Web version of a profile of author Hunter S. Thompson in *Atlantic Monthly* was accompanied by audio excerpts from the Thompson interview.

News sites from traditional media are particularly effective when there is breaking news. The Web site can provide immediate updates in much the way that television does, but the Web can reach workers at their desks. The other advantage of Internet news is that heavy coverage of a breaking story does not prevent the Web site from covering the rest of the news. Television is more limited because covering one major story prevents stations from devoting time to other stories.[37]

Newspapers have been able to create good Web sites in part because they already have the staff to gather news. In Internet terms, they have a good source of content. In some ways, newspaper Web sites have come to resemble miniature television networks.

Despite the name World Wide Web, one reason newspapers succeed is that they are local. Most people work, buy cars, and rent or buy housing in the city in which they live, making local classified ads an important component of the newspaper. When news Web sites were first launched, they were expected to lose money, but the media conglomerates that control many of the most popular Web sites expect to make profits. Whereas banner advertising is the most prominent form of advertising on the Web, employment ads (want ads) and classified ads are the most important source of revenue for newspapers.[38]

The main advantage that online media offer consumers is that they can customize the site to deliver only the news they want. Your sports page leads with the teams you follow, your weather forecast is local, and you don't have to wade through the international news if you aren't interested in it. Cyberpunk author William Gibson likes the idea of being able to control the information coming in to him, but he is also concerned about how such limits will affect him:

> We have access to so much information, the problem is really valving it down and selecting the bits. Eventually we'll all have very specialized software agents that spend their time pre-sorting that stuff for us. That worries me a bit because I know if I had one of those, there are things I would utterly ignore that I should know about. There's something to be said for a certain amount of randomness in your news intake.[39]

*Movies, TV, and the Net.* The first use of the Internet by the movie industry was to promote films through brochure-like Web pages. Then came *The Blair Witch Project*, which showed how interaction on the Web could draw in viewers. Finally, the Internet started being used as the screening venue for short films. Film sites on the Web have become the minor leagues of the movie and television industry. Aspiring filmmakers first establish themselves with a short, low-cost Internet film in the hope that someone in the industry will notice them.[40] Of course, on user-generated content sites like YouTube, the short films can be beyond low budget.

One thing the Internet can do is air films that may be too avant-garde for conventional media. The Web site UbuWeb, for example, is a repository of a wide range of avant-garde and experimental films, interviews, and e-books. Says Dave Garrett, who broke into Hollywood with an Internet film about elderly women playing Russian roulette,

> The Internet is not the place to look for mainstream fare; that's something you can find on television or at the movies. Our film was perfect for the Internet. You couldn't see it on TV because it had old women shooting themselves.[41]

Among the first big hits on the Internet was *405*, a short film that tells the story of an airliner landing on a highway, which was downloaded more than 2 million times in 2000. The film was created by Bruce Branit and Jeremy Hunt, who worked during the day at the special-effects house Digital Muse. *405* had no budget—allegedly the only significant expense was the traffic ticket the moviemakers got for filming illegally on the highway—though it did make use of Branit and Hunt's special-effects skills and some of the software and equipment to which they had access at work.[42]

As we discussed in Chapter 9, audience members, especially younger audience members, are moving away from regarding television sets as the primary way to view video. They can now get both video podcasts and digital downloads of movies and television shows through online services such as iTunes or Amazon.com, or from file-sharing services such as Limewire. From there, they can view their video on computers, smartphones, Playstation Portables, or portable video players. Back in 2000, Martin French, who worked for the Internet film site MeTV, put it this way: "Let's be honest, nobody wants to sit in front of the PC and [watch movies]. It's not a comfortable position."[43] Obviously, people are willing to view video on their computers, and lots of other places, as well. It may be that alternative devices have gotten better, or it may be that there is an ongoing cultural change on how people view video.

*405, created on home computers with specialized video software, was one of the first successful films to be produced for distribution over the Internet.*

The Internet is also being used as a promotional tool for mainstream media content. We saw this early on with *The Blair Witch Project* Web site, followed by the *Lost Experience* alternate reality game. Consider, too, the online scavenger hunt for the 2007 Nine Inch Nails album *Year Zero*, which featured thumb drives containing downloads of CD tracks located around the country, a mysterious Web site located at iamtryingtobelieve.com, and comments on a blog. Music industry trade magazine *Billboard* suggested that all these elements were not so much a promotional campaign for the album but rather additional components of "a new entertainment form."[44]

*New Media.*   Competing with the traditional media on the Web are the Web magazines—publications that look a lot like traditional magazines but don't have a print or broadcast counterpart. The two leading Web magazines are *Slate* and *Salon*, which publish articles similar to those in glossy literary magazines like the *Atlantic* or the *Nation*.[45]

How do these differ from "real" magazines? On the one hand, the Web magazines have low publishing costs and can be updated without the long lead time required for printed magazines. On the other hand, readers expect Web publications to be updated daily, and most of these magazines have no subscription revenue to supplement advertising. Although articles in Web magazines can be of any length, they rarely run longer than 2,000 words, primarily because that's how much people are willing to read.[46] One thing the Web magazines offer that print and broadcast magazines cannot is the opportunity for readers to respond to articles through a message board.

*Aggregator Sites.*   The biggest challenge facing Web surfers is the enormous amount of content on the Internet. How do people find what they are looking for? An easy first step is to rely on sites produced by traditional media companies. But how do people find specialized information? That's where the **aggregator sites** come in. Aggregator sites provide surfers with easy access to e-mail, news, online stores, and many other sites. Among the earliest of these was Excite, which started out as a service for litigation-support departments, political campaigns, and public relations agencies. Its product evolved gradually into a navigation aid—something that would help people to find their way around the Internet. Excite co-founder Joe Kraus says,

> Basically, we call ourselves Publishing on Steroids. Devoid of print, paper, or ink, we do what a publisher does, or a cable provider does. We aggregate consumers around our programming and then we sell that demographic back to advertisers.[47]

With companies like Google, Yahoo, AOL, and Netscape all providing newspaper- or magazine-like content, the Web has turned into a commercial mass medium supported by advertising, just as television, radio, or magazines might be.

*Video Games as Mass Communication.*   In my own media literacy class, I've been questioning for several semesters whether video games and video game consoles count as mass communication and whether they are a new mass medium. I think the answer is a definite yes, for a number of reasons:[48]

- Video game consoles are media content delivery devices. The Playstation 2 was a DVD player as well as a game console, and the Playstation 3 was among the early Blu-ray players. Microsoft's Xbox 360 sells and rents

**aggregator site**
An organizing Web site that provides surfers with easy access to e-mail, news, online stores, and many other sites.

television programs and movies in high definition through Xbox 360 Video Marketplace.[49]

- Video games, like television shows or movies, have stars. They have mascots. The most prominent of these is Super Mario, who has been a force in the gaming world for Nintendo since 1981, but the list also includes characters like Sonic the Hedgehog for Sega and *Halo*'s Master Chief for the Microsoft Xbox.

- Video games are a new venue for advertising. Just like newspapers, magazines, and Web sites funded by ad revenue, many game publishers are turning to the advertising world to help manage costs. Companies like IGA Worldwide are devoted entirely to securing deals for companies to advertise in games, which have a near-perfect saturation in the 18–34 age market. As was mentioned in Chapter 2, Barack Obama advertised in video games during his election campaign, the first presidential candidate ever to do so.[50]

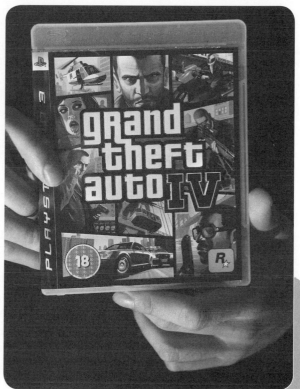

Major video games can bring in more revenue for their publishers than do major motion pictures. Grand Theft Auto IV *earned more than $500 million in its first two weeks of release.*

- Video games, now more than ever, are the site of entire communities. One needs only to look to online-specific games like *World of Warcraft* or online versions of console games like *Halo* or *Left 4 Dead*. The concept of online communities has become commonplace today. Now, instead of gathering around the water cooler to discuss the latest news or entertainment item, people are using Bluetooth headsets to talk to friends and family while playing capture the flag or fighting bosses to help their character rise to the next level.[51]

- Video games can be more profitable than the movies. In summer 2008, the controversial video game *Grand Theft Auto IV* was released at about the same time as the hit movie *Iron Man*. In its first two weeks of release, *Iron Man* grossed approximately $200 million, whereas *Grand Theft Auto IV* grossed $500 million over the same amount of time.[52]

- Video games have become a central part of the synergy used to promote and profit from popular movies, books, and television programs. When the latest *Batman* or *Harry Potter* movie is released, it is almost a given that tie-in video games will be on the shelves sometimes weeks before the movie comes out, in addition to the expected surge in comic or regular book sales. Even television shows such as *Survivor* have games, and game characters like Sonic and Mario have each had their own Saturday morning cartoon show.[53]

Given all this, it's hard not to see video games as a mass medium or a form of mass communication. According to the Pew Internet and American Life Project, 97 percent of teens aged 12–17 play video games in one form or another, with  fully 50 percent reporting having played "yesterday." Of those who play video games, 86 percent play on consoles, 73 percent play on computers, and 60 percent play on portable game systems. As of 2008 the most frequently played games were *Guitar Hero, Halo 3, Madden NFL, Solitaire*, and *Dance Dance Revolution*.[54] Among adults aged eighteen and older, 53 percent play video games and 21 percent play daily. Computers are the most popular place for older users to play video games; consoles are more common among younger players.[55]

## Giving Individuals a Voice

Ultimately the most interesting thing about the Web as a communication medium is that it opens up the world of publishing and broadcasting to anyone who has a computer, an Internet account, and something to say. The line between traditional journalism and newsletter publishing is changing because people no longer need to have a printing press or broadcast station to win national attention for their ideas. If what they write is compelling enough, people will pay attention.

Lawrence K. Grossman, former president of NBC News and PBS, writes in the *Columbia Journalism Review*:

> Gutenberg made us all readers. Radio and television made us all first-hand observers. Xerox made us all publishers. The Internet makes us all journalists, broadcasters, columnists, commentators, and critics. To update A. J. Liebling's classic crack about freedom of the press belonging to those who own one: In the next century freedom of the press could belong to everyone, at least everyone who owns a modem.[56]

*The Changing Nature of News.*    There is a vast flood of information of dubious quality on the Web, and distinguishing what is good from what is nonsense can be difficult. As Internet chronicler Stephen Segaller wrote, information on the Internet is "unregulated and uncensored, and its providers are largely unaccountable."[57] The point here is that the information is truly free. Although people with large amounts of money can have a greater presence on the Internet than can poor people, the Net is open to everyone. An example of this can be seen at the online, user-written encyclopedia Wikipedia. Wikipedia was founded in 2001 by Jimmy Wales. Its one million articles are among the most viewed pages on the Web. Like the Web as a whole, the entries in this free encyclopedia are of varying quality. A recent *New Yorker* article says that Wikipedia has excellent articles on major topics such as author Franz Kafka or the ships of the U.S. Navy but frequently gets bogged down with trivia and political debates.[58]

© 2007 Dave Kellett www.sheldoncomics.com

Because such large amounts of information, accurate and other-wise, are being posted to the Web, the Internet has become a major news source. Many stories start out on the Internet and then creep into the mainstream media. Rumors can start spreading on the Internet and be reprinted without attribution at several sites. Although each version may have the same original source, they can appear to be multiple instances of reporting; thus, the story starts to acquire significance.[59]

When Bill Clinton's White House aide Vince Foster committed suicide, rumors about his death started circulating in politically conservative newsletters. The stories were then discussed on the Internet and spread from there to conservative newspapers and then to more middle-of-the-road media. Media scholar and critic James Fallows writes, "Editors in the mainstream press have sometimes acted as if any fact posted on a Web site were . . . part of the public record, ending all arguments about whether to discuss it in newspapers or on the evening news."[60]

*Weblogs.* When Tim Berners-Lee created the World Wide Web, he viewed it not just as a convenient and inexpensive place to access published materials but also as a forum where people could interact and create their own materials. "We ought to be able not only to find any kind of document on the Web, but also to create any kind of document, easily," he writes in his history of the Web. "We should be able not only to follow links, but to create them—between all sorts of media. We should be able not only to interact with other people, but to create with other people."[61]

Berners-Lee's original idea was that every Web browser would also be an editor that ordinary people could use to create content as well as to view

*You can read the full story of Sheldon's visit with Wikipedia at http://www.sheldoncomics .com/archive/071209.html.*

*Jim Romenesko's blog, The Obscure Store & Reading Room, focuses on news oddities, especially stories about people driving vehicles into buildings.*

it, a vision that the early Web browsers did not support. But the late 1990s brought a new development called the **Weblog** (or **blog** for short), which is a collection of links and commentary in hypertext that can be created and posted on the Internet with relatively little effort. Blogs can be public diaries, collections of photos, or commentaries on the news. They often also allow readers to comment on and annotate what the owner has posted. Blogs are in many ways a throwback to the early days of magazine publishing, when authors wrote without expecting to be paid. While there are subsidized blogs, the vast majority are run simply to give the writers a forum.[62]

I made the case earlier in this book that blogs can be almost as mainstream as what we consider to be the mainstream media. (Truth Two—There are no mainstream media.) One test of the importance of a news source is whether it is included in the Lexis and Nexis online news databases. Lexis and Nexis are part of a giant subscription service that gives clients access to the full text of major newspapers, magazines, financial reports, and court documents. As of 2006 Nexis started including text from selected blogs, including the political gossip site Wonkette.

A prominent example of the influence of bloggers came when Dan Rather, on the CBS newsmagazine *60 Minutes II*, reported on a set of memos that seemed to show that President George W. Bush's superior officer had been critical of his service in the Air National Guard. The story ran a couple of months before the 2004 election, and it drew immediate criticism from the conservative blogs Power Line and Little Green Footballs. The bloggers pointed out inconsistencies in the typefaces used in the memos, suggesting that they looked more like the product of a modern word processor than of a 1970s vintage type-

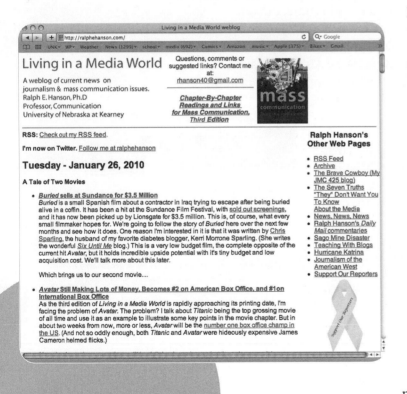

*Blogs have exploded in popularity in recent years, allowing anyone with a computer and an Internet connection (including the author of this text, at http://ralphehanson .com) to publish his or her thoughts on virtually any subject.*

writer. They also raised questions about the motives and honesty of the source of the documents. Criticisms coming from these and other blogs led to Dan Rather's stepping down as the anchor of *The CBS Evening News*.[63]

Blogs have also given readers different perspectives on stories than they might receive otherwise. Army Spc. Colby Buzzell came to national attention when he blogged about fighting in a battle at Mosul, Iraq, in

August 2004.[64] After he returned home, he published articles in *Esquire* and wrote a book entitled *My War.* British writer Julia Darling—a poet, playwright, and fiction writer, and the winner of the Northern Rock Foundation Writer's Award, one of the United Kingdom's largest literary prizes—blogged about her life as she battled cancer. From 2002 until her death in 2005, Darling wrote about writing, her students, and how cancer can be a "pain in the arse."[65] Dallas Mavericks owner Mark Cuban uses his blog to comment on the news and as a way to respond to his critics and those who report on him. But he also writes about digital music and the RIAA (the Recording Industry Association of America); not surprising, given his background in the high-tech industry.[66] He also uses his blog to speak out on issues as diverse as capital punishment and pay for interns.

For links to all the blogs mentioned here, plus many others, visit this author's blog at http://ralphehanson.com.

## Search as a Medium

Are search engines a new part of mass communication? Certainly the Internet and the World Wide Web are a part of our mass media, and search engines, such as Google or Yahoo, are the tools we use to find information on the Web. They might even be considered as news media. Think about Google News. It's in essence a search tool that decides what the major news stories of the day are, collects links to them on a single page, and presents them to the reader. According to Google, Google News draws stories from more than 4,500 English-language news sources from around the world. The articles are evaluated by Google's computers as to how often and on what sites the stories appear. Google claims this leads to an unbiased presentation of the news.[67]

The question of whether the Internet's search capability is a news medium is significant because various governments around the world want to put limits on Internet searching. And companies such as Google, Microsoft, and Yahoo all seem willing to build limits into their portals as part of the price of doing business in countries that have more restrictions on free speech than the United States. Sometimes the censorship of searches is relatively noncontroversial, such as France's attempts to make Yahoo filter out all references to Nazi paraphernalia.[68] But the collaboration of the search companies with the Chinese government has started to raise major questions in the United States. Yahoo gave up the name of blogger Zhao Jing to the Chinese government after the government required the company to do so. Yahoo defended its actions by saying that it had no choice but to comply with local law.[69] Yahoo also says that the Chinese are better served by a censored Internet than by no Internet at all. Google, which operates with the unofficial motto of "Don't be evil," censors its searches in China, but the company does inform users that it has removed items from their searches.

# TEST TEST YOUR MEDIA LITERACY

## Who Protects Free Speech for Chinese Bloggers?

**Zhao Jing**

Chinese journalist and blogger Zhao Jing knew he would likely have trouble from the authorities over the political blog he put online. When he posted an item complaining about the firing of the top editors of a popular Chinese newspaper under the name "Anti," the government filed a complaint with Microsoft, host of the blog, and got it taken down.

According to the *Washington Post*:

> "Anti's Daily Thoughts on Politics and Journalism" tackled a variety of subjects, from public attitudes in Jordan toward the war in Iraq, to the growth of democracy in Taiwan, to the state of Chinese journalism. Zhao generally refrained from topics sure to upset the censors. But his political views were clear.
>
> "I thought of myself as a salesman, and what I was selling was the concept of democracy," he said. "People think discussing politics is dangerous, but I wanted them to relax, to see it was normal and that it's not so sensitive. . . ."
>
> The December incident sparked outrage among bloggers around the world, and in Washington, members of Congress vowed to scrutinize how U.S. firms are helping the Chinese government censor the Internet. But the reaction inside China's growing community of Internet users was strikingly mixed.
>
> Many rallied to support Zhao, but some objected to his "Western" views and said he deserved to be silenced. Others, especially those with a financial stake in the industry, said they worried Zhao's writing could lead officials to impose tighter controls on blogging. And a few said they were pleased that Microsoft had been forced to comply with the same censorship rules that its Chinese rivals obey.[1]

### MORE online

You can find a link to a story about Zhao Jing and blogging in China from the *Washington Post* at **http://ralphehanson.com.** After you've read the story, answer the questions below.

● ● ● ● ● ● ● ● ● ● ● ● ● ● ● ● ●

### Who is the source?

Who is Zhao Jing? What is his background? What did he do?

### What is he saying?

How does Zhao say he was treated by the American companies that hosted his blog? How did the American companies work with the Chinese government to control Zhao's writings?

### What evidence is there?

What evidence does Zhao provide to support his critique of the Internet in China? Do the examples he provides support his arguments?

### What do you think?

What do you and your classmates think about international Internet controls? Should American Internet companies be willing to do business in countries that censor the Net? Why or why not? Have you ever had to deal with controls or censorship of what you can post or search for online? What kind of problems have you experienced?

[1] Philip P. Pan, "Bloggers Who Pursue Change Confront Fear and Mistrust," February 21, 2006, www.washingtonpost.com/wp-dyn/content/article/2006/02/20/AR2006022001304.html.

## The Long Tail of Internet News

The Internet, through blogs, podcasts, and user-video sites like YouTube, has opened up the options for long-tail news that doesn't get out through legacy (or mainstream) channels. Take the concept of **citizen journalism**. Often when we talk about citizen journalism, we're talking about a newspaper-like blog that posts reports about hyperlocal issues such as neighborhood events or elementary school sports. These provide valuable alternatives to stories carried in traditional newspapers or on local television news. But they have more in common with the old-time community newspapers that ran stories about who-had-dinner-with-whom than with cutting-edge journalism.

But news video posted through sites such as YouTube can lead to amateur cell phone video having international implications. Following the disputed elections in Iran during the summer of 2009, a large number of protestors took to the streets. These protests were suppressed by police, who did not allow journalists to cover the events taking place. But that didn't stop people from shooting cell phone video and then posting it to the Internet.

One of the most dramatic examples of this was the news about the murder of Neda Agha-Soltan, a twenty-six-year-old Iranian woman who was studying philosophy and vocal music. Though accurate details about Agha-Soltan are scarce, the *New York Times* reports that she was engaged, valued freedom, and was shot while stopping to get some fresh air after driving home from a singing lesson.[70] When she got out of the car near where protestors were marching, she was shot by a sniper. Her death was captured on cell phone video. The person who captured the video then e-mailed it to a friend, who then forwarded it to the Voice of America, the British newspaper *The Guardian*, and several friends. One of those friends, who lives in the Netherlands, posted the video to Facebook. From there, it moved on to a report on CNN.[71] All of this allowed the person who shot the video to bypass official Iranian censorship efforts to block Internet, cell phone, and text message traffic.[72]

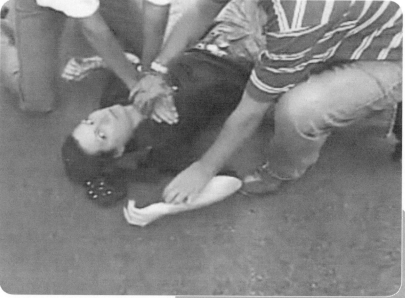

**citizen journalism**
Journalism created by people other than professional journalists, often distributed over the Internet.

*This still image of the murder of Neda Agha-Soltan during the election protests of 2009 in Iran was captured by mobile phone video and distributed worldwide via Facebook and other social media.*

# THE INTERNET AND SOCIETY

Despite having its roots in the world of military research, the Internet works primarily to permit the independent use of computers. The earliest users of time-sharing computer systems, in which several people on separate terminals could share a single computer, started seeing these large institutional computers as "theirs." Stuart Brand, author of the *Whole Earth Catalog*, says that users soon began to understand how they could use computers for their own purposes:

> Kennedy had said, "Ask not what your country can do for you. Ask rather what you can do for your country". . . . Basically we were saying, "Ask not what your country can do for you. Do it yourself." You just tried stuff and you did it yourself. You didn't ask permission.[73]

This would become the rallying cry of the Internet: Take control of it for yourself. This attitude sent shock waves throughout the media industry because it transformed the model of mass communication from one in which a limited number of producers deliver news, entertainment, and culture to a public whose choices are limited to one in which consumers can choose for themselves what news they want to learn about, what movies they want to see, what music they will listen to, and when they will do so.

This uncontrolled information environment is not all bliss, however. Some critics point out that the same giant media companies that dominated the older forms of media produce much of the content available on the Internet. Others complain that information on the Internet is uncontrolled, unreliable, and often unsuitable for young people to view.

## The Hacker Ethic

As a young man, Steve Jobs saw programming computers as a way of rebelling against and controlling an increasingly technological world. Jobs and Steve Wozniak, the co-founders of Apple, built electronic "blue boxes" that would let them place long-distance phone calls free by bypassing AT&T's control system. Beyond allowing the two to steal phone service and play an occasional prank, the boxes taught Jobs that technology could empower individuals: "What we learned was that we could build something ourselves that could control billions of dollars' worth of infrastructure in the world. . . . We could build a little thing that could control a giant thing. That was an incredible lesson."[74]

Jobs's attitude embodied what is known as the **hacker ethic**. The ethic is summed up in Steven Levy's book *Hackers*, originally published in 1984, before the Internet was a public medium and before many of the major Internet tools, most notably the World Wide Web, had been developed. (Levy uses "hackers" to

**hacker ethic**
A set of values from the early days of interactive computing that holds that users should have absolute control over their computer systems and free access to all information contained on those computers. The hacker ethic shaped much of the development of the Internet.

refer to people who like programming computers and using them to their fullest potential and prefers "digital trespassers" to refer to people who break into institutional computers. It appears, however, that many of the "true" hackers are often also digital trespassers.) Understanding the hacker ethic is critical to understanding the development of the Internet because its values shaped so many of the new medium's developers. Levy lists four key principles of the hacker ethic:[75]

1. "Access to computers—and anything which might teach you something about the way the world works—should be unlimited and total." Hackers want to obtain programs, data, and computers, and they do not respect rules that keep them from these tools. They believe that they should be able to directly control any computer system they can find; what's more, they believe that they can probably do a better job of running the system than the people who own it.

2. "All information wants to be free." This translates into a disregard for copyright law. Hackers believe that all information should be available to anyone who wants to make use of it. This was at the heart of file-sharing pioneer Napster and user-video site YouTube. If you have music, photographs, artwork, writings, or programs on your hard drive, why shouldn't you be able to share them? And if those same things exist on other computers, why shouldn't you be able to access them? This idea of universally shared information is at the heart of Berners-Lee's design of the World Wide Web. The problem, as the Napster and YouTube cases showed, remains how the creators of these works are going to be paid for the digital copies that users share. Ironically, Steven Levy got a taste of the "information wants to be free" movement in 2001, when he found the entire text of his book *Hackers* posted on a Web site at Stanford University.

3. "Mistrust authority—promote decentralization." The hacker culture distrusts centralized bureaucratic authority. Bureaucracies hide information and make rules controlling who can have access to it. So the best way to keep information free is to keep it out in the open.

4. You should be judged by your skills and not by "bogus criteria such as degrees, age, race, or position." On the Internet, traditional measures of individuals, such as age, education, sex, or income, matter less than they do under most other conditions because people are able to create identities for themselves that may or may not correspond with their actual identities. In essence, this is an extension of the multiple roles and identities people have always had. You can simultaneously be a teacher, a parent, a spouse, and a child. On the Internet, users can further extend

their identities, changing their sex, race, and background. On a listserv or newsgroup, people can construct entirely new identities for themselves. When all anyone knows about you is your e-mail address, you are free to be whomever you want to be.

The application of the values of the hacker ethic to the Internet in general provides an example of Truth Three—Everything from the margin moves to the center.

## The Notion of Cyberspace

The word *cyberspace* is used extensively to describe the Internet and the interactions that take place there. But the word predates common use of the Internet and the shared culture it has created. The word *cybernetics* (from the Greek *kybernetes*, meaning "pilot" or "governor") has been in use since 1948 to refer to a science of communication and control theory. Science fiction writer William Gibson is generally credited with coupling the prefix *cyber* to the word *space* in his 1984 novel *Neuromancer*, although the authoritative *Oxford English Dictionary* (see Chapter 4) notes that Gibson originally used the word in a magazine story in 1982. Gibson defines cyberspace in this way: "Cyberspace is where the bank keeps your money. It's where a long-distance telephone call happens. It's this ubiquitous, non-physical place where increasingly a lot of what we think of as our civilization takes place."[76]

Gibson sees cyberspace and the culture of the Internet as an expression of the hippie ideals of freedom and self-expression: "Tired as I am with all the hype about the Internet and the info highway, I suspect that from a future perspective it will be on a par with the invention of the city as a force in human culture."[77]

In addition to coining the word *cyberspace*, Gibson is credited with coming up with the idea of the cyberpunk. That word was originally used in the late 1980s to describe the hardboiled style of science fiction that deals with the interface between humans and machines, which Gibson created with *Neuromancer*. In his novels Gibson painted a picture of the future in which nations are in a decline, international corporations are growing in importance, and the world is dominated by consumerism.[78] The word *cyberpunk* has since been extended to describe movies—most notably *The Matrix* series, *Blade Runner,* and *Total Recall*—that raise questions about the differences between humans and machines. For all his talk about the influence of cyberspace, do not assume that Gibson is enamored of high technology. He wrote *Neuromancer* on a 1927-model portable typewriter. By 1995 he had switched to writing on a computer, but it was a castoff from one of his children.

## TEST YOUR MEDIA LITERACY

### A Contrary View of Cyberspace

In a 1994 interview, William Gibson, who invented the term *cyberspace*, talked about how he foresaw the future of the Internet:

> The advent, evolution and growth of the Internet is, I think, one of the most fascinating and unprecedented human achievements of the century. . . . It's really something new, it's a new kind of civilization. And of course the thing I love about it is that it's transnational, nonprofit—it isn't owned by any-one—and its shape is completely user driven. What it is, is determined by the needs of millions and millions of users. So cyberspace is evolving to meet the needs of individuals all over the world.
>
> The American so-called Information Highway . . . is an attempt to cre-ate a commercial version. I think that very, very large interests are looking at the Internet, not really understanding what it is, but thinking, "We can make a fortune if we have one of those!" You know, they want to get in there; it'll be broadcast television again.
>
> But of course that's not going to be it, and I think that the highway metaphor is particularly suspect. A highway is something you can go two ways on, it implies real traffic. Really what they're offering you is a mall. They want to give you an infomall where you pay for every bit of information you download, and you'll download from a menu that some corporation has assembled. . . .
>
> So I have great hopes for the Internet, very little hope for commercial versions, and I profoundly hope that the Internet will continue to be the basis of this sort of growth.[1]

**MOREonline**

Before answering the following questions, make sure you read the accompanying material in the main text about William Gibson. You can find a link to the 1994 interview with Gibson at **http://ralphehanson.com.** After you've read the interview, answer the questions below.

**Who is the source?**
Who is William Gibson? What is his background? What did he do?

**What is he saying?**
How does Gibson describe cyberspace? What does he say happens there? How does Gibson view corporate and individual users of cyberspace? How do their goals differ?

**What evidence is there?**
What evidence does Gibson provide to support his arguments about who controls cyberspace? What evidence does he provide about how he sees the Internet changing society?

**How do you view cyberspace?**
Is your view different from Gibson's vision? Why or why not? Do you think that Gibson's views from 1994 are still relevant today? Or has everything changed to either enhance or reduce the concerns he expressed?

[1] Dan Josefsson, "I Don't Even Have a Modem," josefsson.net, November 23, 1994. Available from www.josefsson.net/gibson/index.html.

## Community on the Net

Before the 1900s, it was relatively easy to define community: The community was made up of the people you interacted with every day. But the growth of the mass media led to changes in our understanding of community. People no longer need to be face-to-face with each other to interact. Larry Tesler, who helped develop the idea of computer communities at the Xerox PARC research center and at Apple Computer, says:

> When we were human beings in small tribes hunting and gathering, everybody you had to deal with was somebody you saw every day. We're a species that's based on communication with our entire tribe. As the population grew and people had to split up into smaller tribes and separate, they got to the point where they would never see each other for their whole lives. The Internet is the first technology that lets us have many-to-many communication with anybody on the planet. In a sense, it's brought us back to something we lost thousands of years ago. So one reason I think the Internet's taken off so fast is that we always needed it. And we finally have it.[79]

*Internet cafes, such as this one in Baghdad, Iraq, provide Web and e-mail access in areas where people could not otherwise afford computers and Internet services.*

***Is It Really a World Wide Web?*** When Tesler claims that the Internet allows people to interact with others anywhere on the planet, he overstates the case. Worldwide, only 24.7 percent of the population has Internet access at all. In many developing countries almost no one has Internet access. Compare North America, which has an Internet access rate of 73.9 percent, with Latin America, which has an access rate of 30 percent, and Africa, with an access rate of 6.7 percent.[80]

One of the major barriers to Internet use in developing countries is the cost. In 1999 it cost $10.50 an hour to use the Internet in the African nation of Chad, where the average annual income was $187. The Web is also largely limited to people who read English, since 80 percent of the world's Web sites are in English.[81] Another barrier in many countries is that there is no way to log on. Consider that in the industrialized nations there are about 50 phone lines for every 100 people, whereas developing nations have an average of 1.4 phone lines per 100 people. According to the United Nations, half the world's population has yet to make a phone call, much less log on to the Internet.[82]

*The Digital Divide.*    Even in the United States, access to the Internet is not universal. Affluent communities have better access to the Internet than do poorer and rural communities. Evidence indicates that whites and Hispanics are more likely to have access to the Internet than are African Americans. Although the percentage of African Americans online has been increasing dramatically, black families still lag behind in overall access levels.[83]

## Conflicts Over Digital Media

For all the benefits associated with the Web, the new medium has been criticized on a number of fronts. For one thing, a great deal of material on the Web is inappropriate for children. Another criticism is that Web surfers give up their privacy when they visit certain sites. Finally, it is argued that people spend so much time with their virtual communities and friends that they forget about their real lives.

*Controlling Content on the Web.*    The World Wide Web differs from all other media in that it is essentially an open forum where anyone can publish anything. More important, anyone can access anything he or she wants to. Because of this lack of control, unsupervised Web surfing is not particularly suitable for children. As computers and the Internet came to classrooms in the 1990s, parents and teachers became concerned about the possibility of students viewing pornography, hate speech, and even instructions on how to build a homemade bomb.

One solution to this problem is the use of filtering software, which can block access to certain kinds of material. This approach has been successful to a degree, but no filtering scheme can block all offensive material and still allow access to a full range of sites. For example, in 1998 the Loudoun County, Virginia, public libraries installed filtering software. The software successfully blocked pornographic material, but it also blocked sites with information on sex education, breast cancer, and gay rights.[84]

The fundamental problem with trying to control information on the Net is that the network of networks was designed specifically to overcome blocks and breakdowns. Once information is on the Net, it is virtually impossible to stop it from spreading. Net pioneer John Gilmore sums up the issue neatly: "The Net interprets censorship as damage and routes around it."[85]

*Privacy and the Web.*    A consumer walking into a conventional bookstore can wander from aisle to aisle, picking up titles of interest. After leaving the store, no one knows what books the consumer looked at. But when that same consumer shops at the online bookstore Amazon.com, the store keeps track of everything looked at. The Amazon software will then make recommendations to the shopper according to previous searches and purchases. Is this a great convenience or a serious loss of privacy?

Web users give up their privacy every time they go online. Each time they fill out a form, join a group, or buy something, information (name, address, interests, etc.) is stored so that the owner of the site will know more about its visitors. Web sites create tiny files called **cookies** to identify Web site visitors and potentially track their actions on the Web. Cookies may identify users so that they don't have to reenter their names and passwords. Or, as Amazon's cookies do, they might keep track of which types of items a visitor likes to look at. Cookies are generally designed to assist users as they go through one particular Web site, but they can also be used to track users' Web surfing habits or to provide evidence of what sites they have visited.

Web site developers can use cookies to tailor sites to a particular visitor. For example, a news site could use information from a cookie to provide the scores of your favorite teams, quotes for the stocks in your portfolio, and reviews of the style of music you like. The tailoring to individual tastes could take a more sinister cast, however. Web creator Tim Berners-Lee speculates that cookies could even be used to tailor propaganda to match the biases of the viewer: "Imagine an individual visiting the Web page of a political candidate, or a controversial company. With a quick check of that person's record, the politician or company can serve up just the right mix of propaganda that will warm that particular person's heart—and tactfully suppress points he or she might object to."[86]

*Clifford Stoll: Silicon Snake Oil.*    Like all new media, the Net has its critics. Clifford Stoll, an astronomer who became famous in the late 1980s when he helped catch a group of German hackers breaking into U.S. military computers, questions how important computers and the Internet should be in people's everyday lives. Central to Stoll's criticism is that for too many people, living in the virtual world of computers and the Internet replaces interactions and experiences in the real world. He argues that the Internet creates a false sense of intimacy without the emotional involvement that leads to true friendships.[87]

Stoll disagrees with the conventional wisdom that the Internet is a powerful and inexpensive way to interact with people around the world and that it's a valuable educational tool:

> It ain't necessarily so. Our networks can be frustrating, expensive, unreliable connections that get in the way of useful work. It is an over-promoted, hollow world, devoid of warmth and human kindness. . . . For all the promises of virtual communities, it's more important to live a real life in a real neighborhood.[88]

**cookies**
Tiny files Web sites create to identify visitors and potentially track their actions on the site and the Web.

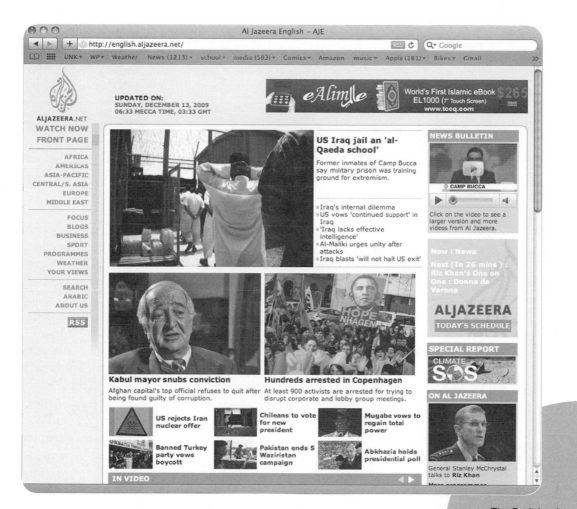

## Convergence of Old and New Media

There is lots of talk these days about convergence and new media, why the Web is the place for news that's going to replace the old dead tree media (newspapers and magazines), broadcast media, and everything else. New media synergy, we are told, will bring together the depth of text, an abundance of photos, audio, and video. You get all of the advantages of the old media in one package.

There are signs that this is happening. National Public Radio launched its new NPR.org Web site in July 2009, with the goal of enabling journalists to present photos, video, audio, and written stories to go with streaming copies and transcripts of all the stories that have aired on NPR since May 2005. The new site also makes these resources available on mobile media, such as the iPhone or Blackberry.[89]

Convergence is also delivering media that wouldn't be available otherwise. The Arab news channel Al Jazeera started its English-language service in November 2006, but it had trouble finding any U.S. cable or satellite services willing to carry it. For the time being, Americans who are interested in watching Al Jazeera must do so primarily over the Internet.

*Reverse Synergy.* Sometimes you get reverse synergy—the worst of the old and new media in one new package. A prime example of reverse synergy happened in 2008 when Bloomberg's online financial news service posted a six-year-old news story about United Airlines (UAL) filing for bankruptcy. The story was true—it was just six years out of date. What happened is this: An undated story about UAL's 2002 bankruptcy filing showed up on a Google search on "bankruptcy 2008" done by a reporter working for Income Security Advisors. The story from the *South Florida Sun-Sentinel* dated back to December 10, 2002, when UAL did file for bankruptcy. The reporter who performed the search then posted the story to Bloomberg News Service. In response to the story, investors started dumping their shares in UAL, dropping the stock from $12.17 a share to approximately $3 a share. Not realizing what had happened, United Airlines was baffled by the tanking of its stock, but it quickly posted an online denial of the story. By the time the market closed, UAL stock was back up to $10.92.[90]

What can we learn from this? Think about Truth Seven—There is no "they." The story that sent the stock price crashing was a single story from a single Web site. Wouldn't you think that if a major corporation had filed for bankruptcy twice in six years the story would be playing on every major news site, not just a single Florida paper that has no local connection to the story? At the risk of oversimplifying things, the story was posted because someone—a "they"—said it was so. This resulted in a huge destruction of wealth, albeit a temporary one, because of a story that had no truth value and apparently was posted completely by accident.

*From Newspapers to Brands.* Old media are certainly not going away, but they are changing, going from being a particular medium to becoming a brand. Consider the *New York Times.* Over the past several years, *New York Times* owner and publisher Arthur Sulzberger has been talking about how the *New York Times* will be changing. He set off a storm of controversy in spring 2007 with his comment at the World Economic Forum in Switzerland: "I really don't know whether we'll be printing the *Times* in five years, and you know what? I don't care either. . . . The Internet is a wonderful place to be, and we're leading there."[91]

This statement generated comments on almost every major press blog, but what few people noticed was that Sulzberger had been saying the same thing for at least eight years. When he was part of an *Advertising Age* roundtable in 1999, Sulzberger was asked about the future of the *Times*. He answered:

> I don't care how they get it 100 years from now. And the key is not caring. It goes back to knowing the audience, and being, not ambivalent, but agnostic, rather. Agnostic about the methods of distribution. Because we can't afford to be tied to any production process. . . . There will still be communities of interest. There will still be a need, both socially and politically, for common and shared experiences.[92]

Now there is a big difference between "I don't care how they get it 100 years from now" and "I really don't know if we'll be printing the *Times* five years from now." But the basic thought, the real point of his comments, is the same—the *New York Times* is no longer in the business of putting black ink on white paper. Instead, the *Times* is in the news business and the ad sales business, and it is going to be delivering news and advertising in whatever forms will turn a profit. His remarks in Switzerland don't mean that the *New York Times* is going to stop printing a newspaper within the next 5, or even 100, years. It means that the *New York Times* is going to keep on selling its two basic products, news and advertising, for a long time, regardless of what happens to the ink-on-paper newspaper business.

## CHAPTER Summary

The Internet arose in the late 1960s out of efforts to share expensive computer resources provided by the military to universities across the United States. The initial network, called ARPAnet, went online for the first time in the fall of 1969. The network operated using packet switching, a method of transferring information that breaks down messages into small packets that are transmitted separately across the network and reassembled once they are received. Through e-mail and file sharing, ARPAnet soon became a tool used by academics to collaborate and communicate across the country.

As the number of incompatible networks grew in the 1970s, Bob Kahn and Vint Cerf developed the TCP/IP protocols that would allow the networks to communicate with each other. In 1983 ARPAnet started using the TCP/IP protocols. This is commonly seen as the true beginning of the Internet.

The Internet is unique among the mass media in allowing interpersonal communication through e-mail and instant messaging; group communication through listservs, newsgroups, and discussion boards; and mass communication through the World Wide Web.

The World Wide Web was developed in 1989 by British physicist Tim Berners-Lee while he was working at the European Organization for Nuclear Research in Switzerland. His goal was to produce a decentralized system for creating and sharing documents anywhere in the world. The Web has three major components: the uniform resource locator (URL), the hypertext transfer protocol (http), and the hypertext markup language (HTML). Berners-Lee published the code for the World Wide Web on the Internet in 1991 for anyone in the world to use at no cost.

The Internet in general and the Web in particular were based on a set of values known as the hacker ethic. This ethic holds that information should be freely distributed and that individuals should have as much control over computers as possible.

The World Wide Web has turned the Internet into a major mass medium that provides news, entertainment, and community interaction. The Web offers a mix of content providers, including traditional media companies, new media companies offering publications available only on the Web, aggregator sites that offer help in navigating the Web, and individuals who have something they want to say.

The Web has been criticized for elevating rumors to the level of news, making inappropriate material available to children, collecting private information about users, and creating a false sense of intimacy and interaction among users.

Over the past several years, users have moved increasingly from slow dial-up connections to high-speed "always on" connections that have changed how people view and use the Internet. Media are making use of these high-speed connections to deliver content that includes a rich mix of video, audio, photos, and text.

## KEYTerms

## CONCEPT Review

The merging of the different levels of communication
Tim Berners-Lee's idealistic conception of the World Wide Web
How the Internet gives voice to individuals
The long-term effect of the hacker ethic
How convergence is changing the media industry

# Advertising
## Selling a Message

**Spike Lee** is best known as the director of films such as *Malcolm X*, *Do the Right Thing*, and *Inside Man*. But he also has a lengthy record of directing commercials for clients such as Levi Strauss, American Express, and Nike. He has even formed his own advertising agency, Spike DDB.

Lee came to prominence in the advertising business with a successful series of ads for Nike shoes that featured Lee not only as a director but also as the character Mars Blackmon from his movie *She's Gotta Have It*. The commercials paired the Blackmon character with NBA superstar Michael Jordan. Lee's Blackmon was obsessed with Jordan and his Nikes and continually argued that the secret of Jordan's success has "gotta be the shoes." Jordan would then respond, "It's not the shoes, Mars."[1] The ads, which mocked the entire shoe marketing process, were a great success with viewers, and they sold shoes as well.

Lee started his own ad agency in the mid-1990s when he got frustrated with just being a director. He wanted to be in charge: "I got tired of just being the hired gun. I wanted more creative input. I tell young people, especially African Americans, that it's about ownership."[2] The agency is a partnership between Lee and DDB Needham World Wide.[3]

Lee says that his agency was hampered initially by its reputation for producing ads for African Americans. "No matter what you do or say, they say Spike DDB is just a black agency that has expertise in the black market," Lee told the *New York Times*. "It's just a shame and it hurts us, but we'll just let the work speak for itself."[4] Lee wasn't satisfied with going after only one segment of the advertising business. "I don't want any crumbs," he told *Marketing* magazine. "I want the whole enchilada, the steak, the wine, the beer, and the champagne on top of that."[5] Lee argues that his agency creates messages that transcend racial categories:

> Race still plays a very important part in how we operate in this country and how people perceive you. They see people who are called minorities and say they have no universal appeal, they're very limited, and if you want to reach everybody that's not the way to go. People who think like that have lost a lot of money. Nike would not be paying Michael Jordan the money they're paying him if only kids from the ghetto were wearing his sneakers.[6]

Spike Lee

Although Lee has his own agency, he still directs commercials for others as well. In 2005, he reunited with Michael Jordan for the twentieth anniversary of Nike's Air Jordan shoes while working for the Wieden+Kennedy agency.[7] Drawing on his skills as a feature film director, Lee depicted people in places that had special meaning to Jordan throughout his basketball career.

In 1999 Lee produced a series of commercials for the U.S. Navy that featured sailors talking about their experiences and how the Navy changed their lives.[8] The commercials were shot with real people telling their stories; no scripts were used. Part of Lee's talent is his ability to listen to people. Navy Seal Shawn Carrizales told *AdWeek*, "I expected him to tell us what to do, but we would tell him exactly how Seals operate, and we would work together from there."[9] The impetus for Lee's campaign came out of problems the Navy was having in recruiting enough new sailors. The ads ran during NFL and NBA games, on cable networks, and even in movie theaters.[10]

Recent clients include Pepsi, Mountain Dew, Topps baseball cards, and Nokia mobile phones. He's also directed a spot promoting Black History Month for VH1-Soul. For some recent examples of Spike Lee's advertising work, take a look at http://ralphehanson.com.

Why does a successful filmmaker produce commercials? Lee sees his ads, no less than his movies, as an expression of his creativity:

I never saw a reason to limit myself to anything. And advertising always seemed like something fantastic to me. You know, new, different, fast. What I do is about telling a story. You can do

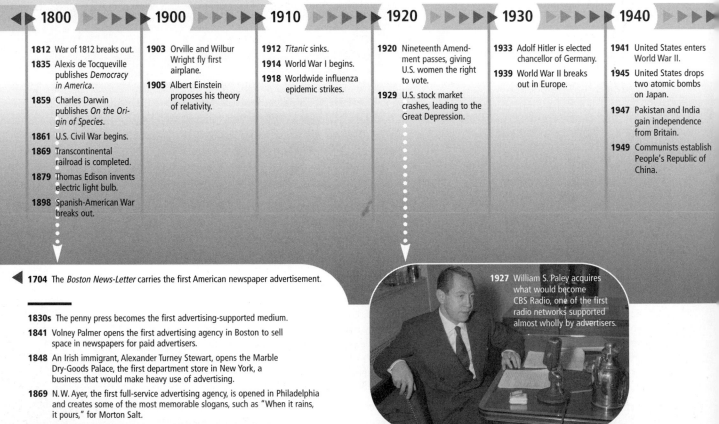

| **1800** | **1900** | **1910** | **1920** | **1930** | **1940** |
|---|---|---|---|---|---|
| **1812** War of 1812 breaks out. | **1903** Orville and Wilbur Wright fly first airplane. | **1912** *Titanic* sinks. | **1920** Nineteenth Amendment passes, giving U.S. women the right to vote. | **1933** Adolf Hitler is elected chancellor of Germany. | **1941** United States enters World War II. |
| **1835** Alexis de Tocqueville publishes *Democracy in America*. | **1905** Albert Einstein proposes his theory of relativity. | **1914** World War I begins. | **1929** U.S. stock market crashes, leading to the Great Depression. | **1939** World War II breaks out in Europe. | **1945** United States drops two atomic bombs on Japan. |
| **1859** Charles Darwin publishes *On the Origin of Species*. | | **1918** Worldwide influenza epidemic strikes. | | | **1947** Pakistan and India gain independence from Britain. |
| **1861** U.S. Civil War begins. | | | | | **1949** Communists establish People's Republic of China. |
| **1869** Transcontinental railroad is completed. | | | | | |
| **1879** Thomas Edison invents electric light bulb. | | | | | |
| **1898** Spanish-American War breaks out. | | | | | |

**1704** The *Boston News-Letter* carries the first American newspaper advertisement.

**1830s** The penny press becomes the first advertising-supported medium.

**1841** Volney Palmer opens the first advertising agency in Boston to sell space in newspapers for paid advertisers.

**1848** An Irish immigrant, Alexander Turney Stewart, opens the Marble Dry-Goods Palace, the first department store in New York, a business that would make heavy use of advertising.

**1869** N.W. Ayer, the first full-service advertising agency, is opened in Philadelphia and creates some of the most memorable slogans, such as "When it rains, it pours," for Morton Salt.

**1887** The magazine *Ladies Home Journal* is designed as a medium for consumer advertising.

**1927** William S. Paley acquires what would become CBS Radio, one of the first radio networks supported almost wholly by advertisers.

that in three hours, you can do it in 30 seconds. . . . Being creative means . . . you're looking for a feeling, in advertising as much as in movies.[11]

Of course, in addition to the creativity, there is also the money. As Lee says, "Commercials pay well."[12] Among the many feature film directors who also produce commercials are the brothers Ridley and Tony Scott (we'll talk more about Ridley Scott at the end of this chapter), Baz Luhrmann (*Moulin Rouge*), and Michael Mann (*Heat* and *Miami Vice*).[13]

One reason advertising agencies seek out talented directors like Spike Lee is to build and sustain viewer interest in an increasingly fragmented market.

"What I do with my work is universal," Lee says. "I've always felt the African-American experience is universal. Minorities know a lot more about the majority than vice versa. You're exposed to it. You're bombarded."[14]

Although advertising has been a part of American media since the 1700s, the challenge today is to get consumers to pay attention to the messages that pay for so much of the media we receive. In this chapter we look at the development of the advertising industry in the United States, the major players in the advertising process, and the influence advertising has had on contemporary culture.

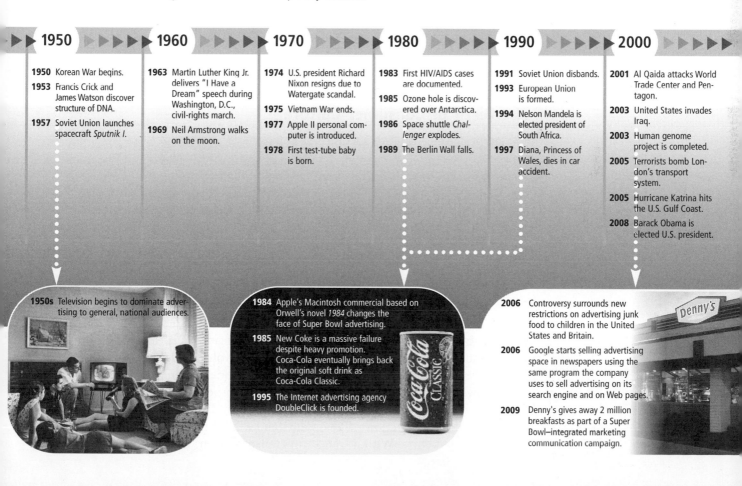

**1950**

**1950** Korean War begins.
**1953** Francis Crick and James Watson discover structure of DNA.
**1957** Soviet Union launches spacecraft *Sputnik I.*

**1960**

**1963** Martin Luther King Jr. delivers "I Have a Dream" speech during Washington, D.C., civil-rights march.
**1969** Neil Armstrong walks on the moon.

**1970**

**1974** U.S. president Richard Nixon resigns due to Watergate scandal.
**1975** Vietnam War ends.
**1977** Apple II personal computer is introduced.
**1978** First test-tube baby is born.

**1980**

**1983** First HIV/AIDS cases are documented.
**1985** Ozone hole is discovered over Antarctica.
**1986** Space shuttle *Challenger* explodes.
**1989** The Berlin Wall falls.

**1990**

**1991** Soviet Union disbands.
**1993** European Union is formed.
**1994** Nelson Mandela is elected president of South Africa.
**1997** Diana, Princess of Wales, dies in car accident.

**2000**

**2001** Al Qaida attacks World Trade Center and Pentagon.
**2003** United States invades Iraq.
**2003** Human genome project is completed.
**2005** Terrorists bomb London's transport system.
**2005** Hurricane Katrina hits the U.S. Gulf Coast.
**2008** Barack Obama is elected U.S. president.

**1950s** Television begins to dominate advertising to general, national audiences.

**1984** Apple's Macintosh commercial based on Orwell's novel *1984* changes the face of Super Bowl advertising.
**1985** New Coke is a massive failure despite heavy promotion. Coca-Cola eventually brings back the original soft drink as Coca-Cola Classic.
**1995** The Internet advertising agency DoubleClick is founded.

**2006** Controversy surrounds new restrictions on advertising junk food to children in the United States and Britain.
**2006** Google starts selling advertising space in newspapers using the same program the company uses to sell advertising on its search engine and on Web pages.
**2009** Denny's gives away 2 million breakfasts as part of a Super Bowl–integrated marketing communication campaign.

# THE DEVELOPMENT OF THE ADVERTISING INDUSTRY

One element of the media that is almost inescapable is advertising. The American Marketing Association defines **advertising** as "any paid form of nonpersonal communication about an organization, product, service, or idea by an identified sponsor."[15] Advertisements are the commercial messages that pay for an article about cardiovascular health in *Prevention*, an editorial about foreign policy in the *New York Times*, and the block of Rolling Stones hits on the local classic rock radio station. Advertising makes possible the vast array of inexpensive media available worldwide. But there is more to advertising than just cheap media. Advertising drives the size and diversity of the world's economy by telling consumers the multimedia functions they can perform by using a new computer, the image they will project by wearing a brand of clothing or driving a particular car, or the eating pleasure and health benefits they will experience by sampling a new variety of breakfast cereal. Advertising has been a key element of the American economy and culture of consumption and acquisition for more than 100 years and has existed since before the United States was a nation. With the pervasiveness and importance of advertising in our society, we see once again Truth One—The media are essential components of our lives.

## The Birth of Consumer Culture

The earliest American advertising was published in newspapers and was targeted at a narrow, elite audience, just as the papers were. Advertising was not a major source of income for the early papers, but it was still important. The *Boston News-Letter*, one of the first successful colonial newspapers, solicited advertising as early as 1704. Most ads were simple announcements of what a merchant or shop had for sale. There was little point in promoting particular products because most manufacturers produced similar goods. Consumers judged the quality of the goods they bought by inspecting them, taking into account the reputation of the individual merchant. There were no brand names.[16]

*Industrialization and the Growth of Advertising.*   Major societal changes had to occur before advertising could become a significant social force. The most important of these changes was the industrial revolution. The 1800s were a period of rapid **industrialization**, in which work done by hand using muscle or water power in small shops was replaced by mass production of goods in large factories that used steam power or, later, electricity. Industrialization brought about the mass production of low-cost, standardized products that had never been available before. With advances in transportation, these goods could be manufactured in a single location and then distributed over a wide area. Personal conversations between shop owners and their customers were beginning to be replaced by sales messages placed in newspapers and magazines or posted on signs. Standardized goods were sold using standardized messages—advertisements. In essence, the mass production of consumer goods was developing along with the mass production of messages promoting those goods. Advertising grew explosively during this period as the responsibility for transmitting marketing information passed into the hands of the media.[17]

*Modernization: Satisfying Needs Through Shopping.* Along with industrialization, the nineteenth century was characterized by **modernization**, the social process by which people go from being born with an identity and a role in life to being able to decide who they want to be, where they want to live, what they want to do, and how they want to present themselves to the world.

As more products became available, advertising was used to promote them and what they stood for. People could now adopt a certain style and purchase the items necessary to portray that style to others—the clothes they wore, the food they served, the soap they washed with, and so forth. Each of these goods was associated with an image that was supposed to rub off on its user. How did people learn about these meanings? Through the advertising that gave meaning to the products.[18]

Media historian Michael Schudson writes that in modern societies people believe they can satisfy their social needs by buying and using mass-produced goods.[19] The late 1800s brought department stores that received new merchandise frequently and then sold it quickly, in contrast to the older dry-goods and clothing stores, which might receive new goods twice a year. As people moved into new communities where their old family identities had little meaning, they could create a new identity for themselves through the products they chose. For example, in the 1920s people started to buy more ready-made clothes rather than sewing clothes for themselves. This ready-made clothing, which they learned about through advertisements, allowed them to be fashionable and "modern" and to "put on" the identity that went with the clothes.

*With the coming of transcontinental railroads in the late nineteenth century, products like beer went from being predominantly locally produced to national brands produced for a larger market.*

**modernization**

The process of change from a society in which people's identities and roles are fixed at birth to a society where people can decide who they want to be, where they want to live, what they want to do, and how they want to present themselves to the world.

*Manufacturers of patent medicines promising cures for almost anything— internal ailments, weight gain and weight loss, debility, the common cold—were among the biggest of the early national advertisers.*

**economy of abundance**
An economy in which there are as many or more goods available as people who want to or have the means to buy them.

**brand name**
A word or phrase attached to prepackaged consumer goods so that they can be better promoted to the general public through advertising and so that consumers can distinguish a given product from the competition.

## The Growth of Brand Names

With the growth of industry allowing more production and the construction of transcontinental railroads and steamships making possible better distribution, more and more prepackaged consumer goods came on the market, ready to be promoted through advertising. Among the first were patent medicines—manufactured remedies that often consisted primarily of alcohol and laudanum (opium). Instead of being shipped to stores in large containers and bottled at the point of sale, these products arrived bottled and ready to be sold to the consumer. These were the first products of the **economy of abundance**, in which there are as many or more goods available as people who want to buy them.[20]

Brand-name goods became popular at the end of the nineteenth century. A **brand name** is a word or phrase attached to prepackaged consumer goods so that they can be better promoted to the general public through advertising. In a highly mobile society, these standardized, branded products became a source of stability for consumers. The idea of stability coming from a brand-name product has persisted into the twenty-first century: For example, wherever they are, weary travelers are likely to stop for a meal at a familiar and comfortable landmark such as a McDonald's or a Pizza Hut.[21]

The development of brand-name goods was a driving force behind the growth of advertising. Brands were necessary to distinguish the new mass-produced products from one another. The names made it possible for people to ask for goods produced by a specific manufacturer, and advertising let people know what these brands were and what they stood for.

Quaker Oats, among the first prepackaged cereals, was typical of early brand-name products. It was sold in a multicolored box illustrated with the trademarked "man in Quaker garb." The cereal was a product of consistently high quality that was manufactured in Cedar Rapids, Iowa, and distributed to the entire country. Wherever you purchased the product, it would be the same. Quaker Oats promoted its trademark everywhere: "on billboards, streetcars, newspapers, calendars, magazines, blotters, cookbooks, Sunday church bulletins, metal signs on rural fences, company-sponsored cooking schools, free samples given away house-to-house, booths at county fairs and expositions."[22]

Thomas J. Barratt developed the first branded soap. "Any fool can make soap," he commented. "It takes a clever man to sell it."[23] Barratt created the Pears'

Soap brand and promoted it with outdoor and newsprint ads asking, "Have you had your Pears' today?" Other versions included "How do you spell soap? Why, P-E-A-R-S', of course," and "Good Morning! Have you used Pears' Soap?" Pears' became one of the most talked-about brands of its era and was even mentioned by prominent writers like Mark Twain. The Pears' Soap catchphrases were the "Where's the beef," "Keeps on going and going," or "Just do it" of its day.

## Advertising-Supported Media

The growth of products that needed advertising to succeed brought about a similar growth in advertising-supported media. Beginning in the 1830s, newspapers became much easier and cheaper to produce with the coming of inexpensive wood-pulp paper and the steam-powered rotary press. The new penny papers (see Chapter 5) were sold to large numbers of people. These large audiences appealed to advertisers, so newspapers moved from depending on subscription revenue to advertising revenue as their primary form of support. The change was dramatic. Instead of merely tolerating advertising, newspapers began to encourage it and even created special advertising sections to seek it out.

Magazines also started out with an uneasy relationship with advertising. In the 1800s publications like *Harper's* ran only limited advertising, trying to preserve their elite image. Another reason early magazines carried little advertising was that their circulation was national, whereas most advertising was done in local publications. Because there were few national brands at the time, few companies wanted or needed to reach a national audience.

Once manufacturers needed to reach the magazines' national audiences, the economics of magazine publishing changed. No longer were publishers selling magazines to subscribers; instead, they were selling subscribers to advertisers. The *Ladies' Home Journal*, which began publishing in 1887, was designed specifically as a medium for consumer advertising. Publisher Cyrus H. K. Curtis put it this way in a speech to advertisers:

> Do you know why we publish the *Ladies' Home Journal?* The editor thinks it is for the benefit of American women. That is an illusion, but a very proper one for him to have. But I will tell you; the real reason, the publisher's reason, is to give you people who manufacture things that American women want and buy a chance to tell them about your products.[24]

Curtis also used advertising to promote his magazine and build its circulation.

*Pears' Soap was one of the earliest national brands. Pears' ads encouraged consumers to ask not for soap, but for Pears'.*

Although the radio industry flirted with revenue options such as taxes and profits from selling radios, it soon became clear that the only way to make enough money to pay for top-notch entertainers and make a profit was to sell advertising. William Paley founded the CBS radio network after he saw how successful radio advertising was for his family's cigar company (see Chapter 7). Paley understood that good programming could attract a large audience that advertisers would want to reach. Sponsors frequently bought not just advertising time but the entire program, giving rise to shows like the *Maxwell House Hour*, the *Lucky Strike Dance Orchestra*, and the *General Motors Family Party*.

There was never any debate about whether television would be driven by advertising. Television grew quickly in the 1950s, and advertisers recognized its potential as a powerful tool for reaching all Americans. By 1960, 90 percent of all homes had television sets.[25] As with the rest of the media, television's "product" is the audience watching its programs. Thus, the primary purpose of the Super Bowl, from television's point of view, is not to choose a professional football champion but rather to deliver 45 percent of the American audience to advertisers for one evening each year. Robert Niles, a network marketing executive, echoed Cyrus Curtis's promise to deliver an audience to American manufacturers almost a century earlier when Niles stated, "We're in the business of selling audiences to advertisers. [The sponsors] come to us asking for women 18 to 49 and adults 25 to 54 and we try to deliver."[26]

*Consumer Advertising.* **Local advertising** attempts to induce people to go to a local store or business to buy a product or service, whether it be a new Toyota truck, a gallon of milk, or a travel agent's services. These ads announce the product or service and its price, and tell consumers where they can buy it. The local ad is also looking for immediate, direct action. Thus, a **direct action message** is designed to get consumers to purchase a product or engage in a behavior. For example: "Hurry down, these prices won't last, buy today!"

**National advertising** is designed to build demand for a nationally available product or service but does not send consumers out to a particular store to buy a can of Pepsi, a movie video, or a bag of cat food. National advertising assumes that the consumer knows where to buy the product or service or can be told in a local ad where and how to do so. The national advertiser is also more patient and can wait for consumers to take action. Thus, an **indirect action message** is designed to build the image of and demand for a product. Perhaps a consumer won't buy a new washing machine this week, but he will eventually, and that's when he should buy a Maytag.

*Advocacy Advertising.* **Advocacy ads** are intended to promote a particular point of view rather than a product. In 1993, for example, the state of California

---

**local advertising**
Advertising designed to get people to patronize local stores, businesses, or service providers.

**direct action message**
An advertising message designed to get consumers to go to a particular place to do something specific, such as purchasing a product, obtaining a service, or engaging in a behavior.

**national advertising**
Advertising designed to build demand for a nationally available product or service and that is not directing the consumer to local retail and service outlets.

**indirect action message**
An advertising message designed to build the image of and demand for a product, without specifically urging that a particular action be taken at a particular time and place.

**advocacy ads**
Advertising designed to promote a particular point of view rather than a product or service. Can be sponsored by a government, corporation, trade association, or nonprofit organization.

ran a $28 million antismoking campaign financed through a cigarette tax. U.S. unions and businesses have fought foreign competition with advocacy ads. Companies express their concerns directly to the public through advocacy ads, bypassing traditional news channels. Such advertising has a long history in the United States, dating back to 1908, when AT&T ran a campaign arguing that it was natural that the phone company should be a monopoly.

*Public Service Advertising.* Some of the most iconic advertising in the United States comes not from business but from long series of **public service ads** created by the Advertising Council. The Ad Council got its start as the War Advertising Council back in 1942 with such memorable messages as the Rosie the Riveter "We Can Do It" campaign designed to promote women working in factories producing goods for the war effort. The best known creation of the Ad Council would likely be Smokey the Bear, who has stayed on message for more than sixty-five years, telling the public that only they can prevent forest fires. He is the second most recognized image in the United States, falling just behind Santa Claus. What is more, generations of children have taken great joy in delivering his basic message of fire prevention to their parents and other adults. Other prominent Ad Council campaigns include the 1971 Crying Indian antipollution campaign, support for the United Negro College Fund, and McGruff the Crime Dog taking "a bite out of crime."[27]

The editorial and opinion pages of the prestigious national newspapers are popular spots for placing advocacy ads. This is partly due to the credibility associated with appearing on those pages and partly because it's a good place to reach the target audience of influential decision makers. These ads might, for example, support or oppose a piece of legislation. Sometimes the target of an advocacy ad in the *Washington Post* might be senators or representatives who are being reminded of the support they have received in the past from a given company or industry.[28]

*Trade Advertising.* **Business-to-business (trade) ads** promote products directly to other businesses rather than to the consumer market. Business-to-business advertising is a critical part of the advertising industry. Consider the fact that General Electric earns 80 percent of its revenue from nonconsumer business.[29] Business customers can be reached through trade magazines like *Electronic Engineering Times*, business-oriented cable news channels like CNBC, or local weekly business newspapers.

*Smokey the Bear has been getting the word out about fire safety for more than sixty-five years. This poster dates from the 1960s.*

**public service ads**
Advertising designed to promote the messages of nonprofit institutions and government agencies. The messages are typically produced and run without charge by advertising professionals and the media. Many of these ads are produced by the Ad Council.

**business-to-business (trade) ads**
Advertising that promotes products and services directly to other businesses rather than to the general consumer market.

# THE ADVERTISING BUSINESS

Advertising is a multifaceted business that involves four major groups. First, there's the *client*, the person or company that has a product or an idea to promote. Then there's the *advertising agency or department* that researches the market, creates the advertising, and places it in the media. Next, there's the *medium*, be it television, the Internet, a newspaper, a magazine, or some other medium, that carries the advertisement. Finally, there's the *audience*, the people who see or hear the advertisement, whom the client hopes to influence.[30]

For a product to be successful in the marketplace, all four of these groups must work together successfully. There must be a good product backed by advertisements that have a strong sales message delivered through well-chosen media to an appropriate audience. If any part of this process is flawed or even seriously miscalculated, the product is likely to fail.

## The Client

The first component of advertising is the client, the company with something to sell. The client may want to increase awareness of a new product, encourage people to use an existing product more often, build a positive image of the product, convince users of competitors' products to switch brands, promote a benefit of the product, or demonstrate some new use for the product. The 3M Company increased its sales of its Scotch brand cellophane tape by suggesting other uses for the product beyond repairing torn paper. Arm & Hammer baking soda's original purpose was to make cakes rise, but the company increased sales by promoting the product as a cleaner and deodorizer. One of Arm & Hammer's best ads tells consumers to buy a box of baking soda and pour it down the drain to clean and deodorize the sink. In essence, the company was suggesting that people buy its product to throw it away! Arm & Hammer's research showed that people used baking soda to freshen laundry and to brush their teeth, so the company introduced detergent and toothpaste enhanced with baking soda.[31] Begun in 1993 on behalf of the California Milk Processor Board, the "Got milk?" advertising campaign succeeded at boosting milk sales and has become one of America's longest running and most celebrated ad series.

For details on America's top advertisers, take a look at Table 11.1.

*Actress and singer Beyoncé (along with her mother) has been featured in the long-running milk mustache "Got milk?" campaign aimed at promoting the consumption of a wide range of milk and dairy products.*

| TABLE 11.1 | TOP ADVERTISERS IN THE UNITED STATES, BY BRAND | |
| --- | --- | --- |
| **Rank** | **Brand** | **2008 U.S. ad spending (in millions)** |
| 1 | Verizion | $2,205 |
| 2 | AT&T | $1,957 |
| 3 | Macy's | $892 |
| 4 | Sprint | $868 |
| 5 | Walmart | $840 |
| 6 | Toyota | $824 |
| 7 | McDonald's | $814 |
| 8 | Chevrolet | $797 |
| 9 | Target | $760 |
| 10 | Ford | $667 |

*Source:* Data from the *Advertising Age Top 200 Megabrands*. Reprinted with permission from *Advertising Age/American Demographics.* Copyright, Crain Communications Inc. 2009.

For a product to be successful, it needs more than a good advertising campaign. It also needs to be a good product at the right price and has to be available for consumers to buy. When Sony launched its PlayStation 2 video game system, it did relatively little initial advertising and held off releasing popular games because it couldn't manufacture enough of the consoles to satisfy public demand. Customers were ready and willing to buy, but the product simply was not available.[32] Once there was a sufficient quantity of the product, Sony started advertising.

No amount of advertising can save a product that the public just doesn't want to buy, as Coca-Cola discovered when it launched New Coke in 1985. Coca-Cola spent $4 million on research that seemed to indicate that consumers would like the new formula better than the original recipe. But consumers reacted to the change with anger and frustration, and Coca-Cola eventually had to bring back the old drink under the name Coca-Cola Classic.[33] The research may have shown what people liked best in blind taste tests, but it didn't take into account how people felt about the product, what meaning they assigned to it, and the fond memories they associated with it.[34] What the research missed was "the abiding emotional attachment" Coke drinkers had for the product in its familiar form. One Coke executive told *Advertising Age* magazine, "We obviously tried to do psychological research, but it wasn't adequate."[35]

## The Agency

The advertising profession originated in the 1840s when agents started selling ad space to clients in the new advertising-supported newspapers. At first the advertising agents worked directly for the newspapers, but before long they became more like brokers dealing in advertising space for multiple publications. George Rowell, the leading advertising agent of the 1860s and 1870s, was the first agent to buy large amounts of newspaper advertising space wholesale and sell it to his customers as they needed it. Rowell was also the first to publish a directory of newspaper circulation numbers, thus providing clients with an independent source of this vital information. Before Rowell's innovation, newspapers could, and did, lie about the size of their circulation.

The early agents earned a 15 percent commission on the space they sold for the newspapers. This is why advertising agencies were traditionally paid by commission on the media space and time they sold; initially, that was all they were selling.[36]

Before long, advertising agents moved beyond just selling space in the media. Their clients wanted help developing the ads for the space they were purchasing. In 1868, twenty-one-year-old Francis W. Ayer opened N. W. Ayer and Son (giving his father a 50 percent share in the company and the lead name), one of the first agencies to write copy, put together the artwork for an ad, and plan campaigns. The agency recognized that providing the associated services that would make advertising easier for clients would help the agency sell more space for the media.

Gradually, ad agencies came to represent their clients rather than the media in which they sold advertising space. This shift resulted from the **open contract**, which enabled the agency to provide advertising space in any publication (and eventually broadcast outlets as well) rather than in only a few. The agent was now handling the advertising services for the client, not selling space for the media.[37]

In the 1920s and 1930s advertisers increasingly recognized that there were different market segments and that ads should be tailored to those segments. Agencies also realized that they needed to use a different mix of media for each of their target audiences. Eventually they began offering clients three major services: research, creative activity, and media planning.

**open contract**
An arrangement that allows advertising agencies to sell space in any publication (and eventually broadcast outlets as well) rather than just a limited few.

*Research and Planning.*    Agencies typically use research throughout the entire advertising campaign. The initial research activity is aimed at identifying the characteristics of the target audience and what they are looking for in a product. Ads are then tested to see how well members of the target audience respond to them. After the campaign, the agency will evaluate its success. How many people remembered seeing the ad? How many people clipped the coupon or called the phone number? How much did sales go up or down?

The process starts with objectives. What does the client want to accomplish with the ads? These objectives could be increasing sales, increasing awareness, or getting people to clip a coupon or make a phone call. The agency may also study characteristics of the product's target audience, a process that is discussed later in the chapter.

Finally, the agency may test the ads themselves, either as a pretest before the ads are run or as a recall test after the campaign. One problem advertising researchers face is that the people they want to reach may be unwilling to participate in the research. And the people who are willing to participate may be trying to give the agency the answers they are looking for. Although advertising research continues to be a powerful tool for reducing uncertainty, it is still a difficult process at best.[38]

*Creative Activity.* There is more to marketing a product than advertising, but advertising is the most visible aspect of marketing, and it has to provide what legendary advertising executive David Ogilvy called **the big idea**—an advertising concept that will grab people's attention, make them take notice, make them remember, and—most important—make them take action. Leo Burnett, founder of one of the nation's biggest agencies, agrees with Ogilvy:

> The word "idea" is loosely used in our business to cover anything from a headline to a TV technique. [But] I feel that a real idea has a power of its own and a life of its own. It goes beyond ads and campaigns. Properly employed, it is often the secret of capturing the imagination of great masses of people and winning "the battle for the uncommitted mind," which is what our business really is about.[39]

A tension often exists between creativity and salesmanship in advertising campaigns. An ad may look beautiful and be exciting; people may love the commercial and remember seeing it. But if the ad doesn't have a solid sales message, consumers won't remember what product or service it was promoting. In 1996, for example, automaker Nissan started running a popular ad called "Toy Story" that featured a Barbie-like doll going out for a ride with a G. I. Joe–like action figure while the music of Van Halen played in the background. Audiences loved the ad, but they didn't buy the car. Adman Hank Seiden puts it this way: "All good advertising consists of both idea and execution. All bad advertising consists of just execution."[40]

Ogilvy believed that all advertising should be created to sell a product or promote a message. It does not exist to be innovative, exciting, creative, or entertaining. Good ads may be all of those things, but the central principle is that they must achieve the client's goals: "A good advertisement is one which sells the product *without drawing attention to itself*. It should rivet the reader's attention on the product. Instead of saying, 'What a clever advertisement,' the reader says, 'I never knew *that* before. I must try this product.'"[41]

For products that are similar, the **brand image** attached to them is often critical. This image gives a brand and the associated product a personality, an

**the big idea**
The goal of every advertising campaign—an advertising concept that will grab people's attention and make them take notice, remember, and take action.

**brand image**
The image attached to a brand and the associated product that gives the product a personality or identity that makes it stand out from similar products and stick in the mind of the consumer.

identity, and helps it stand out from the pack. Ogilvy once headed a campaign to give Hathaway shirts a personality when the company's competitor, Arrow, was spending almost 100 times more on advertising than Hathaway, a smaller company, could. Ogilvy's solution was to buy a black eye patch in a drugstore for $1.50. A model wearing the eye patch was shown conducting an orchestra, driving a tractor, and sailing a boat. This simple bit of brand identity boosted Hathaway out of 116 years of obscurity and turned it into a leading brand.

Ogilvy argues that at the heart of all advertising is an appeal based on facts that are of interest to consumers. As he wrote in the early 1960s, "The consumer isn't a moron. . . . You insult her intelligence if you assume that a mere slogan and a few vapid adjectives will persuade her to buy anything. She wants all the information you can give her."[42]

For print ads, the most important element is the headline because five times as many people read the headline as read the rest of the copy. This means that 80 percent of the ad's effectiveness comes from the headline. The headline must tell readers whom the ad is for, what the product is, what the product does for the consumer, and why he or she should buy it. That's a lot of responsibility for eight to fifteen words. Ogilvy says that the most powerful headline words are *free* and *new*. Other words favored by Ogilvy are "how to, suddenly, now, announcing, introducing, it's here, just arrived, important development, improvement, amazing, sensational, remarkable, revolutionary, startling, miracle, magic, offer, quick, easy, wanted, challenge, advice to, the truth about, compare, bargain, hurry, last chance."[43]

Although these phrases are overused, they do work. Look at what Ogilvy considered to be the greatest headline he ever wrote: "At Sixty Miles an Hour the Loudest Noise in the New Rolls-Royce Comes From the Electric Clock." It uses the word *new*, it contains a fact that also sells a benefit, and it is true.

*Media Planning.* **Media planning** involves figuring out which media to use, buying the media at the best rates, and then evaluating how effective the purchase was. It is the least glamorous part of the advertising business, but it is central to a successful campaign. No matter how brilliant the idea or how beautiful the execution, if the ad doesn't reach the target audience, it can't accomplish anything. Typically, advertisers try to pick a mix of media that will deliver the highest percentage of the target audience at the lowest cost per thousand views, or **CPM**. (M is the Roman numeral for 1,000.) Selecting the right media involves identifying the audience for the ad and knowing which media they use.[44]

*Agency Size and Income.* Advertising agencies have grown immensely since their modest start selling newspaper advertising space. According to *Advertising Age*'s 2009 advertising agency report, the 900+ agencies studied brought in approximately $16 billion for advertising and media buying services for 2008.[45] Keep in mind that this is just the portion of the income that goes to the agency. This figure doesn't include the amount that goes to pay the media for advertising time and space. According to *Advertising Age*'s 2009 annual report, advertisers in

---

**media planning**
The process central to a successful ad campaign of figuring out which media to use, buying the media at the best rates, and then evaluating how effective the purchase was.

**CPM**
Cost per thousand exposures to the target audience—a figure used in media planning evaluation.

2008 spent a total of $142 billion on advertising in the United States using media for which the size of the audience is measured. (This does not include, for example, direct mail advertising.) Of that, magazines had the largest amount at $28.58 billion, followed by broadcast television with $26.71 billion, newspapers with $25.06 billion, and cable television with $18.83 billion. Online advertising, by way of comparison, totaled $9.73 billion. Overall, advertising spending among the 100 top advertisers fell by 2.7 percent in 2008 and was expected to drop more than 5 percent for 2009.[46]

Several major trends have emerged in the agency business since the 1980s. One trend is toward the purchase of independent agencies and small groups of agencies by larger holding companies. The biggest of these are Omnicom Group, WPP Group, Interpublic Group of Companies, and Publicis Groupe, which accounted for more than 56 percent of all advertising spending in the United States.[47] A second trend is toward greater specialization of agency functions. One agency may do research and creative work, whereas another agency (known as a media buyer) develops the media plan and buys the time and space. Because of this specialization, agencies are moving from the commission structure to charging fees for their services. After all, if an agency is just doing creative work, it can't charge a commission on media space that it isn't buying.[48]

## The Media

The third group in the advertising business is made up of the media that carry advertisements. These include newspapers, magazines, radio, television, outdoor sites like billboards and metro buses, and the Internet. The two media that do not receive large amounts of advertising revenue are movies and books, although movies are increasingly using paid product placements and theaters run advertisements before showing movies. Books initially did not carry ads because advertising was not common when books were first published. In the nineteenth century, when advertising became popular, there were other, cheaper media in which to advertise. Postal regulations also pose a barrier to advertising in books: Materials containing advertising can't be shipped using the post office's inexpensive book rate. But advertising scholar James Twitchell suggests that as delivery options expand through companies like FedEx and UPS, advertising in books may become commonplace, especially in expensive academic books.[49] This textbook doesn't yet contain advertisements in its pages, but you probably found a few advertising pieces for credit cards or magazine subscriptions in the bag the bookstore clerk gave you.

*Newspapers.*  Newspapers were the original advertising medium, but they have been suffering major declines in advertising revenue. Between 2006 and 2008, ad revenue declined by an average of 23 percent, with major metropolitan dailies falling significantly more. Nevertheless, newspapers remain the third largest advertising medium, carrying a majority of local advertising as well as a significant amount of national advertising. They allow advertisers to present detailed information (such as grocery prices) that would be confusing on radio or television, and they give audience members plenty of time to interpret the information. Newspaper ads make it easy to include coupons, Web addresses, and 800 numbers that readers can clip and save. They also allow advertisers to target not only specific cities but also specific areas of the city (this is known as **zoned coverage**). Cities typically have only one or two newspapers, so advertisers can cover the entire market with a single purchase. Finally, newspapers allow advertisers to buy space at the last minute.[50]

*Magazines.*   Magazines are an excellent medium for reaching a specific niche audience. Before the 1950s, general-interest magazines were the best way to reach a mass, national audience. Since the 1960s, however, that role has fallen to television. The response of magazines was to seek ever narrower audiences—there are magazines for motorcyclists, computer users, young women, retired people, knitters, and video game players. Whatever audience an advertiser wants to reach, it is likely to find a magazine to help it do so. For business advertisers, magazines may be the only alternative to direct mail for reaching their target audiences. Magazines offer higher print quality than newspapers do but have a much longer lead time, so magazine advertising requires careful planning.

*Digital billboards with changing messages, such as these in New York City's Times Square, have revitalized the outdoor advertising business.*

*Outdoor Advertising.*   Outdoor ads catch people in a captive environment—such as in a car surrounded by slow-moving traffic on the way to work—but they are limited to short, simple messages. The biggest change to have happened to outdoor advertising is the advent of the digital billboard. Essentially giant video screens, digital billboards display a static image that stays up for six to eight seconds before going to a new image. Digital billboards can include changing information like time or temperature, or even the day's television schedule for a local station.[51] In major cities there are transit signs—posters on bus-stop shelters, on subway platforms, and on the buses and in the subway cars themselves. Ads have also been placed in the bottom of golf holes so that you see them when you pick up your ball. Overall, $6.99 billion was spent on outdoor advertising in 2008.[52] New York City's Times Square is one of the most valuable places in the United

States for outdoor advertisements because of the large number of people who pass through there each day, its frequent coverage on television, and the nearly constant presence of tourists who are photographing the area.[53]

*Radio.* Radio enables advertisers to broadcast their message repeatedly and to target a narrow audience. Advertisers can choose stations with programming aimed at teens, women ages 25 to 54, young adult males, Spanish speakers, or almost any other demographic group. Like outdoor advertising, radio ads can be very effective in big cities where advertisers can reach a captive audience in their cars during the morning and afternoon commute known as **drive time**. Radio also offers a short lead time and relatively low costs.

*Video rental company Netflix relies heavily on online advertising messages to reach consumers.*

*Television.* Although the most popular television shows remain an appealing place to advertise to a general, national audience, the remote control, the mute button, and the proliferation of cable channels have made it difficult to get viewers to pay attention to commercials. The audience for broadcast television has been declining, but the Big Four networks (see Chapter 9) can still reach a mass audience quickly and effectively. Television offers sound, motion, and visuals. A drawback, however, is that many of the best advertising time slots on the networks, like the Super Bowl, are sold nearly a year in advance. There is also the problem of viewers channel surfing during commercial breaks or skipping commercials using the fast forward on their digital video recorders (DVRs).

The new television environment allows targeted advertising, such as ads aimed at the youth market on MTV or CW, the Hispanic market on Univision, or the African American market on BET. For local television advertising, there are independent stations along with the network affiliates. In many communities local advertisers can buy time on a range of cable stations with local commercial breaks as well. The biggest problem facing television advertisers is that of clutter, which is discussed later in this chapter.

**drive time**

The morning and afternoon commute in urban areas; the captive audience makes this a popular time to advertise on radio.

*The Internet.* Internet advertising has been the fastest growing segment of the advertising market, increasing by double-digit percentages for several years. But in 2009 Internet advertising saw its first decline since 2002, when the dot.com bubble burst, sending numerous Web properties into bankruptcy. *Advertising*

*Age* estimated 2009 online advertising spending at about $22.8 billion, down from $23.4 billion for 2008. The biggest areas of growth for online advertising include video, search, and banner ads.[54] (For more on Internet advertising, look ahead to the section of the chapter on long-tail advertising.)

## The Audience

The audience is made up of the people advertisers want to reach with their messages. The audience is also the central "product" that media sell to advertisers. In yet another example of **targeting**, advertisers try to make a particular product appeal to a narrowly defined group. Ads for Starburst candies, for example, target the teen and preteen audiences, whereas ads for Godiva chocolates target upscale adult women. The people appearing in an ad are chosen carefully to make members of the target audience say, "This is a product made for someone like me." Advertising executive Robert Meury notes that his agency carefully selects the celebrities who appear in Miller Lite ads: "We make sure our stars are guys you'd enjoy having a beer with. And the locations we film in are always real bars."[55]

As with other types of media such as radio and television, audience members for advertising are often defined by the "graphics": demographics, geographics, and psychographics. As you may recall from Chapter 2, demographics are the measurable characteristics of the audience, such as age, income, sex, and marital status, whereas geographics involve measurements of where people live. Psychographics combine demographics with measurements of psychological characteristics such as attitudes, opinions, and interests.

*Psychographics and the VALS System.*    In advertising, it's not enough to know the demographics of the client's target audience (age, income, sex, etc.). Advertisers also want to know what the target audience dreams about, aspires to, and feels. These are the topics covered by psychographic research.

The term *psychographics* was first used in the 1960s to refer to a measure of consumer psychology. Depending on the project, researchers may look at people's lifestyle, relationship to the product, and personality traits.[56]

Emanuel Demby, one of the first users of the term, defines *psychographics* as the use of psychological, sociological, and anthropological data to segment a market into relevant groupings. The way the income variable is conceived is more sophisticated than just grouping markets by income levels. Demby argues that it is just as important to know whether someone's income is increasing, decreasing, or remaining stable as it is to know the person's actual income. Why? Because how things are going in people's lives will say something about how they see themselves. If advertisers understand how members of the target audience see themselves, they can craft ads that will more readily appeal to the target.[57]

The best-known psychographic system, VALS™, was developed by SRI International and is currently run by Strategic Business Insights. Now in its third generation, VALS places people in one of eight categories according to their

**targeting**
The process of trying to make a particular product or service appeal to a narrowly defined group. Groups are often targeted using demographics, geographics, and psychographics.

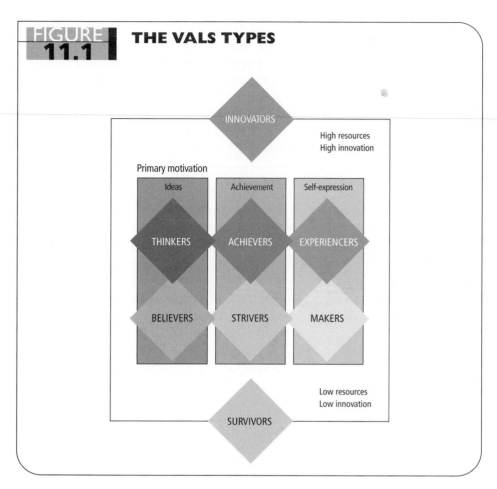

*Source:* Strategic Business Insights (SBI), www.strategicbusinessinsights.com/vals. Reprinted by permission.

primary motivation and level of resources (see Figure 11.1). Resources are the tangible and intangible things that people have to draw on as they seek success: their education, income, health, and self-confidence, among other factors. Primary motivation is the person's approach to life. Ideas-motivated consumers ("thinkers" and "believers") are guided by knowledge and principles; achievement-motivated consumers ("achievers" and "strivers") look for products that will demonstrate their status and success to others; and self-expression-motivated consumers ("experiencers" and "makers") seek action, variety, and risk.

At the top of the VALS hierarchy are the innovators, described as being "successful, sophisticated, take-charge people with high self-esteem." These are people who have established careers and value the image of a product as "an expression of their taste, independence, and personality." At the bottom of the VALS hierarchy are the survivors, who have few resources and believe "the world is changing too quickly." VALS describes them as cautious consumers with little to spend but with high brand loyalty.[58]

How might a company use psychographics and these personality types to target its advertising? As an example, a Minnesota medical center used VALS to identify and understand consumers who were interested in and able to afford cosmetic surgery. The resulting ad campaign targeted to these individuals was purportedly so successful that the clinic was fully booked.[59]

To see targeting in action, we can look at some real-world examples. The first example discusses the targeting of a product (Mountain Dew); the second, a particular audience (gays and lesbians); and the third, some instances of targeting failures.

*Targeting a Product: Mountain Dew.*   Advertising soft drinks can be a particular challenge because all the drinks are basically the same thing—sweetened carbonated water and a small amount of flavoring—with just a few variations—regular or diet, caffeinated or caffeine free. Since the products are so similar, the key to promoting the brand is selling not just a drink but an entire attitude and approach to life, thus making the product appeal to a particular audience. Television scholar Joshua Meyrowitz describes the basic message of a diet soda commercial as "Drink this and you'll be beautiful and have beautiful friends to play volleyball with on the beach."[60]

Mountain Dew has existed as a product since the 1940s and has always projected a rebellious and irreverent image, according to Scott Moffitt, who was director of marketing:

> We have a great unity of message and purpose that has been consistent over time about what we are and what we aren't. The brand is all about exhilaration and energy, and you see that in all that we do, from advertising and community to grassroots programs and our sports-minded focus. We have a very crystal clear, vivid positioning.[61]

In keeping with its young, energetic image, Mountain Dew sponsors events such as ESPN's X-Games because they project the same image the soft drink does. It also goes after heavy consumers, who drink three or more cans of Mountain Dew a day.

Mountain Dew now holds a coveted spot among the top four or five soft drinks, behind Coke, Pepsi, and Diet Coke, but it started out as a bar mix consisting of lemon-lime juice, orange juice, low carbonation, and caffeine. It cultivated a hillbilly image and logo, and was billed as "zero-proof hillbilly moonshine." In the 1960s Pepsi bought the brand and started giving it more of a hip image. Following a period of confused advertising images in the 1980s, Mountain Dew came into its own in 1992. Bill Bruce, who was the creative director on the Mountain Dew account, describes Mountain Dew's coming of age process:

> Seattle grunge music was happening at the time. Extreme sports were happening. So there was this subculture that we wanted to tap into. The idea was to show the most extreme things. We created these four characters, the Dew Dudes, who represented what was happening at the time musically and culturally.[62]

(The Dew Dudes as a part of the extreme sports culture provide yet another example of Truth Three—Everything from the margin moves to the center.)

This approach was first used with Diet Mountain Dew, but given its success, it eventually became the central theme of the entire campaign.

The ongoing challenge to Mountain Dew as it grows in popularity is to maintain its edginess and youth appeal, so that it can maintain both its sales and its image. Most recently Mountain Dew has been engaging its "fans" to help the company select the new flavor variations, what the company refers to as the first "user generated soda." Mountain Dew even has its own recording label, Green Label Sound, which gives away free music downloads online.[63]

*Targeting an Audience: Advertising to the Gay Market.* One audience that advertisers are increasingly targeting is the gay and lesbian market. Gays are desirable as a market to advertisers because they are perceived to be relatively upscale and highly educated.[64] "Because they primarily don't have children and there is one income for each person in the household, you are talking about a population with large sums of disposable income that non-gay families with children wouldn't have," says Rick Dean of the research firm Overlooked Opinions.[65] Media company Rivendell Media estimates that the gay and lesbian market has an annual buying power of $641 billion.[66]

As early as 1994, vodka producer Absolut was among the first major companies to place ads in gay publications, including *Out* and *The Advocate*.[67] In addition to advertising in gay publications, companies are using gay couples in ads. Some advertisers have gone further, experimenting with gay-specific ads. Hyatt Hotels and Resorts has targeted the gay and lesbian market since the late 1990s and has depicted same-sex couples in its messages.[68] Although advertising to the gay community has carried the risk of antigay groups organizing boycotts of companies that do so, the effectiveness of such boycotts has been limited.[69]

The gay advertising market has grown considerably in the twenty-first century, with the launch of at least three gay-themed cable television channels,

The Greater Philadelphia Tourism Marketing Corporation is promoting the city to gay travelers as a gay-friendly destination. In addition to the text in this ad, the illustration features the gay pride flag.

## TEST YOUR MEDIA LITERACY

### Advertising to Targeted Markets

It's pretty obvious, given demographic trends, that major corporations are going to need to target racial and ethnic communities if they want to stay relevant in today's market. The census estimates that approximately 65 percent of Americans identify themselves as "white only." The exact figures get a bit confusing, given that Hispanic is an ethnic category, not a racial category. But that means if companies make their advertising primarily relevant to white people, they're leaving 35 percent of the market out there on the table.

As companies try to market to Hispanic, African American, and Asian American audiences, they need to appeal to their target and avoid offensive and dated stereotypes. McDonald's, for example, has targeted the African American market though efforts often called "urban marketing." One ad that has attracted both positive and negative attention for the fast food chain is an ad called "McNuggets Love" that features an R&B singer crooning about his lady sneaking out at night to meet with her true love—a ten-piece box of Chicken McNuggets. The campaign was a major success for McDonald's, increasing McNuggets sales by 20 percent.[1] But some consumers found the ad offensive or annoying, with one saying, "It's sad that this is how the marketing execs at the McDonald's corporate office think they can attract the urban consumer."[2] McDonald's spokesperson Danya Proud had this to say about the company's urban marketing efforts:

> We have a responsibility to all of our customers to effectively reach them. We certainly take pride in all of our advertising and try to make it relevant and appealing.
>
> We work with a dedicated African-American advertising agency that works with us to develop relevant, contemporary creative for our brand, that will resonate with this demographic. Again, as with all our advertising, these commercials reflect a light-hearted, fun approach to our brand, our menu and our customers' experience with our brand.[3]

**MOREonline**

You can find a link to McDonald's urban ads, including "McNuggets Love," at http:// ralphehanson.com.

**Who are the sources?**
What kind of a company is McDonald's? Who is it trying to reach with its urban marketing campaign?

**What are they saying?**
How is McDonald's attempting to reach the urban audience? What does McDonald's mean by "urban marketing"?

**What evidence is there?**
Why is McDonald's trying to target ethnic and racial minority groups? What can it gain? What can it lose? Do ads targeting specific minority groups appeal to the wider population as a whole?

including MTV Networks' Logo. These go along with 145 separate gay and lesbian publications, including both newspapers and magazines. The *2007 Gay Press Report* estimates ad spending in the gay press to total $181.9 million. Roughly half of the ads appearing in the gay press had "gay specific" content. This compares with only 9.9 percent of the ads in the gay press in 2002.[70] This continued growth of advertising in gay magazines and of gay-themed ads is another example of Truth Three—Everything from the margin moves to the center.

*Failures of Targeted Advertising.* Efforts to target specific audiences are not always successful. When Hornell Brewing launched its western-themed Crazy Horse malt liquor, the company thought it had a product to complement its Dakota Hills Black Sunday brand. The beer was targeted not at Native American groups but rather at people on the East Coast who were interested in western culture. But Native American groups expressed outrage at the use of the venerated chief's name to sell alcohol.[71] Crazy Horse, a leader of the Oglala Sioux in the nineteenth century, was opposed to drinking.[72] Objections by the Native American community eventually led the U.S. Commerce Department to refuse Hornell a trademark on the product; in addition, the beer was banned in Minnesota and Washington, and its sale was discouraged in Nebraska.[73]

R. J. Reynolds Tobacco's Uptown brand met a similar fate in 1990. Uptown was targeted at urban African American smokers and promoted primarily through black-oriented media. The cigarette was designed to appeal to African American smokers through its packaging (a black-and-gold box), name (Uptown), slogan ("Uptown. The Place. The Taste."), and light menthol content.[74] African American leaders and federal health officials criticized both the brand and its promotion, saying that it was unethical to target a group that already had higher-than-average rates of health problems attributable to smoking. Canceling the product cost R. J. Reynolds $10 million. Similarly, Dakota, a cigarette targeted at young women with little education, was soon removed from the market.[75]

R. J. Reynolds, of course, has not given up on the African American market. The company is appealing to this market more subtly with the brands Salem Gold and Salem Box, which have many of the same attributes as Uptown, but because they are not new brands, they have not attracted as much critical attention.[76]

# ADVERTISING IN CONTEMPORARY CULTURE

Advertising is much more than a part of the marketing and media business; it is a central element of American culture. Children sing advertising jingles the way they once sang nursery rhymes. In the 1970s the music from a Coca-Cola commercial even became a hit single, "I'd Like to Teach the World to Sing."

Critics argue that advertising places a burden on society by raising the cost of merchandise and inducing people to buy things they don't need. The American Association of Advertising Agencies has defended the ad business, claiming that there are four common misconceptions about the industry:[77]

1. Advertising makes you buy things you don't want—The industry responds by saying that no one can make you buy things you don't want. People are free to do as they please.

2. Advertising makes things cost more—Advertisers claim that advertising builds demand for products, which can then be manufactured in larger quantities, more efficiently, and at a lower cost. (This defense ignores the idea of the prestige brand, however. Advertising does not make a bar of Clinique soap cost more to produce, but the premium image attached to the soap allows the company to charge more for it. Consumers apparently want to be able to buy better, more expensive products.)

3. Advertising helps sell bad products—The industry responds that a good ad may lead people to buy a product once, but it won't sustain demand for a product they don't like. In fact, the industry argues that good advertising for a bad product will kill the product faster than if it hadn't had a good campaign behind it. M. Night Shyamalan, director of the movies *The Sixth Sense* and *Signs*, says that with enough advertising, studios can buy a good opening weekend for a movie, but only good word-of-mouth reports by fans will make the movie a long-term success.[78]

4. Advertising is a waste of money—The ad industry counters that advertising strengthens the economy by helping to move products through the marketplace and supporting the mass media.

Throughout this section of the chapter you will see numerous examples of Truth Six—Activism and analysis are not the same thing. In many of the following cases, you will see activism and analysis continually intertwined. See if you can sort out the two from each other.

## The Problem of Clutter

When critics complain that there are too many ads on television, few would be quicker to agree than advertising agencies and their clients. They are very concerned about the huge number of commercials and other messages—collectively referred to as **clutter**—that compete for consumer attention between programs.

Advertisers dislike clutter because the more ads and nonprogram messages there are on television, the less attention viewers will pay to any given message. A study conducted by the Cabletelevision Advertising Bureau found that viewers are much more likely to remember the first ad in a group (called a *pod*) than the fourth or fifth.[79] The clutter problem is not limited to television; each day the average American adult is exposed to 150 advertisements in one form or another.

According to a study commissioned by advertising agencies and their clients, clutter is reaching record levels. In 2005 U.S. network television averaged about fifteen minutes of advertising and promotional clutter per hour during prime time.[80] Cable television rates were even higher, with MTV averaging 16 minutes, 13 seconds of clutter per hour. Clutter is generally defined as anything that is not part of the program itself: ads, public service announcements, network promotions, and other gaps between programs. In the spring of 2009, Fox Broadcasting experimented with what the network called "Remote-Free TV," in which the network cut the commercial load during shows such as *Fringe* and *Dollhouse* to only ten minutes as a way of keeping viewers from channel surfing or fast-forwarding through the breaks. The network charged advertisers a 40 to 50 percent premium for spots that ran during Remote-Free TV.[81] Despite the problems of higher clutter, lower-rated network programs, and increasing CPM rates, networks continue to sell advertising time, and advertising experts say that clutter won't disappear until clients stop buying time from the networks.

Advertising clutter in the United Kingdom has also grown dramatically over the past several years, though it's still nowhere near the level seen in the United States. In 2001 the average Briton saw 258 television commercials per week. By 2005 that total had risen to 311. But this was still dramatically lower than the 789 ads per week seen by typical U.S. viewers. Ad clutter in the United Kingdom is lower partly because of legal restrictions on the number of minutes of commercials per hour and because the BBC, a state-supported media entity, doesn't carry ads.[82]

Breaking through the clutter is a continuing challenge for advertisers, who have come up with a variety of solutions to the problem. Tire maker Goodyear

**clutter**
The large number of commercials, advertising, and other nonprogramming messages and interruptions that compete for consumer attention on radio and television, and now also on the Internet.

breaks through the clutter by putting its message on the Goodyear blimp, which flies over sporting and other entertainment events that draw large audiences.[83] Drug companies fight clutter by using celebrities in their advertisements. Former senator and presidential candidate Bob Dole served as an early spokesman for the impotence drug Viagra; NBA star Alonzo Mourning talked about the anemia drug Procrit that's used to treat a kidney disorder that almost ended his career; and actress Lorraine Bracco, who played a psychiatrist on *The Sopranos*, discussed depression in ads for drugs manufactured by Pfizer Inc.[84]

## Debunking Subliminal Advertising

**subliminal advertising**
Messages that are allegedly embedded so deeply in an ad that they cannot be perceived consciously. There is no evidence that subliminal advertising is effective.

With all the concern about advertising clutter, it is ironic that there is substantial public concern about **subliminal advertising**—messages that are allegedly embedded so deeply in an ad that they cannot be perceived consciously. The concept has been popularized by several writers, but no research has ever been done to demonstrate that advertising audiences can be influenced by messages they don't perceive consciously.

Although there is no evidence that it works and little evidence that any advertisers try to create ads with hidden messages, much of the public believes that subliminal advertising is used and is effective. A survey published in 1993 found that among people who were familiar with the concept of subliminal advertising, 72 percent thought it was effective.[85] The concept of subliminal advertising came to public attention in 1957, when Jim Vicary, a market researcher, claimed to have exposed movie audiences to the words *Drink Coca-Cola* and *Eat popcorn* flashed on the screen so quickly (less than .03 of a second) that they could not be perceived consciously. Vicary claimed that popcorn sales increased by an average of 57.5 percent and Coke sales went up 18.1 percent. Vicary claimed that people could be influenced strongly by things they didn't see. It turned out, however, that Vicary had not conducted the tests but had simply made up the precise statistics on increased sales of popcorn and Coke. Throughout 1957 and early 1958 Vicary collected more than $4 million in consulting fees; in June 1958 he disappeared.

In 1970 Wilson Bryan Key, a university professor in Canada, revived the idea of subliminal advertising. While looking at a photo in an article in *Esquire,* he thought he saw an image of a phallus. From that point on Key has been arguing that Madison Avenue hides images of death, fear, and sex in advertisements to increase sales.[86] It is unclear how these hidden images are supposed to influence viewers, who presumably are ignoring the clutter of overt advertising.

## When Advertisements Are More Important Than the Program

Sometimes television ads are as interesting as the programs during which they appear. Commentators have even argued that people sometimes stay tuned to a boring Super Bowl broadcast just to see the commercials. Ridley Scott, best known as the director of blockbuster movies like *Gladiator, Hannibal,* and *Blackhawk Down,* made a name for himself by directing the 1984 Super Bowl commercial that introduced Apple's Macintosh computer. Scott's commercial, known as "1984," changed the world of advertising. Not only was it one of the most talked-about commercials of all time, but it also showed that good commercials can be more memorable than the shows they accompany.[87] It is no accident that Phil de Vellis selected this particular commercial to parody in his YouTube Obama video (discussed in Chapter 2).

The commercial, created by the Chiat/Day agency, was a success on a number of levels. It portrayed a dramatic image of a young woman athlete rebelling against an Orwellian "Big Brother" situation. It generated talk among the 100 million viewers who saw it, and it transmitted the central message that Apple wanted to get across: that there was an alternative to what was perceived at the time as the all-encompassing power of IBM (a role that has since been taken over by Microsoft).[88]

The commercial aired once on network television during the third quarter of the Super Bowl. After the Super Bowl, the commercial was broadcast free on the Big Three network news shows, and the trade magazine *Advertising Age* named it the commercial of the decade. Steve Hayden, who wrote the spot while employed at Chiat/Day, says that the agency wanted to sum up the whole philosophy of the computer in one commercial: "We thought of it as an ideology, a value set. It was a way of letting the whole world access the power of computing and letting them talk to one another."[89]

Ironically, the commercial almost didn't run at all. When it was previewed for Apple's board of directors, several members were horrified by it and wanted the spot scrapped. John O'Toole, former president of the American Association of Advertising Agencies, explained the significance of the ad as follows:

> What "1984" as a commercial for Apple really signified was the first time somebody could put a great deal of production money into a single commercial and run it only once and get tremendous benefit from running it only once. It took great coordination with PR. It was really event marketing, with sales promotion and PR built in. That was the beginning of the new era of integrated marketing communications.[90]

## Advertising to Children

Few aspects of advertising raise more concerns than commercials targeted at children. Yet children (and through them, their parents) are a highly desirable audience and market for advertisers. If your parents tell you that there weren't as many commercials targeted at children when they were young, they're right. In 1983 companies were spending $100 million a year to reach children. But by 2008 spending on advertising directed at children had grown to $17 billion a year. That means that marketers today are spending 170 times more today to reach children than they were a generation ago.[91]

*Television Advertising to Children.* A U.S. Federal Trade Commission study published in 1978 under the title *Television Advertising to Children* found that children between the ages of two and eleven see approximately 20,000 television commercials a year, the equivalent of about three hours a week, or slightly less than half an hour per day. The study was highly controversial at the time because it called for bans (never implemented) on all advertising in programs for which a "significant" portion of the audience was under the age of eight, and on television ads for sugary foods targeted at children ages eight to eleven.[92]

Marketing to children in the twenty-first century goes far beyond the traditional print and thirty-second television ads. Companies are instead pouring money into product placement, in-school programs, mobile phone ads, and video games.[93] In 2006 the advertising industry revised its guidelines for advertising to children for the first time in thirty-two years. The new guidelines require companies to distinguish between advertising and programming content, show mealtime foods as part of a single balanced meal rather than as part of a larger balanced diet, and identify when online games contain advertising.[94]

*Food Ads Directed at Children.* In recent years the biggest criticism of advertising directed at children has moved from cigarettes to junk food. The U.S. federally chartered Institute of Medicine says that there is "strong evidence that exposure to television advertising" is connected with obesity, which can lead to numerous illnesses including diabetes.[95] The Institute goes on to say that ads for junk food targeted at children under age eight can help establish a lifetime of poor eating patterns.[96] Of course, what constitutes a healthy food is subject to some debate. Would a high-fiber granola bar with significant levels of sugar qualify as health food or junk?

Richard Martin, a spokesman for the Grocery Manufacturers Association, said at a U.S. Federal Trade Commission hearing that the association does not believe there are bad foods: "Any food can be responsibly consumed by everyone, including kids."[97]

The advertising industry has been critical of the report's recommendations to regulate food ads targeted at children. Daniel L. Jaffe, an executive with the Association of National Advertisers, told the *Washington Post*, "[The] government stepping in and saying what should be in messages on TV is a very radical proposal. . . . If you do it for food, there's no reason it can't be done for other controversial product categories. People are already trying to restrict the advertising for prescription drugs."[98]

In response to the report and other criticism from activist groups, the U.S. advertising and food industries say they are working to limit the advertising of junk food to children. A group of ten of the largest food and beverage companies—including Kraft, Coca-Cola, PepsiCo, and Hershey's—has pledged to use at least half of its ads directed at children under age twelve to promote

# TEST YOUR MEDIA LITERACY

## Limits on Advertising Food to Children

Advertising to children in general has been controversial for years, but as of late the criticism has become more focused on children's food ads. As mentioned earlier in this chapter, the controversy is a great example of Truth Six—activism and analysis are not the same thing. In a nutshell, a recent research study conducted by the Institute of Medicine found that, in respect to food preferences and diets,

- There is strong evidence that television advertising influences the food and beverage preferences of children ages 2–11 years. There is insufficient evidence about its influence on the preferences of teens ages 12–18 years.

- There is moderate evidence that television advertising influences the food and beverage beliefs of children ages 2–11 years. There is insufficient evidence about its influence on the beliefs of teens ages 12–18 years.

- There is strong evidence that television advertising influences the short-term consumption of children ages 2–11 years. There is insufficient evidence about its influence on the short-term consumption of teens ages 12–18 years.

- There is moderate evidence that television advertising influences the usual dietary intake of younger children ages 2–5 years and weak evidence that it influences the usual dietary intake of older children ages 6–11 years. There is also weak evidence that it does *not* influence the usual dietary intake of teens ages 12–18 years.[1]

### MORE online

You can read the entire executive summary of the report issued by the Institute of Medicine of the National Academies, entitled, "Food Marketing to Children and Youth: Threat or Opportunity?" at **http://ralphehanson.com.**

### Who are the sources?

You have read about groups in the United States and Great Britain who have both advocated and opposed advertising food products to children. Who are these groups?

### What are they saying?

Why do critics oppose food advertisements targeted at children? What types of food ads do they object to? How have supporters of this advertising responded? How have the responses in Great Britain and the United States differed?

### What evidence is there?

What evidence has been presented that food advertising directed at children is harmful? What evidence has been presented that it is benign or even helpful? Who is sponsoring and funding the studies?

### What do you and your classmates think about food advertisements directed at children?

What kinds of effects do you think food advertisements have on children? Do you think that the arguments that advocates and opponents are presenting are sincere? Or are the advocates just trying to advance their own agenda?

[1] J. Michael McGinnis, Jennifer Appleton Gootman, and Vivica I. Kraak, *Food Marketing to Children and Youth: Threat or Opportunity?* (Washington, D.C.: Institute of Medicine of the National Academies, 2005), books.nap.edu/openbook.php?record_id=11514&page=1.

healthier foods or encourage healthy lifestyles. It will also take junk food promotions out of online interactive games.[99]

Televised advertising of junk food to children has been a major issue in the United Kingdom as well, with the government putting in place strong new regulations of the practice. The new restrictions would limit the promotion of high-fat, high-sugar, and high-salt foods to children under age sixteen to certain hours of the day. The ban has been controversial in Britain because these food ads provide funding for popular children's programming such as *Bob the Builder* and *My Parents Are Aliens.* Producers argue that without the revenue from food ads, the commercial broadcast networks will stop producing high-quality children's content.[100] Critics of the ban say that this would leave British children with the choice of commercial-free BBC programming or imported satellite programming from companies such as Disney.[101] Anne Wood, creator of the popular *Teletubbies* series, told the *Guardian,* "I am horrified and, believe me, it's not from a personal or self-interested position. . . . The health lobby seems to have won the day, but what about the other cultural side, protecting the rights of children to have television made for them, as adults do?"[102]

Because the restrictions include ads targeted at children under sixteen, the ban will also affect MTV, costing the network as much as 8.8 percent of its income.

# THE FUTURE OF ADVERTISING

With the rise of new advertising media, including computers connected to the Internet, mobile phone screens, and video games, the older media, such as television, newspapers, and magazines, are going to be facing substantial challenges.

## Integrated Marketing Communication

**integrated marketing communication**

An overall communication strategy for reaching key audiences using advertising, public relations, sales promotion, and interactive media.

One response to the rapidly changing marketing environment advertisers are facing is **integrated marketing communication**, or IMC. The idea is that there should be an overall communication strategy for reaching key audiences and that this strategy could be carried out using advertising, public relations, sales promotion, and interactive media. Dating back to the 1980s and 1990s, IMC is a long-term approach to building the value of a brand or an organization.[103]

We can see how IMC gets used to build a brand by looking at how Denny's worked to "re-introduce" the restaurant to America and to bring "light and lapsed" Denny's customers back into the fold in the winter of 2009.[104] At the center of the IMC campaign was a creative ad that ran during the Super Bowl featuring a group of wise guy–gangsters planning a hit while a waitress delivers clown-faced pancakes. The message? Serious people deserve a serious breakfast. The ad then closed out with the announcement that the chain was giving away breakfast to everyone who came to Denny's on the following Tuesday between 6 a.m. and 2 p.m.[105]

The result? Roughly 2 million people came in for their free Grand Slam breakfast of two eggs, two strips of bacon, two sausages, and two pancakes. That's an effective message. Especially when you consider that most of the people who took advantage of the free food also paid for a drink that came close to covering the cost of the meal.[106]

*Hungry customers across the United States lined up outside of Denny's for free Grand Slam breakfasts given away as part of the restaurant chain's 2009 Super Bowl promotion.*

Brian Quinton, an editor at large for *Promo* magazine, views the Denny's campaign as a mixed success from an IMC point of view. Denny's had a clever ad that ran twice during the Super Bowl, a full-page ad that ran in *USA Today*, an e-mail sent out to Denny's customers, and a compelling promotional offer. Denny's also sent out press kits about the promotion, placed signs within the stores, and highlighted the promotion on the company Web site. The campaign was discussed on NBC's *Today Show*, and it received extensive media attention elsewhere.[107] But while the Denny's campaign was a success, the integration of it was not as well done as it could have been. The biggest problem was that the company did not have enough capacity on its Web site to handle the sudden 1700 percent increase in viewership during the game. The Web site crashed as soon as the first ad ran and stayed down throughout the game. The company also didn't include its Web address in the commercials.[108]

Despite these difficulties, Denny's IMC campaign would have to be considered a success from a results point of view. Denny's estimates that the promotion, including the ads and food, cost $5 million, while Denny's claims the promotion generated $50 million in publicity, though it did not elaborate on how that was measured.[109] The Super Bowl ads were seen by 98 million viewers, and millions more saw local news stories generated by the promotion on the two days following the ads.[110] What's more, it appears Denny's did a good job of hitting its target audience of light and lapsed customers, with follow-up research showing that approximately 60 percent of the customers for the Tuesday promotion fell into that group.[111]

You can view the Denny's Super Bowl commercial and read more about the IMC campaign at http://ralphehanson.com.

## Is Anyone Watching Television Ads?

There is only a fixed amount of spending available for advertising and marketing products. And as companies move their advertising dollars to new media—online for ads and streaming content and to mobile phone screens—there will be less money for older media such as television. If that were not enough, television is facing declining audience sizes and new technologies, such as DVRs, that allow viewers to skip watching commercials altogether. As of 2009, DVRs were in 32 percent of American households.[112]

The broadcast networks are responding to this threat in various ways. CBS is selling Web ads as a package with broadcast ads. These aren't the simple banner ads of the 1990s; they are video ads that come before streaming Web content. Sneaker manufacturer Converse used its broadcast ads to get consumers to generate short videos featuring Converse sneakers, and the company then featured the videos on its Web site.[113]

*Mobile Phone Advertising.*    Mobile phones have become the latest frontier for advertising, with their bright color screens and their ubiquitous use among the notoriously hard-to-reach population of 18–34 year olds. Although many companies are simply using banner ads to go with wireless Web content, others are creating short **mobisodes**, or mobile-phone-delivered video episodes.

Despite having small screens, cell phones have several key advantages to advertisers. They are always on, they are always with the person, and the phone belongs to an identifiable individual. This lets advertisers send out highly targeted messages that can contain time-sensitive offers. Another popular use of mobile phone advertising is to get consumers to participate in activities like voting for contestants on reality shows.[114]

## Product Placement

Product placement has long been with us. When Paul Newman drank a beer in the 1981 movie *Absence of Malice*, it was a Budweiser. And when Steve McQueen played cop Frank Bullitt back in 1968, he chased criminals through San Francisco in a Ford Mustang GT. But in recent years product placement has gotten considerably more sophisticated, rising occasionally to the level known as plot placement, branded entertainment, or **product integration**, where the product or service being promoted is not only seen, but is central to the story.[115]

One of the forces driving the growth of this expanded form of product placement is that multitasking consumers are increasingly ignoring television ads by skipping past them on the DVR, surfing other channels during commercial breaks, or just leaving the room to get a snack.[116]

The biggest challenge to product placement is making it seem natural rather than intrusive, which tends to put off consumers, according to *New York Times* advertising columnist Stuart Elliott. That may be why so much of the product placement is in reality shows, where the use of products as rewards and prizes makes them fit in better.

**mobisodes**
Short video episodes designed to be viewed on the small screens on mobile phones or personal digital assistants (PDAs). These can be brief entertainment, news, or commercial programs.

**product integration**
The paid integration of a product or service into the central theme of media content. This is most common in television programming or movies, but it can be found in books, magazine articles, Web pages, or even songs.

There seem to be no limits now to which products can get placed in prime-time programs. Pregnancy was an unmentionable topic on television in the 1950s, but pregnancy tests are showing up frequently in product placements in shows ranging from *Gossip Girl* to *Sex and the City.*[117]

Television and movie writers have rebelled against product integration, complaining that it interferes with their creative integrity; they've also called for getting a cut of the placement income if they're going to be writing the placements into the stories. Patric Verrone, president of a movie and broadcast writers' union, explained why writers were concerned about product integration: "Product placement is simply putting a branded box of cereal on the kitchen table in a show. Product integration is having the characters talk about the crunchy deliciousness of the cereal."[118]

*Will Ferrell's comedy Talladega Nights parodies NASCAR's high level of product placement with . . . more than ninety distinct product placements. Ferrell (right) is seen here with actress Jessica Alba and* Talladega Nights *costar John C. Reilly at the 2006 MTV Movie Awards.*

## The Long Tail of Advertising

For all the talk about the importance of Internet advertising, it remains a relatively small part of advertising spending, accounting for 6.9 percent of all advertising spending in the United States. Despite recent declines in spending, online advertising is expected to resume growth and should be more and more important in the years to come.[119]

Among the best known of the long-tail advertising tools are Google's AdWords and AdSense programs. Rather than buying a particular Web site, advertisers instead buy certain keywords, which place their ads next to particular content. Under AdWords, when surfers do a Google search that includes the keyword, the ad appears next to the search result. With AdSense, Web sites have a code on them that searches the content of the site and puts ads relevant to the subject matter next to the content posted there. So if I had AdSense on my site and wrote about DVDs in a blog entry, ads that sold DVD players would start coming up. The advertisers pay for each person who clicks on the served-up ad, with a portion of the money going to the owner of the site where the ad appeared.[120] Although this tool can be used to market any product, it is especially useful for advertising long-tail media. If I were trying to sell punk polka CDs, for example, I would try to maximize the return on my advertising money by reaching only people who were already reading about punk polka bands. (You think I'm making this up? Check out the punk polka link at http://ralphehanson.com.)

One of the big problems with Internet advertising is documenting how many people have actually clicked on the ad. Major advertisers have complained that "click fraud" drives up their cost of online advertising. The owner of a Web site with online ads may pay friends to click on the ads repeatedly to generate more page views and hence more income.[121] Or competitors of a particular advertiser will click on a competitor's ad to run up his bill.[122] There are even automated programs known as clickbots or hitbots that will click away twenty-four hours a day, running up the bill for advertisers.

In an interesting move, Google in 2006 started selling advertising space in newspapers using the same program the company uses to sell advertising on its search engine and on Web pages.[123] As discussed in Chapter 3, Google is rapidly moving into becoming more and more of a general purpose media company, once more illustrating Truth Three—Everything from the margin moves to the center.

## CHAPTER Summary

Advertisements are paid messages about an organization, product, service, or idea that appear in the mass media. Advertising provides numerous benefits to society, including making media less expensive and contributing to a large and diverse economy. While advertising has existed in the United States since colonial times, it was industrialization, urbanization, and the growth of national transportation networks in the nineteenth century that allowed advertising to become a major industry. Advertising transformed the media industry from one supported primarily by subscribers to one supported by advertising revenues. Publishers (and later broadcasters) were no longer sellers of content to audience members; they were now sellers of audiences to advertisers.

Advertising can be broken down into consumer advertising, advocacy advertising, and trade (business-to-business) advertising, according to the audience the client is attempting to reach and the idea or product it is trying to sell. The advertising industry encompasses four main groups: the client who has something to advertise, the advertising agency or department that creates the advertising, the media that carry the ads, and the audiences targeted by the advertisements.

Advertisers use a variety of strategies to reach their audiences. They may attempt to understand the needs, wants, and motivations of audience members through psychographic research. They also target products to specific demographic groups.

Critics argue that advertising raises the cost of merchandise, that many ads are tasteless, and that they exploit young people and other vulnerable audiences. Advertisers join the critics in complaining that there are too many advertisements in the media, creating the problem referred to as clutter. Although there have been complaints of advertisers embedding subliminal messages in ads, there is no evidence that such messages have been used or that they are effective.

Advertising is going through a period of significant change as new technology emerges that allows consumers to bypass viewing commercials on television. But technology is also providing numerous new venues for advertising, including the Internet and mobile phones. Companies are increasingly making use of integrated marketing communication strategies that bring together multiple forms of marketing communication to promote their brands. Advertisers are also looking at promoting their products through elaborately developed product placement schemes.

## KEYTerms

advertising   382
industrialization   382
modernization   383
economy of abundance   384
brand name   384
local advertising   386
direct action message   386
national advertising   386
indirect action message   386
advocacy ads   386
public service ads   387
business-to-business (trade) ads   387
open contract   390

the big idea   391
brand image   391
media planning   392
CPM   392
zoned coverage   394
drive time   395
targeting   396
clutter   403
subliminal advertising   404
integrated marketing
   communication   408
mobisodes   410
product integration   410

## CONCEPTReview

Industrialization, modernization, and the growth of consumer advertising
The importance of brands
Advertising-supported media
Types of advertising
The players in advertising: clients, agencies, media, and audiences
Advantages and dangers of targeted advertising
The use of demographics and psychographics in targeting markets
The challenge of advertising in a cluttered market
The growth of integrated marketing communication

# Public Relations

## Interactions, Relationships, and the News

**When Chris Martin** was growing up in working-class Pennsylvania, she was taught to dream big, but never dreamed of becoming a marketing/public relations vice president for a major university. "But who in the world does?" she asks.

The daughter of a World War II veteran and a Westinghouse "factory girl," Martin dreamed of being a military general. "When I was really little, I had Girl Scout paper dolls, and I imagined these women in uniform were directing the vast armies of the free world." Martin says that once she was old enough to think about what she really wanted to do, she "dreamed of working in a field that involved writing, thinking, creating and performing" but wasn't sure exactly what that job would be. Now as the top public relations professional at West Virginia University

(WVU), she marshals a staff of seventy-five people who handle everything from news and information, to marketing, to communication through social media and broadcasting. "If we write it, print it, publish it on the Web, or deal with the traditional media, that's us," Martin says.[1]

The biggest challenge Martin faces is the wide range of publics with which she has to communicate and build relationships. WVU is a big institution, with approximately 10,000 employees across all of its campuses, 5,000 employees at its hospital and health sciences program, and nearly 30,000 undergraduate and graduate students. And that's just the beginning of Martin's list of publics. There are parents for these students, more than 160,000 alumni supporters, not to mention prospective students and opinion leaders throughout the state. . . .

**Chris Martin**

Although Martin started out her career as a newspaper reporter, she doesn't view the switch to public relations as that much of a stretch for someone who has done a wide range of jobs. "I graduated with a degree in English, which was enormously informing but prepared me for nothing specific in the job market," Martin says. "One day I looked across a street in a small town and saw the big, gray building that housed the local newspaper. I told myself that if I got a job as a reporter there, it would be the best job in the world. It was." Martin moved on from there to a succession of "best jobs in the world," including being a journalism professor, a dean of a journalism school, and eventually the vice president for university relations, the job she holds now.

Her central responsibility is telling the story of the university to that long list of publics. "The exciting part of this job is that as a public university we are at ground zero of telling the story of the American dream for many people," Martin says. "We are a nexus of journalism, multimedia storytelling, and traditional communication."

For her staff, Martin looks for people with journalistic talent who understand storytelling, marketing, communication strategy skills, and technical skills. "I need people who can tell stories on various platforms," she says, pointing out that it's no longer enough to send out press releases to legacy media and hope the stories get broadcast or published. Increasingly, Martin says the university is communicating directly with its publics. This means it has to establish a relationship of trust with the wide-ranging audiences on Martin's list. It means the university has to be willing to talk openly and honestly about the bad news as well as the good. For examples of WVU's public relations programming, go to http://ralphehanson.com.

One of the toughest things Martin has to do is prepare for crises that might hit the institution: "We do crisis planning for communication and work with the university for planning on the physical response." Martin is quick to point out that a key skill is understanding the difference between a "crisis" and an "issue." To Martin, a crisis is something like the campus shooting at Virginia Tech in 2007.

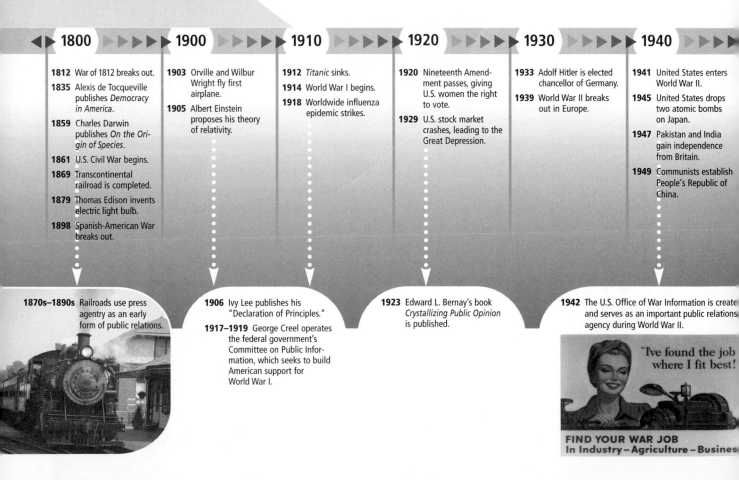

**◀▶ 1800 ▶▶▶▶▶ 1900 ▶▶▶▶▶ 1910 ▶▶▶▶▶ 1920 ▶▶▶▶▶ 1930 ▶▶▶▶▶ 1940 ▶▶▶▶**

**1812** War of 1812 breaks out.
**1835** Alexis de Tocqueville publishes *Democracy in America*.
**1859** Charles Darwin publishes *On the Origin of Species*.
**1861** U.S. Civil War begins.
**1869** Transcontinental railroad is completed.
**1879** Thomas Edison invents electric light bulb.
**1898** Spanish-American War breaks out.

**1903** Orville and Wilbur Wright fly first airplane.
**1905** Albert Einstein proposes his theory of relativity.

**1912** *Titanic* sinks.
**1914** World War I begins.
**1918** Worldwide influenza epidemic strikes.

**1920** Nineteenth Amendment passes, giving U.S. women the right to vote.
**1929** U.S. stock market crashes, leading to the Great Depression.

**1933** Adolf Hitler is elected chancellor of Germany.
**1939** World War II breaks out in Europe.

**1941** United States enters World War II.
**1945** United States drops two atomic bombs on Japan.
**1947** Pakistan and India gain independence from Britain.
**1949** Communists establish People's Republic of China.

**1870s–1890s** Railroads use press agentry as an early form of public relations.

**1906** Ivy Lee publishes his "Declaration of Principles."
**1917–1919** George Creel operates the federal government's Committee on Public Information, which seeks to build American support for World War I.

**1923** Edward L. Bernay's book *Crystallizing Public Opinion* is published.

**1942** The U.S. Office of War Information is created and serves as an important public relations agency during World War II.

"I've found the job where I fit best!"

**FIND YOUR WAR JOB**
**In Industry – Agriculture – Business**

An issue, by contrast, is something that might upset people, such as when WVU announced that, for the second time, the school's Mountaineer mascot would be a woman. Based on some of the reactions the last time a woman had won the competition to carry the rifle and wear the buckskin suit at football games and other events, Martin knew she would need to reach out to key publics.

"You think about who are the people you need to share this information with most immediately," she said. "You don't want it breaking as a big story, so we communicated with older alums and found out from people how they felt about the Mountaineer. This time the focus was not on dealing with the traditional media but with our direct stakeholders. Some of the biggest issues are the most emotional ones that a university deals with and that the alumni are most invested in."

Chris Martin and her work for WVU highlights many of the key issues we look at in this chapter. In addition to examining the development of the public relations industry, we also discuss how the public relations process works, the various publics that organizations need to work with, and how public relations professionals have used public relations to protect and advance their employers' interests.

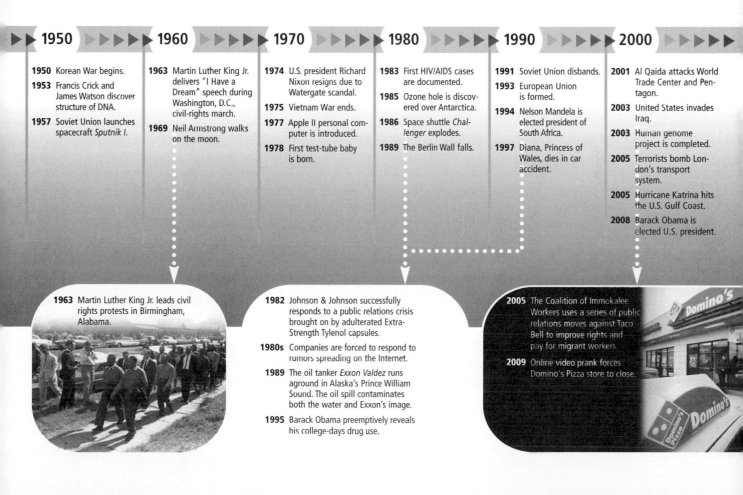

**1950** ▶▶▶▶ **1960** ▶▶▶▶ **1970** ▶▶▶▶ **1980** ▶▶▶▶ **1990** ▶▶▶▶ **2000** ▶▶▶▶

**1950** Korean War begins.

**1953** Francis Crick and James Watson discover structure of DNA.

**1957** Soviet Union launches spacecraft *Sputnik I.*

**1963** Martin Luther King Jr. delivers "I Have a Dream" speech during Washington, D.C., civil-rights march.

**1969** Neil Armstrong walks on the moon.

**1974** U.S. president Richard Nixon resigns due to Watergate scandal.

**1975** Vietnam War ends.

**1977** Apple II personal computer is introduced.

**1978** First test-tube baby is born.

**1983** First HIV/AIDS cases are documented.

**1985** Ozone hole is discovered over Antarctica.

**1986** Space shuttle *Challenger* explodes.

**1989** The Berlin Wall falls.

**1991** Soviet Union disbands.

**1993** European Union is formed.

**1994** Nelson Mandela is elected president of South Africa.

**1997** Diana, Princess of Wales, dies in car accident.

**2001** Al Qaida attacks World Trade Center and Pentagon.

**2003** United States invades Iraq.

**2003** Human genome project is completed.

**2005** Terrorists bomb London's transport system.

**2005** Hurricane Katrina hits the U.S. Gulf Coast.

**2008** Barack Obama is elected U.S. president.

**1963** Martin Luther King Jr. leads civil rights protests in Birmingham, Alabama.

**1982** Johnson & Johnson successfully responds to a public relations crisis brought on by adulterated Extra-Strength Tylenol capsules.

**1980s** Companies are forced to respond to rumors spreading on the Internet.

**1989** The oil tanker *Exxon Valdez* runs aground in Alaska's Prince William Sound. The oil spill contaminates both the water and Exxon's image.

**1995** Barack Obama preemptively reveals his college-days drug use.

**2005** The Coalition of Immokalee Workers uses a series of public relations moves against Taco Bell to improve rights and pay for migrant workers.

**2009** Online video prank forces Domino's Pizza store to close.

# FROM PRESS AGENTRY TO PROFESSIONALISM

The field of **public relations** (also called **PR**) has had an uneven image in the United States. (The term *public relations* is discussed more extensively later in this chapter.) In his book on corporate public relations, Marvin Olasky notes that practitioners have been called "high-paid errand boys and buffers for management."[2] Other names have been less flattering. Despite such criticisms, public relations is critical to industry, government, and nonprofit organizations. These organizations need to deal with the people who work for them, invest in them, are served by them, contribute to them, regulate them, or buy from them. They need to interact with the world. Ultimately, that's what public relations is all about—relating with a wide range of publics. A **public** is a group of people who share a common set of interests. An *internal public* is made up of people within the organization. An *external public* is made up of people outside the organization.

## The Origins of Public Relations

The origins of public relations go back as far as the American Revolution, with pamphlets like Thomas Paine's *Common Sense*, which built up the case for the colonies' break with England. In the early 1800s author Washington Irving used publicity to build excitement for his latest book. But the PR profession is generally seen as having grown out of the industrial revolution. As companies and their accompanying bureaucracies grew, so did the need to manage their image.[3] Advances in communications also made publicity campaigns more feasible. It wasn't until the penny press of the 1830s and 1840s produced widespread newspaper circulation that publicity began to be particularly effective. Circus entrepreneur P. T. Barnum raised publicity to a fine art, building interest in his shows by writing letters to the editor under fake names and accusing himself of fraud. Thus, this early publicity process, known as **press agentry**, was a one-way form of public relations that involved sending material from the press agent to the media with little opportunity for interaction and feedback. Press agentry was used to support causes such as temperance with speakers, books, and songs. It was also practiced effectively by the abolitionist movement.

*One-Way Communication.* As noted in the preceding section, press agentry consisted of one-way communication. For the most part, press agents before the 1920s worked at building publicity for their clients rather than managing or creating a specific image. Standard Oil's efforts in the 1890s were typical of the time. The oil giant's advertising agency sent out news articles as paid advertisements, but the agency paid for the ads only if they looked like articles or

---

**public relations (PR)**

Public relations is "the management function that establishes and maintains mutually beneficial relationships between an organization and the publics on whom its success or failure depends."

**public**

Any group of people who share a common set of interests and goals. These include *internal publics*, made up of people within the organization, and *external publics*, consisting of people outside the organization.

**press agentry**

An early form of public relations that involved sending material from the press agent to the media with little opportunity for interaction and feedback. It often involved conduct that would be considered deceptive and unethical today.

editorials.[4] In the early years of the twentieth century, however, companies started realizing that they needed to respond to criticism from various populist and progressive political groups and to muckraking investigative reports by magazines like *McClure's* (see Chapter 5).

*The Beginnings of Image Management.*  The first major users of public relations were railroads, which had numerous reasons for working on their image.[5] In the 1870s many railroads wanted to divide freight traffic among themselves according to predetermined percentages so as to avoid competition. The railroads did not want criticism of their monopolistic practices in the press, so they bribed reporters and editors, either by making cash payoffs or, more subtly, by giving free passes for travel on the railroad to cooperative members of the press. The Illinois Central Railroad realized that praise of the railroads coming from academics would do more good and be more persuasive than puffery coming from the industry itself, so it funded university research on the railroads, whose findings could then be quoted by the press.

Like the railroads, the utility and telephone industries saw the value of public relations. Chicago Edison argued to both the government and the public that providing electricity was a "natural monopoly" and should not be open to competition. In the early 1900s AT&T required newspapers in which it advertised to run positive articles about its actions. Both the utilities and the phone company made use of publicity firms to write articles and editorials that would be placed in newspapers around the country, promoting the companies' points of view.

COMMON SENSE;

ADDRESSED TO THE

INHABITANTS

OF

AMERICA,

On the following interesting

SUBJECTS.

I. Of the Origin and Design of Government in general, with concise Remarks on the English Constitution.

II. Of Monarchy and Hereditary Succession.

III. Thoughts on the present State of American Affairs.

IV. Of the present Ability of America, with some miscellaneous Reflections.

Man knows no Master save creating HEAVEN,
Or those whom choice and common good ordain.
THOMSON.

PHILADELPHIA;

Printed, and Sold, by R. BELL, in Third-Street.

MDCCLXXVI.

*Thomas Paine's famous* Common Sense *pamphlet is an example of an early PR effort, which was used to build the case for the American Revolution.*

*Ivy Lee.*  Ivy Lee, one of the two key founders of modern public relations, brought to the business a strong understanding of both economics and psychology. Lee recognized that the public often reacted more strongly to symbols and phrases than to rational arguments, and he built his campaigns around the importance of symbolism.[6] He also saw that it was important to put a human face on corporations.[7]

Lee was the first PR professional to deal with crisis management, and although *spin control* did not become a popular term until the 1980s, he was practicing it as early as 1910. Lee wanted to do much more for his clients than just send out favorable publicity; he wanted to manipulate public opinion in favor of his clients. That meant actively working with the press.

Circus promoter P. T. Barnum built publicity for his shows through posters such as this one, as well as by staging protests and complaints about his circus.

Among the problems faced by the railroads was reporting on accidents. The accepted practice of the industry in the late 1800s was either to cover up accidents or to bribe reporters not to write about them. Lee suggested that it might be in the railroads' best interests to deal with the press openly. When his client, the Pennsylvania Railroad, had a wreck, Lee invited reporters to visit the scene of the accident at the company's expense. After they arrived, he helped them report on the story. Company officials were amazed to see that the publicity they received when they cooperated with the press was a vast improvement over what they received when they fought with it.[8]

Lee also recognized the importance of telling the truth. Although the arguments he presented clearly supported his clients' viewpoints, Lee was always careful to be accurate in any factual claims. This was not so much because telling the truth was right or moral as because doing so was effective.[9] Lee once told oil giant John D. Rockefeller Jr., "Tell the truth because sooner or later the public will find it out anyway. And if the public doesn't like what you are doing, change your policies and bring them into line with what the people want."[10]

In 1902 American coal mine operators were facing a strike. The mine owners ignored the press, but the unionized miners worked with reporters to their advantage, with the public strongly supporting the workers. When the mine owners faced another strike in 1906, they hired Lee's publicity firm, Parker and Lee.[11] Lee convinced the mine operators that they could no longer ignore public opinion. A former business reporter, he started giving newspapers all the information they asked for. Supplied with clear and accurate statements from the mine owners, reporters started writing stories that were considerably less antagonistic to the mine owners.

At about this time, Lee developed his "Declaration of Principles," which outlined how he thought public relations ought to be carried out. These principles can be summarized quite simply: Openly and honestly supply accurate and timely news to the press.[12]

Lee himself suffered from bad public relations late in his career: In the 1930s he was accused of being a Nazi propagandist because he had worked for the German Dye Trust. The damage to his reputation from this association came at least in part from the many enemies he had made over the course of his career.[13]

*Edward L. Bernays.*    Along with Ivy Lee, the other founder of public relations was Edward L. Bernays, who was the first person to apply social-scientific research techniques to the field. Bernays, a nephew of Sigmund Freud, promoted the use of psychology to manipulate public opinion, a technique that he called "**engineering consent**":

> This phrase means, quite simply, the use of an engineering approach—that is, action based only on thorough knowledge of the situation and on the application of scientific principles and tried practices in the task of getting people to support ideas and programs. Any person or organization depends ultimately on public approval and is therefore faced with the problem of engineering the public's consent to a program or goal.[14]

**engineering consent**
The application of the principles of psychology and motivation to influencing public opinion and creating public support for a particular position.

In addition to promoting his clients, Bernays actively promoted the concept of public relations as a profession. To that end, he wrote the first books on the practice, *Crystallizing Public Opinion* (1923) and *Propaganda* (1928). In 1923 Bernays taught the first course in public relations, which he offered at New York University.

Like Lee, Bernays recognized the importance of the crowd in modern life. He found that the best way to influence the public was to arrange for messages to be delivered by credible sources. "If you can influence the leaders, either with or without their conscious cooperation, you automatically influence the group which they sway," he commented.[15] While the guaranteed influence of leaders over groups may be a bit of an overstatement, the use of credible or admired individuals to speak on behalf of a company is certainly central to public relations.

To Bernays, the chief characteristic distinguishing public relations from the press agentry of the past was that public relations was a two-way interaction between individuals or organizations—communication that involved listening as well as speaking. Bernays wrote that by the 1920s it became clear to practitioners that words alone did not constitute public relations; there had to be actions to go with the words.

## World War I: The Federal Government Starts Using Public Relations

The years 1914–1918 were a period of major growth for public relations. According to Bernays, during this time governments figured out how

COMMITTEE ON PUBLIC INFORMATION

*The Committee on Public Information had 75,000 "Four-Minute Men" who would give brief speeches about the war to churches and civic groups across the United States.*

**opinion leadership**

A two-step process of persuasion that uses respected and influential individuals to deliver messages with the hope of influencing members of a community, rather than just relying on the mass media to deliver the message.

important persuasive communication could be to mobilize popular support for a major war: "Ideas and their dissemination became weapons and words became bullets."[16] The U.S. government used public relations extensively during World War I. Within a week of the U.S. entry into the war, President Woodrow Wilson established the Committee on Public Information (CPI) under the direction of George Creel, the former editor of the *Rocky Mountain News*. The committee operated from April 6, 1917, until June 30, 1919, building American support for the war. Although the committee lacked many of the modern tools of mass communication—radio was still in its infancy, and the movie industry was just taking its first steps—it was still able to use advertising, billboards, and posters, as well as newspaper opinion pieces, articles, and pamphlets.

The committee also used interpersonal channels. It enlisted 75,000 "Four-Minute Men" who would take the committee's messages to churches and civic groups with four-minute speeches. Research conducted in the 1940s later proved the effectiveness of this technique, by confirming that people often turn to individuals they know and trust when they are looking for guidance about an important topic. So if an organization wants to influence a particular public, the best way may be to use influential local individuals along with the mass media.[17] Bernays referred to this process as **opinion leadership**—using "journalists, politicians, businessmen, scientists, professional men, authors, society leaders, teachers, actors, women of fashion and so on" to deliver influential messages to the public.[18]

Woodrow Wilson's use of public relations was not limited to the war effort. He was the first president to have regular press conferences, and under Wilson the Federal Trade Commission used publicity to force the food industry to adopt more sanitary practices.

The federal government turned to public relations once again during World War II. The Office of War Information served much the same purpose that the CPI had during World War I. The main difference was that the new group could use talking films and radio to supplement the print and interpersonal communications used by the CPI.

## Public Relations Becomes a Profession

During the 1940s and 1950s public relations continued to grow as a profession, and colleges and universities began offering degrees in the field. Advances in polling made it easier to measure public opinion, and clients began to realize that PR firms could help shape how people felt about companies and issues. Clients were also looking for help in making use of the emerging medium of television.

Throughout the 1960s the media became more critical of both business and government as the United States became caught up in the Vietnam War, the civil rights movement, the student and women's movements, environmentalism, and consumerism (for example, groups such as Ralph Nader's consumer activist organization). This trend continued into the 1970s with the rise of Watergate-inspired investigative reporting. It was a time when institutions had to actively manage their images, and they realized the importance of communicating with individuals, businesses, governments, and social organizations.[19]

*Rosie the Riveter was a creation of the War Production Coordinating Committee, and she became an enduring symbol of the importance of women's work, both at home and abroad, during World War II.*

# THE BUSINESS OF PUBLIC RELATIONS

There is a popular misconception among students that public relations is primarily about talking and meeting with people. Although it certainly includes these elements, there is much more to the profession. Public relations involves managing an organization's image through planning, research, communication, and assessment.

## What Is Public Relations?

Edward Bernays described three major functions of public relations:[20]

1. Informing—Sending out information to a variety of publics, ranging from the people who work in a company's office to its customers on the other side of the world. An example of information would be a press release announcing a new product line to stores that sell the company's products.

2. Persuading—Attempting to induce members of various publics to change their attitudes or actions toward an idea, product, or institution. An example of persuasion would be a lobbying campaign to persuade the government to remove a tax on the company's product.

3. Integrating—Attempting to bring publics and institutions together with a shared set of goals, actions, and attitudes. An example of an integrative event would be a charity auction designed to raise funds for a park in the city where the company has its offices as the company works to become a vital part of the community.

Bernays saw public relations as a public good, necessary for the proper functioning of society. He argued that society was moving too fast and becoming too complex for the average person to cope with, and that the only hope for a functional society was to merge public and private interests through public relations.

This two-way model of interaction between the institution and its publics is the central notion of modern public relations, which can be defined as follows: "the management function that establishes and maintains mutually beneficial relationships between an organization and the publics on whom its success or failure depends."[21]

This definition has three basic segments:

1. Public relations is a *management function*. This means that it is central to the running of a company or organization and not merely a tool of the marketing department.

2. Public relations establishes *mutually beneficial relationships*. This means that public relations is an interaction that should benefit both sides—the organization and the public(s).

3. Companies depend on *various publics* to succeed. One of the primary reasons PR campaigns fail is that they neglect these relationships and consider only the company's point of view.

One mistake companies must avoid is to assume that glib communication can be a substitute for real action when solving a public problem. This can be seen clearly in the case of the film industry in the 1920s and 1930s. As discussed in Chapter 8, during that period movies were being criticized for their immorality. Industry leaders responded by hiring former U.S. postmaster Will Hays to supervise the moral content of movies. Throughout the 1920s Hays preached a message of corporate responsibility to the press while the industry made no significant changes in response to criticism of the portrayal of sex, violence, and drug use in the movies.[22]

By 1934 critics had had enough of soothing words without action, and the Catholic Legion of Decency started a movie boycott. With the threat of government censorship growing, the movie industry finally adopted a production code that put strict limits on what directors could portray. Public relations historian Marvin Olasky argues that if the movie industry had dealt with its critics in a meaningful way in the 1920s, it might have avoided the restrictions forced on it in the 1930s.[23]

## The Public Relations Process

Although there are a number of different ways of looking at the PR process, we are going to look at it using a model known as ROPES: research, objectives, programming, evaluation, and stewardship.[24]

1. Research—Researching the opportunities, problems, or issues the organization is facing.

2. Objectives—Setting specific and measurable objectives for the PR campaign.

3. Programming—Planning and implementing the activities necessary to carry out the objectives.

4. Evaluation—Testing the messages and techniques before using them, monitoring the programming while it's being delivered, and measuring the results of the programming.

5. Stewardship—Maintaining the relationships created through the previous steps.

Central to the ROPES process is the notion that public relations is concerned primarily with creating, developing, and nurturing relationships between an organization and its key publics.[25] To see how this process is carried out, let's look at how Breathe Right used public relations both to build awareness of its nasal strips and to promote alternative uses of the product.

*Research.*    CNS, the original parent company of Breathe Right, was looking to broaden the market for its nasal strips, and through research found that customers were using the product in new ways. Breathe Right strips were initially designed to hold people's nostrils open while they sleep to help prevent snoring. But athletes, especially professional football players, soon began using the nasal strips to get more air into their lungs during competition. At the 1995 Super Bowl, players wearing Breathe Right strips scored eight of the game's ten touchdowns.[26] CNS wanted to capitalize on this positive publicity. So the company commissioned research to measure various publics' initial perceptions of their product. This could include the following elements:

■ Public opinion research—Finding out how the public views the company or product, its actions, and its image.

■ Content analysis—Analyzing what is being written or said about the company in the media.

■ Focus groups—Bringing together members of a particular public to talk about how they perceive an organization, a product, or an issue.[27]

Football player Jerry Rice became a spokesman for Breathe Right nasal strips after CNS Inc. noticed that the wide receiver always wore the company's products during games to improve his breathing.

Through consumer research, Breathe Right's manufacturer found that the visibility of the strips during the 1995 Super Bowl had helped build public awareness of the product. According to marketing manager Kirk Hogdon, "After the game, three out of every four adults had heard of Breathe Right, compared to one in four a year earlier."[28]

*Objectives.* A successful PR campaign depends on a clear definition of what the client wants to accomplish. This depends on having clearly measurable objectives for the campaign. In the case of Breathe Right, CNS wanted to build awareness of the product and identify it with athletic performance. Among the objectives CNS set would be raising the percentage of the target public that was aware of the Breathe Right brand and raising the percentage of the audience who knew that athletes used the strips to improve athletic performance.

*Programming.* The company decided to build on its campaign of working with NFL trainers. In 1996 it advertised on the Super Bowl, gave strips to everyone attending the game, and publicized its advertising and promotion. CNS, the parent company of Breathe Right, combined advertising, promotion, and media relations to build awareness of its product. The promotion involved building relationships directly with football fans by distributing Breathe Right strips at the game. The company also advertised during the game to highlight the product so that fans would be likely to notice the players wearing the strips.[29] The media relations campaign emphasized the players who wore the strips and publicized the company's status as one of the smallest Super Bowl advertisers. (CNS has since been acquired by pharmaceutical giant GlaxoSmithKline.)

*Evaluation.* Evaluation of the campaign happened at every stage of the process. Campaign materials were tested during development, while they were being delivered, and at the conclusion of the campaign. This involved seeing how well the campaign met the objectives that had been set earlier in the campaign.

Breathe Right's evaluation showed that CNS had gained a great deal from its 1996 Super Bowl campaign. Not only did it reap the advertising benefit of reaching the big game's massive audience, but it also generated a significant amount of good publicity for the company. Breathe Right received coverage on the front page of *USA Today*'s money section, which mentioned it as one of the smallest companies to advertise during the Super Bowl.[30] The product also received unpaid endorsements from athletes who said that the product improved their performance by giving them more oxygen, a claim the company itself did not make.

*Stewardship.* Breathe Right's communication campaign based on working with professional football players and football fans continues today. As of 2009, Breathe Right was partnering with five professional football teams to promote the nasal strip as a drug-free alternative to promote better breathing for improved athletic performance and sleeping. Breathe Right had plans to hand out more than 400,000 samples to fans at NFL games in fall 2009.[31]

## Who Are the Publics?

The term *public relations* seems to imply that there is a single monolithic group of people—"the public"—with whom the client needs to communicate. But in reality there are many such groups, since a public is any group of people who share a common set of interests.[32] These could include the company's employees, customers, stockholders, government regulators, or even people who live in the community where a new factory is to be built. In general, however, these publics can be divided into two main groups: internal publics and external publics, as we mentioned earlier.

*Internal Publics.* An important audience for companies, and one that is easy to forget, is the internal public—the people who work for the company. Not only are good relations with employees important for morale and responsiveness, but employees are also an important informal source of news about the company. Through e-mail, chat rooms, phone calls, and media contacts, employees are a central part of a company's communication environment.[33] When Chris Martin at West Virginia University makes plans to communicate with her internal publics, she first looks at university employees and students.[34]

Corporations use a variety of media to communicate with their internal publics. In the case of employees and managers, this communication could be done through something as simple as a weekly photocopied newsletter or as elaborate as a four-color company newspaper. But internal communication is not limited to printed materials. Videotapes, closed-circuit television, and even satellite conferences can be used to bring important news to employees. When the Three Mile Island nuclear plant suffered a major accident in 1979, a neighboring utility used videotaped programs to help its employees learn more about nuclear power. This form of education decreased the likelihood that the employees would spread misleading information when they talked with friends and family members.[35]

**intranets**

Computer networks designed to communicate with people within an organization. They are used to improve two-way internal communication and contain tools that allow for direct feedback. They are a tool for communicating with internal publics.

**media relations**

Two-way interactions between PR professionals and members of the press. These can involve press conferences, press releases, video news releases, or interviews. Typically, media relations involve the placement of unpaid messages within the standard programming or news content of the medium.

Many organizations have started **intranets**, computer networks that are open only to members of the organization. An intranet also allows a company to obtain direct feedback from employees. Bass Brewers, a British company, had long depended on a biweekly newsletter to communicate with its employees, but it had much more success with an intranet that could deliver fresh news daily.[36]

Universities typically use tools such as text messages, e-mails, and announcements at electronic campus kiosks to communicate with internal publics.[37]

*External Publics.*    Whereas internal publics are well known to an organization, the range of external publics is far larger and relatively less well known. The press is one of the most important external publics because it is through the press that organizations communicate to many of their publics. Building a good relationship with the press is critical. Public relations practitioners as early as Ivy Lee and Edward Bernays found that working with the press during good times would lead to better relations during bad times.[38] Ian Monk, a British journalist turned PR practitioner, says that the relationships he built up as a reporter help him immensely in the PR business: "I deal with former colleagues and protégés all the time, and the relationships I have already built with them are invaluable."[39] For WVU, external publics would include alumni, state legislators, people of the state, and even members of Congress.

**Media relations** can be defined as two-way interactions with members of the press. Typically, media relations involve the placement of unpaid messages within the standard programming or news content of the medium. Good media relations, ultimately, are good relations with the public at large. A positive image with the press will often become a positive image with the general public. And a company that the public likes to begin with tends to weather a crisis much better than one that is disliked. According to PR practitioner Susanne Courtney, "Corporate PR is about building up an 'equity' account with groups like the investment community, customers, media, employees and others that a company may need to draw on in a time of need."[40]

Presenting a company to the press is the most visible part of public relations. Press conferences, feature stories for the trade press, photographs, news releases, and even video news releases (discussed in the next subsection) are all tools that PR practitioners use to help manage the messages they send out to various publics through the media. Sometimes the press activities of an agency may be more subtle. A PR firm may encourage a prominent leader to write an opinion piece favorable to its client's point of view for publication on the editorial page of a major newspaper. Or it may arrange for a reporter to interview a company president. Or it may simply provide useful background material to reporters.

For WVU, communication with the professional media is an ongoing relationship. In addition to talking directly with the press, Martin and her staff use the Web site wvutoday.wvu.edu to provide journalists with a reliable source of university news and sources. Through the site WVU can provide photos, videos, suggested story ideas, and sources, as well as press releases and kits.[41]

These unpaid messages gain credibility because they come through the press rather than directly from the corporation. When a company wants to directly control the message it sends to the public, it uses advertising as a part of its PR plan.

*Video News Releases.*    Press releases, press conferences, media events—these traditional tools of media relations date back to the days of Edward Bernays and Ivy Lee. But the rise of television and Internet streaming video has created a new opportunity for media relations: the **video news release (VNR)**. The VNR is a taped or digital audio and video message that serves as a press release to the broadcast and online media. When companies want to control their coverage on television, they often turn to VNRs. After the *Exxon Valdez* oil spill (discussed in detail later in this chapter), Exxon became frustrated with the endless images of wildlife covered with oil appearing on the nightly news. The company hired a film crew to shoot stories showing its beach and animal cleanup efforts in an attempt to improve relations with stockholders and the public at large. The company distributed these VNRs to television stations around the United States via satellite. Jim Morakis, who worked in public affairs for Exxon at the time of the oil spill, told the *St. Louis Post-Dispatch*, "The positive aspects of the oil spill cleanup have not been addressed, and we wanted the public to see our side of the story."[42]

Other VNRs have been used to provide quotes to the broadcast media in the same way that a press release would provide quotes to newspapers or magazines. Companies hope that if they do not provide a spokesperson for interviews, the taped response will be aired in the interest of providing balanced coverage of the story.

Increasingly companies are using corporate-produced online video to bypass the legacy media altogether and talk directly to the public. Apple always accompanies new product announcements with video demonstrations of the product's features on its corporate Web site, and as we discuss shortly, Domino's Pizza fought back against an offensive online video by having the company president appear in his own YouTube video.[43]

## Crisis Communication

Nothing tests an organization's PR ability more than a **crisis**, an event perceived by the public as being damaging to the organization's reputation or image. Al Tortorella, an executive with the PR firm Burson-Marsteller, says, "A crisis is what the media says it is."[44] What he means is that a problem can be defined as a crisis when it becomes public and begins to be perceived as a crisis. This means that it is possible to prevent a problem from becoming a crisis, but companies

**video news release (VNR)**

A taped or digital video message that serves as a press release to the broadcast and online media. VNRs are often broadcast or streamed without notice of who produced the program.

**crisis**

Any situation that is perceived by the public as being damaging to the reputation or image of an organization. Not all problems develop into crises, but once a situation develops into a crisis, it can be damaging to an organization's reputation even if information behind the crisis is false.

## TEST YOUR MEDIA LITERACY

### Party School Publicity

It's the sort of publicity any university could do without. The headline in *USA Today* proclaims, "Penn State is life of the party." A parental advice column in a New Jersey paper suggests that Mom and Dad have a talk with their student about beer bongs and Jell-O shots before heading off to Penn State University. The reason for this press? Penn State had the "honor" of being named the "Number One Party School" in the nation in the 2009 edition of the Princeton Review's college guidebook, *The Best 361 Colleges.*[1]

The "honor," based on a casual survey of the schools rated by that company, is one of a number of silly ratings done to generate publicity for the guidebook. The book also ranks schools on such qualities as "Stone Cold Sober Schools," "Most Beautiful Campus," "Where Students Study Least," "Top Jocks Schools," "Lots of Beer," "Reefer Madness," and "Birkenstock-Wearing, Tree-Hugging, Clove-Smoking Vegetarians."[2] But none of these categories generate the amount of publicity that the party-school ranking does. The ranking puts the honored school in a no-win position. "There's no way not to come off being defensive when you get that ranking," a spokesperson for Florida State University (1997's winner) told *USA Today.*[3]

What is the Princeton Review? According to its corporate Web site, the company's main business is to sell test preparation services to help students get ready for college admissions tests such as the ACT, SAT, or GRE. The Review operates a Web site that helps students prepare to apply to colleges and universities, and it also publishes and sells a wide range of books on getting into college.[4] In short, the Princeton Review is in the business of coaching students on preparing to go to college.

A key PR issue for the company is attracting attention to its annual college guidebook, *The Best 361 Colleges.* Ideally, the Review would like the guide to be featured in all of the nation's leading newspapers. But merely publishing a college guide is unlikely to generate that kind of attention. So, starting in 1992, the Review began surveying students on lifestyle issues, including the notorious party-school ranking. The results have grown to sixty-three separate rankings, each of which can be counted on to draw, at the very least, local attention from the media in the towns housing the ranked schools.[5]

Schools "honored" with a place on the party-school list generally fight back hard with a PR effort of their own, all the while pointing out that the ranking is meaningless. A *Houston Chronicle* article that appeared in 2006, when the University of Texas landed in the hated number-one spot on the list, outlines the typical party-school story:

Nervous parents shipping their freshmen off to classes next week may wonder if the rankings have any merit. Princeton Review apparently surveyed more than 115,000 students at schools across the country, randomly asking students about their party habits. No word on how many students at UT were surveyed or whether the survey's authors randomly selected them or targeted specific groups.[6]

Except that the Princeton Review does not randomly survey anyone. It simply has about 300 students at each school complete the lifestyle survey. The purpose of the rankings is, after all, to generate stories about the company, not to establish which schools are (or are not) good for partying.

The one school that doesn't have to worry about its reputation being damaged by the annual party-school list is Brigham Young University in Utah. It has topped the "Stone Cold Sober" list for the past twelve years in a row.

• • • • • • • • • • • • • • • •

### Who are the sources?

What is the Princeton Review? What does the company do? Who is it trying to get to read its guide? Who is publishing stories about the Princeton Review? Who is being critical of the Princeton Review?

### What are they saying?

What are some of the lists that the Princeton Review publishes? What do these say about the schools on the lists? What do schools on the lists have to say about them? Why do critics say the Princeton Review publishes its lists?

### What evidence is there?

How does the Princeton Review compile its lists? What does it mean when it claims a university is "the number-one party school?" What evidence is there that schools are harmed by these lists?

### What do you and your classmates think about the Princeton Review lists?

How do you and your classmates feel about the Princeton Review lists? Has your school been rated on any of the lists? Would you or your parents feel differently about your school if it showed up on the top party-school list? Why or why not? Should colleges and universities respond to being on the Princeton Review lists, or are they better off ignoring them? Why?

---

[1] Carrie Stetler, "Princeton Review Lists Top Party Schools: Kegger-Proof Your Teen?" July 27, 2009, www.nj.com/parenting/carrie_stetler/index.ssf/2009/07/princeton_review_lists_top_par.html; Jillian Berman, "Princeton Review Rankings: Penn State Is Life of the Party," *USA Today*, July 28, 2009.

[2] Sara Lipka, "And This Year's Top 'Party School' Is . . . ," *Chronicle of Higher Education*, September 1, 2006.

[3] Mary Beth Marklein, "WVU 'Top Party School' Campus Acquires Dreaded Rating from College Guide," *USA Today*, August 20, 1997.

[4] The Princeton Review, "Who We Are," princetonreview.com/footer/companyinfo_overview.asp.

[5] Jay Rey, "Princeton Review Dishes It Out Again to Bona in Culinary Survey," *Buffalo News*, August 22, 2006.

[6] Andrew Guy Jr., "So, How Do You Get to Be the No. 1 Party School?" *Houston Chronicle*, August 23, 2006.

*Student revelers are shown here at the annual Mifflin Street block party in Madison, Wisconsin. The University of Wisconsin–Madison fought hard to get itself off the Princeton Review's top-ten party school list. The party school list, based on student surveys from across the country, is used to help market the company's college guidebook.*

should never count on problems being kept secret; they need to have a plan for handling them if they turn into crises.

For example, in 1994 computer programmers discovered that the Pentium computer chip designed by Intel could, in certain rare cases, compute a wrong answer. The flaw in the chip was a minor problem affecting only a very few scientists, but no one wanted to have a computer that "made mistakes." Public relations consultant Susan Thomas says that the flurry of negative publicity about the flaw created a crisis for the company:

What Intel learned from the original Pentium crisis is [that] the difference between the perceived size and actual size of a problem is irrelevant. Just because the chance of the miscalculation happening was slim, it didn't matter. Customers were upset. They wanted responsiveness and answers. . . . When Intel said "only a very small percentage would be affected," it sounded like the company was saying "this isn't worth bothering about."[45]

Intel eventually resolved the crisis by offering all of its customers a "no-questions-asked" replacement chip.

*Principles of Crisis Communication.* What should a company do when it faces a crisis? In general, it should communicate promptly and honestly with all its publics. More specifically, there are five principles of crisis communication:[46]

1. Be prepared—The most important principle is to have a crisis plan. For every company there are certain things that are unlikely to happen but would be enormously damaging if they did. Such events could, if serious enough, put the existence of the company at risk by damaging its most important assets: its credibility and reputation.[47] Airlines should have a plan in the event of a plane crash; universities should have plans in the event of an academic or athletic scandal; a factory should be prepared for a chemical spill. These events might be unlikely to occur, but they can and should be prepared for.

2. Be honest—One of the problems with lying is that liars are often caught. Cover-ups almost always end up being exposed, and the cover-up looks worse than the original problem. Instead, get the story out and over with quickly. President Richard Nixon's lies about the break-in to the

Democratic Party's headquarters at the Watergate building created far more problems for him than did the actual burglary itself. For President Bill Clinton, lying about his relationship with Monica Lewinsky was infinitely more damaging to his reputation than was the affair itself.[48] Public relations consultant Bob Wilkerson says, "The truth is going to get out. I want it out of my lips. It's bad enough I've had an incident. It's even worse if it looks like I was trying to cover up."[49]

3. Apologize, and mean it—The company should respond with real action, not just words. In 2006 motorcycle manufacturer Yamaha got caught claiming that its new middleweight sport bike had an engine that would rev up to 17,500 RPM. This was significantly higher than any competing motorcycle. It turned out that both the tachometer and the marketing department were a little optimistic because the motorcycle's true redline was 16,200 RPM. In real life, this discrepancy probably doesn't matter much. But when complaints about the overstated redline started surfacing on the Internet, Yamaha made a simple decision to completely neutralize the crisis. The company sent a letter to everyone who had bought the motorcycle, apologized for the discrepancy, and offered to buy back the bike—including tax, setup, and interest—no questions asked.[50] In addition to having done the right thing, Yamaha squelched the crisis immediately and kept it from damaging the company's otherwise good reputation with motorcyclists.

4. Move quickly—Public relations critics say that how a company reacts in the first few hours after a crisis occurs will determine how the crisis is perceived from that point on. "All crises have a window of opportunity to gain control of 45 minutes to 12 hours," says crisis communication expert Paul Shrivastava.[51] Beyond that point, people will have already decided what they think about the crisis, and once they have made up their minds, they are reluctant to change them. In the past, companies could build their response around the time the morning newspapers were published or the nightly news was broadcast, but cable news channels and newspaper Web sites can publish news at any time, and gossip Web sites are willing to print unfounded and unverified speculations that traditional news outlets might avoid. Bad news can also spread rapidly over the Internet.[52] Even when things move quickly, the company still needs to act carefully. Crisis management decisions are much more difficult to make than conventional decisions because they deal with things that have important consequences. They also need to be made quickly, while the whole world watches.[53]

5. Communicate with the press and other constituencies—These include the company's own employees and management, stockholders, government regulators, and customers, as well as the press. It was immediate communication with all publics that helped minimize Yamaha's problems with its advertising misinformation.

*Johnson & Johnson had to handle the recall of millions of containers of Tylenol in 1982 after tainted capsules led to the deaths of seven people in the Chicago area.*

The application of these principles can be seen in two examples of crisis communication, discussed in the following subsections. In the first, the company handled both the physical response and the communication response almost perfectly and emerged from the crisis with a good market position and a stronger image than it started with. In the second, mishandled communications led to a blot on the company's reputation that has endured for more than twenty years.

*The Tylenol Scare.*   In September 1982 the consumer products giant Johnson & Johnson faced a crisis that could have destroyed one of its most important brands, Tylenol. Seven people in the Chicago area died after taking cyanide-laced Extra-Strength Tylenol capsules. The deaths set off what the *New York Times* called "the biggest consumer product scare in history."[54] (The perpetrator was never caught.) But Johnson & Johnson, with the help of the PR agency Burson-Marsteller, managed to preserve the brand and the company's reputation with a combination of appropriate ethical action and good public relations.

The first thing the company did right was to be entirely honest with the media and public. In fact, praise for its openness improved its image.[55]

The next thing the company did right was to take immediate action in response to the tampering. As soon as Johnson & Johnson learned of the problem, it immediately stopped advertising the product and took it off the market in Chicago.[56]

Throughout the crisis, Burson-Marsteller did nightly telephone surveys to measure public opinion. When those polls showed that the public feared that other Tylenol capsules might be tampered with, Johnson & Johnson took the product off the market nationwide.[57] The company was perceived as acting responsibly, and in fact it was acting responsibly.

Johnson & Johnson had clearly won the first PR battle and was being perceived as a responsible company that had been the victim of a vicious attack. The second battle would be the campaign to rebuild trust in the Tylenol brand.

In November 1982 Johnson & Johnson announced the relaunch of Extra-Strength Tylenol with the news that the product would now be sold in a triple-sealed container. Along with the expected marketing support, Johnson &

Johnson engaged in an extensive PR campaign that utilized educational advertising, media appearances, and personal contacts.

The company sent out more than 2,000 sales representatives to meet with major retailers and doctors. An advertising campaign told about the new tamper-resistant packaging, and Johnson & Johnson announced the relaunch of the brand in a thirty-city teleconference delivered via satellite. Simultaneously, it held a press conference that was attended by nearly 600 journalists. Finally, Johnson & Johnson's CEO, James Burke, appeared on both *60 Minutes* and the daytime talk program *The Phil Donahue Show*.

The campaign was a success. Before the crisis, Tylenol had had a 37 percent share of the pain reliever market; this number dropped to 7 percent during the tampering scare. But within a month of the relaunch Tylenol was back to 28 percent of the market, and it eventually regained its status as the industry leader.[58]

Johnson & Johnson succeeded in protecting its brand and reputation for a number of reasons. First, few people blamed the company for the tampering; the fault appeared to lay with an individual beyond the span of the company's control. Second, the company acted quickly and responsibly in the interests of consumers. It was also open with its various publics, freely admitting what it did and didn't know. Finally, the company actively worked through the difficult situation and engaged the press by viewing it as an ally instead of as an adversary.

*The* Exxon Valdez *Oil Spill.* On March 24, 1989, the oil tanker *Exxon Valdez* ran aground in Alaska's Prince William Sound, spilling 240,000 barrels of crude oil into the ocean. This oil soon washed up on shore, coating beaches, birds, and sea life in an environmentally sensitive area. Exxon spent more than $2 billion on the cleanup of the oil spill, but it still ended up with a tarnished image. Former reporter and network news president William Small notes that no company ever spent as much as Exxon did following the oil spill and still came out looking so bad.[59]

Exxon's post-spill image problem had numerous causes that illustrate the difference between Johnson & Johnson's response and Exxon's:

*The Exxon Valdez oil spill in 1989 was not just an ecological disaster, it was also a PR nightmare for Exxon that has lingered for decades.*

- Perception of fault—Unlike the Tylenol tampering case, Exxon was considered at fault for the oil spill. Exxon's first problem was that it was the company's tanker that had run aground. It is difficult from a PR point of view to defend a company that has done something wrong.[60]

■ Lack of effective crisis plan—Exxon never developed a crisis plan for dealing with such a serious oil spill. Although Exxon shared responsibility with the Coast Guard for the lack of proper facilities, the fact that it did not have cleanup equipment in Alaska forced it to shoulder the blame after the spill.[61]

■ Failure to take immediate control—Exxon did not take immediate control of the flow of information. Not until a week after the spill did Exxon's CEO, Lawrence Rawl, make public comments. Meanwhile, numerous heartbreaking images of fouled wildlife started coming from the area. Almost all the press coverage of the spill was negative. In fact, Exxon made it actively difficult for reporters to get the company's point of view. The company's initial response was reportedly handled by a one-person PR office in Houston that had trouble coping with all the requests for information. Moreover, Exxon held all its news briefings for reporters in Valdez, Alaska, which had limited communication channels, instead of in a more accessible location like New York.[62]

■ Failure to accept responsibility immediately—Exxon didn't initially accept ethical responsibility for the spill and apologize. The company started off by trying to spread the blame, claiming that the Coast Guard, Alaska environmental officials, and the weather were also responsible. Whether or not these claims were valid, the press and the public saw Exxon as responsible. As one Alaska official put it, "I would suggest it's Exxon's tanker that ran up on the rocks."[63]

The final blow to Exxon's image came in the fall after the oil spill, when a memo from a company official was leaked to the press saying that Exxon would end the cleanup effort whenever it chose to, that it would do nothing in the winter, and that it did not promise to return in the spring. The memo made the company look arrogant and uncaring.[64] Exxon eventually accepted responsibility for the oil spill and the cleanup, but by then the company's image was damaged irrevocably. Even twenty years after the accident, the ship's name is the standard to which environmental disasters are compared. A current news search found 136 stories mentioning the spill and more than 600,000 Web sites.

## Public Relations and the Internet

In the late 1980s and early 1990s, the PR industry acquired a new friend and enemy—the Internet. The Internet gave PR practitioners a new way to research and to distribute information, but it also provided a powerful new channel for the spreading of rumors that had the potential to develop into crises.

*A New Information Channel.*    Among many other things, the Internet has given the PR industry a new tool. Now companies can distribute press releases, background information, and photos to the media through e-mail and Web sites.

If a company's Web site has a good reputation, it may be the first place reporters go to for information. Since reporters often use the Web to research articles, placing statistics and facts on a Web site can affect the way the company is covered.

The Internet has also given companies a means of bypassing the traditional media and communicating directly with various publics. Customers, stockholders, and even critics may go to a company's Web site in search of information. A Web site also ensures that a company's point of view is being presented the way the company intends it to be. Along with having a good Web site, companies need to make sure that their site will show up at the top of searches about their company. It can be embarrassing if a company's critics appear above the company itself in a Web search.[65]

The Internet also allows companies to find out what people are saying about them. Many organizations conduct regular searches of Web sites and bulletin boards to see what complaints and kudos are coming their way. Public relations practitioners may join in with chats and discussion groups to help shape what is being said about their clients. Of course, with millions of Web sites in existence, just finding out what is being said about a company can be a massive undertaking.[66]

Crisis management consultant Jonathan Bernstein says that blogs and other Web sites create significant new PR challenges. He writes that organizations need to consider the following:

- The Internet gives critics access to the world without the checks and balances of traditional journalism. Prior to the Internet, the only way to reach a broad, general audience was through the professional media, which might not always be a fan of your company but would probably treat you fairly. Many Internet sites can be biased or don't engage in editorial oversight or fact checking.

- Once a crisis hits the Internet, it can't be contained. It used to be that a local news story would stay local. Now, once a story is posted to a newspaper's or television station's Web site, it's gone national.

- The Internet makes it easy for critics to leak confidential information. This can include not just reports of confidential information but also images of original documents or recordings of phone calls.

- In the absence of good information, rumors will flourish on the Internet. This problem isn't unique to the Internet. Any time an organization doesn't provide creditable information, rumors and gossip will fill the gap.[67] But the Internet can accelerate the process by which rumors travel.

- These considerations illustrate perfectly the importance of Truth Five— New media are always scary. You can read more about handling crisis management on the Web at http://ralphehanson.com.

*Domino's: Fighting Back Against Social Media.* It used to be that the worst media a company had to worry about was a scathing story by an investigative

**Workers fired for Domino's prank video**

FAST FOOD SHOCKER
DOMINO'S WORKERS FIRED FOR PRANK

0:43 / 2:24

*Domino's Pizza faced an enormous image crisis in 2009 when two employees at a North Carolina store posted a prank video of themselves tampering with pizzas and subs.*

journalist on a program like *60 Minutes.* But today a corporation's worst PR nightmare can come from amateur-produced video posted on video-sharing sites like YouTube and then publicized through social media such as Twitter and YouTube. That's what Domino's Pizza discovered in April 2009, when two employees in Conover, North Carolina, posted a video showing one of them putting cheese up his nose and then placing it on a sandwich, blowing his nose on a sandwich, and farting on a sandwich. The other employee narrated the video with comments like, "In about five minutes it'll be sent out on delivery where somebody will be eating these, yes, eating them, and little did they know that cheese was in his nose and that there was some lethal gas that ended up on their salami."[68] Once the video was posted on YouTube, word about it spread rapidly online through Twitter and other social media, and the video quickly racked up more than one million views.

The Domino's Pizza chain attempted to respond quickly and responsibly but may have spoken out too late in the rapidly changing environment of the Internet. The company responded publicly to the video within forty-eight hours of finding out about it, delaying its response reportedly to keep from giving attention to the video. Domino's eventual response included a YouTube video featuring Domino's president Patrick Doyle, a complete cleaning of the store where the video was shot, and a revision of the company's hiring practices. The company also started a Twitter account with which to respond to customers.[69]

Richard Levick of the PR firm Levick Strategic Communications told *Advertising Age* that Domino's handled the crisis well after its initial delay in responding: "After the first 24 hours, they were largely textbook. They started a Twitter account, separated themselves from the villains, shut down the store, apologized, went to their demographic, went to YouTube—I think all of that is great."[70]

Levick said that companies need to do several things to prepare for online crisis communication:

- Identify your crisis team—This includes PR professionals, lawyers, and digital communication specialists.

- Imagine your nightmare scenarios—Make sure that you have the online resources so that when a crisis hits and people start searching for information they come to your Web site first.

- Track the blogosphere and other social media—Make sure you know what people are saying about you, and be responsive to the people who are talking about your company.

- Don't wait—You have a very limited time to respond.[71]

Following the posting of the video, the two employees were identified by bloggers, arrested, and charged with distributing prohibited foods. Although the Domino's Pizza chain has largely recovered from the crisis created by the video, the North Carolina store where the video was shot has not. After closing briefly for cleaning following the posting of the video, the story closed for good five months later.[72]

To read more about this case and see the videos mentioned, go to http://ralphehanson.com.

*Rumors on the Internet.* Controlling the spread of rumors has always been a problem for the PR industry, but the growth of the Internet has allowed rumors to spread faster and more frequently than ever before.

Seattle-based coffee giant Starbucks faced an Internet rumor that the company did not support the war in Iraq or anyone who was fighting in it. According to the *Seattle Times*, the rumor got started when a Marine sergeant sent an e-mail to friends, in which he claimed that Starbucks had written a letter saying the company did not support the troops or the war in response to another Marine who had asked for free coffee. The e-mail then circulated extensively on the Internet. Several months later, the sergeant sent out an e-mail apologizing for the incorrect statement, but the apology didn't get near the attention that the initial accusation did. Starbucks has since responded to the rumor through a rumor-control page on its Web site and through an entry on Snopes.com, the urban legend debunking site. Despite the company's active response, the rumor continues to circulate more than two years after it got started. As a precautionary measure, Starbucks monitors blog and Web coverage of the company, but it doesn't respond to every rumor.[73] You can read more about corporate rumor control at http://ralphehanson.com.

# PUBLIC RELATIONS AND SOCIETY

This chapter has so far looked at public relations largely from the point of view of either PR firms or their clients. But it is also useful to look at it from the public's perspective. Public relations shapes the news we receive through newspapers, magazines, television, radio, and even the Internet; in the form of "spin control," it attempts to shape our view of politicians and public policy; and it is a central component of social movements.

## Public Relations Supports the News Business

Public relations plays a significant role in what is presented as news in the media. Sociologists David Altheide and Robert Snow argue that public relations is an integral part of the news business because most of the events—including crime and disaster reporting—covered by the media were created by PR practitioners to obtain coverage for their clients.[74] Just how much of the news originates with public relations?

Depending on how it is measured, anywhere from 40 to 90 percent of all news starts out as public relations. The *Columbia Journalism Review* (*CJR*) tried to answer the question by studying an issue of the *Wall Street Journal*. The researchers selected 111 stories from the paper. The companies mentioned in the stories were then contacted and asked to send a copy of their original press releases. *CJR* found that 72 percent of the stories they were able to analyze were based almost exclusively on material from a press release. The study estimated that 45 percent of all the stories in the *Wall Street Journal* that day had been based on press releases, and that 27 percent of the actual news space was devoted to press releases.[75] The newspaper's executive editor estimated that 90 percent of the stories in the paper started with a company's announcement.

How does this happen? Think about a typical news day. Most news coming from Washington, D.C., involves a press conference, a speech, a press release, or an event created specifically to be covered by the media. A scientific report on an environmental issue is published, and both environmentalists and industry groups hold press conferences to provide background information. A bank robber is arrested, and the police hold a media briefing. Even a basketball game will be reported using statistics provided by the sports information office and quotes from an official postgame interview session hosted for the media.

Although news may originate in PR efforts, executives and other individuals covered by the media sometimes have an exaggerated sense of what public relations can accomplish. One movie studio boss reportedly told an applicant for a PR position, "Your responsibility will be, if I step out of my limousine and my pants fall down, you make sure that no one gets a photo to the press."[76] That's a guarantee no PR practitioner can make.

## Public Relations and the Government

Along with the general public and media, the various levels of government are major external publics. With their government relations departments, PR firms represent their clients before the federal government and agencies, state legislatures, and even municipal bodies. As businesses face increasing government regulation, they have increased their efforts to work with government to shape legislation and regulations that are favorable to their interests.[77] Government relations includes lobbying for laws that will best meet the needs of the organization, as well as simply building goodwill with legislators and regulatory bodies. The

*Washington Post* reported that, as of 2005, more than 34,000 lobbyists were registered to work in the nation's capital, more than twice the number there were in 2000.[78]

The government itself is a major practitioner of public relations. All elected federal officials have a press secretary and many have a communications director, and the various agencies themselves have PR offices. The role of the political press secretary is a challenging one, in which the spokesperson has to serve his or her boss while still dealing honestly with the press and the public. Sometimes this involves being evasive. As one congressional press secretary told the Washington, D.C., paper *The Hill,* "It is a matter of practice and experience and being able to steer a conversation toward issues you are looking to advance.... The golden rule is you don't answer the question you are asked, you answer the question you want to answer."[79]

*Press secretary Robert Gibbs (right) is responsible for making sure that President Barack Obama gets his message out to reporters in a way that portrays the administration in the best possible light.*

Lanny Davis, who advised President Bill Clinton on damage control, said that when the press and the public are interested in an issue, the spokesperson only has one option: "Tell the truth, tell it all, tell it early, tell it yourself."[80] During the Monica Lewinsky sex scandal, President Clinton ignored the "tell the truth" rule, and the scandal stuck with him throughout the remainder of his second term in office. Had he acknowledged the affair when the story first broke rather than denying it, the story might well have blown over quickly. That's what happened when President Barack Obama revealed his college-days drug use in his 1995 memoir *Dreams From My Father.* The book allowed him to time the revelation of his drug use early in his political career and kept others from using it against him.[81]

By contrast, the British royal family was portrayed very negatively in the press for failing to respond publicly when Princess Diana was killed in a 1997 car crash in France.[82]

The U.S. military has been actively involved in public relations since World War I. Although the military's initial PR efforts were intended to recruit volunteers, they were also interacting with the press. Today the Armed Forces Radio and Television Service provides internal public relations in the form of radio and television broadcasts for service people overseas. There are also public information activities and community relations for the areas surrounding military bases.[83]

# Spin Control: A More Personal Form of Public Relations

A new kind of public relations, known as spin control, has come to the forefront since the 1970s. Rather than simply providing press releases, events, and background information, so-called spin doctors attempt to influence how a story will be portrayed and discussed. Newspaper columnist and former speechwriter William Safire suggests that the word *spin* came from the idea of spinning a yarn—that is, telling a story. It may also have a sports connotation, as in putting a spin on a tennis or billiard ball.[84]

John Scanlon, a New York City publicist, is often cited as a top spin doctor. He is acquainted with many members of the national press corps and will call them when he considers a story unbalanced—or at least contrary to his client's interests. He also sends out frequent mailings to influential people in which he presents his point of view regarding events in the news. Scanlon's goal is not so much to give information to the press as to influence how stories are interpreted—that is, to control the spin put on them.

Here are some of the things spin doctors do:

- Selectively leak information in advance, hoping that reporters will pay more attention to it than to information received later.

- Contact members of the press immediately after an event in an effort to get them to adopt the desired spin or interpretation of the event.

- Push the idea that there are always two sides to every story. As Scanlon notes, "What seems to be true is not necessarily the case when we look at it and we dissect it and we take it apart, and we turn it around and we look at it from a different perspective."[85]

---

### "Tricks of the Trade" for Government Press Secretaries

*The Hill* reporter Betsy Rothstein lists the following common "tricks of the trade" press secretaries use in dealing with reporters they don't want to talk to:

- Say "I will call you back" and then don't.

- Repeat the same phrase over and over.

- Try to talk the reporter out of writing the story.

- Act brusque and distant.

- Don't return phone calls until the day after the deadline.

- Talk in short sentences.

- Act as though you are in a hurry and need to get off the phone as soon as possible.

*Source:* Betsy Rothstein, "Capital Living: The Fine Art of Flacking," *The Hill,* February 22, 2006.

---

# Public Relations and Political Activism

Not all public relations is practiced by professionals working for large agencies. As numerous political activists have shown, public relations can be an

# TEST YOUR MEDIA LITERACY

## Saving the Polar Bear

Public relations as a part of political activism involves telling your story honestly while making sure that your target publics understand and sympathize with your point of view. That's what the Center for Biological Diversity was trying to accomplish with its "Save the Polar Bear" initiative, a campaign to build public awareness of global warming.

Kassie Siegel, director of the Center for Biological Diversity's climate, air, and energy program, started pushing to have the polar bear listed as an endangered species in 2004 as a way of drawing the public's attention to the problem of global warming. Under Siegel's leadership the Center spearheaded a petition drive of scientists and a lawsuit. Along with all the scientific arguments, the campaign also pushed what Siegel calls the "pop cultural iconic status of the polar bear."[1]

That portion of the effort was apparently successful. Consider what the *Washington Post* wrote in an editorial on the topic: "Cuddly, loveable animals— even ferocious ones that can kill a seal with a single blow of a monster-strong paw—have a way of precipitating steps that non-furry creatures just can't manage."[2] After two years of work, the Environmental Protection Agency proposed listing the polar bear as a threatened species. The polar bear still has to make it through a series of hearings before it becomes officially endangered, but the campaign seems to have been a success.[3]

**MORE online**

You can find links to several articles about the "Save the Polar Bear" campaign at **http://ralphehanson.com.**

• • • • • • • • • • • • • • • • • • •

### Who are the sources?
What is the Center for Biological Diversity? What is the group's purpose? Who funds the Center?

### What are they saying?
What is the Center saying about polar bears and their habitat? How do they connect the polar bears' plight with the problem of global warming?

### What evidence is there?
What evidence does the Center present that the polar bear is endangered? What evidence does it present on the causes and consequences of global warming? Does it present contrasting points of view, or does it speak with a single voice?

### What do you and your classmates think about the campaign?
Do you think it is "fair" to use cute animals to promote awareness of global warming? Is it effective? Why or why not? What other approaches could the Center for Biological Diversity use to build awareness of global warming?

[1] "Flock of Siegel," Grist: Environmental News and Commentary, January 15, 2007, www.grist.org/comments/interactivist/2007/01/ 15/siegel.

[2] "Threatened by Warming," *Washington Post,* January 7, 2007, B06.

[3] Dan Joling, "Critics Take Aim at Polar Bear Listing," *Washington Post,* March 2, 2007.

*Kassie Siegel of the Center for Biological Diversity makes use of the popularity of the polar bear to help attract attention to the Center's attempts to protect endangered species and build public awareness of global warming.*

effective tool for social change as well. In 2005 the farm labor group the Coalition of Immokalee Workers won a battle with Yum Brands, the parent company of Taco Bell, over the rights and pay for migrant workers. The workers engaged in a work boycott against Taco Bell's produce farmers, held an extended hunger strike to draw attention to their cause, organized a 230-mile protest walk, and organized a boycott against Taco Bell. Despite the fact that migrant farm workers are typically seen as a relatively powerless group, the workers were able to force a change in the fast food business.[86]

## Public Relations and the Civil Rights Movement

Civil rights leader Martin Luther King Jr. displayed a brilliant understanding of public relations throughout the campaign to integrate the South in the 1950s and 1960s. King knew that it would take a combination of action, words, and visibility in the media to eliminate segregation laws and integrate lunch counters, restrooms, water fountains, and businesses. He practiced public relations in churches, hotel rooms, and even jail.

In 1963 King and the Southern Christian Leadership Conference, a civil rights group, wanted to do something highly visible that would let the entire nation see the evils of segregation. The goal of the campaign was to hold nonviolent demonstrations and resistance that would force segregated stores and businesses to be opened to African Americans.

King and his colleagues picked Birmingham, Alabama, as one of their targets, in part because the city's police commissioner was Eugene "Bull" Conner. Conner was a racist who could be counted on to attack peaceful marchers. King's campaign was called Project C, for confrontation, and it included press conferences, leaflets, and demonstrations in front of hundreds of reporters and photographers. Starting in April 1963, African American volunteers marched in the streets, held sit-ins at segregated lunch counters, and boycotted local businesses. As the protests started, so did the arrests. The story was covered by the *New York Times* and the *Washington Post*. King and his colleagues knew that all the protests in the world would be ineffective if they were not covered by the press, and that being beaten up by police would accomplish little if no photographers were present to document the event.

David Halberstam, who was a newspaper reporter in the South at the time, commented on civil rights leaders' understanding of public relations:

> The key was to lure the beast of segregation out in the open. Casting was critical: King and his aides were learning that they needed to find the right venue, a place where the resistance was likely to be fierce, and the right local official to play the villain. Neither was a problem: King had no trouble finding men like . . . Bull Connor, who were in their own way looking for him, just as he was looking for them.[87]

*In 1963 Americans were shocked by images, such as this one from photographer Bill Hudson, of police attacking civil rights marchers with dogs, fire hoses, and clubs.*

On Good Friday, King and Ralph Abernathy joined in the marching so that they would be arrested. While King was in jail, he wrote the "Letter from Birmingham Jail," which was smuggled out and published as a brochure. His eloquent words, given added force by having been written in jail, were reprinted across the country.

After King was released, he and his followers raised the stakes. Adults would no longer march and be arrested; instead, children became the vanguard of the movement. The images, which appeared in print media throughout the world, were riveting. In his biography of King, Stephen Oates writes, "Millions of readers in America—and millions overseas—stared at pictures of police dogs lunging at young marchers, of firemen raking them with jet streams, of club-wielding cops pinning a Negro woman to the ground."[88]

King faced criticism for allowing young people to face the dangers of marching in Birmingham. But he responded promptly by criticizing the white press, asking the reporters where they had been "during the centuries when our segregated social system had been misusing and abusing Negro children."[89]

Although there was rioting in Birmingham and King's brother's house was bombed, the campaign was ultimately successful. Business owners took down the "WHITE" and "COLORED" signs from drinking fountains and bathrooms, and anyone was allowed to eat at the lunch counters and sit on the buses. The successful protest in Birmingham set the stage for the March on Washington in August 1963, where King would give his famous "I Have a Dream" speech.[90]

# CHAPTERSummary

Public relations (PR) developed out of the press agentry of the late 1800s. Publicity firms used one-way communication, deceptive techniques, and bribery. By the beginning of the twentieth century, large corporations such as railroads and utilities realized that they needed to develop more sophisticated relationships with the press if they hoped to control their images.

Ivy Lee and Edward L. Bernays are generally considered to be the founders of public relations as a profession. Lee was among the first press agents to recognize that dealing with the press promptly and truthfully was the best way to obtain positive coverage for his clients. In 1906 he codified this approach in his "Statements of Principles." Bernays wrote the first book about public relations and taught the first college course on the subject.

During World War I the federal government realized the value of public relations and used a variety of techniques to build support for U.S. participation in the war. Public relations continued to grow as a profession as businesses were increasingly regulated and the public began to distrust both businesses and the government.

Public relations can be seen as performing three main functions: informing, persuading, and integrating (bringing together) publics, both internal and external. Among the most important publics are the media. Effective public relations generally includes both communication and action. The PR process consists of four steps: 1) defining the problem, 2) planning, 3) communicating, and 4) evaluating. Successful companies work at communicating with their publics during both good times and times of crisis. The rise of the Internet and instantaneous communication not controlled by major media has forced the public relations industry to speed up its rate of response to problems and to deal with a wider range of problems. Public relations is used by a wide range of organizations ranging from major corporations, to the government, to activist groups.

# KEYTerms

public relations (PR)   418
public   418
press agentry   418
engineering consent   421
opinion leadership   422

intranets   428
media relations   428
video news release (VNR)   429
crisis   429

# CONCEPT Review

One-way versus two-way communication

The professionalization of public relations

The public relations process

Managing a public relations crisis

The impact of the Internet on public relations

The relationship between public relations and the news business

The uses of public relations by the government and government officials

The uses of public relations by advocacy groups

# Media Law
## Free Speech and Fairness

**CHAPTER 13**

**When you record** a television show on your digital video recorder (DVR), include a quote from a book in a newspaper review, or register the copyright of an article you have written, chances are you are benefiting from the work of Barbara R. Ringer. Ringer, who went to work for the Copyright Office in the Library of Congress in 1949 right after she graduated from law school, had as much influence on American copyright law as anyone in the twentieth century.

The copyright laws Ringer faced when she started at the Library of Congress were written in 1909, not long after Mark Twain had been fighting for international copyright protection for his books. As Matt Schudel of the *Washington Post* points out, the 1909 version of the law was written before there was television, commercial radio, copying machines, or the recording industry.[1] This was an era in which the hot new music distribution technology was the player piano. There were no DVRs, no iPods, no file sharing.

Although her work pre-dated the Internet and digital distribution, Ringer could see new media technology was coming. In a 1975 speech Ringer said, "The basic human rights of individual authors throughout the world are being sacrificed more and more on the altar of . . . the technological revolution."[2] Ringer worked with a simple premise—authors, songwriters, and performers ought to be protected. For example, the Copyright Act of 1909 exempted owners of coin-operated music boxes from having to pay royalties to composers and performers. As a result, when the jukebox came on the scene, composers and performers were cut out of royalties from that source as well.[3]

Ringer also fought to make sure that the law would protect authors and artists even if they didn't follow every proper step in registering their copyright. "My philosophy has always been to reward authors for what they do, not to punish them for what they don't do," she said.[4]

Ringer worked for twenty-one years on the legislation that would become the Copyright Act of 1976. Among the provisions Ringer put into the law were the following:

- The concept of fair use—Authors and reviewers could quote briefly from works without having to secure permission.
- Extension of copyright—Copyright protection for an individual would last fifty years after the author's death (previously, the copyright term was twenty-eight years).
- Protection for new media—Copyrighted works were protected from duplication by "means not yet devised."[5]

Law professor Pamela Samuelson called Ringer "one of the most important contributors to copyright law during the 20th century."[6] How important? Samuelson

Barbara Ringer, the only woman in the room at this hearing in the 1960s on copyright revision, sued the Library of Congress successfully for sex discrimination after she was passed over for the top position in the copyright office.

449

noted that Ringer, testifying before Congress in 1971, told a representative "that his son wouldn't infringe on copyright if he recorded a song from the radio." That comment became part of the U.S. Supreme Court ruling in 1984 that it was legal for people to record television shows on their videocassette recorders for home use.

In addition to being a pioneer on copyright law, Ringer was also an ardent defender of women's and minority rights.[7] She was passed over for promotion to be the head of the Copyright Office in 1971, despite stellar evaluations and the recommendation of the retiring head. Instead, a man with much less experience was named as register of copyrights. At the encouragement of her friends, Ringer filed and won a sex and racial discrimination suit. The reasoning behind the sex discrimination was fairly obvious. But the racial discrimination was a bit more complicated, given that Ringer was white. The federal hearing examiner in her case ruled that Ringer had been discriminated against because she had been an outspoken supporter of African Americans at the Copyright Office and the Library of Congress.[8]

In 1977, three years before she retired, Ringer was given the President's Award for Distinguished Federal Civilian Service, the highest honor for a federal worker.

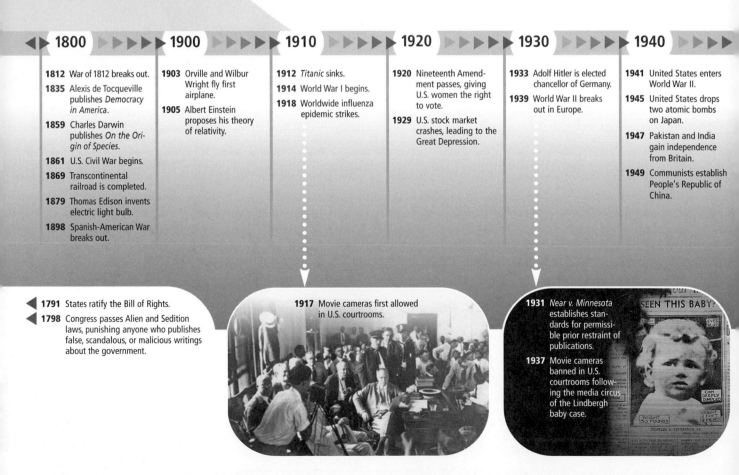

**1800**

**1812** War of 1812 breaks out.

**1835** Alexis de Tocqueville publishes *Democracy in America*.

**1859** Charles Darwin publishes *On the Origin of Species*.

**1861** U.S. Civil War begins.

**1869** Transcontinental railroad is completed.

**1879** Thomas Edison invents electric light bulb.

**1898** Spanish-American War breaks out.

**1900**

**1903** Orville and Wilbur Wright fly first airplane.

**1905** Albert Einstein proposes his theory of relativity.

**1910**

**1912** *Titanic* sinks.

**1914** World War I begins.

**1918** Worldwide influenza epidemic strikes.

**1920**

**1920** Nineteenth Amendment passes, giving U.S. women the right to vote.

**1929** U.S. stock market crashes, leading to the Great Depression.

**1930**

**1933** Adolf Hitler is elected chancellor of Germany.

**1939** World War II breaks out in Europe.

**1940**

**1941** United States enters World War II.

**1945** United States drops two atomic bombs on Japan.

**1947** Pakistan and India gain independence from Britain.

**1949** Communists establish People's Republic of China.

**1791** States ratify the Bill of Rights.

**1798** Congress passes Alien and Sedition laws, punishing anyone who publishes false, scandalous, or malicious writings about the government.

**1917** Movie cameras first allowed in U.S. courtrooms.

**1931** *Near v. Minnesota* establishes standards for permissible prior restraint of publications.

**1937** Movie cameras banned in U.S. courtrooms following the media circus of the Lindbergh baby case.

Ringer returned briefly to the Library of Congress to be the interim register of copyrights from 1993 to 1994. At the time, she recognized the enormous changes taking place with the rise of digital media and urged the Copyright Office to embrace digital records that could be accessed freely by all interested persons.[9]

Ringer retired at age fifty-five from the Copyright Office and joined a Washington, D.C., law firm. She also bought land in rural Virginia, where she built her home. During her retirement, she volunteered at her local library, cataloguing the new books that came in. Following an extended illness, Barbara Ringer died in 2009 at the age of 83.[10]

In this chapter we look at the laws that both protect and restrict the press. We start by examining the First Amendment to the U.S. Constitution, which established a minimally restrictive system of media law. We then look at media law in terms of how it protects individuals through laws governing libel, invasion of privacy, and the right to a fair trial. Next, we look at the controls that can be placed on the press, including requirements that the press tell the truth, restraints on publication, and regulation of obscenity. Finally, we look at how the broadcast industry is regulated by the government in a somewhat stronger fashion than the rest of the media.

---

## 1950 ▶▶▶▶ 1960 ▶▶▶▶ 1970 ▶▶▶▶ 1980 ▶▶▶▶ 1990 ▶▶▶▶ 2000 ▶▶▶▶

**1950** Korean War begins.

**1953** Francis Crick and James Watson discover structure of DNA.

**1957** Soviet Union launches spacecraft *Sputnik I.*

**1963** Martin Luther King Jr. delivers "I Have a Dream" speech during Washington, D.C., civil-rights march.

**1969** Neil Armstrong walks on the moon.

**1974** U.S. president Richard Nixon resigns due to Watergate scandal.

**1975** Vietnam War ends.

**1977** Apple II personal computer is introduced.

**1978** First test-tube baby is born.

**1983** First HIV/AIDS cases are documented.

**1985** Ozone hole is discovered over Antarctica.

**1986** Space shuttle *Challenger* explodes.

**1989** The Berlin Wall falls.

**1991** Soviet Union disbands.

**1993** European Union is formed.

**1994** Nelson Mandela is elected president of South Africa.

**1997** Diana, Princess of Wales, dies in car accident.

**2001** Al Qaida attacks World Trade Center and Pentagon.

**2003** United States invades Iraq.

**2003** Human genome project is completed.

**2005** Terrorists bomb London's transport system.

**2005** Hurricane Katrina hits the U.S. Gulf Coast.

**2008** Barack Obama is elected U.S. president.

---

**1957** *Roth v. the United States* establishes the standard for obscenity.

**1964** *New York Times v. Sullivan* establishes the standard for libel of public officials.

**1971** The Pentagon Papers case leads to first instance of prior restraint of a specific newspaper article; the Supreme Court later overturns the lower court's ban on publication.

**1994** Intense media attention during the O. J. Simpson murder trial highlights the conflict between the right to a free press and the right to a fair trial.

**1996** The Communications Decency Act attempts to prohibit pornography on the Internet; the Supreme Court strikes down most of its provisions.

**1998** The Digital Millennium Copyright Act expands protection of movies, music, and software.

**2001** Congress passes the USA Patriot Act, permitting domestic surveillance and wiretapping to combat terrorism.

**2005** *New York Times* reporter Judith Miller (pictured) is released from jail after 85 days and testifies to a grand jury investigating the leak of a CIA operative's identity.

**2006** Debate arises about whether bloggers deserve protection as journalists after blogger Josh Wolf is jailed.

# THE DEVELOPMENT OF A FREE PRESS

The First Amendment to the U.S. Constitution is at the core of all American laws concerning the media. It says simply, "Congress shall make no law respecting an establishment of religion, or prohibiting the free exercise thereof; or abridging the freedom of speech, or of the press; or the right of the people peaceably to assemble, and to petition the Government for a redress of grievances."

Although the First Amendment states that "Congress shall make no law," the U.S. Supreme Court has long upheld certain limits on both speech and the press. People do not have "the right to say anything they please, any way they please, anywhere or under any circumstances."[11] In this section we look at how the notion of freedom of expression and of the press has developed and what regulations and restrictions the government can place on that freedom.

## The First Amendment: "Congress Shall Make No Law"

According to First Amendment scholar Fred Cate, the First Amendment is an essential component of a representative democracy because a democracy cannot function unless the people have the right to freely and openly discuss matters of public concern. It is through free and open speech that change takes place within society. The First Amendment does not just protect popular or conventional ideas; it protects all forms of expression, including offensive ideas. Even some level of false expression is allowed because the truth is not always clear. Thus the solution to the expression of dangerous ideas is to permit more, rather than less, communication.[12]

The most basic right guaranteed by the First Amendment is freedom of speech without constraint by the government. The right of freedom of the press is an extension of the rights of individuals to express themselves.[13] In addition to its explicit mention of the press and speech, the First Amendment provides a wide range of rights, including freedom of religious practice, the right to assemble, and the right to petition the government.

## The Roots of American Free Speech

Speech was not always free in the American colonies. Colonial newspapers were published under licenses granted by the British colonial government, with the phrase "Published by Authority" printed at the top of each edition. This notice implied that the British government approved of what was being published, and editors violated that approval at their peril.

*The Zenger Case.*   John Peter Zenger and his wife, Anna Catherine Zenger, were independent editors, printers, and small-business owners in the American colonies. Zenger started his *New York Journal* in 1733, and like many editors of that time, was soon in trouble with the authorities. Zenger accused Gov. William Cosby of political corruption for replacing New York Supreme Court justices with whom he disagreed.[14] The governor retaliated by throwing Zenger in jail on a charge of seditious libel (writing things critical of the government). When the case went to trial in 1735, Zenger, who was represented by prominent lawyer Andrew Hamilton, defended himself against the charge by claiming that what he had written was the truth. The shocked judge argued that the truth of the statement didn't matter. But Zenger and Hamilton refused to back down, and the jury found Zenger not guilty, thus establishing truth as a defense against libel.

While her husband was in prison, Anna Catherine took over the operation of the paper, thus becoming one of the first women newspaper publishers in the country.[15]

*Limits on Free Speech.* In 1791 the states ratified the first ten amendments to the Constitution, commonly known as the Bill of Rights. But making the Bill of Rights a part of the Constitution did not end the government's efforts to limit people's right to freedom of expression.

In 1798, just seven years after the ratification of the Bill of Rights, Congress passed, and President John Adams signed, the **Alien and Sedition Acts**. These laws punished anyone who published "false, scandalous, or malicious writings against the government of the United States, or either house of the Congress of the United States, or the President of the United States" with substantial fines, jail time, or deportation. One editor went to prison for accusing Adams of corruption, and a second went to prison for supporting the critical editor. All those charged under the acts were eventually pardoned by Thomas Jefferson when he became president.[16]

Sedition became a crime once again during World War I, when more than 1,900 people were prosecuted under sedition statutes for criticizing the government, the military draft, or American involvement in the war. Following the war, some but not all of the anti–free speech provisions were repealed.[17] Again, in 1940, in the run-up to American involvement in World War II, Congress passed the Smith Act, which made it a crime to advocate the violent overthrow of the government or to belong to a group that advocated the violent overthrow of the

*The Bill of Rights, ratified in 1791, established protection for all forms of expression, not just popular ideas.*

**Alien and Sedition Acts**

Laws passed in 1798 that made it a crime to criticize the government of the United States.

government. The central purpose of the act was to suppress the Communist Party of the United States.[18]

## Limits on Free Speech in the Post-9/11 Era

Forty-five days after the September 11, 2001, terrorist attacks, Congress passed the USA Patriot Act, with a name that is an acronym standing for "Uniting and Strengthening America by Providing Appropriate Tools Required to Intercept and Obstruct Terrorism."[19] The Patriot Act follows in the tradition of previous wartime laws in changing the balance point between maximizing our civil liberties and protecting the United States from perceived threats. The act is one more example of Truth Four—Nothing's new: Everything that happened in the past will happen again.

The law permitted a host of activities by the Justice Department including wiretaps and increased domestic surveillance, as well as widening the definition of what constitutes terrorism. Most of the objections to the act fall under the Fourth Amendment to the U.S. Constitution, which protects against "unreasonable searches and seizures."[20] But there are First Amendment implications as well. One of the biggest is that Section 215 of the act allows the FBI to examine individuals' media use by obtaining "library records, health-care records, logs of Internet service providers and other documents and papers."[21]

Jameel Jaffer of the American Civil Liberties Union (ACLU) says that the fact that people may be watched can keep them from looking at things they might otherwise view: "If people think that the government is looking over their shoulders to see what books they are reading or what Web sites they are visiting, many are not going to read those books or visit those Web sites."[22] The law also makes it a crime for anyone to provide "expert assistance" to any group designated as being a terrorist organization, even if there is no evidence that the advice leads to further terrorism.

The Patriot Act may have been used to identify journalists' confidential sources. Brian Ross and Richard Esposito of ABC News wrote in their blog, The Blotter, that the federal government was tracking the phone numbers they called after they had reported on the CIA's secret prisons in Romania and Poland.[23] Ross charges that this tracking of his calls was done under Section 215 of the Patriot Act. "It's a provision of the Patriot Act designed to fight terrorism—and it's being used to fight journalists," Ross said. "That's what it really comes down to."[24]

Most controversial was the provision that those people served with Patriot Act warrants couldn't tell anyone that they had received them. That is, anyone served with a Patriot Act warrant lost his or her free speech rights when it came to discussing the warrant. Since the Patriot Act was originally passed in 2001, it has undergone changes that have scaled back the free speech limits. The most important of these changes is that people served with warrants under the act now have permission to consult an attorney.

A number of communities, along with the states of Alaska, Hawaii, Maine, Montana, and Vermont, have passed resolutions opposing the Patriot Act because it infringes on people's civil liberties. In a case in Stamford, Connecticut, librarians refused to cooperate with the warrants. Following an investigation, the FBI found that there had been no terrorist threat. One of the librarians told the Associated Press, "I'm glad that we're vindicated in resisting the request for the records. We're just protecting our patrons to the extent we can."[25]

You can read more about how libraries have been affected by and responded to the Patriot Act at http://ralphehanson.com.

# PROTECTION OF INDIVIDUALS

Although the press is censored only rarely in the United States, individuals do have a right to protect themselves from being harmed by the media. Rather than exercising prior restraint to prevent the press from printing or broadcasting potentially damaging material, U.S. law allows individuals to sue the press for any damage they feel they have suffered. Protection of individuals from the press focuses on three main issues: libel, invasion of privacy, and the right to a fair trial.

## Libel

Although in general the press cannot be restricted from publishing something, it can be held accountable for what it does publish. This is accomplished primarily through libel law. **Libel** is any published statement that unjustifiably exposes someone to ridicule or contempt. In general, for a statement to be libelous it needs to contain three elements: defamation, identification, and publication.

**libel**
A published statement that unjustifiably exposes someone to ridicule or contempt; for a statement to be libel, it must satisfy the three elements of defamation, identification, and publication.

1. Defamation—To defame is to damage a person's reputation in some way. This can involve calling someone, for example, a criminal, a communist, or a drunk. If a student newspaper ran an article falsely accusing Dr. Smith, a journalism professor, of selling a grade of A in his Introduction to Mass Communication class for $100, Dr. Smith would probably have been defamed.

2. Identification—No person can sue for libel unless the defamation can be proved to apply to him or her; another reader or viewer must agree that the comment applies to the person who is suing. Just leaving that person's name out of the article isn't enough. If a person can be identified, he or she can sue. Going back to the example of Dr. Smith, suppose that the

article did not mention his name but merely said that the teacher of the Introduction to Mass Communication course at Big State University was taking bribes for grades. If Dr. Smith was the only person teaching the course at Big State U, he would have been identified.

3. Publication—To be libelous, the statement must be published or broadcast and seen by someone other than the author and the person who was defamed.[26]

How can the media defend themselves against libel suits? After all, much of what gets printed or broadcast in the news has the potential to damage a person's reputation. There are at least two approaches. When an article is genuinely false and defamatory, the media look to a landmark 1960s case, *New York Times v. Sullivan*; this case is discussed later in this chapter. First, let's look at approaches that are used when the material in an article is true, privileged, or a statement of opinion.

*The Defense of Truth.*    The Zenger case from the early 1700s established truth as an absolute defense against libel. It is not always an effective defense, however, because the truth is not always clear. In the article about Dr. Smith, it may well be true that a student accused Dr. Smith of selling grades, but it would be much more difficult to prove that Dr. Smith actually sold the grades.

**privilege**
A legal defense against libel that holds that statements made in government meetings, in court, or in government documents cannot be used as the basis for a libel suit.

*The Defense of Privilege.*    Asserting privilege is a much better defense than truth in a libel case. As a legal defense against libel, **privilege** is the idea that statements made in government meetings, in court, or in government documents cannot be used as the basis for a libel suit. What is more, any fair and accurate report of what happened at the meeting, in court, or in a government document is also protected from libel.[27] For example, the privilege defense protects a reporter who is covering a murder trial. The journalist is privileged to give a fair and accurate report of any testimony, no matter how inflammatory, without fear of being sued.

*Opinions.*    Opinions are neither true nor false, so a statement of opinion cannot be used as the basis of a libel suit. Calling someone an idiot or a jerk would probably not be considered libelous; both words are expressions of opinion. Editorial cartoons, parodies, and reviews are all generally considered to be opinion and are given fairly broad latitude in their protection from libel. But remember that, to be protected, statements need to be clear expressions of opinion. An article that states "Dr. Smith, in my opinion, is selling grades" would most likely be considered libelous: Claiming that a fact is a statement of opinion does not protect the writer.

**New York Times v. Sullivan.**    The defenses of truth, privilege, and opinion arise from the notion that the press has published something it is entitled to publish. But there are times when the press gets a story wrong, runs an advertisement containing factual errors, or makes a mistake in a headline. In these cases the press is likely to look to the 1964 case of *New York Times v. Sullivan.*[28]

The 1960s was a period of racial unrest in the United States, with protests and rioting over efforts to integrate schools, lunch counters, and other public facilities. White segregationists claimed that the national media were interfering with local issues that were none of their business,[29] a prime example of Truth Six—Activism and analysis are not the same thing.

On March 29, 1960, a civil rights group ran a full-page ad in the *New York Times* to raise money for Dr. Martin Luther King Jr. The ad included the names of numerous well-known individuals such as Harry Belafonte, Marlon Brando, Nat King Cole, Jackie Robinson, and former first lady Eleanor Roosevelt, and was paid for by the Union Advertising Service for the Committee to Defend Martin Luther King and the Struggle for Freedom in the South.[30]

Among the sections of the ad that created trouble was the following:

> In Montgomery, Alabama, after students sang "My Country 'Tis of Thee" on the State Capitol steps, their leaders were expelled from the school, and truckloads of police armed with shotguns and teargas ringed the Alabama State College Campus. When the entire student body protested to state authorities by refusing to reregister, their dining hall was padlocked in an attempt to starve them into submission.[31]

This passage contained several false statements. The students did not sing "My Country 'Tis of Thee," and the police did not literally surround the building.

Although Montgomery police commissioner L. B. Sullivan, who was in charge of the police department, was not mentioned by name in the advertisement, he felt that any accusations against the police department were accusations against him. He also charged that the advertisement contained numerous factual errors. He asked the *Times* to retract the ad, but the paper responded that it did not see how the ad reflected negatively on Sullivan's reputation. So Sullivan filed suit, joining eleven other libel cases that were pending against the *Times.*[32]

In the initial three-day trial, the *Times* admitted that the ad contained errors, but friends of Sullivan testified that they did not think less of him as a result because they did not believe what they had read in the ad. Nevertheless, the judge instructed the jury that they could presume that the material in the ad was libelous and that it had damaged Sullivan's reputation. The jury returned a verdict in favor of Sullivan, awarding him $500,000 in damages. The verdict was upheld by the Alabama Supreme Court.

The case then went before the U.S. Supreme Court, which reversed the lower courts with a sweeping ruling in favor of the *Times.* The Court could have overturned the lower court judgment simply by ruling that Sullivan had not been identified in the ad or by saying that Sullivan's reputation had not suffered any damage. But it decided instead to use the case to consider whether the public had the right to criticize the government.[33] The Court ruled that it was not enough to protect true statements; false statements against public officials made in good faith should also be protected.

With the *Sullivan* case the Court established a new standard for libel. It ruled that public officials would have to show that the media had acted with **actual malice**, and displayed a reckless disregard for the truth or falsity of a published account. In the *Sullivan* case, the Court ruled, the paper had not acted with malice; at worst it had been negligent. One of the goals of the Court's judgment was to help protect against self-censorship—to prevent publications from being so afraid of making a mistake that they would not print anything that might be controversial. The Court was attempting to balance the right of a public official to protect his or her reputation versus a critic's right to speak out against that official.

*Libel and Public Figures.*   In 1967 the Supreme Court extended the actual malice standard to apply to public figures as well as public officials. The theory behind this extension of the *Sullivan* standard was that these people have voluntarily exposed themselves to public scrutiny and thus to the threat of being libeled.

The standard was settled by the case of *Gertz v. Robert Welch, Inc.*, in 1974.[34] The John Birch Society's magazine had run an article accusing Elmer Gertz of being a communist. The question was whether Gertz, an attorney, was a public figure. The Court ruled that private individuals deserve more protection because they have not voluntarily submitted themselves for public attention and because they are less able than public figures to defend themselves.[35]

## Invasion of Privacy

What magazines do you subscribe to? What books do you check out from the library? How much money do you have in the bank? What movies have you rented from the video store? What do you buy at the grocery store? Why did you see the doctor last week? Are you uncomfortable with these questions? Most people would like to keep such information private.[36]

With all this information potentially available, what legal expectation do people have of maintaining a private life in the information age? The Constitution offers no explicit protection of privacy, but a right to privacy has been implied and the issue shows up in a number of ways. The "freedom to associate" clause of the First Amendment prevents the government from requiring a group to release its membership list to the public. It also protects the right of an individual to possess any type of literature in the privacy of his or her own home. The Fourth Amendment limits searches and seizures, and the Fourteenth Amendment limits disclosure of personal information. In cases involving privacy, the courts try to balance an individual's right to protect his or her privacy and reputation versus the public's interest in a news or feature story that the press might publish.

**actual malice**
A reckless disregard for the truth or falsity of a published account; this became the standard for libel plaintiffs who were public figures or public officials after the Supreme Court's decision in *New York Times v. Sullivan*.

In general, there are four types of legal protection against invasion of privacy: intrusion, embarrassment, false light, and misappropriation. Let's look briefly at each of these.[37]

*Intrusion.*    **Intrusion** is invasion of privacy by physical trespass into a space surrounding a person's body or onto property under his or her control. Reporters and photographers are not allowed to go onto private property to collect news without the permission of the owner, but in some cases, the news-gathering function and the right of the public to know can conflict with the rights associated with private property. For example, a reporter and a photographer were sued for intrusion when they pretended to be patients at a private California medical clinic that was being run by a plumber practicing medicine without a license. Their visit to the clinic was ruled to be trespass, but the story won numerous prizes and resulted in the clinic's being shut down.[38]

The courts have generally held that undercover reporting is legal, if not necessarily ethical, as long as it does not involve trespass. (For more about intrusion, see the section on *Food Lion v. ABC* later in this chapter.)

> **intrusion**
> Invasion of privacy by physical trespass into a space surrounding a person's body or onto property under his or her control.

*Embarrassment.*    Sometimes reporters come across true information that is so embarrassing and private that a person has reason to expect that it will not be published, especially if he or she is not well known. In general, embarrassment cases are difficult to win. If the information is true, it will often be considered newsworthy, which is the press's strongest defense in privacy cases.

One of the best-known embarrassment cases arose in 1975, when Oliver "Bill" Sipple, a former U.S. Marine, helped save President Gerald R. Ford by knocking aside Sara Jane Moore's gun as she attempted to shoot the president. Two days later a columnist for the *San Francisco Chronicle* implied that Sipple was gay. Sipple sued the *Chronicle* for giving unwanted publicity to that information. The court ruled against Sipple, however, because he had been written about in gay magazines and had marched in gay pride parades. The court also ruled that the information about Sipple was legitimate news.

So when is something that is private not newsworthy? On October 13, 1961, an Alabama woman went to a fun house at the local county fair. As she came out, an air jet blew her skirt up, exposing her underwear, and

*In 1975, Oliver "Bill" Sipple (left) helped save President Gerald R. Ford by foiling an assassination attempt by Sarah Jane Moore (see arrow). After the San Francisco* Chronicle *revealed Sipple was gay, he sued the paper, but the courts ruled that information about Sipple was newsworthy and, therefore, not an invasion of his privacy.*

a photographer from the local newspaper took her picture. The woman was recognized by friends and relatives, who teased her about the picture. She called the paper at least twice but found no sympathy. The paper's editor says that had he apologized at that point, the case would have likely ended. But he didn't, and the woman sued and won.[39] What distinguishes this case from the Sipple case? Sipple had just saved the president's life and hence was a part of the news. In the Alabama case, however, the woman had done nothing to make herself newsworthy.

*False Light.*    **False light** is similar to libel, and people who file libel suits often simultaneously file false light suits. False light doesn't really seem to be an invasion of privacy, but that's how the law treats it.[40] False light occurs when a journalist publishes untrue statements that alter an individual's public image in a way that he or she cannot control. The *Cleveland Plain Dealer* lost a false light suit when reporter Joe Eszterhas (who went on to fame for writing the screenplay for the movie *Basic Instinct*) described a poverty-stricken widow whose husband had been killed in a bridge collapse several months earlier in West Virginia—even though he had neither met nor spoken with the woman. He wrote:

> Margaret Cantrell will talk neither about what happened nor about how they are doing. She wears the same mask of non-expression she wore at the funeral. She is a proud woman. Her world has changed. She says that after it happened, the people in town offered to help them out with money and they refused to take it.[41]

Regardless of whether the woman's reputation was damaged, the portrayal was clearly false because Eszterhas had never been in contact with her.

False light often arises more from context than from a deliberate attempt to deceive. For example, a television story about street prostitution might show men and women walking down the street, with the implication that the women are prostitutes and the men are their customers. ABC television settled multiple lawsuits over just such a story (though without admitting guilt).

*Misappropriation.*    The final form of invasion of privacy is quite different from the preceding three. **Misappropriation** is using a person's name or image for commercial purposes without his or her permission. The right to control the commercial use of their name and image is of great importance to athletes and celebrities, who may make more money from endorsements than they do from competing or acting. For example, in 1997 basketball legend Michael Jordan earned $31.3 million in pay from the Chicago Bulls and over $40 million from endorsements.[42] Clearly it is in Jordan's economic and financial interest to control the use of his name and image.

What of the paparazzi armed with telephoto lenses who make a business out of stalking celebrities? Television and movie star Jennifer Aniston has filed

**false light**
Invasion of privacy in which a journalist publishes untrue statements that alter a person's public image in a way that he or she cannot control.

**misappropriation**
Invasion of privacy by using a person's name or image for commercial purposes without his or her permission.

numerous invasion-of-privacy lawsuits to stop distribution or publication of topless photos that had been taken of her. It is not clear how a court would rule on her cases, as most of them have been settled out of court. Aniston has used a range of legal strategies in her cases, including copyright infringement, intrusion, and misappropriation.[43] She apparently did not have a problem with her officially sanctioned topless photo that ran on the cover of *GQ* magazine in 2005, at the same time as one of her lawsuits.[44] In 2009 California governor Arnold Schwarzenegger signed a bill into law that would allow lawsuits against media outlets that publish photos that were shot illegally. In general, freelance photographers can be sued for violating privacy laws, but the publications that buy their photos have been shielded from liability. Free-speech advocates argue that California's new law could interfere with legitimate news gathering. Legal experts have questioned whether California's law is enforceable because it can be difficult to prove when and where a photo was taken.[45]

*Privacy Law in Europe.* When Britain's beloved Princess Diana died in a car crash on August 30, 1997, the entire world mourned, and many people in Europe and the United States blamed the accident on overly aggressive photographers chasing the car in which she was riding. Although evidence soon came to light that Diana's driver had been drunk at the time, the high-speed chase through the streets of Paris brought the privacy rights of the rich and famous to the forefront of the public's attention.[46]

France has relatively strict privacy laws that "each individual has the right to require respect for his private life. . . . Privacy revolves around the secrecy of one's intimate life and the right to oppose investigation and revelation of this domain."[47] This protects against coverage of a person's family life, sexual activity and orientation, illness, and private leisure activities. The person suing does not need to show that he or she has been damaged; the law presumes that invasion of privacy, by its very nature, is damaging.

Despite the strength of the restrictions, the penalties for violating the laws are relatively mild.[48] Most fines are under $50,000, and the French press view them largely as a cost of doing business. Although the law also allows the courts to confiscate the publications containing the offending photographs, in practice the courts almost never do so.[49]

Whereas France has relatively strict laws, until recently British law did not recognize an individual's right to privacy. For example, in 1987 British actor Gordon Kaye suffered a serious head injury in an accident. Kaye was subsequently interviewed while he was semiconscious and recovering from brain surgery. The British courts ruled that the only thing legally wrong with the article was that it implied that the actor had consented to the interview. Thus the article was published without penalty.[50]

In 2000, the British Parliament passed the Human Rights Act, which requires the press to observe a "proper balance" between privacy and publicity.[51] It is too soon to tell exactly how the vague standard set out in this new law will be

*Paparazzi, such as these in Milan, are independent photographers who shoot pictures of celebrities and public figures, often in embarrassing situations.*

applied. So far, actors Michael Douglas and Catherine Zeta-Jones have sued under the act to prevent a magazine from running photos of their wedding. (The celebrity couple had sold exclusive rights to the wedding pictures to a competing publication for a reported £1 million.) The British courts finally ruled seven years later that Douglas and Zeta-Jones had the right to sell photo access exclusively to a single publication.[52] Model Naomi Campbell won her case against the *Mirror* tabloid for running a picture of her leaving a Narcotics Anonymous meeting, while singer Elton John lost a case claiming a newspaper photo taken on the street made him look bald.[53] How much protection the law will provide and what balance it will strike between the rights of the press and the rights of individuals remain to be seen, however.

At the other end of the spectrum, neither Spain nor Germany has laws governing the actions of the press regarding the private lives of public officials and celebrities. Italy, which gave the world the word *paparazzi*, has limited privacy laws, but they are not enforced with significant penalties.[54]

## Free Press/Fair Trial

The right to a free press often conflicts with the right to a fair trial. The Sixth Amendment to the U.S. Constitution guarantees accused individuals the right to be tried by an impartial jury, and the Fourteenth Amendment requires that criminal defendants be tried fairly before an unprejudiced jury. Supreme Court justice Hugo Black wrote, "Free speech and fair trials are two of the most cherished policies of our civilization, and it would be a trying task to choose between them."[55]

Over the years there have been repeated charges that pretrial publicity interferes with the ability to select an impartial jury and that media coverage turns trials into circuses. These complaints became particularly loud during O. J. Simpson's 1994 murder trial, which attracted an inordinate amount of media attention. Media scholar Matthew D. Bunker argues that the conflict between a free press and a fair trial does not require that one right be sacrificed for another. Instead, he suggests that creative decisions by judges can lead to fair trials and open media coverage at the same time.[56] The general rule is that the First Amendment must be upheld unless there is a compelling state interest in regulating the speech. If speech is regulated, it must be done in the least restrictive way possible. The reasoning is that there should be no official version of the truth. Instead, people should be able to put forward contrasting ideas that compete for attention.

*The Case of Dr. Sam Sheppard.*   One of the most spectacular collisions between the right to a free press and the right to a fair trial involved the murder trial of Dr. Sam Sheppard. The case, later fictionalized in the television series and movie *The Fugitive*, involved the murder of Sheppard's wife, Marilyn, who was found beaten to death in their home in 1954. In his defense, Sheppard, a prominent Cleveland doctor, claimed to have been awakened by his wife's screams and to have fought with his wife's attacker, who left him unconscious.

Sheppard's story did not convince the police, and he soon became the leading suspect in his wife's murder. Reporters found out that Sheppard had been having an affair with a woman named Susan Hayes. A newspaper headline demanded "Why Isn't Sam Sheppard in Jail?" As the trial began, the Cleveland newspapers printed the names and addresses of prospective jurors, along with their pictures. Jurors were also allowed to view the media during the trial, despite a "suggestion" by the judge that they avoid doing so.

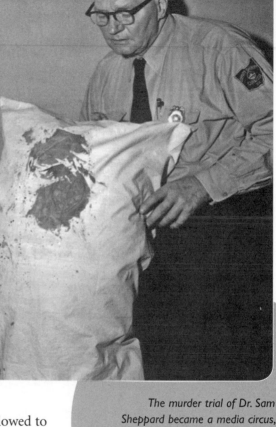

*The murder trial of Dr. Sam Sheppard became a media circus, with jurors seeing prejudicial stories and photos in the news such as this one of the coroner holding up the blood-stained pillow found on Marilyn Sheppard's bed.*

Sheppard was convicted of murder, but his conviction was overturned by the Supreme Court and he was given a new trial. This time he was acquitted. The Supreme Court, in *Sheppard v. Maxwell*,[57] said that the "carnival atmosphere" surrounding Sheppard's trial had denied him due process. But the Court also noted that it was the judge's responsibility to make sure the defendant received a fair trial. If stopping coverage of the trial was not an option, what could the courts do to avoid this problem? The Supreme Court suggested a number of possibilities:[58]

- Put a gag order on participants in the trial to keep them from talking to the press in the first place. (But the press would be free to report on anything that happened in the courtroom itself.)

- Sequester the jury.

- Postpone the trial until the publicity dies down.

- Change the venue for the trial.

- Order a new trial.

**United States v. Noriega.**   Can the press ever be stopped from printing information about a court case? In general, the Supreme Court has held that it is the government's job, not the job of the press, to protect a defendant's right to a fair trial. The only major case in which the press has been restricted from covering a court case occurred in the fall of 1990 in *United States v. Noriega.*[59] In this case the court issued a temporary restraining order against CNN to prevent the network from broadcasting tapes of former Panamanian leader Manuel Noriega talking with his lawyers. The judge felt that broadcasting the tapes would unduly benefit the government in designing its strategy for prosecuting the former leader on drug charges. Nevertheless, CNN did broadcast one of the conversations. The restraining order was lifted eventually, but CNN was found guilty of contempt of court for broadcasting the original tape.[60]

*Cameras in the Courtroom.*   While there is no question that reporters and the public are entitled to view trials, there has been considerable debate over whether television and other cameras ought to be allowed in the courtroom.

The central argument in favor of allowing cameras is that the right to an open trial belongs to the public, not to the participants in the trial. Steven Brill, founder of the cable network Court TV, argues that television coverage of trials

> offer[s] the public the chance to see the legal system at work and to judge with their own eyes whether it has performed properly. They can heighten public understanding of the system, counter rumors and speculation, and provide important insurance against abuses of defendants' rights.[61]

Movie cameras were first allowed in courtrooms in 1917. But in 1935, when Bruno Richard Hauptmann was on trial for the kidnapping and murder of aviator Charles Lindbergh's baby, the trial became a media circus. As a result, in 1937 a general ban was placed on movie and still photography in courtrooms. The fraud trial of the flamboyant Texas financier Billie Sol Estes in 1965 led to a Supreme Court decision that the time had not yet come for cameras to be allowed in the courtroom. But the Court went on to say that this might change when cameras became smaller and less intrusive.

In the 1970s and 1980s, electronic technology led to small, remote-controlled cameras. In 1977 the Florida Supreme Court started experimenting with allowing televised coverage of state court proceedings; by 1981 twenty-nine states had laws allowing partial television access.[62] By 1999 the vast majority of states had begun to allow cameras in their courtrooms under certain circumstances, although the judge generally retained the discretion to control when they can be used. Most states limit coverage of jurors, and many allow witnesses to refuse to be shown on television.[63]

# CONTROLLING THE PRESS

Despite the First Amendment, Congress has repeatedly placed restrictions on speech and the press. These restrictions include bans on false advertising, libel, perjury, obscenity, troop movements during time of war, and solicitation of murder.[64] This section looks at some of these limits in detail as illustrations of Truth Four—Nothing's new: Everything that happened in the past will happen again.

## Honesty and the Press

The law clearly states that the press can be held responsible for printing material that is libelous or invades a person's privacy, but can it require that the press behave ethically? Journalists certainly should behave ethically, but can the law require them to keep a promise or tell the truth? This question has been tested in a number of cases.

### Cohen v. Cowles Media.

In 1982 Republican Wheelock Whitney was running for governor of Minnesota. With just one week to go before the election, the campaign discovered that the Democratic candidate for lieutenant governor had been arrested and convicted of a minor theft eleven years earlier. What could the campaign managers have done with this information? Simply revealing it to the public would have made them look as if they were engaging in a smear campaign. Instead, they hired local public relations practitioner Dan Cohen to leak the information to the press. Cohen spoke to a series of reporters, offering them a deal:

> I have some documents which may or may not relate to a candidate in the upcoming election, and if you will give me a promise of confidentiality—that is, that I will be treated as an anonymous source, that my name will not appear in any material in connection with this, and you will also agree that you're not going to pursue with me a question of who my source is—then I'll furnish you with the documents.[65]

Four reporters from the Minneapolis/St. Paul media agreed to Cohen's terms, and all received copies of the court documents. But once they had the documents, the media responded in three different ways. Television station WCCO decided not to run a story at all. The Associated Press distributed a brief story outlining the charges against the candidate that did not identify Cohen as the source of the story. But against the wishes of their reporters, both the *Star Tribune* and the *Pioneer Press*, the Twin Cities' leading newspapers, ran stories that identified Cohen as the source of the story. In the end, the Democratic candidates won handily and the information about the lieutenant governor seemed to have no effect on the election. There was, however, fallout for Cohen: He was immediately fired by his employer, who did not want to risk offending the new administration that Cohen had helped attack.

Cohen then sued the newspapers. He argued that the newspapers had entered into a verbal contract with him, exchanging a promise of confidentiality in return for the information he provided. The newspapers argued that they had done nothing wrong by printing Cohen's name. Instead, they had simply printed a true and accurate story about dirty tricks during a political campaign. Although the papers clearly broke an agreement with Cohen, they said that they were entitled to do so because they were printing the truth, which was protected by the First Amendment.

The trial court found in favor of Cohen and awarded him $200,000 in damages for being fired, as well as punitive damages of $500,000. The state court of appeals, however, struck down the punitive damages. When the case reached the U.S. Supreme Court, the justices ruled by a five-to-four vote that the First Amendment did not excuse the media from having to live up to the contracts into which they entered.[66]

Controversy over the verdict arose within the press. Although it was the source who sued the press, the conflict lay primarily between editors and reporters. Could editors overrule promises made by reporters? The local reporters' union started urging reporters not to reveal their confidential sources to their editors unless the sources agreed to it. The newspaper publishers argued that the courts ought not to make judgments about journalistic ethics.

### Food Lion v. ABC.

At times, the courts have not punished the press for deceptive behavior. In 1992 the ABC television newsmagazine *Prime Time Live* sent undercover reporters Lynn Dale and Susan Barnett to apply for jobs as food handlers at a Food Lion grocery store. The network had been tipped off by disgruntled union officials that the store had been cleaning, bleaching, and repackaging beef, chicken, and fish that had passed its freshness date. The reporters (who did not reveal their true occupation) wore hidden microphones and cameras to document the store's misconduct. When the story ran, ABC charged that Food Lion had mixed old hamburger with new, sold improperly packaged chicken, and engaged in other unsanitary practices.[67]

Food Lion sued ABC, but not for libel as might be expected. Instead, it sued the network and producers for résumé fraud and trespass. Although the story was substantially true, Food Lion was trying to punish ABC for its aggressive—some would say unethical—reporting techniques. In the initial trial, Food Lion won its case and was awarded $5.5 million in damages. But the judge reduced the award to $316,402, saying that $5.5 million was excessive for lying on a job application and entering a closed area of the store.

The U.S. Court of Appeals, Fourth Circuit, reduced the damages to a symbolic $2—$1 for trespass and $1 for breach of loyalty (not serving their employer properly).[68] The court made it clear that this was not really a résumé fraud or trespass case but a libel suit in disguise (in which truth would be an absolute defense). Food Lion argued that the broadcast had damaged its reputation and that it deserved compensation, but the court held that the reporters' only offense was lying on their résumés. The judgment, although technically ruling against ABC with the award of symbolic damages, preserved the right of journalists to report truthful information.

## Prior Restraint

The most extreme and least accepted form of control of the press in the United States is **prior restraint**, a judicial order that stops a media organization from publishing a story or image. In the American colonies, prior restraint was the rule rather than the exception. All newspapers were published by the approval of the crown; if they did not have that permission, they could not publish. But since the ratification of the First Amendment, in only a handful of cases have stories been barred from being published or broadcast.

**prior restraint**
A judicial order that stops a media organization from publishing or broadcasting a story or image.

**Near v. Minnesota.**   The landmark case on prior restraint is the 1931 case of *Near v. Minnesota.* Jay Near was the publisher of the *Saturday Press,* a racist, anti-Semitic newspaper. Among other things, Near used his paper to charge that the police were controlled by a "Jewish gangster" and therefore were not going after gamblers and bootleggers. A Minnesota court stopped publication of the paper, using a state law allowing prosecutors to suppress publications that were "malicious, scandalous, and defamatory."

On appeal, the U.S. Supreme Court ruled that the government did not have the right to suppress an entire publication merely because it was offensive. Instead, the Court said that the government could engage in prior restraint only to suppress military information during time of war, incitement to overthrow the government, or obscenity. Since none of Near's material fell into those categories, he could not be restrained from publishing it. The case established a major precedent: Although obscenity and publication of military secrets were not protected by the First Amendment, virtually everything else, no matter how offensive, was.[69]

**The Pentagon Papers.**   The second major case of prior restraint arose in 1971, when the federal government tried to suppress newspaper stories about a top-secret forty-seven-volume report with the irresistible title *History of U.S. Decision-Making Process on Vietnam Policy.* The report, which came to be known as the Pentagon Papers, contained extensive background information about how America had become involved in the Vietnam War, going as far back as the Truman administration's assistance to France in its colonial war in Indochina. Along with this lengthy commentary were copies of the original documents on which the report was based.[70]

Among the authors of the report was Daniel Ellsberg, a former U.S. Marine who worked for the Rand Corporation think tank. Although he made only minor contributions to the massive report, he was one of the few familiar with its entire contents. Ellsberg became convinced that if the report was publicized, the public outcry would bring the war to a quicker end. So he started leaking copies of the papers to members of Congress and a few academics. Finally, in March 1971, he gave *New York Times* reporter Neil Sheehan nearly 7,000 pages from the report, withholding only the four "diplomatic" volumes, which he thought should be kept confidential.

Sheehan headed a team of reporters from the *New York Times* that read and verified what was in the papers. There was considerable debate at the *Times* about the ethics of publishing the papers.

On June 13, 1971, after three months of work, the *New York Times* started publishing stories about the Pentagon Papers. On June 14 President Richard Nixon's attorney general asked the paper to stop publishing the information, but it politely declined to do so. On June 15 the third installment of the series was published and the Justice Department obtained a restraining order against the *Times* to prevent it from publishing any additional stories. It was, as journalist Sanford Ungar put it, "the first time in the nation's history that a newspaper was restrained in advance by a court from publishing a specific article."[71]

Ellsberg started looking for another news organization to cover the story. All three of the major broadcast networks turned him down, but the staff of the *Washington Post* was eager to obtain a copy of the papers. Lawyers for the *Post* cautioned the paper not to run the stories because the *Times* had already received a court order not to publish. But to *Washington Post* managing editor Ben Bradlee, not publishing was unthinkable—a violation of what journalism was all about: "Not publishing the information when we had it would be like not saving a drowning man, or not telling the truth."[72] So on Friday, June 18, the *Post* published its first Pentagon Papers story, and on June 19 the government obtained a restraining order against the *Post*.

At this point the documents and stories were spreading across the country. Although approximately twenty newspapers published articles based on the Pentagon Papers, only four were taken to court: the *New York Times*, the *Post*, the *Boston Globe*, and the *St. Louis Post-Dispatch*.[73]

The U.S. Supreme Court heard arguments on the restraining orders on Saturday, June 26, and voted six to three to allow the newspapers to resume publishing their stories. Justice Potter Stewart raised the central issue in the case: Did the publication of the Pentagon Papers pose "such a grave and immediate danger as to justify prior restraint?" Stewart said that it did not: "The only effective restraint upon executive policy and power . . . may lie in an informed and enlightened citizenry—in an informed and critical public opinion which alone can here protect the values of democratic government."[74]

Justice William O. Douglas wrote that one of the primary goals of the First Amendment is to stop the government from covering up embarrassing information. In fact, the reason the First Amendment was ratified in the first place was to put a stop to random charges of seditious libel against people who were exposing embarrassing information about the government. The court pointed out that the government had been engaging in activism, not analysis, when it sought to control the release of the Pentagon Papers, in other words, an illustration of Truth Six.

Now, nearly forty years later, the lessons of *New York Times Co. v. United States*[75] (informally known as the Pentagon Papers case) are still relevant. While the Pentagon Papers were classified "top secret," the secrets they contained were embarrassing political secrets, not dangerous military secrets.[76] In 1989 Erwin Griswold, who had argued the government's case before the Supreme Court, said that he had "never seen any trace of a threat to the national security" from publication of the papers.[77]

But what about Daniel Ellsberg, the man who leaked copies of the Pentagon Papers to the press? The legality of Ellsberg's releasing the documents was never really resolved. Ellsberg was indicted on charges of conspiracy, misappropriation of government property, and violating the Espionage Act. But the court eventually declared a mistrial and dismissed the charges against him after it was revealed that the Nixon administration had Ellsberg's psychiatrist's office burglarized and made illegal recordings of the sessions there. In recent years, Ellsberg has spoken out against the Persian Gulf War and before the invasion of Iraq.[78]

*Daniel Ellsberg (left) was cleared of espionage charges for leaking copies of a top-secret Pentagon report to the press after it was revealed that the Nixon administration had authorized a break-in of Ellsberg's psychiatrist's office.*

*The Progressive Case.* In the Pentagon Papers case, the newspapers were desperately trying to publish their articles. But eight years later author Howard Morland and the *Progressive* magazine *wanted* to have an article censored. Morland was an Air Force pilot turned antinuclear activist who maintained that the government was concealing details about how hydrogen bombs operate—not for security reasons but to stifle public opposition to the weapon. Morland used unclassified documents and interviews with scientists to write an article explaining how these weapons of mass destruction worked. Morland and the *Progressive* knew that censorship would transform the article from an obscure piece in a radical magazine into a cause célèbre that would receive nationwide publicity.

They got their wish. A former professor of Morland's submitted an early draft of the article to the U.S. Department of Energy (DOE), which manages nuclear material in the United States. In addition, the magazine's editor sent the article and drawings to the DOE to have them checked for accuracy. On March 1, 1979, a district court judge in Wisconsin issued a temporary restraining order against the *Progressive* because the article presented a "clear and present danger" to the United States.

It initially appeared that the government might have a good case against Morland and the *Progressive*. The *Near* case (discussed earlier in this chapter) had established that the government could censor a publication that published "the sailing dates of transports or the number and location of troops." Although the types of information involved in national security had changed since *Near*, the same argument might be made—that the article would compromise national security by giving away military secrets. (It should be noted that although the article explained how a hydrogen bomb worked, it did not provide instructions for building one.)

Central to the *Progressive*'s defense was the argument that there were no secrets in the article because all the material it contained was available from nonclassified sources. The government argued that Morland's organization of the material into an article made it a security problem.[79] While the *Progressive* case was under appeal, a number of people started working on similar articles. *Milwaukee Sentinel* reporter Joe Manning re-created Morland's research and published a two-part story that covered the three "secrets" from Morland's article in fairly simple terms. Then nuclear hobbyist Charles Hansen wrote an eighteen-page letter to the editor of the *Madison Press-Connection* that outlined much the same information as Morland's article. On September 17, 1979, the day after the Hansen letter appeared, the government dropped its case, declaring that its attempt to suppress the information was "meaningless, superfluous, unnecessary, inconsequent."[80]

The *Progressive* finally ran Morland's article in November 1979 under the headline "The H-Bomb Secret: How We Got It, Why We're Telling It," but it was a somewhat hollow victory for the magazine.[81] Its editors had gotten the attention they sought, but unfortunately for them everyone saw the case as a freedom-of-the-press issue—not the important debate over nuclear weapons they were hoping for.

The Pentagon Papers and *Progressive* cases have two important implications. The first is that much information that the government would like to believe is secret is actually public knowledge. The second is that in a free and open society it is very difficult to keep secret information that determined people want to make public. And with the addition of the Internet to the range of available media, virtually anyone is able to publish any information widely and easily. Although it is still possible to punish individuals and media corporations after the fact for publishing or broadcasting inappropriate material, prior restraint is becoming virtually impossible in the United States and the Western democracies.

## Free Speech and Students

Do the rights that protect adult journalists also protect student reporters working on high school newspapers? According to the U.S. Supreme Court, the answer is no. In 1988 a group of high school students in Hazelwood, Missouri, sued the school system because their principal had barred articles about

## TEST YOUR MEDIA LITERACY

### Free Speech and Students

Back in 2002–2003, Houston, Texas, high school student newspaper editor Tina Macias found that her high school principal was censoring her student-run newspaper. She had tried to run an article in the paper about a gay-straight alliance (GSA), but the principal suppressed the story to prevent "division in the classroom."[1] In an essay she wrote for the PBS *NewsHour* Web site, she talked about what it was like working at a paper subject to prior review:

> While on staff I have seen countless stories censored. Curfews, street racing, dress code, bathroom use, and a story with quotes "demeaning" student trainers are among the credible stories censored. It outrages the staff every time stories are pulled by the administration. Issue after issue we watch other schools run fascinating controversial articles while we dish out stories about how great our academic team is.
>
> Mandatory by our district, every article the staff writes must be read and approved by an administrator. If a story runs without being checked by our liaison, the reporter must undergo detention. Along with our articles, school organization and events T-shirts must be approved by an administrator, as well as flyers and posters that are posted on school walls. What are the administrators protecting their students from? That question still baffles the newspaper staff. Our prior review policy will always sicken me. Why can't they allow a flow of information and trust the journalism students and sponsors to make decisions on what's newsworthy?
>
> . . . [N]ot until a quote from me and a Student Press Law Center (SPLC) lawyer about the censorship of the story ran in the *Houston Chronicle* was I allowed to run the article. . . .
>
> Students received the story well, but it didn't matter. They already knew. Newspapers—even amateur school newspapers—are meant to inform while stories are time worthy, not after the fact. Students read about the GSA issue in the *Houston Chronicle* or saw it on TV. Why did they have to watch a middle-aged news anchor mispronounce students' names instead of hearing it through the school's information source?

### MORE online

You can find the complete text of Tina Macias's article at **http://ralphehanson .com**. (In case you were wondering, Ms. Macias went on to be a journalism major in college.) After you've read the article, answer the questions below.

• • • • • • • • • • • • • • • • • •

**Who is the source?**
Who is Tina Macias? Where is she from?

**What is she saying?**
What story did she want to run? What did she do to get the story published? Why did she think it important that the story run in the student paper?

**What evidence is there?**
What did the school administrators do about her story? What reasons did they give for the prior review process?

pregnancy and divorce from the student newspaper. The Supreme Court in *Hazelwood v. Kuhlmeier*[82] ruled that a principal could censor a student newspaper when it was produced as part of a class. It wrote, "The First Amendment rights of students in the public schools are not automatically co-extensive with the rights of adults in other settings. . . . A school need not tolerate student speech that is inconsistent with its 'basic educational mission,' even though the government could not censor similar speech outside the school."[83] The Court ruled that the student newspaper is a classroom exercise rather than a vehicle for free speech, and hence administrators may censor any content that is "reasonably related to legitimate pedagogical concerns."[84]

One way students have reacted against this censorship is by starting Web-based newspapers that are not sponsored by the school. In addition, at least six states have passed laws that restore to high school students the rights they had prior to the *Hazelwood* decision. These laws limit the circumstances under which student newspapers can be censored, generally only if they are "libelous, obscene or will create a substantial disruption of school activities."[85]

There have also been several cases that deal with schools trying to limit the free speech of students in other venues. Some schools have attempted to limit what students can post to either blogs or social networking sites such as Facebook and MySpace. Three middle-school students in the Chicago area were suspended after they posted "obscene and threatening" comments about a teacher in their blog. Schools in the Washington, D.C., area have banned students from using their school-provided e-mail accounts to register with Facebook.[86]

Student Joseph Frederick was suspended from a Juneau, Alaska, high school in 2002 by the principal, Deborah Morse, for holding up a giant sign saying "BONG HiTS 4 JESUS" across the street from his high school as the Olympic torch passed through his town.[87] The school district in the case claims that the student was promoting drug use. The student responded, "I wasn't trying to say anything about drugs. I was just trying to say something. I wanted to use my right to free speech, and I did it." The case, known as *Morse v. Frederick*, was heard by the U.S. Supreme Court in 2007, which ruled on June 25, 2007, that principals could punish speech that could "reasonably be viewed" as promoting the use of illegal drugs.[88]

Interestingly enough, the student received support from the ACLU, gay rights advocates, and the Christian Legal Society (CLS). (The CLS and gay rights groups were concerned that other school districts might use the case as a way of limiting speech about religious or gay rights issues.) You can read more about this case at http://ralphehanson.com.

Many students may not be aware that their rights are being limited or what their rights entail. A survey of more than 100,000 high-school-aged students found that three-fourths of them believed incorrectly that flag burning was a crime. The survey also found that 36 percent of students said newspapers should get government permission before publishing stories and that 32 percent said the press has "too much freedom to do what it wants."[89]

*Student Joseph Frederick was suspended from high school in 2002 for displaying a sign reading "Bong Hits 4 Jesus" across the street from the school when the Olympic torch came through his town of Juneau, Alaska. The U.S. Supreme Court supported his suspension in a five-to-four ruling.*

## Journalists Going to Jail

Many states have **shield laws** protecting journalists from having to testify in court (and divulge sources) under certain circumstances, but there is currently no federal shield law in place. Many journalists are lobbying strongly for one.

The U.S. Senate has been considering bills creating a federal shield law for several years. The 2009 version would only cover a reporter or blogger who "obtains the information sought while working as a salaried employee of, or independent contractor for, an entity."[90] In other words, only professional, paid journalists would be covered. Citizen journalists, student journalists, or anyone who had a day job not in journalism would be excluded. Some journalists find shield laws of concern because they seem to define who is a journalist—and is thus protected—while excluding others who are not considered journalists. First Amendment attorney David Bodney says, "Any attempt to legislate the scope of our First Amendment rights is unsettling business." Despite these concerns, Bodney does support the proposed federal law.[91]

**shield laws**
Laws that give journalists special protection from having to testify in court about their stories and sources.

*Reporter Judith Miller testifies before the Senate in 2005 in support of a federal shield law. Miller spent eighty-five days in jail after refusing to testify about the identity of her confidential sources.*

Since the 1960s, a number of journalists have either been fined or sent to jail for refusing to testify in federal courts. These include journalists who had witnessed drug crimes or the actions of the Black Panther Party and those who had interviewed murder suspects.

More recently, journalists Matt Cooper and Judith Miller faced fines and jail time for refusing to testify to a federal grand jury about who had leaked information to them about the identity of a covert CIA agent. Both were eventually granted permission to testify by the source they sought to protect, vice presidential adviser I. Lewis "Scooter" Libby Jr. *Time* magazine's Cooper testified without serving jail time after his employer ordered him to do so. *New York Times* reporter Miller went to jail for eighty-five days for refusing to testify in the same case. Miller finally accepted the release by Libby from her promise of confidentiality and testified.[92] For the latest on the status of the federal shield law, go to http://ralphehanson.com.

*Are Bloggers Protected?*    As concerned journalists are aware, the big question is who is entitled to shield law protection. There is no question that shield laws protect newspaper, television, and radio reporters, but what about independent bloggers? Are they journalists, too? Possibly, but this isn't a certainty. A California judge ruled that three blogging sites had to reveal their sources of company secrets about Apple Inc., but that decision was overturned on appeal, when the court ruled that bloggers were protected by California's shield law.[93]

San Francisco blogger Josh Wolf spent close to eight months in jail after refusing to testify about an anarchists' demonstration he witnessed, the longest sentence to date served by a member of the media. Wolf answered two questions for prosecutors and released a copy of videotape he had shot, something he had been willing to do all along. What he was not willing to do was testify about all he had seen at the demonstration.[94] While Wolf was in jail, a debate raged as to whether he deserved protection as a journalist. He had not made a promise of confidentiality, nor was he employed by a mainstream media outlet. But Wolf maintained that when he was shooting video, he was acting as a journalist. "It was journalism to the extent that I went out to capture the truth and present it to the public," Wolf said. "It has nothing to do with whether or not I'm employed by a corporation or I carry a press pass."[95]

# TEST YOUR MEDIA LITERACY

## Can Bloggers Be Journalists?

Blogger Josh Wolf spent seven-and-a-half months in jail on contempt-of-court charges, the longest of any media person in contemporary America.[1] He was being held for refusing to testify about an anarchists' demonstration he covered for his blog. He was released at long last after he posted all the video he shot on his Web site, turned over copies of it to prosecutors, and answered two brief questions under oath. In return, he was not required to testify further about whom he had spoken with at the protest. Wolf told the *San Francisco Chronicle* that the dropping of the demand for him to testify was the key element of the deal he made: "Journalists absolutely have to remain independent of law enforcement," he said. "Otherwise, people will never trust journalists."[2]

According to the *Chronicle*, the Wolf case has prompted a nationwide discussion as to who is a journalist in the twenty-first century:

> The federal appeals court that upheld Wolf's imprisonment last September said he would not be considered a journalist in California because he was not employed by any publication or news agency. But a state appeals court ruled in an unrelated case last May—the only case to address the issue under California law—that bloggers can be protected by the state's shield law when they act like traditional reporters or editors by developing sources, collecting information and publishing it.
>
> Wolf said Tuesday he considers himself a journalist in the same tradition as independent pamphleteers like Thomas Paine.
>
> "A journalist's mission is to provide the truth to the public," he said. "I came out to the protest to document it and to provide the truth to the public."
>
> Wolf said he plans to go to Congress and lobby for a shield law that would protect bloggers and independent journalists as well as media employees. "We shouldn't have government deciding who is or isn't a journalist," he said.[3]

**MORE online**

You can find a link to a story from the *San Francisco Chronicle* about Wolf's case at **http://ralphehanson.com.** After you've read the article, answer the questions below.

- - - - - - - - - - - - - - -

### Who is the source?
Who is Josh Wolf? What is his background? What did he do?

### What is he saying?
What reasons does Wolf give for refusing to testify? How did he feel about going to jail?

### What evidence is there?
What evidence is there that Wolf deserves protection as a journalist? Why did prosecutors argue that he did not deserve protection?

### What do you and your classmates think about the Wolf case?
Do bloggers deserve the same legal protection as mainstream journalists do? What makes someone a journalist? Why do you think Wolf was willing to go to jail for so long?

[1] Bob Egelko and Jim Herron Zamora, "The Josh Wolf Case: Blogger Freed After Giving Video to Feds," *San Francisco Chronicle*, April 4, 2007, B1.
[2] Ibid.
[3] Ibid.

## Obscenity

The *Near* case, in addition to allowing prior restraint of sensitive military information, also established that obscene material is not protected by the First Amendment. The term **obscenity** describes sexually explicit material that is legally prohibited from being published, but it also raises the question of what kinds of material can be considered obscene. Finding the answer has proven difficult, both for the courts and for society.[96]

**Roth v. United States.**    The Supreme Court made its first contemporary attempt to answer the question of what constitutes obscenity in 1957 in *Roth v. United States*.[97] Samuel Roth, who ran a business selling sexually explicit books, photos, and magazines, had been convicted of mailing obscene material through the U.S. Postal Service. He appealed his case to the U.S. Supreme Court, which eventually upheld his conviction. But more important, the Court used the case to start establishing standards for what was and was not protected by the First Amendment. The *Roth* case reaffirmed that the courts could regulate obscenity and that obscenity is not protected by the First Amendment. But the justices also cautioned that "sex and obscenity are not synonymous."[98]

With Roth, the court established a three-part test to help determine whether something is obscene: "Whether to the average person, applying contemporary community standards, the dominant theme of the material taken as a whole appeals to prurient interests."[99] The three parts of this test can be analyzed as follows:

1. The standard for obscenity is set by individual "community standards" using the view of an "average person." This means that neither the most liberal nor the most conservative view should be used, nor should there be a national standard.

2. The work must be "taken as a whole." It's not enough for there to be a single sexually explicit section; the work as a whole must be explicit to be obscene.

3. The work must appeal to "prurient interests." This is the most difficult point. Prurient interest means, according to the Court, an "exacerbated, morbid or perverted" interest in nudity, sex, or excretory functions.[100]

**Miller v. California.**    The standards established in the *Roth* case were refined with the Supreme Court's ruling in *Miller v. California*. Like Roth, Miller had been convicted of sending obscene material through the mail. The *Miller* case upheld the basic standard from *Roth* but added two key points. The first is that states have used this right to ban child pornography, and many states have laws that ban other types of content.

The second key point is that material that has "serious literary, artistic, political, or scientific value" cannot be banned. This protects, for example, information about sexual health and birth control or literature, like D. H. Lawrence's novel *Lady Chatterley's Lover. Miller* also reaffirmed that local communities could set their own standards. There is not an expectation, the Court said, that "the people of Maine or Mississippi accept public depiction of conduct found tolerable in Las Vegas or New York City."[101]

*Obscenity in the Information Age.*    The *Roth* and *Miller* standards both assume that obscene material is being sold at a particular location in a particular community. Neither case anticipated the problems raised by the growth of the Internet and satellite television. What can the courts do about sexually explicit material that is located on a Web server in New York City but is viewed by a person in Morgantown, West Virginia? Attorney Rieko Mashima's piece in *Computer Lawyer* explains the problem: "On the Internet, which is available to a nationwide audience, a sender of information can neither control where it will be downloaded or through which places it will travel, nor tailor contents for different communities."[102]

Pay-per-view cable and satellite television provide a similar problem. In 1999 Larry W. Peterman, owner of a video store in Provo, Utah, was charged with renting obscene films and appeared to be headed to jail. Then his lawyer came up with the idea of recording all the erotic movies that could be seen on pay-per-view at the Provo Marriott Hotel across the street from the courtroom. A little more research found that far more people in Provo were buying adult movies from cable and satellite providers and in hotels than from Peterman's video store. The jury promptly acquitted Peterman on all charges.[103]

The courts have yet to rule definitively on how to handle local control of pornography delivered by satellite or Internet, although Congress made an attempt to do so with the Telecommunications Act of 1996, discussed later in this chapter. And as of 2004, the Federal Communications Commission (FCC) started cracking down on what it called "indecent" communication on broadcast television, as we discussed in Chapter 9.

# REGULATION OF THE MEDIA INDUSTRY

The print media have been largely unregulated throughout the history of the United States beyond copyright and fair use provisions. But broadcast media have been necessarily controlled from the beginning, for two reasons: radio and television stations have to meet certain technical standards to keep from interfering with each other's broadcasts, and the government has an interest in making sure that the limited number of broadcast frequencies available are used in the public interest. In this section, we look at how these controls of the media industry have been applied.

## Copyright and Fair Use

Creators of books, newspapers, magazines, music, and other media products have been protected from having their works appropriated by others since the first U.S. copyright law was passed in 1790. In the law's original form, works were protected for fourteen years and copyright could be renewed for an additional fourteen years. This protection was extended only to American authors and artists, however. It wasn't until the 1890s that copyright was extended to works by authors and artists from other countries. Under the leadership of Barbara Ringer in the 1960s and 1970s (discussed at the beginning of this chapter), the length of copyright increased from the original twenty-eight years to fifty years after the creator's death for an individual copyright. In 1998 the Copyright Extension Act extended individual copyright to seventy years after the creator's death, and extended corporate copyrights to ninety-five years. Why ninety-five years for the corporate copyright? If not for that extension, Mickey Mouse would have entered the public domain in 2003.[104] The 1998 Digital Millennium Copyright Act expanded the copyright on materials that are recorded digitally, such as electronic books, CDs, and DVDs. It has long been illegal to distribute duplicate copies of electronic material without permission, but the act also makes it a crime to produce software or hardware designed to break the copy protection on movies, music, or other software. The act leaves users in an odd position: It is legal to make a backup copy of a DVD movie for personal use, but it is illegal to use a computer program that will make a copy of the protected movie.[105] In 2002 a group led by Sanford University law professor Lawrence Lessing created an alternative set of copyright licenses known as Creative Commons that allow authors and artists to reserve a limited set of rights for a creative work without using all the restrictions of a conventional copyright. For example, a photographer could license her photo so that anyone could use the image without permission as long as he or she attributed the photo to the original creator. The main advantage of Creative Commons is that it allows creators a middle ground between full copyright and placing their work in the public domain.[106]

## The Rise and Fall of Broadcast Regulation

Broadcast regulation began with the Radio Act of 1912, passed immediately after the sinking of the *Titanic*. But this regulation dealt only with point-to-point communication such as ship-to-shore radio. Meanwhile, commercial broadcasting got its start in 1920 when radio station KDKA went on the air in Pittsburgh. By 1925 broadcasters were calling for regulation by the government to bring stability to the new industry.

The Radio Act of 1927 created the Federal Radio Commission. This act was also the first to charge broadcast stations with acting in the "public interest, convenience, and necessity." With the Communications Act of 1934, the Radio Commission evolved into the Federal Communications Commission. The 1934 act brought all electronic communication, wired and wireless, under the control of the FCC, but the basic tenets of the 1927 act remained in place:[107]

- The airwaves are licensed to broadcasters, but the broadcasters do not own them.

- The FCC has the power to regulate broadcasters to ensure that they act in the public interest.

- The FCC can tell broadcasters what frequencies and power to use and where their transmitters can be located.

## Mandating Fairness on the Air

In addition to attempting to regulate the murky area of indecency, the FCC has regulated how broadcasters handle political campaigns and controversial issues.

*The Equal Time Provision.*   The FCC's **equal time provision** requires broadcast stations to make equivalent amounts of broadcast time available to all candidates running for public office. The rule does not require stations to provide time to candidates, only to ensure that all candidates have equal access. So if a station sells time to one candidate, it must be willing to sell an equal amount of similarly valuable time to all candidates who can afford it. The rule also states that if a station gives free non-news time to one candidate, it must provide similar amounts of free time to all candidates. The purpose of the rule is to prevent stations from favoring one candidate over another while making use of a valuable public resource.[108]

The equal time provision has come under controversy when candidates have sought to run ads that are either offensive or libelous. Because stations cannot edit or censor anything in political advertisements, the FCC has ruled that broadcasters are not responsible for libelous statements made in political ads. There has also been conflict over explicit antiabortion ads. In 1992 and 1994 some stations channeled the graphic messages and images contained in such ads to a "safe harbor" time between midnight and 6:00 a.m., when children were unlikely to see them. Indiana congressional candidate Michael Bailey objected to the channeling, saying that the explicit ads were an essential part of his campaign; he persuaded stations to run the ads during prime time, although the stations ran disclaimers before many of them. The FCC has since said that ads dealing with abortion could be channeled into the "safe harbor" time periods.[109]

There are limits to what candidates can do. When *Hustler* publisher Larry Flynt declared that he would run for president and would broadcast pornographic campaign commercials under the equal time provision, the FCC said that the "no censorship" clause would not apply to "obscene or indecent political announcements."

*The Fairness Doctrine.*   More controversial than the equal time provision was the **fairness doctrine**. Under this 1949 rule, stations were required to cover controversial issues of public interest and to present contrasting views on those issues. The fairness doctrine did not require that stations give the same amount of time to all sides of an issue, but rather that they "afford reasonable opportunity for the discussion of conflicting views on issues of public importance."[110]

---

**equal time provision**
An FCC policy that requires broadcast stations to make equivalent amounts of broadcast time available to all candidates running for public office.

**fairness doctrine**
A former FCC policy that required television stations to "afford reasonable opportunity for the discussion of conflicting views on issues of public importance."

The major objection to the fairness doctrine was that stations might avoid covering controversial issues because they did not want to present extreme viewpoints or cover every aspect of an issue. For example, stations would argue that they did not want to cover problems with racism for fear of having to give the Ku Klux Klan an opportunity to respond. Critics argued that the public suffered because they received no coverage of issues rather than every possible variation.

A 1985 study by the FCC found that the fairness doctrine tended to inhibit free speech and was no longer needed because of new media outlets such as cable television. Moreover, the FCC had had to deal with thousands of complaints filed under the rule each year. Following publication of the 1985 study, the FCC essentially stopped enforcing the fairness doctrine, and it was repealed in 1987.[111]

## The Telecommunications Act of 1996

The Telecommunications Act of 1996 has been called the biggest reform of broadcast regulation since the formation of the FCC in 1934.

*Revising Broadcast Regulation.* The section of the Telecommunications Act that attracted the most attention was one calling for the creation of the V-chip, which allows parents to electronically block material with a particular content rating. But the act's greatest impact was to relax most of the rules that restricted how many broadcast stations a particular company could own. This led to the rapid turnover of many broadcast properties and an increasing concentration of ownership, completing a trend that began in the 1970s and 1980s.[112] (For more about concentration of media ownership, see Chapter 3.)

*Regulation of the Internet.* In addition to calling for the V-chip, the Communications Decency Act provision of the Telecommunications Act of 1996 attempted to regulate the Internet in a similar way to the regulation of broadcasting.

Figuring out what kind of medium the Internet is from a legal standpoint has been a problem for both Congress and the courts. On the one hand, the Internet looks something like television because it comes in over a wire and is displayed on a screen, and many Web sites are maintained by the same companies that operate television networks. On the other hand, the Internet can be seen as more like a newspaper or magazine. There's a great deal of print on the Internet, and newspapers have a strong presence there. Also, the number of channels on the Internet is not limited, as is the case with broadcast or even cable television. But unlike both television and print, the Internet has strong elements of interpersonal communication, resembling the telephone network in this respect. There is no central authority controlling what can and cannot be said on the Internet. Some observers argue that perhaps regulation of the Internet should model regulation of the telephone system. Others say the Internet might qualify as an open public forum, without any need for regulation at all.[113]

In reality, the Internet has elements of all these media—radio, broadcast and cable television, telephone, newspapers, and magazines. The companies that provide high-speed Internet service to the home are regulated to a degree, as are phone or cable television companies. First Amendment protection for media sites on the Web is similar to that given to print media. Individuals have the same levels of responsibility for what they say through the Internet as they would have anywhere. In general, Internet bulletin boards and chat rooms are treated in much the same way as telephone communication. The people who post to the bulletin boards, not the company providing Internet access, are responsible for what they say, just as a phone company is not responsible for a libelous or defamatory phone call or fax sent over its lines.

In fall 2009, the FCC started working on writing rules on **Net neutrality**, rules that would require Internet providers to provide equal access to content from all providers. Under Net neutrality, telecommunication providers could not favor their own products over those of others. For example, without Net neutrality regulations, a company that provided its own online video service could slow down access to video provider YouTube. Internet providers argue that forcing them to give unlimited bandwidth to applications such as streaming video could slow down access for the majority of their customers who don't use such services.[114]

The many levels of communication on the Internet make it extremely difficult to control. The Communications Decency Act attempted to ban Internet messages that are "obscene, lewd, lascivious, filthy or indecent." The law was opposed by the American Library Association, the Electronic Frontier Foundation (an electronic communication rights group), and the ACLU, among others. Although the law banned only the transmission of indecent messages to minors, it seemed impossible to keep minors out of discussions involving adults.

In 1997 the Supreme Court struck down the Communications Decency Act as an unconstitutional limit on the free speech of adults. It ruled that the possibility of a minor being present in a chat room did not remove the adults' First Amendment rights. Justice John Paul Stevens wrote in the majority opinion, "The interest in encouraging freedom of expression in a democratic society outweighs any theoretical but unproven benefit of censorship."[115] The only certainty is that Congress will continue to consider how to regulate communication on the Internet.

Since 1997 attempts have been made to pass new legislation that would control "indecent" content on the Web without infringing on the free speech of adults. As of this writing, the Child Online Protection Act (a follow-up law that attempted to deal with weaknesses in the Communications Decency Act) was still working its way through the courts.[116] You can find a link to the latest status of this and other decency legislation at http://ralphchanson.com.

*Regulating young people's access to indecent material on the Internet is a difficult issue for Congress and the U.S. Supreme Court. Most schemes that successfully restrict minors' access to questionable Web pages also limit adult access, which the Court has ruled is protected.*

**Net neutrality**
Rules that would require Internet service providers to give equal access to all online content providers.

# CHAPTERSummary

The First Amendment to the U.S. Constitution says, "Congress shall make no law respecting an establishment of religion, or prohibiting the free exercise thereof; or abridging the freedom of speech, or of the press; or the right of the people peaceably to assemble, and to petition the Government for a redress of grievances." This statement is at the core of all media law in the United States. The purpose of the amendment is to protect the free and open discussion necessary to a democratic society. Although the First Amendment guarantees the right of free speech, Congress has passed several laws that limit this freedom. These include the Alien and Sedition Acts of 1798; the Espionage Act of 1917; the Smith Act of 1940; the USA Patriot Act of 2001; and laws controlling libel, invasion of privacy, publication of military secrets, and obscenity.

The rights of individuals are protected from actions of the media through libel law, invasion of privacy law, and guarantees of a fair trial. Libel is a statement that unjustifiably exposes someone to ridicule or contempt. For a statement to be libelous it must include defamation, identification, and publication. In general, the media are allowed to publish defamatory material that is true, privileged, or a statement of opinion. *New York Times v. Sullivan* established that public officials seeking to win a libel suit must show that the media acted with actual malice in publishing a false defamatory statement.

There are four basic forms of invasion of privacy: intrusion, embarrassment, false light, and misappropriation. In some cases journalists can defend themselves against charges of invasion of privacy by showing that the story was newsworthy. There is often a conflict between an individual's right to a fair trial and the press's right to cover that trial. The Supreme Court has generally ruled that the judge, not the press, is responsible for guaranteeing the defendant a fair trial. The Court has also ruled that protection of the right to a fair trial should require as few limits on the freedom of the press as possible. This can be done by imposing gag orders, sequestering the jury, postponing or changing the venue of a trial, or ordering a new trial.

Since 1977 courts in the United States have been experimenting with allowing cameras in the courtroom. Proponents of such a policy argue that televising trials allows the public to better understand how the justice system works. Opponents argue that cameras are intrusive and turn trials into media circuses.

Although the press is subject to the same laws as society as a whole, it is protected from censorship in most cases. The government is allowed to prevent publication of certain information only if the material is obscene or gives away military secrets during time of war. There have been only three major cases involving prior restraint: *Near v. Minnesota*, the Pentagon Papers, and the *Progressive* H-bomb story. High school newspapers published as a classroom activity are not afforded the same level of protection, however.

The courts have ruled that obscenity is not protected by the First Amendment, and they have established that the standard for obscenity will be set using state law and local community standards.

The broadcast media traditionally have been regulated much more heavily than the print media because they make use of the public airwaves. They are regulated both for technical reasons and to ensure that they serve the public interest. Major legislation controlling the broadcast media was passed in 1927, 1934, and 1996. Standards for regulating the Internet are still evolving, but they appear to be more similar to print regulations than to broadcast regulations.

## KEYTerms

Alien and Sedition Acts   453
libel   455
privilege   456
actual malice   458
intrusion   459
false light   460
misappropriation   460

prior restraint   467
shield laws   473
obscenity   476
equal time provision   479
fairness doctrine   479
Net neutrality   481

## CONCEPTReview

Conflict between right of free speech and protection of individuals' reputations
Elements of the First Amendment
Defenses against libel
Defenses against invasion of privacy suits
Conflict between the right to a free press and the right to a fair trial
Obligations of the press
Ways in which the press may be controlled
Students' rights to free speech
Differences between obscenity and indecency (see also discussion in Chapter 9)
Changes in broadcast regulation

# Media Ethics
## Truthfulness, Fairness, and Standards of Decency

**Photographer Richard Drew** got up on September 11, 2001, to work the 7:00 a.m. to 4:30 p.m. shift covering New York City for the Associated Press. His assignment for the morning was to photograph a maternity fashion show featuring pregnant models. Around nine o'clock his cell phone rang and his editor told him, "Bag the fashion show—you have to go." An airplane had hit the south tower of the World Trade Center. No one yet knew that this was the start of a day of terrorist attacks on the United States that would include two planes hitting the twin towers of the World Trade Center in New York, a plane crashing into the Pentagon near Washington, D.C., and a plane crash landing in a field in rural Pennsylvania.[1]

When Drew got to the World Trade Center, he faced a chilling sight. People who were trapped in the towers above the floors where the airliners had struck the buildings faced an impossible choice: flames and jet fuel explosions behind them, or a plunge of eighty stories or more from the windows in front. Drew said, "I saw people coming down from the building. We were watching people falling from the building."[2]

He did what any news photographer had to do—he started taking pictures. By the end of the day, he had shot 215 frames.

Among those frames were dozens of images that would become all too familiar to Americans in the ensuing days and weeks: the buildings collapsing in a cloud of dust, the explosions and flames, a person clinging to the debris as it falls from the collapse.

As long as he could, Drew kept shooting pictures of what would come to be known as Ground Zero. He was pulled back by emergency workers when the first tower collapsed. When the second tower collapsed, Drew finally left the area, running from the cloud of ash that enveloped the site.

No other picture would capture the day's events as did Drew's photo of "the falling man," initially identified as pastry chef Norberto Hernandez, who worked at the Windows on the World restaurant at the top of the doomed building. The photo showed a man in a white jacket and black pants, falling from the tower, head down. The image was so clear that friends of the chef identified him in the photo.[3] The photo appeared on page 7 of the New York Times and in hundreds of papers around the world, though at the time the man in the photo had not been identified.

AP photographer Richard Drew (right) shot many iconic images in downtown Manhattan on September 11, 2001, including this image of the World Trade Center's north tower collapsing.

Drew recalled taking photos of a dozen or more people falling from the World Trade Center towers. But, he said:

> I didn't really see what I had till I got back to the office. It was [Norberto Hernandez's] last day on the job; he'd just gotten a new, better job at another restaurant. He had gone in early that day and was preparing whatever he was making for that day's fare, and ended up being the subject of one of my photographs.[4]

More recently, there has been some debate over the identity of "the falling man." An article in *Esquire* by Tom Junod suggests that he was really Jonathan Briley, who also worked at Windows on the World.[5] The man's true identity will likely never be known. You can read more about the controversy surrounding this photo at http://ralphehanson.com.

Drew says that too many of the photos taken on September 11 were sterile, showing buildings and wreckage but not people. The photos he shot of people falling gave viewers a sense of what had really happened. "It has to do with putting a human element with this story. My recollection of watching these buildings fall was like a movie. And all the pictures we've seen don't show the human element except for these people falling."[6]

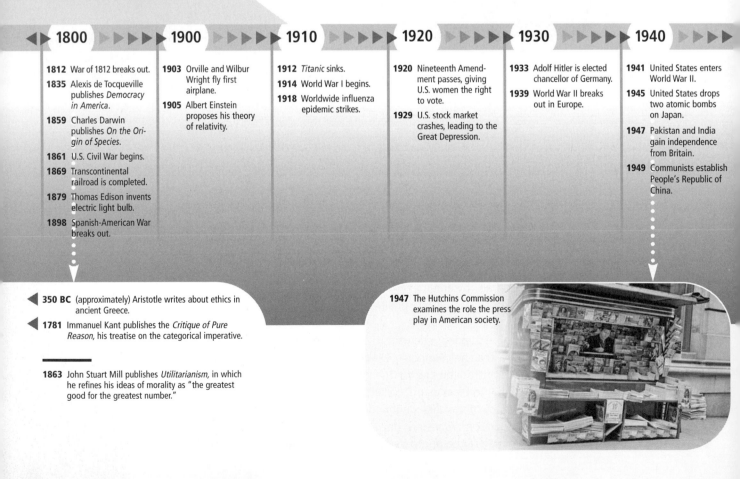

**1800** ▶▶▶▶   **1900** ▶▶▶▶   **1910** ▶▶▶▶   **1920** ▶▶▶▶   **1930** ▶▶▶▶   **1940** ▶▶▶

**1812** War of 1812 breaks out.

**1835** Alexis de Tocqueville publishes *Democracy in America*.

**1859** Charles Darwin publishes *On the Origin of Species*.

**1861** U.S. Civil War begins.

**1869** Transcontinental railroad is completed.

**1879** Thomas Edison invents electric light bulb.

**1898** Spanish-American War breaks out.

**1903** Orville and Wilbur Wright fly first airplane.

**1905** Albert Einstein proposes his theory of relativity.

**1912** *Titanic* sinks.

**1914** World War I begins.

**1918** Worldwide influenza epidemic strikes.

**1920** Nineteenth Amendment passes, giving U.S. women the right to vote.

**1929** U.S. stock market crashes, leading to the Great Depression.

**1933** Adolf Hitler is elected chancellor of Germany.

**1939** World War II breaks out in Europe.

**1941** United States enters World War II.

**1945** United States drops two atomic bombs on Japan.

**1947** Pakistan and India gain independence from Britain.

**1949** Communists establish People's Republic of China.

◀ **350 BC** (approximately) Aristotle writes about ethics in ancient Greece.

◀ **1781** Immanuel Kant publishes the *Critique of Pure Reason*, his treatise on the categorical imperative.

**1863** John Stuart Mill publishes *Utilitarianism*, in which he refines his ideas of morality as "the greatest good for the greatest number."

**1947** The Hutchins Commission examines the role the press play in American society.

In the days following the attacks, Drew would continue to shoot Ground Zero, taking pictures of the piles of flowers, the many dozens of teddy bears people left behind, and the hundreds of posters and pictures people posted of their missing friends and loved ones. Two days passed before Drew could slow down enough to feel the impact of the attacks and their aftermath. He got a call on his mobile phone from his four-year-old daughter, who said, "I just want to tell you I love you." Molly Gordy, Drew's wife, said that his daughter's call broke through Drew's emotional wall. He called the office, said he had to take a day off, and went to see his family. "[He] accepted the fact that in order to take a moving picture, you have to be moved," Gordy said.[7]

Drew says that he records history every day, although some days contain more history than others. He was one of the first photographers on the scene when presidential candidate Robert Kennedy was assassinated in 1968, and he photographed the first World Trade Center bombing in 1993. But nothing he had ever experienced was as monumental as September 11:

> My peers have told me that I photographed the death of these people. But I feel that I've captured a piece of these people's lives. I photograph what happened, and, in turn, I record and document history, and this is what happened. This is history.[8]

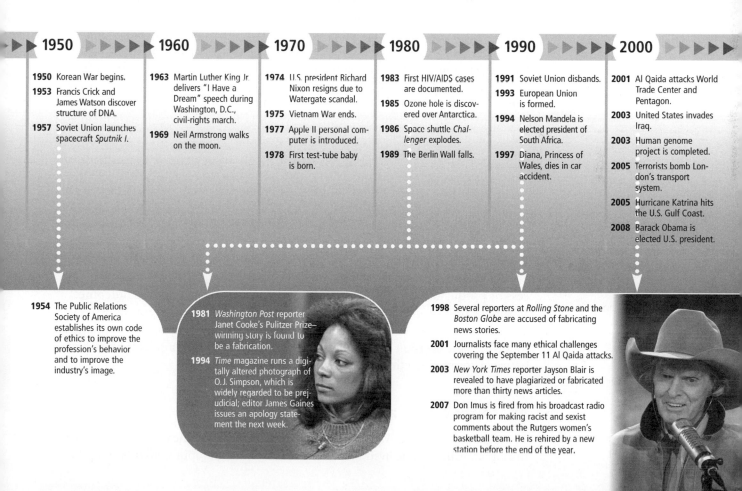

**1950**

**1950** Korean War begins.

**1953** Francis Crick and James Watson discover structure of DNA.

**1957** Soviet Union launches spacecraft *Sputnik I*.

**1960**

**1963** Martin Luther King Jr. delivers "I Have a Dream" speech during Washington, D.C., civil-rights march.

**1969** Neil Armstrong walks on the moon.

**1970**

**1974** U.S. president Richard Nixon resigns due to Watergate scandal.

**1975** Vietnam War ends.

**1977** Apple II personal computer is introduced.

**1978** First test-tube baby is born.

**1980**

**1983** First HIV/AIDS cases are documented.

**1985** Ozone hole is discovered over Antarctica.

**1986** Space shuttle *Challenger* explodes.

**1989** The Berlin Wall falls.

**1990**

**1991** Soviet Union disbands.

**1993** European Union is formed.

**1994** Nelson Mandela is elected president of South Africa.

**1997** Diana, Princess of Wales, dies in car accident.

**2000**

**2001** Al Qaida attacks World Trade Center and Pentagon.

**2003** United States invades Iraq.

**2003** Human genome project is completed.

**2005** Terrorists bomb London's transport system.

**2005** Hurricane Katrina hits the U.S. Gulf Coast.

**2008** Barack Obama is elected U.S. president.

**1954** The Public Relations Society of America establishes its own code of ethics to improve the profession's behavior and to improve the industry's image.

**1981** *Washington Post* reporter Janet Cooke's Pulitzer Prize–winning story is found to be a fabrication.

**1994** *Time* magazine runs a digitally altered photograph of O. J. Simpson, which is widely regarded to be prejudicial; editor James Gaines issues an apology statement the next week.

**1998** Several reporters at *Rolling Stone* and the *Boston Globe* are accused of fabricating news stories.

**2001** Journalists face many ethical challenges covering the September 11 Al Qaida attacks.

**2003** *New York Times* reporter Jayson Blair is revealed to have plagiarized or fabricated more than thirty news articles.

**2007** Don Imus is fired from his broadcast radio program for making racist and sexist comments about the Rutgers women's basketball team. He is rehired by a new station before the end of the year.

Media ethics are a difficult subject because the news media are not always polite or nice, nor should they be. Their job is to keep the public informed, increase people's understanding of the world, and help the functioning of a democratic society. And as photographer Richard Drew has pointed out, journalists sometimes must show things that are uncomfortable, disturbing, and upsetting.

In this chapter we look at and attempt to understand why media practitioners behave the way they do, and how their behavior can be judged by the media-consuming public.

# ETHICAL PRINCIPLES AND DECISION MAKING

**morals**

An individual's code of behavior based on religious or philosophical principles. Morals define right and wrong in ways that may or may not be rational.

**ethics**

A rational way of deciding what is good for individuals or society. Ethics provide a way to choose between competing moral principles and help people decide where there is a clear-cut right or wrong answer.

The words *morality* and *ethics* are often used interchangeably, but they are distinctly different concepts. Media ethics scholars Philip Patterson and Lee Wilkins explain that **morals** refer to a religious or philosophical code of behavior that may or may not be rational. **Ethics**, by contrast, come from the ancient Greek study of the rational way to decide what is good for individuals or society. A moral decision depends on the values held by a particular individual, but an ethical decision should be explainable to others in a way that they will appreciate, regardless of whether they accept it. In short, ethics consist of the ways in which we make choices between competing moral principles.[9]

Journalists in the United States have a wealth of competing ethical principles to draw upon beyond the basic Judeo-Christian values that constitute the core of American morality. (This is not to deny that there are many other significant religious traditions in the United States. But a recent survey of journalists showed that they come overwhelmingly from either Christian or Jewish households.[10]) Franklin Foer, writing in the *New Republic*, suggests that there are two approaches to judging journalistic ethics. The first considers the journalist's process of producing the product. If the process has moral failings, such as conflicts of interest, then the product will be flawed. The other approach, which he advocates, suggests that the product itself should be judged. Apart from the process of production, what can be said about the ethical quality of the outcome?[11] In this section we examine the major ethical principles affecting journalism (all of which fall within Foer's two categories), consider how they might be applied to journalistic decision making, and look at a contemporary model for deciding between competing ethical principles.

## Aristotle: Virtue and the Golden Mean

The Greek philosopher Aristotle was a student of Plato and the tutor of Alexander the Great. Although he lived more than 2,300 years ago (approximately 350 BC), his writings on ethics, logic, natural science, psychology, politics, and the arts contain insights that are still relevant, especially his comments on ethics and human endeavor. Aristotle argued that the ultimate goal of all human effort is "the good," and the ultimate good is happiness. To Aristotle, achieving happiness involved striking a balance, a "just-right point between excess and defect."[12] Popularizers have labeled this valued midpoint the **golden mean**.

The classic example of the golden mean is courage, which strikes a balance between the inaction and timidity of cowardice and the recklessness of foolhardiness, both of which are unacceptable behaviors. The example of courage also illustrates how the acceptable ethical middle ground is not a single defined place, but its parameters depend on the abilities and strengths of the individual.[13]

To behave ethically, according to Aristotle, individuals must do the following:

- Know what they are doing

- Select their action with a moral reason

- Act out of good character

In other words, Aristotle emphasized the character and the intent of the actor and how those determine the way in which he or she acts.

Media ethics scholar David Martinson cautions journalists not to take an overly simplistic view of the golden mean and assume that it refers only to compromise. Instead, they must recognize that finding the mean requires virtue. Martinson writes:

> A virtuous journalist is one who communicates truthfully in a manner which will enable the reader or listener to better understand the reality of the community, nation, and world in which he or she lives. In that communication, the journalist will show respect for human dignity and individual circumstances.[14]

*Among the most disturbing images to come out of the September 11 terrorist attacks was Richard Drew's photo of "the falling man" plunging to his death.*

To test this principle, consider the photo of a person falling from the World Trade Center, discussed in the chapter-opening vignette. A newspaper editor trying to decide whether to run the photo might want to hit a mean between sensitivity and the need to report what happened. One extreme would be not running the photo at all; the other would be running a graphic image of a body after it hit the ground. A possible middle ground would consist of running the photo of the person falling. Other forms of balance might be reducing the size of the photo so that it would have less impact than a large photo and placing it on an inside page rather than on the front page. The decision to run the photo could also be justified by the argument that the editor was acting out of good character by feeling an obligation to help readers understand an event that is otherwise incomprehensible.[15]

## Kant: The Categorical Imperative

The German philosopher Immanuel Kant published his most important writings during the final decades of the eighteenth century. Kant differs from Aristotle in that Kant suggested that morality lies in the act itself and not in the character of the actor or the intent behind the action. He also put forward the Judeo-Christian value of seeing people as ends, never as a means to an end. In short, Kant emphasized that you can't use people to achieve your goals.

Kant's ethics begin with the notion that we have the ability to reason and hence are able to base our actions on moral reasoning. Because of this, people are responsible for their own actions and are obliged to act in a moral way.

The basic summary of Kant's **categorical imperative**, written in the 1780s, states: "Act as if the maxim of your action were to become through your will a universal law of nature."[16] In simpler terms, Kant asks people to consider what would be the result of everyone acting the same way they themselves wish to act. Kant does not worry particularly about the consequences of an action; rather, he looks at the act itself. This does not mean that Kant doesn't consider outcomes important, only that he believes unethical behavior cannot be justified by its possibly desirable outcomes.

In the case of the World Trade Center photo, the philosopher might ask what moral decision the photographer made. The photographer's decision was to tell the truth about the events of the day. Would we be willing to accept the consequences of everyone telling the truth? What problems might arise out of a position of absolute truth?

**categorical imperative**
Kant's idea of a moral obligation that we should act in a way in which we would be willing to have everyone else act; also known as the principle of universality.

**principle of utility**
John Stuart Mill's principle that ethical behavior arises from that which will provide the greatest good for the greatest number of people.

## John Stuart Mill: The Principle of Utility

In the movie *Star Trek II: The Wrath of Khan*, the emotionless Spock performs a rational yet selfless act. He saves the crew of the starship *U.S.S. Enterprise* by entering a reactor room to prevent an explosion that would have killed everyone on board the ship. But in doing so he absorbs a lethal dose of radiation. As he dies, he justifies his actions to his friends with the maxim, "The good of the many outweighs the good of the few, or the one." In this moment, Spock sums up the central tenet of the nineteenth-century ethical philosopher John Stuart Mill's **principle of utility**: the greatest good for the greatest number.

Mill did not create the idea of utility, but he did do a great deal to refine and promote the philosophy known as utilitarianism. Mill wrote that the consequences of actions are important in deciding what is ethical: "An act's rightness is [a] desirable end."[17]

Looking back to the Aristotelian notion of happiness as the ultimate public good, utilitarianism holds that that which is virtuous is that which provides the greatest happiness for the greatest number. Or, looked at another way, that which causes the least pain is best. The challenge in applying this principle is that the same act can cause both happiness and pain. NBC News faced extensive criticism when it decided to air excerpts from a multimedia disk created by Seung-hui Cho, who shot and killed thirty-two students and faculty at Virginia Tech in April 2007. Family and friends of the victims said that they felt victimized all over again when they saw the video. NBC News president Steve Kapas said the network ran the excerpts from the disk so that the public might better understand what had happened, "This is as close as we'll ever come to being in the mind of a killer."[18] The network accepted the additional suffering it caused a smaller number of people who knew the victims in order to accomplish the greater good of informing the public at large.

Mill also held that some forms of pleasure or happiness are morally superior to others. He suggested that actions and decisions that improve the lot of society as a whole may be superior to those that merely provide the most physical or emotional pleasure.[19]

Employing utilitarian reasoning, an editor might decide not to run the photo of a person falling from the World Trade Center because of all the pain it would cause viewers of the image. Since the photo would likely cause a great deal of pain, there is a strong argument against running it.[20]

## John Rawls: The Veil of Ignorance

The contemporary philosopher John Rawls builds on the ideas of utilitarianism. His argument is that which is just is also that which is fair:

> First: Each person is to have an equal right to the most extensive basic liberty compatible with a similar liberty for others. . . . Second: Social and economic inequalities are to be arranged so that they are both (a) reasonably expected to be to everyone's advantage, and (b) attached to positions and offices open to all.[21]

To decide what is fair, the journalist must hide behind Rawls's **veil of ignorance**, a principle of ethics that says that justice emerges when we make decisions without considering the status of the people involved and without considering where we personally fall in the social system. In other words, we shouldn't ask, "How does this affect me?" Behind this veil, everyone is equal. Journalists following this principle would not question whether they or their subjects were powerful or powerless, rich or poor, black or white, male or female.

Reporters deciding how to treat sources should make the same decision whether they like or dislike the person. They should imagine how they would want to be treated if they were the source and would have to live with the

**veil of ignorance**
John Rawls's principle of ethics that says that justice comes from making decisions that maximize liberty for all people and without considering which outcome will give us personally the biggest benefit.

outcome of the story. The value of freedom of the press must be considered on an equal level with the protection of individual privacy, as reporters behind the veil of ignorance do not know whether they are a reporter or a source.[22]

It is difficult to say what a photo editor would decide to do with the World Trade Center photo using the veil of ignorance. On the one hand, taking the perspective of the family of the person in the photo, he or she might decide that publicizing the view of that final fall is asking too much of the grieving family. On the other hand, the editor might say that the photo gives the family an unambiguous last view of the person, thus removing all doubt about what happened.[23]

## Hutchins Commission: Social Responsibility Ethics

In 1947 widespread concerns about the ethical behavior of the press led Henry Luce, the founder of *Time* magazine, to form a commission to study the responsibility of the press in the United States. Chaired by scholar Robert M. Hutchins, the commission concluded that the First Amendment, by itself, might not be enough to protect the free speech rights of the public because a small number of corporations controlled a large number of the available communication outlets. Although the government might not be limiting free speech, corporations might do so. The report reached two major conclusions:

1. The press has a responsibility to give voice to the public and to society.

2. The free press was not living up to that responsibility to the public because of its need to serve its commercial masters.

The social responsibility theory of the press, holding that the press has an ethical obligation to society, arose from the Hutchins report. (This theory is discussed further in Chapter 15.) The Hutchins Commission listed five requirements for a responsible press:

1. The media should provide a truthful, comprehensive, and intelligent account of the day's events in a context that gives them meaning.

2. The media should serve as a forum for the exchange of comment and criticism (that is, the press should present the full range of thought and criticism).

3. The media should project a representative picture of the constituent groups within the society.

4. The media should present and clarify the goals and values of the society.

5. The media should provide full access to the day's news.

Today, the range of long-tail media, including blogs and podcasts, allow both professional and citizen journalists to bypass legacy media (traditional big media) and go directly to the public, though it is hard for the long-tail news outlets to have the impact that a newspaper or television station can. Nevertheless, this is one more example of Truth Two—There are no mainstream media.

Using a social responsibility approach, running the photo of a person falling from the World Trade Center can be defended, assuming that it is run with the goal of giving readers a better understanding of what happened on September 11, 2001.

## The Bok Model for Ethical Decision Making

Given the many competing ethical principles journalists have to consider, it can be difficult to decide what is right or wrong, as our consideration of the decision about running a disturbing photo illustrates. But contemporary ethicist Sissela Bok provides a fairly straightforward three-step model for analyzing an ethical situation:

1. Consult your conscience—How do you feel about the action? What does your conscience tell you is right?

2. Seek alternatives—Is there another way to achieve the same goal that will not raise ethical issues? Is there an expert to whom you can turn for advice?

3. Hold an imaginary ethical dialogue with everyone involved—Ask, "How will my action affect others?" Discuss the issues involved from the point of view of each of the people whom it will affect. Think about who will be involved: the source, the news consumer, the public at large, a special interest group, and so forth.[24]

In her book *Lying: Moral Choice in Public and Private Life*, Bok suggests consulting experts and holding a public dialogue. It may not be practical for a working reporter or editor to apply her method fully, but the basic approach of consulting one's conscience, considering alternatives, and taking the point of view of all affected parties is reasonable.[25]

## ETHICS AND NEWS

Journalists only rarely face ethical dilemmas on the scale of those surrounding the September 11 attacks. But they face many smaller choices every day. These can involve deciding how to report information from an authoritative source whom the journalist knows to be lying, balancing the rights of various individuals, deciding how to present a story, or deciding which photograph to run.

Some of these decisions are routine, but all of them require ethical choices. Of course, journalists and the people with whom they work don't always live up to high ethical standards, so we look here at how news organizations deal with those problems.

## Truthfulness

Journalists have always claimed that they feel obliged to report the truth,[26] and reporters or editors who violate this commitment to truth have paid dearly. As was discussed in Chapter 6, the *Washington Post*'s credibility suffered a major blow when the paper discovered in 1981 that a Pulitzer Prize–winning story by reporter Janet Cooke was fabricated. In spring 2003, the young *New York Times* reporter Jayson Blair created shock waves throughout the news business when it was revealed that he had fabricated or plagiarized at least thirty-six stories for the nation's most prestigious newspaper. The controversy concerns not only the poor behavior of particular journalists but also the implications of that behavior for the publication and the resulting lack of trust in the institution. At issue, too, is the lack of commitment to the truth on the part of publications and editors that put exciting stories ahead of making sure those stories are true.

In her book on the nature of lying, Bok states that there are at least two factors to weigh when considering a lie. The first is whether the speaker is intending to transmit the truth or attempting to deceive people. The second is whether the statement itself is true or false. Bok argues that the major ethical problem related to truth-telling is intentionally deceiving someone, to "make them believe what we ourselves do not believe."[27]

Media ethics scholar David Martinson argues that telling the truth entails more than just stating facts that are not false. Instead, the press needs to report "the truth about the fact." In the early 1950s, when Sen. Joseph McCarthy—without any evidence—started accusing people of being communists, the press reported his charges without giving any indication that the charges he was making might be false or without conducting independent verification. It was true that McCarthy had made the statements, but the statements themselves were not true. Martinson suggests that the press too often asks whether the story is factually true instead of asking whether the story helps the public understand the truth.

As we discussed in Chapter 4, the truthfulness of nonfiction books has been called into question. The instances of fabrication have gone beyond such notable cases as James Frey's memoir, *A Million Little Pieces.* In his memoir, a former U.S. secretary of labor fabricated testimony that he supposedly had given before Congress.[28] And a prominent writer admitted including imagined conversations in a biography of Ted Kennedy. Presidential biographer Edmund Morris went so far as to insert himself as a fictional character in his biography of Ronald Reagan (a fact that he acknowledged in the introduction to the book).

*Catching Fabrications: How Stephen Glass Fooled the Fact Checkers.* With the exception of tabloid stories about space aliens having Elvis's baby, articles in magazines and newspapers are generally assumed to be true, or at the very least based on fact. But occasionally that basic assumption is called into question.

Consider the following case: A twenty-five-year-old writer named Stephen Glass had written incredible stories for the *New Republic, Rolling Stone, George,* and *Harper's.* Other writers, some would say jealous colleagues, thought Glass's stories, with their customary wow

*Stephen Glass became notorious in the late 1990s for fabricating a series of spectacular magazine stories.*

opening paragraphs to set the scene, were too good to be true. Unfortunately, they were. In 1998 Glass was caught fabricating an article for the *New Republic* about teenage hackers, and his subsequent firing sent shock waves throughout the magazine industry.[29] Follow-up investigations suggested that Glass had fabricated material for dozens of articles without the magazines' fact checkers catching on.

Says Charles Lane, then editor of the *New Republic,* "I don't wish [Glass] ill . . . I just don't want him to be in journalism."[30] After becoming the poster boy for bad journalism, Glass left the magazine business, went to law school, and wrote a novel. Following the critical and commercial failure of his novel, Glass has reportedly worked as a paralegal and as an occasional member of a Los Angeles comedy troupe.[31]

How did Glass get away with his fabrications? First, the magazines didn't conduct fact checking as well as they should have. Second, Glass would submit articles late so that they couldn't be checked, and he would fabricate substantiation for them, such as a phony Web page and voicemail message for the beleaguered high-tech company in the hacker story.[32] In an article for the political magazine *George,* Glass wrote a description of presidential advisor Vernon Jordan based on anonymous sources. He avoided the fact checking by saying that his sources would be fired if they were contacted at work. After editors found out that Glass had been fabricating articles, fact checkers discovered that the sources he had cited didn't exist. To be fair to the fact checkers, their procedures were designed to catch mistakes, not outright fabrications.[33]

One result of the fallout from Glass's fabrications was a renewed commitment to fact checking at magazines; another was increased skepticism toward sensational stories, especially by young writers.

*Who Gets Fired for Fabrication?*   In addition to the scandal surrounding Stephen Glass's many fabrications, that same year brought questions about the truthfulness of the work of two popular *Boston Globe* columnists, a white man and an African American woman. Both writers faced allegations of having fabricated characters in their columns.

Patricia Smith resigned from the *Boston Globe* after being asked to do so by the editor. The winner of numerous writing awards during her eight years at the *Globe*, Smith admitted she had simply made up names and quotes in some of her columns. In her farewell column, she apologized to her readers:

> From time to time in my metro column, to create the desired impact or slam home a salient point, I attributed quotes to people who didn't exist. I could give them names, even occupations, but I couldn't give them what they needed most—a heartbeat. As anyone who's ever touched a newspaper knows, that's one of the cardinal sins of journalism: Thou shall not fabricate. No exceptions. No excuses.[34]

That same summer, another *Boston Globe* writer came under fire. Mike Barnicle, a long-time columnist for the paper and one of its best-known writers, came under suspicion for a number of reasons. In one case, jokes that had appeared in George Carlin's book *Brain Droppings* also showed up, unattributed, in Barnicle's column. Barnicle denied that he had read Carlin's book, yet it was soon pointed out that he had reviewed the book for a local television station. He was left in the uncomfortable position of having to either admit that he had lied about not reading the book or confess that he had given a rave review to a book he hadn't read.[35]

Barnicle was originally given a lengthy suspension from the paper rather than being fired, largely because he was popular with readers. But then a second fabrication was discovered. Several years earlier, Barnicle had written a touching column about two boys—one black, one white—who shared a hospital room while they were being treated. When the black child died, Barnicle wrote, the white parents gave the black parents $10,000. In preparing to reprint the article, *Reader's Digest* fact checkers investigated the story but found no one at any Boston hospital who could remember such a case taking place. After this became public knowledge, Barnicle resigned from the *Globe*. (Barnicle later moved to hosting radio commentary on WTKK in Boston; being a regular guest on MSNBC's *Morning Joe* program; and writing for a number of different publications, including the *Boston Herald*, *Time* magazine, and Huffington Post.[36] Since leaving newspaper journalism, Smith has been a successful poetry writer and performer.[37])

In addition to the shame of dealing with two ethical lapses in one summer, the *Globe* also had to confront charges that it had been harsh with Smith, a black woman, while giving Barnicle, a white man, a second chance. *Brill's Content*, a media criticism magazine, even suggested that problems with Smith's columns had been ignored for several years because confronting them would have forced editors to address similar charges that had been leveled against Barnicle.[38]

*Who Writes Those Letters?*    Readers expect magazine and newspaper articles to be authentic, but do they have the same expectation for the advice letters that run in magazines? A lawsuit against *YM* magazine (whose target audience is young women) raised that question. A photo of an underage model was used as an illustration to go with a letter under the headline "I Got Trashed and Had Sex With Three Guys." The magazine argued that no one would really think the photo was of the girl who sent the letter, which the editors said had been sent anonymously and signed "Mortified." However, a second issue surfaced when the magazine's editors could not produce the letter at the trial: Are such letters "real?"[39]

Questions on *YM*'s advice page are not signed, and the editors admit that often they combine comments from multiple letters and present the compilation as if it came from one person. *Teen* magazine also admits to generalizing from several letters to create one that will appeal to as many readers as possible. So even if the problems being written about are real, the specific letters may not be. Journalism professor Carolyn Kitch notes that charges of made-up quotes and sources surface frequently in the women's magazine business, and editors justify the practice as producing a more true-to-life account: "If sometimes an anecdote is a composite of real people . . . and yet the details of the issue are intact . . . it is truer than a single experience can be."[40]

## Corporate Conflict of Interest

Being fair and balanced are core journalistic values that have been discussed extensively in earlier chapters. At times, however, other factors can overwhelm that value, especially when the interests of the news organization's owners are in conflict with the values of balance and fairness. This problem of a conflict of corporate interest extends beyond suppressing stories; it also involves actively promoting the company's interests.

At the peak of the Internet boom in the late 1990s, for example, one of the highest-profile dot-com Web sites was Pets.com, a seller of pet supplies. The site's "spokesthing" was a sock puppet that appeared on a number of programs, including *Good Morning America* and ABC's *Nightline,* to eulogize comic strip artist Charles Schulz. The puppet was introduced on *Good Morning America* as the Pets.com sock puppet. This widespread use of the Web site's name was likely the result of Disney, the owner of the ABC broadcast network, also owning 5 percent of Pets.com. The appearance of the puppet on the shows led to coverage of the appearance in the *New York Times* as well as in several other media outlets.[41] The promotion of Pets.com by a major media channel that co-owns the site is a clear example of synergy (discussed in Chapter 3), but it also illustrates conflict of interest.

Until 2009 the Chicago Tribune, WGN television, and the Chicago Cubs major league baseball team were all owned by the same parent company.

Traditionally, such conflicts of interest are recognized when reporters give favorable coverage to a company in which they have an interest or to a person who is their friend. Or a conflict could involve the negative coverage of someone they dislike. With the growth in size and concentration of media companies in the past decade, an increasing issue is conflict of interest by the owners themselves. For example, the *Washington Post* and NBC joined together to share materials through their various Web sites (especially MSNBC's cable news Web site), *Newsweek* (owned by the *Washington Post*), and the *Post* itself. But, as explained in Chapter 3, NBC is owned by megacorporation General Electric, and computer software giant Microsoft is the MS in MSNBC. So the *Washington Post*, which is generally seen as an independent voice in the press, is cooperating with at least two major nonmedia companies.

Conflicting investments don't just occur with megacorporations. Newspapers have been investors in local professional sports teams, which can also raise conflict-of-interest issues. The best-known case of a sports team–newspaper investment is that of the *Chicago Tribune*, which purchased the Chicago Cubs in 1981 and then sold the team in 2009. Even though the paper owned the team for close to three decades, the *Tribune*'s sports staff was often hard on the Cubs. (Of course, some observers argue that, given the Cubs' performance over the past 100 years, it would be hard not to be critical of the team.)[42]

Newspapers always claim that they keep the business side of their operations separate from those of the newsroom, but it is sometimes hard for the public to see things that way.

## Sensationalism

Along with political, international, economic, and other significant news, journalists sometimes focus on news that may not be important but is certainly interesting, largely because that's what audience members seem to enjoy. Cable television commentator Chris Matthews defends such news coverage on the basis of what he calls "the watercooler principle." He says, "If people are talking about it at the office around the water-cooler, then it should be on the show."[43] Pulitzer Prize–winning reporter Edna Buchanan describes it this way: "The best day is one when I can write a lead that will cause a reader at his breakfast table the next morning to spit up his coffee, clutch at his heart, and shout, 'My God! Martha, did you read this?' That's my kind of day."[44]

Sometimes such stories can move beyond being merely interesting and enter the realm of **sensationalism**—coverage of events that are lurid and highly emotional. In the winter of 2006–2007, celebrity starlets Britney Spears, Lindsay Lohan, and Paris Hil-

The story of Tiger Woods's multiple affairs moved from tabloids to respected media in late 2009 as news outlets such as Newsweek magazine started covering the sensationalistic story.

ton became the big story. The three, famous primarily for being famous, were in the news continually for getting into catfights, being arrested for driving under the influence, and going in and out of rehab. Photos of them flashing various body parts to paparazzi showed up first on celebrity Web sites and in the tabloids. But the stories, if not the photos themselves, soon migrated into the mainstream press, and so we saw stories in every media outlet from ABC News to Fox News. Even the *New York Times* ran a bylined story on Spears's "lack of wardrobe" malfunctions.[45] *USA Today* ran a story on when it's appropriate to "go commando." And the *Toronto Star* in Canada gave the apparent trend story a political twist by noting that Margaret Trudeau, the wife of Canada's former prime minister, inadvertently flashed a photographer at Studio 54 back in 1977.

Sensational news clearly attracts viewers and readers, especially when it's truly out of the norm. When Michael Jackson died unexpectedly in 2009, the coverage of his death and memorial service dominated the media for several weeks, matching that of British princess Diana's death in 1997. And when golfer Tiger Woods had a minor car accident in late 2009, the media coverage began to explode when the news started breaking that Woods had been having affairs with at least eleven different women.[46]

The mainstream media use occasions such as Michael Jackson's death or Tiger Woods's infidelity as an opportunity to engage in **tabloid laundering or tabloidization**, which is when respectable media report on what the tabloids are reporting (without doing the reporting themselves). Journalist and commentator Margaret Carlson says, "We take what the tabloids do and write about, and that way get what we wouldn't write about originally into the magazine. And then we run pictures of the pictures to show how terrible the pictures are."[47]

**sensationalism**

News coverage that panders to audiences with lurid and highly emotional accounts of crime, sex, violence, or celebrity missteps.

**tabloid laundering or tabloidization**

When respectable media report on what the tabloids are reporting as a way of covering sensationalistic stories on which they might not otherwise report.

But *Newsweek* editor Mark Whitaker defends his magazine's reporting on the work of the tabloids:

> When the subject of a legitimate news story is the paparazzi phenomenon, and you're running these pictures in a way that's used to illustrate . . . that news story, and not just titillate people with exclusive photographs that have never been seen that you pay a lot of money for, then I think that that is still a defensible and legitimate use of the photographs.[48]

Why has there been such a move toward tabloidization? The editors of the *Columbia Journalism Review* suggest that there are two major reasons for this:

1. Competition—With increased competition and more players in the field, newsmagazines feel compelled to release stories that they might have avoided in the past. Former television reporter Robert MacNeil, speaking in the 1990s, said, "I tremble a little for the next sizable crisis with three all-news channels, and scores of other cable and local broadcasters, fighting for a share of the action, each trying to make his twist on the crisis more dire than the next."[49]

2. The Internet—Competition from the Internet has quickened the process by which rumors fly. Because anyone is able to publish, stories move quickly to being "out there." Journalist Jonathan Fenby says, "The Internet has a gun to the head of the responsible media. If you choose not to report a story, the Internet will."[50]

Although the 1990s saw an unusually high level of tabloid journalism, this wasn't the only period of questionable taste in the news profession. In the 1830s the biased partisan press ran real or imagined stories about political sex scandals. One paper, for example, claimed that President Andrew Jackson's mother "was a common prostitute, brought to this country by the British soldiers."[51] And the wild stories published by Joseph Pulitzer's and William Randolph Hearst's papers (see Chapter 6) don't seem all that different from the rumors printed by TMZ or Perez Hilton on the Internet.[52] (This brings to mind Truth Four—Nothing's new: Everything that happened in the past will happen again.)

The ethical problem with sensationalism is multifaceted. First, there is the question of whether it lowers politics, public events, and public discourse to the level of crude entertainment that is not to be taken seriously, as Neil Postman pointed out.[53] Second, tabloid-style stories can displace significant news—politics, economics, international affairs, war, genocide, famine, environmental issues—about which people need to be concerned. Finally, tabloid stories appeal to people's basest feelings and instincts rather than to their intellect and sense of decency.

## Whose Deaths Matter?

Whose deaths really matter when it comes to journalism? If an American pop star dies, all mass media entertainment programming is replaced by around-the-clock coverage of the death. But James Warren, an editor at the *Chicago Tribune*, posed the question, "How many Africans have to die for the story to go on page 1?"[54]

Warren raised this question in 2002, when an explosion in Nigeria killed more than 1,000 people. Warren argued unsuccessfully at an editorial meeting that the story should run on the front page of the *Tribune*. But on the same day the death of two people in a bombing in the Middle East did make it onto the front page.

Why is the question of which stories go on the front page an important issue? The front page is "prime real estate" in the newspaper business, and generally the *Tribune* runs no more than six stories on that page. All the stories that ran on the front page that day had a direct connection to people in Chicago. They dealt either with the actions of the president of the United States or with events happening in the state of Illinois.[55] Why were two deaths in the Middle East considered so important? Because they were part of the United States' ongoing battle against terrorism. In addition, many Americans are concerned about the political situation in the Middle East.

The story about Nigeria ended up running on page three with a page one "refer box" telling readers to turn to page three to see the full report. *Tribune* columnist Don Wycliff says that on a day when the president did not dominate the news or there was less important local news, the story might have made it onto page one.

*In 2002 an explosion killed more than 1,000 people in Nigeria. On the same day, two people died when a bomb exploded in the Middle East. The Chicago Tribune decided to run the Middle East story on the front page because of the connection to broader terrorism issues. The Nigeria story ran on page three.*

## There Is No "They": The Sago Mine Disaster

Few journalistic mistakes have been as cruel as the headlines that ran in newspapers across the country on Wednesday, January 4, 2006. The papers trumpeted that all of the coal miners trapped in West Virginia's Sago Mine had been found alive after having been trapped for two days below ground, when, in reality, all but one of the thirteen had died.

Newspapers and television news outlets across the United States struggled with tight deadlines and inaccurate information from the Sago Mine disaster in West Virginia. Though initial stories reported that all thirteen miners survived, the tragic truth was that twelve of them had died.

In the early morning hours of Monday, January 2, an explosion, likely triggered by lightning, trapped thirteen miners deep below ground in the Sago Mine. About 9:00 p.m. Tuesday, the first body was discovered in the mine, according to a timeline in the *Washington Post*.[56] At 11:45 p.m., one miner was found alive more than two miles into the tunnel.

At this point, confusion reigned. According to the *Post*, at 12:18 a.m. the rescue command center heard a report from a rescue worker that twelve miners were found alive. Apparently this early report was overheard and spread instantly through a crowd that had been praying for a miracle. Church bells started ringing. People cried, sang, and cheered.

According to the *Charleston Daily Mail*, West Virginia governor Joe Manchin had come out to the mine to wait with family members and had asked for confirmation of the good news. Although he didn't get the confirmation, Manchin said he was quickly caught up by the joyous mood: "[W]e went out with the people and they said, 'They found them.' We got swept up in this celebration. I said, 'The miracle of all miracles has happened.'"[57]

A statement from the governor would seem to signal some level of official confirmation. But within the next half-hour, reports started coming into the command center that only one miner was alive—reports that were not passed on to families or the press until nearly 3:00 a.m.

Morning papers, such as the *Charleston Gazette* in West Virginia and Denver's now-defunct *Rocky Mountain News*, started printing around midnight (if not a little earlier). Newspapers have to make really tough calls on a breaking story, and unlike television, they leave a permanent reminder of the times that they get a story wrong. For example, the early edition of the *Rocky Mountain News* carried the headline, "They're Alive." The headline was corrected in the final edition.

National papers were every bit as likely to have problems with the story. *USA Today*, which has perhaps the best national distribution of any newspaper in the country, devoted one-third of its front page to the rescue story on Wednesday. On Thursday, the press started an intense examination of how the story was botched.

According to industry newsweekly *Editor & Publisher*, the *Inter-Mountain*, an 11,000-circulation afternoon daily out of Elkins, West Virginia, managed to get the story right, not only in its print edition but also on its Web site. *Editor & Publisher* quotes *Inter-Mountain* editor Linda Skidmore's account of the paper's handling of the story: "I feel lucky that we are an afternoon paper and we have the staff that we do. We had a reporter there all night at the scene and I was on the phone with her the whole time." Skidmore also described how the false story started snowballing: "I was on the phone with her [reporter Becky Wagoner] and I was hearing things on CNN and FOX that she was not hearing there. . . . She heard that the miners were alive just before it was broadcast, around midnight. She talked about hearing church bells ringing and people yelling in jubilation—but nothing official."[58]

"We heard that they were found alive through CNN, then it snowballed to ABC, then FOX and it was like a house afire," recalled Wagoner, who said she was at the media information center set up by the mine's operators, International Coal Group Inc., when the reports spread. "A lot of the media left to go to the church where family members were located, but I stayed put because this was where every official news conference was given—and we never got anything official here," she said. "Something was not right. Then we were hearing reports that 12 ambulances had gone in [to the mine area] but only one was coming out. There was so much hype that no one considered the fact that there was no [official] update."[59]

Then a resident of West Virginia, I went to bed Tuesday night with reports on the Internet announcing that the miners had been found alive. When I sat down to breakfast and my local paper on Wednesday morning, though, it was immediately obvious that something was wrong with the story. The report from the Associated Press read:

> Twelve miners caught in an explosion in a coal mine were found alive Tuesday night, more than 41 hours after the blast, family members and Gov. Joe Manchin III said.
>
> Bells at a church where relatives had been gathering rang out as family members ran out screaming in jubilation.
>
> Relatives yelled, "They're alive!"
>
> Manchin said rescuers told him the miners were found.
>
> "They told us they have 12 alive," Manchin said. "We have some people that are going to need some medical attention."
>
> A few minutes after word came, the throng, several hundred strong, broke into a chorus of the hymn "How Great Thou Art," in a chilly, night air.[60]

What clues tipped me off? How could a reader, reading between the lines, tell there were problems with the story?

- There were no official sources cited, other than the governor. Why didn't reporters also have a source from the coal company?

- When the governor made his statement, he noted, "They told us. . . ." Not a name—just "they." My high school journalism teacher Judith Funk always took us to task about that word, asking, "Who's 'they'?" And the Sago story is probably one of the saddest examples of Truth Seven—There is no "they."

- Later on the story said, "The company did not immediately confirm the news."

- There were no details on the miners' condition or where they were found.

In short, the story read like it was passing along secondhand accounts. How did the press go so wrong with this story?

- There was the understandable problem of midnight deadlines. It's very difficult to handle a breaking story under these circumstances. But news organizations certainly could have been clearer in emphasizing the unconfirmed nature of the information in their reports.

- News organizations have gotten way too comfortable passing on unconfirmed stories that originate in the realm of blogs and rumors, because they are afraid of being "scooped." No longer does a story have to be true; it just has to be true that the story is out there. When we are dealing with rumors about misconduct by politicians, whose realities are more subject to interpretation, perhaps this is okay (though I don't really think so). But when we are talking about the lives of ordinary people, this irresponsibility just doesn't cut it.

- The facts of the news didn't match the story reporters were looking for. Journalists, especially the national press, were looking for a "miracle story" where people's prayers would be answered and everything would turn out fine. When reporters thought they found that story, they reported it. Tragically, that wasn't the way the story turned out.

So what can journalists do to make sure this doesn't happen again? *USA Today*'s Mark Memmott, speaking as part of a panel at West Virginia University on the press coverage of Sago, said:

> Our responsibility was to ask a lot of questions and be very, very careful about attributions and sourcing, and to make sure we told people not just about what we knew, but what we didn't know. We hadn't seen anybody come out of that mine. We hadn't really talked to anybody who knew what was going on inside there. We had heard from family members, who had heard from somebody else, who in some cases couldn't even tell reporters on the scene exactly who it was they had heard it from.[61]

# Photography

Photos seem to be at the heart of many of the most troubling ethical cases that journalists face. Whether it is showing live television video of the shooting at Columbine High School, moments of private grief following a drunk-driving accident, or the horrors of September 11, 2001, editors have always had to strike a balance between sensitivity toward readers, consideration for sources, and dedication to reporting the news accurately. Now they also have new tools, like Adobe Photoshop, that allow them to manipulate photos digitally, sometimes producing quite different images from those they started with.

*"An Incredibly Disturbing Thing Happened."*  Eric Meskauskas, director of photography for the tabloid *New York Daily News,* had to make a tough call on September 11, 2001. For Meskauskas, the Richard Drew photo was not just a national issue; it was a local, hometown story involving events that many of his readers had witnessed directly:

> We did know that our images would disturb people. Look, an incredibly disturbing thing happened and that is the truth of the matter. We did not take this lightly for one minute, but we agreed to run [the Drew image]. . . . This was a tragedy of epic proportions and if we [newspapers] are not going to show the horrible pictures now, when will we ever do so? Sure, we did get some calls and they said that they were upset. But what about all of those that don't call, but are moved to do something about the situation and volunteer?[62]

*How Much Photo Manipulation Is Too Much?*  Photographs have always been prone to manipulation. Photographers choose their films, lenses, and angles with a particular image in mind. Darkroom techniques extended the photographer's ability to control the image. But now photographs are altered electronically in ways that can be almost undetectable. In fact, all photos published today are manipulated digitally in terms of size, shape, color, and contrast. For example, the light and dark contrasts in many of the photos in this book have been adjusted in preparation for the printing process so that they will look better.

So the question becomes "How much manipulation is too much?" Keep in mind that there are several issues here:

- What is an acceptable level of photo manipulation?

- Should viewers know to what degree a photo has been altered?

- Does intentionally making changes in a photo change the viewer's response to the image?

# TEST YOUR MEDIA LITERACY

## Images of War

Few things challenge the ethical decision making of a photo editor more than images of war. Run images that are too harsh, and you will be accused of sensationalizing the war, being antiwar, inflaming readers against the enemy in the war, being unpatriotic, or upsetting young children who might see the image. Run images that are too toned down, and you will be accused of covering up the realities of war, promoting the war, or pandering to advertisers who don't want to upset readers or viewers. (Remember Truth Six—Activism and analysis are not the same thing. Critics often use anything journalists print as evidence of their bias.) The horror of war in photographs is nothing new. Look back at page 156 in Chapter 5. The images from the American Civil War and the war in Afghanistan are startlingly similar.

Kenny Irby, group leader for the Poynter Institute's visual journalism group and an award-winning photo editor, writes that photos can change how people perceive wars:

> The decision to publish dramatic and tragic photographs that depict the horrors of war is never easy.... We do know that throughout the modern era of warfare and photography, journalists have struggled with achieving a balance between maximizing truthful reporting and minimizing unnecessary harm, and the graphic images from Iraq have ignited that struggle anew.[1]

Irby points out that iconic war images such as Nick Ut's 1972 photo of the naked nine-year-old Kim Phuc burned by napalm and the 1968 photo of South Vietnamese national police chief Nguyen Ngoc Loan executing a Viet Cong officer with a pistol shot to the head defined a generation's view of the war in Vietnam. During the current war with Iraq, the images of the mistreatment of prisoners at Abu Ghraib prison or the horrific images of the burned bodies of contractors hanging from the bridge after the 2004 battle of Fallujah similarly define current views of the war. These photos illustrate Truth Four—Nothing's new: Everything that happened in the past will happen again.

Sometimes the images are more subtle. Irby describes the impact of photos the *Seattle Times* ran, of a long line of flag-draped coffins coming home from Iraq, which stirred up a nationwide controversy:

> Such images are articles of visual information that convey messages of truth and report authentic facts in immeasurable ways. Journalists know that, citizens understand this, the American government tries to control this ..., and terrorists seek to abuse this.[2]

When photo editors decide which photos to run, Irby suggests they consider the following questions:

> How would a person react to this image over a bowl of Cheerios or a glass of orange juice? Does the photo show dead bodies? Does the photo show blood? Does the photo show people naked? What if my child saw this?[3]

**MOREonline**

You can find links to more of Kenny Irby's analysis of war photography and see more of the images at **http://ralphehanson.com.**

**Who is the source?**
Who is Kenny Irby? What does he do? What is the Poynter Institute, and what does it do?

**What is he saying?**
Why are war photos controversial? Why are they important to readers? Why can they be offensive?

**What evidence is there?**
What examples does Irby provide of photos changing our perceptions of war? Do the examples he provides support his arguments? Can photos be used to advocate or attack a particular agenda?

**What do you and your classmates think about war photography?**
What war photos stand out in your mind? Where did you see them? Why should the newspaper have run those photos? Why not? Why do you think that photographs can lead people to support or oppose a war?

1 Kenneth Irby, "War Images as Eyewitness," May 10, 2004, poynter.org/content/content_view.asp?id=65426.
2 Ibid.
3 Ibid.

In 2008, there was an intense discussion at a photojournalism online bulletin board about a college newspaper adviser who insisted that a photographer needed to make the sky bluer in a photo of a Martin Luther King Day march. Most of the photographers on the bulletin board were outraged at the demand, saying that deepening the sky's color would be completely unethical. But how many photographers, seeing the pale winter sky, would have boosted the blue in the sky without a moment's thought? Or if the photo had been taken in the predigital era, how many photographers would have chosen to shoot with Kodak's Kodachrome film, which is known for giving intensely vibrant colors?[63] You can find a link to the complete discussion of this case along with the photo in question at http://ralphehanson.com.

Photo manipulation by magazines first came to the public's attention in 1982, when *National Geographic*'s editors "moved" one of the Egyptian pyramids so that a photo of the pyramids would fit on the magazine's cover. The change had no lasting moral significance—a similar effect could have been created by having the photographer reshoot the picture from a slightly different angle—but it forced the magazine industry to confront the implications of journalists altering images.[64]

In 1994 *Time* magazine created a furor when it ran what it called a "photo illustration" based on O. J. Simpson's mug shot, taken the week he was arrested as a suspect in the murders of Nicole Brown Simpson and Ron Goldman. *Time*

News photos from war zones can often shape public opinion in ways that verbal descriptions cannot. Nick Ut's image of Kim Phuc running naked down the road after being hit by napalm during the Vietnam War and Khalid Mohammed's photo of Iraqis rejoicing in front of the charred bodies of four foreigners in Fallujah during the war in Iraq became iconic images that represent their respective wars.

had prepared three covers. One was a straightforward presentation of the mug shot with no manipulation. One was an artist's portrait—an obvious painting. The third was a photo illustration—a computer-manipulated version of the mug shot. In the manipulated photo—which, to *Time*'s credit, was listed as an illustration, not a photo—the prisoner number was reduced, the image was made fuzzier, and the highlights were removed from O. J.'s face. It was the darkening of Simpson's face that was controversial. You can find a link to this controversial magazine cover at http://ralphehanson.com.

In a note to readers the following week, editor James Gaines talked about what had happened:

> I have looked at thousands of covers over the years and chosen hundreds. I have never been so wrong about how one would be received. In the storm of controversy over this cover, several of the country's major news organizations and leading black journalists charged that we had darkened Simpson's face in a racist and legally prejudicial attempt to make him look more sinister and guilty, to portray him as "some kind of animal," as the NAACP's Benjamin Chavis put it. A white press critic said the cover had the effect of sending him "back to the ghetto." Others objected to the fact that the mug shot had been altered at all, arguing that photographs, particularly news photos, should never be altered.[65]

Conflicts over digital manipulation of photographs emerge on a regular basis. In June 2006, *El Nuevo Herald*, the leading Spanish-language paper in the United States, ran a photo that appeared to show four Cuban prostitutes soliciting tourists in Havana while two police officers looked on. The only problem was that the hookers weren't actually there—they had been added digitally by an editor.[66] In another case, a *Los Angeles Times* photographer was fired in 2003 after he combined two images of an American soldier supervising a group of refugees in Iraq to make the image more dramatic. But sometimes the alterations are on a smaller scale and are intended to help rather than to deceive. After a terrorist bombing of a train in Spain, some newspapers digitally removed a severed arm lying next to the tracks because they felt the image was too horrifying for a family newspaper.

> ## Standards for Digital Photo Manipulation
>
> The *Charlotte Observer* has put together a very specific set of guidelines for how digital photos can be edited. Among its criteria are the following:
>
> - "Dodging and burning," similar to what could be done in a conventional darkroom, are acceptable.
> - Colors can't be changed.
> - Backgrounds can't be eliminated or "aggressively toned."
> - The original unedited image files need to be downloaded.
> - Digital retouching (cloning) can be used only to remove things such as dust spots on the image.
> - The only time these rules can be violated is with a photo illustration that is clearly labeled as such, and can be clearly seen as an illustration.
>
> *Source:* Kenny Irby, *Charlotte Observer* Photo Correction/Editing Guidelines, September 25, 2003, poynter.org/content/content_view.asp?id=46958.

## Enforcing Ethics

How should the media address ethical issues? Are such issues the responsibility of the individual journalist? Of his or her editor? Should there be a single person in charge of ethics? Perhaps a code of ethics, applied properly, could provide sufficient guidance. In reality, various methods are used. This section looks briefly at some of the choices for systematically handling ethics issues.

*The Ombudsman.*    The **ombudsman**, also known as the reader's representative or audience advocate, takes the point of view of those who purchase or consume the news. Sanders LaMont, former ombudsman for the *Sacramento Bee*, argues that the ombudsman is an essential part of the journalism ethics process because the ombudsman connects the news consumer with the news outlet, be it a magazine, newspaper, Web site, radio station, or cable news operation.

The term *ombudsman* is derived from the word for a person who mediated between citizens and the government in Sweden in the early 1800s. Since that time it has been used to describe anyone who mediates between two groups. News ombudsmen have a variety of tasks to perform:

**ombudsman**
A representative of a publication's readers who takes the point of view of those who purchase or consume the news; also known as a reader's representative or audience advocate.

- Listening to the concerns of readers or audience members—Readers tend to be enthusiastic about someone taking their point of view, whereas newsroom employees may be less so. Shinika Sykes, the ombudsman for the *Salt Lake City Tribune*, says, "Readers like having someone they can call about concerns . . . and they get to speak to a live person."[67]

- Writing a regular column or commentary—The ombudsmen at papers such as the *San Diego Union-Tribune* or the *Washington Post* have regular spots in the news columns, and the ombudsman for the MSNBC cable network writes a column that appears on the network's Web site.

- Writing a regular memo for the news staff—The *Washington Post*'s ombudsman writes a blog on a regular basis that praises and criticizes the staff; he also writes a column for the Sunday editorial page.[68]

Until summer 2003, the *New York Times* did not have an ombudsman because management believed that the job should be done by the editors. However, following the scandal surrounding reporter Jayson Blair's fabrications, publisher Arthur Sulzberger Jr. appointed two editors to function as ombudsmen and enforce newsroom standards.[69] The position of ombudsman has been in a decline in recent years. When I was updating the Web resources that accompany this book's blog in 2008, I found that about one-third of the newspapers that had had ombudsmen no longer did. Simon Dumenco, writing in *Advertising Age*, suggests that newspapers no longer need to be spending money on ombudsmen since excellent press criticism sites are available online, such as Jim Romenesko's Poynter Institute media blog (discussed in Chapter 10).[70]

*Codes of Ethics.* News organizations have a variety of codes of ethics to consider. The Society of Professional Journalists has an extended code of ethics with three main principles:

1. Seek truth and report it as fully as possible.

2. Act independently.

3. Minimize harm.

Beyond those principles and the accompanying code, the organization's ethics handbook contains a series of case studies and a collection of other codes of ethics to help journalists make ethical decisions. In their introduction, the authors argue that ethics are not merely a set of ideals; they are something journalists do that lead to good reporting.[71] Obviously, a single code of ethics cannot cover all the issues encountered by the many different news outlets in the United States. "Can you even hope to have a common set of standards for the *New York Times*, the *National Enquirer*, and *People* magazine?" asks journalism professor Alex S. Jones, writing in the *Columbia Journalism Review*.[72]

If codes of ethics are to be effective, they need to be more than static documents, writes Jeffrey L. Seglin, an ethics columnist for the *New York Times*. A code of ethics must be central to the way the news outlet does business day-to-day.[73]

Unless that happens, ethics problems will continue to arise, Seglin warns. The *New York Times* management clearly had not followed up on a lower-level editor's complaints about Jayson Blair a year before the young reporter was caught fabricating and plagiarizing stories for the paper.

The *Cincinnati Enquirer* ran into trouble for an exposé it had run on the banana company Chiquita. The story may or may not have been accurate, but the highly critical article about the company's business practices was based on 2,000 voicemail messages the reporter had listened to using stolen access codes. The paper ended up apologizing to the company and paid an out-of-court settlement of $14 million. But prior to writing the story, the reporter had each year signed a copy of the paper's corporate code of ethics.

In these and other cases, the people involved clearly knew that their behavior was wrong and that it violated their publications' codes of ethics. According to Seglin, codes of ethics are often ineffective for two reasons:

1. Pressure from the parent company for profits—If reporters and editors believe that the most important goal of the company is profits rather than truthful news, they may be willing to violate ethical principles.

2. Nonenforcement—At the *Boston Globe*, both Patricia Smith and Mike Barnicle had been warned two years earlier that their columns would be watched closely for fabrications, but as Seglin points out, that warning clearly wasn't followed by action.

# ETHICS AND PERSUASIVE COMMUNICATION

Many of the items we see in the media are not messages created by members of the news staff, but rather are persuasive images created by advertising and public relations (PR) professionals seeking to influence people's behavior. The question of what constitutes ethical behavior for people who are attempting to manipulate public opinion then arises.[74] In this section we examine ethical principles applied in the fields of advertising and public relations.

## Advertising

During World War II the advertising industry formed the Advertising Council in response to charges of unethical behavior. The organization's purpose was to promote both advertising and business in general. One of its first functions was to help build support for wartime austerity. The Ad Council worked on a communication campaign to stop the hoarding of scarce resources, promote the buying of war bonds, and build morale. After the war, it worked on a variety of

# TEST YOUR MEDIA LITERACY

## Don Imus and Race

When CBS Radio and cable news channel MSNBC fired long-time host Don Imus for calling the Rutgers women's basketball team a group of "nappy-headed hos" on the air, it appeared to be an issue of what the public would tolerate from a "shock jock" radio host. But the networks were also under pressure from advertisers who no longer wanted to be associated with Imus's show. Advertisers such as office supply store chain Staples, Bigelow Tea, and consumer products giant Procter & Gamble pulled their ads.[1] The networks also faced considerable pressure from civil rights activists, including Al Sharpton and Jesse Jackson, as well as from the networks' own employees.

Controversy surrounding Imus's show was nothing new.

Back in 1993, Imus said on his show, "Isn't the *Times* wonderful. It lets the cleaning lady cover the White House." The "cleaning lady" he was referring to was Gwen Ifill, an African American woman who was the *New York Times* White House correspondent.[2] He made offensive and racist jokes about former secretary of defense William Cohen having an African American wife, and he described *Washington Post* media reporter Howard Kurtz as a "boner-nosed . . . beanie-wearing Jewboy."[3] (It should be noted that Kurtz was a frequent guest on the more serious portion of Imus's show.)

But there was another side to Imus and his show. Along with the segments of rude talk and bigoted commentary, Imus was also known for extended conversations with a wide range of important newsmakers and journalists. His guests—including Tom Brokaw, Rudy Giuliani, Sen. John Kerry, Sen. John McCain, and, yes, Howard Kurtz—were allowed to talk about serious issues at length instead of just in sound bites. He also runs a camp for children with cancer and has been an advocate for autism research.[4]

CBS had kept the show on the air for years despite the occasional bouts of controversy because it was profitable—making $20 million a year just for his primary station, WFAN-AM in New York. But in the end the network calculated that the cost of carrying the show was greater than the cost of dropping it.[5] In December 2007, approximately eight months after he was fired from WFAN, Imus was back on the air, this time at New York's WABC. And in 2009, cable news channel Fox Business News started running Imus's show on television again. Unlike many media figures who get caught saying something they wish they hadn't, Imus was fairly straightforward in talking about his return to the airwaves. He told trade magazine *Radio Ink*:

> I think what happened is about what should have happened. . . . You don't get to decide, nor should you, how the news media is going to treat a remark you make. You don't get to decide if they will put it in context, and you can't whine and complain if you pick up the *New York Times* and an essay rates what you said as a racist tirade. Every time I would get pissed off, I'd remind myself that if I hadn't said what I said, I wouldn't have to deal with it, the women at Rutgers would have to deal with it. I always remembered that it began with that remark.[6]

**MORE online**

You can read more about the fallout from Don Imus's comments at **http://ralphehanson.com.**

**Who is the source?**

Who is Don Imus? What does he do? What are some of the things he is known for? What kind of show did he host? Who were his listeners?

**What was he saying?**

What did Imus say that got him fired from CBS Radio and MSNBC? What other controversial comments has he made in the past? Why does he say the things he says? What does Imus have to say about the comments that got him in trouble?

**What evidence is there?**

Were Imus's comments about the Rutgers team an isolated incident or part of a general pattern of behavior? Was Imus's show different from those of other shock jocks?

**What do you and your classmates think?**

Do you think that Imus deserved to be fired for his racially loaded comments about the Rutgers women's basketball team? Do you find his comments offensive? Why do such comments matter now, when he's made other racist remarks in the past? Were his racially insensitive comments different from those made by others who use similar language? Why would advertisers use their influence to get programming that they find offensive eliminated?

[1] Paul Farhi and Paul Ahrens, "Advertisers Pull Out of Imus Show," *Washington Post,* April 11, 2007, A01.

[2] Gwen Ifill, "Trash Talk Radio," *New York Times,* April 10, 2007, A21.

[3] Timothy Noah, "The Wit and Wisdom of Don Imus; A Guide for Washington's Power Crowd," April 10, 2007, www.slate.com/id/2163872.

[4] Farhi and Ahrens, "Advertisers Pull Out of Imus Show."

[5] Paul Farhi, "Don Imus Is Fired by CBS Radio," *Washington Post,* April 13, 2007, A01.

[6] "Imus: CBS Firing 'Is What Should Have Happened'," *Radio Ink,* December 3, 2007.

public interest campaigns to maintain the positive image the group had fostered during the war. In recent years, the Ad Council has been responsible for a wide range of memorable public service ads, most notably the "Just say no" and "This is your brain on drugs" campaigns.[75]

A number of ethical issues concern the advertising industry today, including truth in advertising and the level of control advertisers can expect to have over the news content surrounding their ads.

*Truth in Advertising.*   Snapple claims to make its drinks from the "best stuff on earth." But what is the "best stuff?" Papa John's says "Better Ingredients, Better Pizza." Is this true? Just as important, do consumers expect such claims to be true?

Typically, ads for prescription drugs and medicines are held to high standards of truthfulness, whereas claims that one article of clothing is more fashionable than another are held to a much lower standard of proof. However, a dog food

CBS Radio fired morning host Don Imus from his nationally broadcast show in 2007 after he made sexist and racially derogatory comments about the Rutgers women's basketball team. Imus was back at work at a new station before the end of the year.

company was once required to prove that dogs really did prefer one brand over another by showing how much of two competing brands dogs would eat.[76]

A number of groups keep tabs on honesty in ads. The Federal Trade Commission (FTC) investigates many complaints, and consumer groups such as the Center for Science in the Public Interest may pursue complaints when the FTC doesn't act. The group investigated health claims made by Campbell Soup in the company's "Soup Is Good Food" campaign and persuaded the New York attorney general's office to force the company to make several changes to the campaign.[77]

The National Advertising Division of the Council of Better Business Bureaus also investigates claims of false advertising. Says council representative Gunnar Waldman, "We care even about the seemingly frivolous or 'less-important' cases. The issues at stake—truth in advertising—are always broader than the products themselves."[78]

Advertising executive Michael Dweck says that claims of being "best" are dangerous: "So the only claims we'd make ought to be sufficiently humorous, exaggerated, and far-fetched that no one will take them seriously."[79] Chris Wall of advertising giant Ogilvy & Mather says that as long as companies are truthful in their ads, they have nothing to worry about: "The most powerful advertising tends to be fundamentally truthful anyway. The trick is finding an honest point of advocacy for a product and then presenting it in a way that moves people, catches their attention, that they remember."[80]

*Good Taste and Calvin Klein.*   No single advertiser has created more controversy than fashion king Calvin Klein. He and his company have been accused of creating ads that are essentially child pornography, that make models look like heroin addicts and are simply in bad taste. The biggest controversy involving Klein's ads arose in the mid-1990s as a result of a campaign that featured young children in their underwear standing on a couch. Some critics accused the ad of glamorizing child pornography and encouraging pedophilia. Other observers, in contrast, compared the photos to those that might show up in a family photo album.[81]

The controversy likely arose from the fact that the Klein brand is associated with sexually explicit advertising. In 1980 fifteen-year-old Brooke Shields posed for Calvin Klein jeans ads with the headline "Nothing comes between me and my Calvins."[82]

Yet another Calvin Klein campaign, this one for jeans in 1995, led to a Justice Department investigation into whether Klein was using underage models in a series of provocative ads. The $6 million campaign featured television, print, and outdoor ads with young-faced models, all of whom Klein claimed were at least eighteen years old. The campaign was dropped after running for two months, but not before it had attracted massive attention.[83] The campaign was criticized by President Bill Clinton as well as by religious leaders. What pushed this campaign over the limit? Marketing professor Kirk Davidson, writing for *Marketing News*, says that the extremely young-looking models were at the root of the criticism. Klein could get away with naked and near-naked models when they were clearly adults. It was his use of child-like models that created the controversy.[84]

Mark Crispin Miller, a media professor at New York University, sees the criticism of Klein's ads as criticism of the advertising industry as a whole. "It sounds like Calvin Klein is being scapegoated for the general excesses of our commercial culture," Miller told the *Christian Science Monitor*. "I don't simply mean the near nudity or sexual innuendo; I mean the intensifying emphasis on shock value and the sheer omnipresence of advertising. What's immoral is not necessarily [advertising's] occasional lapse in taste, but its reduction of all of life to . . . pursuit of fulfillment in mere products."[85]

*Advertising and Media Control.*    Sometimes concern about media content comes from advertisers themselves rather than from critics of the media. Advertisers may want to control the kind of material that surrounds their messages, hoping to avoid stories that are critical of their products or simply associating themselves with high-quality content. For example, a group of car dealers in California pulled all their advertising from the *San Jose Mercury News* after the paper ran an article that explained to buyers how to read the factory invoices on new cars so that they would be in a better negotiating position.[86] At other times, advertising boycotts are driven by public advocacy groups that want to get a particular radio or television show off the air. In 2000, women's groups and gay activist groups led an effort to get advertisers to boycott conservative commentator Dr. Laura Schlessinger's radio and television programs because of the negative opinions she expressed about those groups.[87]

Magazine editors have long offered warnings to advertisers when potentially offensive articles will be included in a forthcoming issue. *Better Homes and Gardens* warned cigarette makers before running an article on the dangers of secondhand smoke and offered them the option of moving their advertising to another issue. "That's just consideration," said the magazine's editor-in-chief. "You don't want to purposely slap advertisers in the face."[88]

It can also work the other way: Sometimes advertisers are contacted when positive articles are scheduled to appear. An energy company was solicited to advertise in the *National Review* when an article included a favorable mention of the company.

Occasionally companies want to know in advance what kind of content is going to be included in forthcoming issues of magazines so that they can decide whether to include their advertising with it. Some publishers view this simply as a way of keeping important advertisers informed about how their advertising will look. However, the American Society of Magazine Editors warns "that some advertisers may mistake an early warning as an open invitation to pressure the publisher or editor to alter, or even kill, the article in question."[89]

In 1995 Ford pulled all its advertising from the *New Yorker* for six months because one of its ads appeared next to a column by Ken Auletta that quoted an explicit song by Nine Inch Nails. And *Esquire* reportedly cancelled a sixteen-page story about gay sex for fear that Chrysler would pull four pages of advertising from the magazine. In 1996 Chrysler sent a letter to 100 major magazines requiring them to notify the car maker "in advance of any and all editorial content that encompasses sexual, political, social issues or any editorial that might be construed as provocative or offensive."[90] Chrysler defended its policy in *Advertising Age*, saying, "We think we have a right to determine how and where we want to place our advertising. . . . We are not trying to get in the way of the editorial integrity of any magazine, but we do have the right to determine the editorial environment where our ads appear."[91]

Advertisers have also attempted to influence programming on television. Finding "family-friendly" shows to sponsor on television, especially broadcast television, is becoming increasingly difficult. The hit program *Friends* delivered a huge audience for NBC, but it did so with racy story lines and risqué humor. Companies like consumer product giant Johnson & Johnson want to sponsor shows that parents and children can watch together so that they'll see commercials for Band-Aids, baby powder, Motrin, and Mylanta. To combat this problem, Johnson & Johnson, along with companies like Procter & Gamble, Coca-Cola, and Ford, formed a group called the Family Friendly Programming Forum to promote the development of shows that are acceptable to the entire family. The forum isn't boycotting or criticizing adult-oriented shows; it just wants to promote shows on which its members won't be embarrassed to advertise.

The group funds the development of new shows that will meet these needs; in return, it receives the first right to advertise on them. The companies that belong to the forum control $11 billion worth of advertising, so their voices are important to television networks. In 2000 the first show whose development had been funded by the forum came on the air: *Gilmore Girls*.[92] Since then they have been responsible for the development of shows such as *The New Adventures of Old Christine*, *Ugly Betty*, and *Friday Night Lights*.[93]

# Ethics in Public Relations

It is easy to joke about a lack of ethics in public relations, but PR firms ignore ethical behavior at their own peril. The Public Relations Society of America (PRSA), founded in 1948, established its own code of ethics in 1954 not only to improve the profession's behavior but also to improve the industry's image at a time when practitioners were "generally . . . perceived as slick con artists." In its original form, the code said, "We pledge to conduct ourselves professionally, with truth, accuracy, fairness, and responsibility to the public." The code was substantially revised and clarified in 1999.

*Conducting War Through Public Relations: Citizens for a Free Kuwait.*  The ethical challenge of balancing the needs of truthfulness, the public interest, and the client's interests became a major issue for one PR firm during the 1991 Persian Gulf War. Foreign governments often hire PR firms to represent their interests in the United States, but few have hired a major firm to promote the nation's involvement in a war.[94]

Hill & Knowlton, the nation's largest PR firm at the time, was hired by Citizens for a Free Kuwait, a group made up of members of the Kuwaiti government. The campaign was designed to create sympathy for Kuwait, opposition to Iraq and Saddam Hussein, and support for American involvement in fighting Iraq. The campaign followed a typical pattern of lobbying Congress, calling press conferences, sending out press releases, and producing video news releases.[95]

What really attracted controversy, and raised ethical questions throughout the industry, was testimony that Hill & Knowlton arranged to have given before the Congressional Human Rights Caucus. This group of U.S. representatives held hearings on October 10, 1990, on the Iraqi invasion of Kuwait. The centerpiece of these hearings was the eyewitness testimony of a fifteen-year-old Kuwaiti girl identified only as Nayirah. Nayirah told the caucus that she had personally seen atrocities committed following the invasion: "While I was there, I saw the Iraqi soldiers come into the hospital with guns, and go into the room where . . . babies were in incubators. They took the babies out of the incubators, took the incubators, and left the babies on the cold floor to die."[96]

Her testimony certainly was effective. President George H. W. Bush mentioned the "twenty-two babies 'thrown on the floor like firewood' " on six separate occasions.[97]

Two years later, journalist John R. MacArthur revealed that Nayirah, who had not previously been identified, was actually the daughter of the Kuwaiti ambassador—himself a member of the Kuwaiti royal family—to the United States. He, and others, charged that the incubator story was not true. Amnesty International found no evidence that the story was true, and ABC News reported that the story was "almost certainly false."[98]

# Public Relations Society of America's Statement of Professional Values

The following is the Public Relations Society of America's Statement of Professional Values:

> This statement presents the core values of PRSA members and, more broadly, of the public relations profession. These values provide the foundation for the Member Code of Ethics and set the industry standard for the professional practice of public relations. These values are the fundamental beliefs that guide our behaviors and decision-making process. We believe our professional values are vital to the integrity of the profession as a whole.

## Advocacy

- We serve the public interest by acting as responsible advocates for those we represent.
- We provide a voice in the marketplace of ideas, facts, and viewpoints to aid informed public debate.

## Honesty

- We adhere to the highest standards of accuracy and truth in advancing the interests of those we represent and in communicating with the public.

## Expertise

- We acquire and responsibly use specialized knowledge and experience.
- We advance the profession through continued professional development, research, and education.
- We build mutual understanding, credibility, and relationships among a wide array of institutions and audiences.

## Independence

- We provide objective counsel to those we represent.
- We are accountable for our actions.

## Loyalty

- We are faithful to those we represent, while honoring our obligation to serve the public interest.

## Fairness

- We deal fairly with clients, employers, competitors, peers, vendors, the media, and the general public.
- We respect all opinions and support the right of free expression.

Since Nayirah's testimony had not been given under oath, no questions were raised about the legality of Hill & Knowlton's actions. The firm has defended its actions on behalf of Citizens for a Free Kuwait, but the fact remains that it did not investigate Nayirah's claims to see if they were true.[99] Whether true or false, the testimony itself was certainly not enough to send the United States to war with Iraq; rather, it was a well-planned PR effort intended to make Iraq seem evil and Kuwait appear to be a victim in need of assistance.

*Whom Do You Serve: The Client or the Public?*    One of the most difficult ethical problems facing PR practitioners is the conflict between serving the client's interests and serving those of the public. David L. Martinson, a professor of journalism, argues that PR practitioners can internalize important ethical principles of honesty and serving the public interest by practicing them daily in small ways. Then, when the rare moral dilemmas arise, the practitioner is used to behaving in an ethical manner.[100]

As noted earlier, Aristotle suggested that ethical behavior arises from a golden mean, or balance, between two extremes of behavior or belief. Does this mean that PR practitioners can strike a balance between lying and telling the truth? No. Martinson says that PR practitioners must always be fully committed to the truth but that it is possible to compromise between serving the public's interests and the client's. The PR practitioner must serve the client's best interests, but not to the extent that his or her professional and ethical obligations to the public are compromised.

# CHAPTERSummary

Media ethics are a complex topic because they deal with an institution that must do things that ordinary people in ordinary circumstances would not do. Media ethics draw on a range of philosophical principles, including basic Judeo-Christian values, Aristotle's ideas about virtue and balanced behaviors (the golden mean), Kant's categorical imperative, Mill's principle of utility, Rawls's veil of ignorance, and the Hutchins Commission's social-responsibility ethics. One way contemporary journalists can resolve their ethical problems is by using the Bok model for ethical decision making.

Reporters face a range of ethical issues on a regular basis. Those issues include the following:

- *Truthfulness.* Journalists need to make a commitment to telling the truth. This includes not giving false or made-up reports, and telling truthful stories that are not intended to deceive the audience. This may require reporters to provide not only the facts but also the context surrounding them. Truthfulness requires a commitment not only from the journalist but also from the organization he or she works for.

■ *Conflicts of interest.* The interests of a corporation that owns a news organization may sometimes be at odds with the nature of the news being reported. Journalists need to be careful not only to portray their parent company in an accurate light but also to give no special favors to companies connected to the organization's parent company.

■ *Sensationalism.* News organizations sometimes emphasize news that is interesting but unimportant. This happens when reporters put more effort into attracting and pleasing an audience than into reporting on the critical issues of the day. This can happen because of the increased pace of the news business brought about by cable television, the Internet, and the parent company's desire for profits.

■ *Authenticity and appropriateness of photographs.* Photos can be among the most controversial media materials, both because of their disturbing content and because they can be altered with digital editing tools.

Journalists and their employers can apply a variety of methods for enforcing and implementing ethical behavior. These include employing an ombudsman, requiring commitment to ethical behavior on the part of all employees, and adhering to a code of ethics.

The advertising industry became concerned with protecting its image during World War II. Among the major ethical issues in advertising are the following:

■ *Truthfulness.* How important is it that claims such as "Tastes great" or "It's the best" can be demonstrably true?

■ *Taste.* Is it appropriate for ads to attract attention by shocking audiences?

■ *Media control.* Do advertisers have a right to control the editorial material that surrounds their advertisements?

In the public relations industry, practitioners need to work at balancing their clients' interests against those of the public at large. This can become problematic when a client is attempting to influence the public to support an issue such as going to war.

## KEYTerms

## CONCEPTReview

Ethical principles from Aristotle, Kant, Mill, Rawls, and the Hutchins
   Commission

The Bok model for ethical decision making

The difference between morals and ethics

Corporate conflict of interest

Digital alteration of photographs

Advertiser influence on media content

# Global Media

## Communication Around the World

**On the night** of November 26, 2008, a group of terrorists engaged in a series of ten attacks at locations across Mumbai, the heart of India's film industry. The terrorists killed 171 people and held the city hostage for more than sixty hours.[1] As the story broke over the next three days, coverage came from bloggers and tweeters who were caught up in the attacks as well as professional journalists from India's television news channels.

Arnab Goswami, chief editor of Times Now, India's largest satellite news channel, says that the Indian government got very nervous about media coverage of the attacks, fearing that the reports were helping the terrorists. At one point, during the early phases of the attacks, the government shut down television news for forty-five minutes. But Goswami says that when the government cut off the

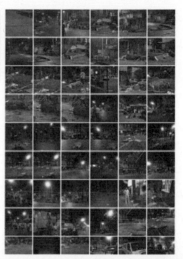

news flow, the response from viewers was "Massive, massive. . . . Every single phone was ringing. People were watching us so closely that if we were off for five seconds they would react, because cable and satellite television is largely the only form of receiving information at a time like this."[2]

Goswami says that he and his reporters often did not report everything they knew for fear of endangering people and drawing government censorship. He told National Public Radio's *On the Media*,

> India has had a largely . . . closed media with only state-run television for 40 years after its independence—that's 1947 to '87. The television media in its present form and private TV channels are only 10 years old. And the power of the television media and news channels is something that sometimes even scares the government. . . . We are fighting for self-regulation, and it is very important that we don't give the opportunity for anyone in the government to accuse us of giving away these kinds of details. That was uppermost in my mind when, on several occasions, I stopped my reporters from giving away such information.[3]

In one case, there were reports of explosives found at a railway station. Nearby was a gathering of thousands of people at the Gateway of India. Goswami said that if the news of the explosives had been televised, there might have been a deadly panic. Instead, he called editors at half a dozen other television stations, and they all agreed not to report it.

But television news channels weren't the only source of news over those days. Indian social media expert Gaurav Mishra says that Twitter feeds and blog posts from people in Mumbai were a major source of news to Western journalists in the early hours of the attacks. Twenty-seven-year old photographer Vinukumar

Photographer Vinukumar Ranganathan (Vinu) distributed his photos of the Mumbai terror attacks via Flickr.

Ranganathan (who goes by Vinu) went out that night to take pictures of the attacks. He then uploaded his images to the photo-sharing service Flickr and started tweeting links to them.[4] Vinu told the Associated Press, "I was just updating online because I could see the buildings from my house. I just felt that there were lots of people I was communicating with who were also my friends, so it was about the personal connection."[5]

Vinu's photos went far beyond his "personal connection," however. Mishra and others started posting links to his Flickr photo pool, and soon news operations from around the world, including CNN, started using Vinu's photos. "That was clearly citizen journalism, in its best sense," Mishra says. "What was happening on Twitter was not analysis but, yes, there were elements of breaking news on Twitter."[6]

Vinu also used his blog to ask people about which photos he ought and ought not to post. Another photo blogger delayed posting photos for an hour after they were taken to keep from passing on sensitive information to the terrorists.

Eyewitness accounts of the attacks came from three bloggers stranded in a hotel near the center of the attacks. Blogger Amit Varma's accounts led CNN and the BBC to interview the writer on their global news broadcasts. Although a limited number of

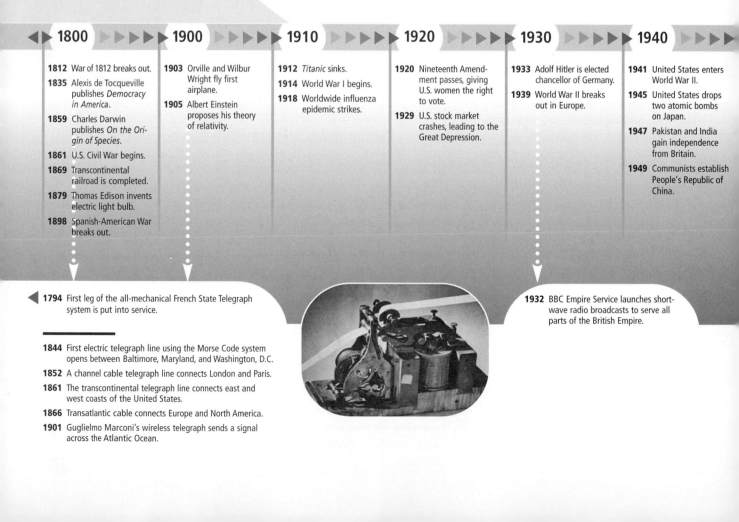

## 1800 ▶▶▶▶ 1900 ▶▶▶▶ 1910 ▶▶▶▶ 1920 ▶▶▶▶ 1930 ▶▶▶▶ 1940 ▶▶▶

| | | |
|---|---|---|
| **1812** War of 1812 breaks out. | **1903** Orville and Wilbur Wright fly first airplane. | **1912** *Titanic* sinks. |
| **1835** Alexis de Tocqueville publishes *Democracy in America*. | **1905** Albert Einstein proposes his theory of relativity. | **1914** World War I begins. |
| | | **1918** Worldwide influenza epidemic strikes. |
| **1859** Charles Darwin publishes *On the Origin of Species*. | | |
| **1861** U.S. Civil War begins. | | |
| **1869** Transcontinental railroad is completed. | | |
| **1879** Thomas Edison invents electric light bulb. | | |
| **1898** Spanish-American War breaks out. | | |

**1920** Nineteenth Amendment passes, giving U.S. women the right to vote.

**1929** U.S. stock market crashes, leading to the Great Depression.

**1933** Adolf Hitler is elected chancellor of Germany.

**1939** World War II breaks out in Europe.

**1941** United States enters World War II.

**1945** United States drops two atomic bombs on Japan.

**1947** Pakistan and India gain independence from Britain.

**1949** Communists establish People's Republic of China.

**1794** First leg of the all-mechanical French State Telegraph system is put into service.

**1844** First electric telegraph line using the Morse Code system opens between Baltimore, Maryland, and Washington, D.C.

**1852** A channel cable telegraph line connects London and Paris.

**1861** The transcontinental telegraph line connects east and west coasts of the United States.

**1866** Transatlantic cable connects Europe and North America.

**1901** Guglielmo Marconi's wireless telegraph sends a signal across the Atlantic Ocean.

**1932** BBC Empire Service launches short-wave radio broadcasts to serve all parts of the British Empire.

bloggers were covering the attacks, the Twitter traffic went through the roof, generating as many as 1,000 messages per hour.[7]

For Mishra, news coverage of the Mumbai attacks was a story not about old versus new media but rather about them working well together. "[T]he story is that many people, thousands of people, came together and tried to make sense of what was happening, using a new service like Twitter, and new media and mainstream media complemented each other in covering this story."[8]

News breaking via Twitter and other social media has become the standard, not the exception. (Remember Truth Three—Everything from the margin moves to the center?) Writing in his social media blog, Mishra says,

> Let's get used to it. From this moment onwards, every accident worth reporting, anywhere in the world, will be reported first, via SMS [text message], by a bystander who has a mobile phone. In most cases, the first photos or videos of the accident will be taken by a bystander who has a camera phone. If the accident occurs in a developed country, or a metro city in a developing country, the SMS will be sent to a microblogging service like Twitter and the photos and videos will be uploaded to photo- and video-sharing services like Flickr and YouTube. From this moment onwards, we will do well to expect it to happen, and reserve our surprise for the cases where it doesn't happen.[9]

## ▶▶ 1950 ▶▶▶▶ 1960 ▶▶▶▶ 1970 ▶▶▶▶ 1980 ▶▶▶▶ 1990 ▶▶▶▶ 2000 ▶▶▶▶

**1950** Korean War begins.

**1953** Francis Crick and James Watson discover structure of DNA.

**1957** Soviet Union launches spacecraft *Sputnik I.*

**1963** Martin Luther King Jr. delivers "I Have a Dream" speech during Washington, D.C., civil-rights march.

**1969** Neil Armstrong walks on the moon.

**1974** U.S. president Richard Nixon resigns due to Watergate scandal.

**1975** Vietnam War ends.

**1977** Apple II personal computer is introduced.

**1978** First test-tube baby is born.

**1983** First HIV/AIDS cases are documented.

**1985** Ozone hole is discovered over Antarctica.

**1986** Space shuttle *Challenger* explodes.

**1989** The Berlin Wall falls.

**1991** Soviet Union disbands.

**1993** European Union is formed.

**1994** Nelson Mandela is elected president of South Africa.

**1997** Diana, Princess of Wales, dies in car accident.

**2001** Al Qaida attacks World Trade Center and Pentagon.

**2003** United States invades Iraq.

**2003** Human genome project is completed.

**2005** Terrorists bomb London's transport system.

**2005** Hurricane Katrina hits the U.S. Gulf Coast.

**2008** Barack Obama is elected U.S. president.

**1956** Siebert, Peterson, and Schramm publish *Four Theories of the Press.*

**1962** Marshall McLuhan introduces the concept of a "global village" that is linked through media.

**1985** News media in the Soviet Union experience a brief period of openness during *glasnost,* a policy promoted by Mikhail Gorbachev.

**1995** John Nerone and his colleagues publish *Last Rights: Revisiting* Four Theories of the Press.

**2000** There are more than 430 privately owned television stations in Europe.

**2006** Al Jazeera launches an English edition, Al Jazeera English, which is only available in the United States online.

**2006** Fifty-five journalists are killed worldwide "in direct connection" to their work. Thirty-two of these deaths were in Iraq.

**2008** News about the Mumbai terror attacks travels worldwide by social media.

You can find links to Vinu's photos, Mishra's blog, and interviews with Times Now editor Goswami at http://ralphehanson.com.

The notion of being able to print or broadcast almost any kind of news is central to the ideal of free speech in the United States and the democracies of the West. But the ideal of a marketplace of ideas where the media are controlled by private industry is not universal. Different countries and cultures have differing ideas as to what constitutes the proper form for the media to take. In this chapter we look at ideals of how the media ought to behave and how the media function in different societies around the world. Finally, we consider what it means to live in a world with such a wide range of media.

# MEDIA IDEALS AROUND THE WORLD

So far in this book we have primarily discussed the development of the media in economically developed democracies. But the relationship among politicians, citizens, and the press can take very different forms in other nations, depending on the country's culture, government, and level of development.

In 1956 three journalism professors—Fred S. Siebert, Theodore Peterson, and Wilbur Schramm—outlined what they considered to be the major forms the press could take around the world in *Four Theories of the Press.* They built their argument around two basic value-oriented theories of how the press ought to behave: *authoritarian* and *libertarian.* They then created two variations on these: *Soviet/communist* and *social responsibility.*[10]

The authors argue that the nature of the press depends on the political and social structures of the society it serves. In other words, the structure and function of the press mirrors the society it portrays. Since 1956, however, much has changed. The Cold War has ended, and the Soviet Union has collapsed. We've gone from talking about the influence of the press to the influence of the media. The media industry has come to be dominated by a limited number of large owners. We have seen the rise of the Internet, which allows many more voices to be heard, though they can easily get lost in all the digital noise. And the importance of developing nations is recognized increasingly.

In response to these changes, and many others, scholars started questioning whether the ideas from the book needed to be revisited. John Nerone and his contributing authors did just that in 1995 with *Last Rights: Revisiting* Four Theories of the Press. Nerone and his colleagues, as well as Siebert and his colleagues, were faculty at the University of Illinois. As the authors of *Last Rights* point out, "When *Four Theories* was written, many U.S. newspapers carried ads for segregated housing, it was still legal in a number of states for a husband to divorce his wife for being a bad housekeeper, and no one had ever seen what the earth looked like from outer space."[11]

Nerone and his colleagues suggest several things that contemporary readers of *Four Theories* should think about, primarily that the four theories were not a timeless set of categories. Rather, they were a critique set within a particular time period that reflects the politics and economics of its day. Other critics have suggested that there should be a fifth theory of the press—*development theory*—to deal with countries that are in the process of building modern economies.[12] In this section we look at the four original theories, along with development theory, and see how well they apply to press systems today.

## Authoritarian Theory

The **authoritarian theory** is the oldest theory of the press. It says that the role of the press is to be a servant of the government, not a servant of the citizenry. Authoritarian theory has its roots in royal control of societies during the era when the printing press was first developed. Monarchs were believed to derive their authority to rule directly from God, and therefore they had the right and responsibility to control all aspects of society, including the printing press. Rulers felt that the proper role of the press was to provide the public with the information the rulers deemed appropriate. Keep in mind that the reach of the press was still fairly limited because relatively few people were literate. So the monarch gave formal permission to the publisher, who in return had a monopoly on the publishing business.

Today countries that are developing mass media often start by taking an authoritarian approach. Authoritarian rule is also practiced in most totalitarian states, which seek to control the press along with all other aspects of social life.

Authoritarian control of the press is carried out by the following means:

- Giving permits to only certain printers—However, as the number of trained printers grows and an increasingly literate public demands more and more printed materials, the ability of the government to control "outlaw" printers can become problematic.

- Prosecuting anyone who violates generally accepted standards for the press.

*Yugoslavian newspaper owner and editor Slavko Curuvija, pictured here in 1998, was shot to death by two gunmen in 1999. His paper, the Dnevni Telegraf (Daily Telegraph), had been banned and heavily fined for criticizing Yugoslavian president Slobodan Milosevic.*

**authoritarian theory**
A theory of appropriate press behavior that says the role of the press is to be a servant of the government, not a servant of the citizenry.

Totalitarian governments have been ruthless in controlling the press through arrests, torture, arson, and imprisonment, along with more subtle methods such as controlling the availability of supplies. For example, in the 1990s Serbian president Slobodan Milosevic shut down the capital city's only independent radio station, Radio B92, and the opposition newspaper had trouble publishing because of newsprint shortages—which didn't seem to affect the official state newspaper.[13] During the 1970s and early 1980s, the military government in Argentina pressured most newspapers into self-censorship through death threats and imprisonment.[14]

Nerone's major critique of authoritarian theory is that it is more a description of the procedures a government uses to control the press than a philosophy of press behavior.[15]

## Communist Theory

**communist theory**
A theory of appropriate press behavior that says the press is to be run by the government to serve the government's own needs.

Although the Soviet Union no longer exists, a variety of governments around the world, including in Cuba and China, continue to hold to communist ideals. The **communist theory** of the press is similar to the authoritarian theory but goes a step further. Instead of just being a servant of the government, the press is run by the government to serve the government's own needs. The communist press is supposedly free to publish the truth. However, in the Soviet Union the press was not free, nor did it speak the truth. The communist view is that there is only one valid political and social philosophy, so there is no need for competing "false" ideals to be portrayed in the media. Moreover, communists argue that the American press is no freer than the communist press because the American media serve the needs of capitalist owners rather than those of society. Communist media theory proposes the following principles:

- The media are an instrument of the government and the Communist Party—An independent press is undesirable and should be suppressed.

- The media should be closely tied to other sources of government power and authority—In the United States, the executive, legislative, and judicial branches of the government serve as checks and balances on each other, all overseen by the press. But communist theory holds that all elements of the state, including the press, should work toward a common goal.

- The media's main purpose is to act as a tool for government propaganda.

The communist notion of absolute right and wrong leaves no room for the media to debate the proper role of government. The press is not a watchdog but rather a supporter of the Communist Party's efforts to create a perfect state. Since the responsibility for enforcing this truth lies within the leadership of the state, the leadership should control the mass media. So the role of the press is to put forward the official party line. This is almost directly counter to the Western notion of the press as an outside observer keeping watch on the government.[16]

In *Last Rights*, the authors point out that what we've been referring to as "the communist theory" was supposed to represent a generalized Marxist response to libertarian theory (discussed below) but really represented the Soviet approach at a given time.[17] The communist theory of the press was an ideal that Soviet communists never came even close to obtaining. The Soviets may have had an ideal of a communist press, but in reality it was generally just authoritarian controls. The only time when the Soviet media came close to acting as a force for the people and not just for those in power was under the leadership of Mikhail Gorbachev in the 1980s during his campaign for *glasnost*, or openness. *Glasnost* allowed citizens and the media to express their opposition to the official government position and to criticize corrupt local leaders. Since then, however, the Russian media have gone back to a level of authoritarian control, as we discuss later in this chapter.

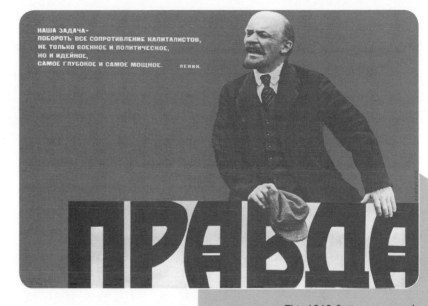

*This 1968 Soviet propaganda poster depicting Vladimir Ilyich Lenin reads: "Pravda: Our task is to overcome capitalist resistance—not only military and political resistance, but ideological resistance, which is the most profound and powerful."*

## Libertarian Theory

The opposite of authoritarian theory is the **libertarian theory**. In this view, the press does not belong to the government but is instead a separate institution that belongs to the people and serves as an independent observer of the government. Libertarian philosophy views people as moral beings who can tell the difference between truthfulness and falsity. Because of this, they need a free and open press so that they can decide for themselves what is true and what is false. The libertarian theory thus holds that there must be a marketplace of ideas in which both true and false statements can compete for the hearts and minds of audience members. This is the basic idea of the First Amendment to the U.S. Constitution.[18] Libertarian theory is the basis of free speech in the democracies of the West and is the most well developed of the theories in *Four Theories*.[19]

Most noncommunist countries pay at least lip service to the libertarian ideal of the press, although many do not adhere to it. Again, even in the United States there tends to be much more government control of the broadcast media than of print.

**libertarian theory**
A theory of appropriate press behavior that says the press does not belong to the government but is instead a separate institution that belongs to the people and serves as an independent observer of the government.

The free press of a libertarian society is based on the following principles:

- People want to know the truth and be guided by it.

- The only way to arrive at the truth is for ideas to be freely and openly discussed.

- Different people will have different opinions, and everyone must be allowed to develop their own.

- The most rational ideas will be the most accepted.

*Leaders of countries with a libertarian press, such as President Barack Obama, pictured here, routinely face questions from a range of reporters who will provide for the "marketplace of ideas" competing accounts of what the leaders' comments might mean.*

In the libertarian view, the major functions of the press are to inform, entertain, and advertise (to support itself). Overall, though, the goal of the media is to help people discover the truth. The press should be free of government control, and every idea, no matter how crazy or offensive, should be allowed a forum for expression. As Fred Siebert wrote in *Four Theories*, the ideal is "to let the public at large be subjected to a barrage of information and opinion, some of it possibly true, some of it possibly false, and some of it containing elements of both."[20]

A key problem with libertarian media theory is that it assumes that the primary threat to freedom of speech and communication comes from the government rather than from the marketplace. However, under the American system, the voices that are profitable to present will be heard much more loudly than those that do not produce a profit. The ideas that attract advertising revenue and sales draw much more attention from the press than do those about the poor or disenfranchised. Hence we hear more in the news about the stock market than about job programs for the unemployed. *Four Theories* argues that the free market is the ultimate in freedom rather than media owned by "community groups, nonprofit corporations, universities, religious groups, and municipalities."[21] The debate is framed in terms of external controls rather than access. There is a presumption that the ideal of freedom is corporate or individual ownership with no government intervention. But what about the BBC? Arguably one of the greatest broadcast news operations in the world, it is run with government funding, albeit with a relatively hands-off approach.

## Social Responsibility Theory

The **social responsibility theory** of the press is an outgrowth of libertarian theory. This theory is based on the concern that, although the press may be free from interference by the government, the press can still be controlled by corporate interests. For example, in principle anyone can start up a newspaper, but in reality it is an expensive and difficult proposition. Moreover, only a limited number of radio and television station licenses are available. So, although the government does not control the press in a free society, the control exercised by a limited number of corporations and individuals can be as effective as that of any government. Social responsibility theory says that the high level of concentrated power in the hands of the media requires that they be socially responsible in covering all sides of controversial issues and providing voters with all the information they need to make considered choices. If the press is not sufficiently vigilant, it is the duty of some representative of the public to force it to be responsible.[22]

Under social responsibility theory, the press is obliged to serve several social functions:

- Provide the news and information needed to make the political system work.

- Give the public the information needed for self-governance.

- Serve as an overseer of the government.

- Serve the economic function of bringing together buyers and sellers through advertising.

- Provide entertainment.

- Be profitable enough to avoid outside pressures.

Social responsibility theory essentially advocates nonauthoritarian media controls. France, Israel, and Sweden all operate under some form of social responsibility controls. The governments own and operate television channels, and the programming tends to promote the government's point of view.[23] The alternative is for the press to be in the hands of private business, which may allow for more political views but limits the media to carrying programming that is profitable. Government ownership frees the media from the constraint of having to make a profit.

The social responsibility theory was a response to the Hutchins Commission report from the late 1940s on the social responsibility of the press, which we discussed in Chapter 14. However, it does describe an approach to the press that is common in the world, for example, in the Israeli press, which we discuss later. The press do not necessarily like the idea that they have responsibilities to go with the freedoms they claim. The question really is, to whom does the freedom of the press belong? Is it to a corporate institution or is it to people with voices

**social responsibility theory**
A theory of appropriate press behavior based on the concern that, although the press may be free from interference from the government, it can still be controlled by corporate interests. It is an outgrowth of libertarian theory.

wanting to be heard? Does giving a voice to one limit the voice of the other? Should we automatically favor the rights of those who can afford the press over those who cannot?[24]

## Norms for the Press in the Twenty-first Century

Perhaps the biggest problem with these normative theories of the press is that it may take two or more of them to describe a given country's media system. For example, theocratic countries whose media operate under a strong social-responsibility theory may incorporate elements of the communist media theory, substituting the values of the state religion for those of the Communist Party.

Several authors have suggested a fifth theory of the press, **development theory,** to address the special needs of emerging nations, whose governments may feel that they need to restrict freedom of the press in order to promote industry, national identity, and partnerships with neighboring nations. Media theorist Dennis McQuail writes that less developed societies undergoing the transition from colonial rule to independence have different needs than do developed nations such as those of North America and Western Europe. These developing nations "lack the money, infrastructure, skills, and audiences to sustain a free-market media system."[25] Thus, in many cases leaders in those nations resort to using authoritarian controls. In May 2007, for example, Venezuelan president Hugo Chávez revoked the broadcast license of the country's oldest and most watched television network, Radio Caracas Television, or RCTV. The network had been severely critical of Chávez and his administration, and lifting the network's broadcast license would effectively silence it.[26]

## The Internet in the Twenty-first Century

The Internet, the most recent of the mass media, perhaps poses some of the most interesting questions in terms of the roles media play around the world. The Internet is still rapidly evolving and changing, just as radio did in the 1920s and television in the 1950s. (Truth Four—Nothing's new: Everything that happened in the past will happen again.) Like radio, the Internet was not initially conceived of as a mass medium. Instead, the first wide-area computer networks were designed to enable academics and military researchers to share data. But these early users soon found that the most useful part of the network was being able to send electronic mail to one another instantly.

Author Tom Standage, in *The Victorian Internet*, argues that the nineteenth-century telegraph, too, was a significant global development, serving many of the same purposes as the Internet at the end of the twentieth century and the beginning of the twenty-first:

> [The telegraph was] a world-wide communications network whose cables spanned continents and oceans, it revolutionized business practice, gave rise to new forms of crime, and inundated its users with a deluge of information.[27]

**development theory**
A theory of appropriate press behavior that states that developing nations may need to implement press controls in order to promote industry, national identity, and partnerships with neighboring nations.

# TEST YOUR MEDIA LITERACY

## Updating the *Four Theories*

John Nerone and the contributing authors of *Last Rights*[1] say that *Four Theories of the Press*[2] was a map of the world's media drawn at a specific time—the mid-1950s. And although it was a good map for its day, it was limited by what could be seen at that time and does not take into account the massive transformations that have taken place since then—the fall of communism, the end of the Cold War, globalization, and media consolidation. So they ask, "Do we need to draw a new map?" Or an even bigger question, "Can we draw a new map?"[3] This new map will need to deal with the issues surrounding the press in developing nations, as well as the norms surrounding the controlled press in many Islamic nations.

Reread the section of this chapter describing the *Four Theories* and pay particular attention to the critique of the theories. Then, answer the following questions.

● ● ● ● ● ● ● ● ● ● ● ● ● ● ● ● ●

**Who is the source?**
Who is John Nerone? What have he and his colleagues written?

**What is he saying?**
According to Nerone, what made *Four Theories* such a significant book? What are the major questions he raises about the theories for the current media world? Are there other notions of a free press than that of the libertarian theory?

**What evidence is there?**
What evidence does Nerone provide that *Four Theories* needs to be updated to apply to the present media world? How does new media—the Internet, Web sites, bloggers, and social networking sites—fit within these theories? What other critiques are there of the *Four Theories*? What evidence is there that the categories are still useful?

**What do you and your classmates think?**
What role do you think the media should play within society? Should the media be forced to be responsible? If so, who should decide what it means to be responsible? Should the role of the media be to support the government or to be a watchdog over the government? Can they do both?

[1] John C. Nerone, ed., *Last Rights: Revisiting* Four Theories of the Press (Urbana and Chicago: University of Illinois Press, 1995).

[2] Fred S. Siebert, Theodore Peterson, and Wilbur Schramm, *Four Theories of the Press* (Urbana, Ill.: University of Illinois Press, 1956).

[3] Nerone, *Last Rights.*

*In the nineteenth century, the telegraph served to transmit news across the United States and around the world far faster than any vehicle could travel. It was the first step toward the creation of global electronic media.*

The telegraph system was followed by both radio and the telephone as media that could tie large areas of the world together. While the earliest components of the Internet were in use by 1969, the Net was limited largely to interpersonal communication until 1991, when Tim Berners-Lee released the World Wide Web as an easy and uniform way to access material on the Internet. Although the Internet owes a historical debt to the early telegraph and telephone systems, it has grown into a new medium unlike any other because it is the only one that incorporates elements of interpersonal, group, and mass communication. The unique nature of the Internet, especially in a global context, poses new moral dilemmas concerning national boundaries, corporate control, freedom of the press, and the rights of individuals. As you read about global media in different countries later in this chapter, keep in mind some of these issues.

## GOING GLOBAL: MEDIA STANDARDS AROUND THE WORLD

There is a presumption that a direct connection exists between a country's media system and its political system. Central to this presumption is the idea that a free press is essential for a functional democracy. But what constitutes a free press? Broadcasters in countries with commercially run media, like the United States, presume that the freest press is that run by private-sector corporate control. Broadcasters in countries with strong traditions of public ownership, such as the United Kingdom, might argue that the commercial broadcasters are beholden to stockholders and advertisers and are no freer than the media in totalitarian states.

Alan Wells suggests that the four theories of the press might be replaced by five dimensions over which media could be rated:

- Control—Who controls the media system? This could be the state, a public corporation, a private enterprise, or corporate sponsorship.
- Finance—How do broadcasters pay the bills? Options include license fees, taxes, advertising, private subsidies, subscription charges, or a combination of them.

- Programming goals—What are the media trying to accomplish with their programming? Providing entertainment, educating the audience, selling products, promoting cultural goals, promoting a political ideology, or just putting up the cheapest possible imported material are all possibilities of programming goals.

- Target audience—For whom are the media producing and distributing content? These could be social or economic elites, the masses, or specialized/targeted audiences.

- Feedback mechanism—How do media organizations hear back from their audiences? Such feedback could be in the form of field reports, audience participation rates, polls and ratings, or response from critics and sponsors.[28]

As you can see, these five properties can be combined in an endless number of ways to describe a wide range of media systems. As we travel around the world looking at the various approaches to running the media, think about how these properties are being applied. You might also consider which of the normative theories of the press discussed previously would apply.

## Canada, Western Europe, and Great Britain

Canada, Western Europe, and Britain have liberal democracies that have free speech and media that are relatively free to criticize their governments. But their media differ in significant ways from the media in the United States, if only because the United States has the largest media industry in the world.

*Canadian Media.*    Canada has a free press patterned in part on the United States' model modified by a desire to preserve a Canadian culture in the face of the massive U.S. media industry. Canada can be characterized as a country with a large geographic area offset by a relatively small population, which makes media transmission relatively expensive. Canada's vastness means that it has strongly regional media, amplified by the fact that both English and French are official languages.

One area of resentment has been the somewhat one-way direction of media influence from the United States. A major Canadian mass communication text points out:

> In Canada, more American television programming is available to the vast majority of Canadians than is Canadian programming. On most Canadian commercial radio stations, more American material is available to listeners than Canadian material. On virtually all magazine racks in Canada more American magazines are available to the reader than Canadian magazines, in spite of the fact that about 2,000 magazines are published in Canada. More American authors than Canadian authors are read by the average Canadian school child.[29]

Little Mosque on the Prairie *is a popular Canadian television comedy that tells the story of a rural Muslim community in small-town Canada. It's an example of Canadian-produced broadcast programming.*

The attitudes expressed in this Canadian text might be seen as an example of Truth Five—New media are always scary.

Despite these issues, the Canadian media industry has been seeing growth. Canada's recording industry has been increasing steadily for the past two decades, as has the book publishing industry. The Canadian film industry has benefited from U.S. movie and television productions going north of the border, with Canada now being the second largest producer of television programming in the world, second only to the United States. Cost is a big factor for this migration. Popular American dramas like the 1990s hit *X-Files* cost half as much to film in Vancouver as in Los Angeles.[30]

In an effort to protect and enhance Canada's media industry, the government has put in a number of "Canadian content" regulations requiring broadcasters to carry a given level of Canadian-produced material. For example, programming on Canadian radio must be at least 35 percent domestically produced. Canadian television attracted widespread attention in spring 2007 when the Canadian Broadcasting Corporation put a sitcom on the air called *Little Mosque on the Prairie*, which tells the travails of a rural Muslim community in small-town Canada.[31] (No, I'm not making this up. It's a hit series in Canada that as of this writing is in its fourth season. You can find a link to more about the show at http://ralphehanson.com.)

These policies put the country at odds with the North American Free Trade Agreement (NAFTA), which calls for products to flow freely across the borders of Canada, the United States, and Mexico. The problem Canada faces is that the United States' largest export is not wheat or steel, but rather media content. Nevertheless, Canada has worked hard at maintaining its cultural production, exporting media content produced by authors such as Margaret Atwood and Douglas Coupland; filmmakers such as James Cameron and Jason Reitman; musicians like Bryan Adams, Sarah McLachlan, Celine Dion, and Alanis Morissette; actors such as Jim Carrey and Michael J. Fox; and magazine editor Bonnie Fuller (see Chapter 5).[32]

*Western Europe and Britain.*  Western Europe covers a wide range of countries, from Spain and Portugal, up through France, Germany, and Scandinavia.

These are the countries of the new European Union.[33] Cable television is common in some regions, such as Belgium and Germany, while satellite programming is more common in Scandinavia. European broadcasting was dominated by state-run monopolies until the 1980s and 1990s, when commercial alternatives became more common. With this switch, broadcasters started moving away from subsidies to advertising revenues. But even the commercial stations remain heavily regulated with strong controls and guidelines on the amounts and placement of advertisements. Part of the drive to privatize broadcasting came from pirate radio stations located offshore on ships that would broadcast into the countries.

Broadcasting in France typifies the European approach, with networks having a strong public service obligation and a desire to preserve French culture from foreign encroachment. According to broadcast scholar Matthew Rusher, "Each country in Western Europe seeks to preserve its own culture and language and sees the foreign produced programming on the international channels as a threat to its cultural integrity."[34] These stations want to attract audiences and make money, but they also want to preserve their distinctive national culture.

Globally, the BBC may well be the best-known non-U.S. broadcaster. Britain, a pioneer in broadcasting from its earliest days, used radio to reach out to its far-flung empire, which once covered a quarter of the globe.[35] As we discussed in Chapter 7, this reputation comes from the BBC World Service, much of which is now carried digitally via the Internet. The BBC operates under a public service model in which audience members pay the cost of the programming through equipment licensing fees. Although the BBC is the best known of the British broadcasters, it also competes with several commercial channels, though these channels have not had the worldwide influence of the BBC. Alan Wells argues that the public service orientation of the BBC has helped it deliver more innovative and less bland programming than the American commercial model. (Though it should be pointed out that international viewers only see the best of the BBC's programming, missing out on the more routine soap operas and game shows.[36])

Media are pervasive throughout Western Europe, with almost every household owning at least one television set and close to half owning two or more. Most homes also have a radio, and two-thirds have VCRs. Computers and the Internet are not as pervasive as in the United States; roughly one-third of homes in Western Europe have a personal computer. The big change in European media is the growth of privately owned television channels. As recently as 1980, Europe had only three privately owned stations; by 2000 there were more than 430.[37]

As we discussed in Chapters 2 and 6, European newspapers tend to take a more obvious political point of view than the detached, objective approach of U.S. papers. These papers have a clearly understood viewpoint designed to appeal to members of particular political parties.[38] While newspaper readership is higher in Europe than anywhere else in the world, papers in European countries are still facing the same kinds of declines experienced by those in North America.[39]

The Danish newspaper Jyllands-Posten set off a worldwide controversy when culture editor Flemming Rose commissioned a series of cartoons depicting the prophet Muhammad.

**The Danish Cartoons.** The biggest controversy surrounding European newspapers took place in the fall of 2005 when Flemming Rose, the culture editor of the Danish newspaper *Jyllands-Posten,* became concerned about what he saw as acts of self-censorship in Europe to avoid offending Muslims. In response, he commissioned a dozen cartoonists to portray the prophet Muhammad in any way that they saw fit.[40]

The cartoons were drawn in a range of styles. One made fun of the editors of *Jyllands-Posten* for trying to provoke attention, another put a Danish anti-immigration politician in a police lineup, and one portrayed the prophet with a bomb in his turban with a quote from the Koran printed on the front.

At the time the cartoons were published, they drew relatively little attention. But in the winter of 2006, a number of European and American newspapers reprinted the cartoons. Following these reprints came rioting throughout the Middle East that led to dozens of deaths.[41]

So why was half the world infuriated over cartoons published in the conservative Danish newspaper? The answer is both simple and complex. At the heart of the controversy is Islam's prohibition on depicting the prophet Muhammad. According to news accounts, it is a sin for a Muslim to create such an image and the "ultimate sort of insult" for a non-Muslim. The *Washington Post's* culture critic Philip Kennicott gives a compelling explanation of why the cartoons have been so controversial and why he believes that publishing them was a bad idea:

They were created as a provocation—Islam generally forbids the making of images of its highest prophet—in a conservative newspaper, which wanted to make a point about freedom of speech in a liberal, secular Western democracy. Depending on your point of view, it was a stick in the eye meant to provoke debate, or just a stick in the eye.[42]

He points out that we would be unlikely to see many cartoons quite that offensive toward Christianity in the United States:

No serious American newspaper would commission images of Jesus that were solely designed to offend Christians. And if one did, the reaction would be swift and certain. Politicians would take to the floors of Congress and call down thunder on the malefactors. Some Christians would react with fury and boycotts and flaming e-mails that couldn't be printed in a family newspaper; others would react with sadness, prayer and earnest letters to the editor. There would be mayhem, though it is unlikely that semiautomatic weapons would be brandished in the streets.[43]

The response to the cartoons was massive: At least four people were killed when Afghan troops fired on demonstrators; the cartoonists themselves went into hiding for fear of being killed; two Jordanian newspaper editors who reprinted the cartoons were arrested; the cartoons were banned in South Africa, where the editor who published them received death threats; protesters burned the Danish embassy in Beirut; and American commentators have written lengthy pieces on the controversy.

After the debate wore down over whether the *Jyllands-Posten* should have commissioned and run the original cartoons, the question then became whether newspapers and magazines ought to reprint the cartoons so that readers could see for themselves what the controversy was about. It wasn't a question that most major newspapers or newsmagazines could avoid. The cartoons were obviously newsworthy, and they were just as obviously offensive and likely to provoke a violent response somewhere in the world.

William Powers at the *National Journal* raised the question as to what editors stood for. Powers says that it is not so much whether newspapers publish the cartoons, but why:

> As I read the various explanations, I was struck by how sensible most of them were—on both sides. Among those who didn't publish the cartoons, the *Boston Globe* offered one of the strongest retorts to those who argued that it was cowardly to withhold the images. "Newspapers," it said in an editorial, "ought to refrain from publishing offensive caricatures of Muhammad in the name of the ultimate Enlightenment value: tolerance."
>
> Yet when I saw the *Austin-American Statesman*'s rationale for publishing the turban-bomb image, I was, frankly, just as impressed. That paper put the cartoon inside, with a front-page note informing readers where to go to "see an example of a drawing that offended Muslims and find out why it has."[44]

Through these arguments, we can see an example of Truth Six—Activism and analysis are not the same thing.

The *Philadelphia Inquirer* did reprint the most offensive of the images. Muslims in the Philadelphia area responded by picketing the paper, thus illustrating the common-sense idea that the proper response to offensive speech is more speech, not less. In fact, *Inquirer* editor Amanda Bennett told the protesters: "Neither I nor the newspaper meant any disrespect to their religion or their prophet. I told them I was actually really proud of them for exercising their right to freedom of speech."[45] The cartoons also ran in the University of

Illinois student paper, the *Daily Illini*, which sparked debate about the issue on the campus and led to peaceful protests.

But far more papers decided against running the cartoons. The *Boston Globe*, in an editorial, explained the paper's reasoning:

> Depicting Mohammed wearing a turban in the form of a bomb with a sputtering fuse is no less hurtful to most Muslims than Nazi caricatures of Jews or Ku Klux Klan caricatures of blacks are to those victims of intolerance. That is why the Danish cartoons will not be reproduced on these pages.[46]

You can read more about the Danish cartoons at http://ralphehanson.com.

## Central and Latin America

Most of Latin American commercial broadcasting is dominated by North American, Mexican, and Brazilian programming. Brazil and Mexico have among the largest and most sophisticated broadcasting operations of any nation in the world. In fact, Mexico and Brazil export culture back to the United States through sports programming and the extremely popular *telenovelas*. Latin American broadcasters tend to follow the American for-profit model rather than the BBC's public-service orientation. One reason for the larger scope of South American broadcasting is that unlike Africa (which we discuss shortly), Latin America has only two dominant languages to deal with—Spanish and Portuguese.[47]

Since the 1990s, Latin American governments have grown more stable and less repressive, and the economies of these countries have grown. All these factors have contributed to the growth of the media industry in Latin America. Unlike much of the world, newspaper circulation has been growing in Latin America, with more than 1,000 newspapers being published and daily readership exceeding 100 million.[48]

## Islamic Countries and the Middle East

The press in the Middle East seems to straddle the fence between social responsibility and authoritarian media control. For example, although Israel is a modern, liberal democracy, reporters there are required to submit stories on sensitive military issues to the government for approval.[49] During the 1991 Persian Gulf War, all news coming out of Israel via commercial media had to be cleared by military censors. Israeli authorities are also quick to control the dissident Palestinian press.

In Syria, Sudan, and Libya, the press is under authoritarian control. Jordan and Egypt have a so-called opposition press, although reporters often are limited in how far they can take their opposition to the official story.[50] Along with the official state-controlled media, many Arab nations also have *Al Hayat*, a regional Arabic newspaper published in London, and the Al Jazeera satellite channel, which originates in Qatar. The other alternative is to listen to news from a neighboring Arab state, which will not hesitate to criticize the government of its neighbor. By listening to a range of reports, one can gain a more complete picture of the news.[51]

Satellite and the Internet have vastly changed media in the Middle East, and they bypass authoritarian rule. During the 1991 Persian Gulf War, people in the Middle East got news from CNN, which they believed was being censored by the U.S. government. But Western media are not that influential in Arab-speaking countries. First, not everyone speaks English or French, the languages typically spoken on international channels. But the middle class and members of Islamist movements have an understandable thirst for local media.[52]

Kai Hafez, a scholar at American University in Cairo, has distinguished three types of press in the Arab world: the "mobilized press," which is controlled by the government to promote the government; the "loyalist press," which is run by private industry but is supportive of people in power, especially those who can control their access to resources such as paper and electricity; and finally the "diverse press," which is relatively free.

Many of these countries will espouse freedom of the press, and the level of criticism of the government that a country will tolerate varies from administration to administration, from year to year. However, even in countries without an Islamist government, such as Egypt, it can be a crime to "insult" the country, which puts definite limits on what can be reported.

*The Importance of "Small" Media.* The question of what passes as mass media is becoming increasingly complicated, however, with the importance of **small media**, such as fax machines, photocopy machines, video cameras, computers, the Internet, and mobile phone media such as Twitter and SMS text messages. Hafez has written about the importance of alternative independent media—of which small media are a crucial component—in the Middle East:

> If we use the very vague and tentative definition of a mass medium as a means to communicate texts or programs on a regular basis to large audiences, then there is another important sector of the mass media that is often ignored or underestimated: the "alternative-independent" media.[53]

These alternatives have taken the spot formerly occupied by cheaply produced short-run magazines. But the alternative-independent media provide for a range of voices, even in countries like Iran with strict Islamic control of the mainstream media. (Which shows us that even in other parts of the world, Truth Two—There are no mainstream media—still holds.)

Although Palestinian media in the West Bank have been subject to Israeli censorship, Palestinians have been able to use the Web to post accounts and images of demonstrations and violence that bypass government censorship.[54]

**small media**
Alternative media such as fax machines, photocopiers, video cameras, and personal Web sites used to distribute news and information that might be suppressed by the government if it were published through traditional mass media channels.

Religion professor Fred Strickert notes that while the Israelis and Palestinians are still capable of manipulating the news, the Internet allows for the expression of a wider range of views:

> Yes, the Palestinian Authority can still censor damaging video footage, as it did in the case of the mob lynching of two Israeli soldiers, and the Israeli government can put its spin on the news. But the truth is on the Internet for anyone who cares to find it.[55]

Whereas the Internet and satellite dishes receive a great deal of popular attention, the small media have also done a good job of transmitting messages outside the realm of censorship. Following the disputed Iranian presidential elections in 2009 (discussed in Chapter 10), the Iranian government began to crack down on news media, going so far as to kick reporters out of the country all together.[56] The government blocked many forms of social media, reduced Internet speed to block online video, shut down mobile phone towers, and threatened retaliation against those who would use new media like mobile phones and the Internet to transmit information out of Iran. Legacy media such as CNN, Fox News, MSNBC, and even the BBC had to turn to online video, blogs, and Twitter feeds of questionable reliability to report on what was happening within Iran. As social media expert Gaurav Mishra pointed out at the beginning of this chapter, mobile phone–based social media are increasingly going to be the medium through which news breaks.[57]

*Television in the Islamic World.* Broadcasting in the Arab world is heavily controlled by the government, though the presence of satellite broadcasting is challenging governmental control. Egypt, which is more secular than much of the Arab world, has a large media industry, producing movies, music, and television programming for much of the Arab and Islamic world.[58] Access to television, especially direct broadcast satellite signals, varies significantly throughout the Islamic nations of the Middle East.

The Saudi Arabian monarchy built a substantial television network in the 1960s, in part to respond to anti-Saudi broadcasts coming into the country from Egypt. In March 1994 Saudi Arabia officially banned ownership of satellite receivers to satisfy religious conservatives who objected to Western programming. The ban has not been enforced, however, and both the dishes and the receivers are readily available.

Little is known about television audience behavior in Saudi Arabia, as the government has shown little interest in commercial broadcasting, which would lead to audience measurement.[59] A 2007 Gallup Poll found that 82 percent of Saudis relied on pan-Arab satellite television channels to stay informed about their own countries, and 93 percent used these cross-border channels to find out what was happening in other countries. As important as satellite television is as a news medium, however, 59 percent of Saudis said word of mouth was a "very important source of information" about their country.[60] According to the survey, the most popular first sources for satellite news were Al Jazeera (30 percent), the Middle East Broadcasting Center (24 percent), and Al Arabiya (23 percent).

The small amount of academic research that has been done on Saudi broadcast consumption shows that most households own television sets and video recorders. In addition to Western networks such as CNN, Saudi subscribers can receive Turkish, French, and numerous Arab-language channels. The most popular programming came from the twenty-one ARABSAT channels. (ARABSAT is a broadcast satellite launched by the Arab League.) The biggest motivation to go to the direct broadcast satellite service was to get news from a variety of viewpoints rather than being limited to the official government position available via the two broadcast channels.[61]

*Al Jazeera.* According to a 2007 forum on Arab broadcasting, the average television viewer in the Arab world watches about four hours a day, much of which comes from the 10 most popular of the 250 free satellite stations. Although there are advertising-supported TV channels, most of the channels rely on state funding.[62] The most significant of these channels is **Al Jazeera**. Broadcast via satellite from the small Arab country of Qatar since 1997, the channel is not censored by the government.[63] The channel has carried interviews with everyone from Osama bin Laden to Colin Powell and has been criticized for doing so by both the United States and Arab countries. During the current war in Iraq, Al Jazeera came to worldwide attention, presenting an Arab point of view to the fighting between the United States and Iraq. It has a regular audience of 40 million, which dwarfs CNN or Fox in scope.[64]

In the Arab Middle East, satellite news channels that can cross over national borders are clearly the top source of international news, and Al Jazeera is the most popular of the many Arab-language satellite channels. It is the most watched, or perhaps the most important, though many claim to dislike the controversial channel. According to NPR's *On the Media*, a recent survey shows that only 10 percent of Arabs who have access to satellite TV never watch Al Jazeera. In Iraq, the Saudi Arabia–based Al Arabiya is popular. But American channel Alhurra is clearly the last choice, with

**Al Jazeera**
The largest and most viewed Arabic-language satellite news channel. It is run out of the country of Qatar and has a regular audience of 40 million viewers.

*Al Jazeera is by far the most popular of the Arabic-language satellite news channels throughout the Arab world. This Iraqi man, while at a sidewalk café in Baghdad, watches a news broadcast about a shooting in a Fallujah mosque.*

## TEST YOUR MEDIA LITERACY

### Al Jazeera English

While Al Jazeera is best known for its Arabic-language news broadcast via satellite throughout the Middle East, it launched Al Jazeera English (AJE) in 2006. The English-language service was designed to provide Westerners with news from an Arab perspective. Lawrence Pintak, the director of the Adham Center for Electronic Journalism at the American University in Cairo, says that AJE is trying to become a worldwide force in broadcasting, much as CNN and the BBC are.

Pintak, a thirty-year veteran reporter who has covered world news on four different continents, writes that while much of what you see on AJE are feature stories you would see on any broadcast news operation, AJE's coverage of the funeral for assassinated Lebanese cabinet minister Pierre Gemayel showed off what the network could do:

> Both BBC World and CNN International (a completely separate channel from the CNN domestic U.S. service) quickly switched away to other programming. CNN-I's anchors looked a little uncomfortable with a segue from Lebanon and the latest carnage in Iraq right into a fluff piece about the Macy's Thanksgiving Day Parade, without so much as a commercial to buffer the jarring contrast.
>
> AJE stayed with Lebanon, interviewing a Hezbollah spokesman, a perspective not heard on the other channels—one in a comprehensive series of interviews with the key players in the drama not seen elsewhere. AJE's Lebanon specialist Omar al-Jassawi dug deeper into the impact on the country and region as a whole, while Middle East analyst Lamis Andoni noted that although Syria is widely presumed responsible for Gemayel's death, plenty of other players in the region had reason to want him dead. . . . The discussions were facilitated by intelligent and knowledgeable prompting by Sami Zeidan, an Egyptian anchor most recently with CNBC Arabia.[1]

You can find a link to the rest of Lawrence Pintak's commentary on Al Jazeera English and to the broadband stream of AJE at **http:// ralphehanson .com.**

Americans wanting to see this coverage would have to go to AJE's Web site to get a broadband stream of the coverage, however, because no U.S. or Canadian cable companies have been willing to carry the channel.[2]

Al Jazeera's first English anchor, Dave Marash, who was with ABC's *Nightline* for sixteen years and is Jewish, defends the sometimes controversial content from Al Jazeera this way:

> Al Jazeera is one of the most positive and significant cultural events in the Arab world in centuries. . . . Do they broadcast hate speech? Yes, they do. Is it put in context and is it discussed as hate speech? Yes, it is. Hate speech is part of the dialogue of the Middle East. To censor or to exclude it would be to lose all credibility.[3]

Marash left Al Jazeera in 2008, citing increased levels of control of the network from corporate headquarters in Doha, Qatar.[4]

### Who is the source?
Who is Lawrence Pintak? What is his background?

### What is he saying?
According to Pintak, what makes Al Jazeera English's news coverage different from that of the BBC or CNN? How is it similar?

### What evidence is there?
What evidence does Pintak provide to support his point that AJE is different? What support does AJE anchor Dave Marash provide for Pintak?

### What do you and your classmates think about Al Jazeera English?
Have you or your classmates ever watched Al Jazeera English? Would you watch it if your cable service provided it? Is it helpful for Westerners to get an Arab perspective on the news? Why or why not?

[1] Lawrence Pintak, "Will Al Jazeera English Find Its Groove?" Columbia Journalism Review Daily, November 30, 2006, www.cjrdaily.org/behind_the_news/will_aljazeera_english_find_it.php.

[2] Paul Farhi, "Al Jazeera's U.S. Face," *Washington Post*, November 15, 2006, C01.

[3] Ibid.

[4] Brian Stelter, "American Anchor Quits Al Jazeera," *New York Times*, March 28, 2008, http://www.nytimes.com/2008/03/28/business/media/28anchor.html.

53 percent saying they never watch it. Interestingly enough, the Hezbollah channel, Al-Manar, is similarly unpopular.[65]

Although some observers accuse Al Jazeera of being a pro-Arab propaganda channel, others have described it as the CNN of the Arab world. Perhaps neither label is completely fair or completely accurate. It would seem instead that Al Jazeera is committed to presenting an Arab view of the world. That is, it works at telling the news accurately, but it tells it from a clear point of view. (Interestingly enough, taking a play from the American media synergy department, there is also an Al Jazeera Sports Channel.) What makes Al Jazeera interesting is that while its headquarters are in Qatar, it tends to take a broad Arab point of view rather than that of one particular country. Too often all Arab or Muslim countries are seen in the West as being the same, rather than having distinctly different views. It's easy for Americans to forget that Iraq and Iran were at war with each other for at least ten years.[66]

Al Jazeera was founded by Sheik Hamad bin Khalifa al-Thani, the emir of Qatar, in an effort to diversify his nation's economy. He started the satellite news channel following the failure of a 1994 BBC experiment with an Arab-language Saudi-financed station. Hiring 120 of the unemployed journalists from the project gave Al Jazeera its start. Although Western governments have been highly critical of Al Jazeera, the network has carried criticism of Qatar's government, the Palestinian Authority, the Jordanian government, the Kuwaiti government, and the Israeli government.[67]

## Africa

The African continent provides a prime example of the range of approaches to development media theory—from a strong social responsibility approach to out-and-out authoritarian controls. The mass media first came to Africa through the European colonial powers; they were created to serve the needs of the colonists. Newspapers and early broadcast stations covered only white news and ignored black Africans, or else treated them as "subhuman beings."[68] After independence, colonial media continued to exist in some countries, whereas in other countries the press was taken over by the new governments, which did not permit private media. Although the media were serving a new population, they continued to focus on the needs of the elite.

Africa is still largely rural, but newspapers are located predominantly in the cities. According to Tawana Kupe, a media scholar at the University of Zimbabwe, most countries have a dominant daily newspaper that is distributed primarily in the capital city. Newspaper circulation is limited by high levels of poverty and illiteracy.[69]

Radio is the most important medium in Africa, but both radios and the batteries to run them are expensive, and transmission equipment often is not good enough to reach the entire country. Television is not available in many countries. Even where there are broadcasts, television can be received only where there is reliable electrical service, primarily in urban areas. Most of the programming consists of old European, American, and Australian reruns. Although many African countries seek to use television and radio to foster development by teaching people how to improve their standard of living, most of the development programming consists of speeches by politicians calling for development.

The Committee to Protect Journalists reports that press freedom varies wildly across the continent. For example, during the 2005 elections in Burundi, local media were able to discuss abuses by those in power. But in Zimbabwe the government clamped down on the press during elections. You can find a link to this report at http://ralphehanson.com.

Language continues to be an issue for African media. Many African nations use the former colonial language (typically French or English) in their nation-building efforts, but this tends to be the language of the educated class, not of the majority of the people.[70] Except in Kenya and Tanzania, which have a Swahili press, virtually no major newspapers are published in African languages.

It is tempting in the West to view Africa as something akin to South America, but unlike South America, Africa as a continent does not share common languages or cultures. Africa is exceedingly culturally diverse, with more languages spoken there than on any other continent in the world.[71] Politically, many of the countries are dominated by single-party or military governments, though there are notable exceptions, such as South Africa, Mali, and Ghana.

South Africa was the first country in sub-Saharan Africa to have radio, and today it has the best-developed system in that area of the world. Most of the country's radio is handled by the South African Broadcasting Corporation. Following heavy censorship in South Africa during the apartheid era, the South African press in the early twenty-first century has an organization of publishers, journalists, and members of the public that can reprimand newspapers when necessary. A committee made up of lawyers and media professionals regulates the broadcast industry.[72]

South Africa's vibrant pop music scene has found fans around the world. Groups such as Mahlathini and the Mahotella Queens, pictured here, and Ladysmith Black Mambazo routinely draw crowds in the United States and Europe.

South African television broadcasts in seven different languages: English, Afrikaans, northern and southern Sotho, Tswana, Xhosa, and Zulu. As you can see, language is a big barrier, when you consider the linguistic diversity within just a single country—South Africa has eleven language groups. African media expert Osabuohien P. Amienyi recognizes this dilemma: "This plurality [of languages] presents broadcasting with the dilemma of how to fulfill the natural desire of every community to be addressed in its own language or dialect."[73]

If stations hope to reach a large group with a single language, they are likely going to have to transmit in the languages of the colonial whites, typically English, French, Portuguese, or Spanish. This furthers the problem of programming that will be accessible primarily to urban elites and not the rural population who need the service the most.

South Africa has also been a major source of inspiration for Western pop music. Among the Western musicians who have worked at bringing African music to the forefront of American pop culture are Paul Simon, Peter Gabriel, and Talking Heads leader David Byrne.[74] Simon, a singer and songwriter, was captivated by the sounds of South Africa's township jive and in 1985 traveled to Johannesburg to record there with artists such as Miriam Makeba.[75] This collaboration resulted in the best-selling album *Graceland* and a world tour. Township jive emerged as a style during the apartheid era in South Africa. The music combines traditional African drumming and rhythms with Western instruments to create a unique musical style. Among the South African musicians who have found success in the West are the a cappella men's choir Ladysmith Black Mambazo, the group Mahlathini and the Mahotella Queens, and musician Johnny Clegg and his band Juluka. Groups such as Bongo Maffin have combined the South African pop music style with rhythm and blues, reggae, and rap.[76]

African pop music is no newcomer to the United States. In 1961 the Tokens recorded a hit single, "The Lion Sleeps Tonight," based on an African chant.[77]

One thing that has inhibited world music's popularity in the United States is the language barrier, though language differences have not stopped people in other countries from listening to American music. "People around the world have been listening to American and British music for the last thirty years, very often not understanding the words but enjoying the ways people put things together," says producer D. A. "Jumbo" Vanrenen. "As Third World artists have access to the same recording studios, it's becoming easier to present their music in a clear way. Language becomes less important. People go for the dance rhythms and the fine quality of people's vocals."[78] You can hear this branch of world music on Public Radio International's Afropop World Wide or on the BBC's world music programming. There are links to these at http://ralphehanson.com.

## Russia and the Former Soviet Republics

Media developed slowly in the old Soviet Union if for no other reason than the vast scale of its empire, which covered one-sixth of the world at its peak, inhibited its development. Along with the more conventional media such as radio, the Soviet Union also made use of alternative media such as sending broadcasts out over phone lines that would then be played in communities over a loudspeaker system. Under communism, there was no ideal of an independent press. The goal of newspapers and broadcasters was to support the goals of communism, not to be a detached and critical external observer. Janis Overlock, who specializes in study of the media of the old Soviet empire, describes the problem:

> One of the main problems of the media in the countries of the former Soviet Union is a basic lack of understanding of the role of the media in a democracy. After years of Soviet domination, many of the governments as well as journalists view the media as a propaganda tool for the government.[79]

She further explains that even if the government professes a belief in the free press, that freedom simply doesn't exist within the culture.[80]

Since the collapse of the Soviet Union in 1991, the Russian press has had a troubled existence. Although many of the media are now in private hands, they are not necessarily free of government control and they experience very high levels of self-censorship. The independent media in Russia are owned by a small group of businesspeople who support the government and want to maintain control of their own media monopolies.

Moscow has at least twenty daily and weekly newspapers ranging from communist publications to sensationalistic tabloids.[81] Many of these papers sell article space to the highest bidder—a process that even has a name, *zakazukha*, or "news-by-order." Many newspapers are not truly self-supporting and need a patron, or boss, to provide financial support. In return, the paper supports the boss's political agenda. Papers that are critical of the central government can disappear seemingly overnight with no warning to the journalists who work there.[82]

The government-controlled media are emphatically serving the needs of the ruling party. A reporter for Russian Television told an American friend, "Our new executive producer has been going over my copy with a fine-tooth comb. Anything that's in the least bit critical of the government is taken out."[83] Television is the most important medium in Russia because few people can afford the expense of a newspaper subscription. Of the three biggest networks, one is the government's channel, but the government has either direct or indirect investments in the other two, Russian Public Television and NTV. Because of this ownership structure, there is relatively little need for active censorship.

Although Russia today officially has a free press, almost every paper is closely identified with a political ideology. The press is a supporter or cheerleader, not a watchdog.[84]

## Asia

Although Asia has many countries and cultures, in most of its nations the broadcast media are either government controlled or run by public corporations. In many of these countries we see a development philosophy for the media, in which broadcasters are expected to work to support the economic and social development goals of the government. China, Japan, and India stand apart from the rest of the continent as major media forces. Communist and former Soviet bloc countries, such as North Korea, continue to operate under the old Soviet-style communist model. Southeast Asia, including countries such as Indonesia, Malaysia, and the Philippines, tend to operate under a development philosophy. This can be seen in particular in Malaysia, where the Ministry of Information and Broadcasting sets guidelines on how broadcasters can portray Malaysian education, art, culture, and identity.[85]

*India.* As of 2005, approximately 40 percent of India's households—an astonishing 80 million households—had television sets.[86] About 40 percent will see

*Although newspaper circulation has been declining in the United States, the business is booming in India, where more than 150 million people read a paper each day. Every day, Indian publishers sell approximately 11 million English papers, 34 million Hindi papers, and another 28 million papers in other languages.*

a newspaper as well. A handbook on Indian media estimates that 120 million of 220 million households have a radio set. Print media in India are heavily supported by advertising, and hitting a balance between serving the public and making advertisers happy is a major issue.

Newspapers are big business in India, with a daily circulation of 72 million, second only to China with 85 million copies a day. Whereas the big newspapers face the same sort of competitive pressures from newer media that U.S. papers face, community newspapers dealing with local issues are seen as a growth industry.[87]

All India Radio (AIR) is the dominant radio service and the exclusive source of radio news and public affairs programming. There are broadcast television stations in India, but the television market is dominated by cable and satellite networks. As was discussed at the beginning of the chapter, television is going through a period of growth because of the rise of commercially run satellite channels. Internet access is growing, especially through cyber cafés and mobile phones, and India's major newspapers all have major Web presences.

*China.*    Until the 1970s and 1980s the media in China were unapologetically political and propagandistic. The role of the media was not to entertain or market products; instead they promoted public policies such as water conservation programs, provided education to rural areas, and mobilized the public after natural disasters or industrial accidents.[88]

Over the past thirty years, Chinese media offerings and availability have changed rapidly. In 1978 China had fewer than one television set per 100 people. By 2007 that number had grown to twenty-five sets per 100 people. Although a wide range of local television stations are available, they are required to carry the Chinese Central Television network's evening newscast. The number of newspapers has similarly expanded, from 42 papers in 1968, most of which were run by the Communist Party, to more than 2,200 newspapers in 2007.[89]

Talk radio is the most open mass medium in China. Prior to the 1990s, radio provided primarily government propaganda. Now lively call-in programs have audience members talking about controversial topics without having to identify themselves. Although party officials have told talk show hosts what they ought to be talking about, the hosts have violated these rules without punishment.[90]

Mobile phones are common in China, serving as a major channel for the flow of news. Chinese phone users tend to upgrade their phones frequently, so new mobile technology spreads through the country fairly rapidly.[91]

Since the 1970s the press has been freer to criticize the government, though how free the press has been has fluctuated depending on party leadership. All media are ultimately subject to control by the Chinese government, from books, to newspapers, to broadcasting, to the Internet. American corporations such as Yahoo and Google have faced international criticism for cooperating with the Chinese government on censorship efforts. (See Chapter 10 for a description of one such incident.)

Chinese media tycoon Liu Changle represents the changing face of Chinese media. He is the founder of Phoenix Satellite Television, a privately owned Chinese satellite channel.

*Japan.*    Japan is in many ways the technological heart of our modern media world. Many of our essential electronic media devices come from there. Broadcasting started in Japan in 1925 and was run by the government for the next twenty-five years. In the era after World War II, American policy helped shape what Japan would offer, which became a mix of public and commercial broadcasting.[92] NHK is Japan's public broadcasting corporation, and it provides both domestic and international service. It is financed through a fee that all television owners must pay. Japan has relatively high levels of television broadcast viewership. The biggest difference between Japanese and U.S. broadcasting is that Japan has a much more even balance between commercial and public broadcasting.

The most popular category of magazines in Japan is not fashion, lifestyle, or hobbies; it's *manga*, or comic books. The word *manga* means comics or amusing drawings, and according to *Publishers Weekly*, the genre accounts for 40 percent of all books and magazines published in Japan. In the United States, *manga*-style comics are most popular with teenage boys and tend to feature action stories such as *Yu-Gi-Oh!*, *Pokémon*, or *Sailor Moon*. In Japan *manga* cover just about every magazine genre. Douglas Wolk, who has covered *manga* in the United States, writes, "There are hundreds of *manga* for girls and for boys, men's *manga* and women's *manga*, romance *manga*, political *manga*, baseball *manga*, mahjongg *manga*, and more."[93] Plots can range from the story of a teenage girl who becomes a superhero after using a magic eye shadow to one that describes the aftermath of the atomic bombing of Hiroshima. There's even one that gives advice on how to get a divorce. *Manga* targeted at adults often contain violent or pornographic imagery.

*Manga* started out in the tenth century as illustrated Buddhist scrolls. By the seventeenth century, silk-bound books using woodblock printing and featuring text and drawings about actors and actresses became popular. Current *manga* can be the size of a small telephone book.[94] Estimates suggest that 95 percent of Japan's population reads *manga* on a regular basis.[95]

The United States has been accused of imposing its culture on the world by exporting media products, but the same charges have been leveled against Japan, especially in other Asian countries. However, attempts to keep comics out of those countries have only led to the publication of pirate editions.[96]

*Manga* are growing in popularity in the United States. They are based primarily on books connected to animé cartoon programs. Featuring characters with spiky hair, big heads, and big eyes, *manga* are seen by young people as exciting, dynamic, and sexy. Many American translations of Japanese *manga* are printed to be read from the back of the book to the front, just as they would be in Japan. Why? In part because it's cheaper than redoing the pages in the American front-to-back style, but also because teen readers see the reverse style as cool.[97] *Manga* characters have also shown up on a wide range of products from video games, to clothing, to plush toys. *Manga*'s popularity in the United States is also an example of Truth Three—Everything from the margin moves to the center.

## Dangers to Journalists

The job of being a journalist around the world can be a dangerous one. The Committee to Protect Journalists (CPJ) reports that worldwide in 2008 forty-two journalists were killed "in direct connection" to their work; eleven of them were in Iraq.[98] Three or more journalists also died in Pakistan, India, Georgia, and Thailand.

In 2006, when thirty-two journalists died in Iraq, only four of the reporter deaths there were combat related. The remaining twenty-eight were murdered, with half of them threatened in advance. CPJ executive director Joel Simon explains,

> When this conflict began . . . most journalists died in combat-related incidents. Now, insurgents routinely target journalists for perceived affiliations—political, sectarian, or Western. This is an extraordinarily alarming trend because along with the terrible loss of life, it is limiting news reporting in Iraq—and, in turn, our own understanding of a vital story.[99]

Among the most prominent of the many journalists injured in Iraq is former ABC News anchor Bob Woodruff. Woodruff and his cameraman Doug Vogt were severely injured in a roadside bombing by an improvised explosive device in Iraq in January 2006. According to ABC News, Woodruff, Vogt, and their four-person crew were in the lead vehicle with a convoy of Iraqi security forces. They were working at telling the story of the patrol when their convoy was ambushed. Woodruff had just been named ABC's evening news anchor a month earlier, replacing the late Peter Jennings.[100] Woodruff was in a coma for thirty-six days and suffered a traumatic brain injury. As of fall 2009, he had completed a book and a television special on his injuries and recovery.

The risks of death or injury are not the only risks reporters face. BBC journalist Alan Johnston, as of this writing, had been held hostage for months in the Gaza Strip; Fox News's Steve Centanni and Olaf Wiig were held hostage in Gaza for thirteen days; and the *Christian Science Monitor*'s Jill Carroll was held hostage for three months in Iraq.

Fox News journalist Steve Centanni (left) and cameraman Olaf Wiig spent thirteen days in captivity in the Gaza Strip. In this photo their pictures are held up by demonstrators in Gaza City calling for their release.

Fox News cameraman Wiig says that the most serious consequence of attacks on journalists is that the stories from war zones won't get told: "My biggest concern, really, is that as a result of what happened to us, foreign journalists will be discouraged from coming here to tell the story. And that would be a great tragedy for the people of Palestine, and especially for the people of Gaza."[101]

You can find links to accounts of attacks on journalists at http://ralphe hanson.com.

## Marshall McLuhan's Global Village

Marshall McLuhan is often better known for his catch phrases than for what he actually wrote. Aside from "the medium is the message," discussed in Chapter 2, he is best known for popularizing the term "the global village." He first used the term in his 1962 book, *The Gutenberg Galaxy: The Making of Typographic Man*, in which he discusses how electronic media, primarily radio and television, help people live and interact globally. Since the rise of the Internet, it would seem that we are truly living in a world where we can interact with people anywhere at any time. But that global village may be largely an illusion.

There is no question that through our media, what McLuhan would call the extension of our senses, we are able to travel to places we could never reach otherwise. In an IMAX theater we can travel to the bottom of the ocean off the Grand Banks near Newfoundland and visit the wreck of the *Titanic*. Or through the photos from the Mars landing craft, *Spirit* and *Opportunity*, we can see into the craters on Mars. On a more down-to-earth scale, our electronic media take us into war zones, to the aftermath of disasters, and to celebrations in cities or countries we would never otherwise visit. But are we really becoming members of a global village, or are we just sightseers who take a glimpse of something we can't really understand?

Media reporter Ken Auletta, whose work we discussed extensively elsewhere in this book, suggests that perhaps there is not a single wired global village, but rather hundreds or thousands of them, "each broadcasting in its own language, with its own anchor and news team, its own weather and sports and local slant."[102]

Communications scholar W. Russell Neuman suggests that McLuhan's global village concept is misleading: "McLuhan envisioned Americans seeing what was going on live in an African village. But Americans may not want to watch that. And perhaps vice versa."[103]

You can read and see more about McLuhan at http://ralphehanson.com.

# CHAPTER Summary

Not all countries take the same approach to the relationship between the government and the press. This can take a variety of forms, depending on the form of government and the culture of the country. Theories of the press include the authoritarian, communist, libertarian, social responsibility, and developmental theories. Although these normative theories of the press still have considerable value today, they have to be reexamined in terms of how the world has changed since they were first discussed in the 1950s. An alternative to the normative theories of the press is to look at the media dimensions of control, finance, programming goals, target audience, and feedback mechanisms.

Media in Western democracies generally operate under a combination of libertarian and social responsibility theories. Many countries have free speech as a goal but are concerned about preserving their national cultures against the power of the American media industry.

Latin America has a vibrant media industry, especially in Brazil and Mexico. These countries export Spanish-language programming, especially sports and *telenovelas*, to the United States.

The electronic media have a powerful presence in the Middle East, and satellite television is able to bypass national borders and bring outside content into otherwise closed media systems. The most popular source of news in the Arab-speaking countries of the Middle East is the satellite news channel Al Jazeera. Small media also have a significant presence in the Middle East because of their ability to bypass official government censorship.

Media in Africa face a number of problems including the lack of a common language, poor economies, and a lack of newsprint and reliable electricity.

While the news media in the old Soviet Union were designed to serve the needs of the government and Communist Party, they went through a brief period of relative freedom in the 1980s. Since that time, the government has cracked down on free speech and the press has tended to serve the specific goals of its owners.

Media in Asia tend to follow either a social responsibility theory or development theory, depending on the region. The major exception is Japan, which has strong public and private broadcasting businesses. Japan also exports content and media technology to the West and to the rest of the world.

Reporting around the world, especially in the Iraqi war zone, is dangerous for reporters, with forty-two journalists being killed on the job in 2008, including eleven in Iraq. Journalists also face the risks of injury and kidnapping.

Media theorist Marshall McLuhan suggested in the 1960s that the world would become a global village, linked together through electronic media. Although these media have become far more pervasive today than when McLuhan was writing, it is unclear whether the media are bringing the world together or breaking it up into a series of disconnected villages.

## KEYTerms

authoritarian theory   527
communist theory   528
libertarian theory   529
social responsibility theory   531

development theory   532
small media   541
Al Jazeera   543

## CONCEPTReview

Normative theories of the press
Analyzing world media systems by control, finance, programming goals, target audience, and feedback mechanisms
How media standards vary among Western democracies
Media standards in the Middle East
The challenge of media in Africa
Having an activist press in countries with no tradition of a free press
The dangers journalists face reporting around the world
The nature of the global village

# Notes

CHAPTER 1
**LIVING IN A MEDIA WORLD**

1. Dr. Ink, "Ask Dr. Ink: On Wacko Jacko," March 10, 2003, www.poynter.org/column.asp?id=1&aid=21116.
2. Al Tompkins, "Al's Morning Meeting: What Michael Jackson Did for Music and Music Videos," June 25, 2009, www.poynter.org/column.asp?id=2&aid=165797.
3. Brian Stelter, "TMZ Was Far Ahead in Reporting Death," *New York Times*, June 27, 2009.
4. Wailin Wong, "Michael Jackson Death News: Online Activity Heats Up Twitter and Google, Slows Down Some Sites," *Chicago Tribune*, June 26, 2009; Sharon Shahid, "Royal Treatment for Fallen Celebrities," June 26, 2009, www.newseum.org/news/news.aspx?item=nh_CELEB090626&style=f; Brian Stelter, "With Jackson News, a Surge in Web Traffic," *New York Times*, June 26, 2009, mediadecoder.blogs.nytimes.com/2009/06/26/with-jackson-news-a-surge-in-web-traffic.
5. Stelter, "TMZ Was Far Ahead in Reporting Death."
6. Scott Collins and Meg James, "Michael Jackson May Be Turning Point for TMZ," *Los Angeles Times*, June 28, 2009.
7. Jackie Alexander, "Diversity at Work: CNN's Klein on Breaking News: 'Being First Is Overrated'," August 7, 2009, www.poynter.org/column.asp?id=58&aid=168086.
8. Ibid.
9. Pew Research Center Project for Excellence in Journalism, "PEJ News Coverage Index: June 22–28, 2009; Media Swings From Protests in Iran to the Passing of the King of Pop," journalism.org/news_index/99?page=1.
10. Bob Garfield, "A King's Farewell," July 10, 2009, www.onthemedia.org/transcripts/2009/07/10/01.
11. Emily Hedges, "A Look Back at the Death of Elvis," August 16, 2007, www.newseum.org/news/news.aspx?item=nh_081607_Elvis&style=f.
12. David Hinckley, "Media Just Responding to Michael Jackson's Fans' Demands With Staples Center Memorial Coverage," *New York Daily News*, July 7, 2009.
13. David Hinckley and Richard Huff, "Michael Jackson's Memorial 2nd Most-Watched Funeral Ever, After Princess Di, Say Nielsen Ratings," *New York Daily News*, July 8, 2009.
14. Howard Kurtz, "Media Notes: TMZ Gets There First," July 27, 2009, www.washingtonpost.com/wp-dyn/content/article/2009/07/29/AR2009072901110.html.
15. Ralph Hanson, interview, September 4, 2009.
16. George Gerbner, "Mass Media and Human Communication Theory," in *Human Communication Theory: Original Essays*, ed. Frank E. X. Dance (New York: Holt, Rinehart and Winston, 1967).
17. Denis McQuail, *McQuail's Mass Communication Theory*, 5th ed. (London: Sage Publications, 2005).
18. Larry G. Ehrlich, *Fatal Words and Friendly Faces: Interpersonal Communication in the Twenty-First Century* (Lanham, Md.: University Press of America, 2000).
19. Hanson.
20. McQuail, *McQuail's Mass Communication Theory*; Benjamin Compaine et al., eds., *Who Owns the Media?* (White Plains, N.Y.: Knowledge Industry Publications, Inc., 1982); Harold Lasswell, "The Structure and Function of Communication in Society," in *Mass Communications*, ed. Wilbur Schramm (Urbana: University of Illinois Press, 1960); Charles R. Wright, *Mass Communication: A Sociological Perspective*, 3rd ed. (New York: Random House, 1986).
21. Wright, *Mass Communication: A Sociological Perspective*.
22. Adam Sternbergh, "The Spreadsheet Psychic," *New York Magazine*, October 12, 2008.
23. C. W. Mills, *The Power Elite* (New York: Oxford University Press, 1959).
24. Bill Carter, "Analysis: Port-Morten of CBS's Flawed Broadcast," *New York Times*, January 11, 2005.
25. Pamela McClintock, "H'wood's Niche Reach," *Daily Variety*, March 6, 2008.

26. Stuart Elliott, "Making Every Second, or $100,000, Count," *New York Times*, January 23, 2009.
27. Sportcal Global Communications, "World Cup 2006: The Commercial Report *Plus New* Post-Event Supplement," www.sportcal.com/commerce/ProductDetails.aspx?productID=30.
28. W. James Potter, *Media Literacy*, 3rd ed. (Thousand Oaks, Calif.: Sage Publications, 2005).
29. Jon Katz, *Virtuous Reality* (New York: Random House, 1997).
30. McQuail, *McQuail's Mass Communication Theory*.
31. Hinckley and Huff, "Michael Jackson's Memorial 2nd Most-Watched Funeral Ever, After Princess Di, Say Nielsen Ratings."
32. Frank Ahrens, "Anti-Indecency Forces Opposed," *Washington Post*, March 26, 2005.
33. Shankar Vedantam, "Two Views of the Same News Find Opposite Biases," *Washington Post*, July 24, 2006.
34. McQuail, *McQuail's Mass Communication Theory*.
35. Joel Brown, "No Question, He's a Success," *Boston Globe*, August 29, 2008.
36. Jeph Jacques, "Comics, Comics, Comics," February 1, 2009, qcjeph.livejournal.com/100732 .html.
37. David Edelstein, "Revenge of the Nerd," *New York Times*, April 28, 2002.
38. Ben H. Bagdikian, *The New Media Monopoly* (Boston: Beacon Press, 2004).
39. Potter, *Media Literacy*; Newspaper Association of America, "Trends and Numbers," www.naa .org/TrendsandNumbers.aspx; Magazine Publishers of America, *Magazines: The Medium of Action; Handbook 2009/2010* (New York: Magazine Publishers of America, 2009); National Association of Theater Owners, "Number of U.S. Movie Screens," www.natoonline.org/statistics screens.htm.
40. U.S. Census Bureau, Housing and Household Economic Statistics Division, "Families and Living Arrangements," www.census.gov/population/www/socdemo/hh-fam.html; Newspaper Association of America, "Trends and Numbers."
41. Pew Research Center Project for Excellence in Journalism, "The State of the News Media 2009," stateofthemedia.org/2009/index.htm.
42. Potter, *Media Literacy*; Magazine Publishers of America, *Magazines: The Medium of Action; Handbook 2009/2010*; Stephanie Clifford, "A Look Ahead at the Money in the Communications Industry," *New York Times*, August 4, 2009.
43. Bagdikian, *The New Media Monopoly*; Potter, *Media Literacy*.
44. Mireya Navarro, "Complaint to Spanish TV: Not Enough Americans; Few U.S. Plots for Growing U.S. Audience," *New York Times*, August 21, 2000.
45. John Consoli, "The 11.8-Hour Daily Diet," *Broadcasting*, April 20, 1998.
46. Clifford, "A Look Ahead at the Money in the Communications Industry."
47. Ibid.
48. George Gerbner, "TV Violence and the Art of Asking the Wrong Question," Center for Media Literacy, www.medialit.org/reading_room/article459.html.
49. Potter, *Media Literacy*.
50. Arthur Asa Berger, *Media Analysis Techniques*, 3rd ed. (Thousand Oaks, Calif.: Sage Publications, 2005).
51. Emma Forrest, "Iconography: Good for What, Exactly, Will Hunting?" *The Guardian*, March 16, 1998.
52. Dwight Garner, "Storm Over Everest," *Ottawa Citizen*, August 23, 1998.
53. Potter, *Media Literacy*.
54. Linda Pershing and Margaret R. Yocom, "The Yellow Ribboning of the USA: Contested Meanings in the Construction of a Political Symbol," *Western Folklore* 55, no. 1 (1996); Jack Santino, "Yellow Ribbons and Seasonal Flags: The Folk Assemblage of War," *The Journal of American Folklore* 105, no. 415 (1992); George Mariscal, "In the Wake of the Gulf War: Untying the Yellow Ribbon," *Cultural Critique*, no. 19 (1991).
55. Brooke Gladstone, "Never the Same Mainstream Twice," NPR, November 24, 2006, www .onthemedia.org/transcripts/2006/11/24/06.
56. Pew Research Center Project for Excellence in Journalism, "The State of the News Media 2009"; Paul Farhi, "No Rush to Measure Limbaugh's Ratings," *Los Angeles Times*, March 9, 2009.
57. Howard Kurtz, "Does the Right Know Jack?" *Washington Post*, January 6, 2006; Brian C. Anderson, "The Plot to Shush Rush," *Chicago Sun Times*, February 5, 2006; Lisa de Moraes, "Rick

Kaplan Out at No. 3 MSNBC," *Washington Post*, June 8, 2006; Peter Johnson, "CBS' Couric Slides to No. 3; 'NBC Nightly News' Jumps Back on Top," *USA Today*, September 12, 2006.

58. Hoover's Inc., "Hoover's Company Records—In Depth Records: Village Voice Media," (Austin, Texas: Hoover's Inc., 2009).

59. Patricia Romanowski, Holly George-Warren, and Jon Pareles, eds., *The New Rolling Stone Encyclopedia of Rock & Roll*, completely revised and updated ed. (New York: Rolling Stone Press, 1995).

60. Hal R. Varian, "File-Sharing Is the Latest Battleground in the Clash of Technology and Copyright," *New York Times*, April 7, 2005.

61. Erik Barnouw, *Tube of Plenty: The Evolution of American Television*, 2nd revised ed. (New York: Oxford University Press, 1990).

62. Shearon A. Lowery and Melvin L. DeFleur, *Milestones in Mass Communication*, 3rd ed. (White Plains, N.Y.: Longman, 1995).

63. Stan Soocher, *They Fought the Law: Rock Music Goes to Court* (New York: Schirmer Books, 1999).

64. Jesse Sheidlower, "If You Seek Amy's Ancestors," March 18, 2009, www.slate.com/id/2214106.

65. Wright, *Mass Communication: A Sociological Perspective*.

66. Ibid.

67. "Rockefeller Bill on Indecency Spurs Action in Congress to Increase Fines on TV Indecency," Sen. Jay Rockefeller, June 16, 2006, rockefeller.senate.gov/press/record.cfm?id=288297.

CHAPTER 2
**MASS COMMUNICATION EFFECTS**

1. Michah L. Sifry, "Parkridge47: Not an R, and Not Bill Hillsman," Personal Democracy Forum, March 21, 2007, www.techpresident.com/node/173.

2. Larry King, interview with Barack Obama, *CNN Larry King Live*, March 19, 2007, transcripts.cnn.com/TRANSCRIPTS/0703/19/lkl.01.html.

3. Arianna Huffington, "Who Created 'Hillary 1984'? Mystery Solved," Huffington Post, March 21, 2007, www.huffingtonpost.com/arianna-huffington/who-created-hillary-1984_b_43978.html.

4. Phil de Vellis, "I Made the 'Vote Different' Ad," Huffington Post, March 21, 2007, www.huffingtonpost.com/phil-de-vellis-aka-parkridge/i-made-the-vote-differen_b_43989.html.

5. James Wolcott, "The YouTube Election," *Vanity Fair*, June 2007.

6. Bob Garfield, "Ads Garfield Loved," *Advertising Age*, December 15, 2008, adage.com/article?article_id=133200; David Kiley; "Best Message Creation of 2008: The Winner Is Will I. Am," *Business Week*, December 31, 2008, www.businessweek.com/the_thread/brandnewday/archives/2008/12/best_message_cr.html.

7. Sarah Lai Stirland, "Fears of a YouTube Swiftboat," Wired News, March 23, 2007, www.wired.com/news/politics/0,73069-0.html?tw=rss.politics.

8. W. James Potter, *Media Literacy*, 3rd ed. (Thousand Oaks, Calif.: Sage Publications, Inc., 2005).

9. Melvin L. DeFleur and Sandra Ball-Rokeach, *Theories of Mass Communication*, 5th ed. (New York: Longman, 1989); Ferdinand Tönnies, *Gemeinschaft und Gesellschaft*, trans. Charles P. Loomis (East Lansing: Michigan State University Press, 1957).

10. DeFleur and Ball-Rokeach, *Theories of Mass Communication*.

11. Stanley Rothman, "Introduction," in *The Mass Media in Liberal Democratic Societies*, ed. Stanley Rothman (New York: Paragon House, 1992).

12. DeFleur and Ball-Rokeach, *Theories of Mass Communication*.

13. Stephen Ansolabehere, Shanto Iyengar, and Adam Simon, "Shifting Perspectives on the Effects of Campaign Communication," in *Do the Media Govern? Politicians, Voters, and Reporters in America*, ed. Shanto Iyengar and Richard Reeves (Thousand Oaks, Calif.: Sage Publications, 1997).

14. Paul Lazarsfeld, Bernard Berelson, and Hazel Gaudet, *The People's Choice*, 3rd ed. (New York: Columbia University Press, 1968).

15. Brooke Gladstone, "Trail of Years," NPR, February 23, 2007, www.onthemedia.org/transcripts/2007/02/23/07.

16. Ansolabehere, et al., "Shifting Perspectives on the Effects of Campaign Communication."

17. Werner J. Severin and James W. Tankard, *Communication Theories: Origins, Methods, and Uses in the Mass Media*, 5th ed. (New York: Longman, 2001).

18. C. Wright Mills, *The Power Elite* (New York: Oxford University Press, 1959).

19. Ben H. Bagdikian, *The New Media Monopoly* (Boston: Beacon Press, 2004).

20. Colbert I. King, "12 Days of Christmas," *Washington Post*, December 24, 2005; District of Columbia, Metropolitan Police Department, "Major Case/Unsolved Homicides—2005," mpdc .dc.gov/mpdc/cwp/view,a,1243,q,559128,mpdcNav_GID,1533,mpdcNav,|.asp.

21. Mark Memmott, "Spotlight Skips Cases of Missing Minorities," *USA Today*, June 16, 2005.

22. DeFleur and Ball-Rokeach, *Theories of Mass Communication*; Denis McQuail, *McQuail's Mass Communication Theory*, 5th ed. (London: Sage Publications, 2005); Potter, *Media Literacy*.

23. Doris A. Graber, *Processing the News: How People Tame the Information Tide*, 2nd ed. (New York: Longman, 1988).

24. David Hinckley, "Rush and Sean Tops in Talk," *Daily News*, December 10, 2005.

25. Graber, *Processing the News;* Lazarsfeld, et al., *The People's Choice*.

26. Jim Rutenberg, "Obama Aims TV Ads at Younger Voters," *New York Times*, October 8, 2008, thecaucus.blogs.nytimes.com/2008/10/08/obama-aims-tv-ads-at-younger-voters; Nicholas Deleon, "Gaming Gets Political: Obama Ads Appear in EA Games," October 15, 2008, TechCrunch Network, www.crunchgear.com/2008/10/15/gaming-gets-political-obama-ads-appear-in-ea-games.

27. Arthur Asa Berger, *Media Analysis Techniques*, 3rd ed. (Thousand Oaks, Calif.: Sage Publications, 2005).

28. Ibid.

29. Potter, *Media Literacy*.

30. "Interview with John Adams About 'On the Transmigration of Souls,'" September 2002, www .earbox.com/W-transmigration.html.

31. Marshall McLuhan, *Understanding Media: The Extensions of Man* (New York: McGraw-Hill, 1964).

32. McQuail, *McQuail's Mass Communication Theory*.

33. Joshua Meyrowitz, "Shifting Worlds of Strangers: Medium Theory and Changes in 'Them' Versus 'Us'," *Sociological Inquiry* 67, no. 1 (1997): 59–71.

34. Joshua Meyrowitz, *No Sense of Place* (New York: Oxford University Press, 1985).

35. McQuail, *McQuail's Mass Communication Theory*.

36. Jürgen Habermas, *The Theory of Communicative Action*, vol. 1, trans. Thomas McCarthy (Boston: Beacon Press, 1984).

37. Matthew Forney, "Testing Beijing's Limits; In the Quest for China's Lucrative—and Elusive—TV Market, Did Murdoch Bend the Rules?" *Time*, September 5, 2005.

38. Bagdikian, *The New Media Monopoly*.

39. Chris Anderson, *The Long Tail* (New York: Hyperion, 2006).

40. Potter, *Media Literacy*; Shearon A. Lowery and Melvin L. DeFleur, *Milestones in Mass Communication*, 3rd ed. (White Plains, N.Y.: Longman, 1995); McQuail, *McQuail's Mass Communication Theory*.

41. Potter, *Media Literacy*.

42. Elihu Katz, "The Two-Step Flow of Communication," in *Mass Communications*, ed. Wilbur Schramm (Urbana: University of Illinois Press, 1960).

43. Harold Lasswell, "The Structure and Function of Communication in Society," in *Mass Communications*, ed. Wilbur Schramm (Urbana: University of Illinois Press, 1960).

44. Robert K. Merton, *Social Theory and Social Structure*, enlarged ed. (New York: Free Press, 1968).

45. Lasswell, "The Structure and Function of Communication in Society."

46. Charles R. Wright, *Mass Communication: A Sociological Perspective*, 3rd ed. (New York: Random House, 1986).

47. Ibid.

48. Mark Jurkowitz, "PEJ News Coverage Index: Feb. 4–9, 2007; Anna and the Astronaut Trigger a Week of Tabloid News," Pew Research Center Project for Excellence in Journalism, journalism .org/node/4096.

49. "Investors Now Go Online for Quotes, Advice," Pew Research Center for the People and the Press, June 11, 2000.

50. Wright, *Mass Communication*; Meyrowitz, *No Sense of Place*.

51. Meyrowitz, *No Sense of Place*.

52. Everett M. Rogers, William B. Hart, and James W. Dearing, "A Paradigmatic History of Agenda-Setting Research," in *Do the Media Govern?* ed. Iyengar and Reeves.

53. Lowery and DeFleur, *Milestones in Mass Communication*.

54. Mark Jurkowitz, "PEJ News Coverage Index: August 17–23, 2009; Health Care, Afghanistan Emerge as the Summer's Big Stories," Pew Research Center Project for Excellence in Journalism, journalism.org/news_index/99.
55. Lowery and DeFleur, *Milestones in Mass Communication*.
56. Elihu Katz, Jay G. Blumler, and Michael Gurevitch, "Utilization of Mass Communication by the Individual," in *The Uses of Mass Communications: Current Perspectives on Gratifications Research*, ed. Jay G. Blumler and Elihu Katz (Beverly Hills: Sage Publications, 1974).
57. Berger, *Media Analysis Techniques*.
58. Albert Bandura, "Social Cognitive Theory of Mass Communication," in *Media Effects: Advances in Theory and Research*, ed. Jennings Bryant and Dolf Zillman (Hillsdale, N.J.: Lawrence Erlbaum Associates, 1994).
59. DeFleur and Ball-Rokeach, *Theories of Mass Communication*.
60. George Herbert Mead, *Mind, Self, and Society* (Chicago: University of Chicago Press, 1934).
61. Merton, *Social Theory and Social Structure*.
62. Michael J. Socolow, "The Hyped Panic Over 'War of the Worlds'," *The Chronicle of Higher Education*, October 24, 2008; Wright, *Mass Communication: A Sociological Perspective*.
63. Elisabeth Noelle-Neumann, "The Contribution of Spiral of Silence Theory to an Understanding of Mass Media," in *The Mass Media in Liberal Democratic Societies*, ed. Stanley Rothman (New York: Paragon House, 1992).
64. Rothman, "Introduction."
65. Huiping Huang, "A Cross-Cultural Test of the Spiral of Silence," *International Journal of Public Opinion Research* 17, no. 13 (2005).
66. David L. Altheide and Robert P. Snow, *Media Worlds in the Postjournalism Era* (Hawthorne, N.Y.: Aldine De Gruyter, 1991).
67. McQuail, *McQuail's Mass Communication Theory*.
68. Joanne Ostrow, "Authority on Media Violence Says Don't Blame TV for Columbine," *Denver Post*, April 25, 1999.
69. George Gerbner, et al., "Growing Up With Television: The Cultivation Perspective," in *Media Effects: Advances in Theory and Research*, ed. Jennings Bryant and Dolf Zillman (Hillsdale, N.J.: Lawrence Erlbaum Associates, 1994).
70. Lowery and DeFleur, *Milestones in Mass Communication*.
71. Wilson Biographies, "Gerbner, George," Wilson Web, hwwilsonweb.com.
72. Gerbner, et al., "Growing Up With Television."
73. Ibid.
74. Dan Balz and Anne E. Kornblut, "Obama Joins Race With Goals Set High," *Washington Post*, February 11, 2007.
75. Ansolabehere, et al., "Shifting Perspectives on the Effects of Campaign Communication."
76. Howard Kurtz, "Media Notes: Big Day or Non-Event?" *Washington Post*, February 19, 2008, www.washingtonpost.com/wp-dyn/content/article/2008/02/19/AR2008021900844.html?referrer=emailarticle.
77. Doris A. Graber, *Mass Media and American Politics*, 7th ed. (Washington, D.C.: CQ Press, 2006).
78. Peter Johnson, "Fox News Enjoys New View—From the Top," *USA Today*, April 4, 2002.
79. Ibid.
80. Ibid.
81. Pew Research Center Project for Excellence in Journalism, "The State of the News Media 2009: Cable TV" (2009).
82. Richard Reeves, "The Question of Media Bias," in *Do the Media Govern?* ed. Iyengar and Reeves.
83. David H. Weaver and G. Cleveland Wilhoit, "The American Journalist in the 1990s," in *Do the Media Govern?* ed. Iyengar and Reeves.
84. U.S. Census Bureau, "United States—DP-1. General Demographic Characteristics, 2008 Population Estimates," factfinder.census.gov/servlet/QTTable?_bm=y&-qr_name=PEP_2008_EST_DP1&-geo_id=01000US&-ds_name=PEP_2008_EST&-_lang=en&-format=&-CONTEXT=qt.
85. Rothman, "Introduction."
86. Media Matters for America, "O'Reilly Asserted 'Most Journalists Give Money to Democrats'—but Study on Subject Refutes Him," August 24, 2007, mediamatters.org/research/200708240007.

87. Bagdikian, *The New Media Monopoly*.
88. Dana Milbank, "Rove's Reading: Not So Liberal as Leery," *Washington Post*, April 20, 2005.
89. Graber, *Mass Media and American Politics*.
90. Herbert Gans, *Deciding What's News* (New York: Pantheon Books, 1979).
91. Nazila Fathi, "In a Death Seen Around the World, a Symbol of Iranian Protests," *New York Times*, June 23, 2009.
92. James O'Byrne, "Katrina: The Power of the Press Against the Wrath of Nature," September 1, 2006, www.poynter.org/content/content_view.asp?id=106352.
93. Gans, *Deciding What's News*.
94. Rothman, "Introduction."

CHAPTER 3
**THE MEDIA BUSINESS**
1. Hoover's Inc., *Hoover's Company Profile Database: Apple Inc.* (Austin, Texas: Hoover's Inc., 2009).
2. Peter Burrows and Ronald Grover, "Steve Jobs's Magic Kingdom," *BusinessWeek*, January 26, 2006.
3. Tim Berners-Lee, *Weaving the Web* (New York: Harper Collins, 1999).
4. Hoover's Inc., *Hoover's Company Profile Database: Apple Inc.*; John Markoff, "Oh, Yeah, He Also Sells Computers," *New York Times*, April 25, 2004.
5. Jefferson Graham, "Jobs Has a Knack for Getting His Way," *USA Today*, January 25, 2006.
6. Hoover's Inc., *Hoover's Company Profile Database: Pixar Animation Studios Inc.* (Austin, Texas: Hoover's Inc., 2009).
7. Burrows and Grover, "Steve Jobs's Magic Kingdom."
8. Graham, "Jobs Has a Knack for Getting His Way."
9. Burrows and Grover, "Steve Jobs's Magic Kingdom."
10. Yukari Iwatani Kane and Joann S. Lublin, "Jobs Had Liver Transplant," *Wall Street Journal*, June 20, 2009.
11. Steve Jobs, "Advice From Steve Jobs on Living and Dying," January 14, 2009, www.thedailybeast.com/blogs-and-stories/2009-01-14/advice-from-steve-jobs-on-living-and-dying.
12. Lydia Adetunji, "US Cable's Black Media Baron Robert Johnson Became a Billionaire When He Sold Black Entertainment Television. Why Is He Still One of a Kind?" *Financial Times*, October 1, 2002.
13. Hoover's Inc., *Hoover's Company Profile Database: Time Warner Inc.* (Austin, Texas: Hoover's Inc., 2006).
14. Ben Bagdikian, *The Information Machines: Their Impact on Men and the Media* (New York: Harper & Row, 1971).
15. John Tebbel, *The Media in America* (New York: Thomas Y. Crowell Company, 1974).
16. Ibid.
17. Ibid.
18. Michael Schudson, *The Power of News* (Cambridge: Harvard University Press, 1995).
19. Margaret A. Blanchard, ed., *History of the Mass Media in the United States* (Chicago: Fitzroy Deaborn Publishers, 1998).
20. Schudson, *The Power of News*.
21. National Cable and Telecommunications Association, "National Cable and Telecommunications Association 2008 Industry Overview," May 16, 2008, i.ncta.com/ncta_com/PDFs/NCTA_Annual_Report_05.16.08.pdf; Satellite Broadcasting and Communications Association, "Satellite Home Entertainment; Industry Overview," www.sbca.com/receiver-network/index.html; "Newspaper Circulation Ranking Index," Advertising Age Data Center, 2009, adage.com/datacenter/article?article_id=106788; Nielsen Company, "How Teens Use Media; A Nielsen Report on the Myths and Realities of Teen Media Trends," June 2009, blog.nielsen.com/nielsenwire/reports/nielsen_howteensusemedia_june09.pdf.
22. Open Society Institute EU Monitoring and Advocacy Program, *Television Across Europe: Regulation, Policy and Independence*, 2005, www.eumap.org/topics/media/television_europe.
23. Ken Auletta, *The Highwaymen* (San Diego: Harcourt Brace, 1998).
24. Ben H. Bagdikian, *The New Media Monopoly* (Boston: Beacon Press, 2004).

25. David Barsamian, "Ben Bagdikian," *The Progressive*, April 1997.

26. Hoover's Inc., *Hoover's Company Profile Database: Clear Channel Communications, Inc.* (Austin, Texas: Hoover's Inc., 2009); Hoover's Inc., *Hoover's Company Profile Database: Gannett Co., Inc.* (Austin, Texas: Hoover's Inc., 2009).

27. Hoover's Inc., *Hoover's Company Profile Database: Time Warner Inc.* (Austin, Texas: Hoover's Inc., 2009); Hoover's Inc., *Hoover's Company Profile Database: The Walt Disney Company* (Austin, Texas: Hoover's Inc., 2009).

28. Hoover's Inc., *Hoover's Company Profile Database: Time Warner Inc.*; Dean Alger, *Megamedia: How Giant Corporations Dominate Mass Media, Distort Competition, and Endanger Democracy* (Lanham, Md.: Rowman & Littlefield, 1998); AOL Time Warner, "AOL Time Warner 2002 Annual Report," 2002.

29. Bill McConnell and John M. Higgins, "Finally, They've Got a Deal," *Broadcasting & Cable*, January 15, 2001; Hoover's Inc., *Hoover's Company Profile Database: Time Warner Inc.*

30. Johnnie L. Roberts, "All for One, One for AOL," *Newsweek*, December 25, 2000.

31. Hoover's Inc., *Hoover's Company Profile Database: Time Warner Inc.*

32. Steve Case, "It's Time to Take It Apart," *Washington Post*, December 11, 2005.

33. Susan Paterno, "An Ill Tailwind," *American Journalism Review*, September 1998, 22.

34. Anick Jesdanun, "New All-in-One Software From AOL Built With Free Strategy in Mind," *USA Today*, October 4, 2006.

35. Hoover's Inc., *Hoover's Company Profile Database: Time Warner Inc.*

36. Ibid.

37. Hoover's Inc., *Hoover's Company Profile Database: The Walt Disney Company.*

38. Wilson Biographies, "Disney, Walt," vweb.hwwilsonweb.com.

39. Richard Schickel, "Walt Disney," *Time*, December 7, 1998.

40. "The House of the Mouse," *New Internationalist*, December 1998.

41. Suzy Wetlaufer, "Common Sense and Conflict," *Harvard Business Review*, January/February 2000; Wilson Biographies, "Disney, Walt."

42. Auletta, *The Highwaymen*.

43. Hoover's Inc., *Hoover's Company Profile Database: The Walt Disney Company.*

44. Peter Schweizer and Rochelle Schweizer, *Disney: The Mouse Betrayed* (Washington, D.C.: Regnery Publishing, Inc., 1998); Robert F. Hartley, *Marketing Mistakes and Successes*, 7th ed. (New York: Wiley, 1998); Maureen Fan, "A Bumpy Ride for Disneyland in Hong Kong," *Washington Post*, November 20, 2006.

45. Schweizer and Schweizer, *Disney: The Mouse Betrayed.*

46. Jim Puzzanghera and Mark Magnier, "Studios Still Bit Actors in China," *Los Angeles Times*, June 18, 2006.

47. Richard Verrier, "Disney May Add 2nd China Park," *Los Angeles Times*, July 20, 2002.

48. Walt Disney Company, "The Walt Disney Company 2005 Annual Report," corporate.disney.go.com/investors/annual_reports/2005/index.html.

49. Fan, "A Bumpy Ride for Disneyland in Hong Kong"; Hoover's Inc., *Hoover's Company Profile Database: The Walt Disney Company.*

50. Fan, "A Bumpy Ride for Disneyland in Hong Kong."

51. Verrier, "Disney May Add 2nd China Park"; Hoover's Inc., *Hoover's Company Profile Database: The Walt Disney Company.*

52. Alger, *Megamedia*.

53. Shannon Peavey, "Disney Believes It Can Duck Downturn," *Electronic Media*, February 12, 2001; Hoover's Inc., *Hoover's Company Profile Database: The Walt Disney Company.*

54. David Lieberman and Laura Petrecca, "Disney, Pixar to Merge in $7.5B Deal," *USA Today*, January 24, 2006; Hoover's Inc., *Hoover's Company Profile Database: The Walt Disney Company.*

55. Wetlaufer, "Common Sense and Conflict."

56. Jon Swartz, "Disney Gets New Comic Heroes With $4 Billion Deal for Marvel," *USA Today*, September 4, 2009.

57. Hoover's Inc., *Hoover's Company Profile Database: The Walt Disney Company.*

58. Auletta, *The Highwaymen*.

59. Hoover's Inc., *Hoover's Company Profile Database: News Corporation* (Austin, Texas: Hoover's Inc., 2009).

60. Auletta, *The Highwaymen*.
61. Pew Research Center Project for Excellence in Journalism, "The State of the News Media 2009: Cable TV," March 16, 2009, pewresearch.org/pubs/1151/state-of-the-news-media-2009.
62. Hoover's Inc., *Hoover's Company Profile Database: News Corporation*.
63. Ibid.
64. Pew Research Center Project for Excellence in Journalism, "The State of the News Media 2008: Newspapers," March 15, 2008, pewresearch.org/pubs/767/state-of-the-news-media-2008.
65. Hoover's Inc., *Hoover's Company Profile Database: Time Warner Inc.*; Hoover's Inc., *Hoover's Company Profile Database: News Corporation*.
66. Hoover's Inc., *Hoover's Company Profile Database: News Corporation*.
67. Ken Auletta, *Three Blind Mice: How the TV Networks Lost Their Way* (New York: Random House, 1991).
68. Ibid.
69. Hoover's Inc., *Hoover's Company Profile Database: Viacom* (Austin, Texas: Hoover's Inc., 2009).
70. Devin Leonard, "Who's the Boss?" *Fortune*, April 16, 2001.
71. David Lieberman, "Viacom Plans Split to Spur Growth," *USA Today*, June 14, 2005; Hoover's Inc., *Hoover's Company Profile Database: CBS Inc.* (Austin, Texas: Hoover's Inc., 2009); Hoover's Inc., *Hoover's Company Profile Database: Viacom Inc.* (Austin, Texas: Hoover's Inc., 2009).
72. John Eggerton, "FCC Upholds Viacom Indecency Settlement," *Broadcasting & Cable*, October 17, 2006; Krysten Crawford, "Howard Stern Jumps to Satellite," October 6, 2004, money.cnn.com/2004/10/06/news/newsmakers/stern_sirius/index.htm?cnn=yes.
73. Hoover's Inc., *Hoover's Company Profile Database: Viacom*.
74. Bagdikian, *The New Media Monopoly*; Hoover's Inc., *Hoover's Company Profile Database: Bertelsmann AG* (Austin, Texas: Hoover's Inc., 2009).
75. Alger, *Megamedia*.
76. "New Chapter," *The Economist*, February 10, 2001; Hoover's Inc., *Hoover's Company Profile Database: Bertelsmann AG*.
77. Jack Ewing, "Bertelsmann's Creed: Inner Growth," March 18, 2005, www.businessweek.com/bwdaily/dnflash/mar2005/nf20050318_7804_db016.htm?chan=search.
78. Frank Gibney Jr., "Napster Meister," *Time*, November 13, 2000; Hoover's Inc., *Hoover's Company Profile Database: Bertelsmann AG*.
79. Jack Ewing, "Bertelsmann's Slimmer Profile Generates Thinner Profits," September 6, 2006, www.businessweek.com/globalbiz/content/sep2006/gb20060906_498406.htm.
80. Hoover's Inc., *Hoover's Company Profile Database: Bertelsmann AG*.
81. Ewing, "Bertelsmann's Creed: Inner Growth"; Ewing, "Bertelsmann's Slimmer Profile Generates Thinner Profits."
82. Hoover's Inc., *Hoover's Company Profile Database: Bertelsmann AG*.
83. Alger, *Megamedia*.
84. Auletta, *Three Blind Mice*.
85. Bill Carter, "Deal Complete, NBC Is Planning to Cross-Market," *New York Times*, May 13, 2004.
86. Hoover's Inc., *Hoover's Company Profile Database: General Electric* (Austin, Texas: Hoover's Inc., 2009); Hoover's Inc., *Hoover's Company Profile Database: NBC Universal*, Inc. (Austin, Texas: Hoover's Inc., 2009).
87. David Lieberman, Peter Johnson, and Gary Levin, "NBC Universal Plans Cost Cuts, Layoffs; 'Tricky Business' Leads to News, Prime-Time Changes," *USA Today*, October 20, 2006; Rebecca Dana and Sam Schechner, "NBC Plans Prime-Time Slot for Leno," *Wall Street Journal*, December 9, 2008.
88. Hoover's Inc., *Hoover's Company Profile Database: NBC Universal, Inc.*
89. Howard Kurtz, "Comcast-NBC Deal Possible," *Washington Post*, October 1, 2009; Paul Tobin, "Vivendi Wants to Exit NBC, Deal Is Complex, CFO Says," November 19, 2009, www.bloomberg.com/apps/news?pid=20601087&sid=anZaSljci4Z4&pos=7; Shira Ovide and Amy Schatz, "Comcast-NBC Deal Would Draw Lengthy Scrutiny in Washington," *Wall Street Journal*, November 16, 2009.
90. Hoover's Inc., *Hoover's Company Profile Database: Gannett Co., Inc.*
91. Alger, *Megamedia*; Bagdikian, *The New Media Monopoly*.
92. Hoover's Inc., *Hoover's Company Profile Database: Gannett Co., Inc.*
93. Hoover's Inc., *Hoover's Company Profile Database: Clear Channel Communications, Inc.*
94. Ibid.; Clear Channel, "Know the Facts," www.clearchannel.com/Corporate.
95. Chris Anderson, *The Long Tail* (New York: Hyperion, 2006).

96. Ibid.
97. Ibid.
98. Ibid.
99. Ibid.
100. Ibid.
101. Michael Liedtke, "Now Starring on the Internet: YouTube.Com," *USA Today*, April 9, 2006.
102. Charlie Rose, "Charlie Rose: A Conversation With the YouTube Co-Founders, August 11, 2006, www.charlierose.com/view/interview/271.
103. Hoover's Inc., *Hoover's Company Profile Database: YouTube, LLC.* (Austin, Texas: Hoover's Inc., 2009).
104. Ibid.
105. Rose, *YouTube Co-Founders*.
106. Diane Mermigas, "Mermigas on Media," *Hollywood Reporter*, October 24, 2006.
107. Ibid.
108. Schudson, *The Power of News*.
109. "Future Forum," *Advertising Age*, September 20, 1999.
110. Bagdikian, *The New Media Monopoly*.
111. Elizabeth Lesly Stevens, "Mouse-ke-fear," *Brill's Content*, January 1999.
112. Ibid.
113. Johnnie L. Roberts, "Desperately Seeking a Deal," *Newsweek*, January 24, 2000.
114. Ibid.; Todd Gitlin, "Introduction," in *Conglomerates and the Media*, ed. Eric Barnouw (New York: The New Press, 1997).
115. Denis McQuail, *McQuail's Mass Communication Theory*, 5th ed. (London: Sage Publications, 2005).
116. Dave Phillips, "Chrysler Drops Censorship Policy," *Detroit News*, October 14, 1997.
117. Jim Edwards, "Nicetv," *Brill's Content*, March 2001.
118. Roberts, "All for One, One for AOL."
119. Auletta, *The Highwaymen*.
120. Matthew Forney, "Testing Beijing's Limits; In the Quest for China's Lucrative—and Elusive—TV Market, Did Murdoch Bend the Rules?" *Time*, September 5, 2005.
121. Tunku Varadarajan, "Rupert: Taking Stock of Mr. Murdoch," December 8, 2008, www.forbes.com/2008/12/07/murdoch-dow-media-oped-cx_tv_1208varadarajan.html.
122. Ralph Hanson, "Go See What All the Shouting Is About," *Charleston Daily Mail*, February 15, 2006.
123. Herbert Gans, *Deciding What's News* (New York: Pantheon Books, 1979); McQuail, *McQuail's Mass Communication Theory*.
124. Schudson, *The Power of News*.
125. Donna Freydkin, "Celebrities Fight for Privacy," *USA Today*, July 7, 2004.
126. Patrick M. Reilly, "Behind the Covers: How Stars End Up on Those Glossies," *Wall Street Journal*, November 18, 1997.
127. Ben Smith, "Clinton Campaign Kills Negative Story," September 24, 2007, www.politico.com/news/stories/0907/5992.html.
128. Ibid.
129. Becky Yerak, "Editors Turn to Readers for Cover Choices," *USA Today*, September 15, 2000.
130. Alessandra Stanley, "The Oxygen TV Channel Is Bowing to Tastes," *New York Times*, February 25, 2002.
131. Stephen Galloway, "Test Screenings; Looking to Shore Up Box Office Returns, Studios Have Become Increasingly Dependent on Findings from Research Screenings—Whether Filmmakers Like It or Not," *Hollywood Reporter*, July 25, 2006; Box Office Mojo, "Little Miss Sunshine," boxofficemojo.com/movies/?id=littlemisssunshine.htm.
132. Seth Schiesel, "Young Viewers Like Screen Translation," *New York Times*, November 19, 2001.

CHAPTER 4
**BOOKS**
1. Adam Kirsch, "He Wrote What They Wanted," *New York Sun*, January 11, 2006; The Smoking Gun, "The Man Who Conned Oprah," January 8, 2006, www.thesmokinggun.com/jamesfrey/0104061jamesfrey1.html.
2. The Smoking Gun, "The Man Who Conned Oprah."
3. Ibid.

4. Scott Eyman, "It's My Story (and I'll Lie If I Want to)," *Palm Beach Post*, February 21, 2006.

5. Carol Memmott, "Oprah Confronts Frey About Disputed Memoir," *USA Today*, January 25, 2006.

6. Kirsch, "He Wrote What They Wanted."

7. Ibid.

8. Eyman, "It's My Story (and I'll Lie If I Want to)."

9. Motoko Rich, "Gang Memoir, Turning Page, Is Pure Fiction," *New York Times*, March 4, 2008.

10. Motoko Rich, "Tracking the Fallout of (Another) Literary Fraud," *New York Times*, March 5, 2008.

11. James D. Hart, *The Popular Book: A History of America's Literary Taste* (New York: Oxford University Press, 1950).

12. Ibid.

13. Ibid.; Bill Katz, *Dahl's History of the Book*, 3rd English ed. (Metuchen, N.J.: Scarecrow Press, 1995).

14. Katz, *Dahl's History of the Book*.

15. Ibid.; "Exceptional Prices," Christies's 2006, www.christies.com/departments/exceptionalprices.asp?DID=10.

16. Katz, *Dahl's History of the Book*.

17. Ibid.

18. Stephen E. Ambrose, *Undaunted Courage* (New York: Simon & Schuster, 1996).

19. Katz, *Dahl's History of the Book*.

20. Ibid.

21. Hart, *The Popular Book: A History of America's Literary Taste*.

22. Katz, *Dahl's History of the Book*.

23. Hart, *The Popular Book: A History of America's Literary Taste*.

24. Ibid.

25. Katz, *Dahl's History of the Book*.

26. Ibid.

27. Chris Anderson, *The Long Tail* (New York: Hyperion, 2006).

28. Katz, *Dahl's History of the Book*.

29. Doreen Carvajal, "Book Publishers Seek Global Reach and Grand Scale," *New York Times*, October 19, 1998.

30. Random House, "About Us," www.randomhouse.com/about/history.html.

31. David Streitfeld, "Book Report," *Washington Post*, March 14, 1999, BW13.

32. Jim Milliot and Rudiger Wischenbart, "Pearson Stands on Top," *Publishers Weekly*, July 20, 2009.

33. Florence Shinkle, "University Presses Seize Upon a Silver Lining," *St. Louis Post-Dispatch*, October 12, 1998.

34. Edwin McDowell, "New Best-Selling Novel at Naval Institute Press," *New York Times*, November 1, 1986.

35. Ken Fuson, "Prophet Motives; Author: Good-Natured Guru James Redfield Happens by to Promote His Sequel to 'The Celestine Prophecy'," *Baltimore Sun*, November 9, 1996.

36. Motoko Rich, "Self-Publishers Flourish as Writers Pay the Tab," *New York Times*, January 28, 2009.

37. David Tyler, "Digital Wave Overtaking Government Printing," *Rochester Democrat and Chronicle*, September 27, 2006.

38. Hoover's Inc., "Hoover's Company Records—In-Depth Records: Ingram Book Group Inc." (Austin, Texas: Hoover's Inc., 2009).

39. James Shapiro, "Wariness Greets the Latest Round in the Publishing Wars," *The Chronicle of Higher Education*, November 27, 1998.

40. Hoover's Inc., "Hoover's Company Records—In-Depth Records: Barnes & Noble, Inc." (Austin, Texas: Hoover's Inc., 2009).

41. Hoover's, Inc., "Hoover's Company Records—In-Depth Records: Borders Group, Inc." (Austin, Texas: Hoover's Inc., 2009).

42. Paul Collins, "Chain Reaction; Do Bookstores Have a Future?" *The Village Voice*, May 22, 2006; Hoover's Inc., "Hoover's Company Records—In-Depth Records: American Booksellers Association," (Austin, Texas: Hoover's Inc., 2009).

43. Doreen Carvajal, "Triumph of the Bottom Line; Numbers vs. Words at the Book-of-the-Month Club," *New York Times*, April 1, 1996.

44. Jenna Ross, "It's Textbook Economics: Colleges Fight High Prices; Campuses Across the State Try New Techniques and Technology to Fight Soaring Book Prices," *Star Tribune*, December 29, 2008.

45. Hoover's Inc., "Hoover's Company Records—In-Depth Records: Barnes & Noble College Booksellers, Inc." (Austin, Texas: Hoover's Inc., 2009).

46. Associated Press, "Nevada Regents Seek Answers to Rising Textbook Costs," *Las Vegas Sun*, November 6, 2006.

47. Ross, "It's Textbook Economics."

48. Anne Ryman, "Arizona State University to Try Out e-Textbooks," *Arizona Republic*, July 27, 2009.

49. Associated Press, "Nevada Regents Seek Answers to Rising Textbook Costs."

50. Association of American Publishers, "Higher Education Publishing; Charts of Independent Data Sources on Student Spending," www.publishers.org/highered/articles.cfm?ArticleID=45.

51. Hart, *The Popular Book: A History of America's Literary Taste*.

52. Ibid.

53. Katz, *Dahl's History of the Book*.

54. Romance Writers of America, "About the Romance Genre," www.rwanational.org/cs/the_romance_genre/romance_literature_statistics.

55. Dana Flavelle, "Torstar Eyes Convergence," *Toronto Star*, May 3, 2001.

56. Jeff Ayers, "Janet Evanovich Works Hard at Her Easy-to-Read Stephanie Plum Novels," *Seattle Post-Intelligencer*, June 23, 2006.

57. Allen Pierleoni, "Doubling Up; With Her Wisecracking Heroines Stephanie Plum and Alexandra Barnaby, Novelist Janet Evanovich Is on the Move," *Sacramento Bee*, December 5, 2005.

58. Carol Memmott, "Janet Evanovich by the Numbers," *USA Today*, June 25, 2009.

59. Daniel Johnson, "Still a Teen Hero? As J. D. Salinger Turns 80, Daniel Johnson Asks Whether Revelations About His Private Life Change Our View of His Work," *Daily Telegraph*, January 1, 1999; Associated Press, "J. D. Salinger Revealed Again in Daughter's Tell-All Memoir," www.cnn.com/2000/books/news/09/01/arts.us.salinger.ap/index.html.

60. Roger Cohen, "In Re: Marketing Parameters for Great American Novel," *New York Times*, March 25, 1990.

61. Jeff Gordinier, "Elvish Lives!," *Entertainment Weekly*, December 14, 2001.

62. Douglas A. Anderson, "Note on the Text," in *The Lord of the Rings* (New York: Houghton Mifflin, 1994); Brian Bethune, "The Lord of the Bookshelves," *Maclean's*, December 23, 2002; Gordinier, "Elvish Lives!"; Lev Grossman et al., "Feeding on Fantasy," *Time*, December 2, 2002; Karen Raugust, "Licensing Hotline," *Publishers Weekly*, July 2, 2001.

63. Carol Memmott and Mary Cadden, "Twilight Series Eclipses Potter Records; Author Meyer Owns Best-Selling Books List," *USA Today*, August 4, 2009.

64. Doreen Carvajal, "Booksellers Grab a Young Wizard's Cloaktails," *New York Times*, February 28, 2000.

65. Paul Gray, "Wild About Harry," *Time*, September 20, 1999.

66. "Revised *Times* Children's Bestseller List Creates Room for More Titles," *Book Publishing Report*, September 18, 2000.

67. Martin Bentham, "Harry Potter: The Best Children's Stories Ever: J. K. Rowling's Books About the Schoolboy Wizard Top Survey of British Children, Their Parents," *Sunday Telegraph*, September 23, 2002.

68. Editorial board, "Lust and Liberties," *The Indianapolis Star*, October 5, 1998.

69. Ibid.

70. "Book Bans Bring Storm of Debate," *Omaha World-Herald*, September 28, 1998.

71. William Breyfogle, "Librarians See Banned Books Week as a Wake-up Call to Society," *Milwaukee Journal Sentinel*, September 25, 1997.

72. Hart, *The Popular Book: A History of America's Literary Taste*.

73. American Civil Liberties Union, "Most Frequently Banned or Challenged Books of 1997," www.aclu.org/issues/freespeech/bbwlist.html.

74. Amy E. Schwartz, "Huck Finn Gets the Revisionist Treatment," *Washington Post*, January 10, 1996.

75. M. L. Lyke, "Blume Explores Her 'Naughty Streak' in 'Sisters'," *Sacramento Bee*, June 14, 1998.

76. Catherine Flannery, "Still in Blume: What Is It About the Great Judy Blume Novels That All Pre-Teens Want and Need?" *Toronto Sun*, September 21, 1997.

77. Bobbi Battista, "Judy Blume Releases Third Adult Novel," May 19, 1998, www.cnn.com/books/dialogue/9805/blume/index.html.

78. Paul Vallely, "They Will Not Be Silenced," *The Independent*, February 14, 1998.

79. Barbara Crossette, "Iran Drops Rushdie Death Threat, and Britain Renews Teheran Ties," *New York Times*, September 25, 1998.

80. Douglas Jehl, "New Moves on Rushdie Exposing Iranian Rifts," *New York Times*, October 21, 1998.

81. "Author Banned by British Air," *New York Times*, September 26, 1998.

82. Sarah Lyall, "Rushdie, Free of Threat, Revels in 'Spontaneity'," *New York Times*, September 26, 1998.

83. David Leppard, "Muslim Gang Firebombs Publisher of Allah Novel, Martin Rynja," *Sunday Times*, September 28, 2008; Ron Hogan, "Sherry Jones Reacts to UK *Jewel of Medina* Firebombing," Galleycat, September 28, 2008, www.mediabistro.com/galleycat/new_upcoming/sherry_jones_reacts_to_uk_jewel_of_medina_firebombing_95818.asp.

84. Vallely, "They Will Not Be Silenced"; "Write and Wrong—Taslima Has the Courage of Conviction," *Statesman* (India), October 22, 1998; Melvyn Bragg, "Forging Links With the Writers in Chains," *Times* (London), February 9, 1998.

85. Anderson, *The Long Tail*.

86. Ibid.

87. Doug Levy, "Amazon.com Amazes: On-line Gamble Pays Off with Rocketing Success," *USA Today*, December 24, 1998; Elisabeth Bumiller, "On-line Booksellers: A Tale of Two C.E.O.s," *New York Times*, December 8, 1998.

88. "Sony Reader (PRS-500) Video Review," *PC Magazine*, July 24, 2006, www.pcmag.com/article2/0,1759,1983663,00.asp.

89. Jim Milliot, "Audio Sales Slipped 6% in 2008," *Publishers Weekly*, June 24, 2009, www.publishersweekly.com/article/CA6667058.html.

90. J. Gerry Purdy, "Inside Mobile: Why Ebooks and Ebook Readers Will Eventually Succeed," *eWeek.com*, October 13, 2008, www.eweek.com/c/a/Mobile-and-Wireless/INSIDE-MOBILE-Why-eBooks-and-eBook-Readers-Will-Eventually-Succeed.

91. Noor Javed, "Digital Reader Meets Skeptics at Literary Fest," *Toronto Star*, September 29, 2008.

92. Jacob Weisberg, "Book End: How the Kindle Will Change the World," March 21, 2009, www.slate.com/id/2214243/.

93. Charlie Rose, "The Charlie Rose Show: A Conversation With Jeff Bezos," February 26, 2009, www.charlierose.com/guest/view/2618.

94. David Pogue, "Some E-Books Are More Equal Than Others," *New York Times*, July 17, 2009, pogue.blogs.nytimes.com/2009/07/17/some-e-books-are-more-equal-than-others/.

95. Jeffrey P. Bezos, "An Apology from Amazon," July 23, 2009, www.amazon.com/tag/kindle/forum/ref=cm_cd_ef_tft_tp?_encoding=UTF8&cd Thread=Tx1FXQPSF67X1IU&displayType=tagsDetail.

96. Anderson, *The Long Tail*.

97. Hoover's Inc., "Hoover's: Ingram Industries Inc."

CHAPTER 5

**MAGAZINES**

1. Kathryn Flett, "Focus: White House: Profile: Style Genius Who Frames the Stars," *The Observer*, November 22, 1998.

2. Joanne McAllister, "Dare to Go Bare; *Vanity Fair* Magazine Nude Portraits," *Inside Media*, September 25, 1991.

3. Cynthia McMullen, "Artist Bellies Up to Expectant Moms," *Tampa Tribune*, March 4, 2002.

4. John Motavalli, "Tina Talks; Power and Prestige at *Vanity Fair*; Tina Brown; Interview," *Inside Media*, June 24, 1992.

5. Lynda Richardson, "A Parody of a Pregnant Actress Stands Up in Court," *New York Times*, December 20, 1996.

6. Barbara Love, "Annie Leibovitz: Portrait of a Portrait Photographer; She Brings a Point of View That's Surprising, Sometimes Startling—Always Arresting," *Folio: The Magazine for Magazine Management*, July 1988.

7. Alison Roberts, "Suri: The Littlest Big Cover Girl," *Sacramento Bee*, September 7, 2006.

8. Christine Ledbetter, "Annie Leibovitz Book Signings," *Chicago Sun-Times*, November 16, 1999.

9. Lorena Blas, "Liebovitz Apologizes for Cyrus' *'Vanity Fair'* Spread," *USA Today*, April 28, 2008.

10. James Playsted Wood, *Magazines in the United States*, 3rd ed. (New York: Ronald Press Company, 1971).

11. Ibid.

12. Ibid.

13. Ibid.

14. Michael L. Carlebach, *The Origins of Photojournalism in America* (Washington, D.C.: Smithsonian Institution Press, 1992).

15. *Magazines: The Medium of Action; Handbook 2009/2010* (New York: Magazine Publishers of America, 2009).

16. Ibid.

17. Charles P. Daly, Patrick Henry, and Ellen Ryder, *The Magazine Publishing Industry* (Needham Heights, Mass.: Allyn & Bacon, 1997).

18. Jeff Gremillion, "Tough Times for Trades," *Brandweek*, September 20, 1999.

19. Lisa Granatstein, "The Big Deal," *Media Week*, March 6, 2000.

20. Erik Sass, "B2B Ad Pages Down 30%," Media Post Publications, August 26, 2009, www.mediapost.com/publications/?fa=Articles.showArticle&art_aid=112238.

21. Pew Research Center Project for Excellence in Journalism, "The State of the News Media 2009: Magazines," March 16, 2009, pewresearch.org/pubs/1151/state-of-the-news-media-2009.

22. Jeff Garigliano, "Victor Navasky and the State of the *Nation*," *Folio: The Magazine for Magazine Management*, September 1, 1998.

23. Ibid.

24. Pew Research Center Project for Excellence in Journalism, "The State of the News Media 2009: Magazines."

25. Bill Eichenberger, "Early Black Authors Featured in Series," *Columbus Dispatch*, January 27, 1999.

26. Larry Bivins, "NAACP Tries to Revive Once-Weighty Magazine," *Detroit News*, April 13, 1997.

27. James Bock, "Revived *Crisis* to Focus on Wide Range of Ideas; Publishing: The *Crisis*, the NAACP's Official Publication Founded by W. E. B. Dubois, Is to Reappear in July, and Readers May Be in for Stimulating Experiences," *The Sun*, May 18, 1997.

28. Wood, *Magazines in the United States*.

29. Louis Joughin, "Introduction," in *The Shame of the Cities* (New York: Hill and Wang, 1957).

30. Wood, *Magazines in the United States*.

31. Ibid.

32. Vicki Goldberg, *Margaret Bourke-White* (New York: Harper & Row, 1986).

33. Ibid.

34. Ibid.

35. Ibid.

36. "Paid Circulation in Consumer Magazines for Six Months Ended December 31, 2008," Advertising Age Data Center, adage.com/datacenter/datapopup.php?article_id=135166.

37. Wood, *Magazines in the United States*.

38. Ibid.; Patricia Okker, *Our Sister Editors: Sarah J. Hale and the Tradition of Nineteenth-Century American Women Editors* (Athens: University of Georgia Press, 1995).

39. Wood, *Magazines in the United States*.

40. Stuart Elliott, "Stuart Elliott in America," *Campaign*, September 27, 2002.

41. Gregory Boyd Bell, "Is *Family Circle*, et al., Too Square for Today?" *Newsday*, November 25, 2002.

42. "Top 300 Magazines Ranked by Estimated Total Advertising and Circulation Gross Revenue in 2007," Advertising Age Data Center, adage.com/datacenter/datapopup.php?article_id=131422.

43. Paula Span, "Between the Covers; As Their Editors Switch Positions, Women's Magazines Unveil a Familiar Look," *Washington Post*, December 30, 1998.

44. Rita Zekas, "The Perfect Cosmo Girl Editor Bonnie Fuller Has It All—Career, Motherhood," *Toronto Star*, June 8, 1997; Fionnuala McHugh, "Penetrating Asia," *South China Morning Post*, April 27, 1997; "Paid Circulation in Consumer Magazines for Six Months Ended December 31, 2008."

45. Zekas, "The Perfect Cosmo Girl Editor Bonnie Fuller Has It All—Career, Motherhood."

46. McHugh, "Penetrating Asia."

47. Shirley Christian, "But Is It Art? Well, Yes; A Trove of Pinups at the University of Kansas Is Admired by All Sorts, Including Feminists," *New York Times*, November 25, 1998.

48. Bill Steigerwald, "Once-Great *Esquire* Is Paying Price for Too Many Silly Articles," *Milwaukee Journal Sentinel*, July 14, 1997; Antonia Zerbisias, "Shriveled *Esquire* Gets Puffed 'n' Fluffed," *Toronto Star*, June 7, 1997; Alasdair Reid, "Have Men's Titles Stalled or Can They Shift Gear?" *Campaign*, February 14, 2002.

49. Wood, *Magazines in the United States*.

50. Michael Quintanilla, "Stylemaker/Hugh Hefner: The King of Swingers Reenters the Singles Scene," *Los Angeles Times*, February 5, 1999.

51. Greg Lindsay, "Rethinking a Great American Magazine," *Folio*, November 2002; Keith L. Alexander, "*Playboy* Boots Publishing Executives as Ad Market Wanes," *USA Today*, December 4, 2000; "Paid Circulation in Consumer Magazines for Six Months Ended December 31, 2008."

52. Alex Kuczynski, "Seeking More Sizzle, *Details* Magazine Hires *Maxim's* Editor," *New York Times*, February 2, 1999; "Maxim's 'Hot Issue' Is All Wrapped Up," *Toronto Star*, April 24 1999; "Paid Circulation in Consumer Magazines for Six Months Ended December 31, 2008."

53. Alex Kuczynski, "Media; A Magazine for Your 'Inner Guy'," *New York Times*, October 19, 1998.

54. Joseph P. Kahn, "Macho in the Morning: 'Guy Talk'," *Boston Globe*, September 7, 1999.

55. Kuczynski, "Seeking More Sizzle, *Details* Magazine Hires *Maxim's* Editor."

56. David Ward, "Men's Lifestyle Magazines—Thriving Market Captures Attention of Younger Men," *PR Week*, April 1, 2002.

57. Janice Turner, "The Trouble With Boys Is They're Just Too Fickle: Janice Turner on Magazines," *The Observer*, March 4, 2007.

58. Jemima Lewis, "From Loaded Lad to Heteropolitan Man," *The Telegraph*, August 15, 2009.

59. Matthew J. Rosenberg, "Media Talk; Men's Journal Encounters Problems on Mount Rainier," *New York Times*, June 29, 1998.

60. Span, "Between the Covers; As Their Editors Switch Positions, Women's Magazines Unveil a Familiar Look."

61. Lisa de Moraes, "Fighting Words From a Bantamweight," *Washington Post*, July 2, 1999; Eils Lotozo, "Getting Real; No Skinny Models in *Grace* Magazine," *Hamilton Spectator*, September 5, 2002.

62. Arlene Vigoda, "Calvin Cuts Ties with Kate," *USA Today*, February 24, 1999; Reuters, "British Model Admits 'Losing Plot' on Drink, Drugs," CNN Interactive, customnews.cnn.com/cnews/pna .show_story?p_art_id=3436180&p_section_name=world.

63. Karen S. Schneider, et al., "Mission Impossible; Deluged by Images From TV, Movies and Magazines, Teenage Girls Do Battle with an Increasingly Unrealistic Standard of Beauty—and Pay a Price," *People*, June 3, 1996.

64. John Leland, Susan Miller, and Carol Hall, "The Body Impolitic," *Newsweek*, June 17, 1996.

65. Nanci Hellmich, "Do Thin Models Warp Girls' Body Image?" *USA Today*, September 26, 2006.

66. Stuart Elliott, "For Everyday Products, Ads Using the Everyday Woman," *New York Times*, August 17, 2005; Theresa Howard, "Dove Ads Enlist All Shapes, Styles, Sizes," *USA Today*, August 29, 2005; Rebecca Traister, "Move Over, Dove Ads: Nike's Posteriors and Scraped Knees Bring a Greater Dose of Reality to Marketing," *Chicago Sun-Times*, August 23, 2005.

67. Cindi Leive, "On the C.L.: The Picture You Can't Stop Talking About: Meet 'The Woman on p. 194'," *Glamour*, August 17, 2009, www.glamour.com/health-fitness/blogs/vitamin-g/2009/08/ on-the-cl-the-picture-you-cant.html. Copyright © 2009 Condé Nast Publications. All rights reserved. Originally published in Glamour.com. Reprinted by permission.

68. Ibid.

69. Associated Press, "Fashion Magazines Showing More Body Types," *USA Today*, August 9, 2005.

70. Sara Ivry, "Liz Hurley, on the Cover and in the Ads," *New York Times*, August 29, 2005.

71. Katherine Rosman, "Stealth Advertising," *Brill's Content*, September 1998.

72. Abigail Pogrebin, "Looks Can Be Deceiving," *Brill's Content*, September 1998.

73. Joan E. Bertin, "Do Teenage Girl Magazines Belong on Middle School Library Shelves?" *Newsday*, March 1, 1998.

74. Jessica Kowal, "Ban Furor Spreads," *Newsday*, February 26, 1998.

75. John T. McQuiston, "Magazines Found Too Adult for School," *New York Times*, February 13, 1998.

76. Associated Press, "Student Magazine Alleges Censorship over Abortion Stories," May 4, 2006, www.firstamendmentcenter.org//news.aspx?id=16853&SearchString=magazine_censor.

77. Magazine Publishers Association, "Historical Subscriptions/Single Copy Sales," www.magazine.org/circulation/circulation_trends_and_magazine_handbook/1318.cfm.

78. Joe Hagan, "Cover Creation 2002," *Folio*, February 2002.

79. Ibid.

80. Kathleen Hays, "Why Aren't Minorities on More Magazine Covers?" in *The Biz* (CNNFN, 2002); David Carr, "On Covers of Many Magazines, a Full Racial Palette Is Still Rare," *New York Times*, November 18, 2002.

81. Carr, "On Covers of Many Magazines, a Full Racial Palette Is Still Rare."

82. Bill Cooke, "Where Are the Swimsuit Models of Color?" March 3, 2006, poynter.org/forum/view_post.asp?id=11167.

83. Hagan, "Cover Creation 2002."

84. John Johanek, "Crafting Covers That Sell," *Folio*, February 2002.

85. Span, "Between the Covers; As Their Editors Switch Positions, Women's Magazines Unveil a Familiar Look."

86. Staff, "The Many 'Whys' for Magazines," *MMR*, April 22, 2002.

87. Leara D. Rhodes, "Magazines," in *Mass Media in 2025: Industries, Organizations, People, and Nations*, ed. Erwin K. Thomas and Brown H. Carpenter (Westport, Conn.: Greenwood Press, 2001).

88. Ibid.

89. Staff, "Historical Subscriptions/Single Copy Sales."

90. Tony Case, "Triumph of the Niche; General-Interest Magazines Are Looking for a Place Among the Growing Number of Targeted Titles," *Media Week*, March 4, 2002.

91. Michael Scherer, "Does Size Matter?" *Columbia Journalism Review*, November 2002, 32.

92. Ibid.

93. Rhodes, "Magazines."

94. "Ziff Davis Media's *PC Magazine* Going All Digital," FishbowlNY, November 19, 2008, www.mediabistro.com/fishbowlny/magazines/ziff_davis_medias_pc_magazine_going_all_digital_101141.asp.

95. Mark Glaser, "Future of Magazines: Net Could Empower Readers," Online Journalism Review, May 24, 2005, www.ojr.org/ojr/stories/050524glaser/.

96. Ibid.

CHAPTER 6
**NEWSPAPERS AND THE NEWS**

1. James O'Byrne, "Katrina: The Power of the Press Against the Wrath of Nature," Poynter Institute, September 1, 2006, www.poynter.org/content/content_view.asp?id=106352.

2. Brian Thevenot, "Apocalypse in New Orleans," *American Journalism Review*, October/November 2005, 24–31.

3. O'Byrne, "Katrina: The Power of the Press Against the Wrath of Nature."

4. Ted Jackson, "Ted Jackson: Our Lives, Ours to Cover," Poynter Institute, September 1, 2006, www.poynter.org/content/content_view.asp?id=106673.

5. Ibid.

6. O'Byrne, "Katrina: The Power of the Press Against the Wrath of Nature."

7. Bob Garfield, "Second Chance at a First Impression," NPR, December 9, 2005, www.onthemedia.org/yore/transcripts/transcripts_120905_first.html.

8. Brian Thevenot, "Myth-Making in New Orleans," *American Journalism Review*, December/January 2006, 30–37.

9. Ibid.

10. O'Byrne, "Katrina: The Power of the Press Against the Wrath of Nature."

11. Brian McNair, *News and Journalism in the UK* (London: Routledge, 1994).

12. Bill Katz, *Dahl's History of the Book,* 3rd English ed. (Metuchen, N.J.: Scarecrow Press, 1995).
13. James D. Hart, *The Popular Book: A History of America's Literary Taste* (New York: Oxford University Press, 1950).
14. Michael Schudson, *Discovering the News* (New York: Basic Books, 1978).
15. Katz, *Dahl's History of the Book,* 218.
16. Hazel Dicken-Garcia, *Journalistic Standards in Nineteenth-Century America* (Madison: University of Wisconsin Press, 1989).
17. Schudson, *Discovering the News.*
18. George H. Douglas, *The Golden Age of the Newspaper* (Westport, Conn.: Greenwood Press, 1999).
19. McNair, *News and Journalism in the UK.*
20. Ibid.
21. Schudson, *Discovering the News.*
22. Dicken-Garcia, *Journalistic Standards in Nineteenth-Century America,* 52.
23. Paul H. Weaver, *News and the Culture of Lying* (New York: Free Press, 1994).
24. George Juergens, *Joseph Pulitzer and the New York World* (Princeton: Princeton University Press, 1966).
25. Brooke Kroeger, *Nellie Bly: Daredevil, Reporter, Feminist* (New York: Times Books, 1994).
26. Ibid.
27. David Nasaw, *The Chief* (New York: Houghton Mifflin, 2000).
28. Vicki Goldberg, *Margaret Bourke-White* (New York: Harper & Row, 1986).
29. Karin E. Becker, "Photojournalism and the Tabloid Press," in *Journalism and Popular Culture*, ed. Peter Dahlgren and Colin Sparks (London: Sage Publications, 1992).
30. Jon Fine, "Sunday, Bloody Sunday: A New Turn in the Tab Wars," *Columbia Journalism Review*, March/April 1999.
31. Stacy Jones, "Altered Photo Faux Pas," *Editor & Publisher* 130 (1997).
32. William S. Paley, *As It Happened: A Memoir* (Garden City, N.Y.: Doubleday, 1979).
33. Ben H. Bagdikian, *The New Media Monopoly* (Boston: Beacon Press, 2004).
34. Paley, *As It Happened.*
35. Edward Bliss, *Now the News: The Story of Broadcast Journalism* (New York: Columbia University Press, 1991).
36. Richard Zoglin, "Inside the World of CNN; How a Handful of News Executives Make Decisions Felt Round the World," *Time*, January 6, 1992.
37. Ken Auletta, *Three Blind Mice: How the TV Networks Lost Their Way* (New York: Random House, 1991).
38. Peter Johnson, "Fox News Enjoys New View—From the Top," *USA Today*, April 4, 2002.
39. Brian Lowry, "On Cable News, It's All Shoutmanship," *Los Angeles Times*, March 5, 2003.
40. John Maxwell Hamilton and George A. Krimsky, *Hold the Press: The Inside Story on Newspapers* (Baton Rouge: Louisiana State University Press, 1996); Pew Research Center Project for Excellence in Journalism, "The State of the News Media 2009: Newspapers," www.stateofthemedia.org/ 2009/index.htm.
41. McNair, *News and Journalism in the UK.*
42. Hoover's Inc., "Hoover's Company Profile Database: Gannett Co., Inc." (Austin, Texas: Hoover's Inc., 2009).
43. Bagdikian, *The New Media Monopoly.*
44. Pew Research Center Project for Excellence in Journalism, "The State of the News Media 2006," www.stateofthemedia.org/2006.
45. Pew Research Center Project for Excellence in Journalism, "The State of the News Media 2009: Newspapers."
46. Johnnie L. Roberts, "The Paperless Paper," *Newsweek*, October 28, 2008.
47. James McCartney, "*USA Today* Grows Up," *American Journalism Review*, September 1997, 18–25.
48. "Newspaper Circulation Ranking Index," Advertising Age Data Center, March 31, 2009, www .adage.com/datacenter; Hoover's Inc., "Hoover's Company Profile Database: Gannett Co., Inc."
49. McCartney, "*USA Today* Grows Up."
50. John Morton, "Short Term Losses, Long Term Profits," *American Journalism Review*, September 1997.

51. Lori Robertson, "There From the Get-Go," *American Journalism Review*, April 1999, 9.

52. Sinéad O'Brien, "The Last of the Color Holdouts," *American Journalism Review*, December 1997, 15.

53. "Newspaper Circulation Ranking Index."

54. Pew Research Center Project for Excellence in Journalism, "The State of the News Media 2008: Newspapers," www.stateofthemedia.org/2008.

55. Daniel Kadlec and Jyoti Thottam, "Extra! Dynasties Duel!," *Time*, November 4, 2002.

56. David D. Kirkpatrick, "*International Herald Tribune* Now Run Solely by the *Times*," *New York Times*, January 2, 2003; Lucia Moses, "'IHT': Ads Playing in Prime Time," *Editor & Publisher*, March 19, 2001.

57. Harriett Marsh, "The Battle for Business," *Ad Age Global*, February 2001.

58. Ibid.

59. Kirkpatrick, "*International Herald Tribune* Now Run Solely by the *Times*."

60. Rob Lenihan, "Marking *Times*' Color Milestone," *Editor & Publisher* 131, no. 39 (1998).

61. O'Brien, "The Last of the Color Holdouts."

62. Ibid.

63. Mario R. Garcia, "Color for a New Millennium," *Editor & Publisher* 131, no. 39 (1998).

64. Ben Bradlee, *A Good Life: Newspapering and Other Adventures* (New York: Simon & Schuster, 1995).

65. Ibid.

66. Ken Adelman, "You Can't Have Secrets," *Washingtonian*, August 1994.

67. Alicia C. Shepard, "Ben Bradlee," *American Journalism Review*, March 1995.

68. Charles Rappleye, "Are New Ideas Killing the *L.A. Times*?" *Columbia Journalism Review*, November/December 1994.

69. Katherine Q. Seelye, "The Newspaper Publisher Who Said No to More Cuts," *New York Times*, September 28, 2006; Pew Research Center Project for Excellence in Journalism, "The State of the News Media 2009: Newspapers."

70. Joseph S. Coyle, "Now, the Editor as Marketer," *Columbia Journalism Review*, July/August 1998, 37–41.

71. John Leo, "Quoting by Quota," *U.S. News & World Report*, June 29, 1998.

72. Ibid.

73. Keith Woods, "The Essence of Excellence," Poynter Online, October 16, 2001, www.poynter.org/content/content_view.asp?id=5048.

74. Peter Schrag, "Is Doing the Right Thing Wrong?" *Columbia Journalism Review*, February 2002.

75. Charles Bermant, "Hometown Newspapers Use Web to Strengthen Communities," August 21, 1998, cnn.com/tech/computing/9808/21/hometown.idg/index.html.

76. O'Byrne, "Katrina: The Power of the Press Against the Wrath of Nature."

77. Robert E. Park, "The Natural History of the Newspaper," in *Mass Communications*, ed. Wilbur Schramm (Urbana: University of Illinois Press, 1960).

78. George A. Hough, *News Writing*, 4th ed. (Boston: Houghton Mifflin Company, 1988).

79. Richard M. Cohen, "The Corporate Takeover of News," in *Conglomerates and the Media*, ed. Eric Barnouw (New York: Free Press, 1997).

80. Ibid.

81. Coyle, "Now, the Editor as Marketer."

82. Pew Research Center Project for Excellence in Journalism, "The State of the News Media 2006."

83. Committee to Protect Journalists, "Iraq: Journalists in Danger," July 23, 2008, cpj.org/reports/2008/07/journalists-killed-in-iraq.php.

84. Committee to Protect Journalists, "In Iraq, Journalist Deaths Spike to Record in 2006," December 20, 2006, cpj.org/reports/2006/12/killed-06.php.

85. Patricia Ward Biederman, "Services to Mark Death of Reporter," *Los Angeles Times*, February 19, 2003.

86. Nancy Gibbs, "Death in the Shadow War," *Time*, March 4, 2002.

87. Jim Lehrer, "Mariane Pearl," in *NewsHour With Jim Lehrer* (PBS, 2002).

88. Terry Anderson, "He Took a Risk in Pursuit of the Truth," *Los Angeles Times*, February 24, 2002.

89. Charles A. Simmons, *The African American Press* (Jefferson, N.C.: McFarland, 1998).

90. Ibid.
91. Roland E. Wolseley, *The Black Press, U.S.A.*, 2nd ed. (Ames: Iowa State University Press, 1990).
92. Simmons, *The African American Press*.
93. Wolseley, *The Black Press, U.S.A.*
94. Jessica Madore Fitch, "Four Companies Vying for Chicago Defender," *Chicago Sun-Times*, May 1, 2000.
95. Wolseley, *The Black Press, U.S.A.*
96. Pew Research Center Project for Excellence in Journalism, "The State of the News Media 2006."
97. Brooke Gladstone, "Tale of Two *Heralds*," NPR, October 6, 2006, www.onthemedia.org/transcripts/2006/10/06/04.
98. Diana McLellan, "Out in Front," *Washingtonian*, March 1998, 31–35.
99. Richard Pérez-Peña, "*Washington Blade* Newspaper Closes," *New York Times*, November 17, 2009; Erik Sass, "So Over: Window Media Closes," November 16, 2009, www.mediapost.com/publications/?fa=Articles.showArticle&art_aid=117466.
100. Pérez-Peña, "*Washington Blade* Newspaper Closes."
101. Tony Case, "Gay Papers Tangle in N.Y," *Editor & Publisher*, November 8, 1997.
102. Kevin McAuliffe, "No Longer Just Sex, Drugs and Rock 'n' Roll," *Columbia Journalism Review*, March/April 1999, 40–44.
103. Pew Research Center Project for Excellence in Journalism, "The State of the News Media 2006."
104. Lucia Moses, "Consider the Alternatives: Move to Mainstream Ownership a Sign of the Times," *Editor & Publisher* 132, no. 22 (1999).
105. Howard Kurtz, "The *Village Voice*'s No-alternative News: Corporate Takeover," *Washington Post,* October 24, 2005, C1
106. Peter Benjaminson, *Death in the Afternoon* (Kansas City, Mo.: Andrews, McMeel & Parker, 1984).
107. Pew Research Center Project for Excellence in Journalism, "The State of the News Media 2006."
108. Roberts, "The Paperless Paper."
109. Eytan Avriel, "*NY Times* Publisher: Our Goal Is to Manage the Transition From Print to Internet," *Haaretz*, February 8, 2007.
110. David Lieberman, "Newspaper Closings Raise Fears About Industry," *USA Today*, March 19, 2009.
111. Agence France-Presse, "Gannett Cuts Staff, *Christian Science Monitor* Drops Print Edition," October 28, 2008, afp.google.com/article/ALeqM5i5p0GFc9-MtVLoJfln9a-2YzDS-Q.
112. Howard Kurtz, "Final Edition: *Rocky Mountain News* to Shut Down Today," *Washington Post*, February 27, 2009.
113. Steve Outing, "Washingtonpost.com's 'Afternoon' Web Edition," *Editor & Publisher* 132, no. 36 (1999).
114. Roy Reed, "Giant," *American Journalism Review*, September 1998, 62–79.
115. Stacy Jones, "Free Press vs. Fair Trial," *Editor & Publisher*, March 15, 1997; Rem Rieder, "A Breakthrough in Cyberspace," *American Journalism Review*, April 1997, 6.
116. Reed, "Giant."
117. Alicia C. Shepard, "Moving Too Fast," *American Journalism Review*, March 1998, 35.
118. Rick Lockridge, "Web Publishers Wonder: 'Is It Worth Being Online?'," December 9, 1998, cnn.com/tech/computing/9812/09/digital.news.forum.
119. Pew Research Center for the People and the Press, "Online Papers Modestly Boost Newspaper Readership," July 30, 2006, people-press.org/report/282/online-papers-modestly-boost-newspaper-readership.
120. Ibid.

CHAPTER 7
**AUDIO**

1. Ralph Hanson, interview, July 30, 2009.
2. Ibid.
3. "Katrina's Web," http://www.katrinasweb.com.
4. Neil Baldwin, *Edison: Inventing the Century* (New York: Hyperion, 1995).

5. Roland Gelatt, *The Fabulous Phonograph* (Philadelphia: L. B. Lippincott, 1955).

6. Baldwin, *Edison: Inventing the Century*.

7. Gelatt, *The Fabulous Phonograph*.

8. Ibid.

9. Charles Hamm, "The Phonograph as Time-Machine" (paper presented at *The Phonograph and Our Musical Life*, Brooklyn College, New York, 1980).

10. Isaac Asimov, *Isaac Asimov's Biographical Encyclopedia of Science and Technology*, rev. ed. (New York: Avon Books, 1972).

11. Ibid.; Kenneth Bilby, *The General: David Sarnoff and the Rise of the Communications Industry* (New York: Harper & Row, 1986).

12. Bilby, *The General*.

13. Ibid.

14. Ibid.

15. Ibid.

16. Burton Paulu, *Television and Radio in the United Kingdom* (Minneapolis: University of Minnesota Press, 1981).

17. Ibid.

18. Lewis J. Paper, *Empire: William S. Paley and the Making of CBS* (New York: St. Martin's Press, 1987).

19. Muriel G. Cantor and Suzanne Pingree, *The Soap Opera*, ed. F. Gerald Kline, The Sage Commtext Series (Beverly Hills, Calif.: Sage, 1983).

20. Ibid.

21. Geoffrey Wheatcroft and Stephen Sandy, "Who Needs the BBC?" *Atlantic Monthly*, March 2001, 53.

22. Mike McGeever, "Commercial Radio Moves Ahead of BBC," *Billboard*, June 7, 1997, 83.

23. "Africa's Dramas Played Out on the Beeb," *Economist*, January 16, 1999, 44.

24. Kim Campbell, "On Media," *Christian Science Monitor*, June 14, 2001, 14.

25. Bob Garfield, "BBC Arabesque," National Public Radio, November 4, 2005, www.onthemedia.org/yore/transcripts/transcripts_110405_bbc.html.

26. Julius Lester, "Foreword," in *Playing the FM Band* (New York: Viking Press, 1974).

27. James Miller, *Flowers in the Dustbin: The Rise of Rock and Roll, 1947–1977* (New York: Simon & Schuster, 1999).

28. "The Walkman Man," *People Weekly*, October 18, 1999, 132.

29. RiShawn Biddle, "Personal Soundtracks," *Reason*, October 1999, 58–59.

30. Ibid.

31. Ibid.

32. Ronald Byrnside, "The Formation of a Musical Style: Early Rock," in *Contemporary Music and Music Cultures*, ed. Charles Hamm, Bruno Nettl, and Ronald Byrnside (Englewood Cliffs, N.J.: Prentice-Hall, 1975).

33. Miller, *Flowers in the Dustbin*.

34. Gerald Early, *One Nation Under a Groove: Motown and American Culture* (Hopewell, N.J.: Ecco Press, 1995).

35. Miller, *Flowers in the Dustbin*.

36. Ibid.

37. Byrnside, "The Formation of a Musical Style: Early Rock."

38. Miller, *Flowers in the Dustbin*.

39. Ibid.

40. Ibid.

41. Ibid.

42. Ibid.

43. Early, *One Nation Under a Groove*.

44. Ibid.

45. Allan F. Moore, *The Beatles: Sgt. Pepper's Lonely Hearts Club Band* (Cambridge, U.K.: Cambridge University Press, 1997); Patricia Romanowski, Holly George-Warren, and Jon Pareles, eds., *The New Rolling Stone Encyclopedia of Rock & Roll*, completely revised and updated ed. (New York: Rolling Stone Press, 1995).

46. Moore, *The Beatles: Sgt. Pepper's Lonely Hearts Club Band*.

47. Early, *One Nation Under a Groove*.
48. Miller, *Flowers in the Dustbin*.
49. Jon Wilde and David Edwards, "McCartney: I Have Tried Heroin," *Mirror*, June 2, 2004.
50. Moore, *The Beatles: Sgt. Pepper's Lonely Hearts Club Band*.
51. Christopher John Farley, "A Hitmaker and a Gentleman," *Time*, November 11, 1996, 90; "New Babyface/David E. Talbert Musical Set Premiering at Beacon Theater," PR Newswire, May 31, 2001.
52. Romanowski, et al., *The New Rolling Stone Encyclopedia of Rock & Roll*.
53. Ibid.
54. Bruce Feiler, "Gone Country," *New Republic*, February 5, 1996, 19–20.
55. Bobby Reed, "'Murder' Numbers; Country Radio Makes a Killing—Is It Killing Country?" *Chicago Sun-Times*, October 8, 2000; Edward Morris, "Taylor Swift Was America's Best-Selling Album Artist of 2008," Country Music Television, January 2, 2009, www.cmt.com/news/country-music/1602002/taylor-swift-was-americas-best-selling-album-artist-of-2008.jhtml.
56. Feiler, "Gone Country."
57. Brian Longhurst, *Popular Music and Society* (Cambridge, U.K.: Polity Press, 1995).
58. Ibid.
59. Ken Auletta, *The Highwaymen* (San Diego: Harcourt Brace, 1998).
60. Richard Crawford, "Introduction: The Phonograph and the Scholar" (paper presented at *The Phonograph and Our Musical Life*, Brooklyn College, New York, 1980).
61. Chris Bonastia, "Sucking in the '70s," *New Republic*, January 30, 1995, 11–12.
62. Gelatt, *The Fabulous Phonograph*.
63. Ken C. Pohlmann, "The Last Compact Disc," *Stereo Review*, May 1996.
64. Nick Carter, "Prince's Phases Have Steered His Stellar and Rocky 22-Year Reign," *Milwaukee Journal Sentinel*, June 28, 2001.
65. Jodi Mardesich, "How the Internet Hits Big Music," *Fortune*, May 10, 1999, 96–98.
66. Ted Bridis, "Sony to Suspend Making Antipiracy CDs," *Washington Post*, November 11, 2005.
67. Electronic Frontier Foundation, *"Riaa v. The People:* Two Years Later" (San Francisco: Electronic Frontier Foundation, 2005).
68. Miller, *Flowers in the Dustbin*.
69. Brooks Boliek, "FCC Proposal Could Halt Payola Probe," *Mediaweek*, January 11, 2007.
70. Arbitron, "Radio Today: How America Listens to Radio," 2008 edition (Arbitron, 2008).
71. Arbitron, "Hispanic Radio Today," 2008 edition (Arbitron, 2008).
72. Della de Lafuente, "Look Who's Talking: Putting a Face on Hispanic Radio," *Adweek*, September 17, 2007.
73. Walt Albro, "Spanish-Language Ads Sell Comfort," *Bank Marketing*, August 1999.
74. Richard Corliss, "Look Who's Talking," *Time,* January 23, 1995, 22–25.
75. Jennifer Harper, "Big Radio Companies Struggle to Sustain Volume Amid Losses," *Washington Times*, March 4, 2009.
76. Judy Rene Sims, "Talk, Talk, Talk: Opinion or Fact?" *Journalism History* 22 (Winter 1997): 173.
77. Corliss, "Look Who's Talking."
78. Brian Stelter, "For Conservative Radio, It's a New Dawn, Too," *New York Times*, December 22, 2008.
79. Pew Research Center Project for Excellence in Journalism, "The State of the News Media 2009: Audio," www.stateofthemedia.org/2009/narrative_audio_intro.php?media=10.
80. Jonathan Foreman, "Howard's End?" *National Review*, April 7, 1997, 53–54; Jacqui Goddard, "Shock Jocks' Sick Jokes Slay Listeners," *Scotland on Sunday*, November 17, 2002, 26.
81. Paul Farhi, "No Rush to Measure Limbaugh's Ratings," *Los Angeles Times*, March 9, 2009.
82. Jeff Borden, "ESPN Radio Shoots to Rack Up the Score," *Crain's Chicago Business*, September 21, 1998, 1.
83. Joseph P. Kahn, "Macho in the Morning: 'Guy Talk'," *Boston Globe*, September 7, 1999, A1.
84. Ibid.
85. Nina Huntemann, "Corporate Interference: The Commercialization and Concentration of Radio Post the 1996 Telecommunications Act," *Journal of Communication Inquiry* 23, no. 4 (1999): 390–407.
86. Roy Bragg, "Clear Channel: Owning the Waves," *San Antonio Express-News*, February 4, 2003, 1; Kenneth Creech, *Electronic Media Law and Regulation*, 3rd ed. (Boston: Focal Press, 2000).

87. US Fed News, "House Members Call on FCC Inspector General to Investigate Hidden Studies on Media Consolidation," *US Fed News*, September 21, 2006.

88. L. A. Lorek, "FCC Review Could Clip Clear Channel; Commission Might Limit Ownership of Radio Stations," *San Antonio Express-News*, May 17, 2003, 1.

89. Pew Research Center Project for Excellence in Journalism, "The State of the News Media 2009: Audio."

90. Jeff Smith, "*Radio* Automation," Radio, May 1, 2006, 22.

91. Linda Werthheimer, ed., *Listening to America: Twenty-Five Years in the Life of a Nation, as Heard on National Public Radio* (Boston: Houghton Mifflin, 1995).

92. William Buzenberg, "The National Public Radio Idea," *Nieman Reports* 51, no. 2 (1997): 32.

93. Paul Farhi, "Consider This: NPR Achieves Record Ratings," *Washington Post*, March 24, 2009.

94. Ibid.

95. Pew Research Center Project for Excellence in Journalism, "The State of the News Media 2009: Audio."

96. Buzenberg, "The National Public Radio Idea."

97. Paul Farhi, "NPR Cutbacks Include 13 Layoffs," *Washington Post*, April 24, 2009.

98. Catherine Apple Olson, "'Mountain Stage' Brings Roots to Radio," *Billboard*, November 2, 1996, 14.

99. Ibid.

100. John Merli, "AM Holds Its Own in '98: Talk, Personalities to the Rescue," *Broadcasting & Cable*, August 24, 1998, 46.

101. Pew Research Center Project for Excellence in Journalism, "The State of the News Media 2009: Audio"; Arbitron, "Radio Today: How America Listens to Radio."

102. "The Infinite Dial 2009: Radio's Digital Platforms" (Arbitron, Edison Media Research, 2009).

103. Pew Research Center Project for Excellence in Journalism, "The State of the News Media 2009: Audio."

104. Ibid.; "The Infinite Dial 2009: Radio's Digital Platforms."

105. Cecilia Kang, "Liberty Extends $530 Million Loan to Bail Out Sirius XM," *Washington Post*, February 18, 2009.

106. Ana Marie Cox, "Howard Stern and the Satellite Wars," *Wired*, March 2005.

107. Jacques Steinberg, "Stern Likes His New Censor: Himself," *New York Times*, January 9, 2007, E1.

108. Leonard Wiener, "Radio's Next Wave: 9 Kinds of Latin Music," *U.S. News & World Report*, August 2, 1999, 70.

109. Pew Research Center Project for Excellence in Journalism, "The State of the News Media 2009: Audio."

110. "The Infinite Dial 2009: Radio's Digital Platforms."

111. Byron Acohido, "Radio to the MP3 Degree: Podcasting," *USA Today*, February 9, 2005; Marco R. della Cava, "Podcasting: It's All Over the Dial," *USA Today*, February 9, 2005; Erika Gonzalez, "Podcast Power: Diversity of Free Audio Programs Expands as Technology Catches On," *Rocky Mountain News*, September 23, 2005, 26D.

112. Benny Evangelista, "Jobs Announces iTunes Will Accommodate Podcasts," *San Francisco Chronicle*, May 23, 2005.

113. Mary Madden, "Pew Internet Project Data Memo," in *Pew Internet and American Life Project* (Washington, D.C.: Pew Foundation, 2006); "The Infinite Dial 2009: Radio's Digital Platforms"; Pew Research Center Project for Excellence in Journalism, "The State of the News Media 2009: Audio."

114. "The Infinite Dial 2009: Radio's Digital Platforms."

115. Ralph Hanson, interview, January 21, 2007.

116. Kevin Maney, "If Pirating Grows, It May Not Be the End of Music World," *USA Today*, May 3, 2005.

117. Ibid.

118. Jefferson Graham, "Summer Tours Help Bands Pay Bills," *USA Today*, August 5, 2004.

119. James Callan, "U.S. Album Sales Decline 14% While Online Track Sales Surge," Bloomberg.com, January 1, 2009, www.bloomberg.com/apps/news?pid=20601103&sid=aC7ekniUw9Fs&refer=us.

120. Lucas Mearian, "Back to the Future: Vinyl Record Sales Double in '08, CDs Down," Computerworld, January 2, 2009, www.computerworld.com/s/article/9124699/Back_to_the_future_Vinyl_record_sales_double_in_08_CDs_down?taxonomyId=19&pageNumber=1.

121. Mark Glaser, "Music Industry Losing Control Over Album Sales," PBS–Media Shift, January 22, 2007, www.pbs.org/mediashift/2007/01/digital_disruptionmusic_indust.html.

CHAPTER 8
**MOVIES**

1. Dorothy Pomerantz, "Hollywood's Highest-Paid Men," Forbes.com, July 14, 2009, www.forbes
.com/2009/07/14/hollywoods-top-earning-men-business-entertainment-hollywood-men.html.

2. Brandon Gray, "'Diary of a Mad Black Woman' Comes Out Swinging at Number One," Box
Office Mojo, February 28, 2005, http://boxofficemojo.com/news/?id=1736&p=s.htm; Brandon
Gray, "'Brokeback Mountain' Most Impressive of Tepid 2005," Box Office Mojo, February 25,
2006, http://www2.boxofficemojo.com/news/?id=2012&p=.htm.

3. Miki Turner, "The Secret to Tyler Perry's Success," Fandango, September 14, 2008, www
.fandango.com/commentator_thesecrettotylerperry'ssuccess_191.

4. Wesley Morris, "Tyler Perry's Secret to Success," Slate, October 22, 2007, www.slate.com/id/
2176281.

5. "Movies—Tyler Perry's Madea Goes to Jail," Box Office Mojo, http://boxofficemojo.com/movies/?
id=madeagoestojail.htm.

6. Morris, "Tyler Perry's Secret to Success."

7. Kim Masters, "Tyler Perry's Impressive Hollywood Rise," National Public Radio, April 24, 2006,
www.npr.org/templates/story/story.php?storyId=5352352.

8. Ibid.

9. Scott Bowles, "Box Office: Why Did These Films Get Buried? Tyler Perry," *USA Today,* October 14,
2007, www.usatoday.com/life/movies/news/2007-10-14-box-office-analysis_N.htm.

10. Turner, "The Secret to Tyler Perry's Success."

11. Bowles, "Box Office: Why Did These Films Get Buried? Tyler Perry."

12. Neil Baldwin, *Edison: Inventing the Century* (New York: Hyperion, 1995).

13. Eadweard Muybridge, "The Attitudes of Animals in Motion (1882)," in *The Movies in Our Midst:
Documents in the Cultural History of Film in America*, ed. Gerald Mast (Chicago: University of
Chicago Press, 1982).

14. Gerald Mast and Bruce F. Kawin, *A Brief History of the Movies*, 6th ed. (Needham Heights, Mass.:
Allyn & Bacon, 1996); John Fell, *A History of Films* (New York: Holt, Rinehart and Winston,
1979).

15. Mast and Kawin, *A Brief History of the Movies.*

16. National Association for the Advancement of Colored People Boston Branch, "Fighting a Vicious
Film: Protest Against 'The Birth of a Nation'," in *The Movies in Our Midst,* ed. G. Mast.

17. Mast and Kawin, *A Brief History of the Movies.*

18. Linda Arvidson Griffith, "When the Movies Were Young (1925)," in *The Movies in Our Midst*, ed.
G. Mast.

19. Mast, "Introduction," in *The Movies in Our Midst,* ed. G. Mast.

20. Mast and Kawin, *A Brief History of the Movies*; Fortune Magazine Staff, "Loew's Inc. (1939)," in
*The Movies in Our Midst,* ed. G. Mast; New York Center for Visual History, *American Cinema:
The Studio System* (Burlington, Vt.: Annenberg/CBP, 1994), videotape.

21. Steven Bach, *Final Cut: Dreams and Disaster in the Making of 'Heaven's Gate'* (New York: William
Morrow, 1985).

22. Mast, "Introduction," in *The Movies in Our Midst*, ed. G. Mast.

23. Fitzhugh Green, "A Soldier Falls," in *The Movies in Our Midst*, ed. G. Mast.

24. Douglas Gomery, "Warner Bros. Innovates Sound: A Business History," in *The Movies in Our
Midst*, ed. G. Mast.

25. Harry Geduld, "The Voice of the Vitaphone (1975)," in *The Movies in Our Midst*, ed. G. Mast.

26. Ralph L. Henry, "The Cultural Influence of the 'Talkies'," in *The Movies in Our Midst*, ed.
G. Mast.

27. Gilbert Seldes, "Talkies' Progress (1929)," in *The Movies in Our Midst*, ed. G. Mast.

28. *United States v. Paramount Pictures, Inc.* (1948).

29. Mast, "Introduction," in *The Movies in Our Midst*, ed. G. Mast; Michael Conant, "The Paramount
Case and Its Legal Background (1961)," in *The Movies in Our Midst*, ed. G. Mast.

30. House Un-American Activities Committee, "Hearings Regarding the Communist Infiltration of
the Motion-Picture-Industry Activities in the United States (1947)," in *The Movies in Our Midst*,
ed. G. Mast.

31. Gordon Kahn, "Hollywood on Trial (1948)," in *The Movies in Our Midst*, ed. G. Mast.

32. John Cogley, "Report on Blacklisting," in *The Movies in Our Midst*, ed. G. Mast.

33. Leonard Maltin, ed., *Leonard Maltin's Movie and Video Guide*, 1997 ed. (New York: Signet, 2006).

34. Mast and Kawin, *A Brief History of the Movies*.

35. Daniel Engber, "Will the 3-D Revival Go the Way of Pixar's *Up*?" Slate, June 2, 2009, www.slate .com/blogs/blogs/browbeat/archive/2009/06/02/will-the-3d-revival-go-the-way-of-pixar-s-up.aspx.

36. Bob Keefe, "Digital Technology Bringing a 3-D Revival to Theaters," *Atlanta Journal & Constitution*, October 17, 2008.

37. Fortune Magazine Staff, "Color and Sound on Film (1930)," in *The Movies in Our Midst*, ed. G. Mast.

38. Garth Jowett, *Movies as Mass Communication*, 2nd ed., vol. 4, The Sage Commtext Series (Newbury Park, Calif.: Sage, 1989).

39. National Association of Theater Owners, "Number of U.S. Movie Screens," www.natoonline.org/ statisticsscreens.htm; Elwin Green, "Big Screen Boom Goes Bust; Rash of Theater Closings Raises the Question: What to Do with an Empty Multiplex," *Pittsburgh Post-Gazette*, August 4, 2005, C1.

40. Arthur Asa Berger, *Media Analysis Techniques*, 3rd ed. (Thousand Oaks, Calif.: Sage, 2005).

41. Carol Cling, "Room With a View: Audiences Paying for IMAX Experience of Summer Blockbusters," *Las Vegas Review-Journal*, July 17, 2009.

42. Jowett, *Movies as Mass Communication*.

43. Ibid.; Thomas Schatz, "The Return of the Hollywood Studio System," in *Conglomerates and the Media*, ed. Eric Barnouw (New York: The New Press, 1997).

44. Mast and Kawin, *A Brief History of the Movies*.

45. Brandon Gray, "'Dark Knight' Begins Smashingly," Box Office Mojo, July 23, 2008, http:// boxofficemojo.com/news/?id=2504&p=.htm.

46. Leonard Klady, "Tara Torpedoes *Titanic* as the Real B.O. Champ," *Variety*, March 2–8, 1998.

47. J. W. Elphinstone, "Watercooler: DVDs' Popularity Passes VCRs', New Year's Resolutions, Bad Publicity," Associated Press Financial Wire.

48. Dan Frost, "Consumers Changing DVD Buying Habits," *San Francisco Chronicle*, September 5, 2005, E1.

49. Harry Allen, "Can You Digit," *Premiere*, November 1999, 93–103.

50. Scott Bowles, "'Sky Captain' Takes CGI to Limit," *USA Today*, September 14, 2004.

51. William Booth, "The Cyberspace Moviemaker," *Washington Post*, September 15, 2004.

52. Larry Carroll, "Reaching for the Sky," FilmStew.com, January 30, 2004, www.filmstew.com/ showArticle.aspx?ContentID=7827.

53. "Sky Captain and the World of Tomorrow," Box Office Mojo, http://boxofficemojo.com/ movies/?id=skycaptain.htm.

54. Duane Dudek, "'Captain' Director May Have Reinvented the Wheel," *Pittsburgh Post-Gazette*, September 17, 2004.

55. "Movies—*300*," Box Office Mojo, http://boxofficemojo.com/movies/?id=300.htm.

56. Brandon Gray, "Hordes Drive '300' to Record," Box Office Mojo, March 12, 2007, http:// boxofficemojo.com/news/?id=2268&p=.htm.

57. Archie Thomas, "Half of Screens to Be Digital by 2013," *Variety*, November 12, 2007, www .variety.com/article/VR1117975781.html?categoryid=13&cs=1&nid=2564.

58. Kendrick Macdowell, "Reflections on the Kind of Exhibition Industry That Best Serves Movie Patrons, Makers, and Exhibitors in the Digital Era" (Washington, D.C.: National Association of Theater Owners, 2009); MKPE Consulting, "Digital Cinema Technology Frequently Asked Questions (FAQs)," http://mkpe.com/digital_cinema/faqs/tech_faqs.php.

59. Dade Hayes, "Bombs Away: Biz Disavows Duds," *Variety*, March 20–26, 2000, 7–8.

60. "Movies—*The Dark Knight*," Box Office Mojo, http://boxofficemojo.com/movies/?id=darkknight .htm.

61. "Movies—*Iron Man*," Box Office Mojo, http://boxofficemojo.com/movies/?id=ironman.htm.

62. "Movies—*Meet Dave*," Box Office Mojo, http://boxofficemojo.com/movies/?id=meetdave.htm.

63. "Movies—*Fireproof*," Box Office Mojo, http://boxofficemojo.com/movies/?id=fireproof.htm.

64. Susan Wloszczyna, "What Makes a Film a Phenom?" *USA Today*, May 12, 2006.

65. "Movies—*Garden State*," Box Office Mojo, http://boxofficemojo.com/movies/?id=gardenstate .htm.

66. Glenn Kenny, "Martin Scorsese and Spike Lee," *Premiere*, October 1999, 74–77.

67. Glenn Kenny, "The Movies That Changed America," *Premiere*, December 1999, 86.

68. Mast, "Introduction," in *The Movies in Our Midst*, ed. G. Mast.

69. Jowett, *Movies as Mass Communication*.

70. Barbara Mikkelson and David Mikkelson, "The Shirt Off His Back," www.snopes.com/movies/actors/gable.htm.

71. Shearon A. Lowery and Melvin L. DeFleur, *Milestones in Mass Communication*, 3rd ed. (White Plains, N.Y.: Longman, 1995).

72. David Van Biema, "Lie Down in Darkness; Does a Death on the Highway Implicate the Entertainment Industry?" *Time*, November 1, 1993, 49.

73. Ibid.

74. "Movies—*Slumdog Millionaire*," Box Office Mojo, boxofficemojo.com/movies/?id=slumdogmillionaire.htm.

75. Victoria Young, "Bolly Good Show," *Sun Herald*, June 30, 2002, 1.

76. Rama Lakshmi, "Hooray for Bollywood: Oscar Bid Lifts Hopes," *Washington Post*, March 24, 2002.

77. Young, "Bolly Good Show."

78. Elham Khatami, "Is Bollywood Coming to Hollywood?" CNN.com, February 23, 2009, www.cnn.com/2009/SHOWBIZ/Movies/02/23/bollywood.hollywood.

79. Roger Ebert, "'Lagaan' Brings Out the Best of Bollywood," *Chicago Sun-Times*, June 7, 2002, 33.

80. Khatami, "Is Bollywood Coming to Hollywood?"

81. John Collier, "Censorship and the National Board (1915)," in *The Movies in Our Midst*, ed. G. Mast.

82. Ellis Paxson Oberholtzer, "Sex Pictures (1922)," in *The Movies in Our Midst*, ed. G. Mast.

83. J. R. Rutland, "State Censorship of Motion Pictures," in *The Movies in Our Midst*, ed. G. Mast.

84. Mast and Kawin, *A Brief History of the Movies*.

85. Anonymous, "The Sins of Hollywood (1922)," in *The Movies in Our Midst*, ed. G. Mast.

86. Motion Picture Producers and Distributors of America, "The Don'ts and Be Carefuls (1927)," in *The Movies in Our Midst*, ed. G. Mast.

87. Mast, "Introduction," in *The Movies in Our Midst*, ed. G. Mast.

88. Wilson Biographies, "Hays, Will H.," Wilson Web, vweb.hwwilsonweb.com.

89. Raymond Moley, "The Birth of the Production Code (1945)," in *The Movies in Our Midst*, ed. G. Mast.

90. Motion Picture Producers and Distributors of America, "The Motion Picture Production Code of 1930s," in *The Movies in Our Midst*, ed. G. Mast; Amy Wallace, "MPAA's Dozen Judge Movies for Millions," *Los Angeles Times*, July 18, 1999, A1.

91. Charles Lyons, *The New Censors: Movies and the Culture Wars* (Philadelphia: Temple University Press, 1997).

92. Sharon Waxman, "Exclusive: Baron Cohen's 'Bruno' Slapped With NC-17," The Wrap, March 29, 2009, www.thewrap.com/article/2127?page=1.

93. Daniel Frankel, "While 'Potter' Soars, 'Bruno' Fades Fast," The Wrap, July 19, 2009, www.thewrap.com/article/five-day-record-harry-and-pals-bruno-dissolves-73-drop_4401.

94. Gary Arnold, "Between PG & R; Valenti Says New Rating Possible by Next Week," *Washington Post*, June 23, 1984, C1.

95. Ibid.

96. Ibid.

97. "Top-Grossing MPAA Ratings 1995 to 2009," The Numbers, www.the-numbers.com/market/MPAARatings.

98. Jerome Hellman, "Problems With Movie Ratings Go Beyond Categories," *Los Angeles Times*, August 23, 1999, F3.

99. Wallace, "MPAA's Dozen Judge Movies for Millions."

100. Ibid.

101. Pamela McClintock, "MPAA Tries to Remove NC-17 Stigma," *Variety*, March 10, 2007, www.variety.com/article/VR1117960864.html?categoryid=13&cs=1&query=%22hard+r%2.

102. Brooks Boliek, "Parents Use Film Ratings," *Chicago Sun-Times*, September 10, 1999, 52; Janet Maslin, "Is NC-17 an X in a Clean Raincoat?" *New York Times*, October 21, 1990, sect. 2, 1; Staff, "The Silver Screen: Movies Reflect Changes in Society," *USA Today*, December 20, 1990, 13A; David Landis, "NC-17 Rating Bombs With Theaters," *USA Today*, October 7, 1992, 7D.

103. Gray, "'Brokeback Mountain' Most Impressive of Tepid 2005."

104. Michael Medved, "Hollywood's Disconnect," *USA Today*, July 25, 2005.

105. Tim Purtell, "Our Favorite Year," EW.com, April 29, 1994, http://www.ew.com/ew/article/0,, 302014,00.html.

106. "US Movie Market Summary 1995 to 2009," The Numbers, www.the-numbers.com/market.

107. Cogley, "Report on Blacklisting."

108. Schatz, "The Return of the Hollywood Studio System."

109. "Movies—*Transformers: Revenge of the Fallen*," Box Office Mojo, http://boxofficemojo.com/ movies/?id=transformers2.htm.

110. "Digital Domain Collaborates with Michael Bay on 'Transformers: Revenge of the Fallen' Movie Tie-Ins," CGArena, January 7, 2009, www.cgarena.com/archives/news/transformers_tieins.html.

111. Sarah Mahoney, "Kmart Launches Transformers Tie-In," Marketing Daily–Media Post News, June 1, 2009, www.mediapost.com/publications/?fa=Articles.showArticle&art_aid=107088.

112. Garrett Kessler, "2010 Camaro Stars in Transformers: Revenge of the Fallen, the Game," Edmunds Inside Line, June 30, 2009, www.edmunds.com/insideline/do/News/articleId=151628; "Latest Buzz: Chevrolet Unveils Camaro 'Transformers' Edition," *USA Today*, July 22, 2009, http:// content.usatoday.com/communities/driveon/post/2009/07/68495117/1.

113. Richard Corliss, "Blair Witch Craft," *Time*, August 16, 1999, 58–64; Timothy L. O'Brien, "The Curse of the Blair Witch," *Talk*, February 2002, 81.

114. Charlotte O'Sullivan, "Film: Hell Is Other People. We Should Know; The Makers of the Blair Witch Project, Ed Sanchez and Daniel Myrick, on the Nightmare of Collective Filmmaking," *The Independent*, October 22, 1999, 13.

115. O'Brien, "The Curse of the Blair Witch."

116. Glenn Whipp, "Searching for 'Blair Witch' a Decade Later," *Los Angeles Times*, July 11, 2009, http://latimesblogs.latimes.com/herocomplex/2009/07/searching-for-blair-witch-project-a- decade-later.html.

117. Ibid.

118. Chris Anderson, "Briefly Noted From Australia," The Long Tail, December 22, 2006, www .longtail.com/the_long_tail/2006/12/briefly_noted_f.html.

CHAPTER 9
**TELEVISION**

1. Howard Kurtz, "Carlson and 'Crossfire,' Exit Stage Left and Right," *Washington Post*, January 6, 2005.

2. Tucker Carlson and Paul Begala, "CNN Crossfire," October 15, 2004, transcripts.cnn.com/ transcripts/0410/15/cf.01.html.

3. Neil Postman, *Amusing Ourselves to Death: Public Discourse in the Age of Show Business* (New York: Penguin Books, 1985).

4. Stephanie Schorow, "A Stand-up Guy? Fans Campaign for 'Daily Show' Comic to Endorse Prez Candidate," *Boston Herald*, September 29, 2004.

5. Andrew Kohut and Kim Parker, "Today's Journalists Less Prominent," March 8, 2007, Pew Research Center for the People and the Press, people-press.org/report/309/todays-journalists- less-prominent.

6. Pew Research Center Project for Excellence in Journalism, "Journalism, Satire or Just Laughs? 'The Daily Show With Jon Stewart' Examined," May 8, 2008, www.journalism.org/node/10953.

7. Ibid.

8. Thomas R. Eddlem, "Will the Stewart/Cramer Battle Be the Death of CNBC?" March 16, 2009, www.thenewamerican.com/culture/education/885; Howard Kurtz, "Stewart vs. Cramer: A One-Sided Smackdown," *Washington Post*, March 13, 2009.

9. Dan Froomkin, "On Calling Bullshit," Nieman Watchdog, November 30, 2006, blog .niemanwatchdog.org/?p=53.

10. Pew Research Center Project for Excellence in Journalism, "Journalism, Satire or Just Laughs? 'The Daily Show With Jon Stewart' Examined."

11. David Dugan, "Big Dreams, Small Screen," WGBH Educational Foundation, 1997, www.pbs.org/ wgbh/amex/technology/bigdream/bigdreamts.html.

12. Neil Postman, "Philo Farnsworth," Time.com, March 29, 1999, www.time.com/time/time100/ scientist/profile/farnsworth.html.

13. Ibid.

14. Erik Barnouw, *Tube of Plenty: The Evolution of American Television*, 2nd rev. ed. (New York: Oxford University Press, 1990).

15. Postman, "Philo Farnsworth."

16. Barnouw, *Tube of Plenty*.

17. John Carman, "The 20 Series That Changed the Tube," *San Francisco Chronicle*, May 24, 1998; Deborah Felder, *The 100 Most Influential Women of All Time: A Ranking Past and Present* (Secaucus, N.J.: Carol Publishing Group, 1996); Douglas McGrath, "The Good, the Bad, the Lucy: A Legacy of Laughs; The Man Behind the Throne: Making the Case for Desi," *New York Times*, October 14, 2001.

18. Fred Kaplan, "Costs of High-Definition TV Make Its Future Look Fuzzy," *Boston Globe*, July 25, 2000.

19. Christopher Carey, "Ready or Not, High-Definition Television Starts on Sunday," *St. Louis Post-Dispatch*, November 1, 1998.

20. Patrick R. Parsons and Robert M. Frieden, *The Cable and Satellite Television Industries* (Needham Heights, Mass.: Allyn & Bacon, 1998).

21. Robert W. Crandall and Harold Furchtgott-Roth, *Cable TV: Regulation or Competition*? (Washington, D.C.: Brookings Institution, 1996).

22. Ibid.

23. Priscilla Painton, "The Taming of Ted Turner," *Time*, January 6, 1992.

24. Ibid.

25. "Prince of the Global Village," *Time*, January 6, 1992.

26. Parsons and Frieden, *The Cable and Satellite Television Industries*.

27. Ken Auletta, *Three Blind Mice: How the TV Networks Lost Their Way* (New York: Random House, 1991).

28. Parsons and Frieden, *The Cable and Satellite Television Industries*.

29. National Cable & Telecommunications Association, "National Cable & Telecommunications Association 2008 Industry Overview."

30. "The Resurrection of the European Cable TV Industry," *Business and Industry Online Reporter*, 2005.

31. Barnouw, *Tube of Plenty*.

32. J. W. Elphinstone, "Watercooler: DVDs' Popularity Passes VCRs', New Year's Resolutions, Bad Publicity," Associated Press Financial Wire, December 19, 2006.

33. Richard Mullins, "VCR's Demise Fast Forwards in Brave New World of DVDs," *Tampa Tribune*, December 20, 2006; Nielsen Company, "How Teens Use Media; A Nielsen Report on the Myths and Realities of Teen Media Trends," June 2009, blog.nielsen.com/nielsenwire/reports/nielsen_howteensusemedia_june09.pdf.

34. Satellite Broadcasting & Communications Association, "Satellite Home Entertainment; Industry Overview," www.sbca.com/receiver-network/index.html.

35. BSkyB Media Center, "Profile," phx.corporate-ir.net/phoenix.zhtml?c=104016&p=irol-mediaprofile.

36. Mark Dawidziak, "Satellite Television Providers to Include Local Programming," *Plain Dealer*, December 17, 1999.

37. Chet Bridger, "Dish vs. Cable: As Cable Rates Rise, More Viewers Are Turning to Satellite Dishes; But Both Choices Can Be Costly," *Buffalo News*, October 12, 1999.

38. Joelle Tessler, "Senate OKs 4-Month Delay to Digital TV Changeover," *USA Today*, January 27, 2009; Leslie Cauley, "Switch to Digital Television (DTV) Went Remarkably Well," *USA Today*, June 15, 2009; Associated Press, "800,000 Caller Phone Digital TV Hotline," *USA Today*, June 14, 2009.

39. Paul Farhi, "A Defining Moment for TV? As Digital Broadcast Age Begins, the Outlook Is Far From Clear," *Washington Post*, November 1, 1998.

40. Ibid.

41. Peter J. Brown, "Satellite-TV Players Seek Answer to Cable's Triple Play," *Via Satellite*, January 1, 2007; David Goetzl, "Picture This: HD Buyers Get Set, Not HD Service," November 28, 2008, www.mediapost.com/publications/?fa=Articles.showArticle&art_aid=95508.

42. Auletta, *Three Blind Mice*.

43. Anthony Smith, "Television as a Public Service Medium," in *Television: An International History*, ed. Anthony Smith (New York: Oxford University Press, 1995).

44. Laurence Jarvik, *PBS: Behind the Scenes* (Rocklin, Calif.: Prima Publishing, 1997).

45. Ibid.

46. Ken Auletta, *The Highwaymen* (San Diego: Harcourt Brace, 1998).

47. Gary Levin, "Viewers' Shifting Habits Redefine 'TV Hit'," *USA Today*, October 23, 2007.

48. Nicholas Covey, "The State of the Console; Video Game Console Usage Fourth Quarter 2006" (Nielsen Wireless and Interactive Services, 2007); Nielsen Company, "Local Television Market Universe Estimates," 2008.

49. James R. Walker and Douglas A. Ferguson, *The Broadcast Television Industry* (Needham Heights, Mass.: Allyn & Bacon, 1998).

50. Auletta, *Three Blind Mice*.

51. Ibid.

52. Bill Carter, "After Years of Being Off Track, VH1 Hits Its Groove," *New York Times*, June 22, 1998.

53. Neal Gabler, "A Merger or an Evolution?" *New York Times*, September 9, 1999.

54. Bridger, "Dish vs. Cable."

55. Auletta, *Three Blind Mice*.

56. Bill Goodykoontz, "Where Have All the 'Good Times' Gone? Networks Skirt Minority Stars," *Arizona Republic*, August 29, 1999.

57. Robert P. Laurence, "NBC Program Executive Says Network Has Lagged on Ethnic Diversity," *San Diego Union-Tribune*, July 31, 1999.

58. Paul Farhi, "Burns Agrees to Include Latino Veterans in 'the War,'" *Washington Post*, May 11, 2007; Elizabeth Jensen, "Ken Burns and Hispanic Groups Reach Agreement," *New York Times*, May 11, 2007.

59. Johnny Diaz, "Speaking Volumes: Use of Spanish Booms on Network Programs," *Boston Globe*, November 13, 2005.

60. Jennifer Armstrong and Margeaux Watson, "Diversity in Entertainment: Why Is TV So White?" *Entertainment Weekly*, June 12, 2008.

61. Lacey Rose, "Talking TV With 'The Cleveland Show' Co-Creator Mike Henry," October 1, 2009, www.forbes.com/2009/10/01/cleveland-family-guy-business-entertainment-henry.html.

62. Melvin Patrick Ely, *The Adventures of Amos 'n' Andy* (New York: Free Press, 1991).

63. Armstrong and Watson, "Diversity in Entertainment."

64. U.S. Census Bureau, "United States—DP-1. General Demographic Characteristics," U.S. Census Bureau, 2008 population estimates, factfinder.census.gov/servlet/QTTable?_bm=y&-qr_name= PEP_2008_EST_DP1&-geo_id=01000US&-ds_name=PEP_2008_EST&-_lang=en&-format=&-CONTEXT=qt.

65. Patricia Brennan, "The Colorful World of 'Grey's Anatomy'," *Washington Post*, May 22, 2005.

66. Amy Amatangelo, "The Subtleties Behind the Subtitles," *Washington Post*, May 22, 2005.

67. Diaz, "Speaking Volumes."

68. David Adams, "ABC, CBS, NBC, Fox . . . Univision?" *St. Petersburg Times*, June 5, 2005; Michael Schneider, "Novela Energizes Univision," *Variety*, October 4, 2009.

69. Lee Romney, "Markets: Univision Shares Drop Over Azteca News," *Los Angeles Times*, September 9, 2000.

70. Scott Collins, "At ABC, a Hopeful Bet on 'Betty'," *Los Angeles Times*, August 14, 2006.

71. "Univision to Produce a Sitcom in the States," *St. Petersburg Times*, May 24, 2000; Juan Tornoe, "2006 World Cup Gives Univision Ratings Boost," Hispanic Trending, July 7, 2006, juantornoe .blogs.com/hispanictrending/2006/07/2006_world_cup_.html.

72. Hollywood Reporter, "Spanish-Language Network Challenges Regis," *Milwaukee Journal Sentinel*, May 21, 2000.

73. Joanne Ostrow, "Risks, Pitfalls Are Plenty When Dubbing TV Shows," *Pittsburgh Post-Gazette*, January 2, 2006.

74. Dennis Hunt, "BET Gambles on Revamped Framework; Network Chief Lists Challenges at Work," *USA Today*, July 28, 2000.

75. Keith L. Alexander, "Placing BET on the Net; Site Part of the CEO's Plan to Expand," *USA Today*, February 10, 2000.

76. Greg Braxton, "BET on the Past and Future of a Dream," *Los Angeles Times*, May 6, 2000.

77. Leona Thompson, "BET Offers 'Blessings' Without Disguise," *Boston Herald*, April 6, 2000.

78. Stuart Elliott, "General Motors Is Significantly Increasing Its Efforts to Aim Pitches at Black Consumers," *New York Times*, September 23, 1999.

79. Laura R. Linder, *Public Access Television: America's Electronic Soapbox* (Westport, Conn.: Praeger Publishers, 1999).

80. Ibid.

81. Ibid.

82. Barnouw, *Tube of Plenty*.

83. Stephen Seplow and Jonathan Storm, "Window to a Culture: The Television Revolution Has Changed Everything, for Better and Worse," *Arizona Republic*, January 4, 1998.

84. Robert Kubey and Mihaly Csikszentmihalyi, *Television and the Quality of Life: How Viewing Shapes Everyday Experience* (Hillsdale, N.J.: Lawrence Erlbaum Associates, 1990).

85. Vicky Rideout, "Key Findings From New Research on Children's Media Use," Henry J. Kaiser Family Foundation, March 9, 2005, www.kaisernetwork.org/health_cast/hcast_index.cfm?display= detail&hc=1377.

86. Kubey and Csikszentmihalyi, *Television and the Quality of Life*.

87. Shearon A. Lowery and Melvin L. DeFleur, *Milestones in Mass Communication*, 3rd ed. (White Plains, N.Y.: Longman, 1995).

88. Terry Gross, "Interview With Mary Tyler Moore," Fresh Air/NPR, October 30, 1995, www.npr.org/templates/story/story.php?storyId=1108624.

89. Elizabeth Kolbert, "What's a Network TV Censor to Do?" *New York Times*, May 23, 1993.

90. Warren Berger, "Censorhip in the Age of Anything Goes; Where Have You Gone, Standards and Practices?" *New York Times*, September 20, 1998.

91. Stephen Farber, "They Watch What We Watch," *New York Times*, May 7, 1989.

92. David Zurawik, "Ratinges Deal Signed; TV: Starting Oct. 1, Symbols Will Give Parents More Clues About Content. Except on NBC," *Baltimore Sun*, July 11, 1997.

93. Berger, "Censorhip in the Age of Anything Goes."

94. Associated Press, "A Closer Look at Broadcast Indecency," First Amendment Center, March 23, 20004, www.firstamendmentcenter.org/analysis.aspx?id=12915.

95. Ibid.

96. Associated Press, "Some Stations Hesitate to Air 9/11 Documentary," First Amendment Center, September 5, 2006, www.firstamendmentcenter.org/news.aspx?id=17352.

97. Associated Press, "'Saving Private Ryan' Not Indecent, FCC Rules," First Amendment Center, March 1, 2005, www.firstamendmentcenter.org/news.aspx?id=14895.

98. Adam Sherwin, "Amateur 'Video Bloggers' Under Threat From EU Broadcast Rules," (London) *Times*, October 17, 2006.

99. Gene Policinski, "Censorship in the Name of Decency?" First Amendment Center, September 5, 2006, www.firstamendmentcenter.org/commentary.aspx?id=17356.

100. Crandall and Furchtgott-Roth, *Cable TV: Regulation or Competition?*

101. Auletta, *The Highwaymen*.

102. Marc Gunther, "Must-See Whenever You Feel Like It TV," *Fortune*, May 27, 2002.

103. Antonio Perez, "How Netflix Transformed the Home Entertainment Industry," September 30, 2009, http://www.theepochtimes.com/n2/content/view/23225.

104. Staff, "Tune In, Log On, Go Play," *Newsweek*, April 17, 2000.

105. Ibid.

106. Susan Stellin, "Bad News for Old News," Media Post Publications, December 1, 2006, publications.mediapost.com/index.cfm?fuseaction=Articles.showArticle&art_aid=51695.

107. David Lieberman and Laura Petrecca, "Deal Has Some ABC Affiliates Feeling Uneasy," *USA Today*, October 12, 2005.

108. Dawn C. Chmielewski and Meg James, "Will Hulu Make You Pay to Watch?" *Los Angeles Times*, October 5, 2009.

109. Richard Siklos, "Media Frenzy: A Video Business Model Ready to Move Beyond Beta," *New York Times*, September 1, 2006.

110. Wayne Friedman, "CBS Strikes Digital Media Deal with Affiliates," Media Post Publications, June 30, 2006, publications.mediapost.com/index.cfm?fuseaction=Articles.san&s=45143&Nid=21417& p=219965.

111. Paul J. Gough, "Online Streams Help ABC Affils," *Hollywood Reporter,* April 26, 2006, www.hollywoodreporter.com/hr/search/article_display.jsp?vnu_content_id=1002386027.

CHAPTER 10
**THE INTERNET**

1. Nielsen Company, "How Teens Use Media: A Nielsen Report on the Myths and Realities of Teen Media Trends," June 2009, blog.nielsen.com/nielsenwire/reports/nielsen_howteensusemedia_june09.pdf.

2. Kevin Maney, "Short & Tweet," February 11, 2009, www.portfolio.com/executives/features/2009/02/11/Twitter-CEO-Evan-Williams-Q-and-A.

3. Jon Swartz, "Twitter Has Millions Tweeting in Public Communication Service," *USA Today*, May 26, 2009.

4. Bob Garfield, "How Tweet It Is," *On the Media*, August 22, 2008, www.onthemedia.org/transcripts/2008/08/22/05.

5. Ibid.

6. Alex Rudloff, "The Twitterholic.Com Top 100 Twitterholics Based on Followers," twitterholic.com.

7. Bob Garfield, "Micro Reporting," *On the Media*, August 22, 2008, www.onthemedia.org/transcripts/2008/08/22/06.

8. Dominic Rushee, "What Makes Twitter Worth a Billion Dollars?" *Sunday Times*, September 27, 2009.

9. Swartz, "Twitter Has Millions Tweeting in Public Communication Service."

10. Rushee, "What Makes Twitter Worth a Billion Dollars?"

11. "Scientist Who Transformed the Internet," *Irish Times*, June 24, 2000.

12. Peter Grier, "In the Beginning, There Was ARPANET," *Air Force Magazine*, January 1997, 66.

13. Barnaby J. Feder, "Donald W. Davies, 75, Dies; Helped Refine Data Networks," *New York Times*, June 4, 2000.

14. Katie Hafner and Matthew Lyon, *Where Wizards Stay Up Late* (New York: Simon & Schuster, 1996).

15. Stephen Segaller, *Nerds 2.0.1*, revised paperback ed. (New York: TV Books, 1999), 40.

16. Ibid.

17. Ibid.

18. Joseph Gallivan, "A Bit More Backbone: Internet II Is in the Wings," *The Independent*, February 25, 1997; Jeffrey R. Young, "Internet2 Spurs Equipment Upgrades, but Use in Research Remains Limited," *Chronicle of Higher Education*, August 13, 1999; University Corporation for Advanced Internet Development, "Frequently Asked Questions About Internet2," www.internet2.edu/html/faqs.html#.

19. Segaller, *Nerds 2.0.1*.

20. Ibid.

21. Ibid.

22. Lawrence K. Grossman, "From Marconi to Murrow to—Drudge?" *Columbia Journalism Review*, July 1999, 17.

23. William J. Mitchell, *City of Bits: Space, Place, and the Infobahn* (Cambridge: MIT Press, 1995).

24. Leslie Regan Shade, "Is There Free Speech on the Net? Censorship in the Global Information Infrastructure," in *Cultures of the Internet*, ed. Rob Shields (London: Sage, 1996).

25. Segaller, *Nerds 2.0.1*.

26. Tim Berners-Lee, *Weaving the Web* (New York: Harper Collins, 1999).

27. Anick Jesdanun, "From Two Users to 7 Million, Web's Come a Long Way," Associated Press, December 24, 2000.

28. Segaller, *Nerds 2.0.1*, 288.

29. Ibid., 291.

30. Ibid.

31. Lisa Corbin, "Speeding Up the Data Superhighway," *Government Executive*, February 1995.

32. John B. Horrigan, "Home Broadband Adoption 2006," May 28, 2006, www.pewinternet.org/Reports/2006/Home-Broadband-Adoption-2006.aspx; John Horrigan, "Home Broadband Adoption 2009," June 17, 2009, www.pewinternet.org/Reports/2009/10-Home-Broadband-Adoption-2009.aspx.

33. Committee on the Internet in the Evolving Information Infrastructure et al., *The Internet's Coming of Age* (Washington, D.C.: National Academies Press, 2001).

34. John Horrigan, "Wireless Internet Use," July 22, 2009, www.pewinternet.org/Reports/2009/12-Wireless-Internet-Use.aspx.

35. Michelle McGiboney, "Twitter's Tweet Smell of Success," March 18, 2009, blog.nielsen.com/nielsenwire/online_mobile/twitters-tweet-smell-of-success; Maney, "Short & Tweet."

36. Mark Jurkowitz, "Online News Outlets Catch Their Breath; Cyber Slowdown Prompts Rethinking," *Boston Globe*, January 19, 2001.

37. James Fallows, "But Is It Journalism?" *American Prospect*, November 23, 1999.

38. Felicity Barringer, "Rethinking Internet News as a Business Proposition," *New York Times*, January 22, 2001.

39. Richard Morochove, "Cyberpunk Guru Unplugged: When It Comes to the Internet and Computers, Author William Gibson Is Decidedly Low-Tech," *Toronto Star*, June 1, 1995.

40. Gary Gentile, "Hollywood Net Survivor: IFILM Hopes to Build Media Company," Associated Press.

41. Hugh Hart, "New Media, Old Methods," *Los Angeles Times*, February 18, 2001.

42. Roger Ebert, "Is '405' a Home Movie?" *Chicago Sun-Times*, November 1, 2000.

43. Jon Healey, "Pay-Per-View Sites Offer New Options for Computer Movie-Viewing," *San Jose Mercury News*, May 21, 2000.

44. Michael Paoletta, "Online Odyssey Stoking Interest in New NIN Album," March 30, 2007, www.billboard.com/bbcom/news/article_display.jsp?vnu_content_id=1003565585.

45. Fallows, "But Is It Journalism?"

46. Ibid.

47. Segaller, *Nerds 2.0.1*.

48. I would like to thank Charley Reed, a communications graduate student at the University of Nebraska at Omaha, for his research and work on the video game section of this chapter.

49. Steve Smith, "No More Fun and Games," Media Post Publications, March 1, 2007, publications.mediapost.com/index.cfm?fuseaction=Articles.showArticle&art_aid=56216&art_type=100.

50. Jim Rutenberg, "Obama Aims TV Ads at Younger Voters," *New York Times*, October 8, 2008, thecaucus.blogs.nytimes.com/2008/10/08/obama-aims-tv-ads-at-younger-voters.

51. Seth Schiesel, "Finding Community in Virtual Town Squares," *New York Times*, November 5, 2005.

52. Derrick J. Lang, "How Iron Man Was Trounced by a Scruffy Car Thief," *USA Today*, May 8, 2008.

53. John Gaudiosi, "Games, Movies Tie the Knot," December 10, 2003, www.wired.com/gaming/gamingreviews/news/2003/12/61358.

54. Amanda Lenhart et al., "Teens, Video Games and Civics," 2008, www.pewinternet.org/Reports/2008/Teens-Video-Games-and-Civics.aspx?r=1.

55. Amanda Lenhart, Sydney Jones, and Alexandra Macgill, "Pew Internet Project Data Memo: Adults and Video Games," in *Pew Internet and American Life Project* (Pew Foundation, 2008).

56. Grossman, "From Marconi to Murrow to—Drudge?"

57. Segaller, *Nerds 2.0.1*.

58. Stacy Schiff, "Know It All; Can Wikipedia Conquer Expertise?" *New Yorker*, July 31, 2006.

59. David S. Bennahum, "Techno-Paranoia in the White House," *New York Times*, January 25, 1997.

60. Fallows, "But Is It Journalism?"

61. Berners-Lee, *Weaving the Web*.

62. Austin Bunn, "Human Portals," *Brill's Content*, May 2001.

63. Howard Kurtz, "After Blogs Got Hits, CBS Got a Black Eye," *Washington Post*, September 20, 2004; Alessandra Stanley, "The TV Watch; Signing Off, Rather's Wish for Viewers Is Still 'Courage'," *New York Times*, March 10, 2005.

64. Mark Memmott, "'Milbloggers' Are Typing Their Place in History," *USA Today*, May 12, 2005.

65. Julia Darling, "Julia Darling in Person," September 26, 2002, www.juliadarling.co.uk/weblog/archives/archive-092002.html.

66. Howard Kurtz, "Throw Another Blog on the Fire," *Washington Post*, April 11, 2005.

67. Google, "About Google News," news.google.com/intl/en_us/about_google_news.html.

68. Peter Sayer, "Yahoo's Legal Battle over Nazi Items Continues," *Infoworld*, August 24, 2004, www.infoworld.com/article/04/08/24/HNyahoonazi_1.html.

69. Marc Gunther, "Yahoo's China Problem," CNN Money, February 22, 2006, money.cnn.com/2006/02/21/news/international/pluggedin_fortune/?cnn=yes.

70. Nazila Fathi, "In a Death Seen Around the World, a Symbol of Iranian Protests," *New York Times*, June 23, 2009.
71. Ibid.
72. Hiawatha Bray, "Finding a Way Around Iranian Censorship," *Boston Globe*, June 19, 2009.
73. Segaller, *Nerds 2.0.1*.
74. Ibid.
75. Steven Levy, *Hackers* (New York: Penguin Books, 1994); Steven Levy, "The Day I Got Napsterized," *Newsweek*, May 28, 2001.
76. Jamie Portman, "Confronting Cyberspace," *Calgary Herald*, June 11, 1995.
77. Ibid.
78. Douglas Barbour, "Pop Culture on the Cyberfrontier," *Vancouver Sun*, September 14, 1996.
79. Segaller, *Nerds 2.0.1*.
80. Miniwatts Marketing Group, "Internet Usage Statistics," www.internetworldstats.com/stats.htm.
81. Agence France-Presse, "U.N. Fears Divisive Impact of the Internet," *New York Times*, June 29, 2000.
82. Anthony Shadid, "Third World Nations Threatened as Digital Divide Grows, Report Says," *Boston Globe*, January 24, 2001.
83. Bloomberg News, "More Black Americans Using Web, Report Says," *Los Angeles Times*, October 3, 2000.
84. Berners-Lee, *Weaving the Web*.
85. Shade, "Is There Free Speech on the Net?"
86. Berners-Lee, *Weaving the Web*.
87. Clifford Stoll, *Silicon Snake Oil: Second Thoughts on the Information Highway* (New York: Doubleday, 1995).
88. Ibid., 233.
89. Daniel Jacobson, "API Update: New Transcript API and Much More," July 29, 2009, www.npr.org/blogs/inside/2009/07/api_update_transcript_api_and.html.
90. Frank Ahrens, "2002's News, Yesterday's Sell-Off," *Washington Post*, September 9, 2008.
91. Eytan Avriel, "*NY Times* Publisher: Our Goal Is to Manage the Transition From Print to Internet," *Haaretz*, February 8, 2007.
92. "Future Forum," *Advertising Age*, September 20, 1999.

## CHAPTER 11
### ADVERTISING

1. Dave Kindred, "NBA's MVP? Here's a Vote for Spike Lee," *Houston Chronicle*, July 27, 1997.
2. Stuart Elliott, "Spike DDB Is Off to a Fast Start, but Obstacles Remain," *New York Times*, July 9, 1997.
3. Lynn Hirschberg, "Spike Lee's 30 Seconds," *New York Times*, April 20, 1997.
4. Elliott, "Spike DDB Is Off to a Fast Start, but Obstacles Remain."
5. Johanna Redtenbacher, "Spike Lee's Once-Faltering Agency Does the Right Thing," *Marketing Magazine*, December 11, 2000.
6. Elliott, "Spike DDB Is Off to a Fast Start, but Obstacles Remain."
7. Barry Janoff, "Mike and Spike Together Again," *Adweek*, February 7, 2005.
8. "Journey Out to Sea," *AdWeek East* 1999, 22.
9. Ibid.
10. Preston Turegano, "'Do the Right Thing' Navy Hopes Spike Lee Can Attract Recruits for a New 'Journey'," *San Diego Union-Tribune*, May 9, 1999.
11. Redtenbacher, "Spike Lee's Once-Faltering Agency Does the Right Thing."
12. Melanie Wells, "Madison Avenue Goes Hollywood; Directors Break for Commercials and Top Pay," *USA Today*, November 1, 1995.
13. Ellen Groves, "Art and Commerce: Top Directors Go Commercial—Literally," *Women's Wear Daily*, January 12, 2007.
14. Hirschberg, "Spike Lee's 30 Seconds."
15. George E. Belch and Michael A. Belch, *Advertising and Promotion: An Integrated Marketing Communications Perspective* (Boston: Irwin McGraw-Hill, 1998).
16. Pamela Walker Laird, *Advertising Progress* (Baltimore: Johns Hopkins University Press, 1998).

17. James W. Carey, "Advertising: An Institutional Approach," in *Advertising in Society*, ed. Roxanne Hoveland and Gary B. Wilcox (Lincolnwood, Ill.: NTC Business Books, 1989).

18. Laird, *Advertising Progress*.

19. Michael Schudson, "Historical Roots of Consumer Culture," in *Advertising in Society*, ed. Roxanne Hoveland and Gary B. Wilcox (Lincolnwood, Ill.: NTC Business Books, 1989).

20. Laird, *Advertising Progress*.

21. Carey, "Advertising: An Institutional Approach."

22. Schudson, "Historical Roots of Consumer Culture."

23. Laird, *Advertising Progress*.

24. James B. Twitchell, *Adcult USA: The Triumph of Advertising in American Culture* (New York: Columbia University Press, 1996).

25. Ibid.

26. Ibid.

27. Alicia C. Shepard, "Public Service Advertising That Changed a Nation," 2004, www.adcouncil .org/default.aspx?id=307.

28. Eugene H. Fram, S. Prakash Sethi, and Nobuaki Namiki, "Newspaper Advocacy Advertising: Molder of Public Opinion," *USA Today Magazine*, July 1993, 90.

29. Belch and Belch, *Advertising and Promotion: An Integrated Marketing Communications Perspective*.

30. Michael Schudson, "Advertising as Capitalist Realism," in *Advertising in Society*, ed. Roxanne Hoveland and Gary B. Wilcox (Lincolnwood, Ill.: NTC Business Books, 1989).

31. Herschell Gordon Lewis, *Advertising Age Handbook of Advertising* (Lincolnwood, Ill.: NTC Business Books, 1999).

32. Mike Snider, "Hunt for Playstation 2 Becomes Easier for Shoppers," *USA Today*, March 22, 2001.

33. Nancy Giges, "Coke's Switch a Classic," in *Advertising Age: The Principles of Advertising at Work*, ed. Esther Thorson (Lincolnwood, Ill.: NTC Business Books, 1989).

34. Jack Honomichl, "Missing Ingredients in 'New' Coke's Research," in *Advertising Age: The Principles of Advertising at Work*, ed. Esther Thorson (Lincolnwood, Ill.: NTC Business Books, 1989).

35. Giges, "Coke's Switch a Classic."

36. Schudson, "Historical Roots of Consumer Culture."

37. Laird, *Advertising Progress*.

38. Lewis, *Advertising Age Handbook of Advertising*.

39. C. Bruce Bartels, "Ad Agencies Must Look to Customers to Change," *Boston Business Journal*, December 30, 1994.

40. Ibid.

41. David Ogilvy, *Confessions of an Advertising Man* (New York: Atheneum, 1963).

42. Ibid.

43. Ibid.

44. Alf Nucifora, "Advertising 101: How to Get the Best Out of Your Media Buy," *Houston Business Journal*, October 16, 1998.

45. Advertising Age, "Agency Report 2009 Index," April 27, 2009, adage.com/datacenter/ article?article_id=136094.

46. Advertising Age, "100 Leading National Advertisers: 2009 Edition Index," June 22, 2009, adage .com/datacenter/article?article_id=136308.

47. Advertising Age, "2006 Fact Pack," adage.com/images/random/FactPack06.pdf.

48. Esther Thorson, ed., *Advertising Age: The Principles of Advertising at Work* (Lincolnwood, Ill.: NTC Business Books, 1989).

49. Twitchell, *Adcult USA: The Triumph of Advertising in American Culture*.

50. Lewis, *Advertising Age Handbook of Advertising*; Pew Research Center Project for Excellence in Journalism, "The State of the News Media 2009: Newspapers," www.stateofthemedia.org/2009/ index.htm.

51. Outdoor Advertising Association of America, "About Digital Billboard Technology," www.oaaa .org/legislativeandregulatory/digital/aboutdigitalbillboardtechnology.aspx.

52. Twitchell, *Adcult USA: The Triumph of Advertising in American Culture*; Outdoor Advertising Association of America, "Research and Data," www.oaaa.org/press/ResearchandData.aspx.

53. Louise Story, "Times Sq. Ads Spread Via Tourists' Cameras," *New York Times*, December 11, 2006.

54. Michael Learmonth, "Online Advertising Spending Expected to Be Down for 2009," *Advertising Age,* October 19, 2009, adage.com/digital/article?article_id=139785.

55. Schudson, "Advertising as Capitalist Realism."

56. Rebecca Piirto Heath, "Psychographics: Q'est-Ce Que C'est," *Marketing Tools*, November/December 1995.

57. Emanuel H. Demby, "Psychographics Revisited: The Birth of a Technique," *Marketing Research* 6, no. 2 (1994).

58. Strategic Business Insights (SBI), "VALS | Strategic Business Insights (SBI)," www.strategicbusinessinsights.com/vals/.

59. Ibid.

60. Joshua Meyrowitz, *No Sense of Place* (New York: Oxford University Press, 1985).

61. Theresa Howard, "Being True to Dew," *Brandweek*, April 24, 2000.

62. Richard Linnett, "A New Dew; A Soft Drink Finds Deliverance," *Print*, November/December 2000.

63. Cortney Harding, "The Indies: Hear Me, Drink Me," billboard.com, August 30, 2008; "Mountain Dew—The Official Site," mountaindew.com.

64. Barbara Thau, "Courting the Gay Consumer," *HFN*, February 27, 2006.

65. Charles A. Jaffe, "Dealers Say Wooing Gay, Lesbian Customers Is Good Business," *Automotive News*, January 31, 1994.

66. "Marketing to Gay and Lesbian Consumers" (Rivendell Media, 2008).

67. Brett Chase, "Advertisements Land in Gay Publications," *Des Moines Business Record*, August 8, 1994.

68. Thau, "Courting the Gay Consumer"; "Marketing to Gay and Lesbian Consumers."

69. Kate Rockwood, "GLAAD's Helping Hand," *Fast Company*, November 2009.

70. Prime Access Inc., "2007 Gay Press Report" (Rivendell Media Company, 2008).

71. Ira Teinowitz, "Crazy Horse Brew Incenses Sioux," *Advertising Age*, April 6, 1992.

72. Dirk Johnson, "Complaints by Indians Lead to Bans on a Beer," *New York Times*, December 6, 1995.

73. Associated Press, "No Trademark for Crazy Horse Brew," *Marketing News*, August 28, 1995.

74. Staff, "A 'Black' Cigarette Goes Up in Smoke," *Newsweek*, January 29, 1990.

75. D. Kirk Davidson, "Targeting Is Innocent Until It Exploits the Vulnerable," *Marketing News*, September 11, 1995.

76. Judann Dagnoli, "RJR's New Smokes Look Uptown," *Advertising Age*, June 25, 1990.

77. Kim Rotzoll, James E. Haefner, and Charles H. Sandage, "Advertising and the Classical Liberal World View," in *Advertising in Society*, ed. Roxanne Hoveland and Gary B. Wilcox (Lincolnwood, Ill.: NTC Business Books, 1989).

78. M. Night Shyamalan, *The Sixth Sense; A Conversation With M. Night Shyamalan* (Burbank, Calif.: Hollywood Pictures Home Video, 2000), DVD.

79. Chuck Ross, "NBC Blasts Beyond the 15-Minute Barrier," *Advertising Age*, August 7, 2000.

80. "Network, Cable Messages Buried in Commercial Avalanche," *Chicago Sun-Times*, May 30, 2006.

81. Brian Stelter, "Fox TV's Gamble: Fewer Ads in Break, but Costing More," *New York Times*, February 13, 2009.

82. Media Week, "Numbers Don't Lie," *MediaWeek*, September 12, 2006.

83. Dick Morris, "Break Through the Clutter," *Chain Store Age*, December 2000.

84. Diedtra Henderson, "Rise of Celebrity Testimonials Spurs FDA Scrutiny," *Boston Globe*, October 30, 2005.

85. Martha Rogers and Christine A. Seiler, "The Answer Is No: A National Survey of Advertising Industry Practitioners and Their Clients About Whether They Use Subliminal Advertising," *Journal of Advertising Research* 34, no. 2 (1994).

86. J. Leo, "Hostility Among the Ice Cubes," *U.S. News & World Report*, July 15, 1991; J. Levine and J. L. Aber, "Search and Find," *Forbes*, September 2, 1991.

87. Tom O'Sullivan, "Ridley Scott Returns to Ads With Orange Blitz," *Marketing Week*, April 2, 1998.

88. Bob Garfield, "Breakthrough Product Gets Greatest TV Spot," *Advertising Age*, January 10, 1994.

89. Bradley Johnson, "The Commercial, and the Product, That Changed Advertising," *Advertising Age*, January 10, 1994.
90. Ibid.
91. Lenore Skenazy, "Keep Targeting Kids and the Parents Will Start Targeting You," *Advertising Age*, May 19, 2008.
92. Thorson, ed., *Advertising Age: The Principles of Advertising at Work*; Carole Shifrin, "Ban on TV Ads to Children Is Proposed," *Washington Post*, February 25, 1978.
93. Caroline E. Mayer, "TV Ads Entice Kids to Overeat, Study Finds," *Washington Post*, December 7, 2005.
94. Annys Shin, "Ads Aimed at Children Get Tighter Scrutiny; Firms to Promote More Healthful Diet Choices," *Washington Post*, November 15, 2006.
95. Mayer, "TV Ads Entice Kids to Overeat, Study Finds."
96. "Selling Junk Food to Toddlers," *New York Times*, February 23, 2006.
97. Melanie Warner, "Food Industry Defends Marketing to Children," *New York Times*, July 15, 2005.
98. Mayer, "TV Ads Entice Kids to Overeat, Study Finds."
99. Andrew Martin, "Leading Makers Agree to Put Limits on Junk Food Advertising Directed at Children," *New York Times*, November 15, 2006.
100. Dan Milmo, "Media: That's All, Folks: As ITV Shuts Its Kids Production Unit and With a Ban on Lucrative Junk-Food Advertising Imminent, Producers Say Children's Television Is in Mortal Danger," *The Guardian*, July 31, 2006.
101. Maggie Brown, "Media: When the Chips Are Down: The Ban on Junk-Food Advertising in Kids' Shows Is Expected to Cost the Industry £39m," *The Guardian*, November 20, 2006.
102. Ibid.
103. Dawn Edmiston, "An Examination of Integrated Marketing Communication in U.S. Public Institutions of Higher Education," *International Journal of Educational Advancement* 8, no. 3/4 (2009).
104. David Goetzl, "Denny's Super Bowl Ad Value: 'Incredible'," February 18, 2009, www.mediapost.com/publications/?fa=Articles.showArticle&art_aid=100566.
105. Bruce Horovitz, "2 Million Enjoy Free Breakfast at Denny's," *USA Today*, February 3, 2009.
106. Ibid.
107. Brian Quinton, "Bowl Post-Game Pt. 1: The Drive for Integration," Chief Marketer Network, February 17, 2009, bigfatmarketingblog.com/2009/02/17/bowl-post-game-pt-1-the-drive-for-integration; John Sternal, "Integrated PR and Marketing; A Grand Slam," Merit Mile Communication, March 10, 2009, www.meritmile.com/pr/integrated-pr-and-marketing.
108. Quinton, "Bowl Post-Game Pt. 1: The Drive for Integration"; "Denny's Scores a Promotion Touchdown," Stradella Road, February 4, 2009, www.stradellaroad.com/2009/02/04/denny's-scores-a-promotion-touchdown.
109. Goetzl, "Denny's Super Bowl Ad Value: 'Incredible'."
110. Staff, "Denny's Scores a Promotion Touchdown."
111. Goetzl, "Denny's Super Bowl Ad Value: 'Incredible'."
112. Nielsen Company, "How Teens Use Media: A Nielsen Report on the Myths and Realities of Teen Media Trends," June 2009, blog.nielsen.com/nielsenwire/reports/nielsen_howteensusemedia_june09.pdf.
113. Julie Bosman, "TV and Top Marketers Discuss the State of the Medium," *New York Times*, March 24, 2006; Julie Bosman, "A Match Made in Product Placement Heaven," *New York Times*, May 31, 2006.
114. Paul Davidson, "Ad Campaigns for Your Tiny Cellphone Screen Get Bigger; Marketers Leverage Growth in Text Messaging, Wireless Web," *USA Today*, August 9, 2006.
115. Stuart Elliott, "More Products Get Roles in Shows, and Marketers Wonder If They're Getting Their Money's Worth," *New York Times*, March 29, 2005.
116. Ibid.
117. Andrew Adam Newman, "Once a Seldom-Heard Word, Pregnancy Is Now in the Spotlight," *New York Times*, April 2, 2009.
118. Doreen Carvajal, "Placing the Product in the Dialog, Too," *New York Times*, January 17, 2006.
119. *Advertising Age*, "Online Advertising Spending Expected to Be Down for 2009"; *Advertising Age*, "100 Leading National Advertisers: 2009 Edition Index."

120. Jefferson Graham, "Google's Adsense a Bonanza for Some Websites," *USA Today*, March 11, 2005.

121. Louise Story, "Marketers Demanding Better Count of the Clicks," *New York Times*, October 30, 2006.

122. Jefferson Graham, "Google to Experiment With Newspaper Ad Sales Online; Search Giant to Offer Print Options to Customer Base," *USA Today*, November 6, 2006.

123. Ibid.

CHAPTER 12
**PUBLIC RELATIONS**

1. Ralph Hanson, interview, October 20, 2009.

2. Marvin N. Olasky, *Corporate Public Relations: A New Historical Perspective* (Hillsdale, N.J.: Lawrence Erlbaum Associates, 1987).

3. Ibid.

4. Cynthia E. Clark, "Differences Between Public Relations and Corporate Social Responsibility: An Analysis," *Public Relations Review* 26, no. 3 (2000).

5. Olasky, *Corporate Public Relations*.

6. Ibid.

7. H. Frazier Moore and Frank B. Kalupa, *Public Relations: Principles, Cases, and Problems*, 9th ed. (Homewood, Ill.: Richard D. Irwin, Inc., 1985).

8. John C. Stauber and Sheldon Rampton, *Toxic Sludge Is Good for You: Lies, Damn Lies, and the Public Relations Industry* (Monroe, Maine: Common Courage Press, 1995).

9. Olasky, *Corporate Public Relations*.

10. Ray Eldon Hiebert, *Courtier to the Crowd: The Story of Ivy Lee and the Development of Public Relations* (Ames: Iowa State University Press, 1966).

11. Edward L. Bernays, *Public Relations* (Norman: University of Oklahoma Press, 1952).

12. Hiebert, *Courtier to the Crowd*.

13. Ibid.

14. Bernays, *Public Relations*.

15. Stauber and Rampton, *Toxic Sludge Is Good for You*.

16. Bernays, *Public Relations*.

17. Shearon A. Lowery and Melvin L. DeFleur, *Milestones in Mass Communication*, 3rd ed. (White Plains, N.Y.: Longman, 1995).

18. Bernays, *Public Relations*.

19. Moore and Kalupa, *Public Relations: Principles, Cases, and Problems*.

20. Bernays, *Public Relations*.

21. Scott M. Cutlip, Allen H. Center, and Glen M. Broom, *Effective Public Relations* (Upper Saddle River, N.J.: Prentice-Hall, 2000).

22. Raymond Moley, "The Birth of the Production Code (1945)," in *The Movies in Our Midst: Documents in the Cultural History of Film in America*, ed. Gerald Mast (Chicago: University of Chicago Press, 1982).

23. Olasky, *Corporate Public Relations*.

24. Kathleen S. Kelly, "Stewardship; The Fifth Step in the Public Relations Process," in *Handbook of Public Relations*, ed. Robert Lawrence Heath and Gabriel M. Vasquez (Thousand Oaks, Calif.: Sage Publications, Inc., 2001).

25. Ibid.

26. Bloomberg News Service, "Anti-Snore Aids Score Big in Super Bowl of Marketing," *Los Angeles Times*, August 20, 1996.

27. Moore and Kalupa, *Public Relations: Principles, Cases, and Problems*.

28. Bloomberg News Service, "Anti-Snore Aids Score Big in Super Bowl of Marketing."

29. Della De Lafuente, "Pros Breathe Life Into Firm's Profits," *Chicago Sun-Times*, January 26, 1996.

30. Melanie Wells, "Small Ad Budgets Don't Stop Super Bowl Play," *USA Today*, January 23, 1996.

31. Jennifer L. May, "Breathe Right 'Extra' to Help Consumers Sleep Better at Night," October 15, 2009, www.news-medical.net/news/20091015/Breathe-Right-Extra-to-help-consumers-sleep-better-at-night.aspx.

32. Moore and Kalupa, *Public Relations: Principles, Cases, and Problems*.

33. Jerry Lazar, "Foot-in-Mouth Disease," *Electronic Business* 26, no. 6 (2000).
34. Hanson.
35. David P. Bianco, ed., *PR News Casebook: 1,000 Public Relations Case Studies* (Potomac, Md.: Gale Research Inc., 1993).
36. Staff, "Craft—the Colophon Award," *PR Week*, October 27, 2000.
37. Hanson.
38. David E. Williams and Bolanle A. Olanieran, "Exxon's Decision-Making Flaws: The Hypervigilant Response to the *Valdez* Grounding," *Public Relations Review* 20, no. 1 (1994).
39. David McCormack, "Inside Marketing & PR: The Pulling Power of the 'Dark Side'," *The Guardian*, January 22, 2007.
40. Susannne Courtney, "Measuring PR," *Marketing Magazine*, October 30, 2000.
41. Hanson.
42. Judith VandeWater, "Companies Turn to Video News Releases," *St. Louis Post-Dispatch*, June 26, 1989.
43. Raymund Flandez, "Domino's Response Offers Lessons in Crisis Management," *Wall Street Journal,* April 20, 2009, blogs.wsj.com/independentstreet/2009/04/20/dominos-response-offers-lessons-in-crisis-management.
44. Lazar, "Foot-in-Mouth Disease."
45. Ibid.
46. William J. Small, "Exxon *Valdez*: How to Spend Billions and Still Get a Black Eye," *Public Relations Review* 17, no. 1 (1991).
47. Williams and Olanieran, "Exxon's Decision-Making Flaws: The Hypervigilant Response to the *Valdez* Grounding."
48. Wayne L. Pines, "Myths of Crisis Management," *Public Relations Quarterly* 45, no. 3 (2000).
49. Lazar, "Foot-in-Mouth Disease."
50. Alex Edge, "Yamaha Offers Buyback Option for 2006 R6 Owners," *Motorcycle Daily*, February 14, 2006, www.motorcycledaily.com/14february06_r6buyback.htm.
51. John Holusha, "Exxon's Public-Relations Problem," *New York Times*, April 21, 1989.
52. Dana James, "When Your Company Goes Code Blue," *Marketing News*, November 6, 2000.
53. Williams and Olanieran, "Exxon's Decision-Making Flaws: The Hypervigilant Response to the *Valdez* Grounding."
54. N. R. Kleinfield, "Tylenol's Rapid Comeback," *New York Times*, September 17, 1983.
55. Moore and Kalupa, *Public Relations: Principles, Cases, and Problems*.
56. Kleinfield, "Tylenol's Rapid Comeback."
57. Jeff & Marie Blyskal, *PR: How the Public Relations Industry Writes the News* (New York: Morrow, 1985).
58. Ibid.; Kleinfield, "Tylenol's Rapid Comeback."
59. Small, "Exxon *Valdez*: How to Spend Billions and Still Get a Black Eye."
60. Holusha, "Exxon's Public-Relations Problem."
61. Williams and Olanieran, "Exxon's Decision-Making Flaws: The Hypervigilant Response to the Valdez Grounding."
62. Holusha, "Exxon's Public-Relations Problem"; Small, "Exxon *Valdez*: How to Spend Billions and Still Get a Black Eye."
63. Williams and Olanieran, "Exxon's Decision-Making Flaws: The Hypervigilant Response to the *Valdez* Grounding."
64. Small, "Exxon *Valdez:* How to Spend Billions and Still Get a Black Eye."
65. Jonathan Bernstein, "Crisis Manager University: My Top 5 Internet-Related Crisis Management Tips"; Crisis Manager: The Internet Newsletter about Crisis Management, www.bernsteincrisismanagement.com/nl/crisismgr070101.html.
66. Carole M. Howard, "Technology and Tabloids: How the New Media World Is Changing Our Jobs," *Public Relations Quarterly* 45, no. 1 (2000).
67. Jonathan Bernstein, "Who Are These Bloggers, and Why Are They Saying Those Terrible Things?" *Associations Now*, October 2006.
68. Stephanie Clifford, "Video Prank at Domino's Taints Brand," *New York Times*, April 16, 2009.
69. Emily Bryson York, "What Domino's Did Right—and Wrong—in Squelching Hubbub over YouTube Video; Pizza Purveyor Faulted for Waiting to Respond but Did Well in the End," *Advertising Age*, April 20, 2009.

70. Ibid.

71. Flandez, "Domino's Response Offers Lessons in Crisis Management."

72. Alice Gomstyn, "Brown's, Domino's and Beyond: Business Felled by Crime, Scandal," October 1, 2009, abcnews.go.com/Business/browns-chicken-dominos-crimes-hurt-stores-restaurants/story?id=8706183.

73. Melissa Allison, "Corporations Seek to Clean Up Online Rumors," *Seattle Times*, March 4, 2007.

74. David L. Altheide and Robert P. Snow, *Media Worlds in the Postjournalism Era* (Hawthorne, N.Y.: Aldine De Gruyter, 1991).

75. Blyskal, *PR: How the Public Relations Industry Writes the News.*

76. Dana Harris, "Flack Pack Hits Burnout Track," *Variety*, April 17–23, 2000.

77. Moore and Kalupa, *Public Relations: Principles, Cases, and Problems.*

78. Jeffrey H. Birnbaum, "The Road to Riches Is Called K Street," *Washington Post*, June 22, 2005.

79. Betsy Rothstein, "Capital Living: The Fine Art of Flacking," *The Hill*, February 22, 2006.

80. Ibid.

81. Betsy Rothstein, "Capital Living: Doing the Write Thing," *The Hill*, January 3, 2007.

82. Sarah Lyall, "Trying to Know a Queen (Right Down to the Tupperware)," *New York Times*, September 24, 2006.

83. Moore and Kalupa, *Public Relations: Principles, Cases, and Problems.*

84. Randy Sumpter and James Tankard, "The Spin Doctor: An Alternative View of Public Relations," *Public Relations Review* 20, no. 1 (1994).

85. Ibid.

86. Daniel Zwerdling, "Fast-Food Deal a Big Win for Small Migrants' Group," June 16, 2005, www.npr.org/templates/story/story.php?storyId=4706271.

87. David Halberstam, "And Now, Live From Little Rock," *Newsweek*, September 29, 1997.

88. Stephen B. Oates, *Let the Trumpet Sound* (New York: Harper & Row, 1982).

89. Ibid.

90. Martin Luther King Jr., *The Autobiography of Martin Luther King Jr.*, ed. Clayborne Carson (New York: Warner Books, 1998); Steven Kasher, *The Civil Rights Movement: A Photographic History, 1954–68* (New York: Abbeville Press, 1996).

CHAPTER 13
**MEDIA LAW**

1. Matt Schudel, "A Local Life: Barbara A. Ringer, 83; Force Behind New Copyright Law," *Washington Post*, April 26, 2009.

2. Ibid.

3. Stephen Miller, "She Helped Put Her Stamp on Copyright Law," *Wall Street Journal*, May 9, 2009.

4. Judith Nierman, "Barbara Ringer, 9th Register of Copyrights, Dies," *Copyright Notices*, April 2009.

5. Schudel, "A Local Life: Barbara A. Ringer, 83; Force Behind New Copyright Law."

6. Miller, "She Helped Put Her Stamp on Copyright Law."

7. Matt Schudel, "Barbara Ringer's Untold Story," *Washington Post*, April 29, 2009, voices.washingtonpost.com/postmortem/2009/04/barbara_ringers_untold_story.html.

8. Schudel, "A Local Life: Barbara A. Ringer, 83; Force Behind New Copyright Law"; Nierman, "Barbara Ringer, 9th Register of Copyrights, Dies."

9. Nierman, "Barbara Ringer, 9th Register of Copyrights, Dies."

10. Schudel, "A Local Life: Barbara A. Ringer, 83; Force Behind New Copyright Law."

11. Fred H. Cate, *Privacy in the Information Age* (Washington, D.C.: Brookings Institution, 1997).

12. Ibid.

13. Legal Information Institute, "Legal Information Institute," Cornell Law School, www.law.cornell.edu.

14. Kenneth Creech, *Electronic Media Law and Regulation*, 3rd ed. (Boston: Focal Press, 2000).

15. Ben H. Bagdikian, "Not Just Another Business," University of Arizona, journalism.arizona.edu/zenger/bagdikian.html.

16. Herbert N. Foerstel, *Banned in the Media* (Westport, Conn.: Greenwood Press, 1998).

17. Creech, *Electronic Media Law and Regulation*; Foerstel, *Banned in the Media.*

18. Don R. Pember and Clay Calvert, *Mass Media Law*, 2005–2006 ed. (New York: McGraw-Hill, 2005).

19. David L. Jr. Hudson, "Libraries & First Amendment," First Amendment Center, www.first
    amendmentcenter.org//speech/libraries/topic.aspx?topic=patriot_act&SearchString=patriot_act.
20. Ibid.
21. Ibid.
22. Ibid.
23. Brian Ross and Richard Esposito, "Federal Source to ABC News: We Know Who You're Calling,"
    March 15, 2006, blogs.abcnews.com/theblotter/2006/05/federal_source_.html.
24. Patrick W. Gavin, "ABC's Ross: Anti-Terrorism Tools Turned on Journos," May 17, 2006, www
    .mediabistro.com/fishbowlDC/sort_of_serious_stuff/abcs_ross_antiterrorism_tools_turned_on_
    journos_37034.asp.
25. Associated Press, "Feds Drop Demand for Conn. Library Records," June 27, 2006, www.first
    amendmentcenter.org//news.aspx?id=17073&SearchString=patriot_act.
26. Rodney A. Smolla, *Law of Defamation* (New York: Clark Boardman Company, 1988).
27. Barbara Dill, *The Journalist's Handbook on Libel and Privacy* (New York: Free Press, 1986).
28. 376 U.S. 254 (1964).
29. Dill, *The Journalist's Handbook on Libel and Privacy*.
30. W. Wat Hopkins, *Actual Malice: Twenty-Five Years after* Times v. Sullivan (New York: Praeger,
    1989).
31. Ibid.
32. Ibid.
33. Ibid.
34. 418 U.S. 323 (1974).
35. Dill, *The Journalist's Handbook on Libel and Privacy*.
36. Cate, *Privacy in the Information Age*.
37. Deckle McLean, *Privacy and Its Invasion* (Westport, Conn.: Praeger Publishers, 1995).
38. Dill, *The Journalist's Handbook on Libel and Privacy*.
39. Ibid.
40. Pember and Calvert, *Mass Media Law*.
41. Ibid.
42. Oscar Dixon, "Jordan Reclaims Richest Athlete Title," *USA Today*, December 1, 1997.
43. Associated Press, "Jennifer Aniston Settles Lawsuit with 'Invasive' Photographer," September 2,
    2006, www.foxnews.com/story/0,2933,211903,00.html?sPage=fnc.entertainment/aniston; "Blogger
    Sued Over Topless Aniston Photo," February 21, 2007, abcnews.go.com/Entertainment/wireStory?
    id=2893926.
44. "Aniston Warns Over Topless Photos," December 5, 2005, www.thesmokinggun.com/archive/
    1205051aniston1.html.
45. Dionne Searcey, "A New California Law Places Paparazzi Under the Spotlight," *Wall Street
    Journal*, October 29, 2009.
46. Christopher Dickey, Mark Hosenball, and Geoffrey Cowley, "A Needless Tragedy," *Newsweek*,
    September 22, 1997.
47. Larysa Pyk, "Legislative Update: Putting the Brakes on Paparazzi," *Journal of Art and Enter-
    tainment Law* 187, no. 9 (1998).
48. Associated Press, "Magazine Fined Over Picture of Diana and Dodi," *Ottawa Citizen*, April 29,
    1998.
49. Ester Laushway, "What Price Privacy?" *Europe*, October 1997.
50. "Whose Life Is It Anyway?" *Economist*, March 9, 2002.
51. Jane Kirtley, "Privacy for Sale," *American Journalism Review*, March 2001.
52. Steve Doughty and Richard Simpson, "OK! Magazine Wins Appeal Over Zeta-Jones Wedding
    Photos—But at a Price," *Daily Mail*, May 3, 2007.
53. Dan Tench, "When Uncertainty Takes Precedence: Elton John's Failed Injunction Against a
    Newspaper Printing a Photo of Him in the Street Highlights Our Hopelessly Confused Privacy
    Law," *Guardian*, July 24, 2006, 10.
54. Laushway, "What Price Privacy?"
55. Matthew D. Bunker, *Justice and the Media: Reconciling Fair Trials and a Free Press* (Mahwah, N.J.:
    Lawrence Erlbaum Associates, 1997).
56. Ibid.
57. 284 U.S. 333 (1966).

58. 284 U.S. 333 (1966); Kyle Niederpruem, "Big Trials Prompt Judges to Issue More Gag Orders," *Quill*, June 1997.

59. 752 F. Supp. 1032 (1990).

60. Bunker, *Justice and the Media: Reconciling Fair Trials and a Free Press*.

61. Steven Brill, "Cameras Belong in the Courtroom," *USA Today Magazine*, July 1996.

62. Joshua Sarner, "Comment: Justice, Take Two: The Continuing Debate over Cameras in the Courtroom," *Seton Hall Constitutional Journal* (2000).

63. "Cameras in the Courtroom," *Quill*, September 1999.

64. Bunker, *Justice and the Media: Reconciling Fair Trials and a Free Press*.

65. Elliot C. Rothenberg, *The Taming of the Press:* Cohen v. Cowles Media Company (Westport, Conn.: Praeger, 1999).

66. *Cohen v. Cowles Media Company,* 501 U.S. 663 (1991).

67. Lisa de Moraes, "With Appeals Court Ruling, ABC Won't Pay Food Lion's Share," *Washington Post*, October 21, 1999; Sue Anne Pressley, "Food Lion Challenges ABC's Newsgathering; Lawsuit Attacks Hidden Cameras," *Washington Post*, December 12, 1996; James C. Goodale, "Shooting the Messenger Isn't So Easy," *New York Law Journal*, December 3, 1999.

68. Goodale, "Shooting the Messenger." See also *Food Lion v. ABC,* 194 F. 3d 505 (4th Cir., 1999).

69. Bunker, *Justice and the Media*; Creech, *Electronic Media Law*; see also *Near v. Minnesota,* 283 U.S. 697 (1931).

70. Sanford J. Ungar, *The Papers and the Papers* (New York: E. P. Dutton, 1972).

71. Ibid.

72. Ben Bradlee, *A Good Life: Newspapering and Other Adventures* (New York: Simon & Schuster, 1995).

73. Ungar, *The Papers and the Papers*.

74. Ibid.

75. 403 U.S. 713 (1971).

76. Peter Schrag, *Test of Loyalty: Daniel Ellsberg and the Rituals of Secret Government* (New York: Simon & Schuster, 1974).

77. Francis Wilkinson, *Essential Liberty: First Amendment Battles for a Free Press* (New York: Columbia University Graduate School of Journalism, 1992).

78. Duncan Campbell, "'It's Time to Take Risks,'" *Guardian,* December 10, 2002, http://www.guardian.co.uk/books/2002/dec/10/biography.usa.

79. Foerstel, *Banned in the Media*.

80. Howard Morland, *The Secret That Exploded* (New York: Random House, 1981).

81. Foerstel, *Banned in the Media*.

82. 484 U.S. 260 (1988).

83. Ibid.

84. Mark Goodman, "Freedom of the Press Stops at the Schoolhouse Gate," *Nieman Reports*, Spring 2001.

85. Ibid.

86. Tara Bahrampour and Lori Aratani, "Teens' Bold Blogs Alarm Area Schools," *Washington Post,* January 17, 2006, A01.

87. Case argued before the Supreme Court, March 19, 2007; 551 U.S. 393 (2007).

88. Robert Barnes, "Justices to Hear Landmark Free-speech Case," *Washington Post,* March 13, 2007, A03; Charles Lane, "Court Backs School on Speech Curbs, *Washington Post,* June 26, 2007, A06.

89. Liz Harper, "First Amendment Understanding Lacking," February 7, 2005, www.pbs.org/newshour/extra/features/jan-june05/first_2-07.html.

90. Zachary M. Seward, "Shield Law: Definition of 'Journalist' Gets Professionalized," Nieman Foundation at Harvard University, September 23, 2009, www.niemanlab.org/2009/09/shield-law-definition-of-journalist-gets-professionalized/.

91. Casey Murray and Kirsten B. Mitchell, "Would a Shield Law Matter?" *The News Media and the Law* 30, no. 3 (2006): 4.

92. Ibid.; Howard Kurtz, "No More Miller Time," September 30, 2005, www.washingtonpost.com/wp-dyn/content/blog/2005/09/30/BL2005093000363.html.

93. Ina Fried and Declan McCullagh, "Apple Thwarted in Bid to Unmask Leaker," c|net News.com, May 26, 2006, news.com.com/Apple%20thwarted%20in%20bid%20to%20unmask%20leaker/2100-1047_3-6077547.html?tag=item.

94. Howard Kurtz, "Blogger Makes Deal, Is Released From Jail," *Washington Post,* April 4, 2007, C01.
95. Ibid.
96. Edward Donnerstein, Daniel Linz, and Steven Penrod, *The Question of Pornography* (New York: Free Press, 1987).
97. 354 U.S. 476 (1957).
98. U.S. Supreme Court, *"Samuel Roth, Petitioner v. United States of America, David S. Alberts, Appellant,"* Communications & the Law 21, no. 4 (1999).
99. Donnerstein, Linz, and Penrod, *The Question of Pornography.*
100. Ibid.
101. Franklin Mark Osanka and Sara Lee Johann, *Sourcebook on Pornography* (Lexington, Mass.: Lexington Books, 1989).
102. Rieko Mashima, "Problem of the Supreme Court's Obscenity Test Concerning Cyberporn," *The Computer Lawyer* 16, no. 11 (1999).
103. Timothy Egan, "Erotica Inc.—A Special Report; Technology Sent Wall Street Into Market for Pornography," *New York Times*, October 23, 2000.
104. Edward Rothstein, "The Owners of Culture vs. the Free Agents," *New York Times*, January 18, 2003.
105. Amy Harmon, "New Visibility for 1998 Copyright Protection Law, With Online Enthusiasts Confused and Frustrated," *New York Times*, August 13, 2001.
106. Minjeong Kim, "The Creative Commons and Copyright Protection in the Digital Era: Uses of Creative Commons Licenses," *Journal of Computer-Mediated Communication* 13, no. 1 (2007).
107. Creech, *Electronic Media Law and Regulation.*
108. Linda Harowitz, "Laying the Fairness Doctrine to Rest: Was the Doctrine's Elimination Really Fair?" *George Washington Law Review* 58, no. 994 (1990).
109. Creech, *Electronic Media Law and Regulation.*
110. Harowitz, "Laying the Fairness Doctrine to Rest: Was the Doctrine's Elimination Really Fair?"
111. Thomas Blaisdell Smith, "Reexamining the Reasonable Access and Equal Time Provisions of the Federal Communications Act," *Georgetown Law Journal* 74, no. 1491 (1986); Creech, *Electronic Media Law and Regulation*; Dan Fletcher, "The Fairness Doctrine," *Time*, February 20, 2009.
112. Creech, *Electronic Media Law and Regulation.*
113. Ibid.
114. Cecilia Kang, "FCC to Draft Net Neutrality Rules, Taking Step Toward Web Regulation," *Washington Post*, October 23, 2009.
115. Foerstel, *Banned in the Media.*
116. David L. Hudson Jr., "Indecency Online," November 17, 2006, www.firstamendmentcenter.org/speech/internet/topic.aspx?topic=indecency_online.

CHAPTER 14
**MEDIA ETHICS**

1. Richard Drew, text of speech delivered September 11, 2002, to the P.I. Reed School of Journalism, University of West Virginia; Kenny Irby, "Behind the Lens: Part 1," Poynter Institute, October 5, 2001; Jeff Young, interviews with Richard Drew and Richard Pyle, 2002.
2. Irby, "Behind the Lens: Part 1."
3. Ibid.
4. Young.
5. Tom Junod, "The Falling Man," *Esquire*, September 2003.
6. Drew.
7. Irby, "Behind the Lens: Part 1."
8. Mac Daniel, "America Prepares Aftermath of Attack/Images of Loss; Families Scan News Photos for Hope," *Boston Globe*, September 20, 2001.
9. Philip Patterson and Lee Wilkins, *Media Ethics, Issues and Cases* (New York: McGraw-Hill, 2002).
10. Doug Underwood, "Secularists or Modern Day Prophets? Journalists' Ethics and the Judeo-Christian Tradition," *Journal of Mass Media Ethics* 16, no. 1 (2001).
11. Franklin Foer, "The Wayward Critic," *New Republic*, May 15, 2000.
12. Larry Z. Leslie, *Mass Communication Ethics* (Boston: Houghton Mifflin, 2000).
13. Patterson and Wilkins, *Media Ethics, Issues and Cases.*
14. David L. Martinson, "Ethical Decision Making in Public Relations: What Would Aristotle Say?" *Public Relations Quarterly* 45, no. 3 (2000).

15. Jane B. Singer, "The Unforgiving Truth in the Unforgivable Photo," *Media Ethics*, Spring 2002.

16. Leslie, *Mass Communication Ethics*.

17. Patterson and Wilkins, *Media Ethics, Issues and Cases*.

18. Howard Berkes, Barbara Bradley Hagerty, and Jennifer Ludden, "NBC Defends Release of Va. Tech Gunman Video," April 19, 2007, www.npr.org/templates/story/story.php?storyId=9604204.

19. Leslie, *Mass Communication Ethics*.

20. Singer, "The Unforgiving Truth in the Unforgivable Photo."

21. Elizabeth Blanks Hindman, "Divergence of Duty: Differences in Legal and Ethical Responsibilities," *Journal of Mass Media Ethics* 14, no. 4 (1999).

22. Patterson and Wilkins, *Media Ethics, Issues and Cases*.

23. Irby, "Behind the Lens: Part 1."

24. Patterson and Wilkins, *Media Ethics, Issues and Cases*.

25. Sissela Bok, *Lying: Moral Choice in Public and Private Life* (New York: Pantheon Books, 1978).

26. Martinson, "Ethical Decision Making in Public Relations: What Would Aristotle Say?"

27. John C. Merrill, "Needed: A More Ethical Press," in *The Media and Morality*, ed. Robert M. Baird, William E. Loges, and Stuart E. Rosenbaum (Amherst, N.Y.: Prometheus Books, 1999).

28. Steven Brill, "Rewind: What Book Reviews Don't Review," *Brill's Content*, August 1999.

29. Paul Tullis and Lorne Manly, "Slipping Past the Fact Checkers: How Magazines Do and Do Not Check Their Stories," *Brill's Content*, July/August 1998.

30. Ann Reilly Dowd, "The Great Pretender: How a Writer Fooled His Readers," *Columbia Journalism Review*, July/August 1998.

31. "Shattered Glass," *Vanity Fair*, October 2007.

32. Tullis and Manly, "Slipping Past the Fact Checkers: How Magazines Do and Do Not Check Their Stories."

33. Dowd, "The Great Pretender: How a Writer Fooled His Readers."

34. Abigail Pogrebin and Rifka Rosewein, "Not the First Time," *Brill's Content*, September 1998.

35. "*Boston Globe* Columnist Resigns, Accused of Fabrications," June 19, 1998, www.cnn.com/US/9806/19/globe.columnist.resigns/index.html.

36. "Biography," www.mikebarnicle.com/biography.

37. "The Poetic Annex of Patricia Smith," www.wordwoman.ws.

38. Pogrebin and Rosewein, "Not the First Time."

39. John Caher, "Teen Model Loses Privacy Appeal," *National Law Journal*, March 6, 2000.

40. Katherine Rosman, "The Secret of Her Success," *Brill's Content*, November 1998.

41. Charles Davis and Stephanie Craft, "New Media Synergy: Emergence of Institutional Conflicts of Interest," *Journal of Mass Media Ethics* 15, no. 4 (2000).

42. Staci D. Kramer, "Another Newspaper Buys Into a Baseball Team," *Editor & Publisher*, January 6, 1996; Richard Sandomir, "New Owner to Improve Wrigley, and Maybe the Cubs," *New York Times*, October 31, 2009.

43. Lance Morrow, "Journalism After Diana," in *The Media and Morality*, ed. Robert M. Baird, William E. Loges, and Stuart E. Rosenbaum (Amherst, N.Y.: Prometheus Books, 1999).

44. Edna Buchanan, *The Corpse Had a Familiar Face* (New York: Charter Books, 1987).

45. William L. Hamilton, "Low Down; Repulsed, yet Watching All the Same," *New York Times*, December 3, 2006.

46. Jacqueline Sharkey, "The Diana Aftermath," in *The Media and Morality*, ed. Robert M. Baird, William E. Loges, and Stuart E. Rosenbaum (Amherst, N.Y.: Prometheus Books, 1999); Howard Kurtz, "Shakeup at ABC: Coverage of Tiger Woods," CNN.com, December 13, 2009, http://transcripts.cnn.com/TRANSCRIPTS/0912/13/rs.01.html.

47. Sharkey.

48. Ibid.

49. Editors, *Columbia Journalism Review*, "What Do We Do Now?" in *The Media and Morality*, ed. Robert M. Baird, William E. Loges, and Stuart E. Rosenbaum (Amherst, N.Y.: Prometheus Books, 1999).

50. Ibid.

51. Adam Goodheart, "Sleaze Journalism? It's an Old Story," in *The Media and Morality*, ed. Robert M. Baird, William E. Loges, and Stuart E. Rosenbaum (Amherst, N.Y.: Prometheus Books, 1999).

52. Ibid.

53. Neil Postman, *Amusing Ourselves to Death: Public Discourse in the Age of Show Business* (New York: Penguin Books, 1985).

54. Don Wycliff, "Getting Kicked Off Page 1," *Chicago Tribune*, February 7, 2002.
55. Ibid.
56. Tamara Jones and Ann Scott Tyson, "After 44 Hours, Hope Showed Its Cruel Side," *Washington Post*, January 5, 2006.
57. "Manchin at a Loss to Explain Rescue Miscommunication; Governor Says He Got Caught Up in Families' Celebration," *Charleston Daily Mail*, January 4, 2006.
58. Joe Strupp, "Local W.Va. Paper Says Skepticism Helped It Avoid Mining Story Goof," *Editor & Publisher*, January 4, 2006.
59. Ibid.
60. Vicki Smith, "Family Members Report 12 Trapped Miners Are Alive," *Charleston Gazette*, January 4, 2006.
61. Ralph Hanson, "Searching for a Miracle: Media Lessons From the West Virginia Mine Disaster," *Montana Journalism Review* (2006).
62. Kenny Irby, "When the Visual Reality Hurts," Poynter Institute, September 15, 2001, www .poynter.org/content/content_view.asp?id=6161.
63. "Asked to Do Something Unethical," www.sportsshooter.com/message_display.html?tid=28059.
64. Gil Klein, "Computer Graphics Now Allow Subtle Alteration of News Photos," *Christian Science Monitor*, August 1, 1985.
65. James R. Gaines, "To Our Readers," *Time*, July 4, 1994.
66. Chuck Strouse, "Listen up, McClatchy," *Miami New Times*, July 27, 2006.
67. Sanders LaMont, "Lending an Ear," Organization of News Ombudsmen, 1999, www.newsom budsmen.org/lamont4.html.
68. Andrew Alexander, "Welcome to the Omblog," *Washington Post*, May 4, 2009, voices .washingtonpost.com/ombudsman-blog/2009/05/welcome_to_the_omblog.html.
69. LaMont, "Lending an Ear."
70. Simon Dumenco, "Is the Newspaper Ombudsman More or Less Obsolete? Five Reasons Why Having a 'Public Editor' at the *Times* and Other Papers No Longer Makes Much Sense," *Advertising Age*, March 24, 2008.
71. Jay Black, Bob Steele, and Ralph Barney, *Doing Ethics in Journalism* (Birmingham, Ala.: EBSCO Media, 1993).
72. Alex S. Jones, "Facing Ethical Challenges: The Integrity/Judgment Grid," *Columbia Journalism Review*, November/December 1999.
73. Jeffrey L. Seglin, "Codes of Ethics: Why Writing Them Is Not Enough," *Media Ethics*, Spring 2002.
74. Robert Jackall and Janice M. Hirota, *Image Makers: Advertising, Public Relations, and the Ethos of Advocacy* (Chicago: University of Chicago Press, 2000).
75. Patterson and Wilkins, *Media Ethics, Issues and Cases*.
76. Rogier van Bakel, "Tall-Claims Court," *Christian Science Monitor*, February 14, 2000.
77. Bruce A. Silverglade, "FTC Oversight Still Needed," in *Advertising Age: The Principles of Advertising at Work*, ed. Esther Thorson (Lincolnwood, Ill.: NTC Business Books, 1989).
78. Van Bakel, "Tall-Claims Court."
79. Ibid.
80. Ibid.
81. Alexandra Marks, "A Backlash to Advertising in the Age of Anything Goes," *Christian Science Monitor*, February 22, 1999.
82. Suzanne Fields, "Calvin Klein Ads Again Use Kids and Sex to Sell," *Philadelphia Business Journal*, March 5, 1999.
83. Associated Press, "Inquiry Into Calvin Klein Ads Is Dropped," *New York Times*, November 16, 1995; Pat Sloan and Jennifer DeCoursey, "Klein's Risque Jean Ads Dodge Kiddie Porn Rap From the Feds," *Advertising Age*, November 20, 1995.
84. Kirk Davidson, "Calvin Klein Ads: Bad Ethics, Bad Business," *Marketing News*, November 6, 1995.
85. Marks, "A Backlash to Advertising in the Age of Anything Goes."
86. M. L. Stein, "Auto Dealers Banned From Boycotting Calif. Media Outlets," *Editor & Publisher*, April 19, 1995.
87. Heidi Staseson, "Dr. Laura's TV Show Facing U.S. Ad Boycott," *Marketing*, June 5, 2000.
88. Paul D. Colford, "Whose Copy Is It Anyway?" *Los Angeles Times*, June 5, 1997.
89. News Services, "Is *Esquire* Slip a Step Up for Mankind?" *Star Tribune*, July 12, 1997.
90. Dave Phillips, "Chrysler Drops Censorship Policy," *Detroit News*, October 14, 1997.

91. Carol Krol, "MPA Joins Editors to Limit Advertiser Interference," *Advertising Age*, September 29, 1997.

92. Jim Edwards, "Nicetv," *Brill's Content*, March 2001.

93. Valerie Kuklenski, "All in the Family; Advertisers Praise—and Fund—Shows for Everyone," *Daily News of Los Angeles*, December 7, 2006.

94. John C. Stauber and Sheldon Rampton, *Toxic Sludge Is Good for You: Lies, Damn Lies and the Public Relations Industry* (Monroe, Maine: Common Courage Press, 1995).

95. Ibid.; Susanne A. Roschwalb, "The Hill & Knowlton Cases: A Brief on the Controversy," *Public Relations Review* 20, no. 3 (1994).

96. Stauber and Rampton, *Toxic Sludge Is Good for You*.

97. Mary McGrory, "PR Ploy Exaggerated Case against Iraq," *St. Louis Post-Dispatch*, January 16, 1992.

98. Robert L. Koenig, "Testimony of Kuwaiti Envoy's Child Assailed," *St. Louis Post-Dispatch*, January 9, 1992.

99. Cornelius B. Pratt, "Hill & Knowlton's Two Ethical Dilemmas," *Public Relations Review* 20, no. 3 (1994).

100. Martinson, "Ethical Decision Making in Public Relations: What Would Aristotle Say?"

## CHAPTER 15
## GLOBAL MEDIA

1. Gaurav Mishra, "Social Media and Citizen Journalism in the 11/26 Mumbai Terror Attacks: A Case Study," November 28, 2008, www.gauravonomics.com/blog/social-media-citizen-journalism-in-the-1126-mumbai-terror-attacks-a-case-study.

2. Brooke Gladstone, "Detailed Coverage," On the Media, December 5, 2008, www.onthemedia.org/transcripts/2008/12/05/01.

3. Ibid.

4. Mishra, "Social Media and Citizen Journalism in the 11/26 Mumbai Terror Attacks: A Case Study."

5. Sam Dolnick, "Bloggers Provide Raw View of Mumbai Attacks," Associated Press, November 30, 2008, www.msnbc.msn.com/id/27984057.

6. Brooke Gladstone, "The Twitter Wire Service," On the Media, December 5, 2008, www.onthemedia.org/transcripts/2008/12/05/02.

7. Mishra, "Social Media and Citizen Journalism in the 11/26 Mumbai Terror Attacks: A Case Study."

8. Gladstone, "The Twitter Wire Service."

9. Gaurav Mishra, "The Digital News Lifecycle: Why Breaking News on Twitter Isn't News Anymore," January 19, 2009, www.gauravonomics.com/blog/tag/citizen-journalism.

10. Fred S. Siebert, Theodore Peterson, and Wilbur Schramm, *Four Theories of the Press* (Urbana: University of Illinois Press, 1956).

11. John C. Nerone, ed., *Last Rights: Revisiting Four Theories of the Press* (Urbana and Chicago: University of Illinois Press, 1995).

12. Denis McQuail, *McQuail's Mass Communication Theory*, 5th ed. (London: Sage Publications, 2005).

13. "Censorship Has Many Faces," *World Press Review*, April 1997.

14. Mark Fitzgerald, "Welcome to B.A., Y'all," *Editor & Publisher*, September 3, 2001.

15. Nerone, ed., *Last Rights: Revisiting Four Theories of the Press*.

16. Siebert, Peterson, and Schramm, *Four Theories of the Press*.

17. Nerone, ed., *Last Rights: Revisiting Four Theories of the Press*.

18. Siebert, Peterson, and Schramm, *Four Theories of the Press*.

19. Nerone, ed., *Last Rights: Revisiting Four Theories of the Press*.

20. Siebert, Peterson, and Schramm, *Four Theories of the Press*.

21. Nerone, ed., *Last Rights: Revisiting Four Theories of the Press*.

22. Siebert, Peterson, and Schramm, *Four Theories of the Press*.

23. Doris Graber, *Mass Media and American Politics*, 7th ed. (Washington, D.C.: CQ Press, 2006).

24. Nerone, ed., *Last Rights: Revisiting Four Theories of the Press*.

25. McQuail, *McQuail's Mass Communication Theory*.

26. Bob Garfield, "Pulling the Plug," On the Media, May 18, 2007, onthemedia.org/transcripts/2007/05/18/05.

27. Thomas Standage, *The Victorian Internet* (New York: Berkley Books, 1998).

28. Alan Wells, "Introduction," in *World Broadcasting: A Comparative View*, ed. Alan Wells (Norwood, N.J.: Ablex Publishing, 1996).

29. Rowland Lorimer and Mike Gasher, *Mass Communication in Canada*, 5th ed. (Don Mills, Ontario: Oxford University Press, 2004).

30. Ibid.

31. Bob Garfield, "God Is Great (Funny, Too)," On the Media, May 18, 2007, onthemedia.org/transcripts/2007/05/18/08.

32. Ibid.

33. Lorimer and Gasher, *Mass Communication in Canada*.

34. Ibid.

35. Wells, "Introduction."

36. Ibid.

37. Kevin Williams, *European Media Studies* (London: Hodder Arnold, 2005).

38. Graber, *Mass Media and American Politics*.

39. Williams, *European Media Studies*.

40. Flemming Rose, "Why I Published Those Cartoons," *Washington Post*, February 19, 2006.

41. Daryl Cagle, "Cagle's Web Log!," Daryl Cagle's Professional Cartoonists Index, cagle.msnbc.com/news/BLOG/Feb2006.asp.

42. Philip Kennicott, "Clash Over Cartoons Is a Caricature of Civilization," *Washington Post*, February 4, 2006.

43. Ibid.

44. William Powers, " 'Toon Terrific," *National Journal*, February 10, 2006.

45. Angela Charlton, "Depictions Put Press Freedoms to the Test," *Star-Ledger*, February 7, 2006.

46. Staff, "Forms of Intolerance," *Boston Globe*, February 4, 2006.

47. Donnalyn Pompper, "Latin America and the Caribbean," in *World Broadcasting: A Comparative View*, ed. Alan Wells (Norwood, N.J.: Ablex Publishing, 1996).

48. Thomas L. McPhail, *Global Communication: Theories, Stakeholders, and Trends* (Malden, Mass.: Blackwell Publishing, 2006).

49. Nicole Gaouette, "Mideast's Clash of Images," *Christian Science Monitor*, October 21, 2000.

50. Marvin Kalb and Jerome Socolovsky, "The Emboldened Arab Press," *Harvard International Journal of Press/Politics* 4, no. 3 (1999).

51. Ibid.

52. Kai Hafez, ed., *Mass Media, Politics, and Society in the Middle East* (Cresskill, N.J.: Hampton Press, 2001).

53. Ibid.

54. Fred Strickert, "War on the Web," *Christian Century*, May 16, 2001.

55. Ibid.

56. I would like to thank Charley Reed, a communications graduate student at University of Nebraska at Omaha, for his research and work on the new media coverage of the Iranian protests section of this chapter.

57. Ali Arouzi, "Iran to Media: No Cameras Allowed," June 16, 2009, worldblog.msnbc.msn.com/archive/2009/06/16/1967136.aspx; Brian Stelter, "Journalism Rules Are Bent in News Coverage from Iran," *New York Times*, June 29, 2009; Brian Stelter, "In Coverage of Iran, Amateurs Take the Lead," *New York Times*, June 17, 2009, mediadecoder.blogs.nytimes.com/2009/06/17/in-coverage-of-iran-amateurs-take-the-lead; Mishra, "The Digital News Lifecycle: Why Breaking News on Twitter Isn't News Anymore."

58. Hussein Y. Amin, "The Middle East and North Africa," in *World Broadcasting: A Comparative View*, ed. Alan Wells (Norwood, N.J.: Ablex Publishing, 1996).

59. Khalid Marghalani and Philip Palmgreen, "Direct Broadcast Satellite Television—Saudi Arabia," *Journal of Broadcasting & Electronic Media* 42, no. 3 (1998).

60. Magali Rheault, "International Television Receives High Marks in Saudi Arabia," October 11, 2007, www.gallup.com/poll/101737/international-television-receives-high-marks-saudi-arabia.aspx.

61. Marghalani and Palmgreen, "Direct Broadcast Satellite Television—Saudi Arabia."

62. Peter Feuiherade, "Analysis: Politics Affect Funding of Arab Satellite TV Stations," *BBC Monitoring International Reports* (2007).

63. Christophe Ayad, "Middle East Media Pluralism via Satellite," *UNESCO Courier*, January 2000.

64. Isabel Hilton, " 'Al-Jazeera': And Now, the Other News," *New York Times*, March 6, 2005.

65. Brooke Gladstone, "Al-Nielsens," On the Media, December 16, 2005, http://www.onthemedia.org/yore/transcripts/transcripts_121605_neilson.html.
66. Mark Memmott, "Former Marine in Media Glare as He Joins Al-Jazeera," *USA Today*, September 28, 2005.
67. Hilton, "'Al-Jazeera': And Now, the Other News."
68. Tawana Kupe, "New Forms of Cultural Identity in an African Society," *Innovation: The European Journal of Social Science* 8, no. 4 (1995).
69. Ibid.
70. Ibid.
71. Osabuohien P. Amienyi and Gerard Igyor, "Sub-Saharan Africa," *in World Broadcasting: A Comparative View*, ed. Alan Wells (Norwood, N.J.: Ablex Publishing, 1996).
72. Jean Huteau, "Media Self-Control, the South's New Option," *UNESCO Courier*, April 2000.
73. Amienyi and Igyor, "Sub-Saharan Africa."
74. Richard Harrington, "'World Beat' Rattles Pop Music Scene," *Toronto Star*, June 18, 1988.
75. Jim Miller, "Simon's Spirit of Soweto," *Newsweek*, November 17, 1986.
76. Bob Young, "Bongo Mafffin Sets Message to Dance Beat," *Boston Herald*, August 16, 2002.
77. Miller, "Simon's Spirit of Soweto."
78. Harrington, "'World Beat' Rattles Pop Music Scene."
79. Janis E. Overlock, "The Former Soviet Union and Eastern Europe," *in World Broadcasting: A Comparative View*, ed. Alan Wells (Norwood, N.J.: Ablex Publishing, 1996).
80. Ibid.
81. Peter Baker and Susan B. Glasser, "Station Break," *New Republic*, April 23, 2001.
82. Mick Paton Walsh, "The Last Stand for Russia's Free Press," *The Guardian*, April 11, 2005.
83. Beth Knobel, "Boris Yeltsin," *Harvard International Journal of Press/Politics* 3, no. 4 (1998).
84. Hedwig de Smaele, "The Applicability of Western Media Models on the Russian Media System," *European Journal of Communication* 14, no. 2 (1999).
85. Hsiang-Wen Hsiao, "Asia," in *World Broadcasting: A Comparative View*, ed. Alan Wells (Norwood, N.J.: Ablex Publishing, 1996).
86. Uday Sahay, ed., *Making News: Handbook of Media in Contemporary India* (New Delhi: Oxford University Press, 2006).
87. Ibid.
88. Kenneth C. Petress, "China," in *World Broadcasting: A Comparative View*, ed. Alan Wells (Norwood, N.J.: Ablex Publishing, 1996).
89. Central Intelligence Agency, "The Chinese Media: More Autonomous and Diverse—Within Limits," https://www.cia.gov/library.
90. Ibid.
91. Sarah Lacy, "Tudou: A Push Towards Mobile Video and Profits," November 7, 2009, www.washingtonpost.com/wp-dyn/content/article/2009/11/08/AR2009110801808.html.
92. Hiroshi Tokinoya, "Japan," in *World Broadcasting: A Comparative View*, ed. Alan Wells (Norwood, N.J.: Ablex Publishing, 1996).
93. Douglas Wolk, "Manga, Anime Invade the U.S.," *Publishers Weekly*, March 12, 2001.
94. Nicole Gaouette, "Get Your Manga Here," *Christian Science Monitor*, January 8, 1999.
95. Milton Mayfield et al., "Manga and the Pirates: Unlikely Allies for Strategic Growth," *Advanced Management Journal* 65, no. 3 (2000).
96. Ibid.
97. Calvin Reid, "Asian Comics Delight U.S. Readers," *Publishers Weekly*, December 23, 2002.
98. Committee to Protect Journalists, "42 Journalists Killed in 2008/Motive Confirmed," 2009, cpj.org/killed/2008.
99. Committee to Protect Journalists, "In Iraq, Journalist Deaths Spike to Record in 2006," December 20, 2006, cpj.org/reports/2006/12/killed-06.php.
100. "ABC News' Bob Woodruff and Doug Vogt Show Improvement," January 30, 2006, abcnews.go.com/WNT/IraqCoverage/story?id=1556157&page=1.
101. Howard Kurtz, "Mission Impossible," August 28, 2006, www.washingtonpost.com/wp-dyn/content/blog/2006/08/28/BL2006082800239.html.
102. Ken Auletta, The *Highwaymen* (San Diego: Harcourt Brace, 1998).
103. Ibid.

# Glossary

**above the fold**: A term used to refer to a prominent story; it comes from placement of a news story in a broadsheet newspaper above the fold in the middle of the front page.

**actual malice**: A reckless disregard for the truth or falsity of a published account; this became the standard for libel plaintiffs who were public figures or public officials after the Supreme Court's decision in *New York Times v. Sullivan*.

**advertising**: Defined by the American Marketing Association as "any paid form of non-personal communication about an organization, product, service, or idea by an identified sponsor."

**advertorials**: Advertising materials in magazines designed to look like editorial content rather than paid advertising.

**advocacy ads**: Advertising designed to promote a particular point of view rather than a product or service. Can be sponsored by a government, corporation, trade association, or nonprofit organization.

**agenda-setting theory**: A theory of media effects that says that the media don't tell the public what to think but rather what to think about—thus the terms of public discourse are set by what is covered in the media.

**aggregator site**: An organizing Web site that provides surfers with easy access to e-mail, news, online stores, and many other sites.

**Alien and Sedition Acts**: Laws passed in 1798 that made it a crime to criticize the government of the United States.

**Al Jazeera**: The largest and most viewed Arabic-language satellite news channel. It is run out of the country of Qatar and has a regular audience of 40 million viewers.

**alphabets**: A form of writing in which letters represent individual sounds. Sound-based alphabet writing allows any word to be written using only a few dozen unique symbols.

**alternative papers**: Weekly newspapers that serve specialized audiences ranging from racial minorities, to gays and lesbians, to young people.

**American Society of Composers, Authors and Publishers (ASCAP)**: The original organization that collected royalties on musical recordings, performances, publications, and airplay.

**analog recording**: An electromechanical method of recording in which a sound is translated into analogous electrical signals that are then applied to a recording medium. Early analog recording media included acetate or vinyl discs and magnetic tape.

**ancillary, or secondary, markets**: Movie revenue sources other than the domestic box office. These include foreign box office, video rights, and television rights, as well as tie-ins and product placements.

**anonymous audience**: An audience the sender does not personally know. These are not anonymous, isolated people who have no connection to anyone else; they simply are anonymous in their audience status.

**ARPAnet**: The Advanced Research Projects Agency Network; the first nationwide computer network, which would become the first major component of the Internet.

**authoritarian theory**: A theory of appropriate press behavior that says the role of the press is to be a servant of the government, not a servant of the citizenry.

*Bay Psalm Book*: The first book published in North America by the Puritans in the Massachusetts Bay Colony. The book went through more than fifty editions and stayed in print for 125 years.

**Big Four networks**: The broadcast landscape we know today: the Big Three networks plus the Fox Network.

**the big idea**: The goal of every advertising campaign—an advertising concept that will grab people's attention and make them take notice, remember, and take action.

**Big Three networks**: The original television broadcast networks: NBC, CBS, and ABC.

**blacklist**: A group of people banned from working in the movie industry in the late 1940s and 1950s because they were suspected of being communists or communist sympathizers. Some of them, such as a few screenwriters, were able to work under assumed names, but others never worked again in the industry.

**block bookings**: Requiring a theater owner to take a whole series of movies in order to get a few desirable, headliner films. This system was eventually found to violate antitrust laws.

**blockbuster era**: A period from the late 1970s to the present day when movie studios make relatively expensive movies that have a large, predefined audience. These movies, usually chock full of special effects, are packaged with cable deals and marketing tie-ins, and can be extremely lucrative if they are able to attract large, repeat audiences.

**bloggers**: People who post their thoughts, typically with the most recent posts at the top of the page, on a regularly updated Web site.

**brand image**: The image attached to a brand and the associated product that gives the product a personality or identity that makes it stand out from similar products and stick in the mind of the consumer.

**brand name**: A word or phrase attached to prepackaged consumer goods so that they can be better promoted to the general public through advertising and so that consumers can distinguish a given product from the competition.

**breaking news**: An ongoing news story that requires frequent updating.

**bricks-and-mortar stores**: Bricks-and-mortar stores are those that have a physical presence at which you can shop.

**British invasion**: The British take on classic American rock 'n' roll, blues, and R&B transformed rock 'n' roll and became internationally popular in the 1960s with groups such as the Beatles and, later, the Rolling Stones and the Who.

**broadband networks**: High-speed channels for transmitting multimedia content into the home via cable or wireless connections.

**broadband service**: A high-speed continuous connection to the Internet using a cable modem from a cable television provider or a digital subscriber line from a phone company. Broadband service is also available in many offices through ethernet lines. Broadband connections are typically ten or more times faster than dial-up services using a modem.

**Broadcast Music, Inc. (BMI)**: A competitor of ASCAP that has generally licensed new composers and artists who had not been represented by ASCAP, including a lot of what was known as "minority music"—including blues, country, Latin, and unpublished jazz compositions.

**broadsheet newspapers**: Standard-sized newspapers, which are generally 17 by 22 inches.

**business-to-business (trade) ads**: Advertising that promotes products and services directly to other businesses rather than to the general consumer market.

**categorical imperative**: Kant's idea of a moral obligation that we should act in a way in which we would be willing to have everyone else act; also known as the principle of universality.

**chains**: Corporations that control a significant number of newspapers and other media outlets.

**channel**: The medium used to transmit the encoded message.

**citizen journalism**: Journalism created by people other than professional journalists, often distributed over the Internet.

**clutter**: The large number of commercials, advertising, and other nonprogramming messages and interruptions that compete for consumer attention on radio and television, and now also on the Internet.

**communication**: How we socially interact at a number of levels through messages.

**communist theory**: A theory of appropriate press behavior that says the press is to be run by the government to serve the government's own needs.

**community antenna television (CATV)**: An early form of cable television used to distribute broadcast channels in communities with poor television reception.

**community press**: Weekly and daily newspapers serving individual communities or suburbs instead of an entire metropolitan area.

**compact disc (CD)**: A digital recording medium that came into common use in the early 1980s. CDs can hold approximately seventy minutes of digitally recorded music.

**competitive model**: A model of the effects of a political campaign that looks at the campaign as a competition for the hearts and minds of voters.

**concept album**: An album by a solo artist or group that contains related songs on a common theme or even a story, rather than a collection of unrelated hits or covers.

**consumer magazines**: Publications targeting an audience of like-minded consumers.

**cookies**: Tiny files Web sites create to identify visitors and potentially track their actions on the site and the Web.

**correlation**: The process of selecting, evaluating, and interpreting events to give structure to the news. The media assist the process of correlation by persuasive communication through editorials, commentary, advertising, and propaganda, and by providing cues that indicate the importance of each news item.

**country music**: Originally referred to as hillbilly or "old-timey" music, this genre evolved out of Irish and Scottish folk music, Mississippi blues, and Christian gospel music, and grew in the 1950s and 1960s with the so-called Nashville sound.

**coverlines**: Teaser headlines on magazine covers used to shock, intrigue, or titillate potential buyers.

**covers**: Songs recorded (or covered) by someone other than the original artist. In the 1950s it was common for white musicians to cover songs originally played by black artists, but now artists commonly cover all genres of music.

**CPM**: Cost per thousand exposures to the target audience—a figure used in media planning evaluation.

**crisis**: Any situation that is perceived by the public as being damaging to the reputation or image of an organization. Not all problems develop into crises, but once a situation develops into a crisis, it can be damaging to an organization's reputation even if information behind the crisis is false.

**cultivation analysis**: An approach to analyzing the effects of television viewing that argues that watching significant amounts of television alters the way an individual views the nature of the surrounding world.

**decoding**: The process of translating a signal from a mass medium into a form that the receiver can understand and then interpreting the meaning of the message itself.

**demographics**: The study of audience members' gender, race, ethnic background, income, education, age, educational attainment, and the like; a method typically used to analyze potential markets for products and programs.

**development theory**: A theory of appropriate press behavior that states that developing nations may need to implement press controls in order to promote industry, national identity, and partnerships with neighboring nations.

**digital recording**: A method of recording sound—for example, that used to create CDs—that involves storing music in a computer-readable format known as binary information.

**dime novels**: Inexpensive paperback books that sold (despite their name) for as little as five cents and were especially popular during the Civil War era.

**direct action message**: An advertising message designed to get consumers to go to a particular place to do something specific, such as purchasing a product, obtaining a service, or engaging in a behavior.

**direct broadcast satellite (DBS)**: A low-earth-orbit satellite that provides television programming via a small, pizza-sized satellite antenna; DBS is a competitor to cable TV.

**disco**: The name of the heavily produced techno club dance music of the 1970s, which grew out of the urban gay male subculture, with significant black and Latino influences. In many ways, disco defined the look and feel of 1970s pop culture, fashion, and film.

**domestic novels**: Novels written in the nineteenth century by and for women that told the story of women who overcame tremendous problems to end up in prosperous middle-class homes.

**drive time**: The morning and afternoon commute in urban areas; the captive audience makes this a popular time to advertise on radio.

**e-book reader**: A portable device for viewing, and sometimes selling, electronic books and other texts. Among the most popular are the Amazon Kindle and the Sony eReader.

**economy of abundance**: An economy in which there are as many or more goods available as people who want to or have the means to buy them.

**electronic mail (e-mail)**: A message sent from one computer user to another across a network.

**encoding**: The process of turning the sender's ideas into a message and preparing the message for transmission.

**engineering consent**: The application of the principles of psychology and motivation to influencing public opinion and creating public support for a particular position.

**entertainment**: Media communication intended primarily to amuse the audience.

**equal time provision**: An FCC policy that requires broadcast stations to make equivalent amounts of broadcast time available to all candidates running for public office.

**ethics**: A rational way of deciding what is good for individuals or society. Ethics provide a way to choose between competing moral principles and help people decide where there is a clear-cut right or wrong answer.

**fairness doctrine**: A former FCC policy that required television stations to "afford reasonable opportunity for the discussion of conflicting views on issues of public importance."

**false light**: Invasion of privacy in which a journalist publishes untrue statements that alter a person's public image in a way that he or she cannot control.

**feature-length film**: A theatrical movie that runs more than one hour.

**Federal Communications Commission (FCC)**: The federal agency charged with regulating telecommunications, including radio and television broadcasting.

**font**: All the characters of a typeface in a particular size and style. The term *font* is typically used interchangeably today with the word *typeface*.

**format radio**: A style of radio programming designed to appeal to a narrow, specific audience. Popular formats include country, contemporary hits, all talk, all sports, and oldies.

**45-rpm disc**: The record format developed in the late 1940s by RCA. It had high-quality sound but held only about four minutes of music on a side. It was the ideal format for marketing popular hit songs to teenagers, though.

**geographics**: The study of where people live; a method typically used to analyze potential markets for products and programs.

**girl group**: A musical group composed of several women singers who harmonize together. Groups such as the Shirelles, the Ronettes, and the Shangri-Las, featuring female harmonies and high production values, were especially popular in the late 1950s and early 1960s.

**golden age of radio**: A period from the late 1920s until the 1940s, during which radio was the dominant medium for home entertainment.

**golden mean**: Aristotle's notion that ethical behavior comes from hitting a balance, a "just-right point between excess and defect."

**gramophone**: A machine invented by Emile Berliner that could play prerecorded sound on flat discs rather than cylinders.

**group communication**: Communication in which one person is communicating with an audience of two or more people. The roles of communicator and audience can be changing constantly.

**hacker ethic**: A set of values from the early days of interactive computing that holds that users should have absolute control over their computer systems and free access to all information contained on those computers. The hacker ethic shaped much of the development of the Internet.

**halftone**: An image produced by a process in which photographs are broken down into a series of dots that appear in shades of gray on the printed page.

**HD radio**: Sometimes also referred to as high-definition radio, this technology provides listeners with CD-quality sound and the choice of multiple channels of programming but is not yet commonly available in mass-market outlets nor as standard equipment in cars.

**heterogeneous audience**: An audience made up of a mix of people who differ in age, sex, income, education, ethnicity, race, religion, and other characteristics.

**high-definition television (HDTV)**: A standard for high-quality digital broadcasting that features a high-resolution picture, wide-screen format, and enhanced sound.

**high fidelity (hi-fi)**: A combination of technologies that allowed recordings to reproduce music more accurately with higher high notes and deeper bass than was possible with previous recording technologies.

**Hollywood Ten**: A group of ten writers and directors who refused to testify before the House Un-American Activities Committee about their political activities. They were among the first people in Hollywood to be blacklisted.

**House Un-American Activities Committee**: The congressional committee, chaired by Parnell Thomas, that held hearings on the influence of communism on Hollywood in 1947. These activities mirrored a wider effort to root out suspected communists in all walks of American life.

**hypertext**: Material in a format containing links that allow the reader to move easily from one section to another and from document to document. The most commonly used hypertext documents are Web pages.

**hypertext markup language (HTML)**: The programming language used to create and format Web pages.

**hypertext transfer protocol (http)**: A method of sending text, graphics, or anything else over the Internet from a server to a Web browser.

**ideograph**: An abstract symbol that stands for a word or phrase. The written forms of the Chinese, Korean, and Japanese languages make use of ideographs.

**indirect action message**: An advertising message designed to build the image of and demand for a product, without specifically urging that a particular action be taken at a particular time and place.

**industrialization**: The movement from work done by hand using muscle or water power in small shops to mass production of goods in factories that used energy sources such as steam power or electricity. It was part of the modernization process.

**instant messaging (IM)**: E-mail systems that allow two or more users to chat with one another in real time, hold virtual meetings that span multiple cities or even countries, and keep track of which of their "buddies" are currently logged on to the system.

**integrated marketing communication**: An overall communication strategy for reaching key audiences using advertising, public relations, sales promotion, and interactive media.

**Internet**: "A diverse set of independent networks, interlinked to provide its users with the appearance of a single, uniform network"; the Internet is a mass medium like no other, incorporating elements of interpersonal, group, and mass communications.

**interpersonal communication**: Communication, either intentional or accidental, between two people. It can be verbal or nonverbal.

**intranets**: Computer networks designed to communicate with people within an organization. They are used to improve two-way internal communication and contain tools that allow for direct feedback. They are a tool for communicating with internal publics.

**intrapersonal communication**: Communication you have with yourself. How you assign meaning to the world around you.

**intrusion**: Invasion of privacy by physical trespass into a space surrounding a person's body or onto property under his or her control.

**jazz journalism**: A lively, illustrated style of newspapering popularized by the tabloid papers in the 1920s.

**kinetoscope**: An early peepshow-like movie projection system developed by Thomas Edison that could be seen only by an individual viewer.

**libel**: A published statement that unjustifiably exposes someone to ridicule or contempt; for a statement to be libel, it must satisfy the three elements of defamation, identification, and publication.

**libertarian theory**: A theory of appropriate press behavior that says the press does not belong to the government but is instead a separate institution that belongs to the people and serves as an independent observer of the government.

**Linotype**: A typesetting machine that lets an operator type at a keyboard rather than pick each letter out by hand. The Linotype was the standard for typesetting until phototypesetting became common in the 1970s.

**listservs**: Internet discussion groups made up of subscribers that use e-mail to exchange messages between as few as a dozen people to as many as several thousand.

**literary magazines**: Publications that focus on serious essays and short fiction.

**local advertising**: Advertising designed to get people to patronize local stores, businesses, or service providers.

**local cable television systems**: The companies that provide cable television service directly to consumers' homes.

**long-playing record (LP)**: A record format introduced by Columbia Records in 1948. The more durable LP could reproduce twenty-three minutes of high-quality music on each of two sides and was a technological improvement over the 78-rpm.

**long tail**: The portion of a distribution curve where a limited number of people are interested in buying a lot of different products.

**magazine**: A periodical that contains articles of lasting interest. Typically, magazines are targeted at a specific audience and derive income from advertising, subscriptions, and newsstand sales.

**mainstreaming**: The effort by newspapers such as the *Los Angeles Times* to include quotations by minorities and women in stories that aren't about minority issues.

**mass communication**: When an individual or institution uses technology to send a message to a large, mixed audience, most of whose members are not known to the sender.

**mass media**: The technological tools, or channels, used to transmit the messages of mass communication.

**mean world syndrome**: The perception of many heavy television watchers of violent programs that the world is a more dangerous and violent place than facts and statistics bear out.

**media literacy**: Audience members' understanding of the media industry's operation, the messages delivered by the media, the roles media play in society, and how audience members respond to these media and their messages.

**media logic**: An approach to studying the mass media that says the forms the media use to present the world become the forms we use to perceive the world and to create media messages.

**media planning**: The process central to a successful ad campaign of figuring out which media to use, buying the media at the best rates, and then evaluating how effective the purchase was.

**media relations**: Two-way interactions between PR professionals and members of the press. These can involve press conferences, press releases, video news releases, or interviews. Typically, media relations involve the placement of unpaid messages within the standard programming or news content of the medium.

**message**: The content being transmitted by the sender to the receiver.

**misappropriation**: Invasion of privacy by using a person's name or image for commercial purposes without his or her permission.

**mobisodes**: Short video episodes designed to be viewed on the small screens on mobile phones or personal digital assistants (PDAs). These can be brief entertainment, news, or commercial programs.

**modernization**: The process of change from a society in which people's identities and roles are fixed at birth to a society where people can decide who they want to be, where they want to live, what they want to do, and how they want to present themselves to the world.

**morals**: An individual's code of behavior based on religious or philosophical principles. Morals define right and wrong in ways that may or may not be rational.

**Mosaic**: The first easy-to-use graphical Web browser, developed by a group of student programmers at the University of Illinois at Champaign-Urbana.

**MP3**: Short for Moving Picture Experts Group audio layer 3; a standard for compressing music from CDs or other digital recordings into computer files that can be easily exchanged on the Internet.

**muckrakers**: Progressive investigative journalists typically publishing in magazines in the early years of the twentieth century.

**multiplex**: A group of movie theaters with anywhere from three to twenty screens that share a common box office and concession stand. Largely a suburban phenomenon at first, they replaced the old urban Art Deco movie palaces.

**narrowband service**: A relatively slow Internet connection using a modem and conventional copper phone lines. Although it is acceptable for viewing text and graphics, it is generally considered too slow for video and audio service.

**national advertising**: Advertising designed to build demand for a nationally available product or service and that is not directing the consumer to local retail and service outlets.

**Net neutrality**: Rules that would require Internet service providers to give equal access to all online content providers.

**network**: A company that provides common programming to a large group of broadcast stations.

**noise**: Interference with the transmission of a message. This can take the form of semantic, mechanical, or environmental noise.

**non-notated music**: Music such as a folk song or jazz solo that does not exist in written form.

**obscenity**: Sexually explicit material that is legally prohibited from being published.

**ombudsman**: A representative of a publication's readers who takes the point of view of those who purchase or consume the news; also known as a reader's representative or audience advocate.

**open contract**: An arrangement that allows advertising agencies to sell space in any publication (and eventually broadcast outlets as well) rather than just a limited few.

**opinion leaders**: Influential community members who invest substantial amounts of time learning about their own area of expertise, such as politics. Less well-informed friends and family members frequently turn to them for advice about the topic.

**opinion leadership**: A two-step process of persuasion that uses respected and influential individuals to deliver messages with the hope of influencing members of a community, rather than just relying on the mass media to deliver the message.

**packet switching**: A method for breaking up long messages into small pieces, or packets, and transmitting them independently across a computer network. Once the packets arrive at their destination, the receiving computer reassembles the message into its original form.

**paper**: A writing material made from cotton rags or wood pulp; invented by the Chinese between 240 BC and 105 BC.

**papyrus**: An early form of paper made from the papyrus reed, developed by the Egyptians around 3100 BC.

**parchment**: An early form of paper made from the skin of goats or sheep, which was more durable than papyrus.

**payola**: Payoffs to disc jockeys in the form of money or gifts to get them to play a particular record.

**penny press**: Inexpensive, widely circulated papers that became popular in the nineteenth century. They were the first American media to be supported primarily through advertising revenue.

**PeopleMeter**: An electronic box used by the ratings company Nielsen Media Research to record which television shows people watch.

**phonograph**: An early sound-recording machine invented by Thomas Edison; the recorded material was played back on a cylinder.

**phonography**: A system of writing in which symbols stand for spoken sounds rather than objects or ideas. Among the most widely used phonographic alphabets are the Latin/Roman used in English and the Cyrillic used for writing Russian.

**photojournalism**: The use of photographs to portray the news in print.

**pictograph**: A prehistoric form of writing made up of paintings on rock or cave walls.

**plus-sized model**: A female fashion model who wears average or larger clothing size.

**podcast**: An audio program produced as an MP3 compressed music file that can be listened to online at the listener's convenience or downloaded to a computer or an MP3 player. Podcasts sometimes contain video content as well.

**Postal Act of 1879**: Legislation that allowed magazines to be mailed nationally at a low cost. It was a key factor in the growth of magazine circulation in the late nineteenth century.

**press agentry**: An early form of public relations that involved sending material from the press agent to the media with little opportunity for interaction and feedback. It often involved conduct that would be considered deceptive and unethical today.

**principle of utility**: John Stuart Mill's principle that ethical behavior arises from that which will provide the greatest good for the greatest number of people.

**print-on-demand**: A form of publishing in which the physical book is not printed until it's ordered, or when the distributor of the book prints additional copies in small batches.

**prior restraint**: A judicial order that stops a media organization from publishing or broadcasting a story or image.

**privilege**: A legal defense against libel that holds that statements made in government meetings, in court, or in government documents cannot be used as the basis for a libel suit.

**producer**: The person who puts together the right mix of songs, songwriters, technicians, and performers to create an album; some observers argue that the producer is the key catalyst for a hit album.

**product integration**: The paid integration of a product or service into the central theme of media content. This is most common in television programming or movies, but it can be found in books, magazine articles, Web pages, or even songs.

**Production Code**: The industry-imposed rules that controlled the content of movies from the 1930s until the current movie ratings system came into use in 1968.

**proofs**: The ready-to-print typeset pages sent to book authors for final corrections.

**psychographics**: A combination of demographics, lifestyle characteristics, and product usage; a method typically used to analyze potential markets for products and programs.

**public**: Any group of people who share a common set of interests and goals. These include *internal publics*, made up of people within the organization, and *external publics*, consisting of people outside the organization.

**public access channels**: Local cable television channels that air public affairs programming and other locally produced shows.

**Public Broadcasting System (PBS)**: A nonprofit broadcast network that provides a wide range of public service and educational programs, which is funded by government appropriations, private industry underwriting, and viewer support.

**publicity model**: A model of the mass communication process that looks at how media attention can make a person, concept, or thing become important, regardless of what is said about it.

**public relations (PR)**: Public relations is "the management function that establishes and maintains mutually beneficial relationships between an organization and the publics on whom its success or failure depends."

**public service ads**: Advertising designed to promote the messages of nonprofit institutions and government agencies. The messages are typically produced and run without charge by advertising professionals and the media. Many of these ads are produced by the Ad Council.

**publishers**: The companies that buy manuscripts from authors, turn them into books, and market them to the public.

**race records**: A term used by the recording industry prior to 1949 to refer to recordings by popular black artists. It was later replaced by more racially neutral terms such as R&B, soul, or urban contemporary.

**Radio Music Box memo**: David Sarnoff's 1915 plan, outlining how radio could be used as a popular mass medium.

**rap music**: This genre arose out of the hip-hop culture in New York City in 1979. It emerged in clubs with DJs playing and remixing different records and sounds and then speaking (or rapping) over the top.

**rating point**: The percentage of the total potential television audience actually watching a particular show. One rating point indicates an audience of approximately 1.14 million viewers.

**receiver**: The audience for the mass communication message.

**reception model**: A critical theory model of the mass communication process that looks at how audience members derive and create meaning out of media content as they decode the messages.

**resonance model**: A model of political campaign effects that attributes a candidate's success to how well his or her basic message resonates with and reinforces voters' preexisting political feelings.

**ritual model**: A model of the mass communication process that treats media use as an interactive ritual engaged in by audience members. It looks at how and why audience members (receivers) consume media messages.

**rock 'n' roll**: A style of music popularized on radio that combined elements of white hillbilly music and black rhythm and blues.

**rotary press**: A steam-powered press invented in 1814 that could print many times faster than the older, hand-powered flat-bed presses.

**satellite radio**: The radio service provided by digital signal broadcast from a communications satellite. This service covers a wider area than terrestrial radio, is supported by subscribers, and offers programming that is different from corporate-owned terrestrial stations, but is costly and doesn't provide local coverage, such as traffic and weather reports.

**scoop**: A news story that a news organization reports well ahead of its competitors.

**scriptoria**: Copying rooms in monasteries where monks prepared early hand-copied books.

**Sender Message Channel Receiver (SMCR) or transmission model**: A dated model that is still useful in identifying the players in the mass communication process.

**sensationalism**: News coverage that panders to audiences with lurid and highly emotional accounts of crime, sex, violence, or celebrity missteps.

**serial novels**: Novels published and sold in single-chapter installments.

**service magazines**: Magazines that primarily contain articles about how to do things in a better way; such articles include health advice, cooking tips, employment help, or fashion guides.

**share**: The percentage of television sets in use that are tuned to a particular show

**shield laws**: Laws that give journalists special protection from having to testify in court about their stories and sources.

**shock jocks**: Radio personalities, like Howard Stern, who attract listeners by making outrageous and offensive comments on the air.

**short head**: The portion of a distribution curve where a large number of people are interested in buying a limited number of products.

**small media**: Alternative media such as fax machines, photocopiers, video cameras, and personal Web sites used to distribute news and information that might be suppressed by the government if it were published through traditional mass media channels.

**soap operas**: Serialized daytime dramas targeted primarily at women.

**socialization**: The process of educating young people and new members about the values, social norms, and knowledge of a group or society.

**social learning theory**: The process by which individuals learn by observing the behaviors of others and the consequences of those behaviors.

**social music**: Music that people play and sing for one another in the home or other social settings. In the absence of radio, recordings, and later, television, this was the means of hearing music most readily available to the largest number of people.

**social responsibility theory**: A theory of appropriate press behavior based on the concern that, although the press may be free from interference from the government, it can still be controlled by corporate interests. It is an outgrowth of libertarian theory.

**spiral of silence**: A theory that suggests that people want to see themselves as holding a majority opinion and will therefore remain silent if they perceive that they hold a minority opinion. This tends to make the minority opinion appear to be less prevalent than it is.

**standard digital television**: A standard for digital broadcasting that allows six channels to fit in the broadcast frequency space occupied by a single analog signal.

**status conferral**: The process by which media coverage makes an individual gain prominence in the eyes of the public.

**studio system**: A factory-like way of producing films that involved having all of the talent, including the actors and directors, working directly for the movie studios. The studios also had almost total control of the distribution system.

**subliminal advertising**: Messages that are allegedly embedded so deeply in an ad that they cannot be perceived consciously. There is no evidence that subliminal advertising is effective.

**surveillance**: How the media help us extend our senses to perceive more of the world surrounding us.

**sweeps**: The four times during the year that Nielsen Media Research measures the size of individual television station audiences.

**symbolic interactionism**: The process by which individuals produce meaning through interaction based on socially agreed-upon symbols.

**synchronized soundtrack**: Sound effects, music, and voices synchronized with the moving images in a movie.

**synergy**: Where the combined strength of two items is greater than the sum of their individual strengths. In the media business, synergy means that a large company can use the strengths of its various divisions to successfully market its content.

**tabloid laundering or tabloidization**: When respectable media report on what the tabloids are reporting as a way of covering sensationalistic stories on which they might not otherwise report.

**tabloid newspapers**: Newspapers with a half-page (11-by-14-inch) format that usually have a cover rather than a traditional front page like the larger broadsheet papers.

**talkie**: A movie with synchronized sound; these quickly replaced silent films.

**targeting**: The process of trying to make a particular product or service appeal to a narrowly defined group. Groups are often targeted using demographics, geographics, and psychographics.

**TCP/IP**: TCP stands for Transmission Control Protocol, which controls how data are sent out on the Internet; IP stands for Internet Protocol, which provides the address for each computer on the Internet. These protocols provided common rules and translations so that incompatible computers could communicate with each other.

**telegraph**: The first system for using wires to send messages at a distance; invented by Samuel Morse in 1844.

**telenovelas:** Spanish-language soap operas popular in both Latin America and the United States.

**television network**: A company that provides programs to local stations around the country; the local affiliate stations choose which programs to carry.

**terrestrial radio**: AM and FM broadcast radio stations.

**trade books**: General-interest fiction and nonfiction books that are sold in hardback or large-format paperback editions.

**trade magazines**: Magazines published for people who work in a particular industry or business.

**typemold**: A mold in which a printer would pour molten lead to produce multiple, identical copies of a single letter without hand-carving each.

**uniform resource locator (URL)**: One of the three major components of the Web; the address of content placed on the Web.

**university and small presses**: Small-scale publishers that issue a limited number of books covering specialized topics. They are often subsidized by a university or an organization.

**Usenet**: The Users Network is the original Internet discussion forum that covers thousands of specialized topics. It is a worldwide bulletin-board system that predates the World Wide Web.

**uses and gratifications theory**: An approach to studying mass communication that looks at the reasons why audience members choose to spend time with the media in terms of the wants and needs of the audience members that are being fulfilled.

**vanity presses**: Companies that print books and distribute books with the author paying all the costs (a process known as self-publishing).

**veil of ignorance**: John Rawls's principle of ethics that says that justice comes from making decisions that maximize liberty for all people and without considering which outcome will give us personally the biggest benefit.

**vertical integration**: Controlling all aspects of a media project, including production, delivery to consumers in multiple formats, and the promotion of the product through other media.

**videocassette recorder (VCR)**: A home videotape machine that allows viewers to make permanent copies of television shows and, thus, choose when they want to watch programs.

**video news release (VNR)**: A taped or digital video message that serves as a press release to the broadcast and online media. VNRs are often broadcast or streamed without notice of who produced the program.

**video-on-demand**: Television channels that allow consumers to order movies, news, or other programs at any time over fiber-optic lines.

**Watergate scandal**: A burglary authorized by rogue White House staffers of the Democratic National Committee headquarters in the Watergate office and apartment building and its subsequent cover-up led to the resignation of President Richard Nixon in 1974. Bob Woodward and Carl Bernstein, two reporters from the *Washington Post*, covered the Watergate scandal.

**Weblog (blog)**: A collection of links and commentary in hypertext form on the World Wide Web that can be created and posted on the Internet with relatively little effort. Blogs can be public diaries, collections of photos, or commentaries on the news.

**wireless telegraph**: Guglielmo Marconi's name for his point-to-point communication tool that used radio waves to transmit messages.

**World Wide Web**: A system developed by Tim Berners-Lee that allows users to view and link documents located anywhere in the world using standard software.

**yellow journalism**: A style of sensationalistic journalism that grew out of the newspaper circulation battle between Joseph Pulitzer and William Randolph Hearst.

**zoned coverage**: When a newspaper targets news coverage or advertisements to a specific region of a city or market.

# Image Credits

Front cover: iStockphoto.com
Back cover: Joel Beeson

Page vii: Joel Beeson

**CHAPTER 1 LIVING IN A MEDIA WORLD**

Page 3: Gareth Cattermole/Getty Images
Page 4 (left): AP Photo
Page 4 (right): AP Photo
Page 5 (left): Apic/Getty Images
Page 5 (right): AP Photo/Paul Sakuma
Page 15: Reuters/Jim Bourg
Page 17: © Najlah Feanny/Corbis
Page 22: Library of Congress
Page 24: Steve Miller photo
Page 25: Kevin Winter/ImageDirect
Page 30: Sucheta Das/Reuters/Landov
Page 34: AP Photo

**CHAPTER 2 MASS COMMUNICATION EFFECTS**

Page 43: Used by permission from Philip de Vellis
Page 44 (left): Library of Congress
Page 44 (right): AP Photo/Obed Zilwa
Page 45 (left): AP Photo
Page 45 (right): Library of Congress
Page 47: Library of Congress
Page 49: AP Photo
Page 53: AP Photo
Page 58: © Kiley Bishop/Retna Ltd./Corbis
Page 64: © Ricco/Torres/Lion's Gate/Bureau L.A. Collection/Corbis
Page 71: AP Photo/Stephen Chernin

**CHAPTER 3 THE MEDIA BUSINESS**

Page 75 : AP Photo/Paul Sakuma
Page 76 (left): AP Photo
Page 76 (right): AP Photo
Page 77 (top): iStockphoto.com/© Roger Van Bulck
Page 77 (bottom left): iStockphoto.com/© Pali Rao
Page 77 (bottom right): iStockphoto.com/© Gino Santa Maria
Page 88: Imaginechina via AP Images
Page 91: © Roger Ressmeyer/Corbis

**Image Credits**

Page 209: Library of Congress
Page 212: www.csmonitor.com

## CHAPTER 7 AUDIO

Page 221 (left): Photo courtesy of Cody Cheesebrough
Page 221 (right): Serge Thomann/WireImage
Page 222 (left): iStockphoto.com/© Clayton Hansen
Page 222 (right): Library of Congress
Page 223 (left): AP Photo/Victor Boyton
Page 223 (right): iStockphoto.com/© Mariya Bibikova
Page 225: Library of Congress
Page 228: Library of Congress
Page 236: Library of Congress
Page 237: AP Photo
Page 238: Michael Ochs Archives/Getty Images
Page 241: AP Photo/Damian Dovarganes
Page 242: © Chad Batka/Corbis
Page 249: http://espndeportes.espn.go.com
Page 250: © Mark Peterson/Corbis
Page 252: © Brooks Kraft/Corbis
Page 257: http://coverville.com

## CHAPTER 8 MOVIES

Page 265: AP Photo/Peter Kramer
Page 266 (left): AP Photo
Page 266 (right): AP Photo
Page 267 (left): AP Photo
Page 267 (right): iStockphoto.com
Page 268: Library of Congress
Page 269: The Granger Collection, New York
Page 272: Library of Congress
Page 276: Mario Anzuoni/Reuters/Landov
Page 279: © Pictorial Press Ltd./Alamy
Page 284: © Photos 12/Alamy
Page 288: © Photos 12/Alamy
Page 291: Sipa via AP Images
Page 297: Reuters

## CHAPTER 9 TELEVISION

Page 303: Courtesy of Comedy Central
Page 304 (left): AP Photo
Page 304 (right): AP Photo
Page 305: © Bettmann/Corbis
Page 307: AP Photo
Page 309: AP Photo
Page 310: AP Photo/Saurabh Das
Page 311: © Kimberly White/Corbis
Page 314: Aman Mehinli/Reuters/Landov
Page 315: Joe Raedle/Getty Images

Page 317: AP Photo/Mark Lennihan
Page 323: Karen Neal/© ABC/Getty Images
Page 325: AP Photo/Chris Pizzello
Page 328: iStockphoto.com/© Huchen Lu
Page 329: CBS/Landov
Page 336: http://www.apple.com/itunes

## CHAPTER 10 THE INTERNET

Page 341: © Jack Dorsey. Reprinted by permission under Creative Commons license
Page 343 (center): AP Photo/Chitose Suzuki
Page 343 (right): iStockphoto.com
Page 347: BBN Technologies
Page 351: AP Photo/Jason DeCrow
Page 357: http://www.405themovie.com/Home.asp
Page 359: Cate Gillon/Getty Images
Page 361 (top): © 2007 Dave Kellett. All rights reserved. Used by permission of Dave Kellett
Page 361 (bottom): http://obscurestore.com
Page 362: http://ralphehanson.com
Page 364: © Shizhao. Reprinted by permission under Creative Commons license
Page 365: YouTube/Reuters/Landov
Page 370: AP Photo
Page 373: http://english.aljazeera.net

## CHAPTER 11 ADVERTISING

Page 379: AP Photo/Peter Kramer
Page 380: Library of Congress
Page 381 (left): National Archives
Page 381 (center): AP Photo
Page 381 (right): AP Photo/Advantica
Page 383: Library of Congress
Page 384: Library of Congress
Page 385: Library of Congress
Page 387: AP Photo/USDA
Page 388: AP Photo/Milk Processors of America
Page 394: © Alan Schein Photography/Corbis
Page 395: http://www.netflix.com
Page 399: AP Photo/Greater Philadelphia Tourism Marketing Corporation
Page 409: AP Photo/Ben Margot
Page 411: Fred Prouser/Reuters/Landov

## CHAPTER 12 PUBLIC RELATIONS

Page 415: Photograph courtesy of M. G. Ellis, WVU University Relations photographer
Page 416 (left): iStockphoto.com
Page 416 (right): Library of Congress
Page 417 (left): AP Photo/Horace Cort
Page 417 (right): AP Photo/Douglas C. Pizac
Page 419: Library of Congress
Page 420: Library of Congress

Page 422: Library of Congress
Page 423: The Granger Collection, New York
Page 426: AP Photo/Paul Sakuma
Page 432: AP Photo/*Wisconsin State Journal*, John Maniaci
Page 434: AP Photo/Jim Mone
Page 435: AP Photo
Page 441: © Brooks Kraft/Corbis
Page 444: Center for Biological Diversity. Photo by Brendan Cummings. Used with permission
Page 445: AP Photo/Bill Hudson

## CHAPTER 13 MEDIA LAW

Page 449: Library of Congress
Page 450 (left): AP Photo
Page 450 (right): AP Photo
Page 451 (left): AP Photo
Page 451 (right): AP Photo/Dennis Cook
Page 453: The Granger Collection, New York
Page 459: AP Photo/*San Francisco Examiner*, Gordon Stone
Page 462: © Tim Graham/Alamy
Page 463: AP Photo
Page 469: AP Photo
Page 473: © Clay Good/ZUMA
Page 474: Mark Wilson/Getty Images
Page 481: AP Photo/Steven Senne

## CHAPTER 14 MEDIA ETHICS

Page 485 (left): AP Photo/Richard Drew
Page 485 (right): AP Photo
Page 486: AP Photo/Robert Kradin
Page 487 (left): AP Photo
Page 487 (right): AP Photo/Richard Drew
Page 489: AP Photo/Richard Drew
Page 495: © Neville Elder/Corbis
Page 498: AP Photo/M. Spencer Green
Page 499: AP Photo/Lefteris Pitarakis
Page 501: Reuters/George Esiri
Page 502: Karen Bleier/AFP/Getty Images
Page 508 (left): AP Photo/Nick Ut
Page 508 (right): AP Photo/Khalid Mohammed
Page 514: AP Photo/Richard Drew

## CHAPTER 15 GLOBAL MEDIA

Page 524: AP Photo
Page 525 (left): AP Photo
Page 525 (right): AP Photo/Ira Schwartz
Page 527: AP Photo
Page 529: The Granger Collection, New York
Page 530: © Brooks Kraft/Corbis

# Index

*Tables, figures, and note(s) are indicated by t, f, and n/nn, respectively, after the page number.*